ROYAL COMMENTARIES

OF THE INCAS

And General History of Peru

PART ONE

THE TEXAS PAN-AMERICAN SERIES

ROYAL
COMMENTARIES
OF THE INCAS

And General History of Peru

PART ONE

by Garcilaso de la Vega, El Inca

Translated with an Introduction by
HAROLD V. LIVERMORE

FOREWORD BY ARNOLD J. TOYNBEE

UNIVERSITY OF TEXAS PRESS, AUSTIN & LONDON

The Texas Pan-American Series is published with the assistance of a revolving publication fund established by the Pan-American Sulphur Company and other friends of Latin America in Texas. Also contributing to the cost of translating and publishing this book were the Pan American Union, the Rockefeller Foundation (through the Latin American translation program of the Association of American University Presses), and the Ford Foundation.

FOREWORD

In making this translation of Garcilaso de la Vega's *Commentaries*, Mr. Harold Livermore has done a valuable service for the English-reading public. This book is one of the prime sources of our knowledge of the pre-Columbian civilization of the Andean World. Some acquaintance with this civilization is indispensable for an understanding of world history. Furthermore, Garcilaso is a particularly illuminating witness to the character of this Andean civilization that the Spanish *conquistadores* had destroyed in the generation immediately preceding Garcilaso's own. The other chroniclers of Andean history in the Spanish language were European in descent on both sides. The New World civilization that they were describing was alien to them, however actively it may have aroused their curiosity, and however successful they may have been in entering into the spirit of it by an act of historical imagination. Garcilaso spent most of his adult life on the Old World side of the Atlantic, but, in writing about the empire of the Incas, he enjoyed one singular personal advantage. His mother was an Inca princess, and the Andean World, as well as the Western World, was thus part of his personal heritage. Each of these points is worth considering.

The corpus of writing in Spanish on the Andean civilization is notable in several ways. The sheer size of it is impressive, and most of these works were written before the conquerors had completed the destruction of the pre-Columbian society and culture upon which they had made their shattering impact. For several generations enough of the pre-Columbian Andean tradition remained alive to enable even some of the latest of the Spanish chroniclers to make valuable contributions to our knowledge of its history.

One of the strange features of the pre-Columbian civilizations' tragic encounter with the conquerors from the Old World was the ambivalence of the conquerors' attitudes towards these other worlds. The conquerors made a barbarous use of their overwhelmingly superior material power. They shattered the pre-Columbian civilizations—and this so thoroughly that, even today, after the passage of nearly four and a half centuries, the Andean World has not yet fully recovered from the blow. When one meets the surviving unassimilated Indians in the Peruvian and Ecuadorian highlands, they give the impression of being still dazed and out of countenance. When one travels up and down the coast of present-day Peru, one comes across the remains of pre-Columbian irrigation-works that have still not been brought back into operation. As destroyers, the Spanish *conquistadores* have been as baneful as the Assyrians and the Mongols. Yet, while some Spaniards were destroying the pre-Columbian civilizations as fast and as furiously as they could, other Spaniards were eagerly recording the history and institutions of the societies that their compatriots were grinding to powder. In most cases, no doubt, the destroyers and the recorders were different persons in different walks of life: the destroyers were mostly military adventurers; the recorders were largely either ecclesiastics or lawyers. Many of these "clerks" (in the mediaeval sense of the word) deplored and resisted the barbarities that were being perpetrated by the men of the sword, and the Spanish Crown took the lawyers' and the ecclesiastics' side. At least one Spanish ecclesiastic however—the philanthropic Bishop Landa of Yucatán—made a record of Maya culture with one hand while he was extirpating "heathenism" with the other. In his case the conflict between these two Spanish attitudes was being fought, unresolved, in the soul of one and the same individual.

Without this corpus of literary works in Spanish, our knowledge of the pre-Columbian civilizations of the Americas would be still more meager than it is. The literary evidence has, however, serious limitations. In this Spanish picture, pre-Columbian history has been foreshortened to the point of distortion. The latest chapter has eclipsed all its predecessors. Andean history becomes the history of the Incas; Middle American history becomes the history of the Aztecs and of the Mayas in their last phase in Yucatán—and Yucatán is only one among the provinces of the Mayas' geographical domain. Fortunately, this literary picture is now being corrected progressively by archaeological explorations and discoveries. These have revealed that the pre-Columbian civilizations had already passed their peak before the Incas and the Aztecs made their appearance. So far from being the whole story, the careers of these two peoples were merely the latest chapter of it. Archaeology has carried back our knowledge of the pre-Columbian cultures of the Americas into the first, and even the second, millennium B.C.

This is an immense and exciting expansion of our historical horizon in the New World. It is, however, inevitably subject to the limitations that are intrinsic to all archaeological evidence. This evidence is derived exclusively from the material débris of culture. The economic, religious, and political life of the human societies that have deposited this débris has to be reconstructed by inference from the surviving relics of the society's physical artifacts, and there are limits to our power of making stones cry out. Archaeological evidence can be eloquent about economics; it can be illuminating about religion; but it is dumb, more often than not, about politics. Troves of skeletons and weapons may bear witness to the ravages of war, but they will not so readily reveal the political consequences of the fighting. Did this battle result politically in the construction of an empire or in the break-up of one? In the field of politics archaeological evidence is likely to be unrevealing unless it is reinforced by literary evidence. Herein lies the value of the Spanish records of the histories of the pre-Columbian civilizations. But this literary reinforcement of the archaeological evidence extends, as has already been noted, no farther back in time than the latest chapter of pre-Columbian history. For the political history of the earlier chapters, our archaeological evidence leaves us still very much in the dark. All that we can do is to piece together our archaeological and our literary evidence, and to make what we can of the result.

The result, even on the political plane, is not without value for our understanding both of pre-Columbian history in the Americas and of human history as a whole.

The Inca Empire, at the date at which the Spaniards broke in upon it, embraced within its frontiers not only the whole domain of the Andean civilization in what are now Peru and Bolivia, but also some borderline areas on its cultural penumbra—for instance, on the north the territory that now constitutes the Republic of Ecuador, and, on the south, territories that are now included in Chile, as far south as the Maule River, and the northwest corner of what is now Argentina. So far as we know, this was the first time that the entire Andean World had been united politically. There had been at least two occasions on which perhaps the greater part of the Andean World had been brought within a common cultural "horizon" (to use the archaeologists' technical term). First the Chavín horizon, and later the Tiahuanaco horizon, had been widespread. Archaeological evidence tells us this, but it does not also tell us whether, in these two cases, cultural unification was, or was not, accompanied by political unification. Our knowledge that the Andean World was unified politically in the Inca Empire is due to the information given to us about this empire by our copious literary sources in Spanish. There is, of course, also much archaeological evidence dating from the Inca Imperial Age;

but, supposing that our literary evidence for this period had been non-existent and that we had had to depend here too on archaeological evidence alone, this by itself might not have enabled us to know for certain that the Inca horizon was a reality on the political plane, as well as on the cultural plane.

The literary evidence combines with the archaeological evidence to inform us that the political unity of the Inca World, at the time when the Spaniards arrived, had been preceded—and this no farther back in the past than a span of two or three generations—by a quite different political dispensation. Previously the Andean World had been split up, politically, among a number of mutually independent local states; and, as far as we know, this had always been the political situation there since the Andean civilization's beginning. The number and the average size of the local states had varied at different stages of Andean history. During the chapter immediately preceding the establishment of the Inca Empire, the average size had been relatively large and the number relatively small. But, throughout the history of the Andean World, political pluralism seems to have been the normal state of affairs. The Inca Empire seems to have been the first, as well as the last, Andean "world state."

This reconstruction of the Andean civilization's political history is tentative; but, if it is correct, it indicates that the history of this pre-Columbian American civilization followed a course that has been normal in the histories of those Old World civilizations which, like the Andean civilization, are now extinct, so that we are able to survey their histories from beginning to end. When the curtain rises on Andean history we find the Andean World fractured politically into a number of local sovereign states that go to war with each other. As time goes on, these interstate wars become progressively more violent and more destructive, until eventually one of the warring local states—the Inca state—defeats and annexes all its rivals and thereby converts itself into a "world state" in the sense that it includes the Andean World's whole domain. This pattern of political history, which we find in the history of the Andean World, presents itself in the histories of the Sumerian, Chinese, and Graeco-Roman Worlds likewise. The Egyptian World is exceptional, among the civilizations whose political history we can trace, in having achieved political unity at the beginning—at the moment, that is to say, when it emerged out of the precivilizational stage of culture. Usually, political unity is not achieved till late—all too late—in the day. When this latter pattern of political history is found in the New World as well as in the Old World, it looks as if the pattern must be intrinsic to the political history of societies of the species that we call civilizations, in whatever part of the world the specimens of this species occur. If this conclusion is warranted, it illuminates our understanding of civilization itself.

If it is true that a "world state" is the normal last phase of the history of a civilization on the political plane, it is possible, and enlightening, to compare the structure of different "world states" with each other and to take note of their likenesses and differences. The Andean "world state," represented by the Inca Empire, has one feature in common with the Chinese Empire, the Roman Empire, and most other "world states," both those that have arisen and survived, like the Chinese, and those that have come and gone, like the Roman. Like these, the Inca Empire was founded by cumulative military conquest in a series of wars. In the Atomic Age it will be impossible to found any future "world state" by force. A "world state"—this time, literally a world-wide one—may now be the only alternative to mass suicide, but it will have to be established by voluntary agreement.

In another respect the Inca Empire was more like some of the local states of the present day than it was like any of the other would-be "world states" of the past. It was authoritarian, bureaucratic, and socialistic to a degree that has perhaps not been approached by any other state at any other time or place. It would be hard to think of any other regime—except, possibly, the Ptolemaic regime in Egypt—in which the public sector has pushed the private sector so close to the wall. The Inca imperial government dictated to its subjects, in detail, the locality in which they were to live, the kind of work that they were to do there, and the use that was to be made of the product of their labour.

When we think of bureaucracy, we think of scribes, clerks, *paperasserie,* pigeonholes, files, and archives. It is amazing that the Incas should have created and operated one of the most high-powered bureaucracies known to history so far, without possessing the instrument of writing—an instrument that might have been supposed to be indispensable for this purpose if the Inca bureaucracy had not proved that it is not. The Incas worked their bureaucratic administration by an apparatus that bore more resemblance to the tallies used by the mediaeval English Exchequer than to the documents in cuneiform or Chinese characters, or in one of the variants of the alphabet, that have been the usual instrument of bureaucracy in the Old World. They kept their reckoning by *quipus,* which were knotted strings of different lengths, different numbers of knots, and different colours. The abacus is perhaps the nearest thing to this in the Old World's equipment. By this means the Incas dispensed with writing, but they could not dispense with bureaucrats. The *quipus,* like archives in writing, could be operated only by people who had made themselves familiar with the conventions that had been established for the use of these mnemonic devices. Without those conventions, and without officials who were acquainted with them, the *quipus* could not have been made to work. When the *"quipu*-conversant" Inca bureaucrats had been killed off or driven into the wilderness by the Spanish invaders, the Incaic regime came to a sudden standstill. The result was catastrophic. There was an appalling mortality and impoverishment in the Andean World—a loss that has not yet been fully repaired. The Inca administration is worth studying, and this not as one of the curiosities of history. It is relevant to mankind's present-day problems. Light on it is therefore precious, and Garcilaso's *Commentaries* is one of our important extant sources of information.

And, then, in the third place, there is Garcilaso's personal relation to those two worlds—the Andean World and the Western Christian World —in which Garcilaso was at home. Garcilaso is an early representative of a class which has been important throughout the history of the encounters between modern Western civilization and all the other surviving civilizations and precivilizational cultures on the face of our planet, and which is supremely important today, when the impact of the West upon the rest of the world has become the dominant motif in the present phase of world history. Thanks to his mixed Andean-European descent and to his initiation into both his ancestral traditions—a double education which was the privilege, or burden, of his mestizo blood—Garcilaso was able to serve, and did serve, as an interpreter or mediator between two different cultures that had suddenly been brought into contact with each other.

A special name was invented in the Russian language for this interpreter class, after the Russian people had been brought into intimate relations with the West at the turn of the seventeenth and eighteenth centuries. The new class of Western-educated and Western-minded Russians that this encounter called into existence came, in the nineteenth century, to be known as the "intelligentsia." This hybrid word, with a French root and a Russian termination, was coined to denote something that was new in Russian experience. A more potent civilization than Russia's ancestral Eastern Orthodox Christian culture was now impinging on Russian life. The Russian people had to take account of this dynamic and aggressive alien force. They had to come to terms with it. The creation of the intelligentsia was the Russian people's answer to this new demand upon them. Literally, "intelligentsia" means simply a class of people that is distinguished by its wits. In practice, it meant a class that had the wit to cope with the problems raised for Russians by the Western civilization's onset. The intelligentsia's position is not a happy one. Having a footing in two worlds simultaneously, the intelligentsia may become estranged from both worlds and may suffer a kind of spiritual schism of their own souls. Yet, though this may not be a happy class, it is an important one. In every non-Western country today, from Russia to China and from Indonesia to Ghana, as well as in the "Indo-American" countries of the New World, from Mexico to Paraguay inclusive, the intelligentsia is in power—and this not only in politics but in every field of activity.

In many cases the members of the intelligentsia have done their compatriots a valuable service in breaking for them, to some extent, the shock inflicted by the impact of the Western civilization. Garcilaso could not do this for his fellow Andeans. In their tragic case, the shock had been shattering. However, he could, and did, effectively perform the reciprocal part of the intelligentsia's twofold task. He interpreted to the Western aggressors the history and institutions and ideas and ideals of one of the civilizations that those aggressors were victimizing. In this role, Garcilaso had some famous predecessors. The West's impact on the world in and after the sixteenth century of the Christian Era has had a precedent in the Greeks' impact on the world in and after the fourth century B.C. This Greek impact on contemporary Oriental civilizations evoked in each of these an intelligentsia that interpreted its ancestral civilization to the Greeks in Greek terms. The Babylonian civilization was interpreted to the Greeks by Berossus; the Egyptian, by Manetho; the Jewish, by Philo and by Josephus. This is a distinguished company to which Garcilaso belongs; and, in this role, too, Garcilaso has eminent counterparts at the present day. The president of the Indian Union, Shri Radhakrishnan, rose to fame by interpreting Indian philosophy in terms of Western philosophy for Western minds. The famous Mexican mural painters of the last generation have not only interpreted the pre-Columbian civilization of Middle America to their own generation in Mexico and in the world at large; they have revived the Middle American style of art so forcefully that they have reactivated the formidable spirit of the culture that this art originally served to express. They have demonstrated visually that the pre-Christian civilization of Middle America had, after all, not been extinguished but had merely been driven underground—waiting for its first opportunity to re-emerge.

What these Mexican painters have done for the Middle American culture in the romantic-minded twentieth century, Garcilaso could not do for the Andean culture in the fanatical sixteenth century. Yet, though he was unable to reanimate his Inca ancestors' way of life, he did succeed in making a record of it, and, from his day to ours, his *Commentaries* has been an indispensable document for Western students of human affairs. In his role as a personal link between two dramatically different cultures, Garcilaso is a document in himself: one of those human documents that can be more illuminating than any inanimate records in the shape of rows of knots on cords or rows of letters on paper.

ARNOLD J. TOYNBEE

INTRODUCTION

The *Royal Commentaries* of the Inca Garcilaso de la Vega is one of the first American classics—that is, one of the earliest books about America by an American, that has been generally accepted as a major work of the Spanish language. Certainly the other languages of the discovery and con- conquest, Portuguese, French, and English, cannot offer a rival, and if there are earlier American authors in Spanish, none of them can genuinely be said to figure on the great stage of Spanish letters.

The author was born in the ancient Inca capital of Cuzco in 1539, in the very decade of the conquest of Peru, the son of a Spanish conqueror of noble lineage and an Indian princess, a second cousin of the last two Inca rulers, the rivals Huáscar and Atahuallpa. He was therefore one of the first of the new race of mestizos, the fruit of the coming together of two branches of the human race that had remained unaware of one an- other's existence until only a few years before his birth. During his child- hood he heard the traditions of the Indian rulers from his mother's rela- tives and tales of the conquest from his father's comrades, and he himself witnessed the scenes of anarchy and confusion as the Spanish settlers struggled among themselves and against the dispensations of their distant master, the emperor Charles V. But as a young man Garcilaso left his na- tive Peru never to return, and it was in the seclusion of a small Andalusian town that he began to elaborate his great work, a task that was concluded only four years before his death in 1616.

The *Royal Commentaries* sets out to give an account of the birth, growth, and fall of the Inca empire from its legendary origins until the execution of the last independent native ruler, Túpac Amaru, in 1572. It is divided into two parts published separately, one at Lisbon in 1609 and the other at Córdova, posthumously in 1616–1617. Part One deals with the history of the Incas and their civilization, ending with the civil wars between Atahuallpa and Huáscar, which reached a climax only just before the arrival of the Spaniards. Although the Incaic theme is supposedly continued in Part Two, which opens with the organization of Pizarro's expedition and his capture of Atahuallpa, the Indians in fact play no more than a subordinate role in it. They move obediently at the Spaniards' behest and after the first clash their leaders make only occasional and usually tragic appearances: the Second Part is essentially a book about the conquerors.

The tone of each part is different, yet both belong at once to the fields of history and of literature. Although he gave his allegiance to the Queen of Sciences, Garcilaso himself admired great poetry and was profoundly concerned with questions of style. Much of the charm of the *Royal Commentaries* lies in its affinity with autobiography. The Inca is not writing about himself, but he is describing the achievements of the two races from which he springs, and the special quality of this long, detailed, and often prolix tale of two empires seems to derive from a double but simultaneous vision of the events that are being described for us. By turns Indian and Castilian, Garcilaso, as he himself puts it, has engagements to both peoples —*"prendas con ambas naciones."*

The great Spanish critic Don Marcelino Menéndez y Pelayo described the *Royal Commentaries* as "the most genuinely American book that has ever been written, and perhaps the only one in which a reflection of the soul of the conquered races has survived," and it is true that since Garcilaso was writing in Spain to enlighten a European public about an oppressed and ill-regarded people, much of the work is pervaded with sympathy for the Incas and a nostalgic feeling for their vanished glories. The tone of Part One is set by the gradual imposition of order, harmony, and civilization on a naughty world, as the Incas dominate the varied peoples dwelling in the Four Quarters of the Earth extending outwards from their capital (the World's Navel) at Cuzco. There is no question of an idealized innocent state of primitive man. Civilization, law, order, good government, and religion are brought by the Incas as an offering to barbarians living in the unordered squalor of primitive liberty. They either accept these blessings or have them thrust upon them: thus grows the mighty and beneficent empire of Tahuantinsuyu.

Nothing could be in greater contrast to Part Two, with its atmosphere of violence, civil strife, disloyalty, and greed, all of which were, at least in theory, wanting in the collectivist state of the Incas. We are now watching a great panorama of individual ambitions in which social obligations seem to be reduced to a mere acknowledgment of a remote, ill-informed, and apparently vacillating institution, separated by two oceans from the realities of Peru: and even this obligation is momentarily in danger of disappearing.

Although this contrast appears so unfavorable to the Spaniards, Garcilaso does not condemn the Conquest. Its justification, he implies, lies not in the mental or physical superiority of the conquering race, but in their mission to spread the light of the Gospel among a people which, though they have achieved much by their adherence to the principles of natural law, nevertheless lack the final grace of Christianity. Religion alone can bring back peace and order to Peru. Perhaps the real crux of Part Two is the long and exaggerated baroque funeral oration in honor of the author's father, the former corregidor of Cuzco, whose social and civil merits are set up as an ideal for Spanish settlers to aim at.[1]

Part One of the *Royal Commentaries,* consisting of nine books, comprises a short introduction to the discovery and nature of the New World and of Peru, and a narration of the reigns of the Inca kings, ending with the suppression of the legitimate line by the usurper Atahuallpa. This history is interspersed with accounts of Indian religion, culture, customs, and traditions, and includes a long description of the natural resources of Inca Peru and indications of the date and circumstances in which European livestock, crops, and inventions were introduced. In dealing with the political history of the Incas Garcilaso draws upon the accounts he received in his boyhood from his Indian relatives who gathered in his mother's house to recall the greatness of their past; from the lost Latin manuscript of a mestizo Jesuit, Padre Blas Valera; and from narratives already published by Spanish writers. All these versions are limited by the very nature of native historiography which rendered impossible anything in the nature of a documented account of the gradual development of Inca civilization.

Despite their achievements in social organization, in architecture, and in other fields, the Peruvian Indians never discovered how to write, and their only comparable means of communication was the *quipu* or knot-archive, with which they could record quantities by a conventional placing of the knots and a limited number of nominatives by the use of strings of different colors. These fragmentary records were supplemented by traditions handed down by professional memorizers, who reduced the events of each reign, such as conquests and dealings with other peoples, to a conventional epitome, which could perhaps be expanded and embellished in the telling. Such history is necessarily official and acritical, and

---

[1] This piece of rhetoric, so different from Garcilaso's usual simple prose, was omitted from Sir Paul Rycaut's translation (1688) as an "oration filled with Doxologies and Rhodomontadoes after the Spanish manner."

aims at verisimilitude rather than what we regard as historical truth. Its version of Inca origins is frankly legendary, but as Garcilaso shrewdly observes, many of these legends are no more improbable than those of the Greeks and Romans who had mastered the art of letters. The accounts of the later rulers, however, follow a formal and uniform pattern in which monarchs gravely accede, visit their domains to receive the plaudits of their subjects, wed (amidst many other brides) their sisters, beget whole lineages, conduct invariably successful campaigns, and are finally called to rest with their ancestor, the Sun. All is glorious and beneficent, and failure and error are piously expunged from the record. Such adjustments of history have, of course, been perfected by an all-provident state in our own times.

In fact the Inca empire, far from rising suddenly out of a general state of primitive savagery, came at the end of a long succession of more or less comparable civilizations. Nor did the Inca kings begin by subjugating and annexing their neighbors' territories: at first they were content to raid and destroy the villages of their rivals, and it was probably only in the time of Pachacútec, less than a century before the arrival of the Spaniards, that the formal expansion of Inca civilization was truly launched: it was still proceeding while the Spaniards were occupying the islands of the Antilles and entering Mexico. However, the version given us by Garcilaso is evidently what his ancestors had handed down and believed to have happened. His own memory was good, and there is no reason to suppose that he added substantially to what he had heard as a boy. His acceptance of the official history of the Incas is not without reservations, and if his version of the Indian past seems roseate, we must remember that the ideals of the Incas were strictly adjusted to the resources at their command and the gap between their aspirations and their achievements was but small.

If in this political history the Inca kings remain shadowy and uniformly beneficent and victorious, the interpolated matter is on the other hand both varied and vivid. Here again there is some idealization, but it is usually of a kind that we ourselves can appreciate and indeed often indulge in, a preference for a simpler life than our own and an admiration for great achievements with limited resources. The sketch of Inca civilization is deftly done. Indian music, poetry, and other attainments are treated briefly but with great skill, while the classic description of Cuzco in Book VII inevitably recalls Renaissance accounts of European antiquities. There are many curious and illuminating details of social and domestic life, and numerous anecdotes drawn from Garcilaso's own experience—the mummies of the Inca kings exhibited by the corregidor of Cuzco, Indian reactions to their first sight of oxen ploughing, instances of Indian astuteness and simplicity, stray notes on native words and practices.

These realistic details are also found scattered throughout Part Two, though here the aura of idealization is rapidly dispelled. The main facts of the Spanish conquest were already a matter of record. They were available in three major accounts, one by a representative of the royal treasury in Peru, Agustín de Zárate (a keeper of the Spanish *quipus,* as it were); the second by Francisco López de Gómara, a royal chaplain who never visited the New World, but who was entrusted with the official chronicle of its discovery and conquest; and the third by Diego Fernández of Palencia, called *el Palentino,* who had served in Peru and wrote at the behest of the Council of the Indies. All these versions, and some others, were used by Garcilaso, who set himself the task of collating, comparing, and amending them: they are abundantly quoted and Garcilaso adds variants or details he himself heard or saw in Peru or collected later.

In contrast to Part One with its procession of shadowy Incas at the head of their mute race of anonymous warriors and peasants, Part Two is rich in names, and characters, in individual feats and pronouncements. There are the great conquerors, the marquis Don Francisco Pizarro himself, dressed in his old-fashioned tunic and deerskin hat; his rival Don Diego de Almagro; Sebastián de Belalcázar, the conqueror of Ecuador; and Pedro de Alvarado, the dashing interloper from Guatemala; notable rebels such as Gonzalo Pizarro and Francisco Hernández Girón; royal officials; the conquistadors now become great landowners, lords of Indian vassals; famous soldiers; priests; captains; ruffians; seafarers; and a handful of peaceable settlers. Of all this galaxy those who interested Garcilaso most were undoubtedly the rebel leader Gonzalo Pizarro and his aged, brilliant, and brutal commander, Francisco Carvajal, the "Demon of the Andes." For these two, the tragic Don Quixote of the conquest and his grim Sancho Panza, Garcilaso seems to have a special regard, partly because he himself saw them as a young boy and was fed at Gonzalo's table, partly because his father was compromised on Gonzalo's behalf, partly (though he does not confess it) because they were victims to the great machine of Spanish bureaucracy.

Such is the subject matter of the *Royal Commentaries,* in which legend, history, and biography are successively blended together. There is no need to describe in detail the career of Garcilaso's father or to say much of the Inca's own youth in Cuzco, for the *Royal Commentaries* themselves con-

tain accounts of the gallant captain's doings and numerous autobiograph-
ical references that cast light on his son's upbringing and interests. But
it is perhaps necessary to say something of Garcilaso's experiences both in
Peru and in Spain, for they do much to explain his method and his purpose
in writing the book.

As we have seen, Garcilaso was among the first of the Peruvian mestizos. His father, Captain Sebastián de la Vega Vargas, had arrived in the
country with Alvarado in 1534, and, after being entrusted with an expedition to discover and explore the hot seaboard of what is now Colombia,
he was recalled by Pizarro and sent to the relief of Cuzco. But on the way
he was captured by Almagro and held under parole in the Inca capital;
and it was during this period of enforced leisure that he came together
with the princess Ñusta Chimpu Ocllo, baptized as Isabel Ocllo, who gave
birth to their son, the future author of the *Royal Commentaries,* on April
12, 1539.[2]

Garcilaso's father soon acquired extensive estates and a house overlook-
ing the main plaza of Cuzco, from the balcony of which visiting notables
used to watch jousts and processions in the square below. During the dis-
turbances of 1544, while the captain was in hiding in Lima, Chimpu Ocllo
and her children remained at the mercy of the rebels of Cuzco and their
house was even cannonaded from across the square, but it was of solid
stone and suffered little damage. They were however deprived of their
Indian servants and even left without food, so that the little Garcilaso used
every day to run across the square to dine with a charitable neighbor. During the war the boy's father became compromised with the rebel leader
Gonzalo Pizarro in a way which was later to cause serious difficulties
for his son, though he himself, by abandoning Gonzalo at the right moment, acquired a pardon, new estates, and ultimately the office of corregidor of Cuzco. Meanwhile, his young son had been educated, in common
with the other mestizos of the first generation, after the manner of a young
Spaniard of noble birth, with the apparent expectation of inheriting at
least part of his father's estates and Indian serfs. However, the Spanish
government, justifiably preoccupied by the immorality of many of the settlers, induced them to form regular unions with Spanish women, and
when Garcilaso was about fourteen his father contracted such a marriage
with Doña Luisa de los Ríos. At about the same time his mother was married to a certain Juan del Pedroche, apparently a soldier or trader, and
the captain may have contributed to her dowry.

---

[2] He was baptised Gómez Suárez de Figueroa, after several of his father's relatives,
including the future duke of Feria, the husband of Jane Dormer.

The separation of his parents undoubtedly had a deep effect on the young Garcilaso. He now found himself bastardized and deprived of any prospect of inheriting his father's estates. It is evident that he had little affection for his stepmother, and although he remained in his father's house and served as amanuensis during the latter's term of office as corregidor, it was now that he began to be stirred by an interest in his mother's people, repairing to her house to listen to the tales of the old Incas: his uncle Francisco Huallpa Túpac Yupanqui; the aged Cusi Huallpa, who told him the legend of the children of the Sun; and Juan Pechuta and Chauca Rimachi, who had been commanders under the emperor Huaina Cápac. On his mother's behalf he was sent to greet the Inca Sairi Túpac, when he came down from his refuge in the wilds in 1553, and the young Garcilaso saw him wearing the sacred plumes of the corequenque bird.

Despite all this, Garcilaso makes it clear that he was not brought up as an Indian. He and his fellow mestizos played with the Indian boys and flew the Peruvian hawks their native cousins trained for them, but they regarded themselves as of a different race. Garcilaso's chief pleasure was riding, which, as he explains, the Indians never practiced, such was their inveterate fear of horses. He and his companions amused themselves by jousting with canes, tilting at the ring, racing, and similar exercises. On December 8, 1557, when he was eighteen, he took part in a tournament to mark the accession of Philip II; these activities and religious processions and celebrations constituted the chief diversions of life in Cuzco.

In later years Garcilaso wrote that his youth was spent among arms and horses, arquebusses and gunpowder "of which I know more than of letters." It is indeed true that his boyhood was passed amidst continual uprisings, but by the time he had reached adolescence Peru had been largely pacified and military alarms had ceased to be a daily occurrence. When he looked back on his youth in Peru from the erudite society of the cathedral chapter of Córdova, which included among its members that most lucubrative of poets, Góngora, he may well have felt modest about his own early studies. Yet he had the best schooling that Peru could offer, and he was fond of telling how when a canon of the cathedral, Dr. Juan de Cuéllar, opened Latin classes in Cuzco, he was so impressed by the aptitude of his mestizo scholars that he used to exclaim: "How I'd like to see a dozen of you in the University of Salamanca!"

It is possible that Captain Garcilaso recognized a literary bent in his son, for when he died the young man received a sum of money to go to Spain and continue his education. Placing the small coca farm he had in-

herited in the hands of his mother, Garcilaso, now twenty-one, took leave
of his relatives and friends and travelled down to Lima, where he perhaps
had his first sight of a purely Spanish city. His ship put in at Cape Passau,
near the equator, for water and fuel, and during the three days he spent
there, he had the opportunity to observe painted natives diving for fish,
perhaps his first personal experience of primitive Indians whom he carefully distinguished in his book from the peoples who had come under the
influence of the Incas. So he arrived in Panama and passed to Cartagena,
where again he saw naked Indians walking through the streets one behind another "like cranes." This was to be his last sight of America.

On his arrival in Spain he first visited his father's relatives in Andalusia
and Extremadura, and in 1562 went to Madrid to petition at court for
recognition of his father's services. Whatever his hopes, they were dashed
to the ground when the Royal Council of the Indies refused his claims
on the ground that the captain had committed treason by lending his
horse to Gonzalo Pizarro in the crucial battle of Huarina. The imputa-
tion deeply wounded the young mestizo's pride. From his mother, the
princess and cousin of an emperor, he had inherited not rank but bastardy;
and now the legacy of his father, the scion of a noble Spanish family,
proved to be not honor but disgrace. The two humiliations, working in the
young man's soul like grits in the bosom of the oyster, were ultimately to
produce the twin pearls of the *Royal Commentaries*. But, for the moment,
Garcilaso was downcast and disillusioned.

He thought briefly of returning to Peru and even received a license in
1563, but it was never used, and he soon settled down with his father's
brother, Alonso de Vargas, who had recently retired after long service
in the imperial army and had married and established himself in the
quiet Andalusian town of Montilla, where he derived an income from the
estates of the marquis of Priego. Except for brief absences, such as those in
1570 when he took part in the War of the Alpujarras and acquired the
title of captain from Don John of Austria, Garcilaso continued to reside
in Montilla until 1589. After his humiliation at the hands of the Royal
Council, he renounced his ambitions and resigned himself to the pleasures
of a rural existence, "forced," as he says, "to retire from the world and to
conceal myself in the haven and shelter of the disillusioned, which are
corners of solitude and poverty," though "consoled and content with the
paucity of my scanty possessions, I live a quiet and peaceful life (thanks to
the King of Kings and Lord of Lords) more envied by the rich than envious of them." In this serene existence, he found relief from the limitations of rural life in the excellent library he was already beginning to

form. Having surrendered his hopes from Peru, the young Inca was attracted by and began to model himself on his distant kinsman the great Castilian poet who had died besieging the castle of Muey three years before his birth and whose name he now began to assume. Like the other Garcilaso, he was strongly attracted by Italian literature, and "to avoid idleness more wearisome than labor and to obtain greater peace of mind than wealth can bring," he embarked on a translation of the three *Dialoghi d'amore* of Leon Hebreo: this was finished by 1586 and finally published in Madrid in 1590. Meanwhile, the young Inca had begun his second work, the *Florida,* a history of Hernando de Soto's unsuccessful expedition to conquer what is now the deep south of the United States. The choice of subject was inspired by his friendship with a member of Soto's expedition, who, like Soto himself, had also campaigned in Peru. This was Gonzalo Silvestre, now settled at Las Posadas, near Córdova. Silvestre had no literary inclinations himself and was glad to pass on his reminiscences, which formed the groundwork of the *Florida* and contributed various anecdotes to the *Royal Commentaries.* He also felt sufficient animosity against the official historians of the Indies to scrawl peppery comments in the margins of his copy of López de Gómara, and may well have inspired Garcilaso with his own misgivings about the historians.

The tranquility of Garcilaso's life at Montilla was at length disrupted in about 1589, apparently as a result of the death of the old marquis of Priego and the passage of the title to a cousin. Garcilaso now found himself struggling to obtain payment of his *censo* and driven to adopt a number of devices to oblige the administrators of the estate to deliver both the current instalments and arrears. Moreover his friend Gonzalo Silvestre now died, and so did the great chronicler, Latinist, and antiquary, Dr. Ambrosio de Morales, who had lately taken him under his wing. In 1592 we find the Inca residing in Córdova, moving from house to house and living apparently in modest circumstances. When his friend the antiquary Juan Fernández Franco wrote to him about the question of going to Peru, Garcilaso replied in May 1592: "If only to get out of these miseries of Spain, I should think it a good plan to go and try one's luck. Would to God I were younger to go with you!" It is perhaps not without significance that he thought of beginning a work on the *Lamentations* of Job in the following summer.

These difficulties appear to have passed a year or two later, when Garcilaso became steward of the hospital of the Limpia Concepción, a post which included a residence and caused him to take minor orders. From this time he seems to have frequented the group of writers connected directly

or indirectly with the great cathedral-mosque and to have extended the
circle of his acquaintanceship to historians, theologians, and antiquaries
in other parts of Andalusia. But while his material circumstances were
now easier, as the inventory of his possessions at the time of his death
proves, his books did not secure the recognition for which he hoped. The
Dialogues of Love, finished by 1586, did not appear until 1590, and
though accompanied by two letters addressed to Philip II, it seems to have
had little effect on its author's fortunes. Garcilaso twice applied for li-
censes for a second edition, but it did not appear, and the Inquisition
finally prohibited the circulation of the work in the vernacular. The
Florida, completed, but awaiting copying in 1592, was at length published
at Lisbon in 1605. It was dedicated, with an eloquent offer of services,
to Dom Teodósio, future duke of Braganza, whose interest in the Inca
seems to have been no more active than the king of Spain's. Part One of
the *Royal Commentaries,* envisaged in 1586 and completed by 1604, was
finally printed early in 1609. This time there was an appeal to Dom Teodósio's mother, the duchess of Braganza, which again passed unheeded.

These delays undoubtedly conceal disappointments and difficulties of
which we know little. Garcilaso seems to have contributed toward the costs
of both parts of the *Royal Commentaries,* and he had some five hundred
unbound copies of Part One still in his house when he died. But beyond
and above these material difficulties, his interest in the fate of the Incas
seems nearly to have embroiled him with that great bureaucratic machine
of which he stood so much in awe.

Garcilaso's three major works, the *Dialogues of Love,* the *Florida* and
the two parts of the *Royal Commentaries,* correspond to successive stages
in his spiritual development. Disappointed and humiliated by his youthful
reverses, he had taken refuge in the ivory tower of his uncle's house at
Montilla. Naturally fond of literature, he conceived the idea of vindicating himself and the fortunes of his mother's race by demonstrating the
intellectual aptitude of an "Antarctic Indian." To this end he devoted
himself to translating one of the most abstruse and intellectual works of
his day, a neoplatonic treatise on love as the mysterious uniting force of
the soul. It is not difficult to see how Leon Hebreo with his concern for the
metaphysics of harmony and union should have appealed to the young
Garcilaso as he looked back on the problems of his own mestizo origin
and brooded on the destruction of the old Inca order. At the same time he
cherished the illusion that Philip II, to whom the work was dedicated,
might be impressed by these cultural first-fruits of Peru and so decide to
alleviate the lot of the Incas and mestizos. A curious anecdote included

in Part Two of the *Royal Commentaries* shows Philip handing the book to his spiritual advisers for their opinion— not even Garcilaso deluded himself into thinking that the harassed monarch read the work.

In the *Florida* Garcilaso leaves the world of philosophical speculation and comes to the problems of America and the conquest. His tale is not of the civilized Incas of Peru but of an expedition to explore and discover territories occupied by half-savage Indians, many of them cannibals. Perhaps the most striking aspect of Garcilaso's approach to the subject is his treatment of the two parties, Europeans and Indians, as equals. In their powwows the Indians deliver themselves of gracious speeches replete with Renaissance courtliness. Garcilaso explains that his words are not translations of those used by the speakers, but he asserts that their words in their own tongue were just as polished and well chosen as those he puts into their mouths. In their battles, also, Europeans and Indians engage and struggle as though they were taking part in a joust. The book has, in fact, something of the romantic quality of Ginés Pérez de Hita's *Civil Wars of Granada,* in which a ruthless struggle between the peoples of two opposing religions is purged of its brutality to make agreeable reading. But Garcilaso's purpose is not simply to present a pleasant picture of the natives of the New World: he is entering an oblique protest against those who believed that the Indians were inherently bestial and beyond redemption, and he stresses the need for their conversion and its feasibility if due regard is paid to their culture and susceptibilities. "We Indians are a people who are ignorant and uninstructed in the arts and sciences," he says in his preface, adding that if his own work is appreciated "it would be a noble and magnanimous idea to carry this merciful consideration still further and honor in me (though I may not deserve it) all the mestizo Indians and creoles of Peru so that on seeing a beginner receive the favor and grace of the wise and learned they would be encouraged to proceed with similar themes drawn from their own uncultivated geniuses."

The *Dialogues* and the *Florida* (or the greater part of it) were written before Garcilaso's departure from Montilla. His own material difficulties which followed his removal to Córdova inevitably sharpened his sympathy for the vicissitudes of his fellow Incas, and in the *Royal Commentaries* we find him gradually linking hands with them. If in Montilla he had identified himself with the great poet of his father's family, we now see him drawn steadily into the orbit of the Incas whose history he is rehearsing. Even while at Montilla he had kept in touch with the affairs of Peru, receiving not only letters and reports but also the visits of his former school fellows when they came to Spain. Shortly before he completed the manu-

script of the First Part, moreover, the surviving Incas in Peru asked him
to undertake a mission on their behalf. At a meeting held in Cuzco in
March 1603 they had empowered him to seek relief from Philip III for
the surviving members of the imperial caste of Peru, and they supplied
him with a genealogical tree "painted on a vara and a half of white China
taffeta" with a list of 567 names of surviving Incas. Immersed in the *Royal
Commentaries,* Garcilaso excused himself from this duty, though he expressed every sympathy with it—"I would willingly have devoted my life
to this, for it could not have been better employed."

But the existence of 567 petitioners steeled the Spanish government in
its determination not to admit the royal origin of the Incas; and though
Garcilaso seems to have come no nearer than this to engaging in political
activities on their behalf, he was to suffer the final humiliation of having
the proud title of *Royal Commentaries* suppressed by the Royal Council
from his Part Two, which finally appeared seven months after his death
under the innocuous guise of a *General History of Peru.*

The *Royal Commentaries* is not a political book but it is history inspired
with a social purpose, that of vindicating the intellectual capacity of the
Americans and so restoring the credit and revising the fortunes both of
his mother's race and of the new breed of mestizos to which Garcilaso
himself belonged. While the two peoples to which Garcilaso owed his
origin are both suitably exalted in his work, there can of course be little
reference to the new race, which was still growing to maturity in the
period he covers. After discoursing on the things brought to Peru by the
Spaniards, he does insert a chapter in which he explains what a mestizo
is, saying that many of them were ashamed of the word and preferred
the meaningless genteelism *montañés;* he urges them to wear proudly
the name bestowed on them by their fathers. These remarks are of particular interest in view of what had happened to the mixed race since Garcilaso's departure from Peru. He himself had been made to realize its uncertain future by his father's marriage and he expresses his disapproval
of the ousting of the mestizo by white women in a single pungent passage.
During the years that had followed his own dispossession his caste had
been steadily degraded in Peru, sinking in esteem and influence as it increased in numbers. Once the period of the civil wars was over, the royal
representatives in Peru began to give thought to the underlying problem
of the lack of homogeneity of Peruvian society. In particular, Don Francisco de Toledo, who arrived in Lima as viceroy in 1569, and who may
be said to have established viceregal power for 250 years, was disturbed

by the lack of social stability he found. The old Spanish conquerors were dying off and the mestizos were becoming the most numerous non-indigenous class. "As the land is such that men give themselves to the vice of sensuality," wrote Padre Bivero, "a great many mestizos are born, many of whom turn out badly, either because the mixture is not good, or because they are brought up badly among mulattos and Indians." And Toledo himself observed that the mestizos were regarded as intelligent and good soldiers, but they received no education and were often reared among their mother's people: they had neither rights nor duties and he urged the crown to give them some definite station.

It is against this background that we must set the Inca's prologue to Part Two, addressed "To the Indians, mestizos, and creoles of the kingdoms and provinces of the great and wealthy empire of Peru, from the Inca Garcilaso de la Vega, their brother, compatriot, and countryman, health and happiness." Although this recalls the political proclamations of a later age, Garcilaso is only concerned that those he addresses should prove their intellectual equality with the Spaniards: "there is no lack of ability among the native Indians," he asserts, "and there is *excess of capacity* among the mestizos, the sons of Indian women and Spaniards or Spanish women and Indians, and among the creoles, born and brought up there . . . and it is well that the old, political world should realize that the new (which it deems barbarous) is not and never had been so, except for lack of culture . . ."

In all this Garcilaso points to a better future for colonials of all races if they will vindicate themselves. But Toledo and his officials saw that if the dispossessed mestizos should make common cause with the Indians they might constitute a real danger to Spanish power. Far from favoring the policy indicated by Garcilaso, the viceroy's chief thought was to break down the last vestiges of Inca power and destroy their imperial legend. The oppressed Indians looked yearningly toward the independent Inca stronghold at Vilcabamba in the far north, and Toledo decided that it must be extinguished. He therefore sent a force to capture Túpac Amaru, brought him down from his fastness, and had him executed. Garcilaso gives a harrowing description of the scenes at his death in his Part Two, Book VIII, chs. xvi–xviii. Friends of the viceroy justify the deed on the ground of acts of banditry committed by the independent Indians, which Garcilaso minimizes or ignores. But the Incas never ceased to regard Túpac Amaru as a legitimate and independent ruler,[3] and Garcilaso, who saw the

---

[3] When Toledo instituted an enquiry in Cuzco into the nature and extent of the government of the Incas, pictures were produced to show the descent of the native kings,

Royal Commentaries of the Incas

execution through Indian eyes, was convinced that it was a judicial murder prompted by reasons of state, that "new doctrine" of which he speaks with such indignation. There is not the slightest ground, as has been insinuated, for supposing that Garcilaso was wreaking a tortuous plot against the viceroy's good name. But he was undoubtedly concerned to refute the evidence which Toledo had prepared and had sent to Spain to show that the Incas were not the "true rulers" of Peru, but only conquerors, like the Spaniards themselves.

This background helps to explain Garcilaso's sympathetic treatment of his mother's people and the civilization they had built up. He was not alone in his estimate of this civilization. In contrast to the evidence collected by Toledo's bureaucrats whose duty it was to minimize the achievements of the Incas, we may point to the will of Mancio Serra de Leguiçamo, who, as Garcilaso tells, was one of the early conquerors of Cuzco and received the gold disc from the temple of the Sun as his share in its loot. He lived to a ripe age and died in 1589. His testament is preceded by a surprising document addressed to Philip II in which he informs the monarch that he has wished for many years to unburden his conscience: his majesty should know

that we found these lands in such a state that there was not even a robber or a vicious or idle man, or adulterous or immoral woman: all such conduct was forbidden. Immoral persons could not exist and everyone had honest and profitable occupations. . . . Everything from the most important to the least was ordered and harmonized with great wisdom. The Incas were feared, obeyed, respected, and venerated by their subjects, who considered them to be most capable lords . . . We were only a small number of Spaniards when we undertook the conquest and I desire his majesty to understand why I have set down this account; it is to unburden my conscience and confess my guilt, for we have transformed the Indians who had such wisdom and committed so few crimes, excesses, or extravagances that the owner of 100,000 pesos of gold or silver would leave his door open placing a broom fixed to a bit of wood across the entrance to show that he was absent: this sign was enough to prevent anyone from entering or taking anything. Thus they scorned us when they saw among us thieves and men who incited their wives and daughters to sin . . . This king-

---

and the widow of the independent Sairi Túpac (whom the viceroy had married to a common soldier) protested that these showed the collaborator Don Carlos Inca in a more auspicious place than her own line. And when Toledo explained: "Don't you see that Don Carlos and his father served the king and your father and brother have been rebels and are still in the wilderness?" the offended princess replied: "You say my father and brother were traitors when they were not. If they have gone away it is because they were not given anything to live on, though they were lords of this kingdom, as you shall see . . ."

dom has fallen into such disorder . . . it has passed from one extreme to another. There was no evil: now there is almost no good . . .

This denunciation delivered by a Spaniard in the hour of death and framed probably by his priest, though evidently exaggerated, is utterly sincere; compared to it Garcilaso's praise of the Incas seems sober enough. But his reputation as an historian is so inextricably bound up with the question of the beneficence or tyranny of his mother's ancestors that it is impossible to attempt a judgment of his work without bringing this vast and vexed matter into the picture. Those who have praised or condemned Garcilaso have often done so less out of regard for his own merits than out of the judgment they have formed of the Inca empire. And this is, and must be, a variable standard. The almost passive acceptance of Spanish rule by Atahuallpa should not blind us to the fact that we are witnessing the clash of two conflicting, perhaps irreconcilable, forms of society: the ideals of the Incas were not the ideals of the Spaniards. Inca civilization was a collectivist one in which there was little room or need for individual conscience. Order was presumed to be the object of society. All the needs of the individual were taken care of by civil servants duly assigned for the purpose. There was no need for a passing Indian woman to attend to a crying child by the roadside because it was someone else's duty to do so. All power, all responsibility was assumed by a privileged administrative class. Liberty and ambition were unnecessary and unknown: we do not know if they were missed.

The Spaniards by contrast existed by a faith in the value of the individual conscience in the sight of God. Every Spaniard was a natural anarchist, and in Spain, as a nineteenth-century dictator remarked, "To govern is to resist." Nor were the unruly soldiers who came to Peru the choicest specimens of Spanish culture. The very history of the civil wars shows that they would only combine in the face of a dire threat to their interests and when the threat was removed they fell into disorder.

Like Mancio Serra de Leguiçamo on his deathbed, Garcilaso preferred the order and stability of Inca society to the discord and strife brought in by the Spaniards. Indeed what is remarkable is not that he should have espoused the Inca cause, but that he should have written with such dispreoccupation and clarity. He displays no malice: the unworthy are usually forgiven or forgotten. If on the other hand Garcilaso chides those chroniclers who have omitted to rescue from oblivion the names of those who have done well, or to establish their birthplaces so that their compatriots may take pride in their deeds, he is usually ready to suppress the name of the perpetrator of a reprehensible action or to turn aside from a matter that is "odious." Even Francisco de Carvajal's cruelties, he declares, are exaggerated by the Spanish historians, though he does not seek to palliate them. He is prepared to quote the versions of those who have been on either side in any affair, but he does not alter his own position: he cites with approval Carvajal's condemnation of the "shuttlers" who changed sides as they saw fit.

Despite his acute sensibility, Garcilaso was a man of equable, conciliatory, and philosophical temperament. He had moreover trained his mind with a wide range of historical reading. His diffidence about his early education and his anxiety to prove the intellectual capacity of his race should not obscure the fact that he was no ordinary "Antarctic Indian." His works, no less than the catalogue of his library, show that he knew his Thucydides, Polybius, Plutarch, Tacitus, Quintus Curtius, Suetonius, Caesar, and Sallust. He was also versed in modern history. In addition to the chroniclers of Castile and the Indies, he knew Guicciardini's Italy, Pandolfo Collennucci's Naples, and Andrea Fulvo's antiquities of Rome.

But if he found inspiration in the great classical historians, his dispassionate approach to the problems of Peruvian history seems to be more directly derived from the temperate atmosphere of Andalusia in which he lived. In the small towns as well as the great cities of Southern Spain, Antonio de Nebrija, "the father of all good Latinity in Spain," as Garcilaso calls him, had left a school of patient and erudite antiquarians. These are the *"curiosos"* to whom the Inca dedicates his remarks from time to time, craving the indulgence of those who are not *"curiosos."* Not a few of these antiquarians have recognized Garcilaso's interest and assistance, and it is curious that many of them were, like himself, men whose erudition is accompanied by an unusual intensity of passion. Ambrosio de Morales had had himself castrated like Origen in order to avoid the temptations of the flesh. Francisco Fernández de Rota, who refers to Garcilaso as "a man of great nobility devoted to the study of good letters," had killed a man in his youth and been condemned to death by his own father, the corregidor of Toledo. Was not Bernardo de Aldrete, to whom the Inca supplied information about his native Peru, involved in the tense polemic arising out of the Lead Books? Did not Don Diego Hurtado de Mendoza compose his *De la Guerra de Granada* in exile for an act of passion committed in the royal palace itself? Was any man of erudition more passionate than the master of Cordovese letters, the great Góngora himself, some of whose poems contain hints of conversations about Peru?

It is indeed to this gallery of writers that Garcilaso belongs, and it is proper that his remains should lie in the cathedral-mosque that represents the greatest material achievement of Andalusian civilization. Yet his spirit belongs to Peru; and as we turn the pages of his long and discursive history we are conscious of listening to a new voice, that "reflection of the soul of the conquered races," and we become aware that the Spanish language has now transcended the limitations of European culture and at last presented a vehicle of expression to peoples who had hitherto found only crude, if elaborate means of staving off the great oblivion around us all.

HAROLD V. LIVERMORE

CONTENTS

Book Two

BOOK THREE

BOOK FOUR

Book Five

Book Six

BOOK SEVEN

BOOK NINE

MAPS

PART ONE *of the* ROYAL COMMENTARIES

which treat[s] of the origin of the Incas, the former kings of Peru, their idolatry, laws, and government in peace and war, and of their lives and conquests, and everything relating to that empire and its society before the arrival of the Spaniards.

Written by the Inca Garcilaso de la Vega, a native of Cuzco, and a captain in His Majesty's service.

Dedicated to the Most Serene Princess, the Lady Catarina of Portugal, Duchess of Braganza, etc.

With licence of the Holy Inquisition, and ordinary
and royal authorization.
With licence of the Holy Inquisition, and ordinary and royal authorization.

In Lisbon, at the press of Pedro Crasbeeck, in the year 1609

To the Most Serene Princess,
The Lady Catarina of Portugal, Duchess of Braganza, etc.

THE COMMON PRACTICE of ancient and modern authors—who always endeavor to dedicate their works, the fruits of their genius, to generous monarchs and powerful kings and princes so that with the countenance and protection of such patrons they may be favored by the virtuous and spared the calumnies of the malicious—has emboldened me, most Serene Princess, to imitate their example and dedicate these *Commentaries* to Your Highness, moved by Your Highness' exalted station and by your generosity toward those who place themselves under your royal protection. Your exalted station is known throughout the world, not only in Europe, but even in the remotest parts of the east, west, north, and south, where those glorious princes, Your Highness' ancestors, have planted the standard of our salvation and that of their own glory at so great a cost in blood and lives, as is well known. Your Highness' generosity is patent to all, since you are the daughter and descendant of the illustrious kings and princes of Portugal; and though you yourself may not prize this merit highly, when the enamel of such heroic virtues covers the gold of such high birth it should be greatly esteemed. For when we behold the great grace with which our Lord God has enriched Your Highness' soul, we find that it exceeds those natural qualities of piety and virtue of which the whole world speaks with admiration, however much Your Highness modestly withdraws them. I would say more of these virtues, without any taint of flattery, did not Your Highness equally abhor praise of them and desire silence about them. As to Your Highness' favor to all those in Portugal and from abroad who have sought the honor of your royal patronage, it is proclaimed by so many tongues that neither they nor the recipients of favors at your royal hands can be numbered. Wherefore I hope to receive the greater protection for these books of mine: they need your countenance and favor the more as their and my deserts are less. I confess my boldness is much and my service very little, though my wish to serve is great. My will I offer too, most ready to be of service in case it should be found worthy to serve Your Highness, whose royal person and house may Our Lord guard and increase. Amen. Amen.

The Inca Garcilaso de la Vega

Preface to the Reader

THOUGH THERE HAVE BEEN learned Spaniards who have written accounts of the states of the New World, such as those of Mexico and Peru and the other kingdoms of the heathens, they have not described these realms so fully as they might have done. This I have remarked particularly in what I have seen written about Peru, concerning which, as a native of the city of Cuzco, which was formerly the Rome of that empire, I have fuller and more accurate information than that provided by previous writers. It is true that these have dealt with many of the very remarkable achievements of that empire, but they have set them down so briefly that, owing to the manner in which they are told, I am scarcely able to understand even such matters as are well known to me. For this reason, impelled by my natural love for my native country, I have undertaken the task of writing these *Commentaries,* in which everything in the Peruvian empire before the arrival of the Spaniards is clearly and distinctly set down, from the rites of their vain religion to the government of their kings in time of peace and war, and all else that can be told of these Indians, from the highest affairs of the royal crown to the humblest duties of its vassals. I write only of the empire of the Incas, and do not deal with other monarchies, about which I can claim no similar knowledge. In the course of my history I shall affirm its truthfulness and shall set down no important circumstances without quoting the authority of Spanish historians who may have touched upon it in part or as a whole. For my purpose is not to gainsay them, but to furnish a commentary and gloss, and to interpret many Indian expressions which they, as strangers to that tongue, have rendered inappropriately. This will be fully seen in the course of my history, which I commend to the piety of those who may peruse it, with no other interest than to be of service to Christendom and to inspire gratitude to Our Lord Jesus Christ and the Virgin Mary His mother, by whose merits and intercession the Eternal Majesty has deigned to draw so many great peoples out of the pit of idolatry and bring them into the bosom of His Roman Catholic Church, our mother and lady. I trust that it will be received in the same spirit as I offer it, for this is the return my intention deserves, even though the work may not. I am still writing two other books about the events that took place in my land among the Spaniards, down to the year 1560 when I left it. I hope to see them finished, and to make the same offering of them as I do of these. Our Lord, etc.

Notes on the General Language
of the Indians of Peru

FOR THE BETTER UNDERSTANDING of what, with divine aid, we shall write in this history, it will be well to give some notes on the general language of the Indians of Peru, many words of which we shall quote. The first is that there are three different ways of pronouncing some of the syllables. They are quite different from the pronunciation in Spanish, and the differences of pronunciation give different meanings to the same word. Certain syllables are pronounced on the lips, others on the palate, and others in the lower part of the throat, as we shall show later by examples as they occur. To accentuate the words it must be noticed that the stress almost always falls on the penultimate syllable, rarely on the antepenultimate, and never at all on the last syllable. This does not contradict those who say that words of barbarous languages should be stressed on the last syllable: they say this because they do not know the language. It is also to be noted that in the general language of Cuzco (of which it is my purpose to speak, rather than of the local pronunciations of each province, which are innumerable), the following letters are lacking: *b, d, f, g, jota.* There is no single *l*, only double *ll*; on the other hand, there is no double *rr* at the beginning of words or in the middle: it is always pronounced single. There is no *x*; so that in all six letters of the Spanish ABC's are missing, and we might say eight if we include single *l* and double *rr*. The Spaniards add these letters to the detriment and corruption of the language; and as the Indians do not have them, they usually mispronounce Spanish words where they occur. To avoid further corruption, I may be permitted, since I am an Indian, to write like an Indian in this history, using the letters that should be used in these words. Let none who read take exception to this novelty in opposition to the incorrect usage that is usually adopted: they should rather be glad to be able to read the words written correctly and with purity. As I have to quote much from Spanish historians in support of what I say, I shall copy their words as they write them with their corruptions; and I must warn the reader that it does not seem to me inconsistent to write the letters I have mentioned which do not appear in the Indian language, since I only do so to quote faithfully what the Spanish author has written.

It is also noteworthy that there is no plural number in the general language, though there are particles that indicate plurality. The singular is used for both numbers. If I put any Indian word in the plural, it will be a Spanish corruption used to keep the agreement of words, for it would sound wrong to write Indian words in the singular and Spanish adjectives or relatives in the plural. In many other respects the language differs from Castilian, Italian, and Latin. These points will be noted by learned mestizos and creoles, since the language is their own. For my part, it is sufficient that I point out for them from Spain the principles of their language, so that they may maintain its purity, for it is certainly a great pity that so elegant a language should be lost or spoilt, especially as the fathers of the Holy Society of Jesus, as well as those of other orders, have worked a great deal at it so as to speak it well, and have greatly benefited the instruction of the Indians by their good example, which is what matters most.

It must also be noted that the word *vecino* in Peru is taken to mean a Spaniard who has an allocation of Indians, and this is the sense in which it is intended whenever it occurs in our history. It should also be understood that in my time, which was until 1560, and for twenty years after, there was no coined money in the country. In its place Spaniards bought and sold by weighing gold and silver in marks and ounces, and spoke of pesos or castilians in Peru as they speak of ducats in Spain. Each peso of silver or gold, consisting of pure metal, was worth 450 maravedis, so that to turn pesos into Castilian ducats, one reckons five pesos as six ducats. This is mentioned to avoid confusion in counting in pesos and ducats in this history. There was a great difference in quantity between the silver peso and the gold peso, as there is in Spain, but the value was the same. In changing gold for silver they paid a rate of interest of so many per cent. Also in changing assayed silver for the silver called "current," or unassayed, interest was paid.

The word *galpón* is not found in the general language of Peru. It must come from the Windward Islands. The Spaniards have introduced it into their language with many others that will be noted in the course of this history. It means a large hall. The Inca kings had them big enough to serve for festivities when the weather was too rainy to hold these out of doors. This will suffice for preliminary notices.

BOOK
ONE *of the*
FIRST PART

which treats of the discovery of the New World; the
derivation of the name Peru, and idolatry and way of life
of the inhabitants before the Incas; the origin of the
Incas; the life of the first Inca; what he did with his
first vassals, and the meaning of the royal titles.

It contains thirty-six chapters.

CHAPTER I

*Whether there are many worlds; it
also treats of the five zones.*

AVING to treat of the New World, or the best and noblest
parts of it, the kingdoms and provinces of the empire
known as Peru, of whose antiquities and of the origin of
whose kings we propose to write, it seems proper to follow
the usual custom of writers and discuss here at the beginning whether there is only one world or many, whether it is round or flat,
whether it is all habitable or only the temperate zones, whether there is
a way from one temperate zone to the other, whether there are antipodes
and what they correspond to, and similar matters which the old philosophers treated very fully and curiously and the moderns do not fail to debate and describe, each following the opinion that pleases him best. But
as this is not my main purpose, and as experience has, since the discovery
of the so-called New World, undeceived us about most of these doubts,
we will pass them briefly by and go on to another part, whose conclusion
I fear I shall never reach. But trusting in God's infinite mercy, I will say
at the outset that there is only one world, and although we speak of the
Old World and the New, this is because the latter was lately discovered
by us, and not because there are two. And to those who still imagine there
are many, there is no answer except that they may remain in their heretical
imaginings till they are undeceived in hell. And those who doubt (if anyone does) if it is flat or round may be satisfied by the testimony of those
who have gone round it, or the most part of it, such as those who were
on the ship *Victoria* and others who have circumnavigated it since. And
about whether the heavens are flat or round an answer can be given in
the words of the royal prophet: *"Extendens coelum sicut pellem,"* in
which he reveals the form and likeness of the work, using the one as a
similitude for the other, and saying "thou hast stretched out the heavens
like a skin," meaning that they were wrapped round about this great
mass of the four elements, even as God covered round with skin the body
of an animal, not only its main parts but all the rest, however small. And

those who say that of the five parts of the world called zones only the
two temperate are habitable and that the midmost is excessively hot and
the two outermost too cold to be habitable, and that it is impossible to pass
from one habitable zone to the other because of the great heat of the intervening zone, may be assured that I myself was born in the torrid zone,
in Cuzco, and was brought up there till I was twenty, and that I have
been in the temperate zone to the south beyond the Tropic of Capricorn,
at the extreme end of Charcas where the Chichas are, and to reach this
other northern temperate zone, where I am writing these words, I passed
through the torrid zone from one side to the other and was three full days
under the equinoctial line where they say it passes perpendicularly at Cape
Passau, so that I can assert that the torrid zone is habitable as well as the
temperate. I wish I could speak as an eyewitness of the cold zones, as I
do of the other three. This I must leave to those who know them better
than I. But I dare declare to those who say that they are too cold to be
habitable that I hold the contrary view, that they are as habitable as the
rest, for it cannot reasonably be imagined, much less believed, that God
should have made so much of the world useless, when He created the
whole to be inhabited by man, and the ancients are wrong about the cold
zones just as they were about the torrid zone being uninhabitable by reason of its heat. It is much more credible that the Lord, as a wise and powerful father, and Nature, like a universal and compassionate mother,
should have tempered the cold with warmth just as they have tempered
the excessive heat of the torrid zone with much snow, springs, rivers, and
lakes, as there are in Peru. These things temper the torrid zone and produce many variations of climate. Some tend to greater and greater heat,
until there are regions so low and therefore so hot that they are thereby
almost uninhabitable, as the ancients said. Other regions incline to greater
and greater cold, till they rise to points so high that they also are rendered
uninhabitable by the coldness of the perpetual snow upon them. This is
contrary to what the philosophers said of the torrid zone, for they never
imagined there could be snow in it, yet there is in fact perpetual snow on
the very equinoctial line and it never diminishes at all, at least on the
great cordillera, though it may on the slopes and passes. So that in the
torrid zone, or the part of it covered by Peru, heat or cold does not depend
on distance, or how near to or how far from the equator a region is, but
on differences of altitude or lowness in the same region and over a very
small distance, as I shall relate in greater detail presently. I say therefore
that this comparison suggests that the cold zones are also tempered and
habitable, as many sound writers have held, though not from personal

knowledge or experience. It is enough that God Himself has given us to understand so, for when He created man He said: "Increase and multiply, and replenish the earth and subdue it." From this we see that it is habitable, since otherwise it could not be subdued nor filled with dwellings. I hope that in His omnipotence He will in His good time reveal these secrets (as He revealed the New World) to the greater confusion and dismay of those bold spirits who wish with their natural philosophies and human understanding to confine the power and wisdom of God to doing His works only as they imagine them, when there is as much difference between their knowledge and His as between the finite and the infinite. And so on.

CHAPTER II

Whether there are antipodes.

ON THE SUBJECT of whether there are antipodes or not, it can be stated that, because the world is round (as is notorious), it is certain that there are. However, my own opinion is that since the lower world is not wholly discovered, there is no certain way of knowing which provinces are the antipodes of which others, as some say. All this can be verified more easily from the heavens than the earth, as the poles are opposite one another, and the orient is opposite the occident at any point on the equinoctial. Nor do we know for sure how all the different peoples of differing tongues and customs that have been found in the New World passed there. If we suppose they went by sea in ships, the problem arises of how the animals got there and how and why they were embarked, for some of them are harmful rather than useful. If we suppose they could have gone by land, there arise greater problems: if they took the domestic animals they have, why did they not take others that remained behind and have been introduced since? If the answer is that they could not carry them all, how is it they did not leave behind some of the kinds they took? The same may be said of the crops, vegetables, and fruits, which differ so greatly from those here that the land is rightly called a New World, as it really is in everything, in the wild and domestic animals, the food, the men, who are usually smooth-cheeked and beardless. And since it is time

wasted to seek answers to questions so obscure, I shall leave them, especially because I am less competent than others to enquire into them. I
shall deal only with the origin of the Inca kings and their succession,
their conquests, laws, and government in peace and war. But before dealing with them it will be as well to say how the New World was discovered, and to treat of Peru in particular.

CHAPTER III

How the New World was discovered.

IN ABOUT 1484, to within a year or so, a pilot born in Huelva, in the
county of Niebla, called Alonso Sánchez de Huelva, had a small
ship with which he traded by sea and used to carry wares from Spain to
the Canaries, where he sold them profitably and brought back to the island
products from the Canaries and carried them to the isle of Madeira, thence
returning to Spain laden with sugar and conserves. While pursuing this
triangular trade and crossing from the Canaries to Madeira, he ran into
a squall so heavy and tempestuous that he could not withstand it and was
obliged to run before it for twenty-eight or twenty-nine days without
knowing his whereabouts, since during the whole time he was unable to
take an altitude either by the sun or by the north star. The crew suffered
great hardships in the storm, for they could neither eat nor sleep. After
this lengthy period the wind fell and they found themselves near an island. It is not known for sure which it was, but it is suspected that it was
the one now called Santo Domingo. However, it is worthy of note that
the wind that drove the ship so furiously and violently could only have
been the *solano,* or easterly—for the isle of Santo Domingo is to the west-
ward of the Canaries—and this wind usually appeases rather than raises
storms on that voyage. But when the Almighty Lord wishes to show His
great mercy, He mysteriously draws the most necessary effects from opposite causes, as He drew water from the rock and sight for the blind
from the mud placed on his eyes, so that these may clearly be seen to be
the works of divine mercy and goodness. He also displayed His clemency
in sending the true light of His Gospel to all the New World which had
such need of it, since its peoples lived, or rather perished, in the darkness

of the most barbarous and bestial paganism and idolatry, as we shall see in the course of our story.

The pilot leapt ashore, took the altitude and wrote a detailed account of all he saw and all that befell him at sea on the outward and inward voyages, and having taken on board water and fuel, he returned, sailing blind and without knowing the way any more than when he had come, so that he took much longer than was necessary. And because of the delay they ran out of water and supplies. For this reason and because of the great privations they had suffered on both journeys, they began to sicken and die, and of seventeen men who left Spain, no more than five reached Terceira, among them the pilot Alonso Sánchez de Huelva. They stayed at the house of the famous Genoese Christopher Columbus, because they knew he was a great pilot and cosmographer and made seamen's charts. He received them kindly and entertained them lavishly so as to learn the things that had happened on the long and strange voyage they said they had undergone. But they arrived so enfeebled by hardships that Christopher Columbus could not restore them to health despite his attentions, and they all died in his house, leaving him the heir to the hardships that had caused their death. The great Columbus accepted the challenge with such courage and zeal that, having suffered others as great and greater (for they lasted longer), he succeeded in the undertaking that gave the New World and its riches to Spain, as was emblazoned on his arms:

> To Castile and to León
> A New World was given by Colón.

Anyone who wishes to learn the great deeds of this hero should read the *General History of the Indies* written by Francisco López de Gómara. There he will find them, though in abbreviated form. But this very conquest and discovery is the work that gives greatest praise and renown to this most famous among famous men. I wished to add these few lines because they were lacking in what the old historian wrote. He wrote far away from the scene of events, and got his information from those who came and went, and told him imperfectly many things that had happened, but I heard them in my own country from my father and his contemporaries, whose favorite and usual conversation was to repeat the stirring and notable deeds performed in their conquests. They recounted then what I have just said and other matters that I shall repeat presently; for as they had known many of the first discoverers and conquerors of the New World, they heard from them the whole story of these things; and I, as I have said, heard them from my elders, though, being only a boy, with scant attention. If I had listened more closely, I would now be able to set down many other remarkable things very needful to this history. I will relate those that have stayed in my memory and regret those I have lost. The Reverend Father José de Acosta also touches on this story of the discovery of the New World and regrets not being able to give it in full, for his Paternity also wanted a part of this narrative, like some modern authors, since the old conquistadors had already disappeared when he visited those parts. In his Book I, ch. xix, he says:

Having shown that there is no ground for thinking that the earliest dwellers in the Indies reached them by deliberately sailing there, it follows that if they went by sea it would have been by chance and under stress of weather that they got to the Indies, and this, despite the immensity of the Ocean Sea, is not incredible. For this happened in the discovery of our own times, when that seaman whose name is still unknown (so that so great a venture shall not be attributed to any other than God), having reached the New World by reason of a terrible and persistent storm, repaid the generous hospitality of Christopher Columbus by imparting the great news to him. Thus it was rendered possible,

etc. This, word for word, is from Padre Acosta, who is thus seen to have found our story in Peru, if not in full, at least in its essentials. This was the origin and first beginning of the discovery of the New World, and the honor of it belongs to the little town of Huelva, which may boast of having produced a son whose narrative inspired such faith in Christopher Columbus that he persisted in his quest and promised things never seen or heard, but like a wise man keeping the secret of them, though he did describe them in confidence to certain persons who enjoyed great authority with the Catholic monarchs and who helped him to press his undertaking through. But if it had not been for the news that Alonso Sánchez de Huelva gave him he could not have promised so much and so exactly what he did promise merely out of his own imagination as a cosmographer, nor have seen the undertaking of the discovery through so rapidly, for the same author tells us that Columbus took only sixty-eight days on the voyage to the island of Guanatianico, including a few days at Gomera to take in supplies. If he had not known from Alonso Sánchez's narrative what direction to take in so vast a sea, it would almost have been a miracle to have arrived there in so little time.

CHAPTER IV

The derivation of the name Peru.

As WE HAVE to deal with Peru, we may properly say here how this name was derived, since the Indians do not have it in their language. In 1513 Vasco Núñez de Balboa, a gentleman born at Jerez de Badajoz, discovered the Southern Sea, and was the first Spaniard to set eyes upon it. He was granted by the Catholic monarchs the title of *adelantado* of this sea with the right to conquer and govern any kingdoms he might discover on its shores, and in the few years he had to live after receiving this honor—until his own father-in-law, Governor Pedro Arias de Ávila, instead of rewarding him with the many favors his deeds had merited, had him beheaded—this knight strove to discover and know what was the land running from Panama southwards and what it was called. For this purpose he had three or four ships built, which he sent one by one at various seasons of the year to reconnoiter that coast while he made the necessary preparations for its discovery and conquest. These ships made as many investigations as they could and returned with reports of many lands on those shores.

One ship went further than the rest and passed the equinoctial line southwards; and not far beyond it, while hugging the shore—which was the method of navigation then employed on this voyage—sighted an Indian fishing at the mouth of one of the numerous rivers that flow from that land into the sea. The Spaniards on the ship landed four of their number who were good swimmers and runners as quickly as possible some distance from where the Indian was, so that he should not escape by land or water. Having taken this precaution, they passed before the Indian in the ship so that he fixed his gaze on it, unmindful of the trap that had been prepared for him. Seeing on the sea so strange a sight as a ship with all sail set, something never before seen on that shore, he was lost in amazement and stood astonished and bewildered, wondering what the thing he beheld on the sea before him could be. He was so distracted and absorbed in this thought that those who were to capture him had seized him before he perceived their approach, and so they took him on board with general rejoicings and celebrations.

Having petted him to help him overcome his fear at the sight of their beards and unaccustomed clothes, the Spaniards asked him by signs and words what land it was and what it was called. The Indian understood that they were asking him something from the gestures and grimaces they were making with hands and face, as if they were addressing a dumb man, but he did not understand what they were asking, so he told them what he thought they wanted to know. Thus fearing they might do him harm, he quickly replied by giving his own name, saying, *"Berú,"* and adding another, *"pelú."* He meant: "If you're asking my name, I'm called *Berú,* and if you're asking where I was, I was in the river." The word *pelú* is a noun in the language of that province and means "a river" in general, as we shall see from a reliable author. To a like question the Indian in our history of Florida answered by giving the name of his master saying, *"Breços"* and *"Bredos"* (Book VI, ch. xv, where I inserted this passage referring to that incident: I now remove it to put it in its proper place). The Christians understood what they wanted to understand, supposing the Indian had understood them and had replied as pat as if they had been conversing in Spanish; and from that time, which was 1515 or 1516, they called that rich and great empire *Peru,* corrupting both words, as the Spaniards corrupt almost all the words they take from the Indian language of that land. Thus if they took the Indian's name, *Berú,* they altered the *B* to a *P,* and if they took the word *pelú,* "a river," they altered the *l* to an *r,* and in one way or another they turned it into *Peru.* Others, more modern, and priding themselves on their refinement, alter two letters and write *Pirú* in their histories. The older historians such as Pedro de Cieza de León and the treasurer Agustín de Zárate, and Francisco López de Gómara, and Diego Fernández de Palencia, and also the Reverend Father Jerónimo Román, though more modern, all write *Peru* and not *Pirú.* And as the place where this happened chanced to be in the confines of the land the Inca kings had conquered and subjected to their rule, they called everything from there onwards *Peru,* that is from the district of Quito to the Charcas, or the main part over which they reigned. The region is over seven hundred leagues in length, though their empire reached as far as Chile, which is five hundred leagues beyond and is another most rich and fertile kingdom.

CHAPTER V

Authorities in confirmation of the name Peru.

THIS WAS THE origin and beginning of the name *Peru,* so famous in the world, and rightly famous, since it has filled the whole world with gold and silver, pearls and precious stones. But because it was imposed by accident and is not one they have themselves given, the native Indians of Peru, though it is seventy-two years since it was conquered, have not taken this word into their mouths. Through their dealings with the Spaniards they now know of course what it means, but they do not use it because they had no generic name in their language to cover collectively the kingdoms and provinces that their native kings ruled over, such as Spain, Italy, or France, which include many provinces. They could call each province by its proper name, as will be amply shown in the course of this history, but they had no word that signified the whole kingdom together. They used to call it *Tahuantinsuyu,* meaning "the four quarters of the world." The name *Berú,* as has been seen, was the proper name of an Indian and is one used by the Yunca Indians of the plains and seacoast, but not by those of the mountains or in the general language. As there are in Spain names and surnames that show which province they come from, so there were among the Indians of Peru. That *Peru* was a name imposed by the Spaniards and that it did not occur in the general speech of the Indians, we are given to understand by Pedro de Cieza de León in his Part III, ch. iii. Speaking of the isle called Gorgona, he says: "The Marquis Don Francisco Pizarro was there with thirteen Spanish Christians, his shipmates, who were the discoverers of this land we call Peru," etc. In ch. xiii he says: "Therefore from Quito, where what we call Peru really begins, it will be necessary" etc. In ch. xviii he says: "From the accounts the Indians of Cuzco give us, we gather that there was formerly great disorder in all the provinces of the kingdom we call Peru," etc. So many repetitions of "we call" shows that the Spaniards called it so, for he only uses it when referring to them, and that the Indians had not the word in their language, to which I, as an Inca, can testify. Padre Acosta says the same and much more in Book I of his *Natural History of the Indies* (ch. xiii), where, speaking on this subject, he tells us:

It has been the usual custom in these discoveries in the New World to give names to lands and harbors on the first occasion that offered, and this we understand to have happened in the naming of the kingdom of Peru. It is the belief here that they gave the name *Peru* to all this land from a river on which the Spaniards chanced at the very outset, called by the inhabitants *Pirú*. This is borne out by the fact that the native Indians of Peru neither use nor know of such a name for their country,

etc. The prestige of this authority will suffice to confound the novelties that have since been invented about the name. As the river the Spaniards call *Peru* is in the same place and quite near the equator, I dare say that the capture of the Indian took place there, and both river and country are called by his proper name, *Berú,* or that the word *pelú,* which was common to all rivers, was turned into a special name for this river by the Spaniards, who called it in particular the river *Peru.*

Francisco López de Gómara in his *General History of the Indies,* speaking of the discovery of Yucatán (ch. lii), gives two derivations of names very similar to the one of Peru. They are indeed so similar that I have extracted what he says, as follows:

Francisco Hernández de Córdoba then departed, and either because the weather prevented him from going beyond this cape or because of his desire to explore, he reached land untrodden by and unknown to our compatriots, where there are saltpans at a point called Cape of Women, so named because there were stone towers there with steps and chapels roofed with wood and straw, in which many idols resembling women were neatly set out. The Spaniards wondered to see stone buildings, which they had hitherto not observed, and that the people should dress so well and spendidly, for they had shifts and cloaks of white and colored cotton, plumes, bracelets, brooches, and jewels of gold and silver, and the women had their breasts and heads covered. He did not stop there, but went on to another point [now] called *Cotoche,* where there were some fishermen, who fled inland in terror and thinking that they were asked for the village answered, *"cotohe, cotohe"* (which means "a house"). Thus the cape continued to be called *Cotoche.* A little further on they found some men, who, on being asked the name of a large village nearby, said, *"Tectetán, tectetán,"* meaning "I don't understand you." The Spaniards thought it was the name of the place, and corrupting the word, always called it *Yucatán,* a name that will never cease to be used.

This extract is taken word for word from López de Gómara. It proves that what happened in Peru happened in many other parts of the Indies, and that the first words uttered by the Indians when they were spoken to and asked the names of the land, were applied to them, since the true meaning of the words was not understood and it was imagined that the Indians were answering the questions correctly just as if they and the Spaniards spoke the same tongue. The same error was committed in a great many matters in the New World, and particularly in our empire of Peru, as can be observed in many passages of this history.

CHAPTER VI

What a certain author says about the name Peru.

APART FROM what Cieza de León, Padre José de Acosta, and López de Gómara say about the name *Peru,* I have the authority of another illustrious writer, a member of the Holy Society of Jesus, called Padre Blas Valera, who wrote a history of the Peruvian empire in very elegant Latin, and could have written it in many other languages, for he had that gift. But to the misfortune of my country, which did not deserve perhaps to be written about by so noble a hand, his papers were lost in the sack and destruction of Cádiz by the English in 1596, and he died soon after. I received the remains of the papers which were saved from the pillage, and they caused me great regret and grief at the loss of the rest, the importance of which can be deduced from what survived. What is missing is the greater and better part. I was presented with the papers by Padre Pedro Maldonado de Saavedra, of Seville, of the same society, who in the present year of 1600 reads Scripture in this city of Córdova. Speaking of the name *Peru,* he says in his polished Latin, the following, which I, as an Indian, have translated into my rough romance:

The kingdom of Peru, illustrious, famous, vast, contains a great quantity of gold, silver, and other rich metals, from the abundance of which arose the saying, "he possesses Peru," to say that a man is rich. This name was newly imposed on the empire of the Incas by the Spaniards, and imposed inappropriately and by chance. It is unknown to the Indians, who regard it as barbarous and so detest it that none of them will use it: only the Spaniards do so. Its recent imposition does not refer to wealth or to any great event. Its use with reference to riches is as new as the imposition of the name and has proceeded from the good fortune of events there. The name *pelú* is a word that means "a river" among the barbarous Indians who dwell between Panama and Guayaquil. It is

also the name of a certain island, *Pelua* or *Pelú*. As the first Spanish conquerors
sailed from Panama and reached these parts before the rest, the name *Peru* or
Pelua pleased them so much that they applied it to anything they found as
though it had meant some thing grand and noteworthy, and so they called the
empire of the Incas *Peru*. There were many who disliked the name, and they
called the country *New Castile*. The two names were imposed on that great
kingdom, and are commonly used by the royal scribes and ecclesiastical notaries,
though in Europe and in the other kingdoms they prefer the name *Peru* to the
other. Many also affirm that this word is derived from *pirua*, a term of the
Quechuas of Cuzco, meaning a granary for storing crops. I am quite willing to
accept this opinion because the Indians of that kingdom do have a great many
granaries for storing their crops. It was easy therefore for the Spaniards to use
this foreign word and say *Pirú*, leaving off the final vowel and transferring the
stress to the last syllable. This noun with its two meanings was adopted by the
first conquerors as the name of the empire they had conquered, and I shall use
it also in the two forms, *Peru* and *Pirú*, indifferently. Nor should the introduction of this new word be rejected on the ground that it was usurped without
rhyme or reason, since the Spaniards found no other generic native name applicable to the whole region. Before the Inca rule each province had its own
name, such as Charca, Colla, Cuzco, Rímac, Quitu, and many others, without
regard for or reference to other regions; but after the Incas had subjected them
all to their empire, they gave them names according to the order of their conquest and as they submitted and acknowledge vassalage; and finally they were
called *Tahuantinsuyu*, or "the four parts of the kingdom," or *Incap Rúnam*,
"vassals of the Inca." The Spaniards, observing the variety and confusion of
these names, wisely called it *Peru* or *New Castile*,

etc.

This is from Blas Valera, who, like Padre Acosta, says the name was
given by the Spaniards and that the Indians did not have it in their language. Having thus quoted Padre Blas Valera's words, I should add that
it is more likely that the name *Peru* should have originated from the
proper name *Berú* or the noun *pelú,* meaning "a river" in the speech of
that province, than that it should come from the word *birua,* "a granary."
For, as has been said, the name was given by the followers of Vasco Núñez
de Balboa, who did not go inland where they would come across the word
pirua, and not by the conquerors of Peru. Fifteen years before the latter
set out on their conquest, the Spaniards living in Panama called all the
coast south of the equator *Peru.* We are assured of this by Francisco
López de Gómara in his *History of the Indies* (ch. cx), where he says:
"Some say Balboa heard reports of how the land of Peru had gold and
emeralds; whether this be true or not, it is certain that Peru had great

fame in Panama when Pizarro and Almagro prepared to go there," etc. This is from López de Gómara, whence it is clear that the application of the name *Peru* occurred long before the departure of the conquerors who won the empire.

CHAPTER VII

Of other derivations of new names.

S O THAT THE derivation of the name *Peru* shall not stand alone, we will deal with others given before it. Although by so doing we anticipate somewhat, it will not be amiss that they should already have been mentioned when we come to them in their places. The first shall be *Puerto Viejo,* because it is close to the place whence the name *Peru* originated. It is necessary to explain that the voyage from Panama to Lima is performed with great difficulty owing to the numerous currents and the southerly winds that constantly blow on that coast. Because of this the ships making the journey were forced to leave port and sail thirty or forty leagues out to sea, and return to the coast on the opposite tack, and so to proceed up the coast,[1] always sailing on a bowline. It often happened that when a ship did not sail well on a bowline, it fell back beyond the point it had started from, until the English sailor, Francis Drake, entering by the Straits of Magellan in 1579, showed a better way of navigating by lengthening the tacks to two or three-hundred leagues out to sea. The pilots had never dared to do this before, since they were frightened and persuaded that if they went one hundred leagues out to sea, they would find great calms, and so as not to run into these they dared not go far out, though there was neither why nor wherefore to all this except their own imaginings. Because of this fear our ship might have been lost when I came to Spain: a squall brought us under the island called Gorgona, where we feared to perish because we could not get out of that dangerous gulf.

A ship was navigating after the fashion we have mentioned in the early days of the conquest of Peru, and having put out to sea from that port six

---

[1] As Garcilaso explains in the Second Part of this work, Peruvians used the term "up the coast" to refer to the trip from Panama to Peru because the whole trip had to be made sailing against the current. The voyage "down the coast" to Panama, with the current, was a much easier trip.

or seven times only to return always to the same point because she could not get forward, one of those on board, vexed because they could not work to windward, exclaimed: "Here is our old port again!", and so it was called "Old Port."

Santa Elena Point, which is near this port, was so called because it was sighted on the saint's day. Another name was adopted in a similar way long before these. This was in 1500, when a ship whose captain is unknown, but may have been either Vicente Yáñez Pinzón or Juan de Solís—both of them very fortunate in the discovery of new lands—was sailing in search of new regions (and Spaniards thought of nothing else in those days) and was looking for a mainland: till then all that had been discovered was the islands now called the Windwards. Sighting the high hill called Capira, above the city of Nombre de Dios, a sailor in the crow's-nest cried: "In the name of God, I can see the mainland, my mates"—hoping for a reward for the good news. Thus the city founded there was called "Nombre de Dios," and the coast "Tierra Firme," "the main." Nowhere else is called "Tierra Firme," though it may well be so, except that spot, Nombre de Dios, where the name has stuck. Ten years later they called that province "Golden Castile" (Castilla del Oro), on account of the great quantity of gold found there and because of a castle erected there by Diego de Nicuesa in 1510. The island is named Trinidad, and is in the Mar Dulce: it is so called because it was discovered on the day of the Holy Trinity.

The city of Cartagena gets its name from its good port, which greatly resembles that of Cartagena in Spain, and led those who first saw it to exclaim: "This port is as good as Cartagena." Serrana Island, on the way from Cartagena to La Havana, is called after a Spaniard named Pedro Serrano, whose ship was lost nearby. He alone escaped by swimming, and being an excellent swimmer, reached the island, which is uninhabited and has neither water nor fuel. He lived on it for seven years by dint of his industry and skill in obtaining fuel and water, and in making fire. It was a historic feat worthy of the greatest admiration, and we may be able to tell about it elsewhere. From his name the island was called Serrana, and another nearby Serranilla to distinguish them. The city of Santo Domingo, whence the whole island takes the same name, was founded and named as López de Gómara tells in the following passage (ch. xxxv), which is quoted word for word: "The town that has achieved the greatest nobility is Santo Domingo, founded by Bartolomé Colón on the bank of the river Ozama. He gave it that name because he arrived there on a Sunday, the feast of St. Dominic, and because his father was called Domingo. Thus

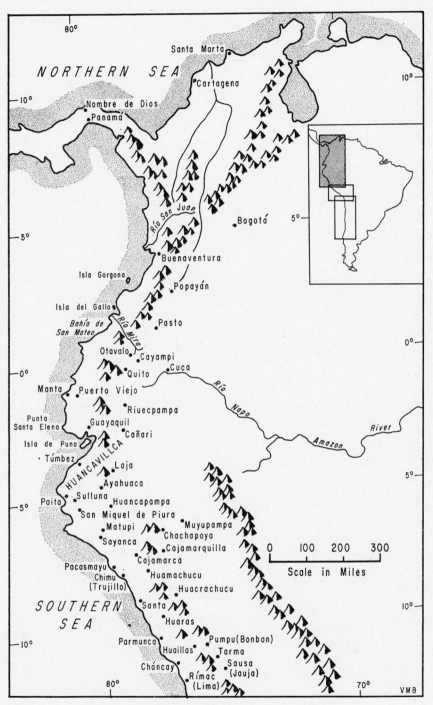

NORTHERN SEA

Santa Marta
Cartagena
Nombre de Dios
Panamá
Bogotá
Río San Juan
Buenaventura
Isla Gorgona
Popayán
Isla del Gallo
Bahía de San Mateo
Río Mira
Pasto
Otavalo
Cayampi
Quito
Cuca
Manta
Puerto Viejo
Río Napo
Riuecpampa
Amazon River
Punta Santa Elena
Guayaquil
Cañari
Isla de Puna
Túmbez
Loja
HUANCAVILLCA
Ayahuaca
Sulluna
Huancapampa
Paita
San Miquel de Piura
Muyupampa
Matupi
Chachapoya
Sayanca
Cajamarquilla
Cajamarca
Pacasmayu
Huamachucu
Scale in Miles
Chimu (Trujillo)
Huacrachucu
0   100   200   300
SOUTHERN SEA
Santa
Huaras
Parmunca
Pumpu(Bonbon)
Huaillas
Tarma
Cháncay
Sausa (Jauja)
Rímac (Lima)

VMB

MAP 1. NORTHWESTERN SOUTH AMERICA

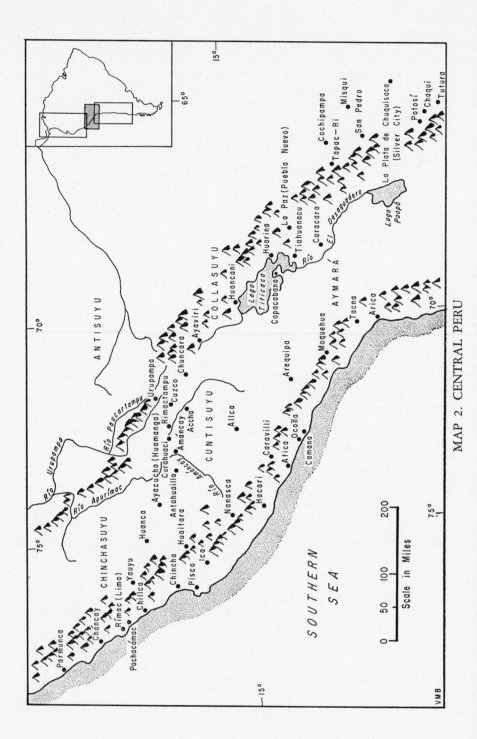

MAP 2. CENTRAL PERU

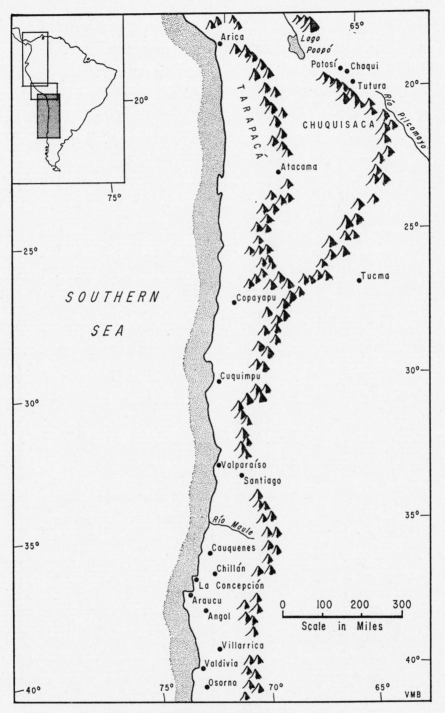

65°

Arica

*Lago
Poopó*

Potosí • Chaqui

Tutura

20°

T
A
R
A
P
A
C
Á

CHUQUISACA

Río Pilcomayo

• Atacama

25°

Tucma

SOUTHERN

SEA

• Copayapu

30°

25°

• Cuquimpu

30°

• Valparaíso

• Santiago

35°

Río Maule

35°

• Cauquenes

• Chillán

• La Concepción

• Araucu

• Angol

0   100   200   300

Scale in Miles

• Villarrica

40°

• Valdivia

• Osorno

75°

70°

65°

VMB

40°

75°

20°

MAP 3. SOUTHERN PERU AND CHILE

three causes concurred to give it that name," etc. This is from López de Gómara.

In the same way all the other names of famous ports, great rivers, provinces, and kingdoms discovered in the New World received their names from those of the saints on whose day they were discovered or from the captain, soldier, pilot, or mariner who discovered them. We have said something about this in the history of Florida in dealing with the description of the place and visitors to it; and in Book VI, after ch. xv, with reference to the subject in hand, derivations were included there together with that of Peru, for I feared I might not live long enough to reach this point. But as God in his mercy has prolonged my life, it seemed best to remove them and put them in their proper place. All I now fear is lest another historian may have robbed me, because that book, owing to my other occupations, was sent off in my absence for his opinion on it and I know it passed through many hands. Moreover, many have asked me if I knew the derivation of the name *Peru,* and though I wished to keep it to myself, I have not been able to refuse it to some of my friends.

CHAPTER VIII

The description of Peru.

THE FOUR BOUNDARIES of the empire of the Incas when the Spaniards arrived were as follows. To the north it stretched to the Ancasmayu River, which runs between the limits of Quitu [Quito] and Pastu [Pasto]. In the general speech of Peru it means "Blue River." It is almost exactly on the equator. To the south the limit was the river called Mauli [Maule], running east and west beyond to the kingdom of Chile, before the land of the Araucanians. It is more than forty degrees south of the equator. Between these two rivers there are just under 1,300 leagues of land. The part called Peru is 750 leagues long north to south by land from the Ancasmayu River to the Chichas, which is the last province of the Charcas. What is called the kingdom of Chile is about 550 leagues from north to south, counting from the province of the Chichas to the river Maule.

To the east it is bounded by the inaccessible chain of snowy peaks, untrodden by man, animal, or bird, and extending from Santa Marta to the

Straits of Magellan. The Indians call it "Ritisuyu," "the land of snows." To the west it is limited by the Southern Sea which extends along the whole length of its coast. The boundary of the empire begins at Cape Passau on the coast and runs beyond the equinoctial line as far as the Maule River, which also flows into the Southern Sea. From east to west the whole kingdom is narrow. At its broadest, crossing from the Muyupampa province over the Chachapoyas to the town of Trujillo on the seacoast, it is 120 leagues wide, and at the narrowest, from the port of Arica to the province called Llaricassa it is 70 leagues long. These are the four boundaries of the realms of the Inca kings, whose history we propose to write, with divine aid.

Before going further, it would be as well to tell here the story of Pedro Serrano mentioned above, so that it is not too far from its place, and in order that this chapter may not be too short. Pedro Serrano swam to the hitherto unnamed desert island, which, as he said, would be about two leagues in circumference. The chart shows this to be so: it gives three small islets with a great many banks round about, and the same appearance is given to the one called Serranilla, which is five islets with more shoals than Serrana: there are many banks in all these parts, and ships avoid them so as not to fall into danger.

It was Pedro Serrano's fate to be wrecked among them and to reach the island swimming. He was in a state of despair, for he found no water nor fuel nor even grass he could graze on, nor anything else to maintain life till some ship might pass to rescue him before he perished from hunger and thirst; this seemed to him a harder fate than death by drowning, which is quicker. So he spent the first night bewailing his misfortune, and was as cast down as one would suppose a man to be in such a plight. As soon as dawn came, he again walked round the island, and found some shellfish from the sea, crabs, shrimps, and other creatures. He caught what he could and ate them raw, having no flame to roast or boil them with. Thus he kept himself going until he saw turtles come forth. Seeing them some distance from the sea, he seized one and turned it over, and did the same to as many as he could, for they are clumsy in righting themselves when on their backs. Drawing a knife he used to wear in his belt, and which saved his life, he beheaded one and drank its blood instead of water. He did the same with the rest, and laid out their flesh in the sun to make dried meat and cleaned out the shells to catch rainwater, for the whole region is, of course, very rainy. Thus he sustained himself during the first days by killing all the turtles he could. Some were as big as and bigger than the biggest shields, and others like smaller shields and targes. They

were in fact of all sizes. The largest of them he could not contrive to turn
over on their backs, because they were stronger than he, and though he
climbed on them to subdue them by tiring them, it was no use because
they could make their way to the sea with him astraddle. So experience
taught him which turtles he could attack and which to abandon. In their
shells he collected a great deal of water, for some could hold two arrobas,
and others less. Finding himself adequately supplied with food and drink,
Pedro Serrano thought that if he could make fire so as to be able to roast
his food and produce smoke in case a ship should pass, he could lack nothing. With this idea, being a man with long experience of the sea (and
they certainly have a great advantage over other men in any sort of task),
he looked for a pair of pebbles that he could use as flint, hoping to use
his knife to strike fire from them. But not finding any such stones on the
island, which was covered with bare sand, he swam into the sea and dived,
carefully searching the sea bottom in all directions, and persisting in his
labors until he found pebbles and collected what he could, picking out
the best and breaking them on one another so as to make edges to strike
the knife on. He then tried out his idea, and seeing that he could strike
fire, made shreds of a piece of his shirt, torn very small like carded cotton.
This served as tinder, and by dint of industry and skill, after great perse-
verance, he made himself a fire. Having got it, he counted himself fortunate and sustained it by collecting the jetsam thrown up by the sea. He
spent hours collecting weeds called sea-pods, timber from ships lost at sea,
shells, fish bones, and other material to feed his fire. So that the showers
should not extinguish it, he made a hut with the biggest shells from the
turtles he had killed, and tended the fire with great diligence lest it should
slip from his hands. Within two months or less, he was as naked as when
he was born, for the great rain, the heat, and the humidity of the region
rotted the few clothes he had. The sun wearied him with its great heat,
for he had no clothes to protect himself nor any shade. When he was very
extenuated, he entered the water and submerged himself. He lived three
years amidst these hardships and cares, and though he saw several ships
pass in that time, and made smoke (the usual signal for people lost at
sea), they did not see him, or else feared the shoals and did not dare to
approach, but passed well out to sea, all of which left Pedro Serrano so
discouraged that he had resigned himself to dying and ending his misery.
Owing to the harshness of the climate hair grew all over his body till it
was like an animal's pelt, and not just any animal's, but a wild boar's. His
hair and beard fell below his waist.

After three years, one afternoon when he was not expecting anything, he saw a man on the island. This man had been wrecked on the shoals the night before and had saved himself on a ship's plank. As soon as dawn appeared, he saw the smoke of Pedro Serrano's fire, and guessing what it was, made for it, aided by the plank and his good swimming. When they saw one another, it would be hard to say which was the more surprised. Serrano thought it was the Devil come in human form to tempt him to some desperate act. His guest thought Serrano was the Devil in his true form, he was so coated with hair, beard, and hide. Each fled from the other, and Pedro Serrano went off crying: "Jesus! Jesus! Oh Lord, deliver me from the demon!"

Hearing this, the other was reassured, and turned towards him saying: "Flee me not, brother, for I am a Christian too," and to prove it, as he still ran away, shouted the Credo. Pedro Serrano heard it, turned back, and they advanced with the greatest tenderness and many tears and groans, seeing that they were both in the same plight with no hope of escape. Each briefly told the other the story of his past life. Pedro Serrano, realizing his guest's need, gave him some of his food and drink, which comforted him a little, and they again discussed their plight. They arranged their life as best they could, dividing the hours of the day and night between the duties of collecting shellfish to eat and sea-pods and wood and fish bones and anything else thrown up by the sea to sustain the fire, and especially the perpetual vigil they had to keep on it, hour by hour, lest it go out. They lived in this way for some days, but it was not long before they quarrelled, and so violently that they lived apart and nearly came to blows (which shows how great is the misery of human passions). The cause of the strife was that one accused the other of not doing the necessary duties properly. This accusation and the words they exchanged were enough to destroy their harmony and divide them. But they themselves soon realized their folly, asked one another's forgiveness, made friends, and lived together again. Thus they continued for four years. During this time they saw some ships pass and made their smoke signals, but in vain, and this so depressed them that they all but died.

At the end of this long time, a ship chanced to pass so near that their smoke was sighted and a boat put out to pick them up. Pedro Serrano and his companion, who had grown a similar pelt, seeing the boat approach, fell to saying the Credo and calling on the name of our Redeemer aloud, so that the sailors should not think they were demons and flee from them. This availed them, for otherwise the mariners would doubtless have fled: they no longer looked like human beings. So they were carried to the ship, where they astounded all who saw them and heard about their labors. The

companion died at sea returning to Spain. Pedro Serrano reached here and
went on to Germany where the emperor then was. He kept his pelt as it
was, as a proof of his wreck and all he had gone through. In every village
he passed through on the way he earned much money whenever he chose
to exhibit himself. Some of the lords and principal knights who liked to
see his figure contributed toward the cost of the journey, and his imperial
majesty, having seen and heard him, gave him a reward of 4,000 pesos in
income, or 4,800 ducats, in Peru. On the way to enjoy this, he died at Panama, and never saw it. All this story, as I have repeated it, is told by a gentleman called Sánchez de Figueroa, from whom I heard it. He knew Pedro
Serrano and warrants that he had heard it from him, and that after seeing
the emperor, Pedro Serrano cut his hair and beard to just above the waist;
and to enable him to sleep at night, he plaited it, for otherwise it spread
out over the bed and disturbed his rest.

CHAPTER IX

The idolatry of the Indians and the gods
they worshipped before the Incas.

FOR THE better understanding of the idolatry, way of life, and customs
of the Indians of Peru, it will be necessary for us to divide those
times into two periods. First we shall say how they lived before the Incas,
and then how the Inca kings governed, so as not to confuse the one thing
with the other, and so that the customs and gods of one period are not
attributed to the other. It must therefore be realized that in the first age of
primitive heathendom there were Indians who were little better than tame
beasts and others much worse than wild beasts. To begin with their gods,
we may say that they were of a piece with the simplicity and stupidity of
the times, as regards the multiplicity of gods and the vileness and crudity
of the things the people worshipped. Each province, each tribe, each village, each quarter, each clan, each house had gods different from the rest,
for they considered that other people's gods, being busy with other people's affairs, could not help them, but they must have their own. Thus
they came to have so great a variety of gods, which were too numerous to

count. They did not understand, as the gentile Romans did, how to create abstract gods such as Hope, Victory, Peace, and so on, for their thoughts did not rise to invisible things, and they worshipped what they saw, some in one way and others in another. They did not consider whether the things they worshipped were worthy of their worship and they had no self-respect, in the sense of refraining from worshipping things inferior to themselves. They only thought of distinguishing themselves from one another, and each from all the rest. Thus they worshipped grasses, plants, flowers, trees of all kinds, high hills, great rocks and nooks in them, deep caves, pebbles, and little pieces of stone of various colors found in rivers and streams, such as jasper. They worshipped the emerald, especially in the province now called Puerto Viejo. They did not worship diamonds or rubies because these stones did not exist there. Instead they worshipped various animals, some for their ferocity, such as the tiger, lion, and bear: and consequently, regarding them as gods, if they chanced to meet them, they did not flee but fell down and worshipped them and let themselves be killed and eaten without escaping or making any defence at all. They also worshipped other animals for their cunning, such as the fox and monkeys. They worshipped the dog for its faithfulness and nobility, the wild cat for its quickness, and the bird they call *cuntur* for its size; and some natives worshipped eagles, because they boast of descending from them and also from the *cuntur*. Other peoples adored hawks for their quickness and ability in winning their food. They adored the owl for the beauty of its eyes and head; the bat for the keenness of its sight—it caused them much wonder that it could see at night. They also adored many other birds according to their whims. They adored great snakes for their monstrous size and fierceness (some of those in the Antis are about twenty-five or thirty feet long and as thick round as a man's thigh). They also considered other smaller snakes—where there were none so big as in the Antis —to be gods, and they adored lizards, toads, and frogs. In a word, there was no beast too vile and filthy for them to worship as a god, merely in order to differ from one another in their choice of gods, without adoring any real god or being able to expect any benefit from them. They were very simple in everything, like sheep without a shepherd. But we need not be surprised that such unlettered and untaught people should have fallen into these follies, for it is well known that the Greeks and Romans, who prided themselves so greatly on their learning, had thirty thousand gods when their empire was at its height.

CHAPTER X

The great variety of other gods they had.

T HERE WERE many other Indians of various nations in this first period
who chose their gods with rather more discrimination than these.
They worshipped certain objects that were beneficial, such as streaming
fountains and great rivers, which they argued gave them water to irrigate
their crops.

Others adored the earth and called it "mother," because it gave them
its fruits. Others the air they breathed, saying that men lived by it; others
fire, because it warmed them and they cooked their food with it. Others
worshipped a ram, because of the great flocks reared in their region; others the great chain of the Sierra Nevada, because of its height and wonderful grandeur and because many rivers used for irrigation flow from
it; others maize or *sara,* as they call it, because it was their usual bread;
others other cereals or legumes, according to what grew most abundantly
in their provinces.

The coastal Indians, in addition to an infinity of other gods they had,
even including those already mentioned, generally worshipped the sea,
which they called *Mamacocha,* or "Mother Sea," implying that it was
like a mother to them in sustaining them with its fish. They also worshipped the whale on account of its monstrous greatness. Besides these
cults, which were common to the whole coast, various provinces and regions worshipped the fish most commonly caught there, holding that the
first fish that was in the upper world (their word for heaven) was the
origin of all other fish of the kind they ate and that it took care to send
them plenty of its children to sustain their tribe. Thus in some provinces
they worshipped the sardine, which they killed in greater quantity than
any other fish, in others the skate, in others the dogfish, in others the gold-
fish for its beauty, in others the crab and other shellfish for lack of anything better in their waters or because they could not catch or kill anything else. In short, they worshipped and considered gods any fish that
was more beneficial to them than the rest. So they had for gods not only
the four elements, each separately, but also the compounds and forms of
them, however vile and squalid. Other tribes, such as the Chirihuanas and

the people of Cape Passau (that is, the southernmost and northernmost provinces of Peru) felt no inclination to worship anything, high or low, either from interest or fear, but lived and still live exactly like beasts, because the doctrine and teaching of the Inca kings did not reach them.

CHAPTER XI

The kinds of sacrifices they made.

T HE CRUELTY and barbarity of the sacrifices of that ancient idolatry were of a piece with the vileness and crudity of its gods. For in addition to ordinary things such as animals and the fruits of the earth, they sacrificed men and women of all ages taken captive in the wars they waged on one another. Among some tribes their inhuman cruelty exceeded that of wild beasts. Not satisfied with sacrificing their captured foes, in case of need they offered up their own children. They performed these sacrifices of men and women, lads and children by opening their breasts while they were still alive and plucking out their hearts and lungs. The idol that had bidden the sacrifice was then sprinkled with still-warm blood, after which the same heart and lungs were examined for omens to show if the sacrifice had been acceptable or not. In either case the heart and lungs were burnt as an offering before the idol until they were consumed, and the victim of the sacrifice was eaten with the greatest pleasure and relish, and not the less merrymaking and rejoicing, even though it might have been their own child.

Padre Blas Valera, as appears from many parts of his torn papers, had the same design as we have in much of what he wrote. He divided the periods, ages, and provinces so as to show clearly the customs of each tribe. Thus in one of his mutilated notebooks he writes as follows, using the present tense, for the people he speaks of still practice these inhumanities:

Those who live in the Antis eat human flesh: they are fiercer than tigers, have neither god nor law, nor know what virtue is. They have no idols nor likenesses of them. They worship the Devil when he represents himself in the form of some animal or serpent and speaks to them. If they make a prisoner in war or otherwise and know that he is a plebeian of low rank, they quarter him and give the quarters to their friends and servants to eat or to sell in the meat market. But if he is of noble rank, the chiefs foregather with their wives and children, and, like ministers of the devil, strip him, tie him alive to a stake, and cut him to pieces with flint knives and razors, not so as to dismember him, but to remove the meat from the fleshiest parts, the calves, thighs, buttocks, and fleshy parts of the arms. Men, women and children sprinkle themselves with the blood, and they all devour the flesh very rapidly, without cooking it or roasting it thoroughly or even chewing it. They swallow it in mouthfuls so that the wretched victim sees himself eaten alive by others and buried in their bellies. The women, crueller than the men, anoint the nipples of their breasts with the unfortunate victim's blood so that their babies may suck it and drink it with their milk. This is all done in a place of sacrifice with great rejoicing and lightheartedness until the man dies. They then finish eating the flesh together with all his inner parts, no longer as hitherto as a feast or delight, but as a matter of the greatest divinity. Thenceforward they regard the flesh with great veneration and eat it as a sacred thing. If while they were tormenting the unfortunate fellow he showed any signs of suffering in his face or body or gave any groan or sigh, they break his bones to pieces after having eaten the flesh, entrails, and tripes, and throw them scornfully into the fields or river. But if he has shown himself firm, composed, and fierce under torture, when they have eaten the flesh and inner parts they dry the bones and sinews in the sun and set them on the top of hills and hold them and worship them as gods, and offer sacrifices to them. These are the idols of these savages. The empire of the Incas did not reach them, nor so far has that of the Spaniards, so they remain in this state to this day. This race of terrible and cruel men came from the Mexican area and peopled Panama and Darien and all the great forests that stretch to the kingdom of New Granada and in the other direction to Santa Marta.

This is all quoted from Padre Blas Valera, who vividly describes such devilries and assists us to give an idea of what happened in those primitive times, and still endures.

There were other Indians less cruel in their sacrifices, who, though they used human blood, did not kill victims, but obtained it by bleeding their arms and legs, according to the importance of the sacrifice: for the most solemn occasions they extracted it from the root of the nose between the eyebrows. This bleeding was common among the Indians of Peru, even after the Incas came, both for their sacrifices (and one kind especially which we shall presently describe), and in case of illness attended by serious headache. Other types of sacrifice were common to all the Indians (those mentioned above were practiced in some provinces and not in others). Those generally used were of animals such as sheep, ewes, lambs, rabbits, partridges and other birds, tallow, the herb they value so highly called *cuca* [coca], maize and other seeds, and vegetables, and scented woods, and similar things, according to what each tribe produced and thought would please its gods, and taking into account the nature of the latter, whether they were animals or birds, and carnivorous or not. They offered up what they usually saw them eat and what seemed to be most agreeable to their taste. This shall suffice so far as our account of the sacrifices of that ancient heathendom is concerned.

CHAPTER XII

The life and government of the ancient
Indians, and the things they ate.

T HESE GENTILES were as barbarous in the style of their houses and villages as in their gods and sacrifices. The more civilized had villages without squares or any order in their streets and houses, but rather after the fashion of a den of wild beasts. Others, because of the wars they waged on one another, dwelt on ridges or high rocks, like fortresses, where they would be least molested by their enemies; others in huts scattered over the fields, valleys, and river bottoms as each happened to find convenient for food and dwellings. Others lived in underground caves, in nooks in the rocks, in hollow trees, each as he happened to find a home, since he was not able to make one. Some of them, like those of Cape Passau and the Chirihuanas and other tribes not conquered by the Inca kings, remain in that state of primitive savagery. They are the most difficult to reduce both to the service of the Spaniards and to Christianity, for as they never had any doctrine, they are irrational beings, who only had a language to make themselves understood within their own tribe, and so live like animals of different kinds which do not meet or deal or communicate between one another.

In these villages and dwelling places the ruler was whoever was boldest and had the will to govern the rest. As soon as he became master, he treated his vassals tyrannically and cruelly, using them as slaves, taking their wives and daughters at will, and making war on his rivals. In some areas they flayed captives and used their skins to cover drums and to terrify their enemies, who, they said, would fly at once on hearing the skins of their relatives. They led a life of banditry, stealing, killing, and burning villages. Thus there arose a multiplicity of chiefs and petty kings, of whom some were good and treated their people well, maintaining peace and justice. The Indians in their simplicity worshipped these as gods for their goodness and nobility, realizing that they were different from and opposed to the horde of tyrants. Elsewhere they lived without rulers or governors, and were unable to form a republic of their own to settle and regulate their lives. They lived in great simplicity like sheep, doing neither good nor harm, though this was due more to ignorance and lack of malice, than to excess of virtue.

In many areas the Indians were so simple and stupid in their way of dressing and covering their bodies that their attempts at dress were laughable. Elsewhere they were astonishingly savage and barbarous in their food and eating; and in many places the two things were found together. In the hottest and consequently most fertile areas they sowed little or nothing, but lived on herbs, roots, wild fruit, and other vegetables that the earth yielded spontaneously or with little improvement from them. As none of them desired more than to sustain their natural lives, they were satisfied with little. In many parts they were extremely fond of human flesh and so greedy that, when they were killing an Indian, they would drink his blood through the wound they had given him before he died: they did the same if they were quartering him, sucking his blood and licking their hands so as not to lose a drop. They had public markets for human flesh, and in order not to waste it they made sausages and polonies of gut which they filled with meat. Pedro de Cieza (ch. xxvi) confirms this and saw it with his own eyes. The passion reached such a pitch with them that they did not spare their own sons by foreign captives taken in war whom they took as concubines. Their children by these women were carefully brought up to the age of twelve or thirteen, and then eaten, and the mothers too, when they were past childbearing. Furthermore, they would spare the lives of many male Indian captives, give them wives from their tribe—the tribe of the victors—bring up the children as their own, and, when they were youths, eat them. It was in fact a cannibals' seminary. They spared none on account of parentage or upbringing, which usually breed affection even among animals of quite various and opposite kinds, as we can affirm from some we have seen and others we have heard about. But among these savages neither the one nor the other availed: they killed the children they had begotten, and the relatives they had reared for the purpose of eating them, treating the parents the same when they no longer served to breed children, without any regard for their close relationship. There was a tribe so strongly addicted to devouring human flesh that they buried their dead in their stomachs. As soon as the deceased had breathed his last, his relatives gathered round and ate him roasted or boiled, according to the amount of flesh he still had: if little, boiled, if much, roasted. Afterwards they assembled the bones and gave them a funeral with great mourning, burying them in crannies in rocks or hollow trees. They had no gods and no conception of worshipping, and are still in the same state. The consumption of human flesh is commoner among Indians of the hot regions than among those of the cold.

In cold and sterile regions where the earth did not bear fruit, roots, and herbs spontaneously, they sowed maize and vegetables, obliged by necessity; but they did this without regard to time or season. They fished and hunted with the same primitive savagery as they displayed in other things.

CHAPTER XIII

How they dressed in those ancient times.

THEIR dress was so indecent that it is rather a subject for silence and secrecy than for discussion and description. But as history obliges one to set down the whole truth, I must beg the modest to turn a deaf ear to this part, and if they censure me in this way, I shall consider their disfavor justified. In this first period the Indians dressed like animals, for they wore no more clothing than the skin nature had given them. Many of them, out of ingenuity or for love of adornment, had a thick string girded round their bodies. They thought that was clothing enough, and we must not go beyond, for it is improper. In 1560, on my way to Spain, I met five Indians in the street in Cartagena without any clothes at all, and they did not walk abreast but one behind the other like cranes, although they had mingled with Spaniards for so many years.

The women went in the same dress, naked. When married they wore a string round the body with a cotton rag about a yard square hanging like an apron from it. Where they could not or would not spin or weave, they made it of the barks or leaves of trees. This covered their modesty. Maidens also wore a string girdle, and instead of the apron they wore something else to show they were maidens. But out of proper respect for our hearers, we had better keep to ourselves what remains to be said. Suffice it to say that this was the dress and costume of the hot regions, so that as regards decency, they resembled irrational beasts, and it can be imagined from this bestiality in adorning their persons alone how brutal they would be in everything else—these Indians of heathen times before the empire of the Incas.

In cold regions they were more decently clad, not indeed out of decency, but obliged by the cold. They covered themselves with skins of animals and a sort of blanket they made of wild hemp and a long, pliable, soft straw that grows in the fields. With these contrivances they covered their nakedness as well as they could. Other tribes had a greater sense of propriety and wore clumsily made cloaks, ill-spun and worse-woven, of wool or wild hemp called *cháhuar*. They wore them fastened about the neck and girded to the body, and were thus adequately covered. The dress we have mentioned used in primitive times in the hot lands—that is going naked—was found by the Spaniards in many regions never conquered by the Incas, and is still today found in many places conquered by the Spaniards, where the Indians are such brutes that they will not dress, except for those who have close intercourse with Spaniards in their houses and wear clothes more because the Spaniards insist on it than from any choice or modesty of their own. The women refuse just as much as the men, and Spaniards often chaff them about their indecency and unwillingness to spin, and ask if they don't dress because they won't spin, or if they don't spin because they won't dress.

CHAPTER XIV

Different kinds of marriage and diverse
languages; their use of poison
and spells.

IN THEIR other customs, such as marriage and cohabitation, the Indians of those heathen days were no better than in their eating and dressing. Many tribes cohabited like beasts without having any special wife, but with anyone they chanced to fall in with. Others married as their fancy directed them without excepting sisters, daughters, and mothers. Among other tribes they excepted their mothers, but no one else. In other provinces it was lawful and even praiseworthy for girls to be as immodest and abandoned as they pleased, and the most dissolute were the surest to marry, since they regarded it as a great quality to have been dissolute. At least girls of that kind were regarded as industrious, while the modest were thought to be feeble since nobody had wanted them. In other regions the custom was the contrary: mothers kept their daughters with great circumspection, and when they were arranging to marry them, they brought them out in public and deflowered them with their own hands before the members of the family who had witnessed the contract so as to prove to all present that they had been taken good care of.

In other provinces the closest relatives of the bridegroom and his best friends violated the maiden who was to be married, and the marriage was so arranged and the husband then received her. Pedro de Cieza (ch. xxiv) says the same. In some regions there were sodomites, though not very openly nor generally, but only among certain individuals and in secret. In some parts they had them in their temples because the Devil persuaded them that their gods delighted in such people, thus treacherously lifting the veil of shame that the gentiles felt about this crime and inuring them to commit it in public and in general.

There were also men and women who gave poison which killed either suddenly or by slow degrees, or stupefied whom they wished, or drove them out of their senses. They could also make their faces and bodies ugly, bring them out in black and white patches, produce white leprosy, and paralyze the limbs. Each district, each tribe, and, in many places, each village had its own language, differing from that of its neighbors. Those who could understand one another in one language regarded themselves as relatives and thus were friends and allies. Those who did not understand one another because of the variety of languages, held one another as enemies and opposites, and waged cruel war and even ate one another as if they were beasts of different kinds. There were also wizards and witches, but this function was performed oftener by women than by men. Many exercised it only to be able to deal privately with the Devil and gain a reputation among their people for giving and taking replies about things to come and making themselves great priests and priestesses.

Other women used the art of bewitching people, more often men than women, from envy or some grudge, and produced with spells the same effect as with poison. And this shall suffice for now about the Indians of that primitive age and ancient barbarism. What I have not described as fully as necessary I leave each one to imagine and supply details: however he stretches his imagination, he will not realize how great was the savagery of these gentiles. In short they were people who had no pride and no master but the Devil. So some were barbarous beyond exaggeration in their life, customs, gods, and sacrifices. Others were simple about everything, like tame animals, or even simpler. Others had something of the two extremes, as we shall see further on in the course of our history, in which we shall say which of the above bestialities existed in each district and tribe.

CHAPTER XV

The origin of the Inca kings of Peru.

WHILE THESE peoples were living or dying in the manner we have seen, it pleased our Lord God that from their midst there should appear a morning star to give them in the dense darkness in which they dwelt some glimmerings of natural law, of civilization, and of the respect men owe to one another. The descendants of this leader should thus tame those savages and convert them into men, made capable of reason and of receiving good doctrine, so that when God, who is the sun of justice, saw fit to send forth the light of His divine rays upon those idolaters, it might find them no longer in their first savagery, but rendered more docile to receive the Catholic faith and the teaching and doctrine of our Holy Mother the Roman Church, as indeed they have received it—all of which will be seen in the course of this history. It has been observed by clear experience how much prompter and quicker to receive the Gospel were the Indians subdued, governed, and taught by the Inca kings than the other neighboring peoples unreached by the Incas' teachings, many of which are still today as savage and brutish as before, despite the fact that the Spaniards have been in Peru seventy years. And since we stand on the threshold of this great maze, we had better enter and say what lay within.

After having prepared many schemes and taken many ways to begin to give an account of the origin and establishment of the native Inca kings of Peru, it seemed to me that the best scheme and simplest and easiest way was to recount what I often heard as a child from the lips of my mother and her brothers and uncles and other elders about these beginnings. For everything said about them from other sources comes down to the same story as we shall relate, and it will be better to have it as told in the very words of the Incas than in those of foreign authors. My mother dwelt in Cuzco, her native place, and was visited there every week by the few relatives, both male and female, who escaped the cruelty and tyranny of Atahuallpa (which we shall describe in our account of his life). On these visits the ordinary subject of conversation was always the origin of the Inca kings, their greatness, the grandeur of their empire, their deeds and conquests, their government in peace and war, and the laws they ordained so greatly to the advantage of their vassals. In short, there was nothing concerning the most flourishing period of their history that they did not bring up in their conversations.

From the greatness and prosperity of the past they turned to the present, mourning their dead kings, their lost empire, and their fallen state, etc. These and similar topics were broached by the Incas and Pallas on their visits, and on recalling their departed happiness, they always ended these conversations with tears and mourning, saying: "Our rule is turned to bondage" etc. During these talks, I, as a boy, often came in and went out of the place where they were, and I loved to hear them, as boys always do like to hear stories. Days, months, and years went by, until I was sixteen or seventeen. Then it happened that one day when my family was talking in this fashion about their kings and the olden times, I remarked to the senior of them, who usually related these things: "Inca, my uncle, though you have no writings to preserve the memory of past events, what information have you of the origin and beginnings of our kings? For the Spaniards and the other peoples who live on their borders have divine and human histories from which they know when their own kings and their neighbors' kings began to reign and when one empire gave way to another. They even know how many thousand years it is since God created heaven and earth. All this and much more they know through their books. But you, who have no books, what memory have you preserved of your antiquity? Who was the first of our Incas? What was he called? What was the origin of his line? How did he begin to reign? With what men and arms did he conquer this great empire? How did our heroic deeds begin?"

The Inca was delighted to hear these questions, since it gave him great pleasure to reply to them, and turned to me (who had already often heard him tell the tale, but had never paid as much attention as then) saying:

"Nephew, I will tell you these things with pleasure: indeed it is right that you should hear them and keep them in your heart (this is their phrase for 'in the memory'). You should know that in olden times the whole of this region before you was covered with brush and heath, and people lived in those times like wild beasts, with no religion or government and no towns or houses, and without tilling or sowing the soil, or clothing or covering their flesh, for they did not know how to weave cotton or wool to make clothes. They lived in twos and threes as chance brought them together in caves and crannies in rocks and underground caverns. Like wild beasts they ate the herbs of the field and roots of trees and fruits growing wild and also human flesh. They covered their bodies with leaves and the bark of trees and animals' skins. Others went naked. In short, they lived like deer or other game, and even in their intercourse with women they behaved like beasts, for they knew nothing of having separate wives."

I must remark, in order to avoid many repetitions of the words "our father the Sun," that the phrase was used by the Incas to express respect whenever they mentioned the sun, for they boasted of descending from it, and none but Incas were allowed to utter the words: it would have been blasphemy and the speaker would have been stoned. The Inca said:

"Our father the Sun, seeing men in the state I have mentioned, took pity and was sorry for them, and sent from heaven to earth a son and a daughter of his to indoctrinate them in the knowledge of our father the Sun that they might worship him and adopt him as their god, and to give them precepts and laws by which they would live as reasonable and civilized men, and dwell in houses and settled towns, and learn to till the soil, and grow plants and crops, and breed flocks, and use the fruits of the earth like rational beings and not like beasts. With this order and mandate our father the Sun set these two children of his in Lake Titicaca, eighty leagues from here, and bade them go where they would, and wherever they stopped to eat or sleep to try to thrust into the ground a golden wand half a yard long and two fingers in thickness which he gave them as a sign and token: when this wand should sink into the ground at a single thrust, there our father the Sun wished them to stop and set up their court.

"Finally he told them: 'When you have reduced these people to our service, you shall maintain them in reason and justice, showing mercy, clemency, and mildness, and always treating them as a merciful father treats his beloved and tender children. Imitate my example in this. I do good to all the world. I give them my light and brightness that they may see and go about their business; I warm them when they are cold; and I grow their pastures and crops, and bring fruit to their trees, and multiply their flocks. I bring rain and calm weather in turn, and I take care to go round the world once a day to observe the wants that exist in the world and to fill and supply them as the sustainer and benefactor of men. I wish you as children of mine to follow this example sent down to earth to teach and benefit those men who live like beasts. And henceforward I establish and nominate you as kings and lords over all the people you may thus instruct with your reason, government, and good works.'

"When our father the Sun had thus made manifest his will to his two children he bade them farewell. They left Titicaca and travelled northwards, and wherever they stopped on the way they thrust the golden wand into the earth, but it never sank in. Thus they reached a small inn or resthouse seven or eight leagues south of this city. Today it is called Pacárec Tampu, 'inn or resthouse of the dawn.' The Inca gave it this name because he set out from it about daybreak. It is one of the towns the prince later ordered to be founded, and its inhabitants to this day boast greatly of its name because our first Inca bestowed it. From this place he and his wife, our queen, reached the valley of Cuzco which was then a wilderness."

CHAPTER XVI

The foundation of Cuzco, the imperial city.

T HE FIRST settlement they made in this valley," said the Inca, "was in the hill called Huanacauri, to the south of this city. There they tried to thrust the golden wand into the earth and it easily sank in at the first blow and they saw it no more. Then our Inca said to his wife: 'Our father the Sun bids us remain in this valley and make it our dwelling place and home in fulfilment of his will. It is therefore right, queen and sister, that each of us should go out and call together these people so as to instruct them and benefit them as our father the Sun has ordained.' Our first rulers set out from the hill of Huanacauri, each in a different direction, to call the people together, and as that was the first place we know they trod with their feet and because they went out from it to do good to mankind, we made there, as you know, a temple for the worship of our father the Sun, in memory of his merciful beneficence towards the world. The prince went northwards, and the princess south. They spoke to all the men and women they found in that wilderness and said that their father the Sun had sent them from the sky to be teachers and benefactors to the dwellers in all that land, delivering them from the wild lives they led and in obedience to the commands given by the Sun, their father, calling them together and removing them from those heaths and moors, bringing them to dwell in settled valleys and giving them the food of men instead of that of beasts to eat. Our king and queen said these and similar things to the first savages they found in those mountains and heaths, and as the savages beheld two persons clad and adorned with the ornaments our father the Sun had given them—and a very different dress from their own—with their ears pierced and opened in the way we their descendants have, and saw that their words and countenances showed them to be children of the Sun, and that they came to mankind to give them towns to dwell in and food to eat, they wondered at what they saw and were at the same time attracted by the promises that were held out to them. Thus they fully credited all they were told and worshipped and venerated the strangers as children of the Sun and obeyed them as kings. These savages gathered others and repeated the wonders they had seen and heard, and a great number of men and women collected and set out to follow our king and queen wherever they might lead.

"When our princes saw the great crowd that had formed there, they ordered that some should set about supplying open-air meals for them all, so that they should not be driven by hunger to disperse again across the heaths. Others were ordered to work on building huts and houses according to plans made by the Inca. Thus our imperial city began to be settled: it was divided into two halves called Hanan Cuzco, which as you know, means upper Cuzco, and Hurin Cuzco, or lower Cuzco. The king wished those he had brought to people Hanan Cuzco, therefore called the upper, and those the queen had brought to people Hurin Cuzco, which was therefore called the lower. The distinction did not imply that the inhabitants of one half should excel those of the other in privileges and exemptions. All were equal like brothers, the children of one father and one mother. The Inca only wished that there should be this division of the people and distinction of name, so that the fact that some had been gathered by the king and others by the queen might have a perpetual memorial. And he ordered that there should be only one difference and acknowledgment of superiority among them, that those of upper Cuzco be considered and respected as first-born and elder brothers, and those of lower Cuzco be as younger children. In short they were to be as the right side and the left in any question of precedence of place and office, since those of the upper town had been gathered by the men and those of the lower by the women. In imitation of this, there was later the same division in all the towns, great or small, of our empire, which were divided by wards or by lineages, known as *hanan aillu* and *hurin aillu,* the upper and lower lineage, or *hanan suyu* and *hurin suyu,* the upper and lower district.

"At the same time, in peopling the city, our Inca showed the male Indians which tasks were proper to men: breaking and tilling the land, sowing crops, seeds, and vegetables which he showed to be good to eat and fruitful, and for which purpose he taught them how to make ploughs and other necessary instruments, and bade them and showed them how to draw irrigation channels from the streams that run through the valley of Cuzco, and even showed them how to make the footwear we use. On her side the queen trained the Indian women in all the feminine occupations: spinning and weaving cotton and wool, and making clothes for themselves and their husbands and children. She told them how to do these and other duties of domestic service. In short, there was nothing relating to human life that our princes failed to teach their first vassals, the Inca king acting as master for the men and the Coya queen, mistress of the women."

CHAPTER XVII

The peoples subdued by the first Inca Manco Cápac.

THE VERY Indians who had thus been recently subdued, discovering themselves to be quite changed and realizing the benefits they had received, willingly and joyfully betook themselves to the sierras, moors, and heaths to seek their inhabitants and give them news about the children of the Sun. They recounted the many benefits they had brought them, and proved it by showing their new clothes they wore and the new foods they ate, and telling how they lived in houses and towns. When the wild people heard all this, great numbers of them came to behold the wonders that were told and reported of our first fathers, kings, and lords. Once they had verified this with their own eyes, they remained to serve and obey them. Thus some called others and these passed the word to more, and so many gathered in a few years that after six or seven, the Inca had a force of men armed and equipped to defend themselves against any attackers and even to bring by force those who would not come willingly. He taught them how to make offensive weapons such as bows and arrows, lances, clubs, and others now in use.

"And to cut short the deeds of our first Inca, I can tell you that he subdued the region to the east as far as the river called Paucartampu, and to the west eight leagues up to the river Apurímac, and to the south for nine leagues to Quequesana. Within this area our Inca ordered more than a hundred villages to be settled, the biggest with a hundred houses and others with less, according to what the land could support. These were the first beginnings of our city toward being established and settled as you now see it. They were also the beginnings of our great, rich, and famous empire that your father and his friends deprived us of. These were our first Incas and kings, who appeared in the first ages of the world; and from them descend all the other kings we have had, and from these again we are all descended. I cannot inform you exactly how many years it is since our father the Sun sent us his first children, for it is so long no one has been able to remember: we believe it is above four hundred years. Our Inca was called Manco Cápac and our Coya Mama Ocllo Huaco. They were, as I have told you, brother and sister, children of the Sun and the Moon, our parents. I think I have expatiated at length on your enquiry and answered your questions, and in order to spare your tears, I have not recited this story with tears of blood flowing from my eyes as they flow from my heart from the grief I feel at seeing the line of our Incas ended and our empire lost."

This long account of the origin of our kings was given me by the Inca, my mother's uncle, of whom I asked it. I have tried to translate it faithfully from my mother tongue, that of the Inca, into a foreign speech, Castilian, though I have not written it in such majestic language as the Inca used, nor with the full significance the words of that language have. If I had given the whole significance, the tale would have been much more extensive than it is. On the contrary, I have shortened it, and left out a few things that might have been odious. However, it is enough to have conveyed its true meaning, which is what is required for our history. The Inca told me a few similar things, though not many, during the visits he paid to my mother's house; these I will include in their places later on, giving their source. I much regret not having asked many more questions so that I might now have information about them from so excellent an archive and write them here.

CHAPTER XVIII

On some fabulous accounts of the origin of the Incas.

ANOTHER FABLE about the origin of their Inca kings is told by the common people of Peru, the Indians of the region south of Cuzco called Collasuyu and those of the regions to the west called Cuntisuyu. They say that it occurred after the deluge, about which they have no more to say than that it took place, without making it clear whether this was the general deluge of Noah's time or some special one (for this reason, we shall omit what they say about it and similar matters, for by the way they have of telling them they make them seem more like dreams or disjointed fables than historical events). According to them, after the flood ended, there appeared a man at Tiahuanacu [Tiahuanaco], to the south of Cuzco, and he was so powerful that he divided the world into four parts and gave them to four men he called kings. The first was called Manco Cápac, the second Colla, the third Tócay and the fourth Pinahua. They say that he gave the northern part to Manco Cápac, the southern to Colla (whence the extensive province was afterward called Colla), the eastern to the third, Tócay, and the western to the fourth, called Pinahua. He ordered each to go to his district, and conquer and govern the people he found there. They do not, however, say if the deluge had drowned them or if the Indians had been resurrected to be conquered and instructed; and so it is with respect to everything they tell of these times. They say that this division of the world was the origin of that which the Incas made of their kingdom called Tahuantinsuyu. They say that Manco Cápac went northwards, reached the valley of Cuzco and founded the city there, and subdued and instructed the surrounding Indians. After this beginning their version of Manco Cápac is almost the same as the one we have given: they assert that the Inca kings were descended from him and cannot say what happened to the other three kings. This is the way with all the stories of those ancient times; and it is hardly to be wondered at that people without letters with which to preserve the memory of their antiquity should have so confused an idea of their beginnings, when the heathens of the Old World, though they had letters and displayed great skill in them, invented legends as laughable as the Indian stories, or more so—for example, there is the fable of Pyrrha and Deucalion, and a great many others we could mention. Moreover the fables of both of these ages of heathendom can be compared, and in many points they will be found to agree. Thus the Indians have something similar to the story of Noah, as some Spaniards have said: of this we shall deal later, and at the end I will say what I myself feel about the origin of the Incas.

Another version of the origin of the Incas similar to this is given by the Indians living to the east and north of the city of Cuzco. According to them, at the beginning of the world four men and four women, all brothers and sisters, came out of some "windows" in some rocks near that city at a place called Paucartampu. The windows are three in number and they came out of the middle one, called the "royal window." Because of this fable they lined this window on all sides with great gold plates and many precious stones. The side windows they decorated only with gold and not with stones. The first brother was called Manco Cápac and his wife Mama Oćllo. They say he founded the city and called it Cuzco, which means "navel" in the private language of the Incas, and that he subdued all those tribes and taught them how to be men, and that from him all the Incas are descended. The second brother they call Ayar Cachi, the third Ayar Uchu, and the fourth Ayar Sauca. The word *ayar* has no meaning in the ordinary tongue of Peru, though it must have had one in the special language of the Incas. The other words occur in the general language: *cachi* is the salt we eat; *uchu* is the condiment they season dishes with, which the Spaniards call *"pimento"* (the Peruvian Indians had no other spices). The other word, *sauca,* means "rejoicing," "satisfaction," or "delight." If we press the Indians for information about what the three brothers and three sisters of the first king did, they invent a thousand foolish tales and find no choice but to explain the fable by an allegory. Salt, which is one of the names, they declare to mean the teaching the Inca gave them about the natural life. The pepper is the relish they took in it, and the word "rejoicing" shows the joy and contentment in which they afterwards lived. Even this is told in such rambling, disjointed, and confused style that one understands what they mean by conjectures rather than by the sense and order of their words. The only thing they are clear about is that Manco Cápac was the first king and that the rest are descended from him. Thus all three accounts ascribe the beginnings and origins of the Incas to Manco Cápac, and say nothing of the other three brothers—on the contrary they are done away with in the allegory and only Manco Cápac remains. This seems likely since no king of this time was ever called by those names, nor has any tribe boasted of descending from them. Some Spanish scholars who have heard these legends think that the Indians heard of the story of Noah, his three sons, his wife, and daughters-in-law, and that the four men and women God spared from the deluge are the four in the fable and that the Indians mean the window of Noah's ark when they spoke of the window of Paucartampu; and the powerful man who, the first version says, appeared at Tiahuanaco and divided the world between the four men, they hold to have been God, who sent Noah and his three sons to people the earth. Other parts of this legend and the other seem to point to those of Holy Writ, which they are thought to resemble. I do not venture on such profound matters: I simply repeat the fabulous accounts I used to hear my family tell in my childhood; let each take them as he wishes and apply whatever allegory he thinks most appropriate. Just as the Incas have the fables we have mentioned, so the other peoples of Peru invent endless stories of the origin and beginning of their earliest ancestors, which distinguish them from one another, as we shall see in the course of this story. For the Indian does not consider himself honorable unless descended from a spring, river, or lake—or even from the sea—or from wild animals, such as the bear, lion, or tiger, or from the eagle, or the bird called *cuntur,* or other birds of prey, or from mountains, moors, peaks, or caverns, each according to his own family, to the greater praise and nobility of his name. This shall suffice for fables.

CHAPTER XIX

The author's declaration about his history.

NOW THAT we have laid the first stone of our edifice, though it be fabulous, it will be proper to proceed from the origin of the Inca kings of Peru to the conquest and subjugation of the Indians, enlarging somewhat the brief account that my uncle the Inca gave me with the accounts of many other Incas and Indians born in the towns that the first Inca Manco Cápac founded, peopled, and added to his empire. I was brought up among these Indians, and as I frequented their society until I was twenty I was able to learn during that time something of all the subjects I am writing about, for in my childhood they used to recount their histories, just as stories are told for children. Later, as I grew up, they talked to me at length about their laws and government, and compared the new rule of the Spaniards with that of the Incas, contrasting especially the crimes and punishments and the severity the latter were dealt with under the two regimes. They told me how their kings acted in peace and war, in what manner they treated their vassals, and how their vassals served them. Moreover, they told me, as if I were their own son, all about their idolatry, their rites, ceremonies, and sacrifices, the greater and lesser festivals, and how they were celebrated. They told me their superstitions and abuses, good and evil auspices, including those they discerned in sacrifices and others. In short, I would say that they told me about everything they had in their state, and if I had written it down at the time, this history would have been more copious. Apart from what the Indians told me, I experienced and saw with my own eyes a great deal of their idolatry, festivals, and superstitions, which had still not altogether disappeared in my own time, when I was twelve or thirteen. I was born eight years after the Spaniards conquered my country, and as I have said, was brought up there till I was twenty: thus I saw many of the things the Indians did in the time of their paganism and shall relate them and say that I saw them.

I have also listened to many accounts of the deeds and conquests of those kings in addition to what my relatives told me and what I myself say, for as soon as I resolved to write this history, I wrote to my old school-mates at my primary school and grammar school, and urged each of them to help me with accounts they might have of the particular conquests the Incas made in the provinces their mothers came from, for each province has its accounts and knots to record its annals and traditions, and thus preserves its own history much better than that of its neighbors. My schoolfellows earnestly complied with my request, and each reported my intention to his mother and relatives, and they, on hearing that an Indian, a son of their own country, intended to write its history, brought from their archives the records they had of their histories and sent me them. Thus I learned of the deeds and conquests of each Inca, which are the same as the Spanish historians obtained, except that this is longer, as we shall point out in various contexts.

And as all the deeds of this first Inca are the beginning and foundation of the history we are to write, it will be very helpful to give them here, or at least the most important of them, so that we do not have to repeat them later in discussing the lives and deeds of each of the Incas descended from him. For all the Incas in general, whether kings or not, took pride in imitating in every way the character, deeds, and habits of the first prince Manco Cápac. Having told about him, we shall proceed to tell about all the rest. Our intention will be to include the most historical deeds and omit others as irrelevant and repetitive. Although some of what has been said and is to be said may seem fabulous, I have thought fit to include it so as not to miss out the foundations on which the Indians rely for the greatest and best things they tell of their empire. For it was from these fabulous beginnings that the magnificent reality that Spain now possesses emerged. For this reason, I shall allow myself to include everything necessary for a full account of the beginning, middle, and end of the Inca monarchy. I declare that I shall simply tell the tales I imbibed with my mother's milk and those I have since obtained by request from my own relatives, and I promise that my affection for them shall not cause me to stray from the true facts either by underestimating the ill or exaggerating the good they did. I am well aware that paganism is a sea of errors, and I shall not write new and unheard of things, but will recount the same things the Spanish historians have written of those parts and their kings, bringing forward where necessary their very words, so as to prove that I have not invented fictitious circumstances to the credit of my relatives, but say no more than what Spaniards have said. I shall merely act as a commentator to reveal and amplify much of what they have begun to say, but have left unfinished for lack of full account. Much will be added that is missing in their histories but really happened, and some things will be omitted as superfluous because the Spaniards were misinformed, either because they did not know how to ask for information with a clear idea of the different periods and ages and divisions of provinces and tribes, or because they misunderstood the Indians who gave them it, or because they misunderstood one another on account of the difficulty of the language. The Spaniard who thinks he knows the language best is ignorant of nine-tenths of it, because of the many meanings of each word and the different pronunciation that a word has for various meanings, as will be seen from some words that I shall have to refer to.

Moreover, in all that I shall have to say about a state that was destroyed before it had been known, I shall plainly tell everything concerning its idolatry, rites, sacrifices, and ceremonies in ancient times, and its government, laws, and customs in peace and war, and make no comparison with other histories divine or human, nor with the government of our times, for all comparisons are odious. The reader can make his own comparisons, for he will find many points of similarity in ancient history, both in Holy Writ and in the profane histories and fables of pagan antiquity. He will observe many laws and customs that compare with those of our own age, and hear many others quite contrary to them. I for my part have done what I could, though not all I desired. I beg the discreet reader to accept my will to give him pleasure and satisfaction, though the strength and skill of an Indian, born among Indians and brought up amidst horses and arms, may be insufficient for the attempt.

CHAPTER XX

The villages the first Inca ordered to be founded.

T O RETURN to the Inca Manco Cápac, we have to say that after found-ing the city of Cuzco in the two parts we have described, he ordered many other towns to be established. Thus to the east of the city, with the people he brought from that direction, in the region that stretches to the river called Paucartampu, he ordered thirteen towns to be settled on either side of the royal road of Antisuyu. We omit their names to avoid prolixity; they are all or almost all of the tribe called Poques. To the west of the city, in an area eight leagues long by nine or ten broad, he ordered thirty towns to be established scattered on either side of the royal road of Cun-tisuyu. These were peoples of three tribes with different names: Masca, Chillqui, and Pap'ri. To the north of the city he settled twenty towns, with four names: Mayu, Çancu, Chinchapucyu, Rimactampu. Most of these settlements are in the beautiful valley of Sacsahuana, where the battle with Gonzalo Pizarro and his capture took place. The remotest of these towns is seven leagues from the city, and the rest are scattered on both sides of the royal road of Chinchasuyu. South of the city thirty-eight to forty towns were set up, eighteen of the Ayamarca tribe, which are scat-tered on both sides of the royal road of Collasuyu for a distance of three leagues beginning from the place called Las Salinas, a short league from the city. Here the lamentable battle between Don Diego de Almagro the elder and Hernando Pizarro was fought. The remaining towns are of people with five or six names: Quespicancha, Muina, Urcos, Quéhuar, Huáruc, Caviña. This Caviña people vainly believed and boasted that its forebears had come out of a lake to which they said that the souls of those who died returned and came forth again to enter into the bodies of those who were born. They had an idol of fearsome appearance to which they made very barbarous sacrifices. The Inca Manco Cápac abolished their sacrifices and the idol, and bade them worship the Sun, as he did the rest of his vassals.

These townships, numbering more than a hundred, were small at the beginning. The biggest had not above a hundred houses and the smaller had twenty-five or thirty. Afterwards, with the favors and privileges Manco Cápac gave them, as we shall presently say, they grew greatly and many came to have a thousand heads of families and the smaller three or four hundred. After, very much later, because of the very privileges and favors the first Inca and his descendants had granted, the great tyrant Atahuallpa destroyed them, some more and others less, and many he completely razed. Now in our own times, during the last twenty years or so, the villages founded by the Inca Manco Cápac and almost all the others in Peru are not in their ancient sites, but in completely different ones, because one of the viceroys, as we shall relate in its place, had them reduced to large towns, bringing together five or six at one place and seven or eight in another, the number varying according to the size of the villages that were concentrated. This led to great misfortunes, which, being odious, I shall not recount.

CHAPTER XXI

The Inca's teachings to his vassals.

THE Inca Manco Cápac settled his vassals in villages and taught them to till the soil, build homes, make irrigation channels, and do all the other things necessary for human life. At the same time he instructed them in the urbane, social, and brotherly conduct they were to use toward one another according to the dictates of reason and natural law, effectively persuading them to do unto one another as they themselves would be done by, so that there should be perpetual peace and concord among them and no ground for the kindling of envy and passion. They were not allowed to have one law for themselves and another for the rest. He enjoined them particularly to respect one another's wives and daughters, because the vice of women had been more rife among them than any other. He applied the death penalty to adulterers, murderers, and robbers. He ordered them not to have more than one wife and to marry within their own family group so as to prevent confusion in the lineages, and to wed after the age of twenty when they would be able to rule their households and work on their estates. He ordered them to round up the tame flocks that wandered ownerless over the countryside and so dressed them in wool, through the industry and skill that the queen Mama Ocllo Huaco had given to the Indian women in spinning and weaving. He taught them to make the footwear they now have, called *usuta.* For each town or tribe he subdued he chose a *curaca,* which is the same as cacique in the language of Cuba and Santo Domingo and means a lord of vassals. He chose them for their merits among those who had labored most in subjugating the Indians and had shown themselves most affable, gentle, and merciful, and most attached to the common good: these he made masters of the rest, so that they should indoctrinate them as fathers do their children. And he ordered the Indians to obey them as children do their fathers.

He ordered the fruits of the earth gathered in each town to be kept in common so as to supply each with his needs, until it should be feasible to give each Indian land of his own. Together with these precepts and ordinances, he taught them the divine worship of his idolatry. He fixed a site for the building of a temple to the Sun, where they were to make sacrifices to it, having persuaded them that they should regard it as their chief deity, whom they should adore and return thanks to for the natural benefits conferred by its light and heat, since they saw that it made their fields produce and their flocks multiply, together with the other mercies they daily received. And they particularly owed adoration and service to the Sun and the Moon for having sent down their children to them to deliver them from the savage life they had led and bring them the advantages of human existence which they now enjoyed. He ordered them to make a house for women of the Sun, so soon as there should be a sufficient number of women of the blood royal to people it. All this he ordered them to observe and comply with out of gratitude for the indisputable benefits they had received, and he promised them on behalf of his father the Sun many other advantages if they did so, assuring them that he did not say these things on his own account, but because the Sun had revealed them to him and bidden him repeat them to the Indians, and in this and everything else he was guided and taught by the Sun as by a father. The Indians, with the simplicity they have displayed then and ever since down to our own times, believed everything that the Inca told them, especially when he said that he was a child of the Sun. For among them too there are tribes that vaunted a similar fabulous descent, as we shall have cause to mention, though they did not make such a good choice as the Inca, but prided themselves on their origin from animals and other low and earthly objects. When the Indians of these and later times contrasted their descent with that of the Inca and saw that the benefits he had conferred on them bore witness to the fact, they believed most firmly that he was the child of the Sun and promised to observe and comply with what he ordered, and in short they worshipped him as a child of the Sun, confessing that no mortal could have done for them the things he had done, and thus they believed that he was a divine man come down from heaven.

CHAPTER XXII

The honorable insignia that the Inca gave to his followers.

THE Inca Manco Cápac busied himself with these and similar matters for many years, to the benefit of his subjects. Having experienced their fidelity, the love and respect with which they served him, and the veneration they bore him, he desired to favor them still further by ennobling them with titles and insignia such as he wore on his head: this was after he had persuaded them that he was a child of the Sun, so that they should esteem it the more. Thus the Inca Manco Cápac and all his descendants in imitation of him went with their heads shorn and wore only a finger's length of hair. They shaved themselves with stone razors, scraping them down the hair and leaving it as long as has been said. They used stone razors because they had not discovered scissors, and they shaved themselves with great trouble, as anyone can imagine. When they afterwards saw how easily and gently it was possible to cut with scissors, an Inca said to a schoolfellow of mine: "If the Spaniards, your fathers, had done no more than bring us scissors, mirrors, and combs, we would have given them all the gold and silver we had in our land."

As well as being shaven, they had their ears pierced, as women usually do for earrings, but they expanded the hole artificially (how I shall say at greater length in the proper place) to a remarkable size which would seem incredible to one who had not seen it, for one would think it impossible for so small a quantity of flesh as the lobe of the ear to be stretched until it could take a hoop the size and shape of the stopper of a jar, for the ear ornaments that they put in the loops they made in their ears were like plugs for pitchers. If the loops happened to break, they hung down a full quarter of a vara in length and half a finger in thickness. Because of this the Spaniards called the Indians "Big-Ears" [*orejones*].

The Incas wore as a headdress a plait they call *llautu*. It was of many colors and a finger's breadth wide and rather less in thickness. They wound it four or five times round their heads like a garland. These three insignia—the *llautu,* the shaving of the hair, and the piercing of the ears— were the chief fashions introduced by the Inca Manco Cápac. There were others we shall mention which were the insignia of the sovereign himself, and no one else was permitted to use them. The earliest privilege that the Inca granted his subjects was to order them to imitate him in all wearing the plait around their heads, though it was not to be of many colors like his own, but of one color only, which was to be black.

After some time had passed, he granted them the favor of another mark of distinction which they esteemed more highly: this was to order them to have their hair shorn, though in different styles for the various tribes of vassals and all theirs different from his, so that there should be no con- fusion in the distinction he had ordered to be made between each province and tribe and no lessening of the difference between him and them. Thus he bade some adopt a tail-plait in the form of an eared cap, that is by let- ting the hair of the scalp grow at the sides till it reached down to cover the ears but wearing it short over the forehead and temples. Others were bidden to wear their hair to reach halfway down the ears, and others even shorter, though none was to wear it so short as the Inca. It is noteworthy that all these Indians, and especially the Incas, took care not to let their hair grow, but wore it always at the same length, so as not to appear to be of one token on one day and another the next. Thus all of them were equally attentive to the marks of distinction they wore on their heads, for each tribe prided itself on its own, and most of them were received from the hands of the Inca himself.

CHAPTER XXIII

Other more honorable insignia and the name Inca.

AFTER SOME months and years, he granted them another favor, greater than the first, which was to bid them pierce their ears. There was however, a limitation as to the size of the hole, which was to be less than half that of the Inca's, and they were to wear different objects as ear-plugs according to their various names and provinces. Some were given as a token a splinter of wood as thick as the little finger, as were the tribe called Mayu and Çancu. Others were to have a little tuft of white wool which stuck out of the ear on both sides the length of the top of the thumb: these were of the tribe called Poques. The Muina, Huáruc, and Chillqui tribes were to have earplugs of the common reed the Indians call *tutura*. The Rimactampu tribe and their neighbors had them made of a plant called *maguey* in the Windward Islands and *chuchau* in the general tongue of Peru. When the bark is removed, the pitch is quite light, soft and spongy. The three tribes bearing the name Urcos, Y'úcay, and Tampu, all dwelling down the river Y'úcay, were given the special privilege and favor of wearing larger holes in their ears than the rest, though they were still to be less than half as large as those of the Inca. He gave them, and all the rest, the measurements of the size of his hole so that they should not exceed it. He also ordered them to make earplugs of the *tutura* reed that they might resemble those of the Inca more closely. They called them earplugs and not earrings, because they did not hang from the ears, but were fitted into the holes like a plug in the mouth of a jar.

According to his subjects themselves, the different tokens the Inca ordered to be made had another significance apart from serving as tokens to prevent tribes and names from being confused, and this was that the tokens most resembling the Inca's were the most honorable and most desirable. Yet he did not distribute them capriciously, affecting some of his subjects more than others, but in conformity with reason and justice. Those who had proved most docile in adopting his teaching and had labored most in reducing the other Indians were allowed to imitate him most closely in their insignia, and were awarded the greatest favor. He explained that what he did was by command and revelation of his father the Sun, and the Indians, believing this, gladly accepted all his orders and his treatment of them, for besides believing everything was done by revelation from the Sun, they experienced the benefits that ensued from obeying him.

Finally, when the Inca was already an old man, he ordered his chief followers to gather at the city of Cuzco and made them a solemn speech in which he said he expected soon to return to heaven to rest with his father the Sun, who was calling him (the word all the kings descended from him used when they felt the approach of death), and as he had to leave them he wanted to bequeath them the crown of all his favors and privileges, the use of his royal name, with which they and their descendants should live honored and respected by the whole world. So, in order that they should see that he loved them as children, he ordered them and their descendants to call themselves Incas, without any difference or distinction among them, as in the case of the past privileges he had given them: all were to enjoy the nobility of the name, since as they were his first subjects and had submitted to his will, he loved them like children and desired to give them his insignia and royal name and call them children, hoping that they and their descendants would serve the present king and his successors in the conquest and subjugation of the other Indians for the increase of their empire. He bade them keep all this in their hearts and memories, and repay it with their service like loyal subjects. He desired that their wives and daughters should not be called Pallas, like those of the blood royal, since women, being incapable of bearing arms in war like men, were also incapable of bearing that royal name.

From these Incas, who were so named by privilege, are descended those who at present exist in Peru called Incas; and their women are called Pallas and Coyas, taking advantage of the devaluation imposed on them and on many other peoples in this and other matters by the Spaniards. For there are very few of the Incas of the blood royal, and in their poverty and need only one is known here and there since their destruction at the hands of the cruel tyrant Atahuallpa. And the few that escaped it, or at least the principal and best known of them, perished in other calamities, as we shall say in due course. The Inca Manco Cápac set aside one of the insignia he wore on his head for himself and the kings who succeeded him: this was a red tassel, like a fringe, which stretched across the forehead between the temples. The heir to the throne wore a yellow one which was smaller than his father's. The ceremonies with which the prince was invested and sworn and the other insignia introduced later by the Inca kings we shall describe in their place, when we speak of the ceremony of knighting the Incas.

The Indians greatly esteemed the privilege of the insignias granted to them by their king because they came from his royal person, and although they had the differences we have mentioned, they accepted them gladly because the Inca persuaded them that he had granted them by order of his father the Sun according to the merits of each tribe. For this reason they were exceedingly proud of them. But when they saw the greatness of the last privilege, that of the name and renown of Incas, conceded not only to them but also to their descendants, they were astonished at the royal spirit of their prince and scarcely know how to extol his liberality and munificence. They said among themselves that the Inca, not content with bringing them from the state of wild beasts and converting them into men nor with showering on them many benefits and teaching them things necessary for human life and natural laws for moral life and the knowledge of their god the Sun, which indeed was sufficient to render them his perpetual slaves, had deigned to give them his royal insignia, and finally, instead of imposing taxes and tributes on them, had transferred to them the majesty of his name, a name so great that they held it to be sacred and divine and which no one dared utter unless with the greatest respect to make reference to their king. Yet now, in order to give them quality and style, he had made it so common that they could all apply it freely to themselves, having become his adopted sons and willing vassals of the child of the Sun.

CHAPTER XXIV

The names and titles the Indians gave to their kings.

THE INDIANS, pondering the greatness of the favors and love the Inca had displayed towards them, praised and blessed him greatly and sought names and titles fit to express the nobility of his mind and signify the sum of his heroic virtues. Such were two in particular among others they invented. One was *Cápac*, meaning "rich," not in estates, for, as the Indians say, this prince did not bring worldly goods but riches of the soul: mildness, mercy, clemency, liberality, justice and magnanimity, the desire to benefit the poor, and good works. Because this Inca had such great store of these riches as his followers relate, they say he was worthily called *Cápac*, which also means "rich and powerful in war." The other name was *Huacchacúyac*, "a lover and benefactor of the poor," as the first name referred to the greatness of his soul, the second signified the benefits he had conferred on his fellows. Thenceforward he was called Manco Cápac, having previously been known as Manco Inca. Manco is a proper name, but we do not know what it meant in the general tongue of Peru. In the private language the Incas used to converse among themselves (which they write to me from Peru is now quite forgotten) it must have had some meaning; for most of the names of the kings had, as we shall see when we give other names. The name *Inca*, applied to the prince, means "lord," or "king," or "emperor," and when applied to others means "lord." To translate its real meaning, it is "a man of the blood royal," for the *curacas,* however great lords they were, were not called Incas. *Palla* means "a woman of the royal blood," and to distinguish the king from the other Incas, they call him *Çapa Inca,* meaning "sole lord," just as the Great Turk is so called by his subjects. Further on we shall explain all the male and female royal names for the information of those who may be curious to know them. The Indians also called this first king and his descendants *Intip Churin,* meaning, "child of the Sun," but this name was given rather with respect to his nature, as they falsely believed it to be, than as a given name.

CHAPTER XXV

The testament and death of the Inca Manco Cápac.

MANCO CÁPAC reigned many years, but they cannot say for sure how many, some say above thirty, others above forty, busying himself with the matters we have mentioned. When he saw that he was near death, he summoned his children, who were numerous, by his wife, the queen Mama Ocllo Huaco, and by the concubines he had taken, saying that it was well that there should be many children of the Sun. He called also the chief of his subjects, and as testament he made them a long speech commending to his heir and his other sons the love and benefit of his subjects, and to his subjects fidelity and service to their king and the preservation of the laws he bequeathed them, declaring them to be ordained by his father the Sun. With this he dismissed his subjects and delivered another discourse to his sons in private. It was the last speech he made, and he enjoined them always to remember that they were children of the Sun, and to respect and worship it as god and father. He bade them imitate him in keeping the laws and commandments: they should be the first to obey them to set an example to the subjects, and they should be mild and merciful, subduing the Indians with love, and attracting them with good works and not by force, for constraint would never make good vassals. He also bade them maintain the rule of justice and suffer no wrongs to exist. Finally he told them to demonstrate by their virtues that they were children of the Sun, proving with works what they declared with words, so that the Indians should believe them: otherwise the Indians would mock them if they saw them say one thing and do another. He ordered them to commend what he commended them to their children from generation to generation, so that what his father the Sun had bidden might be fulfilled and observed, reminding them that these were all the Sun's words, and saying that he left them as his last will and testament. He said that the Sun had called him, and he was going to rest with his father, leaving them in peace, and that he would care for them in heaven and protect them and help them in all their needs. Having said this and similar things, the Inca Manco Cápac died. He left as his heir Sinchi Roca, his eldest son by the Coya Mama Ocllo Huaco, his wife and sister. In addition to the prince the king and queen left other sons and daughters, who married among themselves to preserve the purity of their blood, which was fabulously said to come from the Sun. They did indeed hold in the highest veneration the purity of the blood they received from this king and queen, without admixture of any other, for they held it to be divine and all the rest human, even that of the great lords over vassals called *curacas*.

The Inca Sinchi Roca married Mama Ocllo or Mama Cora, as others call her, his eldest sister, following the example set by their father and their grandparents, the Sun and Moon, for in their heathendom they held that the Moon was sister and wife to the Sun. This marriage was made to preserve the purity of their blood, and in order that the land might belong to the heir to the throne as much from his mother as from his father, and for other reasons we shall presently tell at length. The remaining brothers and sisters, legitimate and otherwise, also wedded one another, to ensure and increase the succession of the Incas. They said that the intermarriage of these brothers and sisters had been ordained by the Sun and that the Inca Manco Cápac had bidden it because his sons had no one to marry so that the purity of their blood might be preserved, but afterwards no one was to marry his sister except only the inheriting Inca. This was duly observed, as we shall see in the course of their history.

The Inca Manco Cápac was greatly mourned by his subjects. The weeping and obsequies lasted many months. They embalmed his body so as to keep it with them and not lose sight of it. They worshipped it as a god, a child of the Sun, and offered it many sacrifices of sheep, lambs, and ewes, tame rabbits, birds, fruits of the earth, and vegetables, confessing it to be lord of all the things Manco Cápac had left behind.

From what I saw of the state and character of these Indians, I suppose that the origin of this prince Manco Inca, whom his subjects called Manco

Cápac on account of his greatness, was that some Indian of good understanding, prudence, and judgment, perceiving the great simplicity of these
tribes, realized the need they had of teaching and instruction about the
natural life, and wisely and cunningly invented the fable to win their
esteem, saying that he and his wife were children of the Sun, that they
had come from heaven, and that his father had sent them to teach and help
those tribes. And in order to ensure their belief he probably adopted the
appearance and dress he used, especially the great ears the Incas affected,
which would certainly have seemed incredible to anyone who had not seen
them, as I have, and anyone who might see them now (if they are still
used) would wonder how they could possibly have enlarged them so.
And since the benefits and honors he conferred on his subjects confirmed
the fable of his genealogy, the Indians firmly believed that he was a child
of the Sun come down from heaven, and they accordingly adored him,
just as the pagans of antiquity, though less savage, gave worship to others
who conferred similar benefits. For those peoples are attentive above all
things in observing whether their teachers conform to what they teach, and
if they find life and doctrine conform, no arguments are necessary to persuade them to do what one wishes. I have mentioned this because neither
the Incas of the royal blood nor the common people know of any other
origin for their kings but what appears in their fabulous chronicles, which
agree with one another, and all concur in making Manco Cápac the first
Inca.

CHAPTER XXVI

The royal names and their meanings.

IT WILL BE well that we should say briefly the meanings of the royal titles
both for men and women, and to whom and how they were given and
how they used them, so as to show the care the Inca took in giving names
and titles, which in any case is a matter worthy of remark. To begin with
the name *Inca*, it must be realized that it means "king" or "emperor," referring to the royal person; but when applied to those of his lineage it
means "a man of royal blood," and the name *Inca* belonged to all of them
with this difference alone, provided that they were descendants in the male
line and not merely the female. They called their kings *Çapa Inca*, which

is "sole king" or "sole emperor" or "sole lord," for *çapa* means "sole," and they gave this name to no one else of his family, even to the heir until he should have inherited; for as the king was unique, the name could not have been applied to others without making many kings. The kings were also called *Huacchacúyac,* "lover and benefactor of the poor," and this title also is not given to any other but the king, by reason of the special care they all had, from first to last, to benefit their subjects. We have already explained the meaning of *Cápac,* "rich in magnanimity and royal qualities toward their followers." This was applied to the king alone and no other, because he was their chief benefactor. They also called him *Intip Churin,* or "child of the Sun," and this name was applied to all males of the blood royal, because according to the fable they descended from the Sun; but not to females. The sons of the king and all those of his parentage by the male line they called *Auqui,* which means "infante," the word used in Spain of younger sons of kings. The name was kept till they married, whereafter they were called *Inca.* These were the names and titles they gave to the king and to men of royal blood, as well as others we shall mention which, as proper names, became family names among their descendants.

Turning to the names and titles of the women of the blood royal, we see that the queen, the legitimate wife of the king, was called *Coya,* meaning "queen" or "empress." She was also called *Mamánchic,"* meaning "our mother," because in imitation of her husband, she performed the office of mother to all her relatives and subjects. Her daughters were called *Coya* after her, but not as their own natural title, for the name *Coya* belongs only to the queen. The king's concubines of his own stock and all other women of the blood royal were called *Palla,* meaning "a woman of royal blood." The remaining concubines of the king who were alien women not of his blood they called *Mamacuna,* which may be translated "matron," but which really means "a woman who is obliged to perform the office of mother." The princesses who were daughters of the king and all other daughters of the royal stock and blood were called *Ñusta,* or "maiden of the royal blood," but the following distinction was made. Those of legitimate royal blood were called simply *Ñusta,* which implied they were of legitimate royal blood. Those who were not of legitimate royal blood were called after the name of the province where their mother was born, as *Colla Ñusta, Huana Ñusta, Yunca Ñusta, Quitu Ñusta,* and so from the other provinces. This name of *Ñusta* they kept till they married, and after marriage they were called *Palla.*

These names and titles were applied to those descended from the blood royal in the male line. If this was wanting, even though the mother might be related to the king—for the kings often gave female relatives of bastard birth to the great lords as wives—the sons and daughters did not take the names of the blood royal, or call themselves *Incas* or *Pallas*, but merely the names of the fathers, for the Incas set no store by female descent so as not to diminish the nobility attributed to the blood royal. Even in the male line it lost a great deal of its royal character by being mixed with the blood of foreign women of a different lineage, quite apart from the question of the female line. Comparing some names with others, we find that the name *Coya,* or "queen," corresponds to that of *Çapa Inca,* or "sole lord"; and the name *Mamánchic,* or "our mother," to *Huacchacúyac,* "lover and benefactor of the people"; and *Ñusta,* or "princess," to *Auqui*; and *Palla,* "woman of royal blood," to *Inca.* Such were the royal names I saw and heard used by the Incas and Pallas, for it was chiefly with these that I conversed as a child. Neither the *curacas,* however great lords they might be, nor their wives nor children, could take these names, for they belonged solely to the blood royal, transmitted in the male line. Although Don Alonso de Ercilla y Zúñiga, in explaining Indian terms in the elegant verse he writes, gives the explanation of *Palla* as a lady of many vassals and estates, he does so because the names *Inca* and *Palla* were improperly applied to many people at the time this gentleman dwelt in those parts. For illustrious and heroic names are coveted by all people, however low and barbarous, and if there is no one to prevent them they soon usurp the noblest names, as has happened in my country.

End of the First Book

BOOK
TWO *of the*
FIRST PART

which describes the idolatry of the Incas and the way in which they glimpsed our true God, and believed in the immortality of the soul and the universal resurrection; It tells of their sacrifices and rites, how for administrative purposes they recorded their subjects in decuria; the office of decurion; the life and conquests of the second king, Sinchi Roca, and of the third Lloque Yupanqui; and the knowledge attained by the Incas.

It contains twenty-eight chapters.

CHAPTER I

The idolatry of the second period and its origin.

HAT WE CALL the second period and the idolatry practiced during it began with the Inca Manco Cápac. He was the first to establish the monarchy of the Inca kings of Peru who reigned for above four hundred years, though Padre Blas Valera says for more than five and nearly six hundred. We have already said who Manco Cápac was and whence he came, how he established his empire, and his subjection of his first Indian vassals, how he taught them to sow, breed stock, and build houses and towns, and other things necessary to sustain a natural life, and how his sister and wife, the Queen Mama Ocllo Huaco, taught the Indian women to spin, weave, bring up their children, and serve their husbands with love and joy, and everything else that a good housewife should do at home. We have said too how he taught them the natural laws and precepts for the moral life for their common good, so that they should not give offence to one another either in their honor or in their possessions.

He also taught them their idolatry and bade them hold and worship the Sun as their chief deity, persuading them to do so on account of his beauty and brightness. He said that the Pachacámac (which is the sustainer of the earth) had not placed the Sun above all the stars in heaven and given him these as his handmaidens for any other reason than that they should worship him and hold him as their god. He represented to them the many benefits the Sun conferred on them and how finally he had sent down his own children to change their state from that of brutes to that of men, as they had seen by experience and would see even more clearly as time went by. On the other hand he undeceived them about the lowness and vileness of their many gods, asking what expectation could they have that such vile objects would succor them in their need and what blessings had they received from those animals comparable with those they received daily from his father the Sun. Let them consider—for their eyes would undeceive them—that those herbs, plants, and trees, and other objects they had worshipped had been created by the Sun for the service of men and sustenance of animals. Let them notice the difference that existed between the splendor and beauty of the Sun and the filth and ugliness of the toad, lizard, frog, and other vermin they regarded as gods. Moreover he bade the Indians hunt out such vermin and bring them to him, and pointed out that such creatures should more properly inspire horror and disgust than esteem and adoration. With these arguments and others as simple the Inca Manco Cápac persuaded his first subjects to worship the Sun and accept him as their god.

The Indians, convinced by the Inca's arguments and by the benefits they had received and undeceived by the evidence of their own eyes, accepted the Sun as their sole god, without the company of father or brother. They regarded their kings as children of the Sun, for they believed very simply that the man and woman who had done so much for them must be his children come down from heaven. So they then worshipped them as divine and continued so to worship their descendants with a much greater venera-ation, both inward and outward, than the ancient gentiles, the Greeks and Romans, bestowed on Jupiter, Venus, and Mars, etc. I should add that even today they worship them as they did then, and on mentioning any one of their Inca kings they first make a great show of adoration. If they are reproached for this and reminded that the Inca kings were men and not gods, as they well know, they reply that they are undeceived with re-gard to their idolatry, but that they worship them for the many great benefits received from them, that those kings treated their subjects as Incas and children of the Sun should, and that if anyone could point out such men to them nowadays they would be no less ready to worship them as divine.

This was the principal idolatry of the Incas and the one they taught their vassals, and though they made many sacrifices, as we shall say further on, and had many superstitions, such as believing in dreams, looking for omens, and other things quite as ridiculous as many of the things they prohibited, at least they had no other gods than the Sun, which they adored for his excellent qualities and natural benefits, as more rational and civi-lized people than their predecessors in that first stage. And they dedicated temples of incredible richness to the Sun, and although they considered the Moon to be the sister and wife of the Sun and the mother of the Incas, they did not worship her as a goddess or offer her sacrifices or build temples to her. They held her in great veneration as the universal mother, but did not go beyond in their idolatry. Lightning, thunder, and thunder-bolts they considered to be servants of the Sun, as we shall see, in the chamber made for them in the house of the Sun at Cuzco, but they were not considered to be deities, as some of the Spanish historians say. On the contrary they abominated, and still do, any house or any place in the fields that is struck by a bolt: they used to shut the door of such a house with stone and mud so that no one could ever get in, and they would mark the place in the field with a landmark so that no one should tread there. They held such places to be ill-fated and accursed, and said that the Sun had marked them out as such by his servant the thunderbolt.

All this I saw in Cuzco, for in the royal house that had belonged to the Inca Huaina Cápac, in the part of it that fell to Antonio Altamirano when the city was divided among the conquerors, there was a room where a thunderbolt had fallen in the days of Huaina Cápac. The Indians shut the doors with stone and mud and took it as an ill omen upon their king, declaring that he would lose part of his empire or suffer some similar misfortune, since his father the Sun had marked his house as a place of ill fortune. I beheld the closed room. The Spaniards later rebuilt it, and within three years another bolt struck the same room and burnt it all up. Among other things, the Indians said that as the Sun had stamped the spot as accursed, why should the Spaniards have chosen to rebuild it instead of leaving it in ruins. If, as that historian asserts, they regarded thunderbolts as gods, they would obviously have worshipped such places as sacred and made their finest temples there, arguing that their gods— lightning, thunder, and thunderbolts—wanted to dwell there and marked them and consecrated them themselves. The three phenomena together are called *illapa*, and they applied the name to the arquebuss, owing to the resemblance. The other names they apply to the thunder and the Sun as a trinity are new inventions of the Spaniards. On this point and on other similar ones the Spanish writers have no real authority for what they say, for such names do not exist in the general language of the Indians of Peru, and even in the new compound language they are not proper compounds and do not mean at all what people think or intend them to mean.

CHAPTER II

The Incas glimpsed the true God, our Lord.

IN ADDITION to worshipping the Sun as a visible god, to whom they offered sacrifices and dedicated great festivals, which we shall describe, the Inca kings and their *amautas,* who were the philosophers, perceived by the light of nature the true supreme God our Lord, the maker of heaven and earth, as we shall see from the arguments and phrases some of them applied to the Divine Majesty, whom they called Pachacámac. The word is composed of *pacha,* "the world, the universe," and *cámac,* present participle of the verb *cama,* "to animate," derived from the noun *cama,* "the soul." Pachacámac means "him who gives life to the universe," and in its fullest sense means "him who does to the universe what the soul does to the body." Pedro de Cieza (ch. lxxii) says: "The name of this demon is intended to mean creator of the world, since *cama* means 'maker' and *pacha* 'world,' " etc. As a Spaniard, he did not know the language as well as I, who am an Indian and an Inca. They held the name in such veneration that they dared not utter it except when they must, and then only with signs and demonstrations of great respect: raising the shoulders, bowing the head and trunk, raising the eyes to heaven and dropping them to the ground, raising their open hands before their shoulders and kissing the air, all of which the Incas and their vassals did as proof of great adoration and reverence suitable for mentioning the name of Pachacámac, for worshipping the Sun, and for venerating the king, and for no other purpose. In all this however there were degrees. Those of the blood royal were honored with part of these ceremonies, and other rulers such as the caciques with other much lesser observances. Inwardly they regarded the Pachacámac with much greater veneration than the Sun, for, as I have mentioned, they did not dare to utter his name and the Sun they alluded to on every occasion. If asked who was the Pachacámac, they would say "he who gave life to the universe and sustained it," but they did not know him because they had never seen him, so they did not make temples to him or offer him sacrifices, but adored him in their hearts—that is, mentally—and held him to be the unknown god. Agustín de Zárate (Book II, ch. v) recounting what Fray Vicente de Valverde said to the king Atahuallpa, that Christ our Lord had created the world, says the Inca replied that he did not know anything about that, nor that anyone had created anything but the Sun, whom they considered to be God, and the earth their mother and her huacas: and that Pachacámac had created everything there was, etc. This shows that those Indians regarded him as the creator of all things.

It is true as I am saying, therefore, that the Indians were on the track of the truth with this name, and gave it to our own true God. The Devil himself testified as much, despite himself, though as the father of lies he disguised the truth with lies and lies with the truth in his own favor. For as soon as he saw our holy Gospel preached among the Indians and saw them accepting baptism, he told some of his familiars in the valley now called Pachacámac (from the great temple erected there to the unknown god) that the God the Spaniards were preaching about and the Pachacámac were one and the same, as Pedro de Cieza de León states in his *Demarcation of Peru* (ch. lxxii). And the Reverend Father Jerónimo Román says the same in his *Republic of the Western Indies* (Book I, ch. v). Both refer to the same Pachacámac, but not knowing the true sense of the word, they apply the name to the Devil. The Devil was right in saying that the God of the Christians and the Pachacámac were one and the same, for the intention of the Indians was to give the name to the Most High God who gives life and being to the universe, as the very name implies. But the Devil was quite wrong in saying that he was the Pachacámac, for the Indians never intended this name for the Devil, whom they called *Çúpay,* meaning "devil," and on naming him, they first spat as a sign of malediction and abomination, but Pachacámac they mentioned with the marks of adoration and the rites we have mentioned. Yet as the enemy had such power among those infidels, he made himself god and insinuated himself into everything they venerated and held holy. He spoke in their oracles and temples and in the corners of their houses and other places, saying that he was Pachacámac and all the other things the Indians looked on as deities. Thus deceived, they worshipped the things out of which the Devil spoke to them, thinking it was the deity of their imagination, for if they had understood that it was the Devil they would have burnt them then as they are doing now, through the mercy of God who desired to reveal Himself to them.

The Indians do not understand or dare not tell these things with the true interpretation and meaning of the words. They see that the Christian Spaniards abominate them all as works of the Devil, and the Spaniards do not trouble to ask for clear information about them, but rather dismiss them as diabolical, as they imagine. This effect is also produced by the fact that they do not know properly the general language of the Incas by which they might understand the derivation, composition, and true meaning of such words. Consequently the Spaniards in their histories give another word for God, *Tici Viracocha,* whose meaning neither they nor I can give. The name *Pachacámac,* which the Spanish historians so abominate because they do not understand it, is "God." On the other hand they are right, because the Devil spoke in that splendid temple pretending to be God under that name, which he adopted for himself. But if anyone should now ask me (who by God's infinite mercy am a Catholic Christian Indian), "What is the word for God in your language?" I should answer, "*Pachacámac,*" because in the general language of Peru there is no word but this for God. All the rest given by the historians are generally incorrect. They are either not from the general speech, or are corrupted from the tongue of some special province, or are merely invented by the Spaniards. Some of the newly invented words are acceptable as renderings from the Spanish, such as the *Pachaya chácher,* which they pretend means "creator of heaven," though it means "teacher of the world"—for creator one would have to say *Pacharúrac,* from *rura,* "to make"—nevertheless they do not fit into the general language for they are not natural to it, but strangers. And also in honest truth they rather lower the name of God from that dignity and majesty to which the correct name of Pachacámac raises it. In order to explain our meaning, we may mention that *yacha* is "to learn," and on adding the syllable *chi* means "to teach." The verb *rura* is "to make" and by adding *chi* is "to have made," and so on with other verbs. And as the Indians paid no attention to abstract speculation, but only to material things, these verbs do not mean "to teach spiritual things or to make great and divine things, such as the world," etc., but "to make and teach trades or humble, mechanical crafts," acts that appertain to men and not to the deity. The name Pachacámac is quite free of these material associations. It means, as we have said, "to do to the universe what the soul does to the body, to give it being, life, growth, and sustenance," etc. This clearly shows the incorrectness of the names newly composed to be applied to God (if they are to be used in the true meaning of the language) owing to the baseness of their meaning. It may be hoped that in time they will become cultivated and more acceptable. The devisers of new names should take care to avoid changing the meaning of the noun or verb in the compound word, since it is important that the Indians should accept them and not turn them to ridicule. This is especially important in the teaching of Christian doctrine for which new words must be devised, though with great care.

CHAPTER III

The Incas kept a ✠ in a sacred place.

T HE INCA KINGS had in Cuzco a cross of fine marble, of the white and red color called crystalline jasper. They cannot say how long they have had it. When I left in 1560 it was in the sacristy of the cathedral church of that city, where it hung from a nail by a cord running through a hole in the top of the cross. I remember that the cord was a strip of black velvet. Maybe in Indian times it had a holder of silver or gold, and whoever found it exchanged it for this strip of silk. The cross was square, as broad as it was high, and would be perhaps three quarters of a vara or a little less in size, each arm being about three fingers in width and the same in thickness. It was all in one piece, very well carved, with its edges perfectly smooth, both sides exactly matched, and the stone polished to a high luster. They used to have it in one of their royal houses, in one of the chambers called *huaca,* "a sacred place." They did not worship it, though they held it in reverence, possibly because of its handsome appearance or for some other reason they could not express. It was so preserved till the marquis Don Francisco Pizarro entered the valley of Túmbez, and because of what occurred to Pedro de Candía there they worshipped it and held it in greater veneration, as we shall mention hereafter.

The Spaniards, when they won the imperial city and made a temple to our Most High God, put this cross in the place I have mentioned, with no more ornament than has been said, though it was fit to stand on the high altar with adornments of gold and precious stones of both of which they found so much. It would thus have disposed the Indians toward our holy faith, for they would have been able to compare its objects with those of their own, such as this cross, and with other points in their laws and ordinances that closely approach the natural law and could be compared with the commandments in our holy law and the works of mercy. These, as we shall see, had close parallels in their gentile faith.

And with reference to the cross, we may mention that here, as is well known, it is usual to swear by God and the cross to affirm a statement, both in a place of judgment and on other occasions, and many do so without any need, but simply from a bad habit. Such people will be confounded to know that the Incas and all the tribes of the empire never knew what swearing was. We have seen with what veneration and respect they uttered the names of Pachacámac and the Sun, whom they only mentioned to adore. When they examined a witness, however grave the matter, the judge said to him instead of administering an oath: "Do you promise the Inca to tell the truth?"

The witness would say: "Yes, I promise."

The judge then said: "See that you tell it without any mixture of falsehood and without concealing anything that took place, but say plainly all you know of this case."

The witness then repeated: "I truly promise."

Then under promise he was left to tell all he knew of the affair, and not interrupted with: "We are not asking you that, but this," or anything else. If it were a question of a civil dispute, even one involving a murder, they said to the witness: "Say clearly what happened in this dispute, and conceal nothing of what either of the two who quarrelled did or said." And the witness did so, saying what he knew for or against both parties. The witness dared not lie, for the people were very humble and devout in their idolatry, and moreover he knew that if his lie were detected he would be punished with great severity and often with death if the case were a serious one. This was not so much because of the harm that he might have done with his words, but because he had lied to the Inca and broken the Inca's royal mandate that no lie should be told. The witness knew that to speak to any judge was to address the Inca himself, whom they adored as a god, and it was chiefly out of regard for this, as well as for other reasons, that they told no lies.

After the Spaniards conquered the empire, a serious case of murder took place in a province of the Quechuas. The corregidor of Cuzco sent a judge to investigate, who, in taking the deposition of a *curaca* (a lord of vassals), placed the cross of his wand of office before him and told him to swear to tell the truth by God and the cross. The Indian said, "I have not been baptized and cannot swear as the Christians do." The judge answered that he was to swear by his gods, the Sun, the Moon, and the Incas. The *curaca* answered: "We only take these names to worship them; it is not lawful for me to swear by them."

The judge said: "What assurance have we of the truth of your deposition if you do not take an oath?"

The Indian replied: "My promise is sufficient, and the fact that I know that I am speaking in the presence of your king, since you have come to do justice in his name; this is what we did before our Incas. But to give you the assurance you seek, I will swear by the earth, bidding it open and swallow me alive as I stand here if I lie."

The judge took the oath, seeing he could get no other, and asked him the necessary questions to establish who were the murderers. The *curaca* replied, but seeing that they asked nothing about the victims, who had been the aggressors in the dispute, he asked to be allowed to say all he knew about it, for his understanding was that if he told one side and was silent about the other it was equivalent to lying, and he had not told the whole truth as he had promised. And though the judge told him it was enough that he should answer what he was asked, he said he was not satisfied nor would he fulfil his promise unless he said in full what both parties had done. The judge completed his investigation as best he could and returned to Cuzco, where the conversation he reported he had had with the *curaca* caused great wonder.

CHAPTER IV

Of many gods wrongly attributed to the Indians by the Spanish historians.

RETURNING to the idolatry of the Incas, we must enlarge upon the assertion already made that they had no other gods but the Sun, which they worshipped outwardly. They made temples to him, the walls of which were lined from top to bottom with gold plates. They sacrificed many things to him. They presented to him great gifts of much gold and all the things they held most precious, in gratitude for what he had given them. They set aside as his own property a third of all the cultivated land in the kingdoms and provinces they conquered and the harvests from them and innumerable flocks. They built cloistered and secluded houses for women who were dedicated to the Sun and preserved perpetual virginity.

In addition to the Sun they worshipped the Pachacámac (as has been said) inwardly, as an unknown god. They held him in greater veneration than the Sun. They did not offer sacrifices to him or make temples for him, for they said that he was not known to them because he had not allowed himself to be seen. Yet they believed he existed. In its proper place we shall mention that famous and wealthy temple there was in the valley called Pachacámac, which was dedicated to this unknown god. Thus the Incas worshipped only the two gods we have mentioned, the one visible and the other invisible. For the princes and their *amautas,* the philosophers and doctors of their commonwealth, although they had no knowledge of letters and never used them, realized that it was unworthy and dishonorable to accord divine honor, power, titles, fame, and virtue to inferior things under heaven. So they established a law and ordered it to be published abroad so that everyone in their empire should know that they were not to worship anyone but Pachacámac, as supreme god and lord, and the Sun, on account of the good he did everyone; and the Moon was to be venerated and honored because she was the Sun's wife and sister, and the stars as ladies and handmaidens of her house and court.

Further on we shall duly treat of the god Viracocha, which was a phantom that appeared to a prince who was heir to the throne of the Incas, and declared that he was a child of the Sun. The Spaniards attribute many other gods to the Incas because they are unable to distinguish the times and idolatries of the first age from those of the second. Moreover they are not well enough acquainted with the language to be able to ask for and obtain information from the Indians, and their ignorance has led them to attribute to the Incas many or all of the gods the latter removed from the Indians they subjected to their empire, and these subject peoples had many strange gods, as we have said. A particular source of this error was that the Spaniards did not know the many diverse meanings of the word *huaca.* This, when the last syllable is pronounced from the top of the palate, means "an idol," such as Jupiter, Mars, or Venus, but it is a noun and does not admit the derivation of a verb meaning "to idolatrize." Beyond this first and main meaning it has many others, examples of which we shall set down so that they may be better understood. It means " a sacred thing," such as all those in which the Devil spoke: idols, rocks, great stones, or trees which the enemy entered to make the people believe he was a god. They also give the name *huaca* to things they have offered to the Sun, such as figures of men, birds, and animals made of gold, silver, or wood, and any other offerings held sacred because the Sun had received them and they were his, and consequently to be greatly venerated. *Huaca* is applied to any temple, large or small, to the sepulchers set up in the fields, and to the corners in their houses where the Devil spoke to their priests and to others who conversed with him familiarly—these corners were held to be sacred and regarded as oratories or sanctuaries. The same name is given to all those things, which for their beauty or excellence, stand above other things of the same kind, such as a rose, an apple, or a pippin, or any other fruit that is better or more beautiful than the rest from the same tree, or trees that are better than other trees of the same kind. On the other hand they give the name *huaca* to ugly and monstrous things that inspire horror and alarm: to the great serpents of the Antis which reach twenty-five and thirty feet in length. They also call *huaca* everything that is out of the usual course of nature, as a woman who gives birth to twins. Both mother and twins were given this name because of the strangeness of the occurrence: the mother was taken out into the streets with great rejoicing and celebration and garlanded with flowers, accompanied with much singing and dancing in praise of her fecundity. Other tribes, however, took it as a mischance, and wept, as though the birth of twins were an ill omen. The same name *huaca* is applied to sheep that bear two lambs at a birth. I refer, of course, to the sheep of Peru, which is large and usually gives birth to only one at once, like cows and mares. They preferred to offer twin lambs rather than others, where possible, in their sacrifices because they considered them of greater divinity, and so called them *huaca.* Similarly double-yolked eggs are *huaca,* and so are children born feet first or doubled up, or with six fingers or toes, or humpbacked, or with any other defect, great or small, of body or face, such as a harelip, which is very common, or a squint, which they call "marked by nature." They apply the word also to great springs that flow like rivers, because they excel the rest in size, and to pebbles and stones found in brooks and streams if they are of unusual shape or many colors, and so different from the rest.

They use the word *huaca* of the great range of the Sierra Nevada, which runs the whole length of Peru down to the Strait of Magellan, on account of its length and height which is certainly truly remarkable to anyone who ponders on it. The same name is given to very high hills that stand above the rest as high towers stand above ordinary houses, and to steep mountain slopes on the roads which may be three, four, or five leagues from top to bottom and as sheer as a wall: these are what Spanish writers call *apachitas,* corrupting the Indian name, and declaring that the Indians worshipped them and made offerings to them. We shall presently speak of these slopes and say who was worshipped and how. All these things and others like them were called *huaca,* not because they were considered gods and therefore worthy of adoration, but because of their special superiority over the common run of things, for which reason they were regarded and treated with veneration and respect. Because of these very various meanings, the Spaniards, who only understood the first and main sense of "idol," think that the Indians regarded as gods everything they called *huaca* and that the Incas worshipped all these things just as the Indians of the first age had done.

To explain the name *apachitas* given by the Spaniards to the crests of steep slopes which they say the Indians worship, it is necessary to note that the correct form is *apachecta*. This is the dative: the genitive is *apachecpa,* whence the present participle *apáchec*, which is the nominative. The syllable *-ta* makes the dative. The sense is "that which causes to rise," without saying who it is or what is raised. But by the nature of the language, as we have already said and shall have occasion to repeat when we discuss the wealth of meaning that the Indians are able to pack into a single word, the word implies "we give thanks and offer something to the one who enables us to carry these burdens and gives us health and strength to scale such rugged slopes as this." They never use the word until they have reached the top, and that is why the Spanish writers call the summits *apachitas*; supposing the Indians meant the latter when they were heard to use the word *apachecta* and not understanding its real meaning, they transferred it to the slopes. The Indians meant, by the light of their natural understanding, that thanks should be given and some offering made to Pachacámac, the unknown god they inwardly worshipped, for having aided them in these labors. Thus, having scaled the slope, they deposited their burdens and, raising their eyes to heaven and dropping them to the ground wih the same gestures of adoration I have already mentioned for the naming of the Pachacámac, they used to repeat two or three times the dative *apachecta*, and in order to make an offering they would pluck their eyebrows and blow any hair that came out toward the sky or they would take the herb called coca, which they so much esteem, from their mouths. The implication was that they offered up what they prized most. And if they could find nothing better, they would offer a stick or some straws if there were any lying about, or if not, a pebble, and if there were no pebble, a handful of earth. And there were great piles of these offerings on the top of the slopes. They did not look at the Sun during this ceremony, for it was not he, but the Pachacámac, they were adoring. The gifts were really rather tokens of their feelings than offerings, for they were well aware that such poor things were not fit for offerings. I myself am a witness to all this, for I have often seen it done when travelling with them. I should add that unladen Indians did not do it, but only those with burdens. Nowadays, through God's mercy, crosses have been placed at the crests of the hills, and they worship them in gratitude that our Lord Jesus Christ has revealed Himself to them.

CHAPTER V

Of many other meanings of the word Huaca.

THE SAME WORD *huaca*, when the last syllable is pronounced deep down in the throat, becomes a verb. It means "to mourn." This has caused two Spanish historians, who did not know the difference, to state that the Indians enter their temples for their sacrifices weeping and wailing, for such is the meaning of *huaca*. Although the difference between this meaning of "mourn" and the others is so great and it is a verb and the other a noun, the difference is really shown by the different pronunciation, without changing any letter or accent, the last syllable being uttered from the top of the palate in one case and from deep down in the throat in the other. The Spaniards, however diligent (as they ought to be), take not the slightest notice of this pronunciation or others in the native language, because they do not exist in Spanish. Their negligence may be illustrated from what occurred to me with a Dominican monk who had been four years in Peru as professor of the general language of the empire. Knowing me to be a native of the country, he got in touch with me and I visited him often at San Pablo in Córdova. It happened one day in discussing the language and the many different meanings of single words, I gave this noun *pacha* as an example: when pronounced straightforwardly, according to the values the letters have in Spanish, it means "world" or "universe" and also means "heaven and earth" and "hell" and "ground."

The friar said: "But it also means 'clothes,' 'utensils,' and 'house furniture'."

I said: "Yes, but tell me, Father, what difference is there in pronunciation in that case?"

He answered: "I don't know."

I explained: "You are a master of the language and you don't know that! Well, let me tell you that when it means 'utensils' or 'clothes,' you pronounce it with the lips tightly pressed together and forcing them open with the breath, so that you hear the plosive." I demonstrated the pronunciation of this word and others viva voce, for there is no other way to teach it. The professor and his fellow monks who were present were astonished. This clearly shows how ignorant Spaniards are of the secrets of the language, for they were unknown to this monk, although he had been a professor of it. Consequently many errors and misinterpretations are written about it, as for example the assertion, made without realization of the various meanings the word has, that the Incas and their vassals worship as gods everything they call *huaca*. We have said enough of the idolatry and gods of the Incas. In their idolatry and in that of the previous age the Indians are greatly to be admired, both in the second age and in the first, since among such a confusion and such a hotch-potch of gods, they never adored pleasures and vices like the olden gentiles of antiquity who paid worship to admitted adulterers, murderers, drunkards, and especially priapism, this in spite of their pretensions to literature and knowledge, while the Indians were remote from all learning.

The idol Tangatanga, which one author says was worshipped at Chuquisaca and was one in three and three in one, I have never heard of, nor does the word exist in the general language of Peru. It may be a word in the speech of that province, which is 180 leagues from Cuzco, but I suspect the word is corrupt, because the Spaniards corrupt all other languages they try to speak, and the word should be *acatanca*, which means a "scarab" or "beetle." It is composed of the noun *aca*, "dung," and the verb *tanca* (the last syllable pronounced down in the throat), "to push"; so *acatanca* is the "dung-pusher."

It would not surprise me that it should have been worshipped as a god in Chuquisaca in the first age of ancient heathendom before the Inca empire, for as we have seen they worshipped other things as vile in those days, but not after the coming of the Incas, who prohibited it. That they should say that the god was three in one and one in three is a new invention of the Indians, made after hearing of the Trinity and of the unity of our Lord God, to win favor with the Spaniards by pretending that they had some things similar to our holy religion, like this trinity, and the trinity which the same author says they imputed to the Sun and to lightning, and the statement that they had confessors and confessed their sins like Christians. All this is invented by the Indians with the object of gaining some benefit from the resemblance. I can affirm this as an Indian who knows the nature of the Indians. And I can declare that they had no idols with the name of the trinity; although the general language of Peru, having relatively few words, comprehends in one word three or four different things—for instance the word *illapa* covers "lightning," "thunder," and "thunderbolt," and *maqui*, "hand," covers "hand," "forearm," and "biceps," and *chaqui*, which pronounced straightforwardly as in Spanish means "foot," covers "foot," "leg," and "thigh," and so on with many words we could mention. This does not prove that they worshipped idols with the name of trinity or had any such word in their language, as we shall see. It would not surprise me that the Devil should seek to get them to worship him under this name, for he had great power over those infidel idolators who were so far from Christian truth. I simply say what those gentiles had in their vain religion. I may mention also that the word *chaqui,* when pronounced with the first syllable in the top of the palate, is a verb meaning "to be thirsty or dry," or "to dry anything that is wet," which is another case of three meanings for one word.

CHAPTER VI

What an author says about their gods.

A MONG THE papers of Padre Blas Valera I found the following, which I have gladly taken the trouble to translate and insert here since it adds the weight of his authority to what I have been saying. Referring to the sacrifices offered up and the gods worshipped by the Indians of Mexico and other countries, he says:

It is impossible to explain in words or to imagine without horror and alarm how contrary to religion, how terrible, cruel, and inhuman were the various sacrifices made by the Indians in ancient times, or the multitude of gods they had, which in the city of Mexico and its district alone exceeded two thousand. These idols and gods in general were called Teutl, though each had its special name. But the statements of Peter Martyr and of the bishop of Chiapas and others that the Indians of the islands of Cozumel who are subject to the province of Yucatán regarded the sign of the cross as God and worshipped it, and that in Chiapas they had heard of the Holy Trinity and of the incarnation of our Lord, are merely interpretations imagined by these and other Spanish writers and applied to these mysteries, just as in their histories of Cuzco they apply the three statues said to have been in the temple of the Sun together with those of thunder and lightning to the Trinity. If in our own day, after receiving so much instruction from priests and bishops, they barely know if there is a Holy Spirit, how could those barbarians sunk in such dense darkness have a clear idea of the mystery of the Incarnation and of the Trinity? The method used by our Spanish historians was to ask the Indians in Spanish what they wanted to know. Their contacts either had no clear knowledge of the old days or had bad memories and told them wrong, or gave incomplete accounts min-gling the truth with poetic inventions and fabulous stories. Worst of all, each side had only a very defective and incomplete knowledge of the other's language as a basis for asking and answering questions. This arose from the great difficulty presented by the Indian language and the little instruction the Indians then had in Spanish, so that the Indian understood the Spaniard's questions badly and the Spaniard understood the Indian's replies even worse. Very often either party understood the opposite of what was said; otherwise something similar but not the exact meaning, and it was only rarely that the true sense was conveyed. In this state of great confusion, the priest or layman asking for information took at his will and pleasure whatever seemed closest to and most like what he wanted to know and what he thought his Indian had said. Thus interpreting things according to the whim of their imagination, they wrote down as true things the Indians never dreamed of. For in the true histories of the Indians none of the mysteries of our Christian religion are to be found. There is no doubt that the Devil in his arrogance has always sought to be esteemed and honored as God, not only in the rites and ceremonies of the heathen, but also in some customs of the Christian religion. These customs he had introduced, like an envious monkey, into many regions of the Indians so that he might be the more honored and esteemed by those wretched men. So in one region they practiced oral confession to purge themselves of their sins; in another they washed the heads of children; and elsewhere they kept very rigorous fasts. Sometimes they willingly gave up their lives for their false faith: just as in the Old World faithful Christians offered themselves to martyrdom for the Catholic faith, so in the New World the heathen offered themselves to death for the accursed Devil. But when they say that Icona is God the Father, and Bacab God the Son, Estruac God the Holy Spirit, and Chiripia the Holy Virgin Mary, and Ischen the blessed St. Anne, and that Bacab slain by Eopuco is Christ our Lord crucified by Pilate, all this and the like is pure invention and fiction on the part of Spaniards, for the natives are quite ignorant of them. The truth is that these were men and women so named whom the natives of the country honored among their gods, for the Mexicans had gods and goddesses they worshipped including some very filthy ones who were looked on as gods of the vices. They included Tlazoltéutl, god of lust; Ometochtli, god of drunkenness; and Vitcilopuchtli, god of strife and murder. Icona is the father of all the gods whom he begot on various wives and concubines: he was the god of fathers of families. Bacab was the god of sons of families; Estruac god of the air; Chiripia mother of the gods and the earth; Ischen, stepmother of the gods; and Tláloc god of the waters. Other gods were honored as the authors of moral virtues, such as Quetzalcoatl, the aerial god, who was the reformer of customs; still others as patrons of human life in its various ages. They had innumerable idols and effigies of gods invented for various duties and purposes. Many of them were very base. Some gods were in common; others were special. They were annual, and every year everyone changed and varied them at will. When the old gods were forsaken as infamous or because they were no good, other gods and household demons were chosen. They had also invented gods to preside over and rule the ages of children, young people, and the old. When children came into their inheritance they could accept or reject their parents' gods, who could not rule over them against their wishes. The old honored other greater gods and also forsook them and created others in their place at the end of the year or age of the world, as the Indians said. Such were the gods of all the natives of Mexico, Chiapas, Guatemala, Vera Paz, and other places, who thought they had chosen the greatest, highest, and most sovereign of all the gods. The gods they worshipped when the Spaniards first set foot there were all born, made, and chosen after the renewing of the Sun in the last age, and according to López de Gómara each Sun consisted of 860 years, though the Mexicans themselves say it was much less. This manner of counting the age of the world in Suns was common to the Indians of Mexico and Peru. According to their count, the years of the last Sun are counted from the year 1043 A.D. There is thus no doubt but that the ancient gods which the natives of the Mexican empire worshipped in the Sun, or age, before the last, or more than 600 or 700 years earlier, were all, as they themselves say, drowned in the sea, and that they invented many other gods in their place. This clearly shows that the interpretation of Icona, Bacab, and Estruac as Father, Son, and Holy Ghost is false.

All the other peoples in the northern parts corresponding to the northern parts of the Old World, that is the provinces of the great Florida and all the islands, had no idols or spell-making gods. They merely worship what Varro calls natural gods—the elements, the sea, lakes, rivers, springs, hills, wild animals, snakes, crops, and similar things—a custom that originated first with the Chaldeans and after spread to many various nations. Those who ate human flesh, who occupied all the Mexican empire and all the islands, and a great part of the territories of Peru, practised this evil and beastly custom until the rule of the Incas and the Spaniards.

All this is quoted from Padre Blas Valera. Elsewhere he mentions that the Incas worshipped only the sun and planets, and that they imitated the Chaldeans in this.

CHAPTER VII

*They apprehended the immortality of the soul
and the universal resurrection.*

THE INCA *amautas* held that man was composed of body and soul, and
that the soul was an immortal spirit, while the body was made of
earth, for they saw it turn to earth. They therefore called man *allpaca-
masca,* "animated earth." To distinguish him from the brutes they called
him *runa,* "a man of understanding and reason," and the brutes in general
were called *llama,* "a beast." They attributed to the latter a vegetative and
sensitive spirit, since they saw that they grew and felt, but had not the
rational spirit. They believed there was another life after this, with punishment for the wicked and rest for the good. They divided the universe
into three worlds. Heaven they call *Hanan Pacha,* "the upper world,"
where they said the good went to be rewarded for their virtues. They
called this world of generation and corruption *Hurin Pacha,* "the lower
world," and they called the center of the earth *Uca Pacha,* meaning "the
world below this," where they said the wicked went, and more explicitly
they called it by another name *Çupaipa Huacin,* "house of the Devil."
They did not consider the other life to be spiritual, but corporeal, like
this. They said that the rest of the upper world was living a quiet life,
free from the labors and cares in which this life is passed. The life of the
lowest world, on the other hand, which we call hell, they considered to be
full of all the sickness and pains, cares and toils that are known here, without remission and comfort. Thus they divided the present life in two, giving all joy, happiness, and content to those who had been good, and all the
torment and toil to those who had been bad. They did not include carnal
delights or other vices among the joys of the other life, but only quietness
of spirit without care and the repose of the body without corporeal labors.

The Incas thus believed in the universal resurrection, not for glory or
pain, but for a temporal life, for they could not raise their minds above
this present life. They took great care to preserve the hair they cut off or
combed and the nails they clipped, placing them in rocks and crannies in
the wall: if they fell down, any Indian who saw them would pick them
up and replace them. I have often asked various Indians in various places
why they did this, to see what they would say. They always replied with
these words: "All we who were born must return to live in the world

(they had no verb for 'to resurrect'), and the souls are to rise from their sepulchers with everything that belonged to their bodies. And so that ours do not have to linger looking for their hair and nails—for on that day there will be great haste and much to-do—we put them together so that our souls will rise sooner. As far as possible, we always spit in the same place." López de Gómara (ch. cxxv), speaking of the burials of kings and great lords in Peru, uses these words which we reproduce verbatim: "When Spaniards open these sepulchers and scatter the bones, the Indians ask them not to do so, so that they may be together for the resurrection, for they do believe in the resurrection of the body and immortality of the soul" etc. This clearly shows what we have said, for this author, though he lived in Spain and never went to the Indies, heard the same account. The treasurer Agustín de Zárate (Book I, ch. xii) used almost the same words as López de Gómara; and Pedro de Cieza (ch. lxii) says the Indians believed in the immortality of the soul and resurrection of the body. I came across these authorities and that of López de Gómara when reading them, after I had written what my relatives believed about this point in their heathendom. I was very glad to find these references, for unless some Spaniard had mentioned it, so strange a thing as the resurrection among gentiles would have appeared to have been an invention of my own: I can however certify that I only found them after I had written what I have, lest it be thought that I have merely followed Spanish writers. Naturally when I do find such references I am glad to quote them in confirmation of what I have heard my own people recount of their ancient tradition. The same thing occurred with the law against sacrilege or adultery with the wives of the Inca or of the Sun (of which we shall speak later): after writing my version I came upon the subject by chance in reading the history of the treasurer Agustín de Zárate, and was delighted to find confirmation of such an important matter in a Spanish historian. I do not know how or by what tradition the Incas may have received the resurrection of the body as an article of faith, nor is it for a soldier like me to investigate it; nor do I think that it can be established for certain until the Most High God be pleased to reveal it. I can only truthfully say that they did believe it. All this I wrote in the history of Florida, taking it from its place in obedience to the venerable fathers of the Holy Society of Jesus, Miguel Vázquez de Padilla of Seville and Gerónimo de Prado of Ubeda, who instructed me to do so. I have now taken it thence, though late, because of certain tyrannical acts, and restore it to its place, so that so important a stone may not be lacking in the edifice. And so we shall place others as they offer themselves, for it is not possible to set down all at once all the childish deceptions the Indians entertained. One of these was that the soul left the body while it slept, for they said the soul could not sleep: what the soul saw in the world are the things we say we dream. Because of this vain belief they attached so much importance to dreams and their interpretation, believing them to be auguries and omens from which much good might be expected or much ill feared, as the case might be.

CHAPTER VIII

The things they sacrificed to the Sun.

THE SACRIFICES offered by the Incas to the Sun consisted of many different things, such as domestic animals, great and small. The chief and most esteemed sacrifice was of lambs, followed by that of rams, and then of barren ewes. They sacrificed tame rabbits and all the birds they ate, tallow alone, crops and vegetables (including the coca plant), fine garments, all of which they burnt in place of incense and offered as a thanksgiving for everything created by the Sun for man's sustenance. They also offered as a sacrifice much of the brew they drank, made of water and maize, and during their ordinary meals when their beverage was brought to them after eating—for they never drank while eating—they would wet the tips of their fingers in the first cup and looking devoutly at the sky, would toss up the drop with a flip of the finger, offering it to the Sun as a thanksgiving for what he had given them to drink, at the same time kissing the air two or three times, which, as we have said, was a token of worship among the Indians. Having made this offering from the first cups, they then drank what they wished without more ado.

This last ceremony or idolatrous practice I have seen performed by unbaptized Indians, for in my time there were still many old ones not yet baptized, and I myself baptized some in case of need. So that in the matter of sacrifices the Incas were almost exactly like the Indians of the first age. The only difference was that they did not have death sacrifices with human flesh or blood, but rather abominated and prohibited them as they did cannibalism. If some historians have said otherwise, this was because their informants deceived them and did not distinguish between the periods and places when and where such sacrifices of men, women, and children were made. So one historian writes, speaking of the Incas, that they sacrificed men, and states the provinces where he says the sacrifices were made. One of these is just under a hundred leagues from Cuzco, the city where the Incas made their sacrifices, another two hundred leagues south of Cuzco, and the third over four hundred leagues north, so that it is clear that the failure to distinguish between time and place often caused the attribution to the Incas of things they prohibited to the subjects of their empire, though the latter practiced them in the first period, before the Inca kings.

I can bear witness to having heard my father and his contemporaries many times compare the two states of Mexico and Peru, with particular reference to the question of human sacrifice and the eating of human flesh. They praised the Incas of Peru for not indulging in or permitting these two practices, and equally abominated the Mexicans who performed both of them, inside and outside the city of Mexico, as devilishly as the history of its conquest says. And it is reported on good grounds, though secretly, that the author of the history was the very man who twice conquered and won the city: I personally believe this, for I have heard trustworthy gentlemen say so on good evidence both in my own country and in Spain. And the work itself shows as much when carefully studied. It is indeed a pity that it was not published under his own name so that the work might have greater authority and the author have imitated in everything the great Julius Caesar.

To return to the sacrifices, we have said that the Incas neither practiced them nor permitted them to be made with men or children, even when their kings were sick (as another historian asserts). They did not in fact consider the sicknesses of kings as the same as those of common people, but held them to be messengers, as they said, from their father the Sun, who came to call his child to rest with him in heaven. Thus it was common for the Inca kings who felt themselves on the verge of death to say: "My father is calling me to rest with him." Because of the vain belief they had taught the Indians, and in order that they should not doubt this and all the similar things about the Incas being children of the Sun, they would not oppose his will by offering sacrifices when they were sick, since they themselves declared that he was calling them to rest with him. This is sufficient to show that they did not sacrifice men, women, and children, and further on we shall relate at greater length the common and individual sacrifices they offered, and the solemn festivals in honor of the Sun.

On entering the temples, or when already inside, the person of highest rank among them would pluck his eyebrows as though pulling hairs out, and whether any came out or not, he would make the gesture of blowing them toward the idol as a token of worship and offering. This form of worship was not performed for the king, but only for idols or trees or other objects into which the Devil entered to speak to them. The priests and witches did the same when entering the secret places and corners to speak with the Devil, as if they obliged their imagined deity to hear and reply to them, since the ritual meant that they offered their persons to him. I too have seen them perform this idolatrous custom.

CHAPTER IX

The priests, rites and ceremonies, and laws
attributed to the first Inca.

THEY HAD priests to offer up their sacrifices. The priests of the House of the Sun in Cuzco were all Incas of the blood royal. The remaining services of the temple were performed by Incas by privilege. They had a high priest, who was an uncle or brother of the king, or at least a legitimate member of the royal family. The priests wore no special vestments, merely the normal dress. In other provinces where there were temples of the Sun (which were numerous), the priests were natives of the province and relatives of the lords or rulers. However, the principal priest (or bishop) had to be an Inca so that the sacrifices and ceremonies should conform with those of the capital, for in all the chief offices of peace or of war Incas were placed in charge, though the natives were not deprived of office or despised or tyrannized over. They had also many houses of virgins, some of whom kept perpetual virginity and never left their houses, while others were royal concubines. I shall have more to say of their rank, reclusion, duties, and devotions.

The Inca kings, wherever they wished to establish laws or sacrifices either for sacred matters in their false religion or for the secular purposes of their temporal government, always attributed it to the first Inca Manco Cápac, saying that he had ordered all the laws, but that some had been drawn up and put into practice by him while others had merely been outlined for his descendants in due time to formulate them. For as they declared that the first Inca was the child of the Sun come down from heaven to rule over the Indians and give them laws, they declared that his father had taught him all the laws he was to make for the common benefit of men and all the sacrifices they were to offer in their temple. They affirmed this fable so as to give authority to all they commanded and ordained. For this reason one can never say with certainty which of the Incas made any particular law, for as they had no writing they similarly lacked many of the things that are preserved in writing for posterity. What is certain is that the Incas made the laws and ordinances, sometimes establishing new ones and sometimes repeating and revising old ones, according to the requirements of the times. One of their kings, as we shall see in relating his life, was held to be a great legislator. They say he gave many new laws and reformed and amplified all the existing ones, and that he was a great priest because he ordained many rites and ceremonies relating to the sacrifices, and enriched many temples with great wealth, and that he was a general who gained many kingdoms and provinces. However, they do not say precisely what laws he instituted or what sacrifices he ordained, and they can find no better solution than to attribute them all to the first Inca, who is thus credited with the foundation of the empire and of all its laws.

Bearing in mind this confusion, we will here mention the first law on which the government of the whole commonwealth was based. After mentioning it and some others, we shall advert to the conquests made by each king, and as we relate their deeds and lives we shall insert other laws and customs, modes of sacrifice, the temples of the Sun, the house of the virgins, the chief festivals, their ceremony of creating knights, the service of their houses, and the greatness of their court, so that the variety of subjects shall render their perusal less wearisome. But first I must substantiate what I have said with accounts of the same matters from the Spanish historians.

CHAPTER X

*The author compares what he has said
with the statements of the
Spanish historians.*

IN ORDER to show that what I have said above of the origins of the Incas
and of the state of things before their time is not my own invention, but
in agreement with the accounts given by the Indians in common to all the
Spanish historians, I have resolved to include a chapter written by Pedro
de Cieza de León, a native of Seville, in the first part of the *Chronicle of
Peru, which treats of the demarcation of its provinces, the description of
them, the foundations of the new cities, the rites and customs of the Indians, and other matters,* such being the author's title for his work. He
wrote it in Peru, and in order to do so with greater accuracy travelled, as
he himself says, the twelve hundred leagues stretching from the port of
Urabá to the town of La Plata, now called the City of Silver. In each
province he set down what he heard of its customs, whether barbarous or
civilized. He wrote them making the proper distinction between different
times and periods. He describes the state of each tribe before the Incas subdued it and what it was like after they began to rule. He spent nine years
in gathering information and writing his account, from 1541 until 1550.
Having set down what he found from Urabá to Pasto, he begins a separate chapter (ch. xxxviii of his work) on entering the boundaries of the
Incas, saying:

As I shall often have to refer to the Incas in this first part, and to mention
their dwellings and other matters of note, I have thought fit to say something
of them here so that my readers may know what these rulers were like, and be
aware of their merits, and not confuse one thing with another, though I have,
of course, devoted a special book to them and their deeds, and it is a very
copious work. From the reports the Indians of Cuzco give us, we gather that in
ancient times there was great disorder in all the provinces of the kingdom we
call Peru, and it is hardly credible how little reason and understanding the
natives had, for they are said to have been most brutelike and to have eaten
human flesh: some took their daughters and mothers to wife and committed
other even greater and graver sins, having much intercourse with the Devil
whom they all served and held in high esteem.

They had also castles and fortresses on the highest hills and peaks and sallied forth from them to make war on one another on the slighest pretext, killing and capturing as many as they could of their enemies. And although they were involved in these sins and committed these wickednesses, some of them are said to have been much attached to religion, so that in many places great temples were built where they prayed and the Devil revealed himself and was worshipped by them with great sacrifices and superstitious ceremonies before their idols. While the people lived thus, there appeared some great tyrants in the province of Collao and other places who made great wars on one another and committed many murders and robberies. Great calamities were suffered at their hands, and many castles and fortresses destroyed, and the rivalry between them continued, to the delight of the Devil, that enemy of humankind, that so many souls should be lost.

While all the provinces of Peru were in this state, there appeared a brother and sister, the name of the former being Manco Cápac, of whom the Indians relate great marvels and very attractive fables. This can be read in the book I have composed, when it is published. This Manco Cápac founded the city of Cuzco and established laws after his own usage. He and his descendants called themselves Incas, a name that means kings or great lords. They were so powerful that they conquered and governed from Pasto to Chile. Their banners saw the river Maule to the south and the river Angasmayo to the north, and these were the limits of their empire, which was so great that it stretched above thirteen hundred leagues from end to end. They built great fortresses and strongholds, and placed captains and governors in all their provinces. Their deeds were so great and their rule so good that few in the world have bettered them. They were intelligent and great computers, though they had no writing, which had not been discovered in that part of the Indies.

They imposed good customs on all their subjects and bade them wear *usutas,* which are a kind of sandal, instead of shoes. They were familiar with the immortality of the soul and other secrets of nature. They believed there is a Creator of all things, and held the Sun to be the supreme god, and made great temples in his honor, but, deceived by the Devil, they worshipped trees and stones, as the heathen do. In the chief temples they had a great many very beautiful virgins, as there were in Rome in the temple of Vesta, and they preserved almost the same regulations as these. For their armies they chose captains from among the bravest and most faithful men they could find. They were also most adroit at winning over their enemies to friendship without war. But those who rebelled were punished with great severity and no little cruelty. And since, as I have said, I have written a book about these Incas, the foregoing shall be enough to give those who may read this book to understand what these kings were like and what their merits were, wherefore I shall return to my path.

All this appears in ch. xxxviii. It will be seen that he gives the sum of what I have said and am about to say concerning the idolatry, conquests, and rule in peace and war of the Inca kings: he goes on with an account

of Peru running to eighty-three chapters and always speaking favorably
of the Incas. And of the provinces where he says they made human sacrifices, practiced cannibalism, went naked, were ignorant of agriculture, or
had other abuses such as the worship of vile and filthy things, he always
mentions that under the rule of the Incas they lost their evil habits and
learnt those of the Incas. Speaking of many other provinces which had the
same abuses, he remarks that they had not yet been reached by the rule of
the Incas. Dealing with the provinces where such barbarous customs did
not prevail, but there was some civilization, he says: "These Indians were
improved under the empire of the Incas." So that he always credits them
with having removed abuses and improved good customs, as we shall show
in due course, quoting his very words. Anyone who wishes to study them
at length should refer to his book, where the devilry of the Indian customs is described. Even if one tried to invent such things, human imagination would boggle at such horrors. But since the Devil was their author,
it is no cause for surprise, for he instilled the same ideas into the ancient
heathens and does so still to those who have not received the light of the
Catholic faith.

In all his history, though he says that the Incas or their priests conversed
with the Devil and had other notable superstitions, he never says that
they sacrificed men or children, except that, in speaking of a temple near
Cuzco, he says they sacrificed human blood there, which they drew by
bleeding from between their brows and poured onto a crust of bread, as
we shall have occasion to say: there was however no question of the death
of men or children. He says that he met many *curacas* who had known
Huaina Cápac, the last of the Inca kings. He received many of the reports
he had written down from them, and they were then (that is fifty years or
so ago) different from the reports received today, for they were more recent and closer to the period under discussion. I have gone into all this
to rebut the opinions of those who say the Incas sacrificed men and children, which they certainly did not. Some may think it does not matter,
for it was all idolatry, yet so inhuman an accusation should not be made
unless it is known for a fact. Padre Blas Valera, speaking of the antiquities
of Peru and of the sacrifices the Incas made to the Sun, recognizing it as
their father, says the following words, which I copy literally: "In whose
veneration their successors made great sacrifices to the Sun of sheep and
other animals, but never of men, as Polo and those who have followed him
falsely assert," etc.

What I have said about the first Incas having issued from Lake Titicaca
is also in Francisco López de Gómara's *General History of the Indies* (ch.

cxx), when he speaks of the lineage of Atahuallpa, whom the Spaniards captured and killed. Agustín de Zárate, the former treasurer of his majesty's revenue, says it too in his history of Peru (Book IV, ch. xiii), and the most venerable Padre José de Acosta, S.J., says as much in the famous work he wrote on the natural and moral philosophy of the New World (Book I, ch. xxv), where he very often speaks in praise of the Incas. So that we are not making new assertions, but merely amplifying and extending with our own account—as a native Indian from those parts —what the Spanish historians, as strangers, have told in brief because they did not know the language properly and could not suck in with their mother's milk, as I did, these fables and facts. Now let us pass on to describe the order established by the Incas in the government of their kingdom.

CHAPTER XI

They divided the empire into four districts; they made a census of their subjects.

T HE INCA KINGS divided their empire into four parts, which they called *Tahuantinsuyu,* meaning "the four quarters of the world," corresponding to the four cardinal points of heaven: east, west, north, and south. They took as the central point the city of Cuzco, which in the private language of the Incas means "the navel of the world." The semblance of the navel is a good one, for all Peru is long and narrow like a human body, and the city is almost in the middle. They called the eastern part Antisuyu, from a province called Anti in the east, whence they called Anti the whole of that great range of snowcapped mountains that runs to the east of Peru, indicating that it is to the east. They called the west part Cuntisuyu from a small province called Cunti. The northern quarter they called Chinchasuyu, from a great province called Chincha, to the north of the city. And the district to the south they called Collasuyu, from a very extensive province called Colla to the south. By these four provinces they implied all the land in the direction of the four parts, even if many leagues beyond the limits of those provinces. Thus the kingdom of Chile, though more than six hundred leagues to the south of the province of Colla was in Collasuyu, and the kingdom of Quito, though above four hundred leagues north of Chincha, was in Chinchasuyu. The names of these quarters were thus the same as saying eastwards, westwards, etc., and the four main highways issuing from the city were also so called because they led to the four parts of the empire.

As the basis and foundation of their government the Incas devised a law which they thought would enable them to prevent and stem all the evils that might arise in their empire. They ordered for this purpose a register of all the towns of the empire, great and small, by decuries of ten, one of the ten, called the decurion, being put in charge of the other nine. Five decuries of these rulers of ten had a superior decurion who commanded fifty; two decuries of fifty had a superior decurion who ruled a hundred. Five decuries of a hundred were subject to another captain-decurion who ruled five hundred. Two companies of five hundred acknowledged a general with command over a thousand. The decuries never exceeded a thousand, for they said that a commission to command a thousand men was enough to bring out the best in a leader. There were thus decuries of ten, of fifty, of a hundred, of five hundred, and of a thousand, each with a decurion or group leader, subordinated one to another, greater and less, up to the last and highest decurion which we have called a general.

CHAPTER XII

Two duties performed by the decurions.

THE DECURIONS of ten were obliged to execute two tasks in relation to the men in their decury or group: first, to act as advocate to assist them with diligence and care in any case of need, taking their case to the governor or any other minister whose duty it might be to succor them, perhaps to ask for grain if they had none to sow or eat, or wool to wear, or the rebuilding of their house if it had collapsed or was burnt, or in any other case of need, great or little. The other duty was to be procurator to report any offence, however slight, which must be referred to the decurion above, whose duty it was to apply a punishment or refer it to the decurion above him. The judges were thus superior to one another and settled cases according to the seriousness of the crime, so that there was never any lack of a judge to deal summarily with a case, and it was not necessary to take each case to higher judges with one or more appeals, and so on to the judges of the supreme court. They held that delay in punishment encouraged crime, and that appeals, proofs, and objections could make civil suits everlasting, and the poor would rather forgo justice and lose their goods than suffer the vexation of delay which cost them thirty to recover ten. They therefore provided that every town should have a judge with powers to give a final decision in suits between the inhabitants, excepting those between one town and another about grazing rights or boundaries, for which the Incas would send a special judge, as we shall say.

Any of the officers, of lower or higher rank, who neglected the performance of his duties as advocate was punished more or less severely, according to the need he had failed by his negligence to meet. Anyone who did not inform on the transgression of any subject, even though it was only an unjustifiable delay of a day, made the fault his own, and was punished on two accounts: for neglecting his own duty and for the other's sin, which he had made his own by not reporting it. And as each officer had a procurator to watch over him he tried hard to do his duty conscientiously and fulfil his obligation. There were therefore no vagabonds or idlers, and none dared do what he ought not do for his accuser was near and his punishment severe—generally a sentence of death, however slight the crime, for they said that the punishment was not for the crime done nor for the wrong given but for the breaking of the commandment and word of the Inca whom they respected as a god. And although the aggrieved person desisted from the suit or did not institute it, justice was applied by obligation as part of the ordinary duties of the officers, and they applied the full penalty prescribed by the law in each case according to the degree of the crime, which might be death, whipping, exile, or the like.

A child was punished for the crimes he committed like anyone else, according to the gravity of his offence, even though it was no more than boyish naughtiness. The penalty was increased or lessened according to the age and innocence of the person, and fathers were severely punished for not having instructed and corrected their children from an early age so that they should not grow up naughty or acquire bad habits. The decurion's duty was to accuse both son and father of any crime, so they brought up their children with great care lest they should be guilty of naughty or wanton acts in the streets or fields. Given the docile nature of the Indians, the boys grew up under the instruction of their parents so well trained that there was no difference between them and gentle lambs.

CHAPTER XIII

On certain laws the Incas had in their government.

THEY HAD no pecuniary fines or confiscation of property, saying that to
punish the offender's possessions and leave him alive was not the
way to rid the state of evil-doing, but merely to rid the evildoer of his responsibilities and leave him the freer to commit greater misdeeds. If any
curaca rebelled—and this was the crime the Incas punished most severely
—or committed any other crime that merited the death penalty, even
though the latter was inflicted, the victim's successor was not deprived of
his estate, but entrusted with it with a warning about the guilt and punishment of his father so that he should beware of a similar fate. Pedro de
Cieza de León says the following of the Incas on this subject (ch. xxi):
"They had a further device so as not to make themselves hated by the natives: they never deprived those who inherited chiefdom by birth of their
powers. If one of them happened to commit a crime or was guilty of some
offence which required that he should be deprived of his office, they presented and entrusted the chiefdom to his children or brothers and commanded the rest to obey them," etc. This is from Pedro de Cieza. The same
principle was observed in time of war: captains from the provinces whence
they brought their troops were never displaced from the command. They
kept their posts even as field commanders, and other generals of the royal
blood were set over them. The local commanders were glad to serve as
subordinates to the Incas, saying they were their limbs, being their ministers and soldiers. The Incas' vassals regarded this service as a great favor.
The judge had no discretion about the penalties required by law, but was
obliged to apply them in their integrity, under pain of death for infringement of the royal command. They held that if the judge had discretion
the majesty of the law, established by the king with the opinion and consent of the gravest and most experienced men of the Council, would be
diminished. Moreover such gravity and experience was wanting in single
judges, and the use of discretion would make them venal and open the
door to the purchase of justice by bribery or importunity, leading to utter
confusion in the state, since each judge would do as he thought fit and it
was not right that anyone should constitute himself a legislator, when his
duty was to execute what the law prescribed, however rigorous. Of course,
when one considers how severe the laws were and that the usual penalty
for even a small infraction was, as has been said, death, it may be main-

tained that they were the laws of barbarians. Yet, if we ponder on the benefit received by the commonwealth from this very severity, we may on the contrary affirm that they were the laws of wise people who wished to extirpate evil-doing from their state. The infliction of the legal penalties with such severity and the love of life and hatred of death natural in men caused them to detest the crimes that led to death. Consequently there was hardly any crime to punish the whole year through in the empire of the Incas, the whole thirteen hundred leagues of it and all its various tribes with their different languages being governed by the same laws and ordinances, as if it were of one house. The fact that the laws were regarded as divine was also important in securing that they were kept with love and respect, for as in their vain faith they held the kings to be children of the Sun and the Sun to be God, they considered any ordinary command of the king to be a divine commandment, and the special laws for the common good even more so. So they said the Sun ordered the laws to be made and revealed them to his child the Inca. Hence lawbreaking was held to be sacrilegious and anathema, even if the crime were committed in ignorance.

It often happened that such delinquents felt the accusations of their own conscience and came to make their hidden sins manifest before the seat of justice. For besides believing that their souls would be damned, they held it as certain that misfortunes would be brought upon the commonwealth by their faults and sins, including sicknesses, death, famine, and other private or public evils. They would say that they wished to appease their god by their deaths, so that he should not send down misfortunes to the earth through their sin. I imagine it to have been on account of these public confessions that the Spanish historians have sought to assert that the Peruvian Indians confessed in secret, as we Christians do, and that they had chosen confessors. This, however, is a false account which the Indians have given to flatter the Spaniards and ingratiate themselves with them, replying to the questions they are asked according to what they think is the wish of the questioner, and not in conformity with the truth. There were certainly no secret confessions among the Indians (I speak of those of Peru and do not meddle with other tribes, kingdoms, or provinces I do not know), but merely these public confessions in which they sought exemplary chastisement.

There were no appeals from one court to another in any suit, whether civil or criminal, for as the judge had no latitude, the law applicable to the case was enforced simply at the first instance and the case was closed, though indeed, owing to the government of those kings and the way of life of their subjects, there were in any case few civil cases. Each town had a judge for the cases that might occur, and he was obliged to carry out the law within five days after hearing the parties. If any case of more importance or greater atrocity than usual occurred for which a higher judge was required, they would go to the capital of the province there to have it settled, for in the chief town of each province there was a higher governor in case of need, so that no plaintiff need leave his own town or province to seek justice. For the Inca kings understood that the poor, because of their penury, could not be expected to seek justice outside their provinces or in many courts because of the expense involved and the inconvenience they would suffer, which often exceed the value of the object of the case. Thus justice perishes, especially if the poor sue the rich and powerful, who crush the justice of the poor with their might. Wishing to remedy these wrongs, the Inca princes gave no occasion for the judges to exercise discretion or for many courts to exist, or for plaintiffs to have to travel beyond their own provinces. The ordinary judges had to report the sentences they gave each moon to superior judges, and these reported to higher judges, for at court there were judges of various ranks, according to the kind and seriousness of the business. Indeed in all the ministries of the Inca state there was a hierarchy from the lower to the higher and so up to the supreme officers, who were presidents or viceroys of the four quarters of the empire. The reports were made to show that due justice had been administered so that the lower judges should not neglect it, or if they did neglect it, that they should be severely punished. This was a kind of secret investigation made every month. The manner of making such reports to the Inca and the members of his Supreme Council was by means of knots tied in strings of various colors which they read as figures. Knots of certain colors meant the crimes punished, and small threads of various colors attached to the thicker strings showed the penalty meted out and the law that had been applied. Thus they made themselves understood without the use of writing. Later we shall devote a separate chapter to a fuller account of the method of counting by means of these knots. It certainly often amazed the Spaniards that their own best accountants went astray in their calculations while the Indians were perfectly accurate in dividing and reckoning, and the more difficult the operation the easier it seemed. Those who operated the system did nothing else day or night, and thus became perfect and highly skilled in it.

If any dissension arose between two kingdoms or provinces about boundaries or grazing rights, the Inca would send one of the judges of the blood royal, who enquired, and saw with his own eyes what the two parties claimed, and tried to reconcile them: the decision was given as a judgment in the Inca's name and became an inviolable law, as if pronounced by the king himself. If the judge failed to reconcile the parties, he reported what had happened to the Inca with his recommendation about the claims of each party and the obstacles. The Inca then pronounced sentence, or if the judge's report did not satisfy him, ordered the case to be suspended until he should next visit the district so that he could see for himself and decide accordingly. Their subjects regarded this as a great grace and favor on the part of the Inca.

CHAPTER XIV

The decurions gave an account of
births and deaths.

RETURNING to the group leaders or decurions, we must mention that, in addition to the two duties they had as advocates and procurators, they were obliged to furnish to their superiors in the hierarchy a monthly account of births and deaths of both sexes: thus at the end of the year the king had an account of the annual births and deaths and of those who had gone to the wars and been killed. The same rule and order was preserved in wartime, with group leaders, ensigns, captains, field commanders, and a general in order of rank. They had the same duties of accusers and protectors toward their men, and for this reason there was as much order in the heat of battle as in the quiet of peacetime or in the midst of the court. They never allowed conquered towns to be sacked, even though they were acquired by force of arms. The Indians said that by taking great care in the punishment of first offences it was possible to avoid the second and third and the host of others that are committed in states which do not take the trouble to root up weeds as soon as they appear. They thought it was not a sign of good government, nor of a desire to suppress evil-doing to wait until complaints were lodged before chastising malefactors, for many of those aggrieved hesitated to complain so as not to make public the wrong they have suffered and wait to take vengeance in their own hands. Thus great scandals arise in the commonwealth, which could be avoided by

watching carefully over everyone and punishing offenders forthwith
without waiting for someone to lodge a complaint.

The decurions had names corresponding to the number of persons subordinated to them. The first decurions were called *chunca camayu,* "having charge of ten," comprised of *chunca, "ten,"* and *camayu,* "one who
has charge"; and so on with the other numbers, which we shall not give in
the native language for fear of prolixity, though it might be agreeable to
the curious to see two or three numbers that form compounds with
camayu: the latter word is also used in many other senses as a compound
with another noun or verb denoting the object of the charge. The same
word, *chunca camayu,* has another sense of "inveterate gambler," one who
has a pack of cards in the hood of his cloak, as the saying is. Any game is
chunca because all games are reckoned with numbers, and as all numbers
go in tens, they use "ten" as a game, and to say "let's play a game" they use
the word *chuncásum,* which strictly means "let's count in tens or by numbers" and thus "play." I mention this to show how many meanings the
Indians derive from a single word; this makes it very difficult properly
to understand the language.

By means of these decurions the Inca and his viceroys and governors of
provinces knew how many subjects there were in each town and could
thus apportion without injustice the contributions they were each obliged
to make in common to the provincial public works, bridges, thoroughfares,
paved roads, royal buildings, and so on, and also the number of men they
were obliged to send in case of war, either as soldiers or as porters. If anyone returned from the war without permission, his captain or lieutenant
or group leader accused him, and his decurion in his own place, and he
was punished with death for treachery in having disloyally abandoned his
comrades, his relatives, and his commander, and finally the Inca or the
general who represented his person.

The Inca ordered the number of vassals of all ages in each town to be
calculated every year for another reason apart from the question of contributions and military service: this was to assess the abundance or want
existing in each province, so that the quantity of supplies necessary to
succor them in years of scarcity and bad harvests might be known and
made provision for: similarly the quantity of wool and cotton needed to
clothe them at all seasons was known, as we shall see. All this the Inca
commanded to be calculated and provided against so that in case of need
there should be no delay in succoring the wants of his subjects. On account of the foresight of the Incas for the good of their subjects, Padre
Blas Valera often says that they should not be called kings at all, but

prudent and careful guardians of wards. The Indians, to express this in a word, called them "lovers of the poor."

Lest the governors and judges or any lesser officials, or those of the treasury of the Sun or of the Inca, should neglect their offices, there were inspectors and investigators who secretly visited the districts to see what the official did wrong, and to report it to the superiors whose duty it was to punish their subordinates. These were called *túcuy rícoc,* "he who looks at everything." These officials, like all others who were concerned in the government of the Inca state, or administration of the royal estates, or the like, were subordinated one to another so that none should neglect his office. Any judge, governor, or lower official who was found to have been guilty of injustice or to have committed any other fault in his office was punished more severely than any private person for a similar crime, and the more severely according to the degree of his office, for they said that it was intolerable that any who had been chosen to give justice should do wrong or that one set to punish crime should commit it, this being an offence to the Sun and to the Inca who had chosen him to be better than all his subjects.

CHAPTER XV

The Indians deny that an Inca of the blood royal has ever committed any crime.

IT DOES NOT appear that any of the Incas have ever been punished, at least publicly, and the Indians themselves deny that such a thing has ever happened. They say that the Incas never committed any fault worthy of public or exemplary punishment because the teaching of their parents and example of their elders and the common repute that they were children of the Sun, born to instruct and benefit the rest, restrained and guided them, and made them an example rather than a scandal to the commonwealth. The Indians said too that the Incas were also free from the temptations that are often the cause of crimes, such as the passion for women, covetousness, or the desire for vengeance, for if they desired beautiful women it was lawful for them to have as many as they wanted, and if they took a fancy to any pretty girl and sent to ask her father for her, he would not only not refuse but would give her up with expressions of the greatest thankfulness that the Inca should have deigned to take her as his mistress or servant. Similarly about property: the Incas had no lack of anything that might impel them to take the goods of others, nor were they suborned by necessity for wherever they were, as governors or not, they had at their disposal all the property of the Sun and of the Inca which was either under their direct control, or if they were not governors, then the governors and magistrates were obliged to give them what they needed, for it was said that as children of the Sun and brothers of the Inca they were entitled to have the part they needed in the estates. They also had no occasion to kill or wound anyone out of vengeance or hatred, for no one could offend them. On the contrary they were adored only less than the royal person; and if anyone, however great a lord, offended an Inca, it was considered sacrilege and an offence to the royal person, and accordingly punished very severely. But it can also be stated that no Indian was ever punished for offending the person, honor, or estate of an Inca, because as the Indians considered them gods the case never occurred, just as there is no record of an Inca being punished for crime. The two cases are comparable, for the Indians will not admit they have ever offended the Incas or that the Incas have committed any serious wrong, and they are scandalized that the Spaniards should enquire about it. Thus the Spanish historians have said that there was a law that no Inca should die for any crime. Such a law would have been scandalous to the Indians, who would have said it would license the Incas to commit any crime they wished and have made one law for them and another for the rest. They would rather have degraded and expelled such a one from the royal blood and then punished him more severely; for, being an Inca, he would have become an *auca,* that is a tyrant, traitor, renegade.

Speaking of the justice of the Incas, Pedro de Cieza de León says of their army in ch. xlix: "And if there was any disturbance or robberies in the surrounding districts, they were at once punished with great rigor, the Incas showing themselves so exact in the rendering of justice that they did not hesitate to carry out the penalty even on their own children," etc. In ch. lx, speaking also of their justice, he says: "Consequently if anyone travelling with him made so bold as to enter the sown fields or houses of the Indians, even though they did little harm, he had them killed," etc. The author says this without making distinction between those who were Incas and those who were not, for their laws were applicable to all. Pride in being children of the Sun was what mainly stimulated them to be good, so as to stand above the rest both in goodness and in blood and persuade the Indians that both things were hereditary in them. They believed it, too, so implicitly that when a Spaniard spoke in praise of anything done by the kings or their families, the Indians would reply: "Do not wonder; they were Incas." And if, on the contrary, they criticized anything badly done, the Indians would say: "Do not believe that an Inca did that, or if so, he was no Inca but an outcast bastard"—as indeed they said of Atahuallpa because of his treachery toward his brother Huáscar Inca, the legitimate heir, as we shall recount fully in due course.

For each of the four districts in which the empire was divided, the Inca had councils of war, justice, and finance. These councils had ministers for each division, in a hierarchy down to the decurions in charge of ten men. These officials reported everything in the empire from rank to rank till it reached the Supreme Council. There were four viceroys, one for each district. They acted as presidents of the councils of their district, and collected reports about all that happened in the kingdom for which they rendered account to the Inca: they were immediately below him and were in supreme control of their districts. They had to be legitimate Incas of the blood and experienced in the affairs of peace and war. These four, and only these, formed the Council of State, to whom the Inca gave commands about what to do in peace and war, and they passed instructions to their officials from rank to rank, down to the lowest. This shall be sufficient for the moment about the laws and government of the Incas. Further on in speaking of their lives and deeds, we shall interweave the things that seem most worthy of note.

CHAPTER XVI

The life and deeds of Sinchi Roca, the second Inca king.

MANCO CÁPAC was succeeded by his son Sinchi Roca. His proper name was Roca, the *r* being pronounced weak. The word has no meaning in the general language of Peru: it must mean something in the special language of the Incas, though I do not know what. Padre Blas Valera says that *roca* means "a prudent and astute prince," though without saying in what tongue. He remarks on the soft pronunciation of the *r* as we have done. He refers to the excellence of the Inca Roca, as we shall see. *Sinchi* is an adjective meaning "valiant," for he is said to have been of brave spirit and great strength, though he never had occasion to prove these qualities in war, since he was never engaged in any. He excelled all his contemporaries, however, in wrestling, running, and leaping, throwing a stone or a lance, and in every other feat of strength.

This prince, having completed the solemn obsequies of his father and assumed the crown (which was the red fringe), resolved to extend his territories. He called together the principal *curacas* appointed by his father and made them a long and solemn harangue, saying among other things that, in fulfilment of his father's last will expressed when he was on the point of returning to heaven, all the Indians should be converted to the acknowledgment and worship of the Sun, and he proposed to go forth and convoke the neighboring tribes: he bade the *curacas* undertake the same duty since, being called Incas after their king, they shared with him the obligations of serving the Sun, the common father of them all, to the benefit and advantage of their neighbors who were in dire need of being delivered from their bestial and squalid way of life. And as they themselves were proof of the advantages and superiority of their present over their former life before the arrival of his father the Inca, they should help him to reduce the savages by demonstrating to them the benefits they had received and so inducing them the more easily to receive the same.

The *curacas* replied that they were prepared and ready to obey their king and even to pass through fire in his service. The Inca then ended his speech and set the day for their departure. At the appointed time, the Inca sallied forth, accompanied by his followers, and reached Collasuyu, to the south of Cuzco. They convoked the Indians, and urged them with fair words and their example to submit to the command and vassalage of the Inca and to worship the Sun. The Indians of the Puchina and Canchi tribes who dwell there are exceedingly simple in their natural state and quite ready to believe any new thing, as all Indians are. Seeing the example of those who had already submitted, for example is always more convincing than anything else, they easily agreed to obey the Inca and accept his rule. Thus during his lifetime the Inca gradually in this manner broadened his boundaries in that direction, as far as the town called Chuncara, twenty leagues beyond the limits of his father's territories. The new territory included many towns on both sides of the highway and was all annexed without the use of arms or any deeds worthy of note. The Inca everywhere imitated his father's procedure in his conquests, teaching them to till the soil and bend their minds toward the natural and moral life, to abandon their idols and evil customs, and to worship the Sun and observe his laws and precepts as revealed and declared to the Inca Manco Cápac. The Indians obeyed and performed everything they were bidden, and were very satisfied with the new government of the Inca Sinchi Roca, who imitated his father in doing everything he could to benefit them with great consideration and love.

Some Indians hold that this Inca won only the district as far as Chuncara, which indeed would be enough, given the small resources the Incas then had. But others say he went far beyond and won many towns and tribes on the Umasuyu road, such as Cancalla, Cacha, Rurucachi, Assillu, Asancatu, Huancani as far as the town called Pucara de Umasuyu to distinguish it from Pucara in Orcosuyu. I name these provinces in detail for the benefit of Peruvians, for it would be useless to do so for those in other kingdoms: I trust this may be excused for I desire to be of use to all. *Pucara* means "fortress." It is said that this prince ordered the present one to be built as a frontier fort to protect what he had won, that in the direction of the Antis he occupied the territory as far as the river Callahuaya (where very fine gold said to exceed twenty-four carats is found), and that he won the other towns between Callahuaya and the royal highway to Umasuyu, where the above-mentioned towns are. Whether the first area or the second is the true one matters little; whether the second Inca won this area or the third, the fact remains that they were won, and won not by force of arms, but by persuasion, promises, and proofs of what was promised. And as the feat was accomplished without warfare, there is little to say of the conquest but that it took many years, though exactly how many is not known, nor is the length of the reign of the Inca Sinchi Roca. Some say he ruled for twenty years. He passed them like a good gardener who, having planted a tree, tends it in every necessary way so that it may bear the desired fruit. This was what this Inca did with all care and diligence, and he saw and enjoyed, in great peace and quietness, the harvest of his toil, for his vassals were very loyal and grateful for the benefits he conferred on them with his laws and ordinance, which they embraced with love and preserved with respect as commandments of their god the Sun, as they understood them to be.

Having lived many years in peace and prosperity, the Inca Sinchi Roca died, saying he was going to rest with his father the Sun from the efforts he had devoted to converting men to a knowledge of their god. He left as his successor Lloque Yupanqui, his legitimate son by his legitimate wife and sister Mama Cora, or Mama Ocllo, as others say. As well as his heir, he left other sons by his wife and by his concubines, his nieces, whose children we shall call legitimate by blood. He left too another large number of bastard sons by foreign concubines of whom he had many, so that many sons and daughters should remain to increase the generation and caste of the Sun, as they put it.

CHAPTER XVII

*Lloque Yupanqui, the third ruler,
and the meaning of his name.*

THE INCA Lloque Yupanqui was the third of the kings of Peru. His name *Lloque* means "left-handed." The neglect of his attendants in rearing him, which led to his left-handedness, was the origin of his name. The name *Yupanqui* was applied to him for his virtues and feats. In order to show the various ways of expressing themselves the Indians had in their general language, it is necessary to explain that *yupanqui* is the second person singular of the future imperfect indicative of a verb, and means "thou shalt tell." The verb thus used above contains and signifies all the good that can be told of a prince—"thou shalt tell his great deeds, his excellent virtues, his clemency, his piety, his mildness," etc.—it is good style and an elegance in their language to express it so.

The native tongue has very few words, as we have said, but they are very expressive, and in applying a noun or verb to their kings in this way, the Indians comprehended all that could be understood by such a noun or verb. We have seen how *capac* meant rich, not in possessions, but in all the virtues a good king can have; and this way of speaking was not extended to others, however great lords they were, but reserved for kings, so as not to vulgarize what was applied to the Incas, which they would have regarded as sacrilege. These names seem to resemble that of Augustus, which the Romans gave to Octavius Caesar for his virtues, and which would have lost all the majesty it contains if applied to anyone but an emperor or great king.

To those who say that the word means "to tell evil things" and that the verb to tell can be applied in both senses, good and bad, I must explain that the Indian language, when used elegantly, does not employ the same verb for good and for evil, but only one part: to give the opposite meaning the Indians used another verb with the contrary sense, applicable to the evil deeds of a prince. In this case it was *huacanqui,* used in the same mood, tense, number, and person to mean "thou shalt mourn for his cruel deeds done in public and in private, with poison or the knife, his insatiable avarice, his general tyranny, without distinction of sacred and profane, and everything else that can be deplored in a wicked prince." And as they say that nothing the Incas did was to be deplored, they used the word *huacanqui* with reference to lovers, meaning that they would have cause to mourn the passions and torments love produces in lovers. The two names *Cápac* and *Yupanqui,* with the meaning we have said, were applied by the Indians to three other kings, as we shall see. They were also taken by many of the royal blood, and the name given to the Inca has become a surname, as in Spain with the name *Manuel,* which was the Christian name of an infante of Castile, but was later used as a surname by his descendants.

CHAPTER XVIII

Two conquests made by the Inca Lloque Yupanqui.

HAVING TAKEN possession of his kingdom and visited it in person, the Inca Lloque Yupanqui resolved to extend its limits, and for the purpose ordered six or seven thousand warriors to be mobilized so that he could advance with greater power and authority than his predecessors. For more than seventy years had passed since they became kings, and he wished not to rely only on petitions and persuasion, but that arms and power should play their part, at least with those who proved stubborn and pertinacious. He nominated two of his uncles as field commanders and chose other members of his family as captains and advisers. Then instead of taking the Umasuyu highway which his father had followed in his conquests, he followed that of Orcosuyu. The two roads diverge at Chuncara and go through the district called Collasuyu, embracing the great lake Titicaca.

After leaving his own district, the Inca entered a great province called Cana and sent messengers to the natives requiring them to submit to and obey and serve the child of the Sun, abandoning their false and wicked sacrifices and beastly customs. The Canas wished to be informed at length about the Inca's demands and to know what laws they were required to adopt and what gods they must worship. On being told, they replied that they were ready to worship the Sun and obey the Inca and observe his laws and customs, which seemed to them better than their own. They thus sallied forth to receive the Inca and offer him their obedience and homage.

The Inca, leaving officials to instruct them in his idolatry and to teach them to divide and till the soil, advanced to the tribe and town called Ayaviri. These natives were so stubborn and rebellious that neither persuasion nor promises, nor the example of the other subjugated Indians availed. They obstinately preferred to die in defence of their liberty—far otherwise than the tribes the Incas had so far met with. So they came out to fight without heeding arguments, and forced the Incas to take arms to defend themselves rather than to attack. The battle was long, and men were killed and wounded on both sides. Undefeated, the Ayaviris entered into their town, fortified it as best they could and made daily sallies to fight the Inca's men. He, following the practice of his forbears, tried as far as possible to avoid conflict with the enemy, and as if he were the besieged instead of the besieger, he endured the insolence of the savages and ordered his men to seek to close the blockade if possible without coming to grips. But the Ayaviri, taking courage from the forebearance of the Inca and attributing it to cowardice, became daily more hard to reduce and fiercer in the fight, and even managed to enter the Inca's camp. In these skirmishes and encounters the besieged always had the worst of it.

Lest other tribes should follow this bad example and have the effrontery to take up arms, the Inca wished to punish the pertinacious Ayaviris, and therefore sent for more men, to display his power rather than because they were needed. Meanwhile the enemy was closely pressed on all sides: none were allowed to leave, to their great distress, for they were beginning to lack food. They tried their fortune in a hand to hand combat, and fought a whole day with great fierceness. The Inca's men resisted valiantly; many were killed and wounded on both sides. The Ayaviris were so badly mauled in the fight that they no longer dared to come out to offer battle. The Incas could have butchered them, but did not wish to do so, and by tightening the siege forced them to surrender. Meanwhile his reinforcements came up, and the enemy's spirit sank and they were glad to give in. The Inca received them unconditionally and, after severely reproaching them for their disrespect to the child of the Sun, pardoned them and ordered them to be well treated without regard to the obduracy they had displayed. Leaving officers to teach them and look after the property to be reserved for the Sun and for the Inca, he advanced to the town now called Pucara, or "fortress," because it had been established as a defence and frontier post to protect the conquests, and also because the town had been defended and it was necessary to conquer it by force of arms: the fortress was thus made because the site was a good one, and a strong garrison was left there. The Inca then returned to Cuzco, where he was received with much celebration and rejoicing.

CHAPTER XIX

The conquest of Hatun Colla and the pride of the Collas.

AFTER a few years the Inca Lloque Yupanqui again turned to the conquest and reduction of the Indians, for the Incas, having from the first propagated the idea that the Sun had sent them to earth to draw men from their wild, primitive life and teach them civilization, gave substance to this belief by taking special pride in reducing the Indians to their rule, concealing their ambition by saying that their acts were commanded by the Sun. With this pretence the Inca ordered an army of eight or nine thousand to be made ready, and having chosen his commander and advisers, set out by way of the district of Collasuyu and journeyed as far as the fortress called Pucara, where later Francisco Hernández Girón was defeated in the battle named after the place. From there he sent messengers to Paucarcolla and Hatun Colla, places from which the district gets the name Collasuyu. This is a very extensive province embracing many peoples and tribes under the name Colla. The Inca summoned them as he had the others and bade them not resist like the Ayaviris who had been punished by the Sun with death and famine because they had dared to take arms against his children, warning them that the same fate would befall them if they resisted. The Collas took counsel and their chiefs met at Hatun Colla, which means "great Colla." They decided that the sufferings of Ayaviri and Pucara had been a punishment from heaven, and wishing to profit by the example, told the Inca that they were content to be his vassals and to worship the Sun and embrace and keep his laws and ordinances. Having sent this answer, they came forth to receive the Inca with much rejoicing and solemnity and with songs and acclamations newly devised to express their feelings.

The Inca received the *curacas* cordially and presented them with clothes from his own person and other gifts they greatly esteemed. Thenceforward he and his descendants showed great favor and honor towards these two places, especially Hatun Colla, for the service they had performed by receiving him with signs of love, for the Incas always rewarded such services with gratitude and recommended those who served them to their successors so that as time went on the town was ennobled with great and splendid buildings, apart from the temple of the Sun and the house of the virgins, which the Indians greatly esteemed.

The Collas are many different tribes and boast of descent from various things. Some say their ancestors came out of Lake Titicaca. They considered it their mother, and before the Incas came, worshipped it among their many gods and performed sacrifices on its shores. Others claimed to descent from a great fountain which they declared was their first ancestor. Others took pride in the appearance of their forefathers from caves and nooks in great rocks, and held these places sacred and visited them in due season with sacrifices and the thanksgiving of children to their parents. Others said the first of them had come from a river and revered and venerated it like a father. It was sacrilege to kill fish in that river, which they said were their brothers. They had thus many fables about their beginnings, and similarly had many different gods according to their fancy, some for one reason and some for another. There was only one god the Collas agreed about. They all worshipped and regarded as their chief god a white ram, for they were the owners of innumerable flocks. They said that the first sheep in the upper world (meaning heaven) had taken more care of them than of any of the other Indians and loved them better, since it had left a greater posterity in the land of the Collas than anywhere else on earth. They said this because in the Collao the native sheep bred more and better than in the rest of Peru, and because of this privilege the Collas worshipped the ram and offered rams and tallow in sacrifice, and prized pure white sheep above the rest of their flocks, saying that they were most like the original sheep and had most divinity. Besides this folly, in many provinces of the Collao they tolerated an infamous practice: the women were allowed to be as shameless and dissolute as they liked before marriage, and the most dissolute married first as though their wickedness was a great quality. The Inca kings stopped all this, especially their worship of many gods, convincing them that the Sun alone deserved to be worshipped for its beauty and excellence and because it created and supported all the things they held to be gods. The Incas did not contradict them in the claims they made about their origin and descent, for as they vaunted descent from the Sun, they were content that there should be other similar fables which would make their own the easier to believe.

Having settled the government of these important places, both with regard to their false religion and to the revenue of the Sun and of the Inca, Lloque Yupanqui returned to Cuzco, preferring not to press his conquests further, for the Incas always thought it better to advance gradually and impose order and reason, so that their subjects should appreciate the mildness of their rule and attract their neighbors to submit, rather than swallow up many lands at once, which would have caused scandal and made them appear ambitious and covetous tyrants.

CHAPTER XX

The great province of Chucuitu peacefully reduced; and many other provinces likewise.

T HE INCA was received in Cuzco with great celebrations and rejoicing and dwelt there several years, devoting himself to the government and general welfare of his subjects. Afterwards he decided to visit his kingdom, since the Indians were glad to receive the Inca in their districts and so that his officials should not neglect their duties owing to his absence. This done, he ordered preparations for war in order to carry forward his previous conquests. He went forth with ten thousand warriors, took chosen captains, and reached Hatun Colla and the borders of Chucuitu, a famous and populous province, which because of its importance was awarded to the emperor in the division made by the Spaniards. He sent out the unusual commands to these and the neighboring peoples, that they should worship the Sun as god. The people of Chucuitu, though they were powerful and their ancestors had subjected some neighboring tribes, did not wish to resist the Inca. They replied on the contrary that they would obey him with love and goodwill as a child of the Sun, to whose clemency and mercy they were attached and whose benefits they desired to enjoy by becoming his subjects.

The Inca received them with his usual courtesy and granted them favors and presents, which were highly esteemed among the Indians. Seeing how successful his conquest had been, the Inca then sent the same demands to the other neighboring towns as far as the river that drains the great lake of Titicaca. All followed the example of Hatun Colla and Chucuitu and readily obeyed the Inca. The chief of these towns were Hillavi, Chulli, Pumata, and Cipita. We do not relate in detail the demands and replies in each case because they were all similar to what we have described, and to avoid repetition, we have given only one case. They also say that the Inca took many years to conquer and subdue these towns, but the manner in which they were won was the same, so there is no point in repeating what adds nothing to the story.

Having pacified these peoples, he dismissed his army, keeping with him only the necessary guard for his person and officers for the instruction of the Indians. He wished to supervise the business personally, both to lend zeal to them and to favor the towns and provinces with his presence, for they were places of importance for the future. The *curacas* and all their subjects were grateful that the Inca should remain among them for the winter, for this seemed to them the greatest favor he could confer on them. He treated them with affability and affection, daily devising new favors and honors, for he saw by his own experience (and by the teaching of his ancestors) how much mildness and bounty and esteem availed in attracting strangers to his obedience and service. The Indians published the excellence of their prince on all sides, declaring that he was truly a child of the Sun.

While the Inca was in Collao, he ordered an army of ten thousand warriors to be prepared for the following summer. In due time the force was gathered, and he chose four field commanders. As general he appointed one of his brothers, whose name the Indians have forgotten, and he ordered him, with the counsel of the captains, to proceed with the conquest he proposed. All five were expressly bidden not to make war on the Indians who did not at once submit, but to follow the advice of his ancestors and attract them with kindness and benefits, proving themselves to be loving fathers rather than warlike captains. He ordered them to go to the west, to the province called Hurin Pacassa and to reduce the Indians they might find there. The general and commanders went as the Inca commanded, and had such good fortune that they reduced the natives of the space of twenty leagues as far as the foothills of the range and the Sierra Nevada, which divides the coast from the mountains. The Indians were easy to subdue, for they were independent and isolated people without order, law, or political organization. They lived like brutes, and were ruled by the boldest with tyranny and arrogance. For these reasons they were easily won over, and most of them being simple people willingly submitted on hearing of the wonders told of the children of the Sun. Nearly three years were taken in reducing them, for it took longer to instruct them because of their brutishness than to subdue them. Once the conquest was finished and necessary officers had been appointed to govern them, and the captains and warriors to garrison and defend what had been won, the general and his four commanders returned to give account of their deeds to the Inca. As long as the conquest lasted, he had been engaged in visiting his kingdom, seeking to improve it by extending the cultivated lands, for which purpose he ordered new irrigation channels to be dug, and such necessary works as barns, bridges, and roads for communication to be executed. On their arrival, the general and commanders were warmly received and rewarded for their labors and accompanied the Inca to his court. He was resolved to end the conquests, deeming the empire to be sufficiently enlarged: from north to south he had added more than forty leagues of land and from east to west above twenty to the foot of the snowcapped range that divides the coastal plain from the uplands, the regions called llanos and sierras by the Spaniards.

In Cuzco he was joyfully received by the whole city, for he was much loved for his affability, mildness, and liberality. He spent the remainder of his life in quiet repose, busying himself with the interests of his subjects and doing justice. He twice sent his heir called Maita Cápac to visit the kingdom, accompanied by experienced elders, so that he might know his subjects and gain practice in governing them. When he felt the approach of death, he called his sons, and among them the heir, and in place of a testament commended to them the welfare of his subjects, the preservation of the laws and ordinances bequeathed by his ancestors by order of their god and father the Sun, and the duty of acting in all circumstances like children of the Sun. He commanded the Inca captains and other *curacas* entrusted with vassals to care for the poor and obey the king. Finally he bade them to remain in peace, for his father the Sun was calling him to rest from his past labors. These and similar things said, the Inca Lloque Yupanqui expired. He left many sons and daughters by his concubines but no male issue by his legitimate wife Mama Cava other than his heir Maita Cápac: he had also two or three daughters by her. Lloque Yupanqui was sincerely mourned throughout his kingdom, for he was much loved for his virtues. He was included in the number of the gods, and so was worshipped as a child of the Sun. In order that the history may not become tedious, from always dwelling on the same theme, we shall interweave between the lives of the Inca kings something of their customs, which will be more interesting to hear than their wars and conquests, almost all of which occurred in the same way. We will therefore say something of the sciences known to the Incas.

CHAPTER XXI

The sciences known to the Incas: first, astrology.

T HE INCAS had little knowledge of astrology and natural philosophy, since they had no letters; and although they had men of notable understanding called *amautas* who philosophized with great subtlety, a science many in their republic practiced, yet as they left nothing written for their successors, their ideas perished with their discoverers. Thus they made little headway in all sciences, or lacked them altogether, except for certain principles perceived by natural enlightenment, and even these were expressed in rough and unpolished terms for people to see and take note of. We shall say what they understood of each subject. In moral philosophy they were strong, and in practice they left it written in their laws, life, and actions, as we shall see in the course of our history. To this end they were aided by the natural law they desired to observe and the experience they acquired in good customs which they accordingly cultivated from day to day in their republic.

Of natural philosophy they had little or nothing, and did not meddle with it. In their simple and natural life there was nothing to oblige them to probe and draw forth the secrets of nature, so they passed them by without searching for them or knowing them. They had thus no practice in them, or knowledge of the qualities of the elements. If they said that the earth was cold and dry and fire hot, it was from experience that fire warmed and burnt, and not a statement arrived at by philosophical science. They merely perceived the virtues of certain medicinal plants and herbs with which they doctored their illnesses, as we shall have cause to say in dealing with their medicine. But this was achieved by experience under the obligation of necessity and not by natural philosophy, for they were little given to speculation about anything they could not touch with their hands.

In astrology they had rather more practice than in natural philosophy, for here there was more to stir them to speculation. They wondered about the sun, the moon, and the various movements of the planet Venus, which they saw sometimes pass before the sun and sometimes behind it. They saw the moon wax and wane, now full, now lost to sight in its conjunction, which they called the death of the moon because they did not see it for three days. They were also stimulated to observe the sun as it approached and receded, and how some days were longer than their nights, others shorter and others equal with them: all these things caused them to observe the heavens, but their observations were purely material in character.

They wondered at the effects, but never sought the causes. They did not therefore discuss if there were many heavens or only one, nor did they imagine there was more than one. They did not know the causes of the waxing and waning of the moon, nor the movements of the other planets, sometimes leisurely and other times rapid. They only noticed these three planets because of their size, splendor, and beauty, and ignored the four other planets. They had no conception of the signs of the zodiac, and less of their influence. They called the sun *Inti*, the moon *Quilla*, and the planet Venus *Chasca*, "curly" or "maned," from its many rays. They recognized the Seven Kids [the Pleiades] because they were relatively close together and different from the other stars, but for no other reason. They did not watch the other stars, for they had no obligation to do so and saw no object to be gained. They had no special names for stars but the two already mentioned. In general the word they used for them all was *cóillur*, "a star."

CHAPTER XXII

They understood the measurement of the year,
and the solstices and equinoxes.

B UT FOR ALL their simplicity, the Incas realized that the sun completed its course in a year, which they called *huata*. The noun means
"a year," but used as a verb, similarly pronounced and accented, it means
"to tie." The ordinary people reckoned the years by harvests. They understood also the summer and winter solstices; these were marked by large
and visible signs consisting of eight towers built to the east and eight to
the west of the city of Cuzco. They were arranged in sets of four: two
small ones three times the height of a man stood between two larger. The
small ones were set eighteen or twenty feet apart, and at the same distance
from them stood the larger, which were much higher than Spanish watch-
towers. The larger towers were observatories from which the smaller could
be more easily watched. The space between the small towers by which the
Sun passed in rising and setting was the point of the solstices. The towers
to the east corresponded with those of the west, according to whether it
was the summer or winter solstice.

To ascertain the time of the solstice, an Inca stood at a certain point at
sunrise and sunset, and watched whether the sun rose and set between the
two small towers to the east and the west. In this way they established the
solstices in their astrology. Pedro de Cieza (ch. xcii) refers to these towers.
Padre Acosta also mentions them in Book VI, ch. iii, though he does not
mention their position.

The Incas could establish the solstices only roughly because they did
not know how to fix them by the days of the months in which the solstices
occur. They counted the months by moons, as we shall see, and not by
days; and although they divided the year into twelve moons, they did not
know how to allow for the difference of eleven days by which the solar
year exceeds the normal lunar year. They therefore relied entirely on the
movement of the sun by the solstices to calculate their year, and not on the
moons. They thus divided one year from another and ordered the sowing
of their crops by the solar and not the lunar year. Some have asserted that
they did adjust the solar and lunar years, but this is a mistake: if they had
known this, they would have fixed the solstices on the proper days of the
month, and it would not have been necessary to raise these towers to serve

as markers by which to observe and establish so laboriously the solstices by daily watching the rising and setting of the sun. I saw these towers standing in 1560, and unless they have since been pulled down, the point from which the Incas observed the solstices can be verified: I cannot say whether it was a tower in the house of the Sun or another place.

They were also acquainted with the equinoxes, which they observed with great solemnity. At the March equinox they reaped the maize in the fields of Cuzco with great rejoicing and celebrations, especially on the terrace of Collcampata, which was regarded as the garden of the sun. At the September equinox they held one of the four principal festivals of the Sun, called Citua Raimi (the *r* is soft). This means the "principal feast," and we shall say how it was celebrated. To ascertain the time of the equinoxes they had splendidly carved stone columns erected in the squares or courtyards before the temples of the Sun. When the priests felt that the equinox was approaching, they took careful daily observations of the shadows cast by the columns. The columns stood in the middle of great rings filling the whole extent of the squares or spaces. Across the middle of a ring a line was drawn from east to west by a cord, the two ends being established by long experience. They could follow the approach of the equinox by the shadow the column cast on this line, and when the shadow fell exactly along the line from sunrise and at midday the sun bathed all sides of the column and cast no shadow at all, they knew that that day was the equinox. They then decked the columns with all the flowers and aromatic herbs they could find, and placed the throne of the Sun on it, saying that on that day the Sun was seated on the column in all his full light. Consequently they especially worshipped the Sun on that day with a greater display of rejoicing and celebration than usual, and offered to him rich presents of gold, silver, precious stones, and other valuable things. It is worthy of remark that the Inca kings and their *amautas* or philosophers discovered as they extended their provinces, that the nearer they approached the equator, the smaller was the shadow cast by the column at midday. They therefore venerated the columns more and more as they were nearer to the city of Quito, and were especially devoted to those of that city itself and in its neighborhood as far as the sea, where the sun is in a plumb-line, as bricklayers say, and shows no shadow at all at midday. For this reason they were held in the greatest veneration, it being thought that they afforded the Sun the seat he liked best, since there he sat straight up and elsewhere on one side. These simple things and many others were included by the Indians in their astrology because their imagination never went beyond what they saw materially with their eyes. The columns at

Quito and those of all that region were very properly pulled down and broken to pieces by the Governor Sebastián de Belalcázar, because the Indians worshipped them idolatrously. The others throughout the empire were demolished by the rest of the Spanish captains as they came across them.

CHAPTER XXIII

They observed eclipses of the sun, and what they did at eclipses of the moon.

THEY COUNTED the months by moons, from one new moon to the next, and therefore called a month *quilla,* the name for the moon. They had a name for each month, and reckoned half-months by the waxing and waning of the moon; they counted weeks by quarters of the moon, but had no names for the days of the week. They observed the eclipses of the sun and moon, but without understanding their causes. When there was a solar eclipse, they said the Sun was angry at some offence committed against him, since his face appeared disturbed like that of an angry man, and they foretold, as astrologers do, the approach of some grave punishment. When the moon was eclipsed, they said she was ill as she grew dark, and thought that if she disappeared altogether, she would die and the sky would fall in and crush and kill them all, and that the end of the world would come. When a lunar eclipse began, they were seized with fear and sounded trumpets, bugles, horns, drums, and all the instruments they could find for making a noise. They tied up their dogs, large and small, and beat them with many blows and made them howl and call the moon back, for according to a certain fable they told, they thought that the moon was fond of dogs in return for a service they had done her, and that if she heard them cry she would be sorry for them and awake from the sleep caused by her sickness.

To account for the spots on the moon they have another fable even simpler than the one about the dogs, which might be added to those invented by the ancient heathens for Diana, whom they thought a huntress. But the Indian story is very bestial. They say that a fox fell in love with the Moon because of her beauty and went up to the sky to steal her. When he tried to lay hands on her, she squeezed him against her and thus produced the spots. This simple and ridiculous fable shows the childishness of the people. They bade boys and small children weep and yell and shout, calling "Mama Quilla," "mother moon," begging her not to die or they would all perish. Men and women did the same, and there was an incredible noise and confusion.

They assessed the sickness of the Moon by the extent of the eclipse. If it was total, they could only think she was dead, and they feared every moment that she would fall and they would perish. Then they wept and wailed with more sincerity, as people who were face to face with death and the end of the world. As they saw the Moon gradually recovering her light, they said she was getting better from her sickness, because Pachacámac, the upholder of the universe, had restored her to health and commanded that she should not die so that the world should not perish. When she was quite bright again, they congratulated her and thanked her for not having fallen. All this concerning the moon I have seen with my own eyes. The day they called *punchau,* the night *tata,* and daybreak *pacari.* They had words for dawn, and other parts of the day and night, such as midnight and midday.

They observed lightning, thunder, and thunderbolts, and called all the three *illapa.* They did not worship them as gods, but honored and esteemed them as servants of the Sun. They held that they resided in the air, but not in heaven. Similar respect was shown for the rainbow, on account of the beauty of its colors and the realization that it came from the Sun. The Inca kings used it in their arms and device. Each of these had its special place in the house of the Sun, as we shall say. They fancied they saw the figure of an ewe with the body complete suckling a lamb in some dark patches spread over what the astrologers call the milky way. They tried to point it out to me saying: "Don't you see the head of the ewe?" "There is the lamb's head sucking"; "There are their bodies and their legs." But I could see nothing but the spots, which must have been for want of imagination on my part.

But they did not make any use of these figures in their astrology beyond seeking to draw them as they imagined them. They did not tell fortunes or make ordinary prognostications from signs of the sun, moon, or comets, but only in very rare and exceptional cases, such as the death of kings or destruction of kingdoms and provinces; we shall, if we get so far, have occasion to refer to some comets. For ordinary things they based their prophecies and prognostications on dreams and sacrifices, not on stars or signs in the air. It is a fearful thing to hear what they foretold from dreams, but to avoid giving offense, I shall not repeat what I could say about this. Venus, which is sometimes a morning and sometimes an evening star, they thought to have been ordered by the Sun, as lord of all the stars, to go near him, sometimes before him and sometimes behind, because she was more beautiful than the rest.

When the Sun set and they saw him sink beyond the sea—for the whole length of Peru has the sea to its west—they said he entered the sea, and dried up a great part of its waters with his fire and heat, but like a good swimmer he dived under the earth and came up next day in the east, whence they supposed that the earth rests on the water. They had nothing to say of the setting of the moon or the other stars. All these follies were included in the Incas' astrology, whence it may be concluded how little they understood. This shall be sufficient about their astrology: we will pass to the medicine they used for their sicknesses.

CHAPTER XXIV

The medicines they had and their way of curing themselves.

THEY CERTAINLY divined that evacuation by bleeding and purging was a salutary and even necessary thing. They therefore bled themselves from the arm or leg, though they did not know how to apply leeches or how the veins were disposed for the treatment of various diseases. They merely opened the vein nearest the place where they felt the pain. If they had a bad pain in the head, they bled themselves between the eyebrows above the bridge of the nose. Their lancet was a flint point in a cleft stick, bound around so that it could not fall out. They put the point on the vein and gave a twist, and so opened the vein with less pain than by using an ordinary lancet.

In applying purgatives they were ignorant of the humors of the urine which they did not examine, and ignored choler, phlegm, and melancholy. Purges were normally taken when they felt heavy and sluggish, more often in health than in sickness. In addition to other purgative herbs, they took some whole roots like small turnips. They say that these roots are male and female, which they take in equal quantities, two ounces or thereabouts of each, ground and mixed with water or anything they are drinking. After taking it, they stretch in the sun so that the warmth may help the purge to work. After an hour or so, they feel so dizzy they can hardly stand. They are like those who suffer from seasickness on first going to sea. The head suffers from dizziness and faintness, and they feel as if ants were swarming over their arms and legs, in their veins and sinews and over all the body. Evacuation is almost always by both ways. While it lasts, the patient is giddy and sick, and anyone who had not experienced the effects of the root would think that they were dying. The patient has no wish to eat or drink. He expels all his humors, and readily yields up worms and other vermin that breed inside. When all is over, he is in such good spirits and has such an appetite that he will eat anything set before him. I was twice purged from a stomach-ache at various times and underwent all this.

These purges and bleedings were performed by the most experienced of them, especially by old women (as midwives are here) and by great herbalists who were very famous in the days of the Incas. These herbalists learnt the virtues of many herbs and taught them by tradition to their sons: they were regarded as doctors, who were not supposed to cure anyone, but only kings, the royal family, and the chiefs and their relatives. The ordinary people cured one another by what they had heard tell of medicine. When unweaned babies fell ill, especially if of a feverish ailment, they washed them all over in urine in the mornings and gave the child its own urine to drink when possible. When they cut a new-born child's navel string, they left a finger's length of the cord, which, when it fell off, they preserved with the greatest care and gave to the child to suck whenever it was ill. To detect illness, they looked at the root of the tongue: if it was whitish, they said that the child was ill and gave him the string to suck: it must be his own, for that of another person was accounted useless.

The natural secrets of these things were not told to me, nor did I ask about them, but I saw the operations done. They did not know how to take the pulse or examine urine. They knew a fever by the excessive heat of the body. They performed purges and bleedings standing rather than lying. When they had given way to their illness, they took no medicine at all, but let nature work and followed a natural diet. They had no knowledge of the usual purging medicine, clysters, or of the application of plasters and ointments, except a few of the very common things. The ordinary, poor people treated illness hardly otherwise than as beasts do.

The chill of a tertian or quartan they call *chucchu,* "trembling," fever is *rupa,* with a soft *r,* "to burn." They feared these illnesses a great deal, because of the alternating extremes of heat and cold.

CHAPTER XXV

The medicinal herbs they used.

THEY UNDERSTOOD the virtues of the juice and resin of a tree named *mulli,* which the Spaniards call *molle.* This has a remarkable effect on fresh wounds: it seems almost supernatural. The herb or shrub called *chillca,* heated in an earthenware pot, has a wonderful effect on the joints if the cold gets into them, and on sprains in horses' legs. A root, like couch-grass, but much thicker, and with smaller but solider knots, whose name I have forgotten, was used to strengthen and clean the teeth. They roasted it on embers, and then while still hot, split it between their teeth: they applied one part of it boiling hot to one gum and the rest to the other and kept it in their mouths till it was cold. Thus they treated all their gums, to the great distress of the patient since his mouth was roasted. The patient applies the root and performs the whole treatment himself. They do it in the evening, and next day their gums are as white as scalded flesh. For three or four days they cannot eat anything that requires chewing and are spoon fed. Then the burnt flesh sloughs off the gums, revealing a new flesh underneath which is very red and healthy. I have often seen them renew their gums like this. I once tried it myself purely as an experiment, but gave up because I could not stand the fiery heat of the burnt roots.

They made many various uses of the herb or plant the Spaniards call tobacco and the Indians *sairi.* They inhaled it as a powder to clear the head. Many have experienced the virtues of this plant in Spain, and it is therefore entitled "holyweed." Another herb they had is excellent for the eyes. It is called *matecllu,* and grows in brooks and has a single stalk with but one round leaf on it. It resembles that plant called "abbot's ear" in Spain which grows on roofs in winter. The Indians eat it raw, and it has a pleasant taste. When it has been mashed, the juice is poured on the ailing eye in the evening and the crushed herb placed like a plaster on the eyelids with a bandage on top to keep it in place. In the space of a night it removes a cloud before the eye and eases any pain or harm they have suffered.

I tried it on a boy whose eye was almost falling out of his head. It was as inflamed as a pepper, so that it was impossible to tell the white from the pupil, and it was half dropping on his cheek. The first night I applied the herb, the eye returned to its place: after the second, it was completely restored. I later saw the boy in Spain and he told me that he sees better with that eye than with the other. I was told about it by a Spaniard, who swore that he had gone completely blind with cataract and that he recovered his sight in two nights with this herb. Whenever he saw it, he would embrace it and kiss it with great affection, and place it on his eyes and on his head, as a token of his gratitude for the blessing our Lord had given him in restoring his sight through it. My Indian relatives used many other herbs, which I have forgotten.

Such was the medicine usually practiced by the Inca Indians of Peru. It consisted of simple herbs and not compounds, and they got no further. Since in matters of such importance as health they had studied and learnt so little, it is understandable that of such things as natural philosophy and astrology which concerned them less, they knew correspondingly less, and less still of theology, since they could not raise their minds to invisible things. The whole theology of the Incas was comprehended in the word *Pachacámac*. Later the Spaniards experimented with many medicinal products, especially maize, which the Indians call *sara*. This was partly due to the information the Indians gave of the little they knew in medicine, and partly because the Spaniards philosophized about what they found and discovered that maize, as well as being such a substantial foodstuff, is of great benefit in diseases of the kidneys, pains in the side, stone, stoppage of the urine, and pains in the bladder and colon. They realized this because very few or no Indians have those diseases, and attributed the fact to the habit of commonly drinking a brew of maize. Many Spaniards who suffer from such diseases therefore drink it. The Indians also use it as a plaster for many other diseases.

CHAPTER XXVI

Their knowledge of geometry, geography, arithmetic, and music.

THEY KNEW a great deal of geometry because this was necessary for measuring their lands, and adjusting the boundaries and dividing them. But this was physical knowledge, obtained with strings and stones used for counting and dividing, and nothing to do with heights in degrees or any other speculative method. As I risk not making myself understood, I shall refrain from saying what I know about this.

In geography they were able to depict, and each tribe could model and draw its towns and provinces as they had seen them. They did not trouble about other provinces. Their skill in this was extreme. I saw the model of Cuzco and part of the surrounding area in clay, pebbles, and sticks. It was done to scale with the squares, large and small; the streets, broad and narrow; the districts and houses, even the most obscure; and the three streams that flow through the city, marvellously executed. The countryside with high hills and low, flats and ravines, rivers and streams with their twists and turns were all wonderfully rendered, and the best cosmographer in the world could not have done it better. The model was made for a visitor called Damián de la Bandera who had a commission from the royal chancery in Lima to ascertain how many towns and how many Indians there were in the district of Cuzco: other visitors went to other places for a similar purpose. The model I saw was made at Muina, which the Spaniards call Mohina, five leagues south of the city of Cuzco. I was there because the visitor was inspecting part of the towns and Indians of my Lord Garcilaso de la Vega.

They knew a great deal of arithmetic and had an admirable method of counting everything in the Inca's kingdom including all taxes and tributes, both paid and due, which they did with knots in strings of different colors. They added, subtracted, and multiplied with these knots, and ascertained the dues of each town by dividing grains of maize and pebbles so that their account was accurate. They had special accountants for all the affairs of peace and war, for the number of vassals, tributes, flocks, laws, ceremonies, and all else that had to be counted. These studied their special branch and its accounts, and could therefore easily provide the necessary information, since everything was recorded on threads and knots, which were like notebooks. Although one Indian, as chief accountant, was the overseer of two or three or more things, each subject was accounted for separately. Further on, we shall describe the method of counting and of reading the threads and knots at greater length.

In music they understood certain modes, which the Collao Indians or others of that area played on instruments of reed pipes. Four or five reeds were bound side by side, each a little higher than the last, like organ pipes. There were four different reeds. One gave the low notes, another higher, and the others higher still, like the four natural voices: treble, tenor, contralto, and bass. When an Indian played one reed, the next answered on the fifth or any other interval; then the next played another note and the last another, some going up the scale and some down, but always in tune. They did not understand accidentals, but all the notes fell within their scale. The performers were Indians trained to provide music for the king and the great lords, and although their music was simple, it was not common, but learned and mastered by study. They had flutes with four or five stops, like those of shepherds. These were not for use together in consort, but played separately, for they did not know how to harmonize them. They played their songs on them. These songs were composed in measured verse and were mostly concerned with the passion of love, its pleasure and pain, and the favor or coldness of the beloved.

Every song had its known tune, and they could not sing two different songs to the same tune. This was because the lover who serenaded his lady with his flute at night told her and everybody else of the pleasure or sorrow produced by her favor or coldness by means of the tune he played, and if two different songs had had the same tune, no one would have known which he meant. One might say that he talked with his flute. Late one night a Spaniard came upon an Indian girl he knew in Cuzco and asked her to return to his lodging, but she said: Let me go my ways, sir. The flute you hear from that hill calls me with such tender passion that I must go toward it. Leave me, for heaven's sake, for I cannot but go where love draws me, and I shall be his wife and he my husband.

The songs they made for their warlike deeds were not played because they were not for singing to ladies nor suitable for rendering on flutes. They sang them at the chief festivals and for victories and triumphs to commemorate brave deeds. When I left Peru in 1560, I left five Indians at Cuzco who could play flutes most skillfully from any book of part-songs that was put in front of them. They belonged to Juan Rodríguez de Villalobos, formerly a householder in the city. At the time of writing, which is 1602, they tell me that there are as many Indians expert in playing musical instruments as may be met with anywhere. In my time the Indians did not use their voices, because they were not very good: this must have been for lack of exercise because they did not know how to sing. On the other hand there were many mestizos with excellent voices.

CHAPTER XXVII

The poetry of Inca amautas, or philosophers, and harauicus, or poets.

THE AMAUTAS, or philosophers, were not wanting in skill in compos- ing comedies and tragedies for performance before the kings and lords attending court on solemn feast days. The actors were not common people, but Incas and nobles, the sons of *curacas,* and the *curacas* and captains themselves, even generals, so that the subjects of the tragedies could be properly represented. Their arguments were always concerned with warlike deeds, triumphs, and victories, and the doings and greatness of past kings and of other heroic worthies. The arguments of the comedies dealt with agriculture, property, and family and household themes. As soon as the comedy was over, the performers took their places according to their rank and office. There were no unseemly, vulgar, or low farces. All the plays were serious and decorous with appropriate sentences and turns of speech. Valuable jewels and favors were given to those who were outstanding for the grace of their performance.

They had also a little poetry, and made long and short lines, measuring the number of syllables in each. These meters were used for the love song with different tunes, as we have seen. They also told of deeds of their kings and other famous Incas and chief *curacas* in verse, and taught these poems to their descendants as a tradition, so that the good deeds of their ancestors should be remembered and imitated. The verses were few, so that the memory might retain them, but full of meaning, like cyphers. Verses did not have assonance or rhyme, but were all blank. They were usually like the native Spanish composition called redondillas. A love song in four lines occurs to me. It will show the style of composition and the concentrated and concise expression of what in their simplicity they wanted to say. Love poems were composed with short lines so that they could be more easily played on the flute. I should have liked to set down the music in parts, so that both might be seen together, but the irrelevance will spare me the trouble.

The song is as follows, with its translation:

Caylli llapi		To this song
Puñunqui	which means	thou shalt sleep:
Chaupituta		In the middle of the night
Samúsac		I will come.

Or more exactly without the pronoun *I*, and with three syllables for the verb, as the Indian has, not naming the subject but including it in the verb to suit the meter. The Inca poets, called *haráuec* which really means "inventor," had many other types of verse. In Padre Blas Valera's papers, I found other verses which he calls spondees: they all have four syllables, while these are four followed by three. He sets them down in Indian and Latin: they deal with astrology. The Inca poets wrote them wondering about the secondary causes that God puts in the region of the air to produce thunder, lightning, thunderbolts, hail, snow, and rain, all of which emerges from the verse. They were composed in accordance with a fable they had, as follows: they say that the Creator placed a maiden, the daughter of a king, in the sky with a pitcher full of water which she spills when the earth needs it, and that one of her brothers breaks it occasionally, and the blow causes thunder and lightning. They say the man causes them, because they are the work of a fierce man and not of a tender woman. The maiden they say causes hail, rain, and snow, which are the works of her gentleness and softness and of such benefit. They say that an Inca, a poet and astrologer, made the verses in praise of the excellence and virtues of this maiden, which God had given her to do good to all the creatures of the earth. The fable and verses, Padre Blas Valera says he found in the knots and beads of some ancient annals in threads of different colors: the Indian accountants in charge of the historical knots and beads told him the tradition of the verses and the fable; and, surprised that the *amautas* should have achieved so much, he copied down the verses and memorized them. I can recall having heard the fable as a child which my relatives told me, with many others, but whose meaning I have lost or they did not tell me. For those who understand neither Indian nor Latin, I have made bold to translate the verses, following the meaning of the language I absorbed with my mother's milk rather than the Latin, for my little Latin was learned in the heat of warfare in my native country among arms and horses, powder and arquebusses, of which I knew more than of letters.

Padre Blas Valera in his Latin has imitated the four syllables in each line of the Indian, and has done it very well. I could not do so; in Spanish it is impossible, for as the meaning of the Indian words has to be explained, some need more syllables and others less. *Ñusta* is a maiden of royal blood, and is not to be interpreted as less; an ordinary maiden is *tázque*; a servingmaid, *china. Illapántac* is a verb which includes the meaning of three, "to thunder, to lighten, and to fall (of thunderbolts)." Thus Padre Blas Valera expressed them in two lines, and suppressed the previous line *cunuñunun,* "to make an explosion," in order to give the three meanings of *illapántac. Unu* is "water," *para* "to rain," *chichi* "to hail," *riti* "to snow." *Pachacámac* means "he does to the universe what the soul does to the body." *Viracocha* is the name of a modern god they worship, whose story we shall tell at length, *Chura* is "to put," *cama* "to give soul, life, being, and substance." This said, we will give the poem as best we can, and keeping close to the meaning of the Indian tongue. The verses are as follows in the three languages:

Súmac ñusta	*Pulchra Nimpha*	Fair maiden,
Torralláiquim	*Frater tuus*	Thy brother
Puiñuyquita	*Urnam tuam*	Thine urn
Paquir cayan	*Nunc infringit*	Is now breaking.
Hina mantara	*Cuius ictus*	And for this cause
Cunuñunun	*Tonat fulget*	It thunders and lightens
Illapántac	*Fulminatque*	And thunderbolts fall,
Camri ñusta	*Sed tu nympha*	But thou, royal maiden
Unuiquita	*Tuam limpham*	Their clean waters
Para munqui	*Fundens pluis*	Shalt give us in rain;
Mai ñimpiri	*Interdunque*	And sometimes too
Chichi munqui	*Grandinem, seu*	Shalt give hail
Riti munqui	*Nivem mittis*	And shalt give snow.
Pacharúrac	*Mundi factor*	The world's Creator,
Pachacámac	*Pacha cámac*	Pachacámac,
Viracocha	*Viracocha*	Viracocha,
Cai hinápac	*Ad hoc munus*	For this office
Churasunqui	*Te sufficit*	Has appointed thee,
Camasunqui	*Ac praefecit*	And has created thee.

I have included these verses to enrich my poor history, for it can be said truly and without flattery that all Padre Blas Valera wrote was pearls and gems. My country did not deserve to be so adorned.

They tell me that nowadays the mestizos have taken much to composing these verses in the Indian tongue, and others of various kinds, both sacred and profane. May God give them his grace to serve him in all things.

Such was the little, and so limited, that the Incas of Peru had attained in these sciences, though if they had had letters, they would have passed gradually further on, inheriting from one another, as the early philosophers and astrologers did. They were only notable in moral philosophy, both in theory and in the exercise of the laws and customs they observed, according to which they treated one another as vassals according to natural law, and obeyed, served, and adored their king and those in authority, and their king in turn ruled and benefited the chiefs and other vassals and inferiors. In the use of this science they excelled so much that it would be hard to exaggerate. Their experience in this drove on to ever greater perfection. But this experience was lacking in other sciences, because they could not treat them in a material way as they did moral science; and they themselves were not given to speculation as those sciences require, being content with their natural law and natural life, like people whose character inclines more toward not doing harm than toward doing good. Pedro de Cieza de León says (ch. xxxviii), speaking of the Incas and their rule: They performed such great deeds and had such good government that few in the world have excelled them, etc. And Padre Acosta (Book VI, ch. i) says the following in favor of the Incas and Mexicans:

Having treated of the religion of the Indians, I propose in this book to write of their customs, institutions, and government. I have two purposes: one is to refute the false opinion commonly entertained of them, that they are a brute and beastly people without understanding, or with so little that it is not worth mentioning: this error has led to many great wrongs being perpetrated on them, to their being treated as little better than animals, and to contempt for any kind of respect for them. How common and pernicious is this error, all those who have been among them and asked with a little zeal and consideration and seen and known their secrets and affairs, must realize, as they will realize that the Indians are held of small account by all those who think they know a great deal (and are usually the most stupid and presumptuous). I see no better way to combat this prejudicial opinion than by explaining the order and way of life they had when under their own law, which, though in many respects barbarous and ill-grounded, had yet other points that are worthy of admiration. From this we can clearly see that they have a natural capacity for instruction, and in many ways even excel many of our states in the old world. It is not to be wondered that they mingled with this grave errors, for such are to be found in the most advanced legislators and philosophers, even Lycurgus and Plato. And we find ridiculous ignorance even in the wisest republics, such as those of Rome and Athens; certainly if the states of the Mexicans and of the Incas had been known in the Greek and Roman times, their laws and government would have been esteemed. But as we have entered by the sword without realizing any of this, or hearing them or understanding them, it does not occur to us that the Indians' affairs deserve any credit, but they are like game, hunted in the wilds and rounded up at our will for our service. The most learned and curious scholars who have learnt and penetrated their secrets, their way of life and their ancient government judge them very differently, and are amazed that they should have such good order and reason.

This is quoted from Padre José de Acosta, whose authority is so great that it will stand for all we have so far said and shall say of the Incas, their laws and government and abilities. One of these abilities was the composition in prose and in verse of short and concise fables of a poetic kind to summarize moral doctrine or preserve some tradition of their idolatry or of the famous deeds of their kings or other great men. Many of these the Spaniards say are not fables but true stories, for they have some semblance of truth. Of many others they make fun, saying they were ill-invented lies, because they do not understand the allegory. Some were indeed absurd, as some we have mentioned. In the course of this history we may have cause to mention some of the good ones.

CHAPTER XXVIII

The few instruments used by the Indians for their crafts.

HAVING SPOKEN of the abilities and sciences attained by the philosophers and poets of the heathen Indians, we must say something of the lack of skill of their craftsmen, so as to show in what misery and want of necessities the people lived. Beginning with silversmiths, we can say that, although they were so many and worked perpetually at their craft, they never made anvils of iron or any other metal. This must have been because they did not know how to found iron, though they had mines. They call iron *quíllay*. They used hard stones of a color between green and yellow as anvils. They planed and smoothed them against one another; and esteemed them highly since they were very rare. They could not make hammers with wooden handles. They worked with instruments of copper and brass mixed together: they were shaped like dice with rounded corners. Some are as large as the hand can grip for heavy work; others are middle-sized, others small, and others elongated to hammer in a concave shape. They hold these hammers in the hand and strike with them like cobblestones. They had no files or graving tools, nor bellows for founding. Their founding they did by blowing down copper pipes half an ell or less in length, according to the size of the work. The pipes were blocked at one end, but had a small hole through which the air came out compressed and with greater force. It might be necessary to use eight, ten, or twelve at once according to the furnace. They walked round the fire blowing, and still do today, for they do not like to change their habits. Nor had they tongs for getting the metal out of the fire. They used rods of wood or copper, and thrust the metal onto a lump of wet clay they had near to temper its heat. There they pushed it and turned it over and over until it was cool enough to pick up. Despite these handicaps they executed marvellous work, especially in hollowing things out, and other admirable things we shall mention. They also realized, despite their simplicity, that smoke from any metal was bad for health, and thus made their foundries, large or small, in the open air, in yards or spaces, and never under roof.

The carpenters were no more skillful, maybe less, for of all the tools those in Spain use in their work, those of Peru only attained copper hatchets and adzes. They did not find how to make a saw, a gimlet, a plane, or any other tool for carpentry, and so could not make chests or doors except by cutting wood and smoothing it for buildings. The hatchets, adzes, and a few billhooks they made were silversmith's work rather than blacksmith's, for all the tools were of copper and brass. Nailing was unknown to them: all the timber in their buildings was bound with esparto ropes and not nailed. Stonemasons similarly worked their stone with some black pebbles called *hihuana,* with which they pounded rather than cut. To lift and lower stone they had no device at all: all was done by hand. Yet they performed such grand works, of such skill and refinement that it seems incredible, as Spanish historians assert and as can be seen from the remains that exist of many of them. They could not make metal scissors or needles. They used some long thorns that grow there, and so could do little sewing: it was indeed darning rather than sewing, as we shall see. The same thorns served as combs. The mirrors used by the women of the blood royal were of highly polished silver, the ordinary ones of brass (they were not allowed to use silver, as we shall see). The men never looked in a mirror: they held it as shameful and effeminate. Thus they lacked many things needful for human life.

They managed with only what was essential, for they were little inventive by nature, though great imitators of what they see others do, as the experience of what they have learnt from the Spaniards in all the crafts they have seen shows. In some they better the Spaniards. The same ability is shown for the sciences, if they are taught them, as is seen from the plays they have acted in various places. Some ingenious religious, of various orders but especially Jesuits, have composed comedies for the Indians to perform so as to give the Indians a feeling for the mysteries of our redemption. They realized that the Indians performed plays in the time of the Inca kings and saw that they had great natural ability, so a Jesuit father wrote a play in praise of our Lady in the Aymará language, which differs from the general speech of Peru. The argument was based on the words of Genesis iii: "I will place enmity between thee and the woman, etc. . . . and she shall break thy head." Indian boys and lads in a village called Sulli performed it. In Potosí a dialogue on faith was done before an audience of twelve thousand Indians. In Cuzco another dialogue of the child Jesus was given before all the notabilities of the city. Another was done in Lima, before the chancery and all the nobility of the place, and innumerable Indians. It was about the Holy Sacrament, composed partly in Spanish and partly in the general language of Peru. The Indian boys acted the dialogues in all four parts with such grace and feeling in their speech and such gesture and appropriate action that they stirred the audience to delight, and they sang the songs so sweetly that many Spaniards wept with pleasure and joy to see the grace and skill and wit of the little Indians, and changed the opinions they had hitherto held that they were uncouth, stupid, and clumsy.

The Indian boys memorize the parts they are given to speak, which they receive in writing, by going to some Spaniard who can read, either a priest or a layman, and maybe a high official, and begging him to read the first line four or five times until they get it by heart. So as not to forget it, though their memories are tenacious, they repeat each word many times, marking it with a colored pebble or a colored pip or seed, one of these the size of chick-peas called *chuy*. Thus they remember the words and easily and quickly fix the parts in their minds by dint of their diligence and care. The Spaniards whom the little Indians ask to read are not contemptuous or angry, however important they are, but encourage and please them, knowing the purpose of it all.

So the Indians of Peru, though they used to be uninventive, are clever to imitate and learn what they are taught. This was proved fully by Licentiate Juan Cuéllar, a native of Medina del Campo, who was canon of the cathedral at Cuzco and taught grammar to the mestizo sons of noblemen there. He was impelled to do it out of charity and at the request of the pupils, for five tutors whom they had had had abandoned them in turn after five or six months work, thinking to earn more in other ways, though each pupil gave them ten pesos (which are twelve ducats) a month: this seemed little, however, as the students were not many, eighteen at most. Among them I knew an Inca Indian called Felipe Inca, belonging to a rich and honored priest called Fray Pedro Sánchez, who, seeing the boy's ability in reading and writing, put him to study, and he did as well in grammar as any student of the mestizos. When the tutor abandoned them, they returned to their primary school until a new tutor arrived, who taught them on different principles from the old and, if they remembered anything of what they had learnt before, told them to forget it because it was all wrong. Thus were the students in my time led on from one tutor to another without learning anything, until the good canon took them under his cloak and read Latin with them for nearly two years amidst arms and horses, bloodshed and the flames of war that then raged when Don Sebastián de Castilla and Francisco Hernández Girón rebelled. Hardly had the first been extinguished than the second flared up: it was the worse and took longer to die down. Then Canon Cuéllar saw the ability his pupils displayed in grammar and their quickness in other branches of knowledge, that had been lacking before owing to the barrenness of the land. Grieving that he was losing such good pupils, he often said to them: "Oh, my sons, what a pity it is that a dozen of you are not in the University of Salamanca!" I have mentioned all this to show the ability the Indians have when they are taught, an ability they share with the mestizos, their relatives. Canon Juan de Cuéllar did not leave his pupils perfect in Latin because he could not go through with the labor of reading four lessons a day with them and devote hours to his choir, so their Latin remained imperfect. Those who are now living should be very grateful to God for sending them the Society of Jesus, which so abounds in all sciences and teaches them so well. With this it is time to return to the successors of the Inca kings and their conquests.

End of the Second Book

BOOK

THREE *of the*

FIRST PART

which contains the life and deeds of Maita Cápac, the
fourth king; the first wicker bridge built in Peru and
the wonder it caused; the life and conquests of the fifth
king called Cápac Yupanqui; the famous bridge of
straw and osier he made over the Desaguadero; the description of the house and temple of the
Sun and its great wealth.
It contains twenty-five chapters.

CHAPTER I

Maita Cápac, the fourth Inca, conquers Tiahuanaco; the buildings there.

THE INCA Maita Cápac (whose name needs no interpretation, since Maita is a proper name with no special meaning in the general language and Cápac has already been explained), having performed the burial rites for his father and the solemn ceremonies of his own accession, now again visited his realms as absolute king. Although he had twice visited them while his father was alive, he was then a ward in the hands of tutors, and could not take cognizance of or settle affairs or grant favors without the presence and consent of his council, whose place it was to frame replies, decide petitions, pronounce sentences, and assess and stipulate the favors the prince was to confer. Even though he was heir, he was not of an age to govern, and this was the law of the kingdom. As soon as he was free of guardians and tutors, he wished to revisit his subjects in their provinces, for, as we have already noted, this was one of the activities of the princes that most pleased their people. For this reason, and to show his liberality, magnanimity, mildness, and affection he made the journey and bestowed great favors on both *curacas* and common people.

The visit over, he turned his mind to the chief glory of the Incas, the conversion of barbarians to their false religion, since they used their idolatry as a cover for their ambition and desire to extend their realms. For either of these objects, or both (for the motives of the powerful are complex), he ordered an army to be raised and in the spring marched forth with twelve thousand warriors and four field commanders, and the officers and ministers of the army, and reached the river that drains the great lake of Titicaca, since all this territory of Collao, being flat, seemed easier to conquer than any other, and also because the natives seemed more simple and docile.

Reaching the Desaguadero, he ordered great rafts to be made and ferried his army over. He sent the usual demands to the first towns he came upon. There is no need to repeat them: the Indians easily obeyed on account of the marvels they had heard tell of the Incas, and among the towns that surrendered was one, Tiahuanaco, of whose large and well-nigh incredible buildings we must now say something. Among other wonderful works, there is an artificial hill or mound, of remarkable height considering it was made by men. They established the hill on great stone foundations so that the heaped earth might not loosen or slide. The purpose of the construction is unknown. Elsewhere at some distance from the hill, were two gigantic figures carved in stone, with headdresses on their heads and long robes reaching down to the ground. They were much worn by the hand of time, and this shows their great antiquity. One can also see a very large wall, the stones of which are so great that it is amazing to think what human force could have put them in place, for there are truly no rocks or quarries from which they could have been hewn for a very great distance around. One can see in another place other strange buildings. The most remarkable are some great stone portals, standing in various places. Some of them are solid stone all in one piece, and the wonder of the portals is increased by the fact that many of them stand on stones that have been shown by measurement to be thirty feet long, fifteen broad, and six deep. These enormous stones and the portals are in one piece, and it cannot be imagined with what instruments or tools they could have been worked. Proceeding from the consideration of their size, one thinks how much bigger they must have been before they were worked.

The natives say that all these buildings and others not described are works dating from the period before the Incas, and that the Incas built the fortress of Cuzco in imitation of them, and that they do not know who built them, but have heard their ancestors say that all those wonderful monuments were erected in a single night. The works seem unfinished, and appear rather to be the commencement of what their founders planned. The above is in Pedro de Cieza de León's *Demarcation of Peru* (ch. cv), where he writes at length of these and other buildings which we have briefly described. I have thought fit to add the description of a priest who was at school with me called Diego de Alcobaça—I could call him my brother, since we were both born in the same house and his father brought me up like a guardian. Speaking of the great buildings of Tiahuanaco in reports he and others have sent me from my native land, he uses these words:

In Tiahuanaco, in the province of Collao, there is one antiquity among others that is worthy of immortal memory. It is by a lake called Chucuito by the

Spaniards: its real name is Chuquivitu. There there are some enormous buildings, including a square courtyard some fifteen fathoms deep with a wall twice
the height of a man running around it. On one side of the yard is a chamber
forty-five feet long and twenty-two wide, roofed like the thatched rooms you
have seen in the house of the Sun here in Cuzco. This courtyard with its walls
and floor, chamber, roof and cover, and the posts and lintels of two doors it
has, and another gate in the yard are all made of solid stone in single pieces,
hewn and worked from a rock. The walls of the courtyard and of the chamber
are three-quarters of a vara wide, and the roof of the room looks like straw
from outside but is actually of stone; for the Indians, who cover their houses
with thatch, have combed and grooved the stone to look as if it were thatched
like theirs. The lake washes one side of the courtyard. The natives say that the
house and other buildings are dedicated to the Creator of the universe. There
is also nearby another great pile of stones carved with figures of men and
women, and so natural that they seem to be alive: some are drinking from cups
in their hands, others sitting, others standing, others crossing a stream that
runs among the buildings; some statues have children on the laps, others are
carrying them on their backs, and others are in many other attitudes. The present Indians say that they were turned to stone for their sins and especially for
stoning a man who passed through that province.

These are the words of Diego de Alcobaça, who has been vicar and
preacher to the Indians in many provinces of that country: his superiors
have sent him to many places, because, as a mestizo born in Cuzco, he
knows the language of the Indians better than strangers from other countries and his work is more fruitful.

CHAPTER II

Hatunpacassa is reduced and
Cac-Yaviri conquered.

T O RETURN to the Inca Maita Cápac, he reduced most of the province
called Hatunpacassa almost without resistance. This is the land to the
left of the Desaguadero. The Indians differ as to whether it fell to one expedition or many: most think it was won gradually by the Incas as they
instructed the people and tilled the soil. Others say that this happened at

first when they were still not powerful, but that later they conquered all they could. It is of no real importance which way it happened. In order not to bore the reader with many repetitions of the same thing it will be best to state at once what each of these kings conquered, otherwise we shall wrong them by omitting each one's expeditions to different places. Proceeding with his conquest, therefore, the Inca reached a people called Cac-Yaviri, with many groups of homesteads scattered over its territory, without being arranged in townships. Each group was governed by a petty chief who lorded it over the rest. Knowing that the Inca was going to conquer them, these agreed and gathered on a hill in that district which is less than a quarter of a league high and as round as a sugarloaf, as though it were made by hand, though the land round about is all flat. This hill, because of its beauty and the fact that it stood alone, the Indians held as a sacred thing, and they worshipped it and offered it sacrifices. They went to it for succor, expecting it, as their god, to protect them and rid them of their enemies. They built on it a fort of dry stone and turfs mingled. They said the women undertook to provide all the turfs that were needed, so as to speed the work, while the men laid the stones. They shut themselves in the fort with their women and children in great numbers with all the food they could collect.

The Inca sent them the usual summons and in particular assured them that he would not deprive them of their lives or property, but would bestow on them the benefits the Sun had commanded he should confer on the Indians. They were not to disrespect the children of the Sun, who were invincible, for he aided them in all their conquests and battles; and they were to recognize him as god and worship him. The message was sent many times to the Indians, who remained obdurate, saying that they liked their own way of life, had no desire to improve it, and had their own gods, one of which was the hill which protected them and would favor them. Let the Incas go away in peace and teach others what they wanted; they did not want to learn anything. The Inca, who had no desire to come to blows with them, but hoped to win them with fair words, or if necessary to starve them out, divided his army into four parts and surrounded the hill.

The Collas continued many days in their obstinacy and prepared for an attack on the fort, but seeing the Incas reluctant to fight, they thought they were afraid and cowardly, and growing bolder day by day, often left the fort to fight them. The Inca's army, however, obeyed the orders of the king and merely resisted, though men were killed on both sides, more naturally of the Collas, who, being wild folk, rushed on their enemies' weapons. It was then a common report among the Collao Indians, which was afterwards widely circulated by the Incas in all their domains, that one day when the besieged Indians came out to fight the Inca's men, the stones and arrows and other missiles they threw against the Incas turned back against themselves, and many Collas died struck by their own arms. We shall later explain this fable, which was one of the ones they most venerated. With the great slaughter that took place that day, the rebels gave in, and especially the *curacas,* who repented of their obstinacy and, fearing a greater punishment, gathered all their people and came in troops to beg for mercy. The children were made to march first, behind them their mothers and the old people among them. Next the soldiers came out, and lastly the captains and *curacas* with their hands tied and ropes round their necks as a token that they deserved death for having taken up arms against the children of the Sun. They came barefoot, which was a sign of humility among the Peruvian Indians, and was intended to show that there was great majesty or divinity in the person they wished to reverence.

CHAPTER III

Those who surrendered are pardoned;
the explanation of the fable.

BROUGHT before the Inca, they cast themselves to the ground in their bonds and adored him as the child of the Sun with great acclamations. After the common people had paid worship to him, the *curacas* came separately, and with their usual signs of veneration begged his highness to pardon them, or if he preferred to slay them, they would be happy to die if he would spare their men who had resisted him by their orders and ill example. They begged forgiveness for the women, children, and old people, who were blameless. They alone were guilty and were ready to pay for all.

The Inca received them seated on his chair and surrounded by his warriors. Having heard the *curacas,* he ordered their hands to be unbound and the ropes to be removed from their necks as a token that he spared their lives and set them free. With gentle words he told them he had not come to take their lives or property, but to do them good and teach them to live by natural law and reason, and, abandoning their idols, to worship the Sun as god, to whom they owed their pardon. The Inca forgave them by the Sun's command and returned their lands and subjects to them as a favor, with no other purpose than to do them good, as they and their sons and descendants would find from long experience, for such were the Sun's commands: so let them return home and look to their wounds, and obey the orders they would receive, all of which would be to their benefit and advantage. That they might be the surer of the forgiveness of the Inca and have proof of his mildness, he bade that the *curacas,* in the name of all the rest, should approach and greet him by touching his right knee, to show that he regarded them as his people by permitting them to touch his person. This merciful favor was inestimable in their eyes, for it was prohibited and indeed sacrilegious to touch the Inca, who was one of their gods, unless they were of royal blood or expressly permitted by him. Seeing thus the merciful disposition of the king, they quite lost their fear of punishment and again abasing themselves, the *curacas* promised to be good subjects so as to deserve such a great favor, declaring that His Majesty showed himself by word and deed to be a child of the Sun since he conferred an unimaginable mercy on those who had deserved to die.

In explanation of the fable, the Indians say that the historic truth is that when the Inca's captains saw that the boldness of the Collas grew daily greater they secretly ordered their men to be ready to fight with fire and the sword, with all the rigor of war, since it was impossible to suffer such insolence towards the Inca. The Collas came out as usual to make their threats and vaunts, regardless of the anger and preparedness of their foes. They were received and attacked with great severity. Most of them died. But as the Inca's men had never before fought to kill, but only to resist, they spread it about that they had not fought that day either, but that the Sun, unable to stomach the disrespect of the Collas for his child, had ordered that their own weapons should turn against them and punished them, since the Incas had been reluctant to do so. The Indians were simple enough to believe this from the Incas as children of the Sun. The *amautas,* or philosophers, allegorized the tale, saying that the Collas' arms had been turned against them because they would not lay them down and obey the Inca when they were bidden. Their arms were thus the cause of their death.

CHAPTER IV

Three provinces are reduced and others conquered;
colonies are established; those who
use poison are punished.

THIS FABLE and the act of mercy and clemency of the prince were made widely known among the neighboring tribes around Hatunpacassa, where they occurred, and caused such wonder and astonishment, and also such admiration, that many peoples came over voluntarily and gave obedience to the Inca Maita Cápac, and adored and served him as a child of the Sun. Among other peoples that thus obeyed him were three great provinces with great wealth in flocks and numerous warlike inhabitants, called Cauquicura, Mallama, and Huarina (where the bloody battle was fought between Gonzalo Pizarro and Diego Centeno). Having granted favors to both those who were conquered and those who submitted, the Inca recrossed the Desaguadero in the direction of Cuzco. From Hatuncolla he sent the army with its four commanders westwards with orders to cross the desert called Hatunpuna, the edge of which had been won by the Inca Lloque Yupanqui, and to reduce to his service the tribes that might be found on the other side of the desert, as far as the shores of the Southern Sea. Under no circumstances were they to offer battle to the enemy: if any were so obdurate and pertinacious as to refuse to give in except to force of arms, they were to be left, since their loss would be greater than the Inca's gain. With these instructions and a great store of supplies assembled daily for them, the captains marched across the snowcapped range, with some difficulty since there was no road and about thirty leagues of waste land had to be crossed. They reached a province called Cuchuna, with a loosely scattered though considerable population. Hearing of the arrival of this army, the natives built a fort and shut themselves up with their wives and children. The Incas surrounded it, but out of respect for the orders of their king, were unwilling to attack it, though it was very weak. They offered peace and friendship. The enemy would accept neither, and the deadlock continued for above fifty days, during which the Incas had plenty of opportunities to cause great havoc to their enemies, yet avoided battle to keep up their tradition and obey the special injunction of the Inca only to press home the siege. But the natives were sorely pressed by hunger, the bitterest foe of the besieged, and it was the greater since the sudden arrival of the Incas had prevented them from laying in provisions; nor had they thought the Incas would persist in the siege, but rather go away on finding them resolute. The older people, men and women, stood the hunger with good cheer, but the children were unable to bear it and went out to find herbs in the fields. Many went over to their enemies, and their parents let them rather than see them die before their eyes. The Incas received them and fed them and even gave them a little food to take back to their parents, sending the usual messages of peace and friendship. Seeing this, the natives, who no longer hoped for relief, decided to surrender unconditionally, thinking that those who had been so full of clemency and mercy when they were rebels and enemies would be much more so if they were humble and penitent. So they surrendered to the Incas' will and were affably received without rancor or reproach for their past obstinacy. On the contrary they were received as friends, given food and undeceived about the Inca's policy, being told that he did not want their lands to oppress them, but to do good to the inhabitants as his father the Sun had ordered. To prove it by experience, they handed out clothes and other gifts to the chief people, saying they were favors from the Incas. The common people were given supplies to take home and all were very satisfied.

The Inca captains reported all that had happened in this conquest and asked for colonists to settle in two towns there, for the land seemed fertile and capable of supporting far more people than it held. It was proposed also to leave a garrison there to assure the possession of what had been won, and for any emergencies that might occur. The Inca sent the required settlers with their wives and families, and the two towns were peopled. One was at the foot of the mountains where the natives had built their fort. It was called Cuchuna, the name of the mountains. The other was called Moquehua. The towns are five leagues apart, and the provinces are now called after the two towns. They are in the jurisdiction of Collasuyu.

While the captains were busy establishing these towns, planning their government, and arranging for the instruction of the inhabitants, it came to their ears that some of the Indians used poison against their enemies, not so much to kill them as to disfigure and injure them in face and body. It was a gentle poison which was only fatal to those of weak constitution. Those who were robust survived it, though at the expense of losing the use of their senses and members and remaining half-witted and deformed in body and appearance. They were indeed repulsive, being covered with patches and blotches of black and white, and in short ruined in body and mind, so that their whole families grieved to see them in such a state. The poisoners delighted in their suffering more than if they had killed them outright. Informed of this wicked practice, the captains reported it to the Inca who ordered that anyone guilty of it should be burned alive and their memory obliterated. The natives of the provinces were so pleased with this order that they themselves sought out the criminals and executed the sentence, burning the guilty alive with everything in their houses, which were pulled down and the site strewn with stones as accursed places. Their flocks were burnt, and their estates destroyed, even the trees they had planted were uprooted; and the land was left abandoned, never to be given to anyone else lest the new occupants should inherit the wickedness of the first owners. The severity of the punishment put such fear into the natives that this evil practice was never known again in the lands of the Inca kings, down to the time of the Spanish conquest, as the natives themselves declare. Having executed this penalty, installed the settlers, and established the government of their new subjects, the captains returned to Cuzco to report what had happened. They were well received and rewarded by the king.

CHAPTER V

The Inca gains three provinces and
wins a hard-fought battle.

SOME YEARS later the Inca Maita Cápac decided to sally forth and reduce the natives of new provinces to his empire, for ambition and the desire to increase their kingdom grew daily among the Incas. Having collected all the warriors he could and supplied them with provisions, he went to Pucara de Umasuyu, the last town won by his grandfather in that direction (others say by his father). From Pucara he advanced to the east to a province called Llaricassa and reduced its inhabitants without resistance: in fact they rejoiced to receive him as their lord. Thence he passed to the province called Sancauan, and just as easily brought it into submission. As his fame had preceded him in those provinces, broadcasting the deeds of his father and grandfather, the natives rushed willingly to offer him their vassalage. The two provinces are more than fifty leagues long and thirty broad in one place and twenty in another. They are thickly populated and rich in flocks. The Inca, having established his idolatry as usual and set up government over his new vassals, passed on to the province called Pacassa, reducing its natives to his service unconditionally and without battle or indeed resistance. All obeyed and venerated the child of the Sun.

This province is part of that we have mentioned as a conquest of the Inca Lloque Yupanqui. It is very large and has many towns, and its conquest was thus completed by those two Incas, father and son. Having completed the conquest, the Inca reached the royal highway of Umasuyu near a town today called Huaichu. He heard there that there was a great crowd of people ahead prepared to make war on him. The Inca advanced in search of the enemy, who came out to bar the passage of a river called the Huichu. Thirteen or fourteen thousand Indians of various tribes (though all included under the name of Collas) came out. The Inca, in order to avoid battle but to pursue his conquests as hitherto, repeatedly offered the enemy peace and friendship, but they would never accept them and grew daily more impudent, supposing that the terms offered by the Inca and his unwillingness to break with them were due to fear they had inspired in him. In this vain supposition they crossed the river in bands in many places and shamelessly attacked the Inca's camp. To avoid death on both sides, he sought in all ways to attract them and suffered their rudeness with such patience that his own men objected that it was not proper to the majesty of a child of the Sun to permit and suffer such insolence from barbarians; or others would scorn them, and they would lose the reputation they had won.

The Inca calmed the indignation of his men, reminding them that he had followed the example of his ancestors and the command of his father the Sun, who bade him look to the welfare of the Indians and not punish them by force of arms: let them wait a day or so without inflicting harm on the army or offering battle to see if some knowledge of the good he desired to do would dawn on them. With these and similar words, the Inca held his captains' patience for many days, without giving them permission to get to grips with the enemy. But at last, giving way to the importunity of his followers and impelled by the insolence of the enemy, now grown insupportable, he ordered preparations for battle.

The Incas, who were extremely anxious for this, promptly went out. The enemy saw the long-provoked battle approach and marched forth with great spirit and eagerness. They came to grips and fought with enormous ferocity and courage on both sides, the one party to keep their freedom and uphold their desire not to be vassals and servants of the Inca, even though he was the child of the Sun, the other to prevent the disrespect shown to their king. They fought with great pertinacity and blindness, especially the Collas, who flung themselves needlessly against the Incas' weapons and fought desperately, like barbarians obstinate in their resistance and without order or plan, so that the mortality among them was great. This bitter fight lasted all day without remission. The Inca was to be found in every part of the field, now urging on his men with his example like a good captain, now fighting with the enemy, so as not to lose the reputation of being a good soldier.

CHAPTER VI

Those of Huaichu surrender; they are courteously pardoned.

ACCORDING to their descendants, above six thousand of the Collas perished, owing to the lack of plan and discipline in their attack. On the Incas' side no more than five hundred were lost, such was their order and good government. When night fell, both sides withdrew to their quarters and the Collas, feeling the pain of their wounds, now chilled, and seeing the number of the dead, lost the courage they had so far shown and did not know what to do or what policy to follow. They had no strength to escape from the place by fighting, and did not see how or where they could escape by flight, for the enemy had surrounded them and cut them off; and they feared to ask for clemency knowing they had forfeited it by their rascality and because they had scorned the many generous offers of terms the Inca had made.

In this state of confusion they took the safest course, which was the advice of the old men, who recommended that, though it was late, they should submit and beg the prince's clemency. Though aggrieved, he would imitate the example of his forefathers, of whose mercy towards enemies, whether rebellious or submissive, they had heard. This agreed, they donned at daybreak the vilest garb they could find, their heads bare, shoeless, without cloaks, covered with only their tunics. The captains and chiefs presented themselves in silence, with their hands bound at the gate to the Inca's lodging. He received them mildly. The Collas knelt and said they came not to beg mercy, which they knew they did not deserve of the Inca because of their ingratitude and obstinacy. They only begged him to order the warriors to be put to the sword as an example to others not to disobey the child of the Sun as they had done.

The Inca ordered one of his captains to answer in his name and tell them that his father the Sun had not sent him down to earth to slay Indians but to confer on them the benefit of raising them from their bestial life, teaching them the knowledge of the Sun, their god, and giving them laws, ordinances, and government so that they could live like men, not brutes. To fulfil this commandment he moved from province to province, though he had no need of them, and attracted the Indians to the service of the Sun. As a child of his, though they did not deserve it, he forgave them and bade them live. As to their rebelliousness, the Inca was sorry for the severe punishment that his father the Sun had to inflict on them; thenceforth let them mend their ways and obey the Sun's commandments so as to live in prosperity and peace enjoying his benefits. Having given this reply, he ordered them to be clad, their wounds to be cured, and good treatment to be shown them. The Indians returned home, declaring what they had suffered on account of their rebelliousness and ascribing their survival to the clemency of the Inca.

CHAPTER VII

Many towns are reduced; the Inca orders the
construction of a bridge of osiers.

NEWS OF THE slaughter in this battle soon spread throughout the region. It was known that the Sun had punished the Indians for disobedience to his children, the Incas, and disregard for the benefits they offered. Consequently many peoples who had hitherto been under arms and encamped to resist the Inca gave up on hearing of his clemency and mercy and addressed themselves to him to ask pardon and beg him to receive them as vassals, which they would be happy to be. The Inca received them very affably, and sent them robes and other gifts which greatly pleased them; and they declared everywhere that the Incas were true children of the Sun.

The tribes that submitted to the Inca were those between Huaichu and Callamarca, to the south, along the road to Charcas for a distance of thirty leagues. The Inca advanced a further twenty-four leagues beyond Calla-marca on the same Charcas highroad as far as Caracollo. All the peoples on both sides the highways as far as the lake of Paria submitted. Thence he turned east towards the Antis, reaching the valley now called Chuquiapu, meaning "chief or leading lance." Here he established many colonies of Indians, realizing that these hot valleys were better for growing maize than all the other provinces included under the name Colla. From the valley of Caracatu he went eastwards to the skirts of the great snowcapped range of the cordillera of the Antis, which are thirty leagues and more from the Umasuyu highway.

He spent three years in these journeys and in reducing the inhabitants and establishing his laws and government among them. Then he returned to Cuzco, where he was welcomed with great festivities and rejoicing. Having rested two or three years, he ordered supplies and men to be brought together for a new conquest, for his spirit could not brook idle-ness, and he resolved to go to the area west from Cuzco, which they call Cuntisuyu, where there are many great provinces. As he had to pass the great river called Apurímac, he ordered a bridge to be prepared for the passage of his army. He drew the plan for it after consulting the best in-telligences among the Indians. As writers on Peru mention rope bridges, but do not say how they are made, it seems well to depict them here, for those who have never seen them, the more so as this was the first rope bridge made by order of the Incas in Peru.

To make one of these bridges, a very great quantity of osier is collected. This is of a different variety from the Spanish, with fine and tough withies. They make three single osiers into a long rope according to the length needed for the bridge. Three ropes each of three osiers are used to make one of nine osiers, and three of these are used for others twenty-seven osiers thick, and three of these make even thicker ones. In this way they increase and thicken the ropes until they are as thick as a man's body or thicker. They make five ropes of the thickest kind; and to get them across the river they swim or use rafts carrying a thin cord to which is attached a cable as thick as the human arm made of a hemp the Indians call *cháhuar*. To this cable they fasten one of the ropes and a great crowd of Indians heaves at it until they get it over the river. Having got all five over, they mount them on two high supports that have been cut out of the living rock in a convenient place, or if these are not available they make the sup-ports, of masonry, as strong as rock. The Apurímac bridge, which is on the highway from Cuzco to Lima, has one support of living rock and the other of masonry. The supports are hollowed out near the ground, and the sides are strengthened with walls. From side to side of these hollow spaces run five or six beams, as thick as bullocks, placed one above another like the rungs of a ladder. Each of the thick osier ropes is twisted round each of these beams so that the bridge will remain taut and not sag with its own weight, which is very considerable. But however much it is stretched, it always sinks in the middle and assumes a curved shape, so that in crossing one first descends and then mounts the other side; if there is a strong breeze at all it rocks.

Three of the great ropes are used for the floor of the bridge, and the other two as handrails on either side. The floor ropes are overlaid with wood as thick as a man's arm, crossing the full width of the bridge, which is about two varas, rather like hurdles. This wood preserves the ropes from wear and is firmly fixed to them. It in turn is strewn with many boughs fixed in rows so as to give a firm footing to beasts of burden which would otherwise slip and fall. Between the lower floor ropes and the handrails they string twigs and thin boards securely fixed so as to make a wall the whole length of the bridge. This is now strong enough to carry men and animals.

The Apurímac bridge, which is the longest, may be about two hundred paces long. I have not measured it, but when I discussed it in Spain with many who have crossed it, they said this is about the length—more rather than less. I have seen many Spaniards cross without dismounting, and some on horseback at a gallop to show how little they were afraid: the feat is rather a rash one. The fabric is begun with only three osiers, but the result is the bold and impressive work that I have described, however imperfectly. It is certainly a marvellous piece of work, and would be incredible if one could not still see it, for its very necessity has preserved it from destruction, or time might have destroyed it like many others which the Spaniards found on the same highways, some as big or even bigger. In the Incas' times the bridges were replaced every year. People came from the neighboring provinces for the work and the supply of materials was divided between them according to their proximity and capabilities. This system is still followed today.

CHAPTER VIII

Many tribes are reduced voluntarily to submission
by the fame of the bridge.

WHEN THE Inca learnt that the bridge was finished, he went forth with his army, consisting of twelve thousand warriors led by seasoned captains, and advanced to the bridge, which was well guarded lest an enemy should try to burn it down. But his enemies were so astonished at the new work that they desired only to acknowledge as their lord the prince who had ordered it to be erected. Even until the coming of the Spaniards, the Indians were so simple that the sight of anything that they had never beheld before was enough to cause them to bow down and recognize the inventor as a divine child of the Sun. Thus nothing impressed them so much, causing them to regard the Spaniards as gods and surrender to them at the beginning of the conquest, as the sight of them fighting mounted on such fierce animals as horses appeared to them, and able to shoot with arquebusses and kill men at a distance of two or three hundred paces. Because of these two things especially, together with others, the Indians thought the Spaniards were children of the Sun and gave in to them with little resistance. They show the same astonishment and awe whenever the Spaniards do something they have never seen before, such as using a mill for grinding corn, ploughing with oxen, or building bridges over rivers with arches of stonework, which seems to them as though a great mass is hanging in the air. For these reasons and others that appear daily they say that the Spaniards deserve that the Indians should serve them. As the simplicity of the Indians was even greater in the days of the Inca Maita Cápac, they were so astonished at the construction of the bridge that it alone sufficed to cause many provinces of the region to submit to the Inca without any reservations, one being the part called Chumpivillca in the district of Cuntisuyu, which is twenty leagues long and more than ten broad. He was welcomed as their lord with a good will because of his face as a child of the Sun and because of the marvellous new work that seemed only possible for men come down from heaven. He was resisted only in a town called Villilli where the natives shut themselves in a fort they had built outside the town. The Inca had them surrounded on all sides so that none might escape, and invited them to come to terms with his usual clemency and mercy.

After a few days, not above twelve or thirteen, those within surrendered and the Inca gave them a full pardon. Leaving the province at peace, he crossed the desert of Cuntisuyu, a distance of sixteen leagues. The army reached a dangerous swamp three leagues across which runs deep into that country and it was unable to cross. The Inca ordered a causeway to be built of large and small stones mingled with turfs. The Inca himself worked on the scheme, both in planning it and in helping to lift the great stones used in it. With the aid of his example his men toiled with such diligence that the causeway, although it was six varas broad and two deep, was finished in a few days. The Indians of the region greatly venerated it, and still do, both because the Inca himself worked at it and because of the advantage they derived from its use, for they were saved a long and arduous journey in making a detour round the swamp on either side. They therefore took great pains to keep it in repair, and hardly had a stone fallen out than they replaced it. They have divided it up between various districts, each of which is entrusted with the repair of a part. They still rival one another in their efforts as if it had just been finished, and this division of responsibility is practiced in all their public works. If the object is a small one, it is divided among families, if larger among villages, and if very large, as in the case of bridges, storehouses, royal palaces, and the like, among provinces. Turfs are much used in making causeways, because the roots can be intertwined among the stones to bind and greatly strengthen the work.

CHAPTER IX

The Inca gains many other great provinces, and dies in peace.

HAVING finished the causeway, the Inca Maita Cápac passed over it and entered a province called Allca, where many armed Indians came from all around to bar the passage between some very rugged slopes and difficult passages in the road. These are so forbidding that even in time of peace they cause fear and horror, let alone when they are infested with hostile opponents. The Inca behaved with such providence, foresight, and military skill in these places that though they were defended and there were losses on both sides, he constantly gained ground. His enemies, seeing their inability to resist him on such rough terrain and their own daily loss of ground, concluded that the Incas were truly children of the Sun and invincible. In this false belief, though they had resisted more than two months, the whole province with common consent now received him as lord and king, promising him the loyalty of faithful subjects.

The Inca entered the chief town of Allca in great triumph. Thence he passed to other great provinces named Taurisma, Cotahuaci, Pumatampu, and Parihuana Cocha, which means "lake of flamingoes." For in an uninhabited part of the province there is a large lake. In the Inca language the sea is *cocha,* and so any lake or pool, and *parihuana* are the birds called "flamingoes" in Spain. These two words give Parihuana Cocha, the name of this large, beautiful, fertile, and auriferous province. The Spaniards abbreviate the name to Parina Cocha. Pumatampu is "lions' store," from *puma,* "a lion," and *tampu,* "a store." There must have been a lair of them at some time in the province, or perhaps it had more lions than the rest.

From Parihuana Cocha the Inca advanced and crossed the desert of Coropuna, where there is a most beautiful and lofty pyramid of snow that the Indians reverently call huaca, for the meanings of this word include that of "wonderful," which it certainly is. In their ancient simplicity the natives worshipped it for its height and beauty, which are remarkable. Passing the desert, he entered the province called Aruni. Thence he passed to another called Collahua which stretches to the valley of Arequipa, which according to Padre Blas Valera means "sounding trumpet."

All these tribes and provinces were reduced by the Inca Maita Cápac and added to his empire with great ease and much willingness on the part of the Indians. For having heard of the deeds of the Incas in passing the rough passes and rugged mountains Allca, they thought them invincible and children of the Sun, and were glad to be their subjects. In each of these provinces the Inca stopped long enough to settle and order the good government and general peace of the place. He found the valley of Arequipa uninhabited, and seeing the fertility of the place and mildness of the air, he decided to settle many Indians from the conquered tribes in this valley. Explaining the suitability of the site to them and the advantages that would follow the colonization and enjoyment of the land, not only to the settlers themselves, but also to the rest of the tribe to whose benefit it would certainly redound, he established three thousand families there, founding four or five towns. One was called Chimpa and another Sucahuaya; and leaving the necessary governors and other officers there, he returned to Cuzco, having taken three years in this second conquest. In this time he incorporated in his empire an area of the district called Cuntisuyu nearly ninety leagues in length and from ten to twelve in width in one part and fifteen elsewhere. All this land was continuous with that already won and added to the empire.

In Cuzco the Inca was received with very great solemnity, festivals, rejoicings, dances, and the singing of songs composed in praise of his great deeds. Having rewarded his captains and soldiers with favors and graces, the Inca dismissed his army. He now thought that his conquests were sufficient and wanted to rest from his past labors and devote himself to laws and ordinances for the good government of his kingdom. He paid particular attention to the care of the poor and widows and orphans; to this he gave the rest of his life. His reign, like those of his predecessors, is thought to have lasted thirty years, more or less: it cannot be certainly established how long he reigned or lived, and I could not learn any more of his deeds. He died full of the honors and glories he had won in peace and war, and was wept and mourned for a year, according to the Inca custom. He was beloved by his subjects. He left as his sole heir Cápac Yupanqui, his eldest son by his wife and sister Mama Cuca. As well as this prince, he left sons and daughters, both those called legitimate by blood and not legitimate.

CHAPTER X

*Cápac Yupanqui, the fifth king, wins many
provinces in Cuntisuyu.*

THE INCA Cápac Yupanqui, the meaning of whose name can be deduced from those of his ancestors, assumed the crimson fringe on the death of his father as a token of his accession. Having performed the obsequies, he went out to visit the whole of his empire, and went from province to province enquiring about the acts of his governors and other officials. This took two years. He returned to Cuzco, and ordered armies and supplies to be made ready for the following year, thinking to conquer the region of Cuntisuyu to the west of Cuzco where he knew there were many large and thickly inhabited provinces. In order to reach them, he ordered the building of another bridge across the great river Apurímac at a place called Huacachaca, downstream from that at Accha, which was duly constructed and proved even longer than the first, since the river is wider at this point.

The Inca left Cuzco with nearly twenty thousand warriors. They reached the bridge eight leagues from the city. The road is rough and difficult, for the slope down to the river alone is three full leagues downhill and almost perpendicular, the actual distance being less than half a league. Beyond the river there is a climb of three leagues. Over the bridge he entered the lovely province of Yanahuara, which today has over thirty towns. How many it then had is unknown, but the first that is reached in that direction is called Piti. There the inhabitants—men, women, and children—came out with feasts and rejoicing and songs and acclamations to receive the Inca as lord and offer him their obedience and homage. The Inca received them warmly, and gave them many presents of garments and other things worn at his court. The people of Piti sent messengers to other towns in the district of the same Yanahuara tribe, advising them of the Inca's arrival and their acceptance of him as king and lord, and the other *curacas* came and imitated those of Piti with due rejoicing.

The Inca received them as he had the first, and gave them honors and presents, and as a great favor desired to see their towns, and visit them all, although they stretch over an area twenty leagues long and over fifteen broad. From the province of Yanahuara he passed to another called Aimara. Between them there is a desert fifteen leagues across. Beyond the desert, on a great hill called Mucansa, he found a great number of people gathered to resist his entry into their province, which stretches for more than thirty leagues and is over fifteen leagues broad and rich in gold, silver, and lead mines and also in flocks. It is thickly populated and had over eighty towns before its conquest.

The Inca bade his army camp at the foot of the hill to cut off the enemy. They, like savages with no military skill, had abandoned their towns and collected on the hills as a strong point without realizing that they could be surrounded like cattle in a stockyard. The Inca lingered many days without wishing to give battle or consenting that any harm should be done them except to prevent the passage of supplies so they would be forced by hunger to surrender. He also peacefully invited them to come over.

For more than a month this defiance continued, until the rebel Indians, driven by hunger, sent messengers to the Inca, saying that they were ready to receive him as king and worship him as a child of the Sun, if as a child of the Sun he would give his word to conquer and annex the province of Umasuyu, next to them, as soon as they had surrendered. Umasuyu was peopled with warlike and tyrannous people who invaded their pastures to the very doors of their homes and molested them in other ways, provoking battles and death and plundering. As often as this strife was appeased, it was rekindled, and always owing to the tyranny and outrageous conduct of those of Umasuyu. They begged him, as they were to be his subjects, to save them from these cruel enemies, and that was their condition for surrendering and acknowledging him as prince and lord.

The Inca answered through one of his captains that he had come there only to right wrongs and grievances and to teach all the barbarous tribes to live under the law of men and not as beasts, and to show them the knowledge of his god the Sun, and since the righting of wrongs and teaching the Indians reason was the duty of an Inca, they had no cause to make it a condition for him to do what it was his duty to do. He received them as subjects, but not the condition. It was not for them to give laws, but for the child of the Sun: let them leave their dissensions, quarrels, and wars to the Inca's will, for he knew what was to be done.

With this reply the ambassadors returned, and next day all the Indians who had withdrawn into the hills came down, to the number of over twelve thousand warriors. They brought their wives and children, exceeding thirty thousand souls; all came in troops, divided according to their towns, and they knelt, as the custom was, to honor the Inca and presented themselves as his vassals, in token of which they offered gold, silver, lead, and everything else they had. The Inca received them with great clemency, ordering them to be fed, since they were fainting with hunger, and gave them supplies until they should reach their towns so that they should not perish by the wayside. He then sent them to their homes.

CHAPTER XI

The conquest of the Aimaras [Umasuyus]; they
forgive the curacas; they place landmarks
on their boundaries.

HAVING dismissed the people, the Inca went to a place in the same
province of Aimara called Huaquirca, which now contains above
two thousand dwellings. Thence he sent messengers to the chiefs of Umasuyu, ordering them to appear before him so that he might settled the differences between them and their neighbors, the Aimaras, about grazing-
rights and common lands: he would expect them at Huaquirca where he
would lay down laws and ordinances in the light of which they should live
as reasonable beings instead of slaughtering one another like beasts about
such a trifle as pasture for their flocks, since it was well known that there
was abundant grazing for both parties. The *curacas* of Umasuyu assembled
to elaborate their reply which, since the Inca's summons was addressed to
them all, should represent their common view. It was that they had no
reason to go to the Inca; if he wanted anything of them, let him come to
their country where they would await him with their weapons in their
hands. They did not know whether he was a child of the Sun and did not
recognize or want the Sun as their god: they had gods of their own land
who suited them well, and needed no others. Let the Inca confer his laws
and orders on those who were willing to obey them: for their part they
found it a good law to take what they wanted from whoever had it by
force of arms, and were ready to defend their lands in the same way
from anyone who came to molest them. This was their reply and if the
Inca wanted any other, they would give him it on the field, like brave
soldiers.

The Inca Cápac Yupanqui and his commanders considered the reply
of the Umasuyus and agreed to strike against their towns as speedily as
possible so as to take them unprepared and crush their shameless insolence with fear and surprise rather than by warfare, since, as we have
said, the first Inca Manco Cápac had expressly ordered all the kings who
descended from him never to permit bloodshed in any conquest they
might make unless it was absolutely necessary and always to try to attract
the Indians with benefits and blandishments, so that they should be loved

by the subjects they had conquered with love, and not perpetually hated by those reduced by force of arms. The Inca Cápac Yupanqui knew how wise it would be to observe this rule in order to keep and extend his kingdom, and prepared with all speed a force of eight thousand men, the flower of his army. Marching day and night, he soon entered the province of Umasuyu, where his unsuspecting enemy did not expect him for at least a month owing to the size of his force and the difficulty of the journey. Seeing him now so suddenly appear in their midst with an army of chosen men and knowing that the rest of his force was following, they realized that before they could assemble and establish their defence, the Inca would have burnt all their homes. They therefore repented of their untoward reply and abandoned their arms. Their *curacas* from all sides hastily advised together by means of messengers and decided to beg for mercy and forgiveness for their crime. They hastened to the Inca and presented themselves as they happened to arrive, first some, then others, and begged him to pardon them; for they confessed that he was the child of the Sun, and that as their child of such a father he might receive them as his subjects who protested they would serve him faithfully.

The Inca, far from justifying the fears of the *curacas* who expected to be executed, received them with great clemency and ordered them to be told he was not surprised that they, as untutored barbarians, should not understand what was good for them in regard to religion and moral life. If they had tasted the good government and rule of his royal forebears, they would gladly be his subjects, and they would similarly scorn their idols if they had considered and recognized the enormous benefits they and the rest of the world would receive from the Sun, his father, who so deserved to be adored as god, instead of the so-called gods of their country, which being images of vile and filthy animals, deserved to be despised rather than deified. He therefore ordered them to obey him in everything and in every way, and to do what he and his governors bade them, both in matters of religion and in their laws, for both were laid down by his father the Sun.

The *curacas* very humbly replied that they promised to have no other god but the Sun, his father, and to observe no laws but those he might vouchsafe: from what they had seen and heard all these were ordained for the honor and benefit of his subjects. To favor his new vassals, the Inca went to one of the chief towns of the province, Chirirqui, and, having informed himself of the facts about the pasturage that had given rise to disputes and wars, took into consideration the interests of both parties, and established landmarks, where he thought fit, so that each province should know its own land and not trespass on its rival's. These landmarks were, and still are today, preserved with great veneration, for they were the first to be set up in all Peru by order of the Inca.

The *curacas* of both provinces kissed the Inca's hands, giving him many thanks for the division he had made to such great satisfaction on both sides. The king visited the two provinces at leisure in order to establish his laws and ordinances; and having done this, returned to Cuzco, preferring not to press on with his conquests, though he could well have done so in view of the success he had had. The Inca Cápac Yupanqui entered his capital with his army in triumph, for the *curacas* and noble people of the three newly conquered province had gone with him to see the imperial city. They carried him in a golden litter on their shoulders as a token of their submission to the empire. His captains marched around the litter, and his warriors before, in military array by companies, that from each province being separate from the last and preserving the order of seniority by which they were conquered and added to the empire, the first to be annexed being closest to the Inca and most recent farthest away. The whole city came out to receive him with songs and dances, according to custom.

CHAPTER XII

The Inca sends an army to conquer the Quechuas; they agree to submit.

THE INCA busied himself for four years with the government and welfare of his subjects. Then, deeming it wrong to devote so much time to the quiet enjoyment of peace without giving an opportunity for martial exercise, he gave orders that supplies and weapons should be collected with special care and his soldiers summoned for the following year. In due course he chose one of his brothers called Auqui Titu as commander-in-chief and four Incas from among his nearest relatives, all men of experience in affairs of peace and war, to be field commanders, each one having under his orders a regiment of five thousand soldiers and all five being in charge of the army as a whole. He ordered them to pursue the conquest he himself had begun in the district of Cuntisuyu, and in order to give the expedition a good start, he accompanied it as far as the bridge of Huacachaca, and having recommended the leaders to follow the example of his Inca forebears in conquering the Indians, he made his return to Cuzco.

The Inca general and his commanders entered a province called Cotapampa. They found its ruler accompanied by a relative of his who ruled another province called Cotanera, both peopled by the Quechua tribe. The chiefs, aware that the Inca had sent an army to their country, had met to offer a willing reception to him as their lord and king, having long desired his coming. So they advanced escorted by many people singing and dancing, and welcomed the Inca Auqui Titu, saying with demonstrations of joy and delight:

"Welcome, Inca Apu (meaning general); you give us new life and new honor by making us servants and vassals of the child of the Sun, wherefore we worship you as his brother and assure you that it is a fact that if you had not come now to induce us to serve the Inca, we were resolved to go next year to Cuzco to deliver ourselves to the king and beg him to give instructions for us to be admitted under his empire, since the fame of the deeds and miracles performed by the children of the Sun in peace and war has so filled us with esteem and desire to serve them and be their subjects that every day seems an age to us. We also desired these things in order to be liberated from the tyranny and cruelty inflicted on us by the Chanca and Hancohuallu tribes and their neighbors. These abuses we have suffered for many years, since the days of our grandfathers and forebears from whom they have taken much land, as they have from us too, committing great wrongs and oppressing us bitterly. For this reason we desired the empire of the Incas to free us from tyranny. May the Sun, your father, guard and protect you for you have crowned our desires."

This said, they performed their obeisance to the Inca and the other commanders and offered them a great quantity of gold for despatch to the king. The province of Cotapampa, after the war of Gonzalo Pizarro, was allocated to Don Pedro Luis de Cabrera, a native of Seville, and that of Cotanera and another of which we shall speak presently called Huamanpallpa were the property of my lord, Garcilaso de la Vega. This was the second *repartimiento* he received in Peru: to the first we shall return in its due place.

General Auqui Titu and the commanders replied in the Inca's name, saying that they rejoiced at the goodwill of the chiefs in the past and at their present desire to serve, of both of which and of every word of their speeches a full account would be presented to his majesty so that he might reward them as he rewarded all services performed on his behalf. The *curacas* were very gratified to know that their words and services would reach the Inca's ears, and daily displayed greater regard for the general and commanders and obeyed them in everything they ordered. Having established the customary order in these two provinces, the commanders passed on to the other called Huamanpallpa. They reduced it too without bloodshed or opposition. The Incas crossed the Amáncay River by two or three branches that run through these provinces, coming together lower down to form the great Amáncay River.

One of these branches flows through Chuquinca, where the battle between Francisco Hernández Girón and the marshal Don Alonso de Alvarado took place, and by the same river, years before, Don Diego de Almagro fought the marshal, who was defeated on both occasions, as we shall tell in due time if God spares us so long. The Incas continued to reduce the provinces on both sides of the river Amáncay, which are numerous and all belong to the Quechua nation. They are all rich in gold and flocks.

CHAPTER XIII

They conquer many valleys on the seacoast,
and punish sodomy.

AFTER HAVING established the order necessary for the government of these places, they set out through the desolate region of Huallaripa, a range of mountains famous for the great quantity of gold extracted from it and for the even greater quantity that remains. Crossing a strip of this desert country, which is thirty-five leagues across in that part, they descended to the plains of the seacoast. Any coastal region or other land with a hot climate the Indians call *yunca,* "hot land." The name *yunca* covers a great many valleys along the whole coast. The Spaniards apply the word *valles* to land watered by the rivers that flow down from the mountains to the sea. This is the only inhabited land on this coast, for except when watered by the rivers the land is quite uninhabitable and consists of dead sand on which neither grass nor anything else of use will grow.

At the place where the Incas reached the coastal plain is the valley of Hacari, a broad, fertile, and thickly populated area that in times gone by had more than twenty thousand Indian settlers, who were easily reduced to obedience and service by the Incas. From the Hacari Valley they passed to those called Uviña [Ocoño], Camana, Caravilli, Picta, Quellca, and others further down the coast on a line running sixty leagues north and south. The valleys mentioned are above twenty leagues long, running downstream from the mountains to the sea, and as broad as the area irrigated by the rivers on both sides, in some cases two leagues and in others more or less according to the greater or less volume of water. There are some rivers on this coast that the Indians do not allow to reach the sea, since they divert them from their beds to water their crops and orchards. When the Inca general Auqui Titu and the commanders had reduced all these valleys to the service of the king without giving battle, they reported what had happened and in particular informed the king that in investigating the secret customs of the natives, their rites and ceremonies and their gods, who were the fish they caught, it had been discovered that there were some sodomites, not in all the valleys, but in some of them, and not including all the inhabitants, but only certain ones, who practiced this vice in secret. They also reported that there was no more land to conquer in that direction, for with the previous conquests they had now reached the coast right down to the south.

The Inca was much pleased with the account of the conquest, and still more because it had been accomplished without bloodshed. He sent orders that after leaving the usual system of government, they should return to Cuzco. In particular he ordered that the sodomites should be sought out with great care and when found burnt alive in the public square, not only those proved guilty but those convicted on circumstantial evidence, however slight. Their houses should be burnt and pulled down, and the trees on their fields pulled up by the roots and burnt so that no memory should remain of so abominable a thing, and it would be proclaimed as an inviolable law that thenceforward none should be guilty of such a crime, or the sin of one would be visited on his whole town and all the inhabitants would be burnt just as single ones were now being burnt.

This was done as the Inca directed, to the great wonder of the natives of those valleys that this unspeakable crime should be dealt with in this new fashion. It was indeed so hated by the Incas and their people that the very name was odious to them and they never uttered it. Any Indian from Cuzco, even though not an Inca, who used it as a term of abuse when roused to anger in dispute with another was automatically regarded as disgraced and looked upon for many days by the rest of the Indians as something vile and filthy for having let the word pass his lips.

Once the general and commanders had accomplished all that the Inca had commanded, they returned to Cuzco where they were received in triumph and granted great honors and favors. Some years after this conquest, the Inca Cápac Yupanqui desired to make a new expedition in person and extend the bounds of his empire in the direction known as Collasuyu, for the last two conquests had been confined to Cuntisuyu. So he ordered an army of twenty thousand chosen men to be assembled for the coming year.

While this force was being prepared, the Inca took the necessary steps for the government of his kingdom. He named his brother, General Auqui Titu, as governor and his lieutenant, and disposed that the four commanders who had accompanied him should now remain as his advisers. He chose for himself four other commanders and other captains for his army, all Incas—for as long as there were Incas available, no others could command, and although each contingent brought captains from its own tribe, as soon as they entered the royal host Incas were placed over them, and they obeyed the orders of the Incas and acted in military affairs as their lieutenants. Thus the whole army came to be governed by the Incas, though the other tribes were not deprived of their particular offices and therefore not disfavored or insulted by being displaced. For the Incas always commanded that the *curacas* and people of every tribe should be gratified and contented in all things that were not contrary to their own laws and ordinances. By reason of this mild form of government, the Indians hastened to serve the Incas with so much readiness and affection. The Inca ordered the prince, his heir, to accompany him in order to obtain experience of warfare, though he was still very young.

CHAPTER XIV

Two great curacas bring their dispute
to the Inca and become his subjects.

WHEN THE TIME for the campaign arrived, the Inca Cápac Yupanqui
set out from Cuzco and marched as far as the lake of Paria, which
was the extreme limit of his father's conquests in that direction. He and
his officers collected the warriors raised from each of the provinces along
the road, and took care to visit the towns that were accessible on either
side, so as to favor the inhabitants with his presence. So great was the
favor they felt that the Inca should enter their provinces that even today
they still preserve the memory of many places where the Incas happened
to stop in the town or among the fields to give orders, or dispense some
favor, or rest on the way. These places are today revered by the Indians
because their kings have been there.

On reaching the lake of Paria, the Inca sought to reduce the peoples of
the district to obedience. Some submitted because of the good news they
had heard of the Incas, and others because they could not resist. In the
course of these conquests, messengers reached the Inca from two great
chieftains in the district of Collasuyu who were engaged in a bitter war
against one another. That the episode may be better understood it is necessary to know that these two *curacas* were the descendants of two famous
leaders who in the days before the Incas had risen up in those parts and
had each gained many towns and subjects, thus becoming great lords. Not
content with what they had each won, they now turned their arms against
one another, according to the common practice of rulers, who cannot brook
an equal. They waged cruel war, each now losing, now gaining, and sustaining themselves courageously like brave captains as long as they lived.
They bequeathed the conflict as an inheritance to their sons and descendants who continued it with no less courage than their ancestors until the
time of the Inca Cápac Yupanqui.

Beholding this continual and cruel war in which they had often been
all but destroyed, and fearing that, since strength and courage were well
matched on both sides, each might finally be destroyed without advantage
to the other, they resolved, in agreement with their captains and kinsmen,
to submit to the will of the Inca Cápac Yupanqui and abide by his decision and order concerning their feud and passions. They reached this

understanding moved by the fame of the Incas, past and present, whose justice and rectitude, together with the wonders said to have been wrought on their behalf by their father the Sun, were so widely noised abroad among those tribes that all desired to experience them. One of these chiefs was called Cari and the other Chipana: their ancestors had borne the same names since the first, who had wished their successors to preserve their memory, passing their names down from generation to generation and therefore remembering their ancestors and imitating them in valor. Pedro de Cieza de León (ch. c) touches briefly on this story, though he attributes it to a much later date, and calls the *curacas* Cari and Çapana. When they knew that the Inca's conquests had brought him near to their provinces, they sent messengers to give him an account of their wars and disputes, begging him to grant them permission to come and kiss his hands and describe their passionate quarrel more fully in his presence, so that his majesty might settle their case and reconcile them. They protested their willingness to perform whatever the Inca ordered, since everyone acknowledged him as the child of the Sun and from his rectitude they hoped for justice to both parties so that henceforth there might follow perpetual peace.

The Inca heard the messengers and replied bidding the *curacas* to present themselves as soon as they would: he would try to reconcile them and hoped to establish peace and friendship between them, for the laws and ordinances he would prescribe would be those decreed by his father the Sun, to whom he would refer the case so that his decision should more certainly be right. The *curacas* rejoiced at this reply, and came to Paria, where the Inca was, within a few days, both arriving on the same day from different directions, as had been agreed. Introduced to the king, they both kissed his hand together, neither seeking to obtain precedence over the other. Then Cari, whose lands were closer to the Inca's, spoke in name of both of them, and gave a long account of their disputes and the causes of them. He said that sometimes they arose out of the envy that one felt at the deeds and successes of the other, sometimes from ambition and covetousness to despoil one another, and sometimes from questions of boundaries and jurisdiction. They besought his majesty to settle the case in whatever way he thought fit: this was the purpose of their visit, for they were long since weary of the wars that had existed between them for many years. Having received them with his usual courtesy, the Inca ordered them to remain some days with his army and commanded that two Inca captains should instruct them in those laws, founded on natural law, with which the Incas governed their realms so that their subjects might live at peace, respecting one another's honor and property. And as to the quarrel between them concerning their boundaries and jurisdiction which was at the root of their strife, he sent two Incas of his family to investigate the provinces of the *curacas* and get to the bottom of the conflict. Now fully informed, the Inca consulted the members of his council, and sending for the *Curacas,* told them briefly that his father the Sun bade them observe the laws taught them by the Incas so as to preserve peace and concord, study the welfare and increase of their subjects—for they were more likely to ruin them and themselves in their strife—and remember that other *curacas,* seeing them at strife, could rise up and overthrow them, finding them weak and incapable. They would thus lose their estates, and the memory of their ancestors would be removed from the face of the earth, whereas peace would preserve and increase it. He ordered them to erect landmarks in certain places and not to alter them. Finally he said that his god, the Sun, gave these orders and dispositions so that they might have peace and live quietly, and that he, the Inca, confirmed this: any infringement would be severely punished since they had made him the judge of their differences.

The *curacas* answered that they would obey his majesty readily, and would remain true friends out of the regard they had acquired for his service. Afterwards the chiefs Cari and Chipana discussed together the Inca's laws, the government of his house and court and of all his kingdom, the mildness of his proceedings in time of war, and the justice he dealt out to all without tolerating the oppression of any. They particularly noted the gentleness and fairness he had shown toward them, and how just his division of their lands had been. Having observed this and pondered it with their kinsmen and subjects, they decided to submit to the Inca and become his vassals. They also did this because they saw that the Inca's empire was so very near their estates and that one day he would take them by force, since they were powerless to resist him. They were prudent enough to become his subjects willingly rather than by force, so as not to lose the merit this would win them in the Inca's eyes. Thus agreed, they presented themselves before him and said they begged his majesty to receive them into his service, for they wished to be subjects and servants to the child of the Sun. They would deliver their estates at once: let his majesty send governors and ministers to teach his new subjects what they were to do to serve him.

The Inca said he thanked them for their good disposition and would make a point of favoring them on all occasions. He ordered them to be presented with many garments, his own for the chiefs and others of less distinction for their families. He granted them other honors of great value and esteem, and the *curacas* were well content. In this way the Inca reduced to his empire many provinces and towns which the two chiefs possessed in the district of Collasuyu. Among them were Pocoata, Murumuru, Maccha, Caracara, and everything to the east of these provinces as far as the great chain of the Antis, including all the vast desert that reaches to the confines of the great province called Tapac-Ri, which the Spaniards call Tapacari. This desert is over thirty leagues across and is so extremely cold that it is quite uninhabited, though its numerous pastures are covered with innumerable flocks, both wild and domesticated, and it has many springs so hot that the hand cannot be held in them for the space of an Ave-Maria. The fountains can be discerned from a distance by the steam from the water as it issues forth, and the hot water stinks of sulphur. It is remarkable that among these hot springs there are others of very frigid and excellent water. Both unite to make a river called Cochapampa.

Beyond the great desert of the springs, there is a slope that continues for seven leagues down to the plain of the province of Tapac-Ri, which was the first allocation of Indians my lord Garcilaso de la Vega had in Peru. It is of very fertile land, well stocked with people and flocks, and is more than twenty leagues long and more than twelve broad. Eight leagues beyond is another splendid province called Cochapampa, whose valley is thirty leagues long and four broad and has a long river which forms it. These two provinces, among others, were included in the territories surrendered by the two chiefs Cari and Chipana, as already described. This acquisition enlarged the empire of the Incas by sixty leagues of territory. On account of its fertility the Spaniards established a town in the province of Cochapampa in 1565. They called it San Pedro de Cardeña, because its founder was a gentleman from Burgos called Captain Luis Osorio.

When these conquests had been made, the Inca ordered two commanders from his escort to go to the estates of the *curacas* with enough officials for the government and instruction of the new vassals. This done, he thought that the conquest was sufficient for that year, for it was greater than he had expected, and he returned to Cuzco, taking the two chiefs so that they might see his court and be entertained and welcomed there. They were very well received in the city, and the two *curacas* were much feasted and honored by the Inca's orders. After some days, they were given leave to return to their own countries, and went very satisfied with the honors and favors done them. On their departure, the Inca bade them be prepared, for he proposed soon to go to their country to reduce the Indians beyond.

CHAPTER XV

*They make a bridge of straw, reeds, and rushes
over the Desaguadero; Chayanta
is conquered.*

THE INCA Cápac Yupanqui was proud of the result of the bridge of Huacachaca across the river Apurímac we have mentioned, and therefore ordered another to be made across the Desaguadero of Lake Titicaca. He expected soon to return to the conquest of other provinces in Collasuyu; and as the country was flat and suitable for the march of armies, the Incas found it favorable for their conquests and therefore persisted in them until they had won the whole area. The bridge of Huacachaca and all the others in Peru are made of osier: that over the river the Spaniards call the Desaguadero is of rushes and other materials. It is not thrown across the river in a span like the osier bridge we have described, but lies across the surface like the bridge of boats at Seville. There is a long, soft, and pliant straw that grows all over Peru: the Indians call it *ichu* and use it for thatching their houses. The sort that grows in Collao is the strongest and makes very good fodder for their flocks. The Collas also use it for hampers, baskets, and what they call *patacas* (a sort of small chest), as well as ropes and cords. In addition to this stout straw there also grows on the shores of Titicaca a very great quantity of rushes and reeds, otherwise called *enea*. In due season the Indians from the provinces charged with the building of the bridge cut a great quantity of these plants and dry them before the building begins. Of the straw they make four ropes as thick as a man's leg. Two are laid on the water across the width of the river. This seems still on the top, but runs with a great current below the surface, according to those who have seen it. Instead of boats, they lay on these ropes great bundles of rushes and reeds as thick as an ox and stoutly bound together and to the ropes. On these bundles of rushes and reeds they then lay two more ropes, lashing them to the bundles so that they are all secure and serve to strengthen one another. In order that these ropes shall not be worn by the feet of animals crossing they strew them with a great quantity of rushes in small bundles no thicker than a man's leg or wrist, all of which are duly stranded together and to the ropes. These smaller bundles the Spaniards call the roadway of the bridge. The bridge is 13 or 14 feet wide and above a vara deep and 150 paces, more or less, in length, so that the immense quantity of rushes and reeds that are necessary for so large a work can readily be imagined. It is remarkable that the bridge is renewed every six months. It is in fact made anew for the materials used, being as perishable as straw, reeds, and rushes, are not used again. To make sure that the bridge is secure it is renewed before the ropes become rotten and break.

The care of this bridge, like that of other important public works, was divided among the neighboring provinces in the time of the Incas. Each knew what quantity of material it was required to furnish, and they were made ready each year for the next; the bridge was finished very rapidly. The large ropes or cables which formed the foundation were buried underground, and no stone posts are set up to secure them. The Indians maintain that this is best for this type of bridge, but it is also a fact that they change the site of the bridge, sometimes putting it further upstream and other times downstream, though not at a great distance.

As soon as the Inca knew that the bridge was done, he left Cuzco with the prince, his heir, and travelled as far as the remotest provinces of the chiefs Cari and Chipana, which were those of Tapac-Ri and Cochapampa already mentioned. The chiefs were ready with soldiers to serve the Inca. From Cochapampa they went on to Chayanta. They crossed a wild desert thirty leagues long where there is not a foot of good land, but merely cliffs, rocks, and stony wastes. Nothing grows in this desert but some cactuses with thorns as long as a man's fingers, from which the Indian women made such sewing needles as they have. These cactuses or *cirios*, grow in all parts of Peru. Beyond the desert they entered the province of Chayanta, which is twenty leagues long and nearly as many wide. The Inca ordered the prince to send messengers with the usual summons.

The Indians of Chayanta differed as to the reply they should make, some saying that it was only proper to receive the child of the Sun as their lord and obey his laws, since it seemed credible that, being ordained by the Sun, they would be good, fair, and mild laws, favorable to the subjects and not framed in the interest of the Inca. Others said they had no need of a king or of new laws: those they had were good, since their ancestors had observed them, and their own gods were sufficient without their taking up a new religion and new customs. It seemed even worse that they would have to submit to the will of a man who came preaching religion and holiness, but who tomorrow when he had them as his subjects, might set up whatever laws he wished, to his own advantage and the detriment of his vassals. Rather than experience these evils, they had better live in liberty as they had done, and die in its defence.

This difference of opinion lasted some days, each party seeking to vindicate its point of view, until the fear of the Inca's arms and the news of his good laws and gentle government induced them to agree. Their reply was neither an absolute surrender nor a defiance, but a mixture of both attitudes. They said they would gladly receive the Inca as their king and lord, but they did not know what laws he would establish, whether to their benefit or detriment. They therefore besought a truce, during which the Inca and his army would enter the province and instruct them in the laws, but if they did not find them satisfactory, he would give his word to depart and leave them free. If the laws proved as good as the Inca said, they could worship him as a child of the Sun and receive him as their lord.

The Inca said he accepted the condition on which they proposed to receive him, though he was well able to oblige them to surrender by force of arms. He liked however to follow the example of his ancestors and win subjects by love and not by force, and gave them his word of honor to leave them in the freedom they previously enjoyed if they did not wish to worship his father the Sun or observe his laws. He hoped that after seeing and understanding these laws they would not only not abhor them, but would like them, and indeed come to regret that they had not known them centuries before.

Having made this promise, the Inca entered Chayanta, where he was welcomed with veneration and respect, but not with the feasting and joy he had received in other provinces, for it was not known how the test would turn out. The Indians remained in mingled fear and hope until the elders chosen by the Inca as advisers and governors of the army unfolded the laws relating to their idolatry and those for the government of the country in the presence of the prince and heir to the throne. The laws were expounded many times for many days until they were clearly understood. The Indians, realizing how much they redounded to their honor and welfare said that the Sun and his children the Incas, well deserved to be worshipped and held as gods and lords of the earth for having conferred such laws and ordinances on mankind. They therefore promised to serve his statutes and rules, and repudiate all the idols, rites, and customs they had. They made this protestation before the prince and worshipped him in place of his father the Sun and of the Inca Cápac Yupanqui.

As soon as the oath had been solemnized, they came out with great dances after their own fashion, all new to the Incas. They were gallantly arrayed and sang songs composed in praise of the Sun, of the Incas, and of their good laws and government, and celebrated them with every possible manifestation of love and good will.

CHAPTER XVI

Various devices used by the Indians
for crossing rivers and fishing.

NOW THAT an account has been given of the two types of bridges the Incas had built for crossing rivers, the first of osier and the second of rushes and reeds, it will be well to mention other devices they adopted for the same purpose. The bridges, owing to their cost in labor and time, could only be used on the royal highways, and as the country is very broad and long, and crossed by so many rivers, the Indians were driven by sheer necessity to invent various contrivances for crossing them according to their different circumstances, and also for navigating at sea to the small extent they ventured to do so. For this purpose the piraguas or canoes of Florida and the Windward Islands and Spanish Main were unknown to them. These boats are like troughs; but in Peru there is no large timber suitable for the purpose. It is true that there are very thick trees, but their wood is as heavy as iron. The Indians therefore had to adopt another sort of wood which is no thicker than a man's thigh but as light as the wood of the fig tree. The best kind, according to the Indians, grows in the provinces of Quito, where it was taken by the Inca's orders to the various rivers. From it they made rafts, large and small, of five or seven poles lashed together. The center pole was the longest, those on either side a little shorter, the next pair shorter still and the outermost pair the shortest. The raft thus cut through the water more easily than if it had been square-fronted, and the stern was the same shape as the bow. Two ropes were then attached by which the raft was drawn from one side of the river to the other. Often if the ferrymen were not there, the passengers pulled themselves over by means of the rope. I remember having crossed rivers in rafts that dated from Inca times, and they were venerated accordingly by the Indians.

Apart from these, they made small boats operated by hand. They take a stout bundle of reeds as thick as an ox, bind it up firmly, taper it from the middle forward and draw it upwards like the prow of a ship so that it breaks the water. The rear two-thirds is broadened out; the top of the bundle is made flat so as to carry the load they wish to transport. A single Indian propels each of these boats. He places himself at the end of the stern, lying with his breast on the boat and using his arms and legs as oars. The boat drifts with the current, and if the water is rough it reaches a point a hundred or two hundred paces below its starting-point. If they are ferrying a man, he lies face downward the length of the boat with his head toward the ferryman. They bid him grip the ropes and bury his face in the reeds and not lift his head or open his eyes to look at anything. I was once passing in this manner across a very swollen and fast river (it is in these cases that the passenger is so bidden, for on quiet streams such instructions are unnecessary) and the Indian boatman went to such lengths in insisting that I should not raise my head or open my eyes that I, being then only a boy, was terrified lest the earth was going to collapse or the skies fall in, and I felt the desire to look up in case I should see something marvellous from the other world. When I felt we were in the middle of the river, I therefore lifted my head a little and looked up at the water, and I really felt we were falling down from the sky. This was because the great rush of the water and the furious speed with which it drove the reed boat turned my head. I was obliged by fear to close my eyes, and to admit that the boatmen are right in telling passengers not to open them.

Other rafts are made of great whole gourds which are bound together in a mesh so as to make a raft more or less a vara and a half square, according to what is needed. They fix a breast band in front like that of the saddle of a horse, and the Indian boatman puts his head through it and begins to swim, pulling the raft behind him, thus ferrying his cargo across a river, bay, or creek. If necessary one or two assistants swim behind helping to push the raft.

On large rivers where the currents are too strong and rough to permit the use of rafts of gourds or rush boats, and where there are too many cliffs and rocks on the banks and therefore no beach to embark and disembark, they throw across one of the thick cables made of the hemp they call *cháhuar,* fastening it to a thick tree or a strong rock high above the stream. An osier basket with a wooden handle as thick as a man's arm runs along the cable and can hold three or four persons. The basket has two ropes, one tied to each side so that it can be drawn to and fro across the river. As the cable is long, it gets slack and sags in the middle. The basket is therefore gradually lowered till it reaches the middle of the cable: from there it is necessary to pull hard to get it up. There are therefore Indians sent in turn by the neighboring provinces to assist travellers in those places, without reward. The passengers help to pull the ropes from the basket and many cross by themselves without help, standing in the basket and hauling on the cable with both hands. I remember crossing two or three times this way as a very small boy: on the road the Indians still carried me on their backs. They also ferried their flocks across in these baskets, though not in large numbers. It was done with some difficulty, for the animals were bound and laid in the basket, and it is tiring work. They do the same with the smaller European animals, such as sheep, goats, and pigs. But larger animals—horses, mules, asses, and cows—are too big and heavy to cross in baskets, but have to be taken to the bridges or fords. This ferry service does not occur on the royal highways, but only on the local roads between the Indian towns: they call it *uruya*.

All the coastal Indians of Peru fish in the sea with the reed boats we have described. They go four, five, or six leagues out to sea, or further if need be, for the sea is calm and can be navigated with frail craft. To carry heavier burdens they use wooden rafts. In sailing the fishermen kneel on bundles of rush. They propel the boat with a rod a fathom in length with a cleft split in the middle. Some of these rods in these parts are as thick as a man's leg or thigh: we shall describe them later. They hold the rod with both hands, putting one at one end and the other in the middle. The hollow of the rod serves as a paddle to give greater force in the water. Having struck the water on the left side they change over hands and swing the rod to give the next stroke on the right side, putting the right hand where the left was and vice versa. This method of rowing by changing hands and swinging over the rod from one side to the other is the most remarkable of the many remarkable things in their sailing and fishing. When such a boat is going at full pelt, it could not be overtaken by a post horse however good. They fish with harpoons and contrive to catch fish as large as a man. This type of fishing, given the poverty of the Indians, is like the Basque whale fishery. They attach a thin cord such as sailors call a *bolantín* to the harpoon. It may be twenty, thirty, or forty fathoms long, and the other end is fastened to the prow of the boat. On striking a fish, the Indian frees his legs and grips his boat with them, paying out his line with his hands as the fish seeks to escape. When the line has run out, he clutches the boat firmly and lets the fish drag it. If it is a very large fish, the boat may go so fast that it looks like a bird flying across the water. In this way the struggle continues until the fish tires and the Indian can get his hands to it. They also fished with nets and hooks, but these were poor and wretched devices. Each man fished by himself and not in company: the nets were small and the hooks clumsily made— they did not use iron or steel, for though they had mines, they could not work the metal. Iron they call *quíllay*. They do not have sails on the reed boats, because there is no mast to support them; nor do I think they would go so fast under sail as they do with a single oar. They hoist sails on their wooden rafts when they go to sea. The devices that the Peruvian Indians had for sailing the sea or crossing large rivers were still in use when I left, and are probably so now, for the people are so poor that they aspire to nothing better than they have. In my *History of Florida,* Book VI, I have said something about these devices, speaking of the canoes used for crossing and sailing on the rivers of those parts, which are as large and full as any in the world. We now return to the conquests of the Inca Cápac Yupanqui.

CHAPTER XVII

Of the conquest of five great provinces,
besides other smaller ones.

FROM Chayanta the Inca marched out, leaving a garrison and the officials necessary to establish his idolatry and deal with taxation. He continued to other provinces that are in the area called Charca. Under this name many provinces of different tribes and different tongues are included, but all are in the district of Collasuyu. The chief of them are Tutura, Sipisipi, and Chaqui. To the east of these, toward the Antis, there are other provinces called Chimuru (where the coca herb also grows, though it is not so good as that from the region of Cuzco), and Sacaca, as well as others which I omit for the sake of brevity. The Inca sent them the usual summons.

Knowing what had already happened in Chayanta, these tribes all replied in almost the same way with but little difference, saying that they regarded themselves as happy to worship the Sun and to have his child, the Inca, as their lord: they had already heard of his laws and good government: they begged him to receive them under his protection for they offered him their lives and property: let him conquer and crush the other tribes next to them so that these people should not wage war against them and molest them for having overthrown the old idols and adopted a new religion and new laws.

The Inca sent to tell them that they should leave the conquest of their neighbors to his care and he would see to it as and when would be most advantageous to his subjects: let them have no fear that anyone would molest them for having submitted to the Inca and received his laws, for when they had had experience of them they would all rejoice to live under them, since the Sun had granted them. After this reply they freely received the Inca in all their provinces. As nothing occurred worthy of memory in particular, I give only a general account. The Inca spent two, some say three, years on the conquest, and having left a sufficient garrison to prevent the neighboring peoples from risking an attack, he returned to Cuzco, visiting on the way the towns and provinces that happened to be on his route. He sent his son and heir by another route so that he too should visit his subjects, on account of the honor they received from seeing their kings and princes in their towns.

The Inca was received with great festivities and rejoicing in his capital, which he entered surrounded by his captains, and preceded by the *curacas* who had come from the newly conquered provinces to see the imperial city. Shortly afterwards the prince, Inca Roca, arrived, and he was received with the same satisfaction, and with dances and the singing of songs composed in praise of his victories. Having rewarded his captains, the Inca bade them return to their homes, and he remained in his palace, attending to the government of his kingdom, which now stretched from Cuzco southwards for more than 108 leagues as far as Tutura and Chaqui. Westwards it stretched to the Southern Sea, which is more than 60 leagues from the city in one direction and more than 80 in another. To the east of Cuzco his realms extended as far as the river Paucartampu, which is 13 leagues from the city due east. To the southeast they stretched to Callavaya, 40 leagues from Cuzco. It thus seemed to the Inca unnecessary to undertake new conquests, but that he should preserve what had been won to the benefit and welfare of his subjects. He thus devoted some years of peace and quiet to this end. He sought to enrich the house of the Sun and that of the chosen virgins founded by the first Inca Manco Cápac. He saw to the erection of other buildings within the city and in many of the provinces where their increase had made it necessary. He caused great channels to be dug to irrigate the cultivable land, built many bridges over rivers and streams for the protection of wayfarers, and opened new roads between the various provinces so that there should be communication between all the parts of the empire. In short he did everything that he deemed would contribute to the welfare and prosperity of his subjects and his own greatness and majesty.

CHAPTER XVIII

Prince Inca Roca reduces many great provinces, both inland and on the coast.

THE INCA was occupied in this and similar ways for six or seven years. At the end of this time he thought it would be well to turn again to military exercises and the extension of his realms. For this purpose he ordered the preparation of an army of twenty thousand with four experienced commanders to accompany his son Inca Roca towards Chinchasuyu to the north of Cuzco. In that direction the Incas had not extended the doors of their empire beyond the point to which the first Inca Manco Cápac had carried them, as far as Rimactampu, seven leagues from the city. As the country was rough and sparsely populated, the Incas had taken no pains to conquer it.

The prince went out of Cuzco and reached the Apurímac River. He crossed it on great rafts they had prepared for him. As the country was uninhabited, he marched on to Curahuaci and Amáncay, eighteen leagues from the city. He very easily reduced the few Indians he found in the area. From the province of Amáncay he turned to the left of the royal highroad from Cuzco to Rímac and passed the desert called Cochacassa which is there twenty-two leagues across, and entered the province called Sura. This is populous, and rich in gold and flocks, and the Inca was received peaceably and obeyed as lord of the people. He passed thence to another province called Apucara where he was also humbly received. The reason for the ready submission of these provinces was that each was the enemy of the other and neither could resist the Inca.

From Apucara he reached the province of Rucana, which is divided in two, Rucana and Hatunrucana, "Rucana the great." The people are handsome and well-disposed, and they willingly submitted. From this point he went down to the seacoast across what the Spaniards call the llanos, and reached the first valley in that direction, called Nanasca. It means "sad" or "afflicted," but no one knows why the name was given—probably not by chance, but on account of some visitation or plague. The Spaniards call it Lanasca. Here too the Inca was received in great peace and readily obeyed. The same occurred in all the other valleys from Nanasca down the coast to Arequipa, a distance of more than eighty leagues and fourteen or fifteen leagues in depth. The chief valleys are those of Hacari and Camana with twenty thousand householders. There are other smaller valleys of less importance, such as Aticu [Atica], Ucuña [Ocoña], Atiquipa, and Quellca. The prince Inca Roca easily reduced them all to obedience, because they had no force to resist him and they were all exposed. Each of the small valleys had one petty chief, and the bigger ones two or three and there were quarrels and disputes among them.

It will be proper since we are on the spot not to pass on without mentioning a strange occurrence that took place in the valley of Hacari soon after the Spaniards took it, although we anticipate the time of the event. Two *curacas,* neither of whom had been baptized, had a bitter dispute about their boundaries and fought a battle in which men were killed and wounded on both sides. The Spanish governors sent a commissioner to do justice and reconcile them. He settled the boundary as he thought right and bade the two chiefs keep the peace and be friendly. They promised to do so, though one of them, who felt wronged by the decision, harbored a grievance and desired to avenge himself on his rival in secrecy under cover of their friendship. So, on the day when the truce was solemnized, they all ate together in an open place, one side facing the other. After the meal, the aggrieved *curaca* rose and raised two bowls of their liquor to drink to his new friend's health after the common custom of the Indians. One of the bowls was poisoned to kill his enemy, and standing before him, he invited him to drink. The other, either seeing some sign in the man's face or not being satisfied that he could trust him, suspected what was afoot and said: "Give me the other bowl and drink this." Not to show cowardice, the *curaca* quickly changed hands and gave his enemy the harmless bowl and himself drank the deadly one. Within a few hours he

died, from the influence of the poison and out of chagrin on seeing that he
had killed himself while meaning to kill his enemy.

CHAPTER XIX

*They take Indians from the seacoast to found
colonies inland; the Inca Cápac Yupanqui dies.*

FROM Nanasca the Inca took local Indians and transported them to the
river Apurímac, since on the stretch between Cuzco and Rímac the
river passes through a district that is so hot that the mountain Indians,
who are used to a cold or temperate climate, cannot survive it, and fall ill
and die. As has been said, the Incas had ordered that when Indians were
moved thus from one province to another, which they call *mítmac*, the regions should also be selected to have the same sort of climate, so that the
change should not cause them harm, it being realized that to transfer them
from a cold climate to a hot, or vice versa, caused them to die. It was
forbidden therefore to move the Indians of the sierra to the llanos, or they
would have certainly died in a few days. Having regard to this danger, the
Inca brought Indians from one hot region to another. Not many were
needed, for there was little land to settle, since the Apurímac passes
through steep and lofty mountains and has little cultivable land on either
side. But the Inca did not want it to be wasted but to have it used for
orchards, so as to enjoy the numerous and excellent fruit that ripens on
the banks of that famous river.

This done, and having established the usual order in the government
of the new conquests, Prince Inca Roca returned to Cuzco where he was
well received by his father and the court. The captains and men were dismissed, duly rewarded for their war service. The Inca Cápac Yupanqui
then decided not to proceed with the conquests for he felt himself growing old, and wished to establish and settle what had been won. He lived
some years in tranquility with much regard for the welfare of his subjects,
who also rallied promptly and affectionately to his service, both in laboring on the house of the Sun and on other buildings, some erected by order of the Inca and others devised by the Indians to serve and please him,
each province building its own.

In this state of peace and tranquility the Inca Cápac Yupanqui died. He was a most valiant prince, deserving the name Cápac so much esteemed by the Indians. He was mourned in the court and throughout his realms with great grief. His body was embalmed and placed with those of his ancestors. He left as his successor the Inca Roca, his eldest son by the Coya Mama Curi-Illpay, his wife and sister. He left many other sons and daughters, both legitimate and bastards. The number of these is not known for certain and therefore is not given, but it is believed they exceeded eighty, for most of these Incas left a hundred or two and some left more than three hundred sons and daughters.

CHAPTER XX

The description of the temple of
the Sun and its great wealth.

O NE OF THE chief idols of the Inca kings and their subjects was the imperial city of Cuzco which the Indians worshipped as a sacred thing because of its foundation by the first Inca Manco Cápac, the innumerable victories it had brought in his conquests and its position as the home and court of the Incas, who were regarded as gods. This veneration was so great that it was displayed even in very small things: if two Indians of equal rank met on the road, one going towards Cuzco and one coming from it, the latter was saluted and greeted by the other as his superior, simply because he had been in the city, and the respect was the greater if he were a resident in it and greater still if he was born there. Likewise seeds, vegetables, or anything else taken from Cuzco to other places was preferred, even if not of better quality, because whatever came from Cuzco was deemed superior to the product of other regions and provinces. It may be deduced to what extent this distinction was applied in things of greater moment. Such was the veneration in which the kings held the city that they ennobled it with splendid houses and palaces, which many of them had built for themselves, as we shall see in describing some of the buildings. Among these was the house and temple of the Sun, to which they devoted special attention, adorning it with incredible riches, to which each Inca added so as to excel his predecessor. The splendor of the building was so incredible that I would not dare to describe it, except that all the Spanish historians of Peru had already done so. But neither what they have said, nor what I shall say, adequately expresses the truth. The building of the temple is attributed to King Inca Yupanqui, the grandfather of Huaina Cápac. He was not the founder, for it existed from the time of the first Inca, but he completed its adornment and brought it to the state of wealth and majesty in which the Spaniards found it.

Coming therefore to the plan of the temple, we should say that the house of the Sun was what is now the church of the divine St. Dominic. I do not give the exact length and breadth because I have not got them, but as far as size is concerned it exists today. It is built of smooth masonry, very level and smooth. The high altar (I use the term to make myself clear, though the Indians did not, of course, have altars) was at the east end. The roof was of wood and very lofty so that there would be plenty of air. It was covered with thatch: they had no tiles. All four walls of the temple were covered from top to bottom with plates and slabs of gold. Over what we have called the high altar they had the image of the Sun on a gold plate twice the thickness of the rest of the wall-plates. The image showed him with a round face and beams and flames of fire all in one piece, just as he is usually depicted by painters. It was so large that it stretched over the whole of that side of the temple from wall to wall. The Incas had no other idols of their own or of any other people in the temple with the image of the Sun, for they did not worship any other gods except the Sun, though some say otherwise.

When the Spaniards entered the city, the figure of the Sun fell to the lot of one Mancio Serra de Leguiçamo, a nobleman, one of the first conquerors, whom I knew. He was still alive when I came to Spain. He was a great gambler, and though the figure of the Sun was so large, he staked it and lost it in a night. Hence we may say, following Padre Acosta, there originated the saying: "The Sun he plays away before the break of day." Later the city council, seeing how he was ruining himself by his gambling, elected him one year as *alcalde ordinario,* hoping to reform him. He served his country with such care and attention (for he had all the qualities of a gentleman) that he never touched a playing card the whole year long. Seeing this, the city reappointed him for a further year and thereafter for many more years to public offices. Occupied in this way, Mancio Serra forgot his passion for gaming and came to hate it ever afterwards, recalling the many embarrassments and difficulties it had involved him in. This clearly shows that idleness fosters vice, and occupation favors virtue.

To return to our story, the fact that that piece fell to a single Spaniard shows how vast was the treasure found by the Spaniards in the whole of the temple and city. On both sides of the image of the Sun were the bodies of the dead kings in order of antiquity as children of the Sun and embalmed so that they appeared to be alive, though it is not known how this was done. They sat on golden chairs placed on the golden daises they had used. Their faces were towards the people. Only Huaina Cápac was distinguished from the rest by being placed before the figure of the Sun which he faced as the most beloved of his children. He had earned this distinction because in his lifetime he was worshipped as a god on account of his virtues and the royal qualities he displayed from boyhood. The bodies were hidden by the Indians with the rest of the treasure, and most of them have never reappeared. In 1559 Licentiate Polo discovered five of them: three kings and two queens.

The main gate of the temple faced north as it does today, but there were other lesser gates for the service of the temple. All were lined with plates of gold. Outside the temple, at the top of the walls, a gold cornice consisting of a plate more than a vara wide, ran round the whole temple like a crown.

CHAPTER XXI

The cloister of the temple and the dwelling places of the Moon, stars, thunder, lightning, and rainbow.

BEYOND the temple, there was a cloister with four sides, one of which was the temple wall. All round the upper part of the cloister there ran a cornice of gold plates more than a vara wide, which crowned the cloister. In its place the Spaniards had a white plaster cornice made of the same width as the golden one, in order to preserve its memory. I saw it before I left on the walls which were still standing and had not been pulled down. Round the cloister there were five halls or large square rooms each built separately and not joined to the others, covered in the form of a pyramid, and forming the other three sides of the cloister.

One of these halls was dedicated to the Moon, the wife of the Sun, and was the one nearest the principal chapel of the temple. All of it and its doors were lined with plates of silver, which by their white color showed it to be the hall of the Moon. Her image and portrait was placed like that of the Sun and consisted of a woman's face drawn on a silver plate. They used to enter this hall to visit the Moon and commend themselves to her as the sister and wife of the Sun and mother of the Incas and all their progeny. Thus they called her Mamaquilla, "Mother Moon." They did not offer sacrifices to her as they did to the Sun. On either side of the figure of the Moon were the bodies of the dead queens, arranged in order of antiquity. Mama Ocllo, mother of Huaina Cápac, was placed in front of the Moon and face to face with her, being thus distinguished from the rest as the mother of such a son.

Another hall, next to that of the Moon, was dedicated to the planet Venus, the Seven Kids and all the other stars. The star Venus they called Chasca, meaning "having long curly hair." They honored it saying that it was the Sun's page, standing closest to him and sometimes preceding and sometimes following him. The Seven Kids they respected for their peculiar position and equality in size. They thought the stars were servants of the Moon and therefore gave them a hall next to that of their mistress, so that they would be on hand to serve her. They said that the stars accompanied the Moon in the sky, and not the Sun, because they are to be seen by night and not by day.

This hall was lined with silver, like that of the Moon, and the gate was of silver. All the ceiling was strewn with stars, great and small, like the starry sky. The room next to the hall of the stars was devoted to thunder, thunderbolts, and lightning, which three phenomena they included together under the name *illapa*. According to the verb they used with it, they distinguished its various meanings, so that by saying, "Did you see the *illapa?*" they implied lightning. If they said, "Did you hear the *illapa?*" they meant thunder; and when they said that the *illapa* fell somewhere or damaged something, they meant a thunderbolt.

They did not worship them as gods, but respected them as servants of the Sun. They felt about them as the ancients felt about the thunderbolt, which was regarded as the instrument and weapon of the god Jupiter. So the Incas assigned a hall in the house of the Sun to the thunder, thunderbolt, and lightning as his servants, and had it decorated with gold. There was no statue or picture of the three phenomena, for as they could not draw them from nature (which they always tried to do in all their images), they simply respected them under the name *illapa* whose triple meaning has so far eluded the Spanish historians. The latter have supposed a god, three in one, and have attributed it to the Indians, likening their idolatry to our holy religion, just as they have made trinities of other objects of even less probability and foundation and invented names which the Indians never imagined in their language. As I have said before, I am writing what I sucked in with my mother's milk, and what I saw and heard my elders do and say. As regards thunder, I have already stated their belief.

Another hall, the fourth, was dedicated to the rainbow. They realized it proceeded from the Sun and the Incas therefore took it as their arms and device to illustrate their boast of descent from him. This room was decorated throughout with gold. On one wall over the gold plates they had a representation of the rainbow, which was very natural and so large that it stretched with its living colors from one wall to the other. They call the rainbow *cuichu,* and as they venerated it so, when they saw it, they used to close their mouth and place their hand in front, for they said that if they exposed their teeth to it, it wore and decayed them. This piece of folly, among others, had no explanation. The fifth and last room was devoted to the high priest and other priests who shared the service of the temple. All these had to be Incas of the royal blood. The room was not used for sleeping or eating, but as an audience room where the sacrifices to be performed were arranged and for other purposes connected with the service of the temple. Like the others, this room was decorated from ceiling to floor with gold.

CHAPTER XXII

The name of the high priest, and
other parts of the house.

THE HIGH PRIEST is called by the Spaniards *vilaoma,* instead of *villac umu,* a word composed of the verb *villa,* "to say," and the noun *umu,* "soothsayer, wizard." *Villac,* with *c,* is the present participle. Adding the word *umu,* it means "the soothsayer or wizard who says," but does not explain what is said, it being understood that he says to the people what he asks the Sun in his capacity as high priest, what the Sun orders him to tell them according to their fables, what the devils may tell him in their idols and sanctuaries, and what he as a priest divines from omens and sacrifices and the interpretation of dreams and other superstitions they had in their paganism. There was no name for priest: they simply formed a word from what the priests did.

Of the five halls, I saw the three that were still standing with their ancient walls and roofs. Only the plates of gold and silver were missing. The other two, those of the Moon and stars, had already been pulled down. In the walls of the rooms giving on to the cloister, four tabernacles were hollowed out in each of the outside walls. They were hollowed into the thickness of the walls which, like the rest of the temple, were of masonry. They had moldings round the edges and in the hollows of the tabernacles, and as these moldings were worked in the stone they were inlaid with gold plates not only at the top and sides, but also the floors of the tabernacles. The edges of the moldings were encrusted with fine stones, emeralds, and turquoises, for diamonds and rubies were unknown there. The Inca sat in these tabernacles when there were festivals in honor of the Sun. He sat sometimes in one and sometimes in another, according to the festivity.

In two of these tabernacles in a wall facing east, I remember noticing many holes in the moldings made in the stonework. Those in the edges passed right through while the rest were merely marks on the walls. I heard the Indians and the religious of the temple say that those were the places in which the precious stones were set in pagan times. The tabernacles and all the doors opening onto the cloister, which were twelve excluding those of the hall of the Moon and of the stars, were all plated with leaves and slabs of gold like portals, while the other two were done in silver in accordance with the white color of their owners.

Besides the five great halls already mentioned, the house of the Sun had many other rooms for the priests and servants, who were Incas by privilege. No Indian who was not an Inca, however great a lord he might be, could enter the house. No women could enter, even daughters or wives of the king. Priests served the temple by the week reckoned according to the quarters of the Moon. During this time they abstained from their wives and never left the temple, either by day or by night.

The Indians who served in the temple as servants, porters, sweepers, cooks, stewards, butlers, keepers of the jewels, woodmen, water-carriers, and others whose offices concerned the service of the temple, came from the same towns which supplied servants to the royal household. The towns were obliged to supply these persons for the palace and for the temple of the Sun. The two houses, like the houses of father and son, were indistinguishable in so far as their service was concerned, except that women did not serve in the house of the Sun and there was no offering of sacrifices in the house of the Inca. Otherwise they were equal in grandeur and majesty.

CHAPTER XXIII

*The places for sacrifices and the threshold where
they took off their sandals to enter the
temple; their fountains.*

T HE PLACES for burnt offerings were in accordance with the solemnity of the rites. Some were burnt in some courtyards and others in others, of the many which in various parts of the house were dedicated to special festivals, according to the obligation and devotion of the Incas. General sacrifices, performed in the principal feast of the Sun called Raimi, were carried out in the main square of the city. Other sacrifices, and lesser festivals took place in a large square before the temple where all the provinces and tribes of the realm performed their dances. They were not allowed to enter the temple and could only appear there barefoot, for this was already within the precinct where no sandals were permitted. We shall describe these precincts.

Three main streets go out of the main square of Cuzco and run north and south toward the temple. One runs down by the side of the stream. The next was known in my time as Prison Street, because the Spanish prison was in it, though I am told this has since been moved elsewhere. The third leaves the corner of the square and runs in the same direction. Another street to the east of all these, now called San Agustín, goes the same way. One could thus reach the temple of the Sun by any of these four roads. But the largest and straightest street which goes to the very gate of the temple is Prison Street which issues from the middle of the square. Along it the Indians used to come and go to worship the Sun, and send him embassies, offerings, and sacrifices. It was the Street of the Sun. All four were crossed by another street running east and west from the stream to San Agustín. This cross street was the threshold and limit where they bared their feet on going to the temple, and even if they were not

going to the temple they still had to take their sandals off there, for no
one was allowed to pass beyond with them on. From this street which we
call the threshold to the gate of the temple is more than two hundred
paces. To the east, west, and south of the temple there were the same
limits on reaching which the Indians took off their sandals.

To return to the decoration of the temple, it had inside five fountains,
the water being brought to them from various directions. They had golden
pipes, and some of the fountainheads were of stone, while others were
tanks of gold and silver in which the sacrifices were washed according to
their quality and the solemnity of the festival. I did not see more than one
fountain which was used to water the vegetable garden the monastery
then had. The others had been lost, either because they had not been
needed or because it was not known whence they came: in any case what
is sure is that they have been lost. Even the one I say I knew, I saw six or
seven months later lost and the garden abandoned for lack of water. Although all the monastery was distressed by the loss, and indeed the whole
city, no Indian was to be found who could tell whence the water of that
fountain came.

This water was lost because it went from the west of the convent
underground and crossed the stream that runs through the city. In the time
of the Incas the stream had banks made of masonry and its bottom was
paved with great flagstones, so that floods did no harm to the bottom or
the walls, and the structure was carried more than a quarter of a league
beyond the city. Because of the neglect of the Spaniards, it was gradually
broken, especially the flagstones, which have been carried away by the
sudden rush of the floods, which are incredibly large in relation to the
little water it usually contains since it rises practically within the city. In
1558 the stones that covered the pipes to the fountain were finally carried
away, and the pipe was broken and spoiled. The silt filled it up and cut
off the water, so that the garden was left dry. Owing to the filth that is
thrown in the stream all the year round the whole place was buried and
no sign was left of the pipes.

Although the friars did what they could to search, they found no trace
at all. To trace the pipe from the fountain would have meant pulling down
many buildings and digging up much land, for the fountain stood on an
elevation. No Indian could be found to trace the pipes, and they therefore
ceased to trouble about the fountain, or about the others that used to exist.
This shows how little tradition the Indians of today have preserved of
their antiquities, since even forty-two years ago they had already lost the
memory of such important things as the waters that went to the house of

the Sun, their god. It would seem impossible that there should not have been a tradition handed down from the masons to their successors and from the priests to their followers so that the memory of the spring should be preserved. But the truth is that the masons and priests of the Inca state had ended and it was they who preserved the tradition of things held sacred since they were concerned with the honor and service of the temples, and so the explanation is missing, as of so many things that the Indians are unable to account for. If the tradition had been preserved by the knots used for recording tribute or in the accounts of the royal administration or in the historical annals of events, which are secular matters, there is no doubt that the details about the fountains would have been saved, like much else of greater or less importance which the accountants and historians who kept records have handed down, though even these things are lost as time goes on with the change to new events and modern histories of the new empire.

CHAPTER XXIV

The garden of gold and other riches of the temple,
in imitation of which there are many others
throughout the empire.

RETURNING to the fountain—at the end of six or seven months, some little Indian boys were playing by the stream when they saw the spring of water coming from the broken and silted-up pipe. At the novelty of the sight they called some others to look until at last the news reached some older Indians, and they told the Spaniards, who suspected that this must be the lost water supply of the monastery nearby and ascertaining the direction taken by the pipes, they verified that they went towards the house, and feeling that their suspicion was right, informed the friars. They joyfully repaired the pipes, though not with the skill of the previous owners, and restored the water to their garden without making any more attempts to find out whence it came or which way it took. It is true, of course, that there was much earth above the water, for the pipes ran very deep underground.

That garden, which now serves to supply the monastery with vegetables, was in Inca times a garden of gold and silver such as existed in the royal palaces. It contained many herbs and flowers of various kinds, small plants, large trees, animals great and small, tame and wild, and creeping things such as snakes, lizards, and snails, butterflies and birds, each placed in an imitation of its natural surroundings. There was also a great maize field, a patch of the grain they call *quinua,* and other vegetables and fruit trees with their fruit all made of gold and silver in imitation of nature. There were also in the house billets of wood done in gold and silver, which were also to be found in the royal palace. Finally, there were figures of men, women, and children cast in gold and silver, and granaries and barns, which they call *pirua,* to the great majesty and ornamentation of the house of their god, the Sun. Each year, at the great festivals they celebrated, they presented the Sun with much gold and silver which was used to decorate his temple. New devices were continually invented for this purpose, for the silversmith assigned to the service of the Sun did nothing else but make these figures, together with an infinite quantity of plate as well as pots, jars, vases, and vats used in the temple. In short, in the whole of the house there was no implement necessary for any function that was not made of gold and silver, even the spades and hoes for weeding the gardens. Thus with good reason, they called the temple of the Sun and the whole building *coricancha,* "the golden quarter."

In imitation of the temple of the city of Cuzco others were made in many of the provinces of the kingdom. Pedro de Cieza de León mentions many of these and the houses of the chosen virgins in the *Demarcation* of that land. In describing it province by province, he says where these were, but he does not include all of them, but only those on the royal highways he travelled on and described, omitting those in the great provinces on either side of the highways. I also will omit them for the sake of brevity. There is no need to mention them since the principal one has been described and the rest were made like it. Each *curaca* strove to decorate the local temple according to his district's resources in gold and silver. Each sought to do everything within his power so to serve his god and to please his kings who boasted of being children of the Sun. Consequently all the provincial temples were also lined with silver and gold plates to vie with that of Cuzco.

The nearest relatives of the *curacas* were the priests of the temples of the Sun. The high priest, or bishop as it were, of each province was an Inca of the royal blood, so that the sacrifices made to the Sun might be in accordance with the rites and ceremonies of Cuzco and not with the superstitions that had existed in some provinces until the Incas prohibited them, such as sacrifices of men, women, and children and the eating of human flesh after the sacrifices and other barbarities which we have mentioned as existing in the first age of heathendom. So that their subjects should not return to these practices, they were obliged to have an Inca of the royal blood as high priest. This was, moreover, an honor to the subjects, who, as we have often had occasion to say, greatly valued the appointment of Incas over them either as priests in peacetime or as captains in war: they thus became inferior members of the body of which the Inca was the head. What has been said of this very rich temple must stand instead of very much more that might have been written by anyone better able to describe it.

CHAPTER XXV

The famous temple of Titicaca and its fables and allegories.

AMONG OTHER famous temples dedicated to the Sun in Peru, which might have rivalled that of Cuzco in their wealth of gold and silver, there was one on the island called Titicaca, meaning "leaden hill." The word is composed of *titi,* "lead," and *caca,* "hill, mountain." Both syllables of *caca* are pronounced at the back of the throat, for if they are said as the letters sound in Spanish the word means "an uncle, one's mother's brother." The island gave its name to the lake called Titicaca in which it stands, about two shots of an arquebus from the shore. It is five or six thousand paces round, and is said to have been the place where the Sun placed his two children, male and female, when he sent them down to earth to instruct and teach the barbarous savages who then dwelt there how to live like human beings. To this fable they add another relating to more ancient times: they say that after the deluge the rays of the Sun were seen on that island and on that lake before any other place. The lake is seventy or eighty fathoms deep in places and is eighty leagues round. Padre Blas Valera writes that it has much loadstone and says that this is why boats cannot sail on its waters: of this I can say nothing.

The first Inca Manco Cápac, taking advantage of this ancient fable, and of his own shrewdness and inventive wit, saw that the Indians be-

lieved this and regarded the lake and island as sacred places, so he made
up the second fable that he and his wife were children of the Sun and
that their father had placed them on that island so that they should go
about the land teaching the people, as was described at length at the beginning of this history. The Inca, *amautas*, the philosophers and wise
men of the state, reduced the first fable to the second, applying it as a
prefiguration or prophecy, so to speak. They said that the fact that the
Sun had cast its first rays on that island to illuminate the world was a
sign and promise that he would place his first two children there to teach
and illuminate the natives, and to draw them out of their primitive savagery, as the Inca kings later did. With these and other inventions made
for their own benefit, the Incas induced the remaining Indians to believe
they were children of the Sun and confirmed it by the good they did.
Because of the fables the Incas and all the peoples of their empire regarded the island as a sacred place, and therefore ordered a very rich
temple to be built on it, completely lined with gold plates, and dedicated
to the Sun. Here all the provinces subdued by the Incas offered up a great
quantity of gold, silver, and precious stones every year as a thank offering
for the two benefits he had conferred on them at this spot. The temple
had the same service as the one in Cuzco. There was such a store of gold
and silver offerings on the island, apart from what was worked for the
use of the temple that the accounts given of it by the Indians are rather
to be wondered at than believed. Padre Blas Valera, speaking of the
wealth of the temple and the quantity of treasure left over from it and
stored there, says that the Indian colonists (called *mítmac*) who live in
Copacabana assured him that the quantity of gold and silver left over
was enough to have made another temple from foundation to roof without using any other material. As soon as the Indians knew the Spaniards
had entered that country and were seizing for themselves all the treasure
they found, they threw it all in the lake.

Another similar story occurs to me. In the valley of Orcos, six leagues
south of Cuzco, there is a small lake less than half a league round, but
very deep and surrounded by high hills. The story is that the Indians
threw a great part of the treasure from Cuzco in it as soon as they knew
about the approach of the Spaniards, and that one of the treasures was
the gold chain Huaina Cápac had ordered to be made, of which I shall
speak in due course. Twelve or thirteen Spaniards dwelling in Cuzco, not
settlers who possess Indians but merchants and traders, were stirred by
this report to form a company to share the risk or profit of draining the
lake and securing the treasure. They sounded it and found it was twenty-

three or twenty-four fathoms of water without counting the mud which was deep. They decided to make a tunnel to the east of the lake, where the river Y'úcay passes and the land is lower than the level of the lake: they could thus run off the water and leave the lake dry. In fact it could not have been drained from any other side because it was surrounded by hills. They did not make the drain by cutting an open channel from above, which would probably have been better, but thought it would be cheaper to tunnel upwards from the bottom. They began work in 1557 with great hopes of getting the treasure, but after tunneling fifty paces into the hillside, they struck a rock and though they tried to break it, they found it was flint, and when they persisted, they found they struck more sparks than stone. So having wasted many ducats of their capital, they lost hope and gave up. I went into the tunnel several times while they were working. It is publicly rumored, as these Spaniards heard, that the Indians hid a great quantity of treasure in lakes, caves, and mountains, but there is no hope of recovering it.

Apart from the temple and its decorations, the Inca kings greatly honored the island as being the first place trodden by their forebears when they came down from the sky, as they said. They flattened the island as much as possible, removing the rocks, and made terraces which they covered with good fertile soil brought from a distance so as to bear maize, for the whole of that region is too cold for growing maize. On these terraces they sowed the seeds and by dint of great care grew a few cobs which were sent to the Inca as sacred objects. He took them to the temple of the Sun and sent them to the chosen virgins in Cuzco, and ordered them to be taken to other temples and convents throughout the kingdom, in some years to some and in other years to others, so that all might enjoy the grain sent from heaven. It was sown in the gardens of the temples of the Sun and houses of the virgins where these existed and the crop was divided among the peoples of the provinces. A few grains were cast in the granaries of the Sun and of the king and in the municipal barns, so that its divine power would protect, increase, and preserve from corruption the grain gathered there for the general subsistence. Any Indian who could get a grain of that maize or any seed to cast in his barn thought he would never want for bread for his whole life, so great was their superstition in any matter relating to the Incas.

End of Book Three

BOOK
FOUR *of the*
FIRST PART

It treats of the virgins dedicated to the Sun and of the law against those who might violate them, how the common Indians married, and the marriage of the heir to the crown; how they inherited their estates; how they reared their children; the life of Inca Roca, the sixth king; his conquests; the schools he founded; his sayings; the life of Yáhuar Huácac, the seventh king, and a strange phantom which appeared to the prince his son.

It contains twenty-four chapters.

CHAPTER I

The house of the virgins dedicated to the Sun.

HE INCA kings had in their vain and heathen religion some great things worthy of much consideration. One of these was the profession of perpetual virginity observed by women in many conventual houses built for them in various parts of the empire. In order that it shall be understood what these women were, to whom they were dedicated, and how they occupied themselves, I shall now say how all this was, for the Spanish historians who mention it have passed over the surface like a cat on hot bricks, as the saying goes. We refer especially to the house in Cuzco, since those established later in the rest of Peru were modelled on it.

A quarter of the city of Cuzco was called Acllahuaci, "house of the chosen women." The quarter is between two streets that run from the main square to the convent of St. Dominic, which used to be the house of the Sun. One of those streets goes out of the corner of the square to the left of the cathedral and runs north and south. When I left Cuzco in 1560 this was the main shopping street. The other leaves the middle of the square, where the prison was, and runs parallel toward the same Dominican convent. The front of the house faced the square between these two streets, and its back gave onto a street running across them east and west, so that it occupied an island site between the square and these three streets. Between it and the temple of the Sun there was a large block of houses and a big square which is in front of the temple. This shows how far off the mark were these historians who say that the virgins were in the temple of the Sun, that they were priestesses and that they aided the priests in the sacrifices. In fact the house and the temple are a great distance apart, and the chief object of the Inca kings was that men should not enter the nunnery, or women the temple of the Sun. They called it "the house of the chosen" because the nuns were chosen for their rank or beauty; they must be virgins, and to ensure this, they were set apart at the age of eight years or under.

As the virgins of the house of Cuzco were dedicated to the Sun, they had to be of his own blood, or daughters of Incas, either of the king or of members of his family, and legitimate and free from all foreign blood.[1] Those with any taint of foreign blood, or bastards, were not admitted into the house in Cuzco of which we speak. The reason they gave was that as only incorrupt virgins were set aside for the Sun, so it would have been unlawful to offer to him a bastard with any taint of foreign blood. They reasoned that the Sun would have children and that they must not be bastards with a mixture of human with their divine blood. The women devoted to the Sun must therefore be of the legitimate royal blood, which was that of the Sun himself. There were usually more than fifteen hundred nuns, but there was no established limit of number.

Within the house there were senior women who had grown old in their vocation. If they had entered it long ago the were called *mamacuna* because of their age and of the office they performed. Superficially this word means "matron," but its real significance is a woman entrusted with the duties of a mother: it is composed of *mama,* "mother," and the particle *cuna,* with no fixed meaning, but in this compound implying what we have said, though it has many other senses in diverse compounds. The name was appropriate, for the functions of some were those of abbesses, and others were mistresses of the novices whom they indoctrinated in the divine worship of their idolatry and in handiwork connected with it such as spinning, weaving, and sewing. Others were portresses and stewardesses, who had to obtain whatever was required: this was provided in great abundance from the estates of the Sun, whose women they were.

CHAPTER II

The rules and duties of the chosen virgins.

THEY LIVED in perpetual seclusion to the end of their days and preserved their virginity. They had no locutory or hatch or any other place where they could see or speak to men or women except one another. As women of the Sun they were not to be made common by being seen by anyone. Their seclusion was so absolute that even the Inca never used the privilege he might have had as king of seeing or speaking to them, lest

[1] Blood other than that of the Incas: *sangre ajena.*

anyone else should have ventured to seek the same privilege. Only the *coya,* or queen, and her daughters had leave to enter the house and converse with the nuns, both young and old.

The Inca sent the queen and her daughters to visit them and ask how they were and what they needed. I saw this house intact, for only its quarter and that of the temple of the Sun, and four other buildings that had been royal palaces of the Incas were respected by the Indians in their general rebellion against the Spaniards. Because they had been the house of the Sun, their god, and of his women, and of their kings, they did not burn them down as they burnt the rest of the city. Among other notable features of this building there was a narrow passage wide enough for two persons that ran the whole length of the building. The passage had many cells on either side which were used as offices where women worked. At each door were trusted portresses, and in the last apartment at the end of the passage where no one entered were the women of the Sun. The house had a main door as convents do in Spain, but it was only opened to admit the queen or to receive women who were going to be nuns.

At the beginning of the passage which was the service-door for the whole house, there were a score of porters to fetch and carry things needed in the house as far as the second door. The porters could not pass this second door under pain of death, even if they were called from within, and no one was allowed to call them in under the same penalty. The nuns and their house were served by five hundred girls, all maidens and daughters of Incas by privilege, those whom the first Inca had reduced to his service and not those of the royal blood. They did not enter the house as women of the Sun, but only as servants. Daughters of foreigners were not admitted for this service, but only those of Incas by privilege. These maids had also their *mamacunas* of their own rank and also virgins, who told them what to do. These *mamacunas* were those who had grown old in the house, and who on reaching this seniority were granted the title and responsibility, as if to say: "Now you can be a mother and mistress of the house." In the division the Spaniards made of the royal houses of Cuzco to supply themselves with dwellings, half of this convent fell to Pedro del Barco, whom we shall mention later. This was the part of the offices. The other half went to Licentiate de la Gama, whom I met as a child, and after passed to Diego Ortiz de Guzmán, a gentleman from Seville whom I knew. He was still alive when I came to Spain.

The various duties of the women of the Sun were spinning, weaving, and making all the clothes and headwear the Inca and the *coya,* his legitimate wife, wore on their persons. They also made the fine garments that were offered as sacrifices to the Sun. The Inca wore on his head a band, the *llautu*, which was as broad as the little finger and very thick, so as to be almost square, being passed four or five times around the head, and the scarlet fringe which stretched across his temples. His dress was a tunic falling to the knees, the *uncu*. The Spaniards call it *cusma*, but this is not in the general language but a word from some provincial dialect. He wore also a blanket two *piernas* square instead of a cloak, the *yacolla*. The nuns also made for the Inca a kind of pouch, about a quarter of a vara square. These pouches are carried under the arm on a highly embroidered band, two fingers in width and passed like a bandolier from the left shoulder to the right side. They are called *"chuspa."* They were used only to carry the coca herb which the Indians chew. It was not then as common as it is now, for only the Inca and his kinsmen and some *curacas*, to whom the king sent a few baskets every year as a special mark of favor, used it.

They also made some small tassels of two colors, yellow and scarlet, called *paicha,* which were attached to a thin band about a fathom long. These were not for the Inca, but for those of the royal blood, and were worn on the head, the tassels falling over the right temple.

CHAPTER III

The veneration they had for things made by the virgins and the law against those who might violate them.

ALL THESE things were made by the nuns in great quantities for their bridegroom the Sun. As the Sun could not wear these garments, they were sent to the Inca as his legitimate son and legal heir that he might wear them. He received them as sacred things, and he and his whole empire held them in greater veneration than the Greeks and Romans would have done if the goddesses Juno, Venus, and Pallas had made them. For these gentiles of the New World, being simpler than those of antiquity, worshipped with extreme veneration and heartfelt affection everything they held sacred and divine in their false faith. Because these things were made by the hands of *coyas,* wives of the Sun, and made for the Sun, and the women who made them were of the Sun's own blood, they held them in the greatest veneration. The Inca likewise could not give them to anyone not of his own blood and kin, for they held that divine things could not be put to human purposes without sacrilege, and it was there-fore prohibited even to the king to offer them to *curacas* and captains, however well they had served him, unless they were of his blood. We shall later say what garments the Inca did give to the *curacas* and viceroys, governors and captains when he wished to show them great honor and favor.

In addition the nuns occupied themselves in due season in making the bread called *çancu* for the sacrifices they offered to the Sun at the great festivals of Raimi and Citua. They also brewed the drink the Inca and his kinsfolk drank on the festivals, called in their language *aca,* the last syl-lable being pronounced in the gullet, for if it is said as the Spanish letters sound, it means "dung." All the vessels of the house, even pots, pitchers, and vats, were of silver and gold, as in the house of the Sun, for they were his wives and were worthy of it by their rank. There was also a garden of trees and plants, herbs and flowers, birds and animals, done in gold and silver like those in the temple of the Sun.

The things we have mentioned were the main occupations of the nuns of Cuzco. Otherwise they lived and conversed like women dedicated to perpetual seclusion and perpetual virginity. There was a law that a nun who forfeited her virginity should be buried alive and her accomplice hanged. As they thought it was a small punishment merely to kill a man for so grave an offence as venturing to violate a woman dedicated to the Sun, their god and father of their kings, the law provided that the guilty man's wife, children, and servants should be slain too, together with his kinsmen, his neighbors, and his fellow townsmen, and all his flocks, with-out leaving a babe or suckling, as the saying is. His village was destroyed and strewn with rocks, and the home and birthplace of so wicked a son left forsaken and desolate and the place accursed, to remain untrodden by the foot of man or beast, if possible.

This was the law. But it was never applied, for no one ever transgressed it. As we have said, the Peruvian Indians were very fearful of breaking the laws and extremely observant of them, especially those relating to their religion or their king. But if anyone did transgress, the law was applied literally without any remission, as if it were merely a matter of killing a puppy. The Incas never made laws to frighten their subjects or to be mocked by them, but always with the intention of applying them to any-one who dared to break them.

CHAPTER IV

There were many other houses of chosen virgins;
the strict application of their laws in proved.

ALL THIS applied to the house of the virgins dedicated to the Sun in
Cuzco. There were many like it in the chief provinces, where the
Inca had ordered them to be built as an honor and privilege. Into these
were admitted maidens of all ranks, both those of the legitimate royal
blood and those called bastards of mixed descent. As a great favor and
honor, the daughters of *curacas*, the chiefs of vassals, were allowed to
enter; and there were also daughters of the common people chosen for
their beauty as wives or concubines of the Inca, but not of the Sun. Their
parents held it to be the greatest happiness to have their daughters chosen
as wives of the king, and so did the girls themselves.

These girls were guarded with the same care and vigilance as the
women of the Sun. They had serving-girls, maidens like the others. They
were supported out of the Inca's revenues, for they were his wives. They
had the same occupations as the women of the Sun: spinning, weaving,
and making a great quantity of garments for the Inca. They also did all
the other things we have mentioned. The Inca shared the fruit of their
handiwork with the members of the royal family, the lords of vassals,
the captains of his armies, and all others on whom he wished to bestow
honors and favors. These he was not prohibited from giving away because they were made by his wives and not those of the Sun; and they
made them for him and not for the Sun.

These houses also had their *mamacunas,* who governed them like those
at Cuzco. In brief, they might have been the same house except that entry
to that of Cuzco was for women of the Sun who were of the legitimate
royal blood and remained permanently cloistered, while into the other
houses throughout the country women of all kinds were admitted so
long as they were maidens and beautiful, for they were for the Inca.
When he asked, the most beautiful of them were selected to be sent
wherever he might be as his concubines.

The same strict law against the violation of the houses of the Inca's
women existed as in the case of the house of the Sun, for the crime was
considered to be the same, but it was never applied because no one

transgressed it. In confirmation of what we have said about the severity of the law against offenders against the women of the Sun or of the Incas, the treasurer Agustín de Zárate, speaking of the causes of the violent death of Atahuallpa (Book II, ch. vii), has the following passage which illustrates this matter and is quoted word for word:

As the evidence about this came from the mouth of Felipillo himself, he interpreted it according to his own intentions. These motives were never clearly understood, but were probably one of two: either this Indian had an intrigue with one of Atahuallpa's women and desired by his death to enjoy her in safety, but Atahuallpa had wind of this and complained to the governor, saying that he felt this insult more deeply than his imprisonment or all the other disasters that had befallen him, even though they should lead to his death—that an Indian of such base birth should scorn and outrage him, knowing the law that existed for such a crime. For if he were found guilty of it, or even merely of attempting it, he would have been burnt alive with the woman, if she were guilty; and his parents, children, brothers, and sisters, and the rest of his near relatives would have been killed, even down to his flocks, and his birthplace would have been depopulated and sown with salt, all the trees and houses being destroyed and other great punishments inflicted in memory of the crime.

This is from Agustín de Zárate, who makes it plain that he had had a full account of the severity of this law. I found the passage after I had written what I myself knew of it. I was very glad to find the law so fully recorded by a Spanish gentleman who thus confirms me with his authority, for although the other historians speak of this law, all they say is that the delinquents were killed, without mentioning that the same penalty was applied to their children, parents, relatives, and fellow townsfolk, even to the extent of killing animals, pulling up trees, laying waste the birthplace, and strewing it with stones or with salt, which amounts to the same thing. All this was contained in the law so as to place due emphasis on the gravity of the offence. And so did it appear to the wretched Inca Atahuallpa when he said he felt it to be a greater outrage than his arrest or all his adversities, even though they led to his death.

Those who had once been sent out as concubines of the king could not again return to the convent, as being now impure. They served in the royal households as ladies or servants to the queen until they were retired or allowed to return to their own country, where they were given houses and lands and served with great veneration, for every tribe took the greatest honor in have one of the Inca's women with it. Those who did not attain the honor of being the king's concubines remained in the house until they were very old, then were given permission to return to their homes where they were treated as we have said, or they remained in the convent until they died.

CHAPTER V

*The service and ornaments of the virgins;
they were never given in marriage
to anyone.*

T HE WOMEN dedicated to the reigning king were entitled "mothers" of his successor on his death, and they were then with more propriety accorded the title of *mamacuna,* since they had become mothers. They instructed and cared for those who were to be concubines to the new Inca, as if they had been their daughters-in-law. Each convent had its governor (who was always an Inca), major domo, steward, and other officers necessary for the service of the king's wives, for although concubines they were called wives for form's sake. In all these houses of maidens set aside for the Inca, the vessels and other utensils were of gold and silver, as they were in the house of the women of the Sun and in their famous temple, and also, as we shall see, in the royal palaces. In short, it can be stated that the whole wealth of gold, silver, and precious stones extracted in that great empire was all devoted exclusively to the adornment and service of the temples of the Sun, which were very numerous, and the houses of the virgins, which were equal in number, and to the sumptuousness and majesty of the royal palaces, of which there were many more. What was used by the lords of vassals was little or nothing, consisting only of drinking vessels, which were limited in number according to the privilege granted by the Inca in each case. Another small quantity was used for the robes and ornaments they wore to celebrate the chief festivals.

The statement that maidens were taken from the houses of the virgins to be given to lords of vassals, famous captains, and others who had deserved well of the Inca and that he himself presented them as wives is an error into which the author of it fell through receiving false information. For when once dedicated as a woman of the Inca and so professed, it was unlawful for anyone to lower herself from that estate. Nor could anyone be allowed to say of the wife of a private person: "She was once a woman of the Inca." This would have been to profane something sacred, since, second only to things dedicated to the Sun, whatever was dedicated to the Inca, especially women, because of their especially close relationship, was considered sacred. The lowering of the women of the Inca to be wives of private persons would have been an outrage and would never have been permitted. Even in small things they permitted no affront from anyone, and would certainly never have tolerated it in a matter of such gravity as this, for they thought it more honorable to be a slave of the Inca than the wife of a private person. As slaves of the Inca (and in using the word we must remember that they had no slaves and did not conceive the idea of a slave) they were venerated as something sacred, as being the Inca's, but as wives of lords of vassals they were of no more consequence than anything private compared with anything of the Inca's. All these matters were considered very attentively by the Indians and observed with the greatest care, because they considered their kings not only to be invested with royal majesty, but to be gods.

CHAPTER VI

The women who were favored by the Inca.

IT IS true that the Incas gave women to those who had deserved well of them by virtue of their services as *curacas,* captains, and the like. But these were the daughters of other *curacas* and captains, whom the Inca took to bestow as wives on those who had served him well. Anyone whose daughter was so sought in marriage was as greatly honored and delighted as the recipient of her hand, because the Inca had lighted on his daughter and made her as it were a jewel of his to bestow with his own hand on one who had served him well: and when the Inca conferred an honor, it was not so much the gift that was valued, however great it was, as the fact that it was received from the majestic hand of the Inca, which was looked upon as a divine, not a human, favor.

The Inca also gave, though rarely, bastard girls of the royal blood as wives to *curacas* who were lords of great provinces, both to do them honor and to oblige them in this way to be loyal subjects. The king had thus so many women to bestow that there was no need for him to give those who had been dedicated to him in the houses of the virgins. It would indeed have been dishonorable to the Inca, the woman, and their religion, which they regarded as inviolable, since those of legitimate birth could become women of the Sun (as has been said), or they could have become wives of the Inca (who took his concubines from those of the royal blood), or they could have become the wives of legitimate Incas without in any of these three states losing their divine nature; it would have been wrong for them to become the wives of human beings, even if these were great lords, for they would thus debase the blood they regarded as divine. But as a bastard was held to have lost this imaginary divinity, no wrong was done by giving her in marriage to a great lord.

CHAPTER VII

*Other women who preserved their
virginity, and widows.*

B ESIDES the virgins who entered monasteries to profess perpetual virginity withdrawn from the world, there were many women of the royal blood who led a similar life in their own homes, having taken a vow of chastity, though not of reclusion. They did not fail to visit their closer relatives in case of sickness or childbirth, or when their first-born children were shorn and named. Such women were greatly respected for their chastity and high-mindedness, and as a mark of their excellence and divinity they were called *ocllo,* a name held sacred in their idolatry. Their chastity was not feigned, but sincerely preserved, on pain of their being burnt alive as traitors and counterfeiters of their false religion or thrown into the lake of lions, if they were shown to have defiled it. I myself knew one of these women when she was extremely old. She had never married and was called *ocllo.* She sometimes visited my mother, and I understood she was her great-aunt, a sister to her grandparents. She was always treated with the respect I have mentioned, and given the seat of honor on all occasions: I can bear witness that my mother treated her so both because she was her aunt and also on account of her age and virtue.

Nor should one omit to mention the chastity of widows, who usually remained in complete retirement for the whole of the first year of their widowhood. Of those who were childless very few married again. Those who had children never remarried, but lived in continence. This virtue was greatly commended in their laws and ordinances, which prescribed that the fields of widows should be tilled before those of the *curaca* or those of the Inca, apart from many similar privileges. It is a fact also that the Indians were reluctant to marry widows, especially those who were not themselves widowers. They thought that anyone who married a widow lost something of his quality. The above remarks contain what is most notable about virgins, virtuous women, and widows.

CHAPTER VIII

How they usually married and set up house.

IT WILL be well to describe the way in which marriages were celebrated throughout all the realms and provinces subject to the Incas. It must be explained that every year or every two years, at a certain season, the king ordered all the marriageable maidens and youths of his lineage to gather together in Cuzco. The girls were between eighteen and twenty years old and the youths from twenty-four upwards. They were not allowed to marry earlier, for they said that it was necessary to be old enough and wise enough to rule their houses and estates, and for them to marry earlier would be childish.

The Inca placed himself in the midst of the contracting parties, who were near to one another, and having looked at them, called a youth and a girl, took each by the hand, united them in the bond of matrimony and delivered them to their parents. They then went to the bridegroom's house and solemnized the wedding in the presence of the nearer relatives. The celebrations lasted two, four, or six days, or longer if they wished. These were legitimate wives, and as a mark of greater honor and favor to them they were said in their language to be "given by the Inca's hand." When the king had married those of his own family, the officials appointed for the purpose married on the following day the sons and daughters of the other residents in the city, keeping separate the two divisions called upper Cuzco and lower Cuzco, which we described at the beginning of our history.

The houses for the dwellings of bridegrooms who were Incas, of whom we are speaking, were made by Indians from the provinces entrusted with the task, according to the division of labor that was set down for everything. The household requirements were provided by the relatives, each bringing a piece. There were no other ceremonies or sacrifices. If the Spanish historians say that other practices existed in their weddings, it is because they have failed to distinguish between the provinces where different usages were found. In this way barbarous customs that existed in many provinces before the Incas took over are commonly attributed to the Incas, who certainly never knew them, but rather stopped them and severely punished the Indians if they practised them.

The Incas had no other marriage ceremony than that we have described, and orders were given to every governor in his district together with the provincial *curaca* to marry disposable youths and girls according to the same rite. The *curacas* had to be present at the weddings or perform them themselves as lords and fathers of their people. For the Incas never oppressed them by usurping the jurisdiction of the *curaca,* and the Inca governor was present at the marriages performed by the chief not to take any active part in them, but to approve in the king's name the proceedings of the *curaca* toward his vassals.

For the marriages of the common people the councils of each village were obliged to have houses built for those who were married, and the relatives provided the furniture. It was not lawful for those of different provinces to intermarry, or even those of different towns. All were to marry within their own towns and their own families like the tribes of Israel, so as not to confuse and mix the lineages and tribes. They were not to marry their sisters. All those of one village regarded themselves as relatives, like the sheep of one fold. Even those of the same province did so, if they were all of one tribe and the same language. It was not permitted for them to go from one province and live in another, or from one town to another, or one quarter to another, so as not to confuse the decuries of the dwellers in each town and quarter. Also the councils had to make the houses and would not make them more than once, and then only in the quarter or parish to which their relatives belonged.

CHAPTER IX

The heir to the throne married his sister;
the reasons they gave for this.

HAVING spoken of the marriage customs of the Indians in general it is appropriate to describe how the heir to the throne was married. Since the first of the Inca kings, the custom and law among them was that the heir to the kingdom should marry his eldest sister, the legitimate daughter of his father and mother. She was thus his legitimate wife, and was called *coya* which means "queen" or "empress." The first-born son of brother and sister was the legitimate heir of the kingdom.

This law and custom was observed from the first Inca Manco Cápac and his wife Mama Ocllo Huaco, who declared that they were brother and sister, children of the Sun and Moon, and this was believed by the Indians, both those who were their subjects and others. This tradition was lent force to by another that in their heathendom they believed, as we have said, namely that the Moon was the sister and wife of the Sun, from whom the Incas boasted of descending. Consequently, in order to imitate the Sun and his children, the first Incas, in every respect, they established the law that the first-born son of the Inca should follow both traditions and marry his sister by his own father and mother. In default of a legitimate sister, he married his closest female relative in the royal line, his first cousin, niece, or aunt, whichever would inherit the throne if a male heir were lacking according to the practice in Spain.

If the prince had no children by his eldest sister, he married the second and third, until he had children. This strictly observed custom and law was founded on the principles already mentioned. They thought that as the Sun had wedded his sister and begotten by this marriage his two first children, it was proper that the first-born of the king should imitate his example. They also had in mind the preservation of the purity of the Sun's blood, saying that it was wrong for it to be mingled with human blood (human blood was any other than that of the Incas). They also said that the princes married their sisters so that the heir might inherit the kingdom as much through his mother as through his father. Had it been otherwise, they would have thought the prince a bastard on his mother's side. So seriously did they consider the succession and the right to inherit the throne. As an additional reason, they considered that the majesty of being queen should not be granted to any woman unless she inherited it in her own legitimate right and not as the king's consort; and if she were not capable of reigning in her own right it was not proper that she should be worshipped and served by others who in other respects were better than she.

Apart from their legitimate wives, the kings had many concubines. Some were relatives within and beyond the fourth degree; others were foreign-born. Children by women related to the Inca were held legitimate because they had no taint of other blood. Purity of descent was highly venerated by the Incas, not only among the kings but among all those of royal blood. Children of foreign concubines were considered bastards; and though respected as children of the king, they did not receive the reverence and internal and external worship which was reserved for those who were of legitimate blood. The Inca king thus had three kinds of children—those by his wife who were legally entitled to inherit the throne, those by his relatives who were of legitimate blood, and bastard children by other women.

CHAPTER X

Various ways of inheriting estates.

IN DEFAULT of the sons of a legitimate wife, the law was that the eldest of the sons who were legitimate by blood should inherit. Thus Manco Inca succeeded Huáscar, as we shall say in due course. In default of the eldest the others were successively eligible, but none of the bastards was permitted to succeed under any circumstance at all. If there was no son who was legitimate by blood, the succession fell to the nearest legitimate male relative.

By the light of this law Atahuallpa destroyed the whole royal blood, male and female, as we shall say, for he was a bastard, and feared lest the crown he had usurped should be taken away from him and given to a legitimate member of the royal family. All those of the royal blood used to marry their relatives within the fourth degree so that there might be many children who were legitimate by blood. They did not marry their sisters, a custom that was only permitted to be practiced by the king. The eldest son always inherited the kingdom, and the succession never failed in the twelve generations of kings before the arrival of the Spaniards.

The *curacas* or lords of vassals had different customs concerning the transmission of their estates. In some provinces the first-born son succeeded, and there was a regular succession from father to son. Elsewhere the son most popular with the subjects, or most beloved for his virtue and graciousness, inherited, a practice savoring of election, rather than heredity. This practice was intended to be a check against the son of a chief becoming a wicked tyrant, and to stimulate each of them to seek to merit the succession to his father's estate and power by displaying goodness and valor and thus persuading the subjects to ask for him to be made chief on account of his merits.

In other provinces all the sons inherited in order of seniority. On the death of the father, the eldest son succeeded, followed by the second, then the third, and so on. When all the brothers were dead, the inheritance went to the sons of the eldest, and then to those of the second and third, etc. For some of them it was a weary wait. Through hearing of this type of inheritance among some of the chiefs, one of the Spanish historians mistakenly says it was the common custom throughout Peru, not only among the chiefs, but also of the kings, and that king's brothers and then their sons inherited in order of seniority. It was not true of the Inca kings, and only of some of the *curacas,* as we have said.

The three different customs or laws which the lords of vassals of various provinces had in the inheritance of their estates were not laid down by the Incas, for their laws and ordinances were general and common to all their dominions. The *curacas* practiced them before the Inca empire. After they were conquered by the Incas, just as they were not deprived of their estates, so they were allowed to keep the customs they had in former times, provided they were not contrary to those the Incas ordered them to observe. On the contrary, many laws that seemed good were confirmed, especially the practice of allowing the most virtuous and beloved of a chief's sons to succeed. This seemed very laudable to the Incas, and so they approved it and ordered it to be observed wherever it had been in force and wherever there was a wish to adopt it. One of their kings sought to take advantage of this law of the chiefs because his eldest son was of a bad and incompatible character for a prince, as we shall see. In one village I knew, of the Quechua race, Sutcunca, about forty leagues west of Cuzco, the following occurred, which illustrates the different customs of inheritance. The *curaca* of the tribe was called Don García. On his deathbed he called four sons he had and the men of rank of his people, and bade them as his last will to observe the law of Jesus Christ which they had newly received and always to give thanks to God for having granted it them, and to serve and respect the Spaniards for bringing it, and especially to serve their master with great love because it had been their fortune that he should become their lord. Finally he said: "You know that according to the custom of our country the most virtuous and best beloved of my sons inherits my estate. I bid you choose the one you think. If you do not find such a one among them, I bid you disinherit them and choose one of yourselves to preserve your honor, safety, and welfare, because I desire the common good of you all more than I desire the private happiness of my sons." This was recounted by the priest who instructed them as a notable deed and testament on the part of the Indian.

CHAPTER XI

The weaning, shearing, and naming of their children.

T HE INCAS used to celebrate the weaning of their first-born sons with a great feast, but not that of daughters or other male children, or at least not with the same solemnity. The dignity of primogeniture, especially in the male sex, was greatly esteemed among the Incas and, by their example, among all their vassals.

They weaned their children when they were two years old or more, and cut off the first crop of hair which they had had since they were born, and which had hitherto not been touched. At the same time the children were given the names they were to bear. The whole family gathered for the purpose, and one of them was chosen to stand godfather and give the first clip to his godchild. The shears used were flint knives, for the Indians did not discover how to make scissors. After the godparent the rest of the family was ranged according to degree, age or dignity and each gave a clip with the shears to the newly weaned child. Once shorn, it was given a name and presented with gifts that had been brought: clothes, cattle, weapons of various kinds, and drinking vessels of gold or silver if the child was of the royal family (the last named could only be used by commoners by special privilege).

After the presentation followed the ceremony of drinking, without which no feast was worthy of the name. They sang and danced until nightfall, and their rejoicing lasted two, three, or four days, or more, according to the child's family. Almost the same procedure was followed when the heir to the kingdom was weaned and shorn, except that it was done with royal solemnity and the godfather was the high priest of the Sun. The *curacas* of the whole kingdom came in person or sent ambassadors. A feast was given that lasted at least twenty days, and great gifts of gold, silver, and precious stones and the best of everything in the provinces were offered. As everyone wished to imitate their ruler, the *curacas* and the whole of the common people of Peru all did the same, each according to his degree and parentage, and this was one of their most joyous feasts.

Those who are interested in philology may like to know that the general language of Peru has two words for children: the father says *churi* and the mother *huahua*—this should be written with the two *h*'s, the four vowels being each pronounced in two diphthongs: I have added the *h*'s so that it is not reduced to two syllables. The two nouns mean "child" or "children," each including both sexes and singular and plural. But they are strictly limited to either father or mother, and cannot be changed round without implying that the male is female and the female, male. To distinguish between the two sexes they add words that mean male or female, but the father says *churi* and the mother *huahua* to indicate child or children. They have four different words to name brothers and sisters. Brother calls brother *huauque*, "brother." Sister calls sister *ñaña*, "sister." If the brother said *ñaña* of his sister, it would imply he was a girl, and if the sister said *huauque* of her brother, it would imply she was a boy. Brother calls sister *pana*, which also means "sister." Sister calls brother *tora*, which means "brother." But one brother cannot call another *tora* though it means "brother," because it would imply he was a girl, and one sister cannot call another *pana*, though it means "sister," since it would imply she was a boy. There are therefore two words with the same gender and meaning, one appropriate for men and the other for women, and they cannot be interchanged without the implications I have mentioned. All this requires to be duly noted in teaching the Indians our holy religion, or they are provoked to mirth by barbarisms. The Jesuit fathers, who are so thorough in everything, and other religious pay great attention to the Indian language in indoctrinating the heathen, as we said earlier.

CHAPTER XII

They brought up their children
without pampering them.

T HEY BROUGHT up their children in a strange way, both Incas and
common folk, rich and poor, without distinction, with the least possible pampering. As soon as the infant was born it was washed in cold
water and swaddled in shawls. Every morning when it was wrapped up it
was washed in cold water, and often exposed to the night air and dew.
When the mother wanted to pamper her child, she would take the water
into her mouth and then wash it all over, except the head, and especially
the crown, which was never washed. It was said that this accustomed
babies to cold and hardship, and also that it strengthened their limbs.
Their arms were kept inside the swaddling clothes for more than three
months, because it was thought that if they were loosened earlier, they
would grow weak in the arm. They were kept lying in their cradles, which
were sort of rough benches on four legs with one leg shorter than the
others so that they could be rocked. The bed on which the baby reclined
was a coarse net which was a little less hard than the bare boards: the same
net was used to hitch the baby to the sides of the cradle and tie it up so
that it could not fall out.

The mothers never took the babies into their arms or on their laps
either when giving suck or at any other time. They said it made them
crybabies, and encouraged them to want to be nursed and not to stay in the
cradle. The mother bent over the baby and gave it her breast. This was
done thrice a day, in the morning, at midday, and in the evening. Except
at these times no milk was given, even if they cried. Otherwise it was
thought they would get used to sucking all day long and develop dirty
habits with vomiting and diarrhea, and grow up to be greedy and gluttonous men. They said that animals did not give their young milk at all
hours of the day and night, but only at fixed times. The mother reared
the child herself, and never gave it out to nurse, even if she were a great
lady, unless she were ill. During this time they abstained from sexual
intercourse, considering that it spoiled the milk and caused the baby to
pine and grow weak. Such weaklings were called *ayusca,* a past participle
which really means "one who has been denied" or more exactly one that
has been changed for another by its parents. The word was similarly used

by one youth to another making fun of another because the girl he was in love with favored someone else more than him. It could never be addressed to a married man, for it was one of the great insults, and anyone who offered it was severely punished. A *palla* of the royal blood I knew was obliged to give her daughter out to nurse. The nurse either cheated her or became pregnant, for the child grew weak and seemed almost consumptive, a mere bag of skin and bones. The mother, seeing her child *ayusca,* eight months after her milk had dried up, brought it back to her breasts with plasters and herbal poultices applied to her back, and resumed suckling her child, and brought it back to health, rescuing it from death. She would not entrust it to another nurse, saying that it was her mother's milk that had saved it.

If the mother had enough milk to feed her child, she never gave it anything to eat until it was weaned, saying that the food would spoil the milk, and the child become dirty and smelly. When it was time to remove them from the cradles, they were still not taken in arms: a hole was made in the ground coming up to the level of their breasts. It was lined with a few rags, and they were put inside with a few toys to amuse them. In this pit the child could leap and play, but it was never taken in arms even though it was the offspring of the greatest chief in the kingdom.

When the child reached the crawling stage, it approached its mother from one side or the other to be suckled, which it did kneeling on the ground, yet it was never lifted on the mother's lap. When it wanted the other breast, it was made to go round the other side to get it so that the mother avoided lifting it in her arms. Mothers pampered themselves even less then they pampered their children, for on giving birth they went to a stream or washed themselves in the house with cold water and resumed their household duties as if nothing had happened. They gave birth without midwives, which were unknown: if anyone undertook the duty, it was a witch rather than a midwife. This was the usual custom of the Indian women of Peru in giving birth and rearing their children, and it was quite natural to them, without distinction between rich and poor or between noblewomen and common people.

CHAPTER XIII

The life and duties of married women.

THE LIFE of married women was generally devoted to the perpetual care of their houses. They busied themselves with spinning and weaving wool in the cold districts and cotton in the hot. Each woman spun and wove for herself, and for her husband and children. They sewed very little, for the garments worn by both sexes required very little sewing. Everything they wore was twisted, either wool or cotton. Every piece of cloth they made, for whatever purpose, was made with four selvages. Cloth was never woven longer than what was needed for a single blanket or tunic. Each garment was not cut, but made in a piece, as the cloth came from the loom, and before weaving it they fixed its approximate breadth and length.

There were no tailors or cobblers or hosiers among the Indians. Ah, how many of the things that there are here in Spain they did not need or simply did without! The women made the clothes for the household and the men the footwear, which, as we have said, they had to know how to do before being admitted to knighthood. Although the Incas of the royal blood and the *curacas* and rich people had servants to make their shoes, they did not disdain from time to time to occupy themselves in making footwear or any kind of weapon that they were required to know how to make, for they prided themselves on fulfilling their duties. Everyone, men and women, joined in working the land and helped one another.

In some provinces remote from Cuzco which were still not well disciplined by the Inca kings, the women tilled the fields and the men sat at home spinning and weaving. But I am speaking of the capital and the tribes that followed its example, which were almost all those of the empire. The others were so barbarous they do not deserve to be remembered. The Indian women were so fond of spinning and so reluctant to waste even a short time that as they came or went from the villages to the city or even from one quarter to another, visiting one another for necessary purposes, they carried equipment for the two operations of spinning and twisting. As they walked along, they twisted what they had spun, this being the easier task. While visiting, they would take out their distaff and spin as they conversed. Spinning and twisting on the road was done by the common people, but the *pallas* who were of the royal blood were accompanied by servants carrying their yarn and distaffs. Thus both the callers and ladies of the house were occupied and not idle while they conversed. The spindles were of cane, like the Spanish iron ones. They have whorls, but not hollow at the point. They cast a loop round the spindle from the thread they are spinning, and as they spin they drop the spindle as they do when they twist. The thread is made as long as possible. They pick it up by the middle finger of the left hand and pass it on to the spindle. The distaff is held in the left hand and not carried at the waist. It is a quarter of a vara long. They hold it with the two smallest fingers, and use both hands to thin the thread and smooth out the burls. They do not draw it up to their mouths, because in my time they did not spin flax, which was unknown, but only wool and cotton. The quantity they spin is little, because the operation is a lengthy and complicated one, as I have said.

CHAPTER XIV

How women visited one another;
how they kept their clothes;
public women.

IF ANY woman who was not a *palla*, even though she was the wife of a *curaca*, or lord of vassals, went to visit a *palla* of royal blood, she did not take her own work to do, but after the first exchange of conversation of the visit or the adoration (for this is what it was), she would ask to be given some work, implying that she was not making a visit for she was not an equal, but serving the *palla* as inferior to superior. As a great favor the *palla* met the request by giving her something of what she was doing herself or one of her daughters, so as not to place her on a level with the servants as she would have if she ordered them to give her something they were doing. This favor was all that could be desired by the visitor, since the *palla* had deigned to put her on a level with herself or her daughters. In the Inca state men and women behaved with this return of affability for humility, and the inferiors studied to serve and please their superiors, and the superiors to reward and favor their inferiors, from the king and Inca down to the wretchedest *llama michec,* or shepherd.

The good custom the Indian women had of visiting one another carrying their work with them was imitated by the Spanish women in Cuzco and preserved in very creditable fashion by them until the rebellion and war of Francisco Hernández Girón, which destroyed this custom, as tyranny usually destroys all virtues that come under its cruel jurisdiction.

I had forgotten to mention how the common people repair their clothes, which is worthy of note. If the dress they are wearing or any other clothes break, not from wear, but by accident such as getting caught on a hook or burnt by a spark or some similar mischance, they take it and re-weave it with a needle made of a thorn (they have no metal needles) and a thread of the same color and the same thickness as the garment. They first passed the threads of the warp among the torn threads, and then those of the web fifteen or twenty threads beyond the place of the tear, where the thread was cut. They then went back with the same thread and by crossing and interweaving the warp with the woof, and the woof with the warp, they left no sign of the rent when the patch was completed. Even if the tear was as big as the palm of the hand or bigger, it was patched in this way, using the mouth of a pot or a broken calabash as a mushroom so as to keep the cloth taut and level. They laughed at Spanish darning. Of course the material is different from that of the Indians, and cannot be repaired in the same way.

It is also noteworthy that the hearths in their houses for cooking were clay ovens, large or small according to the means of the owner. The fire was kindled at the mouth, and on top they made two or three holes according to the number of dishes they would eat, on which they placed the cooking pots. This ingenious device was adopted by these thrifty people so as not to waste the heat or use more fuel than was necessary. They were surprised at the way the Spaniards wasted fuel.

It remains to say something of the public women, which the Incas permitted to avoid worse consequences. They lived in the fields, in poor cabins, each by herself and not together. They were not allowed to enter the towns so as not to communicate with other women. They were called *pampairuna,* a word that indicates their dwelling-place and trade, composed of *pampa,* "open place" or "field," (it has both meanings), and *runa,* which in the singular means "person," man or woman and in the plural "people." Putting the two words together, if the sense of "open field" is taken, *pampairuna* means "people who live in the field, because of their wretched trade"; if the sense of "market place" is taken, it means "a person or woman of the market-place," implying that as the place is public and receives all those who go to it, so do they. In short it means "public woman." Men treated them with great scorn. Women did not speak to them under pain of being given the same title and being shorn in public, and regarded as infamous and repudiated by their husbands, if they were married. They were not called by their real names, but *pampai-runa* or "whore."

CHAPTER XV

Inca Roca, the sixth king, conquers many nations, among them the Chancas and Hancohuallu.

KING INCA ROCA, whose name, as we have already seen from Padre Blas Valera, means "mature and prudent prince," took the scarlet fringe on the death of his father, and having performed the funeral solemnities, began to visit his domains. He spent the first three years of his reign in this way. He then ordered an army to be prepared to press forward his conquest in the direction of Chinchasuyu, to the north of Cuzco. He ordered the building of a bridge over the river Apurímac. This is the one on the royal highway, from Cuzco to Lima. It seemed undignified, now that he was king, for him to cross the river with his army on rafts as he did when he was prince. The previous Inca had not ordered a bridge to be made because he was not then master of the surrounding provinces, as the present Inca was.

When the bridge was finished, the Inca left Cuzco with twenty thousand soldiers and four commanders. He ordered the army to cross the new bridge in companies marching in triple file as a permanent record of its first use. He reached the Amáncay valley, meaning "lily valley," so called from the vast number of these flowers that grow there. The flower differs in shape and smell from the Spanish lily, for the *amáncay* is bell-shaped and has a smooth green stem, and is leafless and odorless; it is called lily by the Spaniards only because of its white and green color. From Amáncay he bore right from the road to the great range of the snowcapped mountains, finding few towns between the road and the range, and incorporating them in his empire. The tribes are called Tacmara and Quiñualla. Thence he passed to Cochacassa, where he ordered a great store to be prepared. He marched next to Curampa, and easily reduced the two towns because they are small in population. From Curampa he went to a large province called Antahuailla, whose inhabitants stretch on both sides of the royal highroad a distance of sixteen or seventeen leagues. They are a wealthy and warlike people. The tribe is called Chanca. They boast of their descent from a lion, which they worshipped and held as god, and in their great festivities both before and after their conquest by the Inca kings, two dozen Indians used to appear in the same guise as Hercules, covered with a lionskin with the Indian's head inside the lion's. I have seen this at the celebration of Corpus Christi in Cuzco.

Many other tribes are included under the name Chanca, such as the Hancohuallu, Utunsulla, Uramarca, Villca, and others. They pride themselves on their descent from various parents, some from a spring, others from a lake, and others from a high hill. Each regarded its parent as its god, and offered it sacrifices. The ancestors of those tribes came from a great distance and conquered many provinces until they reached their present dwelling place in the province of Antahuailla, which they won by force of arms, ejecting the former inhabitants and penning up the Quechua Indians, from whom they took much land, in a corner of their territories. They forced them to pay tribute and treated them tyrannously. They performed other notable deeds in which their descendants now take great pride. King Inca Roca was well informed about all this and therefore, on reaching the boundaries of the province of Antahuailla, he sent the Chancas the usual demand that they should submit to the children of the Sun or have recourse to arms. The tribes met to frame their reply to this demand, and held various opinions which divided them into two factions. Some said that it was right that they should accept the Inca as their lord since he was the child of the Sun. Others, including the descendants of the lion, said on the contrary that they should not accept any foreign domination when they themselves were lords of so many subjects and children of a lion; they knew their own descent, and did not believe that the Incas were really descended from the Sun. According to their honor and the deeds of the Chancas, their forefathers, it was more fitting for them to pretend to subject other tribes to themselves than to confess themselves the subjects of the Inca without having made the final test of the strength of their arms: let them therefore resist the Inca and not obey him so pusillanimously as to surrender to him at the first onset without unfurling their banners or showing their weapons on the field.

The Chancas occupied many days in their dispute, at times tending to submit and at times to resist, without reaching agreement. When the Inca knew this, he determined to invade their province to intimidate them, so that they should not take courage and comfort from his gentleness and humanity. He also hoped that they would not derive confidence from their past victories and rashly presume to insult his person, thus forcing him to inflict cruel war and severe punishment on them. He ordered his commanders to enter the province called Antahuailla, and at the same time sent a messenger to the Chancas warning them to acknowledge him as their lord or prepare their throats, for he would put them all to the knife, to end the intolerable obstinacy and rebelliousness they had hitherto evinced. The Chancas, seeing the Inca's determination and knowing that his army included many Quechuas and other tribes they had offended in the past, abated their arrogance and accepted the yoke of the Incas, more through fear of their forces and of the possible vengeance of their armies than out of love for the Inca's laws and good government. Thus they sent to say that they would obey him completely as their lord and would submit to his laws and ordinances. But they did not lose the rancor of their hearts, as we shall see later.

Leaving the necessary officials, the Inca went on to conquer another province called Uramarca, also peopled by Chancas. It is not very large, but thickly settled with brave and warlike tribes, and was not reduced without some defiance and resistance. If their powers had been equal to their gallant and bellicose spirit, they would have made a real resistance, for the Indians of this region were not so docile and friendly to the Incas as those of Cuntisuyu and Collasuyu. But at length the people of Uramarca grudgingly submitted. The Inca then passed to the province and tribe called Hancohuallu and Villca, which the Spaniards call Vilcas, who submitted with equal reluctance to their sway. These tribes, also Chancas, were masters of other provinces which they had conquered by force of arms: their ambition waxed daily greater, and they treated their new subjects with arrogance and oppression. This King Inca Roca ended by reducing them to obedience to him, but they all resented it and their humiliation rankled in their hearts. In both these provinces children were sacrificed to their gods at the chief festivals. When the Inca knew this, he made them a speech in which he persuaded them to worship the Sun and abandon this cruel practice of theirs. To prevent them from perpetuating it in the future, he established a law, which he promulgated from his own mouth so that it might be the more respected, to the effect that if a child were sacrificed they would all be put to the knife and their lands given to other tribes who loved their children and did not sacrifice them. The provinces felt this very deeply, for the devils they regarded as gods had induced them to believe that this form of sacrifice was the most agreeable to them.

From Villca, the Inca bore to the left, or westwards toward the seacoast, reaching one of two very large provinces, both bearing the same name, Sulla, though they are distinguished by one of them being called Utunsulla. These two provinces include many tribes of various names, some numerous, others scanty, which, to avoid prolixity, I shall not enumerate. There were, however, above forty thousand inhabitants, and the Inca spent many months among them—the inhabitants say three years—in attracting them by kindness and favors, so as to avoid an open breach and recourse to arms. But those Indians, aware of their numerical strength and their rough and warlike qualities, came on many occasions to the brink of open war. But the great skill and tact of the Inca stood him in such good stead that at the end of this long time they submitted to serve him, embraced his laws, and admitted the governors and ministers the Inca appointed. He returned to Cuzco after this victory. In the last two provinces conquered by the Inca, Sulla and Utunsulla, mines of silver and quicksilver were discovered some thirty-two years ago. They are very rich and the latter are of great value in founding the silver.

CHAPTER XVI

Prince Yáhuar Huácac and the
meaning of his name.

AFTER SOME years, which King Inca Roca spent in peace and quiet governing his realms, he decided to send his heir, called Yáhuar Huácac to conquer Antisuyu, which is not far from Cuzco to the east. On that side the empire did not extend beyond what was won by the Inca Manco Cápac, as far as the river Paucartampu.

Before proceeding, we had best explain the meaning of the name Yáhuar Huácac and the reason why it was applied to this prince. The Indians say that when he was a child of three or four he wept blood. They cannot say if this happened often or only once. He probably had some disease of the eyes which brought some blood to them. Others say he was born weeping blood, and this they regard as the best version. It might also be that some drops of his mother's blood remained in his eyes, and as they are very credulous and superstitious they thought they were the child's blood. In any case, they affirmed he wept blood. As the Indians were so concerned with witchcraft, they set much more store by the occurrence since the heir to the kingdom was concerned, and regarded it as an ill omen and unhappy augury, fearing some great misfortune or curse laid on the prince by his father the Sun. Such is the meaning of the name Yáhuar Huácac, which is "he who weeps blood" and not "the tears of blood," as some translate it. The weeping occurred when he was a child and not when he had grown up, or because he was defeated and imprisoned, as others say, for no Inca was defeated or imprisoned until the unfortunate Huáscar, who was captured by the traitor Atahuallpa, his bastard brother, as we shall record, if the Most High God allows us to go so far. Neither was he kidnapped as a child, as another historian says, for these are things quite foreign to the veneration in which the Indians held their Incas. The guardians and servants appointed to serve and protect the prince would never have shown such neglect as to permit him to be kidnapped, nor would any Indian have been so bold as to do so, even if he could. On the contrary, if such a thing had occurred to him, he would have thought that the very idea of it, let alone any attempt to carry it out, would cause the earth to open and swallow him and all his family, town, and province. For, as we have said elsewhere, they adored their kings as gods, and as children of their god the Sun, and held them in the highest veneration, much greater than any other heathens held their gods.

Like the augury of weeping blood and perhaps in confirmation of it, another superstition occurs to me; and as it concerns the eyes it is obviously to the point. The Indians gazed at the eyes and the flickering of the upper and lower eyelids, whence the Incas and all their subjects drew good or ill auguries according to which eyelid twitched. It was a good omen if the upper lid of the left eye twitched: they said the eye would see things of joy and happiness. But it was a vastly better augury if the right eyelid twitched, for it promised that they would see very happy things, prosperity, plenty, pleasure, and peace beyond all belief. If on the contrary the lower eyelids twitched, the right-hand one indicated grief, and would see things that would bring pain and grief, though not to excess. But the twitching of the lower left eyelid was the height of misfortune, threatening an infinite number of tears, and that they would behold the saddest and unluckiest things imaginable. They had such faith in these auguries that, when this last one occurred, they would burst into bitter weeping as if they already found themselves in the midst of all the ills they feared, and to avoid perishing from bemoaning the evils they had still not seen, they had a remedy as ridiculous as the augury itself. This was to take a stalk of straw, wet it with spittle and press it against the lower eyelid. They then consoled themselves by saying that the straw so placed cut off the tears they feared they would weep and so undid the evil omen of the twitching. They had almost the same belief about buzzing in the ears, but I will not repeat it as it is not so much to the point as the superstition about the eyes: I can warrant having seen both.

King Inca Roca determined, as we have said, to send his son to conquer Antisuyu, and ordered the preparation of fifteen thousand soldiers with three commanders who were to be the prince's companions and advisers. He instructed him carefully in everything that was to be done before sending him. The prince successfully reached the river Paucartampu and advanced beyond to Challapampa, reducing the few Indians found in those parts. Thence he passed to Pillcupata where he ordered four towns of settlers to be planted. From Pillcupata he went on to Havisca and Tunu, which are the first coca farms the Indians had (this is the herb the Indians value so greatly). The estate called Havisca afterwards belonged to my lord Garcilaso de la Vega and he did me the favor of granting it to me for life, but I lost it by coming to Spain. To enter the valleys where coca is grown, a pass called Cañac-Huay is used. It has a drop five leagues long on an almost perpendicular slope, the mere sight of which inspires fear and horror, not to mention the climbing of it, for it goes up winding first to one side then to the other like a snake.

CHAPTER XVII

The idols of the Anti Indians and the conquest of the Charcas.

IN THESE provinces of the Antis they commonly worshipped as gods tigers and great serpents called *amaru*. These are much thicker than a man's thigh and twenty-five or thirty feet long. Others are smaller. The Indians worshipped them all for their monstrous size. They are stupid and do no harm. They say that a witch put a spell on them to prevent them from doing harm: before they were very fierce. They worshipped the tiger for his ferocity and courage. They said that the serpents and tigers were the natives of those parts, and as lords of it, deserved to be worshipped; the Indians themselves were new arrivals and strangers. They also worshipped the herb called *cuca,* or coca as the Spaniards say.

On this expedition Prince Yáhuar Huácac added nearly thirty leagues of land to the empire, though it was thinly settled. He did not go beyond because of the great belt of heath, bog, and swamp that lies there on the edge of the province properly called Anti, whence the whole area is called Antisuyu. After the conquest the prince returned to Cuzco. His father the king then ceased to embark on new conquests, for toward Antisuyu, or eastwards, there was nothing left to conquer, and westwards, what is called Cuntisuyu was also all reduced, and the limit of the empire reached the Southern Sea on that side. So that from east to west they had more than a hundred leagues of land at the level of Cuzco, and from north to south, over two hundred leagues. Over all this area the Indians busied themselves with building royal palaces and making gardens, baths, and pleasure houses for the Inca. They also made storehouses on the royal highways where supplies, arms, and clothing for the common people were kept.

After some years of peace, King Inca Roca determined to make a famous expedition in person, by going to complete the conquest of the great provinces called Charcas, which his father Inca Cápac Yupanqui had begun to conquer in the district of Collasuyu. He ordered thirty thousand warriors to be prepared, an army greater than any raised by his predecessors. He named six commanders, as well as captains and officers of lower rank, and ordered Prince Yáhuar Huácac to stay and govern the kingdom advised by four other Incas.

The Inca left Cuzco by the royal highway to Collasuyu. He collected soldiers prepared by all the provinces on the way, and reached the borders of the provinces of Chuncuri, Pucuna, and Muyumuyu, which were nearest to his dominions. He sent them messengers, warning them that he had come to reduce those tribes to live under the laws of his father the Sun, and to recognize him as god, and to abandon their idols of wood and stone, and the many wicked abuses they committed against natural law and human life. The natives waxed wroth: their young and warlike captains took arms with great fury, declaring it was a strange and cruel thing to deny them their own natural gods and force them to adore others, to repudiate their laws and customs, and to submit to those of the Inca, who took land from his vassals and imposed tributes and taxes on them, and even treated them as slaves—all of which was not to be tolerated. They would not have it, but all preferred to die in defence of their gods, their country, and their freedom.

CHAPTER XVIII

The reasoning of their elders and how they received the Inca.

THE ELDEST and most prudent members of the tribe reminded them that they had long known that the Incas' laws were good and their government mild, since neighboring tribes had submitted years before: the Incas treated their subjects like their own children, and not like vassals at all, and the lands they had taken were those that were not needed by the Indians, but left unused because the latter could not till them. The crops from these lands, which were tilled at the Incas' expense, formed the tribute that was levied. The Indians did not pay it; on the contrary, the Inca gave them everything of his that was left over after meeting the needs of his armies and court. As a proof of all this it was only necessary to consider dispassionately how much better off the vassals of the Inca now were than they had been, how much richer and more prosperous, quiet, pacific, and civilized. The disputes and quarrels they had engaged in for trivial causes had ceased. Their property was better protected from robbers, their wives and children from fornicators and adulterers. In short, the whole state was assured that no wrong would be done to rich or poor, great or small. Let them note that many provinces touching those of the Inca had remarked these benefits and freely offered to submit to their empire and overlordship in order to experience the mildness of their government. As they were well aware of all this, they would do well to act in the same way, for it was better and safer to appease the Inca by granting his demands than to provoke him to indignation and wrath by refusing them. If later they had to surrender and obey by force of arms and lose the Inca's favor, it would be much better to secure that favor now by submitting in a friendly fashion. Let them consider that this was the safest policy since it would preserve their lives and property, and their wives and children. As to their gods, reason should show them that the

Sun was more deserving of worship than their idols, without any need for the Inca to tell them. So let them incline themselves and accept the Inca as lord and the Sun as god, for honor and profit was to be gained from both. With these and other similar reasons the elders calmed the young men to such good purpose that all by common consent went out to receive the Inca. The youths with their weapons in their hands and the elders with gifts and presents of the produce of their country, which they said they brought as a token that they delivered the land into the Inca's hands. The young men said they brought their arms in order to serve in the Inca's army as loyal subjects and to assist him to win new provinces.

The Inca received them very graciously. He ordered garments to be presented to the elders. The foremost were given the Inca's own garments as a mark of special favor, the rest common clothes. The captains and youths were permitted to offer a contingent of five hundred in order to show the Inca's appreciation of their demonstration of good will. These were not to be selected or nominated by favor, lest those rejected should think themselves wronged, but chosen by lot, and to content the rest they were told that they could not all be accepted lest their land be left empty and undefended. The Indians, both young and old, were made so proud and happy by these honors and favors, that they all began to acclaim the Inca aloud, saying: "You have indeed acted like a child of the Sun; you alone deserve to be called king. Very properly you are called the lover of the poor, since we had scarcely become your subjects when you loaded us with honors and favors. May the Sun your father bless you, and the peoples of all the four corners of the earth obey and serve you, for you are worthy of the title of Çapa Inca, or sole Lord." With these and similar blessings King Inca Roca was adored by his new subjects. Having appointed the necessary officials, he passed on to reduce other nearby provinces, such as Misqui, Sacaca, Machaca, Caracara, and others as far as Chuquisaca, which is now called Silver City. All are of the Charca race, though they are of different tribes and tongues. They were all reduced to obedience by King Inca Roca as easily as those we have mentioned. On this expedition, the empire was extended above fifty leagues north and south and as many more east and west. Leaving there, according to ancient custom, the officials necessary to implant his idolatry and set up the adminstration of his treasury, he returned to Cuzco. He dismissed his armies to their respective provinces, as he had recruited them. The captains received honors and favors.

This done, he decided to rest from his conquests and attend to the peaceful government of his realms. In this way he spent the remaining years of his life, though we cannot say how many they were. On his death, he had lost nothing of the goodness formerly showed by his forefathers, but rather imitated them in every possible way, both in extending the empire and in rewarding and benefiting his subjects. He founded schools where the *amautas* taught such sciences as they knew, and he made his palace near them, as we shall see in due course. He established laws and solemn judgments: as Padre Blas Valera wrote them down in detail I will say what he has written, and they are certainly noteworthy. He was mourned unusually by all his people, and his body was embalmed according to the custom of the kings. He left Yáhuar Huácac as his heir—the son of his legitimate wife and sister Mama Mícay. He left many other children, both legitimate and bastards.

CHAPTER XIX

Some laws made by King Inca Roca; the schools he founded in Cuzco, and some of his sayings.

WHAT Padre Blas Valera, that great investigator of the affairs of the Incas, says of this king is that he reigned nearly fifty years and established many laws of which the following he considers to be the most important. It was proper that the sons of the common people should not learn the sciences, and that these should be restricted to the nobility: otherwise the populace would grow overweening and overthrow the republic. It was sufficient that the common people should learn the trades of their parents. Thieves, murderers, adulterers, and incendiaries should be hanged without mercy. Children should serve their parents until the age of twenty-five, after which they should apply themselves to the service of the republic. Padre Valera says he was the first to build schools in the royal city of Cuzco where the *amautas* taught the sciences they knew to the Inca princes, to those of royal blood, and to the nobility of the empire. As they had no book-learning, the teaching was by practice, daily use, and experience, and in this way they learned the rites, precepts, and ceremonies of their false religion and came to understand the reason and basis of their laws and privileges, the number of them, and their true interpretation. They attained the knowledge of how to govern and became more civilized and better skilled in the art of war. They learnt about the times and seasons of the year and could record and read history from the knots. They learned to speak with elegance and taste, and to bring up their children and govern their houses. They were taught poetry, music, philosophy, and astrology, or such little as was known of these sciences. The masters were called *amautas,* "philosophers" or "wise men," and were held in high veneration. Padre Blas Valera says all these things were instituted as laws by this king Inca Roca, and that his great-grandson Inca Pachacútec greatly encouraged, clarified, and extended them, adding many new laws. He also adds that Inca Roca used to consider the greatness of the sky and its brilliance and beauty, and often said that this showed that Pachacámac, or God, was a most powerful king in the sky, since he had so beautiful a dwelling. He also said: "If I had to adore anything that is here below on earth, I would adore the wise and discreet man who stands above everything else on earth. Yet he is born as a little child, grows, and dies at the last. Yesterday he had his beginning and today he has his ending. And he who cannot overcome death, or recover the life that death takes away from him, should not be worshipped." This is quoted from Padre Blas Valera.

CHAPTER XX

The seventh king, the Inca "Weeping-Blood,"
his fears and his conquests, and the
disgrace of the prince.

O N THE death of King Inca Roca, his son Yáhuar Huácac assumed the crown. He governed the kingdom with justice, piety, and mildness, caring for his subjects and doing them all the good he could. His desire was to sustain the property his forefathers had handed down to him without seeking new conquests or engaging in disputes, for owing to the ill omen of his name and the forebodings that daily surrounded him, he feared some untoward event and dared not risk trying his fortune for fear of provoking the anger of his father the Sun who might visit him with some grave chastisement, as the omens said. Fearing this, he passed some years, desiring peace and quiet for himself and his neighbors; and in order not to be idle, he visited his realms once, twice, and thrice. He sought to enrich them with splendid buildings. He favored his subjects in general and in particular. He treated them with greater affection and love than his predecessors had shown, as a result of the fear he felt. Thus nine or ten years passed by. But not to seem pusillanimous and to avoid being remembered among all the Incas as a coward who did not increase the empire, he resolved to send a force of twenty thousand soldiers to the southwest of Cuzco to the coast beyond Arequipa, where his ancestors had left unconquered a large though thinly peopled strip of land. He chose as commander-in-chief his brother Inca Maita, who, after being general of this expedition, was always known as Apu Maita, meaning Captain General Maita. He named four seasoned Incas as commanders. The Inca did not dare to take the field in person. Though he greatly desired to do so, he could not decide to go, for his evil omen concerning warlike deeds placed him on such stormy waves of doubt that when the swell of desire drove him forward the ebb of fear drew him back. Because of these fears he named his brother and officers, who completed the conquest briefly and with good fortune and added to the Inca empire everything from Arequipa to Tacoma, which is called Collasuyu and is the boundary and coastal limit of what is today called Peru. The land is broad and narrow and thinly populated, so that the Incas took longer to travel through it than to reduce it to their command.

When the conquest was completed, they returned to Cuzco and reported what had been done to the Inca Yáhuar Huácac. Encouraged by the successful outcome of this campaign, he determined to undertake a conquest of greater honor and fame by adding to his empire some large provinces still unconquered in the district of Collasuyu, by name Caranca, Ullaca, Llipi, Chica, and Ampara. These were both large and thickly populated with brave and warlike peoples. Consequently the previous Incas had not undertaken this conquest by force of arms, not wishing to destroy these untamed and savage tribes, but hoping that they would gradually become tamer and more civilized, and take to the rule and overlordship of the Incas after seeing from the experience of neighboring tribes that their rule was as mild, clement, and beneficial to their subjects as all those who made trial of it discovered.

The Inca Yáhuar Huácac was full of anxiety about the conquest of these provinces. Torn between fear and hope, he sometimes foresaw success such as had attended the expedition of his brother Apu Maita, and sometimes mistrusted the outcome because of his unlucky omen. On account of this he did not dare to risk the dangers of any military undertaking. Thus beset by worry and anguish, he turned his attention to other cares within his family circle which for some time had caused him pain and grief. His eldest son, who would inherit his dominions, was of an unmanageable disposition. Since a child, he had shown himself harsh and cruel, ill-treating boys of his own age whose company he kept and showing signs of roughness and cruelty. Although the Inca made every effort to correct him, and hoped that he would develop self-control as he grew older and lose the wildness of his character, this hope seemed no longer justified, for as he grew older his disposition seemed more rather than less fierce. This caused the Inca, his father, very great anguish, for as all his ancestors had prided themselves on humanity and mildness, it was very grievous to him to see the prince so different. He tried to alter his son by persuasion and by reminding him of the examples of his forefathers, hoping he would come to admire them. He also upbraided the prince and showed him disfavor. But all this was to little or no purpose, for evil inclinations in the great and powerful seldom or never admit of correction.

Thus it happened that all the antidotes applied to the prince's evil disposition themselves turned to poison. His father the Inca saw this, and decided to disgrace him and banish him, with the object of disinheriting him if the disgrace did not bring about any improvement in his character, and choosing another of his sons who followed more after the pattern of his ancestors to succeed. He proposed in this to follow the custom of some of the provinces of the empire where the best-loved sons were those who succeeded; and he wished to apply this rule to his own case, though it had never been followed by the Incas. Consequently he ordered the prince, who was then nineteen, to be excluded from his house and court and taken to some fine pasture lands called Chita, just over a league to the east of the city: I have often been there. There were many flocks belonging to the Sun there, and the Inca ordered the prince to graze them with the shepherds. The prince had no recourse but to accept the banishment and disfavor visited on him to punish his wild and warlike spirit, and duly set about the task of tending the flocks with the other shepherds, and watched the flocks of the Sun, and the fact that they were of the Sun was a consolation to the sad Inca. The disgraced prince performed this task for three years and more, where we shall leave him to bide his time. He will give us much to relate, if we can tell the story well.

CHAPTER XXI

A warning given by an apparition
to the prince to be conveyed to his father.

T HE INCA Yáhuar Huácac had thus exiled his eldest son: the name of
the latter while he was a prince is unknown, for the name he was later
given completely expunged it, and as they had no writing, everything that
was not entrusted to memory by tradition was completely forgotten forever. The Inca therefore decided to abandon all thought of war and the
conquest of new provinces and attend only to the government and peace
of his kingdom. He would no longer keep his son at a distance and out of
sight, but have him at hand and try to improve his disposition, and if this
did not avail, seek other remedies, though everything he could think of,
such as confining him in perpetual imprisonment or disinheriting him and
choosing another in his place, seemed violent and uncertain, owing to the
novelty and importance of the case. Such solutions implied the loss of the
divinity of the Incas, who were held to be divine children of the Sun, and
his subjects would not have agreed to this punishment or any other
against the prince.

In this state of anguish and care, which deprived him of rest and peace
of mind, the Inca spent more than three years, during which time nothing
of note occurred. He twice sent four of his kinsmen to visit the kingdom,
assigning to each the provinces to be visited. He bade them see to the
works that required to be done for the Inca's honor and the common
benefit of his subjects—building new irrigation channels, erecting store
houses, palaces, forts,[1] bridges, roads, and other such works. But he himself dared not leave the capital, where he occupied himself with celebrating the festivals of the Sun and other annual events and in doing justice
for his subjects.

At the end of this long spell, the prince one day shortly after noon
entered his father's palace when he was least expected, alone and un-
attended as befitted one in disgrace. He sent to say that he was there and
had a certain mission which he must discharge. The Inca angrily replied
that he was to go away to his appointed place of residence, unless he

---

[1] Reading *fuertes* for *fuentes*.

wished to be put to death for disobedience to the royal command, for he knew that no one could disregard this, however trivial the thing commanded. The prince answered that he had not come to break his command but in obedience to another Inca as great as he, who had bidden him say certain things that it was of great importance he should know: if he wished to hear them, let him give permission for the prince to enter and tell them, if not, the latter would have fulfilled his mission by returning to the one who had sent him and reporting the answer.

The Inca, hearing mention of another lord as great as himself, ordered him to be admitted to see what nonsense this was and to find who it was who sent him messages by his exiled and disgraced son. He wished to investigate these new heresies and punish them. The prince, brought before his father, said:

"Sole Lord, know that as I was lying down today at noon, I do not know if asleep or awake, under a great rock there is in the fields of Chita, where by your bidding I tend the sheep of our father the Sun, a man appeared before me in a strange garb, and in features different from us, for he had a beard on his chin more than a palm long and his dress was long and loose and covered him down to his feet. He said to me: 'Nephew, I am a child of the Sun and brother to the Inca Manco Cápac and the Coya Mama Ocllo Huaco, his wife and sister, the first of your forefathers. I am therefore the brother of your father and of you all. I am called Viracocha Inca. I come from the Sun, our father, to bid you warn the Inca, my brother, that most of the provinces of Chinchasuyu subject to his empire and others not subject to him are in rebellion and have brought together many people to come with a powerful army and overthrow his throne and destroy our imperial city of Cuzco. Go then to the Inca, my brother, and tell him from me to prepare, forearm, and take the steps necessary to meet the emergency. In particular I tell you that in any adversity that may befall you, fear not that I shall fail you, for I will always succor you as my own flesh and blood. Therefore do not hesitate to undertake any deed, however great it seems, that befits the majesty of your line and the greatness of your empire, for I shall always he ready to favor and protect you, and will seek the aid you may need.' Having said these words," said the prince, "the Inca Viracocha disappeared, and I saw him no more. I took the road to Cuzco, to tell you what he bade me say."

CHAPTER XXII

*The discussions of the Incas about
the apparition's message.*

T HE INCA Yáhuar Huácac was so angry and embittered against his son
that he was unwilling to believe him. He told him that he was an
arrogant madman who claimed that the nonsense he had imagined was a
revelation of his father the Sun; let him return at once to Chita and never
leave it again, under pain of his father's wrath. So the prince went back to
guard his flocks, more deeply in his father's disgrace than ever. The Incas
closest to the king, his brothers and uncles who had access to his presence,
being much addicted to superstitions and auguries, especially dreams,
took quite a different view of the prince's story, and told the Inca that the
message and warning from his brother Inca Viracocha should not be disregarded, since he had said that he was a child of the Sun and brought the
message from him. It could hardly be credited that the prince should have
imagined such a speech taking the Sun's name in vain: it would have been
sacrilege merely to imagine it, let alone recount it before his father, the
king. They should therefore examine the prince's words one by one, make
sacrifices to the Sun and take omens to see if they forbode ill or well, and
take such steps as were necessary in so grave a matter. To leave it unheeded was not only to run a risk, but also to appear to scorn their common father, the Sun, who had sent the warning, and his son, the Inca
Viracocha, who had brought it; it was in fact to heap error upon error.

The Inca, out of the hatred he bore his son for his ill disposition, was
reluctant to accept the advice his kinsmen gave him. He declared that no
notice ought to be taken of a raving madman's words: instead of mend-
ing his ways and checking the violence of his character, the prince had
produced new follies. On this account and because of his oddness he deserved to be deposed and deprived of his rank as prince and heir to the
kingdom, as the Inca had immediately thought of doing; and they ought
to choose one of his brothers who could imitate their ancestors and merit
the title of child of the Sun by his clemency, piety, and mildness. It was
wrong that a madman with wrath and vengeance in his heart should destroy with the knife of his cruelty what all the past Incas had added to the
empire with mildness and benefits; let them recall that it was more important to attend to this and seek a remedy than to attend to the foolish

words of a raving lunatic, which were such as to show the source they came from. If his son had not obtained authority for his folly by saying that his mission was from a child of the Sun, he would have been beheaded for breaking the sentence of exile imposed on him. He therefore ordered them not to discuss the matter, but to keep perpetual silence about it, for it angered him even to remember the subject of the prince. He, the Inca, knew what was to be done with him.

On the orders of the king, the Incas were silent and spoke no more of the matter, though inwardly they continued to fear some untoward event. These Indians, like all heathens, were much addicted to auguries, and paid special attention to dreams, particularly if the dreams happened to be those of the king or the heir or the high priest, who were regarded among them as gods and great oracles. The diviners and wizards asked them to tell their dreams to be explained and interpreted, if the Incas themselves did not say what they had dreamed.

CHAPTER XXIII

The rebellion of the Chancas;
their ancient deeds.

THREE MONTHS after the dream of Prince Viracocha Inca—this name was afterwards given to the prince on account of the apparition he saw—there came news, albeit unconfirmed, of the rising of the provinces of Chinchasuyu from Antahuailla onwards. This is a distance of forty leagues to the north of Cuzco. The news came from no definite source, but as a confused and sinister rumor, as often happens in such cases. So although Prince Viracocha had dreamed it and the news corresponded to his dream, the king took no notice, regarding it as tittle-tattle and the memory of the past dream which seemed almost forgotten. A few days later the same news circulated once more, still doubtful and confused, for the enemy had closed the roads with great care so that their rising should remain unknown and they could appear at Cuzco before their coming was known. The third rumor then arrived, and it was definite. The tribes called Chanca, Uramarca, Villca, Utunsulla, Hancohuallu, and others of their neighbors had rebelled and slain the governors and royal officials.

They were coming against the city with an army of more than forty thousand warriors.

These tribes are the ones we have mentioned as having accepted the rule of King Inca Roca rather from fear of his arms than love for his government, and as we remarked, they preserved a hatred and rancor against the Incas which they were to reveal when the opportunity offered. Finding the Inca Yáhuar Huácac so unwarlike, but rather intimidated by the ill omen of his name and scandalized and bewildered by the cruel disposition of his son, Prince Inca Viracocha, and having learnt something of the renewed displeasure of the king toward his son, though the cause was not known, and of the great disfavor into which the latter had fallen, they regarded it as the best occasion to show their hostility toward the Inca and the hatred they felt for his rule and dominion. So with the greatest possible speed and secrecy they sent out the summons to war and roused their neighbors. Between them all a powerful army of over thirty thousand warriors was raised and it marched in the direction of the imperial city of Cuzco. The instigators of the rising who had stirred up the other lords of vassals were three leading Indians, the *curacas* of three great provinces of the Chanca tribe (many other tribes are included under the same name). The first was Hancohuallu, a youth of twenty-six, the next Túmay Huaraca, and the third Astu Huaraca. These last were brothers and relatives of the first. The ancestors of the three kinglets had been engaged in perpetual war before the time of the Incas against the neighboring tribes, and especially against the people called Quechuas, under which five large provinces are comprised. They had crushed these and other neighbors, and treated them roughly and tyrannically, for which reason the Quechuas were glad to become subjects of the Incas and accepted their rule readily and with affection, as we have said, in order to be rid of the insolence of the Chancas. The latter, on the other hand, regretted that the Incas had put an end to their doughty deeds, and had reduced them from lords of vassals to tributaries. They nursed the ancient hatred inherited from their fathers, and made the present rebellion, thinking that they could easily conquer the Inca because of the suddenness of the attack they had planned, and the state of unpreparedness they imagined they would find him in. They fancied he would be without warriors and that a single victory would make them masters, not only of their ancient enemies, but also of all the Inca empire.

With this hope they summoned their neighbors, both those subjected to the Incas and the rest, promising them a great share of the spoils. It was easy to persuade them, both because of the enormous prize that was offered and because of the ancient reputation of the Chancas as valiant warriors. They chose Hancohuallu as captain general. He was a valiant Indian. His two commanders were the two brothers, and the other *curacas* were leaders and captains of the host, which marched at all speed in search of Cuzco.

CHAPTER XXIV

The Inca abandons the city; the prince saves it.

INCA YÁHUAR HUÁCAC was bewildered by the confirmation that his enemies were on their way. He had never believed such a thing could happen. The experience of the Incas had always been that of all the provinces they had conquered and added to their empire none had rebelled from the time of the first Inca Manco Cápac till the present. Because of this uncertainty and because of his hatred for the prince, his son, who had foretold the rebellion, he had not wanted to believe it could happen or to take the advice of his kinsmen, since passion had blinded his understanding. Now he found himself submerged and had no time to call men together to go out against the enemy and no garrison in the city to hold them off until help arrived. He therefore decided to give way to the fury of the rebels and withdraw toward Collasuyu, where he knew his life would be safe because his subjects were noble and loyal. With this intent he withdrew with the few Incas who could follow him, and reached the ravine called Muina, which is five leagues south of the city. There he halted to discover what the enemy was doing on the road and how far he had advanced.

The city of Cuzco was defenceless in the absence of the king. No captain or leader dared even speak, much less consider defending it, but all sought safety in flight. Those who could scattered in various directions, according to what they thought would be most likely to save their lives. Some of the fugitives came upon Prince Viracocha Inca and told him the news of the rebellion of Chinchasuyu, and how his father, the Inca, had retreated toward Collasuyu, thinking there was no possibility of resisting the enemy because of the suddenness of their onslaught.

The prince greatly regretted that his father should have withdrawn and left the city unprotected. He ordered his informants and some of the shepherds he had with him to return to the city and tell all the Indians they met on the roads and those still left in the city that everyone who could was to try to follow the Inca their lord, with whatever arms they could find. He would do the same, and they must pass his order on from one to another. Having given this order, Prince Viracocha set out to follow his father by a short cut, without entering the city. Hastening, he came upon the Inca in the Muina ravine, for he had still not left the place. Covered with sweat and dust, with a spear he had snatched up on the way in his hand, he presented himself before the king and with a grave and sorrowful face said:

"Inca, why do you let news, whether true or false, that a few of your subjects have rebelled cause you to abandon your palace and court, and turn your back on enemies you have not even seen? How can you bear to deliver the house of your father, the Sun, to enemies who will tread in it with shoes on their feet and commit there the abominations your ancestors taught them to abandon, sacrifices of men, women, and children, and such bestialities and sacrileges? What regard have we for the virgins dedicated as brides of the Sun, with the observance of perpetual virginity, if we leave them unprotected for a brutal and bestial enemy to wreak his will upon them? What honor have we gained if we permit these iniquities to save our lives? I do not want to save my life, and therefore I shall return to take my stand before the enemy, and lose it before he enters Cuzco. I will not live to see the abominations the barbarians will commit in the imperial and sacred city the Sun and his children founded. Those who wish to follow me, come now, and I will show them how to exchange a shameful life for an honorable death."

Having said this with great grief and feeling, he retraced his steps toward the city, without stopping either to eat or drink. The Incas of the royal blood, who had set out with the king, together with their brothers and many nephews and cousins and many other relatives, to the number of over four thousand, all returned with the prince. Only the aged and incapable stayed with his father. On the way they came across many who were fleeing the city. They called on them to return, and encouraged them by telling them the prince Inca Viracocha had returned to defend the city and the house of his father the Sun. With this news the Indians so took heart that all those who were running away returned, especially the stout-hearted. These called to others across the fields, passing the word from hand to hand that the prince had come back to hold the city. The news so stirred them that they returned with great relief to die by the prince's side. His courage and energy were such that they infected all his followers.

Thus he entered the city and ordered that the people who had collected should follow him at once. He marched on up the highway to Chinchasuyu, whence his enemies were coming, so as to take up a position between them and the city. His intention was not to resist them, for he thought his forces were insufficient, but to die fighting before the foe entered the city and trod its streets with their barbarian and victorious feet, without respect for the Sun, which was what touched him most deeply. And as Inca Yáhuar Huácac whose life we are recounting ended his reign here, as we shall see, I thought it right to cut the thread of this story to divide his deeds from those of his son Inca Viracocha. I shall insert information about the government of the empire to vary the story and prevent it from running all on one theme. This done, we will return to the deeds of Prince Viracocha, which were very great.

End of the Fourth Book

BOOK
FIVE *of the*
FIRST PART

It describes how they divided and tilled the land; the tribute paid to the Inca and the provision of arms and supplies for warfare; how they clad their subjects; they had no beggars; laws and ordinances in favor of their subjects and other matters of note; the victories and liberality of Prince Inca Viracocha, their eighth king; the deposition of his father; the flight of a great lord; the prophecy of the coming of the Spaniards.

It contains twenty-nine chapters.

CHAPTER I

How they increased the agricultural land and divided it among their vassals.

HEN THE Inca had conquered any kingdom or province and established the form of government in its towns and the way of life of the inhabitants in accordance with their idolatrous religion and their laws, he ordered that the agricultural land should be extended. This implies, of course, the area under maize. For this purpose irrigation engineers were brought: some of these were extremely skilled, as is clearly demonstrated by their works, of which some survive today and others have been destroyed leaving only traces behind. These engineers made the necessary irrigation channels, according to the amount of land that could be turned to account: the greater part of Peru is poor in grain-bearing land, and the Incas therefore tried as far as possible to extend what there was. Because the country falls within the torrid zone, irrigation is necessary, and great attention was paid to this: not a grain of maize was sown unless channelled water was available. They also dug channels to water their pastures when the autumn rains were delayed: as they had an infinite quantity of flocks, they had to give their pastures the same attention as their grainlands. The channels for the pastures were destroyed when the Spaniards entered Peru, but traces of them are still to be found.

Having dug the channels, they levelled the fields and squared them so that the irrigation water could be adequately distributed. They built level terraces on the mountains and hillsides, wherever the soil was good; and these are to be seen today in Cuzco and in the whole of Peru. In order to make these terraces they would construct three walls of solid masonry, one in front and one at each end. These sloped back slightly (like all the Indian walls) so as to withstand the weight of earth with which they are filled to the level of the top of the walls. Above the first platform they built another smaller one, and above that another still smaller. In this way the whole hill was gradually brought under cultivation, the platforms being flattened out like stairs in a staircase, and all the cultivable and irrigable land being put to use. If there were rocky places, the rocks were removed and replaced by earth brought from elsewhere to form the terraces, so that the space should not be wasted. The first platforms were large, according to the configuration of the place: they might be one or two or three hundred measures[1] broad and long. The second were smaller and they diminished progressively as they were higher up, until the last might contain only two or three rows of maize plants. This shows how industrious the Incas were in extending the area which could be planted with maize. A water channel was commonly brought fifteen or twenty leagues to water a few measures of soil, so that it should not be wasted.

Having thus extended the cultivable land, each settlement in each province measured all the land assigned to it and divided it into three parts, one for the Sun, one for the king, and one for the inhabitants. In the division care was taken that the inhabitants should have enough to sow for themselves, and rather too much than too little. When the population of a town or province increased, part of the area assigned to the Sun or the Inca was transferred to their subjects, so that the only lands reserved by the king for himself or for the Sun were those which would otherwise have remained ownerless and untilled. The terraces were usually assigned to the Sun and the Inca, since the latter had been responsible for constructing them. In addition to the irrigated maize fields, other land without a supply of water was divided among them for dry farming and sown with crops of great importance, such as three they call *papa, oca,* and *añus.* This land was also divided in due proportion between the Sun, the Inca, and a third part for their subjects, but as it was waterless and of low productivity, it was sown only for a year or two and then rested while another part was sown. In this way the poor soil was kept under control, and there was always an abundance of it for use.

The maize fields were sown every year, and as they were always supplied with water and manure like gardens, they always bore fruit. With the maize they planted a seed rather like rice which they call *quinua*: it also grows in a cold climate.

---

[1] *fanegas de sembradura:* usually the ground needed to sow a *fanega* (1.6 bushels).

CHAPTER II

Their system of agriculture; the festival of tilling the land assigned to the Inca and the Sun.

THEY ALSO had an established system in cultivating the soil. They first tilled the part assigned to the Sun and then that of the widows and orphans and those who were unable to work owing to age or ill health. The latter were regarded as the poor, and the Inca therefore bade that their land be tilled for them. In each village, or in each quarter, if it were a large village, there were men appointed exclusively to attend to the cultivation of what we shall call the poor. These men were called *llactaca-mayu,* "aldermen or councillors of a town." When the time came to plough, or sow, or bring in the harvest, it was their duty to go out at night and climb a sort of watch tower or beacon they had for the purpose and sound a trumpet or horn to attract attention, and then announce: "On such and such a day the lands of the disabled are to be tilled: let each attend to the task assigned him." The inhabitants of each quarter knew from traditional practice which land was assigned to them, since it was that of their relatives or nearest neighbors. Each was obliged to take his own food from his home so that the poor should not have the trouble of feeding them. They used to say that the aged, the sick, and widows and orphans had enough troubles of their own, without attending to others. If the poor had no seed, this was supplied from the storehouses, of which we shall speak later. Land belonging to soldiers on campaign was also tilled by the community, like that of the widows, orphans, and poor, for when their husbands were away on military service, wives were reckoned as widows, and received this service as being in need of charity. The children of those killed in war were very carefully brought up until they married.

After the cultivation of the land of the poor, they tilled their own, taking turn and turn about, as the saying is. They then tilled the *curaca's* land, which was always the last to be attended to in each town or province. Once in the time of Huaina Cápac, an Indian *regidor* in a village of the Chachapoyas was hanged for having the land belong to the *curaca,* who was a relative of his, tilled before that of a widow: this was because he had broken the order established by the Inca for tilling the soil, and the gallows were erected on the *curaca's* own land. The Inca ordered that his subjects' land should be given priority over his own, because it was said that prosperity of the subjects redounded to the king's service: if they were poor and needy, they would be of little use in peace or war.

The last land to be cultivated was that assigned to the king. It was tilled communally. All the Indians went out together to the fields of the Inca and of the Sun with great rejoicing and satisfaction. They wore the clothes and adornments they kept for their greatest festivities, covered with gold and silver plates and with feather headdresses. As they ploughed (which was the work that gave them most pleasure) they sang many songs composed in praise of the Incas: their labor thus became a matter for festivity and joy because it was performed in the service of their god and their kings.

Inside the city of Cuzco, on the skirts of the hill where the fortress is, there used to be a large terrace of many *fanegas* of soil: it may still be there today unless it has been built over. It is called Collcampata. The quarter in which it is takes its name from the name of the terrace, which was the special and chief jewel of the Sun, for it was the first to be dedicated by the Incas to him in the whole empire. This terrace was tilled and cared for by those of the royal blood, and none but Incas and Pallas could work in it. The work was done amidst the greatest celebrations, especially at ploughing time, when the Incas came dressed in all their insignia and finery. The songs they recited in praise of the Sun and their kings were all based on the meaning of the word *hailli,* which means triumph over the soil, which they ploughed and disembowelled so that it should give fruit. The songs included elegant phrases by noble lovers and brave soldiers on the subject of their triumph over the earth they were ploughing. The refrain of each verse was the word *"hailli,"* repeated as often as was necessary to mark the beats of a certain rhythm, corresponding to the movements made by the Indians in raising their implements and dropping them, the more easily to break the soil.

As a plough they use a stick two yards long: its front is flat and its back rounded, and it is about four fingers thick. It has a point to pierce the ground and, half a vara above it, a footrest made of two sticks tightly lashed to the main shaft. On this the Indian sets his foot and forcibly drives the plough in up to the footrest. They work in bands of seven or eight, more or less, according to family or neighborhood groups. By all lowering their ploughs at once they can raise clods of earth so large that anyone who has not seen it could hardly credit it. It is remarkable to see them perform such a considerable task with such weak implements, and they work with great speed and ease and never lose the rhythm of the song. The women work opposite the men and help to lift the clods with their hands, turning the grass roots upwards so that they dry and die, and the harrowing requires less effort. They also join with their husbands in the singing, especially in the *hailli* chorus.

The choirmaster of the cathedral in Cuzco, taking a liking to the Indian songs and music, composed a part-song in the year '51 or '52 for the feast of Corpus Christi, in perfect imitation of the Inca singing. Eight mestizo boys, schoolfellows of mine, appeared in Indian dress, each with a plough in his hand, and acted the song and *hailli* of the Indians in the procession, the whole choir joining in the chorus. It greatly pleased the Spaniards, and the Indians were delighted to see the Spaniards solemnize the festivity of our God, whom they call Pachacámac (or "him who gives life to the universe"), with their own songs and dances.

I have mentioned the special festivity of the Incas when the terrace dedicated to the Sun was harrowed since I saw it done two or three times as a child, and it will give an idea of the festivities that took place throughout Peru when the land of the Sun and of the Inca was hoed. However, what I saw was said by the Indians to be only a shadow of what used to be done in the days of the Incas.

CHAPTER III

The quantity of soil given to each Indian, and how it was manured.

EACH Indian was given a *tupu*, which is a *fanega*, of land for growing maize: however, this is a *fanega* and a half in Spain. *Tupu* is also applied to a league's distance, and as a verb it means "to measure." Any measure of water, wine, or other liquid is called *tupu*, and so are the long pins the women use to fasten their garments with. A measure of seed has another name, *poccha*, meaning *"fanega."*

A *tupu* of land was enough to maintain a peasant and his wife without family. As soon as they had children, each boy was given a *tupu* and each girl half a *tupu*. When the male children married, the father gave them the measure of land he had received for their support, and if he turned them out of his house, he could not keep the land.

The daughters did not receive their portions when they married, for their land was not regarded as a dowry, but as a means of support. As their husbands were given land for their maintenance, they themselves could not have any; women were not provided for after marriage, but only before marriage and if they became widows. Their fathers kept the land assigned to their daughters if they needed it; otherwise it was returned to the community for no one could buy it or sell it.

They dealt with the land for growing other crops without irrigation in the same way as the fields provided for maize growing.

Noblemen, such as the *curacas,* lords of vassals, were given land in proportion to the number of their wives and children, concubines, and servants. Similarly Incas, those of the royal blood, received the best of everything wherever they lived, apart from their common share in the property of the king and of the Sun which they all enjoyed as children of the latter and brothers of the former.

They fertilized the soil by manuring it, and in the valley of Cuzco and almost all the highland area they treated their maize fields with human manure, which they regarded as the best. They go to great trouble to obtain it, and dry it and pulverize it in time for the sowing season. In the whole of Collao, which is more than 150 leagues long, the climate is too cold for growing maize, and they sow potatoes and other vegetables: for this they use the manure of the Peruvian sheep, which they regard as more beneficial than any other.

On the seacoast, from below Arequipa to Tarapacá, a distance of over 200 leagues along the coast, they use no other manure but the dung of sea birds, of which large and small varieties occur on the coast of Peru in such enormous flocks that they seem incredible to anyone who has not seen them. They breed on some uninhabited islands off the coast, where they deposit an amount of dung that is no less incredible. From a distance the heaps of it look like the snowy crests of a range of mountains. In the times of the Inca kings these birds were so carefully watched that no one was allowed to land on the islands during the breeding season under pain of death, so that they should not be disturbed or driven from their nests. It was also illegal to kill them at any season either on the islands or elsewhere, under pain of the same penalty.

Each island was assigned, on the Inca's instructions, to a certain province, or if it was a large island, to two or three provinces. Landmarks were set up to prevent the inhabitants of one province from trespassing in the area assigned to another, and a more detailed division was applied to each section, in which each village had its piece and each householder in

the village his part, according to the quantity of manure he was reckoned
to need. He was prohibited from taking dung from the area allotted to
another village, for this was regarded as theft, nor could he take more
than the quantity allocated to him from his own section, for this was
based on the requirements of his land, and the taking of any in excess of
it was punished as an infringement of the law. Nowadays the manure is
used quite differently. The dung of the sea birds produces great fertility.

In other parts of the same coast, such as the basins of Atica, Atiquipa,
Villacori, Malla, and Chillca, and other valleys, they manure with the
heads of sardines and use nothing else. The natives of the parts we have
named and of others like them live precariously, for they have neither
standing water nor rainfall to irrigate with: it is well known indeed that
along the whole coastline of seven hundred leagues it never rains and
there are no rivers in the places we have named. The country is very hot
and full of sandy wastes, and in order to find sufficient moisture for their
maize, the inhabitants build their villages as near the sea as possible and
clearing away the surface sand on top of the soil, they dig down to the
coastal water level, which in places may be the height of a man and in
places two, or more or less. These places are therefore called *hoyas*, "pits,"
by the Spaniards. Some are large and some are small: the smallest may be
about half a *fanega* and the largest three or four *fanegas*. They are not
ploughed or weeded for this is not necessary. They sow them by means
of stakes of appropriate size: with these they make pits in which they burn
the sardine heads with two or three grains of maize among them. This
is the manure they use when planting in the pits, and they maintain that
any other does more harm than good. And Divine Providence, which
abounds in all things, takes care of the Indians and of the birds of the
coast by causing the sea to produce in due season such a vast quantity of
live sardines that there are enough to eat, to manure the soil, and to load
many ships if they should go there for the purpose. Some say that the
sardines come because they are pursued by skate and other larger fish that
live on them. In any case it is to the advantage of the Indians in providing
manure. The Indians are unable to say who invented the system of pits;
and the inventor must have been necessity, which sharpens the wits, for
as we have said there is a great lack of grain land throughout Peru, and
it may well be believed that the pits were devised in the same way as the
terraces. Thus all the natives sowed what they needed for their sustenance
and there was no need to sell supplies or to hoard them; and they did not
know what want was.

CHAPTER IV

How they shared water for irrigation;
they punished idlers and slackers.

IN DISTRICTS where the quantity of water for irrigation was small, they
divided it proportionately (as they did with everything they shared
out), so that there should be no dispute among the Indians about obtaining it. This was only done in years of scanty rainfall when the need was
greatest. The water was measured, and as it was known from experience
how long it took to irrigate a *fanega* of land, each Indian was accordingly
granted the number of hours supply he needed for the amount of land he
had, with plenty to spare. Water was taken by turns, according to the
order of the plots of land, one after another. No preference was given
to the rich or the nobles, or to favorites or relatives of the *curaca*, or to the
curaca himself, or to royal officials or governors. Anyone who neglected
to irrigate his land at the proper time received an ignominious punishment. He was struck on the back with a stone three or four times in
public, or his arms and legs were whipped with osier switches. This was
the penalty for idleness and slackness which they considered very serious
faults. Idlers were called *mizquitullu*, "soft-bones," from *mizqui*, "sweet,
soft," and *tullu*, "bone."

CHAPTER V

The tribute they paid the Inca and
the reckoning of their bins.

HAVING described how the Incas divided the land and benefited their
subjects, we must now refer to the tribute that was paid to the kings.
The principal tribute was the tilling and fertilizing of the lands assigned
to the Sun and the Inca, the harvesting of whatever crops it produced and
their storage in bins and the royal granaries that existed in each village
for collecting the harvest. One of the principal crops was the *uchu*, which
the Spaniards call *ají*, or otherwise, *pimiento*.

The bins are called *pirua*. They are made of trodden clay mixed with plenty of straw. In Inca times they were very skilfully constructed. Their size varied in proportion to the height of the walls of the building in which they were placed. They were narrow, square, and of one piece, and had to be made with moulds of different sizes. They were of various capacities, some bigger than others, some of thirty *fanegas,* or fifty, one hundred or two hundred, more or less as they were required. Each size of bin was kept in a special building, which it had been made to fit. They were placed against the four walls and also in the middle of the building. An alley was left between the rows of bins so that they could be emptied and filled in turn. Once erected they were not moved. In order to empty a bin little holes about an *ochava* in size were made in the front of it. They were made so that it was possible to tell how many *fanegas* had been taken out and how many were left without measuring them. In this way it could easily be reckoned from the size of the bins how much maize there was in each barn and each granary, and the small holes showed what had been extracted and what remained in each bin. I have seen some of these bins which survived from Inca times, and they were some of the first, since they were in the house of the chosen virgins, the wives of the Sun, and were made for the use of these women. When I saw them, the house belonged to the children of Pedro del Barco, who were schoolfellows of mine.

The shares of the crop assigned to the Sun and to the Inca were stored separately, though in the same granaries. The seeds for sowing were supplied by the owner of the land, the Sun or the king, and so was the maintenance of the Indians, for when they were cultivating the lands of either the Sun or the Inca they were fed from the revenue of the respective owners. In this way the contribution of the Indians was limited to their personal service. The Indians paid nothing to the Inca from the crops they derived from their own land. This is confirmed by Padre Acosta, who says in his Book VI, ch. xv:

The Inca gave a third of the land to the community. It has not been ascertained whether this third was greater or less than those assigned to the Inca or the huacas, but it is certain that care was taken to see that it sufficed for the maintenance of the people. No one owned any of this third as personal property, for the Indians never possessed anything as their own, but always as a special concession from the Inca. The land could thus not be alienated or divided as an inheritance. The communal land was divided annually, and everyone was apportioned a piece sufficient for the maintenance of himself, his wife, and his children. He therefore received more or less from year to year in accordance with the size of his family and with a predetermined scale. Consequently no tribute was paid on the land so divided, since the only form of tribute was the labor required for the cultivation of the land assigned to the Incas and the huacas, and the storage of the harvest in the royal granaries,

etc. Thus far Padre Acosta: he applies the word *huacas* to the land of the Sun because it was sacred.

In the whole of the province called Colla, for a distance of over 150 leagues, the climate is very cold and maize does not grow. A great deal of *quinua*, which is like rice, is grown, as well as other plants and vegetables, which give root crops, including what they call *papa*. This is round and damp, and because of its dampness it easily rots. To preserve it from corruption it is spread on the ground on straw, of which there is a good supply in the fields. It is left out for many nights exposed to the frost, which is severe in that province throughout the year. After it has been repeatedly frozen it is as though cooked, and is then covered with straw and gently and skilfully trampled on so as to squeeze out the natural moisture of the *papa* and the dampness of the frost. When it has been well pressed, it is exposed to the sun and protected from the dew until it is thoroughly dry. Prepared in this way, the *papa* can be kept for a long time, and the name given to it in this form is *chuñu*. All the potatoes produced on the lands of the Sun and of the Inca were treated in this way and kept in the storehouses with the other seeds and vegetables.

CHAPTER VI

Clothing, footwear, and arms were supplied for the warriors.

IN ADDITION to the main tribute which took the form of sowing the soil, cultivating, and harvesting the crops of the Sun and of the Inca, they paid also a second tribute which consisted of clothes, footwear, and weapons for use in time of war and for the poor, that is those who could not work through age or infirmity. In assessing and collecting this second tribute they followed the same system as in all their other affairs. Throughout the mountainous region clothing was made from wool which the Inca supplied from the innumerable flocks belonging to him and to the Sun.

On the llanos, or seacoast, where the climate is hot and wool is not worn, they made cotton cloth from cotton grown on the land of the Sun and of the Inca. All the Indians supplied was their labor. They made three kinds of woolen cloth. The coarsest, called *avasca,* was for the common people. Another finer sort was called *compi,* which was worn by the nobility, such as captains, *curacas,* and other officials: it was made in all colors and patterns with a reed or comb such as is used in making Flanders cloth. It was finished on both sides. Other very fine clothes, also called *compi,* were made for those of the royal blood, such as captains, soldiers, and royal officials in peace or war. The fine cloth was woven in provinces where the natives were most ingenious and expert in its manufacture, and the coarser sort was made elsewhere where the natives were less skilled. All the wool for this cloth was spun by the women, who also wove the coarse cloth called *avasca.* The finer sort was woven by men, for the work is done standing. Both kinds were made by the vassals, and not by the Incas, who did not even make their own clothing. I mention this point because there are those who say that the Incas themselves used to spin. Further on, in describing their method of arming knights, we shall explain what the spinning attributed to the Incas was and the reason for it.

Shoes were made in the provinces where hemp was most abundant, for they were produced from the leaves of the plant called *maguey.* Weapons were also furnished by districts that had the most abundant supply of the necessary materials. In some they made bows and arrows, in others lances and darts, elsewhere clubs and axes, and in others slings and ropes for transport, or shields and targets. These last were the only weapons of defence they knew. In short, each province and tribe supplied whatever it produced, and never needed to import from outside what it lacked, for it had no other obligation. Finally, they paid their tribute without having to leave their homes, for the universal law throughout the empire was that no Indian should be obliged to leave his own country in search of what he had to furnish as tribute. The Incas said that it was unjust to demand of their vassals any articles that they themselves did not produce, and that such demands opened the door to idleness, by driving them to wander from place to place. There were thus four things to be supplied to the Inca—supplies from the royal domains, woolen clothing from the royal flocks, arms, and footwear, according to what was available in each province. These requirements were apportioned with perfect order and system. The provinces that were required to supply cloth on account of their great skill in producing it were discharged from the obligation to supply weapons and footwear, and in the same way any who were required to furnish

more of one thing were relieved of demands for others. The same principle was applied in all matters of taxation so that no one could feel any
cause for grievance, either as an individual or in common as a province.
Because of the mildness of their laws, vassals rallied to the Inca's service
with alacrity and satisfaction, and a famous Spanish historian uses these
words in speaking of the subject: "But the greatest source of wealth of
these barbarous kings lay in the fact that all their vassals were their slaves,
whose labor they disposed of as they pleased, and what is most surprising
is that they treated these vassals with such order and good management
that they never regarded it as servitude, but rather as a happy and fortunate existence." Thus far is taken from another author, whom I am glad
to quote here and I shall have occasion in other places to borrow other
words from this very venerable author. He is Padre José de Acosta, S.J.,
whose authority, like that of other Spanish historians, I desire to avail myself of against the words of slanderers who may accuse me of inventing
fables in favor of my country and my relatives. Such in fact was the tribute
the Indians used to pay their idolatrous kings.

Another sort of tribute was given by the infirm we have called poor:
this was that every so many days they were obliged to deliver some hollow
reeds full of lice to the governors of their villages. It is said that the Incas
demanded this tribute so that no one except those who were exempt from
tribute, should avoid paying something, however poor he might be, and
these were required to pay in lice because they were prevented by their
infirmity from offering personal service, which was the general tribute
everyone paid. It is also said that the chief purpose of the Incas in asking
for this tribute was their zealous love of the disabled poor, forcing them
to remove their lice and clean themselves so that they might not perish
miserably devoured by vermin. Because of this zeal, which the kings displayed in everything, they were called lovers of the poor. The decurions
of tens (whom we have referred to in their place) were obliged to see that
this tribute was paid.

All those of the royal blood, priests and ministers of the temples, *curacas* (who were lords of vassals), all field commanders and captains of
high rank down to centurions (even though not of royal blood), and all
governors, judges, and royal ministers were exempt from the payment of
tribute, so long as they held these offices. So were all soldiers actually engaged in war and youths of less than twenty-five, because below that age
they helped their parents and could not marry, and for a year after marry-
ing they were also exempt from paying tribute. So also old people of fifty
years of age upwards and women, whether spinsters, married, or widows

were exempt, though many Spanish writers insist that they did pay tribute, for they say that everyone worked. They are mistaken: if women worked it was because they wanted to, or to help their parents, husbands, or relatives to fulfil their obligations sooner, and not because they were obliged to pay tribute. The sick were exempt until they completely recovered, and the blind, lame, maimed, and limbless. But the deaf and dumb were not exempt, since they were capable of working, so that of a truth the personal service was a tribute that everyone paid. This is confirmed by Padre Blas Valera, as we shall see; and his words are so like mine that one might seem copied from the other. In the whole of the part dealing with tribute he agrees with me in the same way.

CHAPTER VII

Gold, silver, and other objects of value
were not offered as tribute,
but as presents.

T HE GOLD, silver, and precious stones which the Inca kings possessed in such great quantities, as is well known, were not produced by any enforced tribute that the Indians were obliged to pay, nor were they demanded by the rulers, because such objects were not regarded as necessary either for war or for peace, or prized as property or treasure. As we have said, nothing was bought or sold for gold or silver, and these metals were not used to pay soldiers or expended to supply any wants whatsoever. Consequently they were considered to be something superfluous since they were not good to eat nor useful in obtaining food. They were only esteemed for their brilliance and beauty, to adorn the royal palaces, the temples of the Sun, and the houses of the virgins, as we have seen in their place and shall enlarge upon later. The Incas had discovered quicksilver, but never having found any purpose for it, they did not turn it to advantage: on the contrary, they thought it harmful and prohibited its extraction. Further on, in the proper place, we shall speak of it at greater length.

The gold and silver given to the king thus took the form of presents and not of enforced tribute, for the Indians, then as today, never thought of paying a call on a superior without bringing a present, and if they had nothing else, they would provide a small basket of fresh or fried fruit. The *curacas* or lords of vassals visited the Inca on the chief annual festivals, and especially on that great celebration in honor of the Sun called Raimi, and on occasion of the triumphs that marked the celebration of great victories and the shearing and naming of the heir to the throne and many other occasions during the year when they had audience of the king about their private business or the affairs of their districts, or when the king visited the provinces. On all these occasions they never kissed the Inca's hands without bringing him all the gold, silver, and precious stones that their Indians extracted when they had no work to do, for as the occupation of mining was not necessary to sustain life they only engaged in it when they had no other business to attend to. But as they saw that these articles were used to adorn the royal palaces and temples, places which they valued so highly, they employed their spare time in seeking for gold, silver, and precious stones to present to the Inca and the Sun, their gods.

Besides these treasures, the *curacas* used to offer the king many sorts of precious woods for building the palaces. They also presented him with men who excelled as craftsmen, such as silversmiths, painters, stonemasons, carpenters, and builders: the Incas had skilled men in all these trades, and the *curacas* provided such men for them as being worthy of the royal service. The common people had no need of them, for everyone had all the skills necessary for his own household, such as making clothes and footwear and building a poor hut to live in; in those days the council presented them with a hut ready made, but now each Indian makes his own with the help of his relatives or friends. Thus skilled artisans were quite unnecessary to the poorer people, who only sought to sustain their natural lives and never aimed at the superfluity of things that the powerful require.

In addition to good craftsmen, they offered the Inca savage beasts such as tigers, lions, and bears, and smaller animals like monkeys of various sorts, wild cats, parrots, macaws, and larger birds, such as ostriches, and the bird they call *cuntur,* which is by far the largest of birds there or here. They also presented large and small snakes, such as inhabit the country of the Antis. The biggest, called *amaru,* are twenty-five or thirty feet or more in length. They would also bring great toads and wild lizards. The coastal peoples brought seals and the alligators called caimans which also reach twenty-five or thirty feet in length. In short, there was no creature remarkable for its ferocity, size, or beauty which they did not present together with their gold and silver, implying that the Inca was lord of all those things and everything else they brought him, and to demonstrate the love with which they served him.

CHAPTER VIII

The storing of supplies and their use.

WE MUST now explain how the tribute was kept and on what it was used. Throughout the whole kingdom there were three sorts of storehouses to hold the harvest and tribute. Every village, whether large or small, had two storehouses: one was used to hold the supplies kept for the use of the people in lean years, and the other was used for the crops of the Sun and of the Inca. There were other storehouses at intervals of three leagues on the royal highway, and these now serve the Spaniards as inns or taverns.

For a distance of fifty leagues round the city of Cuzco the crops of the Sun and of the Inca were brought in for the use of the court, so that the Inca might have adequate supplies on hand to entertain the captains and *curacas* who came to see him. A certain proportion of the revenue of the Sun was left in every village within the radius of fifty leagues for the common store of the vassals.

The crops of the other villages, outside the orbit of the capital, were collected in the royal storehouses that existed and thence transferred to the stores on the royal roads where garrisons, arms, clothes, and footwear were kept for the armies that marched along to the four quarters of the world, which they called Tahuantinsuyu. The wayside deposits were well stocked with all these things, and although many companies or regiments of warriors went past, there was always ample for all. Soldiers were not allowed to billet themselves on the villages at the cost of the vassals. The Incas used to say that each village had already paid the appropriate tribute and it was unjust to tax it further: thus there was a law that any soldier who took anything from a vassal, however trifling, should be punished with death. Pedro de Cieza de León mentions this in speaking of the highways in his ch. lx, and uses these words:

The Incas had large and imposing storehouses and deposits for military supplies, for they were so much feared that their subjects dared not fail to provide ample stocks. If anything was lacking, a severe punishment was inflicted, and consequently if anyone who was obliged to travel along the road made bold to enter the fields or dwellings of the Indians they were ordered to be put to death, even though the damage they had done was very small.

Thus far Pedro de Cieza. The Indians used to say that the soldiers were given all they needed so as to prevent their harming anyone in the fields or villages and to ensure that the punishment for doing so was just. As the soldiers used the stores in the wayside deposits, these were replenished from the villages with such system and good order that there was never any lack of supplies. Agustín de Zárate, after speaking of the excellence of the royal highways (which we shall describe in due place) says the following in his Book I, ch. xiv:

Besides the labor and expense of these roads, Huaina Cápac ordered that in the sierra spacious palaces should be built at each stage with lodgings where he and his household and the whole army could be accommodated. On the llanos similar buildings were made, though they could not be so close or numerous as those in the mountains, but had to be placed on the banks of the rivers, which, as we have said, are eight or ten leagues apart, or in places fifteen or twenty. These lodgings are called *tambos,* and the Indians from the surrounding district had to stock and supply them with everything required for their army, not only provisions, but also arms, clothing, and all other requirements. Thus if the Inca wished to rearm and clothe twenty or thirty thousand of his warriors at any of these *tambos,* he could do so without going outside his house. The Inca was accompanied by a great force of warriors with pikes, halberds, clubs, and axes of silver and copper, and some of gold, and with slings and hand-arrows[1] with burnt points,

etc. Thus far Agustín de Zárate, describing the storehouses made by the kings for their armies along the highway.

If the expenses of a war were too great to be borne by the royal revenues, the Inca then laid hands on the property of the Sun, whose legitimate son and universal heir he considered himself to be. The supplies that were not consumed in warfare or by the court were kept in the three kinds of storehouses we have mentioned and distributed in years of want among the people, whose well-being was the first care of the Incas.

Throughout the kingdom the estates of the Sun were applied to the maintenance of the priests and ministers of their idolatry while they officiated in the temples, which they did by weekly rotation. But when they were at home they ate at their own expense, for they too were given

[1] *tiraderas de palma*: a catapulted arrow.

land to till like the ordinary people. The expenditure from the estates of the Sun was thus small in proportion to the extent of its income, and a great deal was therefore left over to assist the Inca in case of need.

CHAPTER IX

They supplied clothing for their subjects; there were no beggars.

JUST AS there was an orderly system for supplying abundant clothing for the armies, so also wool was distributed every two years to all the subjects and the *curacas* in general, so that they could have clothes made for themselves and their wives and children; and the decurions saw to it that they were all dressed. The ordinary Indians had few flocks; even the *curacas* had only enough for themselves and their families. The Sun and the Inca however had innumerable flocks, and the Indians used to say that when the Spaniards reached Peru there was no longer any room to graze. I also have heard my father and his contemporaries tell of the great excesses and enormous waste some of the Spaniards practiced with regard to these flocks; we may perhaps refer to this in its due place. Where the climate was hot, cotton from the royal revenues was distributed for the Indians to dress themselves and their households. Thus all that was required for human life in the way of food, clothes, and footwear was available to all, and no one could call himself poor or beg for alms. In the matter of necessities they were amply supplied, as if they were all rich: as regards superfluities they were all exceedingly poor, for they had no more than they needed. Thus Padre Acosta in speaking of Peru says very briefly and concisely what we have set down with such prolixity. At the end of ch. xv of his Book VI, he says:

The flocks were shorn in due season and everyone was given enough to spin and weave clothes for his family. An inspection was made to see that this was done, and those who neglected it were punished. The wool left over was put in storehouses, which the Spaniards on their arrival found full of wool and all other articles necessary for human life. No thinking person can fail to wonder at this noble and provident system of government, for the Indians, though not believers or Christians, observed after their own fashion the highest and most perfect law of having nothing of their own but providing in abundance every-thing that was necessary for the service of religion and their king and lord.

This is the end of his ch. xv, which he entitles: "The Property of the Inca and Tribute."

In the following chapter in speaking of the crafts of the Indians, where he touches on many of the matters we have mentioned and shall refer to later, he says the following which we have copied literally:

Another excellent thing the Indians of Peru had was that everyone learned from boyhood all the crafts that a man needs to sustain human life. They had no specialized craftsmen such as we have—tailors, cobblers and weavers—but all of them learnt how to make everything they needed for themselves and their houses, and they all supplied their own needs. They could all weave and make clothes, and for this purpose the Inca enabled them to clothe themselves by supplying them with wool. They could all plough the soil and cultivate it with-out needing to call in other laborers. They could tend to their own houses, and the women knew most of all, never living a life of ease, but busying them-selves constantly in their husband's service. There were special and qualified artisans for other crafts which are not concerned with the everyday needs of the individual, for example silversmiths, painters, potters, boatbuilders, account-ants, and musicians, and there were also experts in weaving, embroidery, and building who did special work and were employed by the lords. But among the common people, everyone as we have said attended to all the needs of his house and had no need to pay anyone else for this purpose: it is the same even at the present day. Consequently no one requires the help of another for the immediate needs of his household and person, either for making shoes or clothes, or building a house, or sowing or reaping, or making the tools and implements he uses. In all this the Indians seem to copy the institutions of the monks of old, as described in the lives of the Fathers. They are indeed neither covetous nor extravagant people, but are content to live very simply; and cer-tainly if they had adopted their way of life from free choice and not because they were born to it or from habit, we should have said that it was a very per-fect state of life, and one which could not but be an excellent preparation for receiving the teaching of the Holy Gospel, which is so opposed to pride, cov-etousness and vanity. But preachers do not always adjust the example they set to the doctrine they preach to the Indians.

A little further on, he adds:

It was an inviolable law that none of them changed the dress and habit of his own province even if he moved to another: the Inca regarded this as most im-portant for good government, and it still is, thought less care is taken of it than formerly.

Thus far Padre Acosta. The Indians are very surprised to see the Spaniards change their dress every year and attribute it to pride, presumption, and perdition.

The custom that no one begs for alms was still preserved in my own times. Until 1560, when I left Peru, I never saw in all my journeyings there an Indian man or woman who asked for alms, except an old woman in Cuzco called Isabel: she begged, but it was rather as a pretext to go gossiping from door to door as gypsies do than from need. The Indian men and women used to upbraid her, and in the midst of the shindy would spit on the ground, which is a mark of scorn and abomination: the old woman therefore stopped begging from the Indians and limited herself to the Spaniards. As there was no coined money in my country in those days, she was given maize as alms. This was what she demanded and if she perceived that it was granted readily, she would ask for a piece of meat; and if this was given, some of the beverage they drank; and then with a great deal of backchat and jesting, she would ask for a little coca, which is the greatly esteemed herb the Indians chew: in this way she led an idle and worthless existence.

Nor did the Incas forget wayfarers in their commonwealth: on the royal and ordinary roads they had lodging houses built, which they called *corpahuaci*, where food and necessities for the journey were supplied from the royal storehouses that existed in every village. If the traveller fell sick, he was cared for with great solicitude and regard, so that he did not miss his own home, but rather enjoyed much more attention than he could otherwise have had. It is true that they did not travel for pleasure and content or on business for their own profit or for any similar reason, for they had no such private motives: they only travelled by order of the king or of the *curacas*, who sent them from place to place, or by that of the captains and ministers of war and peace. Such travellers were amply supplied: others who went about without any reasonable cause were punished as vagabonds.

CHAPTER X

*The system of stock-raising and division
of the flocks; wild animals.*

IN ORDER to keep a record of the great multitudes of sheep the Incas had, they were divided according to their colors, for these animals are of many different hues like horses in Spain, and there is a name to distinguish each color. Those which are strongly marked in two colors are called *murumuru,* or as the Spaniards pronounce it, *moromoro.* If a lamb is born of a different color from its parents, it is put with those of its own color as soon as it has been reared. In this way the flocks were easily counted and recorded by means of the knots, the threads being of the same color as the flocks in each case.

The droves used for carrying supplies about the country were composed of these animals, to which the Spaniards apply the name of sheep, though they are more like camels without humps than sheep. Although it was a common practice for the Indians themselves to carry loads, the Inca did not allow them to do so in his own service except in case of necessity. He ordered that men were to be exempted from all sorts of labor from which they could be spared, saying that they were to save their efforts for other operations from which they could not be spared and on which they were better occupied, such as building fortresses and royal palaces, bridges and roads, terraces, aqueducts, and other useful works for the benefit of the community on which the Indians were constantly engaged.

We have already spoken of the use made of the gold and silver which the Inca's subjects presented to him for the decoration of the temples of the Sun; and we shall refer to that of the palaces and of the chosen women when we come to them.

The strange birds and wild animals and large and small snakes, and all the other creatures, good and bad, that the *curacas* presented to the Inca, were kept in certain provinces which even today keep their names. Some were kept at court, partly to add to its grandeur and partly to signify to the subjects who had brought them that as the Inca preserved them by him this service had been agreeable to him, which was of the greatest gratification to the Indians.

When I left Cuzco, there was still some recollection left of the parts of the city where these animals were kept. The district where the Jesuit fathers now have their house was called Amarucancha, "district of *amarus*," which are very large snakes. Similarly the districts where they kept lions, tigers, and bears were called Pumacurcu and Pumapchupan, from the name of the lion, *puma*. One of these districts was on the skirt of the hill where the fortress stands, and the other was behind the monastery of St. Dominic.

The birds were kept outside the city where they could be more easily reared. Hence a property about a league to the south of Cuzco is called Surihualla, "the ostrich field": it belonged to my tutor Juan de Alcobaça, and was inherited by his son, Diego de Alcobaça, priest, my schoolfellow.

Wild animals such as lions and tigers, snakes and toads, were kept for the punishment of malefactors as well as to enhance the court: of this we shall deal when discussing the laws they made for various types of delinquents.

This concludes what we have to say about the tributes paid to the Inca kings and the way in which they were used. What follows I have extracted from the papers written by the curious and learned Padre Blas Valera, so as to show how closely what he says about the origins, customs, laws, and government of the Inca state agrees with what I have written. His Paternity wrote more methodically and briefly, and with great beauty of style, and this impels me to reproduce his words, both to corroborate mine and to embellish it and supply its deficiencies from other sources.

CHAPTER XI

*The laws and ordinances of the Incas
for the benefit of their vassals.*

PADRE BLAS VALERA has the following to say of the government of the Incas, which I have translated literally from his most elegant Latin, because it confirms what I have already said and strengthens it with his authority:

"The Indians of Peru began to have some kind of state from the time of the Inca Manco Cápac and King Inca Roca, another of their kings. Until that time they had lived for many centuries in utter sloth and barbarism, with no teaching of laws or any other polity. But thenceforward they educated their children, communicated with one another, made clothing for themselves, not only to meet the requirements of decency, but also with some attempt at elegance and taste, cultivated their fields with industry and in company with one another, began to appoint judges, conversed politely, constructed buildings, both for private and for public and common use, and did many other praiseworthy things of the same kind. They very readily embraced the laws laid down by their princes who were guided by the light of nature, and observed them very faithfully. In all this I consider that the Incas of Peru deserve to be set before not only the Chinese, Japanese, and Indians of the East, but also before the heathen natives of Asia and Greece. For when duly considered, the toils and labors of Numa Pompilius in framing laws for the Romans, or those of Solon for the Athenians, or Lycurgus for the Spartans are less admirable, since these were acquainted with letters and human sciences which showed how to establish good laws and customs and made it possible for laws to be committed to writing for the use of their contemporaries and for posterity. What is really remarkable is that these Indians, though entirely deprived of these aids and contributions, should have contrived to frame such laws (apart from those referring to their idolatry and errors). Innumerable of these laws are still observed today by the faithful Indians: they are systematized and closely resemble those of the greatest lawgivers. The Indians recorded them distinctly by means of the knots or threads of different colors which they used for counting, and taught them to their children and descendants so that the laws that were established by their first kings six hundred years ago are still as clearly remembered as if they were but freshly promulgated.

"They had a municipal law dealing with the particular rights enjoyed by every tribe or village within its own jurisdiction, and an agrarian law dealing with the division and measurement of the land among the inhabitants of each village. This was executed with very great attention and fairness: the measurers reckoned out the land with cords by *fanegas,* which they call *tupu,* and divided it among the inhabitants, assigning to each his part. What they called the 'common law' was that which enjoined on all Indians (except the aged, the children, and the sick) the duty of laboring collectively on all public works, such as building temples and houses for the kings or chiefs, cultivating the soil, constructing bridges, making roads, and similar operations. What they called the 'law of brotherhood' was that which obliged all the inhabitants of every village to assist one another in ploughing, sowing, bringing in the harvest, building their houses, and such things, without any payment whatsoever. The law called *mitachanácuy,* 'changing by turns or by families,' established that in all operations carried out in common the same rules as governed the use of the land should be applied, so that each province, village, family, and person should perform a due meed of work and no more, and that the work should be parcelled out so that everyone did his spell followed by a spell of leisure.

"They had a law about ordinary expenditure which prohibited luxury in the usual dress and the use of precious things such as gold, silver, and fine stones, and prevented excess in banquets and meals: it required that all the inhabitants of each village should eat together two or three times a month in the presence of their *curacas,* and practice military or popular games so as to work off their rivalries and remain in perpetual peace, and in order that the herdsmen and field workers might rest and rejoice. The law and favor of the so-called poor required that the blind, dumb, lame, and paralyzed, the aged and infirm, chronic invalids, and others who were unable to till the soil and feed and clothe themselves by their own labors should be maintained from the public stores. They had also a law that required that guests should also be maintained from the same public stores, and strangers, pilgrims, and travellers should be lodged in public houses which they called *corpahuaci,* 'lodging-houses,' where their needs were supplied free of charge. The same law required that the needy whom we have mentioned above should be invited two or three times a month to the public feasts so that they might forget part of their misery in the public rejoicing.

"Another was called the domestic law. It had two points: the first, that no one was to be idle, on account of which, as we have said, even children of five were given very light tasks suitable for their age; and the blind, lame, and dumb were also given various tasks, provided they had no other ailments, while everyone else, as long as he had good health, toiled each at his own task and business, and it was regarded as a most degrading and dishonorable thing to be punished for idleness. The second part of the same law provided that the Indians should dine and sup with their doors open so that the officials and judges should be able to inspect them freely. There were in fact certain judges appointed to inspect temples, public places and buildings, and private houses, and they were called *llactacamayu.* These officials, either in person or through deputies, frequently visited the houses to see that both husband and wife carefully and diligently kept the household and family in proper order and attended to the obedience, occupations, and needs of the children.

The diligence of the couple was assessed by the adornment, cleanliness, and tidiness of the house, furniture, and clothes, and even the pottery and other domestic utensils. Those who were regarded as careful and neat were rewarded with public commendation, while the careless were flogged on the arms and legs or punished in such other ways as the law established.

"Because of this all that was necessary for human consumption was so abundant that it was practically given for nothing, even things which today are greatly prized. The remaining moral laws and ordinances which they all observed singly and communally were based on reason and can be deduced from what we shall say about their life and customs. We shall also speak at length in ch. viii and ix of the reasons for the disappearance of these laws and rights, or the greater part of them, and of the administration of the Incas, which was so politic and worthy of praise, and of how the Indians now live in greater barbarism and with a greater lack of citizenship and in greater want of everything necessary for human life than they had in former times."

CHAPTER XII

How they conquered and civilized
new vassals.

T HE SYSTEM the Incas adopted in conquering new territories and their method of teaching the inhabitants to adopt a civilized and political way of life are certainly not things which should be omitted or despised. Since their earliest kings, who were imitated by their successors, they never waged war unless moved by causes that seemed to them sufficient, such as the need that the barbarians should be reduced to a human and civilized existence, or offences and injuries inflicted on their subject peoples by untamed neighbors. Before they went to war, they used to warn their enemies one, two, or three times. After a province had been subdued, the first thing the Inca did was to take the chief idol of the region and carry it off as a sort of hostage to Cuzco. He would order it to be kept in a temple until the chief and his men were disillusioned about the deceits of their false gods and had taken to the idolatry of the Incas

who worshipped the Sun. The other gods were not overthrown immediately on the conquest of a new province, out of respect for it; for the
natives would be aggrieved by any disrespect of their own gods until
they had been indoctrinated in the vain religion of the Incas.

"They also carried off the leading chief and all his children to Cuzco,
where they were treated with kindness and favor so that by frequenting
the court they would learn not only its laws, customs, and correct speech,
but also the rites, ceremonies, and superstitions of the Incas. This done,
the *curaca* was restored to his former dignity and authority, and the Inca,
as king, ordered the vassals to serve and obey him as their natural lord.
And so that the victorious and vanquished warriors should be reconciled
and live together in permanent peace and concord, and that any hatred
and rancor that had been generated in the course of the war should be
buried and forgotten, they ordered great banquets to be held with an
abundant supply of good things, to which the blind, the lame, the dumb,
and other disabled people were invited to share in the royal liberality.
At these feasts there were dances by the maidens, games and celebrations for the boys, and military exercises by the grown men. In addition
to this they were given many presents of gold, silver, and feathers to
enrich their dresses and to serve as decorations for their principal feasts;
and other awards consisting of garments and similar prizes which they
greatly esteemed were distributed. The Inca bestowed these and similar
gifts on newly conquered Indians, so that however brutish and barbarous
they had been they were subdued by affection and attached to his service
by a bond so strong that no province ever dreamed of rebelling. And in
order to remove all occasion for complaint and to prevent dissatisfaction
from leading to rebellion, he confirmed and promulgated anew all the
former laws, liberties, and statutes so that they might be more esteemed
and respected, and he never changed a word of them unless they were
contrary to the idolatry and laws of his empire.

"When necessary, he would move the inhabitants of one province to
another, furnishing them with land, houses, servants, and flocks in sufficient abundance; and would replace them in their own area with natives
of Cuzco or other faithful provinces, who would act as a garrison colony
and teach them the laws, rites, ceremonies, and general language of the
kingdom.

"The rest of the mild administration of the Inca kings, which was
superior to that of any other kings or peoples of the New World, is
clearly shown not only from the annual knots and traditions of the Indians, but also from the trustworthy handwritten reports which Viceroy

Don Francisco de Toledo ordered his inspectors, judges, and secretaries to write after many lengthy enquiries among the Indians of each province. These papers are now in the public archives and they give a clear picture of how benignantly the Inca kings of Peru treated their people. For, as we have said, apart from certain matters affecting the security of the whole empire, all the laws and rights of the vassals were preserved without change. Their estates and patrimony, both common and private, were left free and undivided by order of the Incas without any reduction or diminution. Soldiers were never allowed to rob or sack provinces or kingdoms that were reduced by force of arms to surrender: their natives who surrendered were quickly appointed to peaceable offices or entrusted with military commands, as if the latter had been long and trusted soldiers of the Inca and the former his most faithful servants.

"The burden of the tributes imposed by the kings was so light that what we are about to say may well appear to the reader to have been written in jest. Yet, not content or satisfied with all these things, the Incas distributed all that was needful for clothes and food with abundant liberality and gave away many other gifts not only to lords and nobles but also to taxpayers and the poor. They might therefore more properly be called diligent fathers of families or careful stewards than kings, and this gave rise to the title *Cápac Titu* which the Indians applied to them. *Cápac* is 'a prince powerful in wealth and greatness' and *titu* means 'a liberal, magnanimous prince, august demi-god.' This is also the reason why the kings of Peru were so beloved by their vassals that even today the Indians, though converted to Christianity, do not forget them, but rather call upon them in turn by their names with weeping and wailing and cries and shouts, whenever they are in trouble or need. We do not read of any ancient king of Asia, Africa, or Europe having shown himself so careful, affable, beneficent, free, and liberal toward his natural subjects as were the Inca kings toward theirs. Those who read the historical facts as we have written and shall continue to write them will be able to understand what were the ancient laws and rights of the Peruvian Indians, their customs, statutes, occupations, and way of life, which was so reasonable that all these things should be recorded and observed so that they may be reduced to the Christian religion with more ease and mildness."

CHAPTER XIII

How they appointed officials for every kind of duty.

PROCEEDING further with the subject Padre Blas Valera gives the following title to his next chapter: "How the Incas appointed governors and officials in time of peace; how overseers and laborers were assigned to various tasks; how common and personal goods were distributed; and how tribute was imposed."

"When the Inca had subdued some new province and had ordered its principal idol to be taken to Cuzco and had quieted the spirits of the chiefs and their vassals, he gave orders that all the Indians, both priests and soothsayers as well as common people, should worship the god Ticci Viracocha, otherwise called Pachacámac, as the most powerful god and the vanquisher of all other gods. He then ordered them to regard the Inca as their king and overlord whom they were to serve and obey: the caciques were to visit his court by turns every year or every two years according to the distance from it of their respective provinces—for this reason the city of Cuzco was one of the largest and busiest cities in the New World.

"In addition to this he ordered that all the natives and residents of the new province should be counted and listed (even including the children) by age, descent, trade, property, family, crafts, and customs. This information was to be gathered and recorded as if in writing on strings of different colors, so that the burden of tribute and other obligations owed by them in kind or in labor on public works could later be assessed according to their capacity. Various officers were appointed for war: generals, marshals, captains, ensigns, sergeants, and group leaders of from ten to fifty men. The junior captains commanded a hundred men, and others five hundred or a thousand. The marshals commanded three, four, or five thousand soldiers, and generals from ten thousand upwards: they were called *hatun apu,* 'great captain.' Lords of vassals—as it were dukes, counts and marquises—were called *curaca:* they, as true and natural lords, stood over their people in time of peace and war. They had the power to make local laws and to divide the tribute and provide for their families and all their vassals in time of need according to the ordinances and statutes of the Inca. The captains of different degrees, although they did not have the right to make laws or decide cases also acquired office by inheritance: in time of peace they never paid tribute, but were held to be exempt from taxation, and were allowed to satisfy their needs by drawing from the royal storehouses and not the communal. Those of lower rank than the captains, the leaders of groups of ten to fifty, were not exempt from the payment of tribute, for they were not of noble descent. Generals and field commanders could appoint group leaders, but once chosen, could not dismiss them: they held office for life. They paid tribute in the form of undertaking the duties of decurions: they had also to oversee and inspect the fields and properties, the royal palaces and the clothing and feeding of the common people.

"Other governors and officials were selected by the Inca, and given their appropriate place in the hierarchy for all matters concerning the government of the empire and payment of tribute, so that their rights and duties were evident and generally understood, and no one could be deceived. There were shepherds of various ranks to whom the royal and ordinary flocks were entrusted; and they tended them with great care and fidelity so that no sheep was ever missing, for they diligently warded off wild beasts; and thieves were unknown, so that they all slept securely. There were guards and accountants of various degrees for the fields and estates; and also stewards and administrators and inspecting judges. It was the duty of all of them to see that their village as a whole and each inhabitant in particular never lacked anything that was needful, and if there was want of anything to report it immediately to the governors, the *curacas,* and the ruler himself so that steps could be taken to supply it. This they did with wonderful care, especially the Inca, who earnestly desired that his people should not look upon him as king, but rather as the head of a family and a diligent guardian. The judges and inspectors saw to it that all the men attended to their business and were never by any means idle; that the women kept their homes neat, and looked after the rooms and the family's food and clothing, and reared the children, and spun and wove for the whole household; that the girls obeyed their mothers and nurses and were kept busy with work about the house suitable for women; and that the aged and infirm who were incapable of heavy duties should occupy themselves with some useful exercise such as collecting brushwood or straw or catching lice, which they had to deliver to the decurions or group leaders. The task for the blind was to clean cotton of the seeds and bits it has and to remove maize from the husks in which it grows.

"There were craftsmen of various trades who recognized and respected their masters, such as goldsmiths, silversmiths, and workers in copper and brass, carpenters, builders, masons, lapidaries who worked precious stones, and all the other crafts the commonwealth required: maybe if their children still exercised their trades after the system established by the Incas and later confirmed by the emperor Charles V the Great, the state of the Indians would today be more flourishing and abundant in everything required for food and clothing, as indeed it used to be, and thus better prepared for the preaching of the Gospel. How these abuses have arisen from our carelessness and neglect, and how the *curacas* and the Indians who are now in charge often grumble and ridicule the present administration in their assemblies and conversations, contrasting the present times with those of the Incas, we shall mention later in our Second Book, ch. ix, no. 55."

Thus far Padre Blas Valera: the passage he refers to has been lost. Continuing on this subject, his Paternity says as follows:

"In addition to the foregoing there were agricultural officials who inspected the fields, birdcatchers and fishermen on the rivers and the sea, weavers, and shoemakers; there were men who cut timber for the royal houses and public buildings, and blacksmiths who made implements out of copper. In addition there were a great many other mechanics, and despite their vast numbers all applied themselves with great care and diligence to their crafts and handiwork. But now in our own times it is remarkable how the Indians have forgotten the ancient system of public craftsmen, how persistently they cling to the other customs and usages they had, and how ill they take it if our governors change them."

CHAPTER XIV

Their system of dealing with property, *both public and private.*

WHEN THE Inca had conquered a province and had its inhabitants counted, and had appointed governors and teachers of his idolatry, he set about establishing order in the affairs of the region. For this purpose he had a record made on his knots and beads of the pasture lands, high and low hills, ploughlands, estates, mines of metals, saltworks,

springs, lakes, and rivers, cotton fields, and wild fruit-trees, and flocks
of both kinds, including those that produced wool and those that did
not. All these things and many others he had counted, measured, and
recorded under separate headings, firstly the totals for the whole province, and then those for each village and each inhabitant. They measured the length and breadth of the arable land, the cultivable area, and
the pasture land. When all the details were known, a full report was
made of the whole province. This was done, not so that the Inca could
divert to his own use or to that of his treasury any of the things he required to be so meticulously and completely reported, but so that having
a thorough understanding of the fertility and opulence or barrenness
and poverty of the region and its various villages, he could decide what
it should contribute and what its inhabitants should work at, and calculate beforehand what supply of food or clothes or anything else it would
need in time of famine, pestilence, or warfare. Finally he ordered it to
be announced and published to the Indians what they were required to
provide for the service of the Inca, the *curacas,* or the commonwealth.
In this way his subjects could not abate anything of what they were required to do, nor could the *curacas* and royal officials molest or oppress
them. He further required that landmarks and boundaries should be set
up to divide the province from its neighbors, according to the measurements and calculations that had been carried out.

"To avoid the possibility of confusion in the future he applied new
and appropriate names to the mountains, hills, fields, meadows, springs,
and other natural features, one after another: if they had names before,
he confirmed them, adding some new epithet to distinguish them from
other regions. This is very noteworthy as showing the origin of the veneration and respect which the Indians even today feel toward such places,
as we shall mention later. After this the land was divided so that every
village in each province should have its own private territory, and any
confusion of the fields and commons as defined and delineated within
the bounds of each village was prohibited. Pasture, heath, and other land
was to be regarded in common only as between the natives of a given
province or the inhabitants of a given village. Gold and silver mines,
whether ancient or newly discovered, were granted to the *curacas* and
their relatives and subjects for them to take whatever they wished from
them, not as treasure which they rather despised, but to enrich their
dresses and the adornments they wore to celebrate their chief festivals
or to make vessels for the cacique to drink from, though in this case the
quantity was limited. Having supplied these wants, the mines were ig-

nored, and even forgotten or abandoned; and it was for this reason that there were so few miners to extract and found metals, though there were innumerable experts in other arts and crafts. Miners, metal-founders, and those engaged in related tasks paid no tribute but their labor in their occupation. Tools, implements, food, clothes, and other necessities were amply provided from the royal estates or from those of the chief in whose service they were. They were obliged to work for two months and no more as payment of tribute, the rest of the year they could spend as they chose. Not all the Indians of the province worked in this industry, but only those skilled and specialized in the work, who were described as metalworkers. They used copper, which they call *anta,* instead of iron, and from it they made parts for weapons, cutting knives, and the few instruments they had for carpentry, the large pins used by women for fastening their clothes, mirrors, hoes for weeding the fields, and silversmiths' hammers. They therefore set great store by this metal, which was more useful to them than silver or gold, and they mined it in greater quantity than the rest.

"By the Inca's orders, the salt that was collected from salt springs or from sea water, fish from the rivers, streams, and lakes, and the fruit of wild trees, cotton, and hemp was common to all the natives of the province where they grew; no one was allowed to reserve them for himself, but all were to take whatever they needed and no more. Everyone was allowed to plant what fruit trees he liked on his own land and to enjoy their fruits as he wished.

"Cultivable land, whether producing cereals or other fruits and vegetables the Indians grew, was divided by the Inca into three parts, the first for the Sun and its temples, priests, and officials; the second for the royal patrimony, the product of which was used to support governors and royal officials when they were away from their homes and also to contribute to the common storehouses; and the third for the natives of the province and inhabitants of each village. Each householder was given a share sufficient for the maintenance of his house. The distribution was made by the Inca for all the provinces of his empire, so that the Indians were never asked to pay any taxes on their possessions or property, nor were they obliged to render anything more to anyone, either to their chiefs, or to the common storehouses in the villages, or to the royal governors, or to the king himself, or to the temples, or priests, or even for the sacrifices made to the Sun. No one could force them to pay because the quantity due from them for all purposes was already fixed. The fruits left over from the part assigned to the king were added to the common store in each village. What was left over from the lands of the Sun was also assigned to the poor, or disabled, lame, limbless, blind, paralyzed, and on on. This was done after having satisfied the numerous sacrifices they made, and after providing for the innumerable priests and officials of the temples."

CHAPTER XV

How they paid their tribute, the amount of it,
and the laws concerning it.

COMING to the subject of the tribute levied and collected by the Inca kings of Peru from their vassals, this was so moderate that when one realizes what it consisted of and how much it was, it can truthfully be affirmed that none of the kings of the ancients, nor the great Caesars who were called Augustus and Pius can be compared with the Inca kings in this respect. For properly speaking it seems that they did not receive taxes and tributes from their subjects, but rather that they paid their subjects or merely imposed taxes for their benefit, such was their liberality toward their vassals. Considered in relation to the general circumstances of those times, the daily pay of laborers, and the value of commodities, and the expenses of the Incas, the tribute was so small in quantity that many Indians barely paid the value of four reals of the current time. Although there could not fail to be some inconvenience attached to the payment of the tribute or the service of the king or the *curacas*, it was borne cheerfully and contentedly owing to the smallness of the tribute, the perquisites the Indians received, and the numerous advantages that arose from the performance of the tasks. The rights of the tribute payer and the laws in his favor were inviolably preserved so that neither the judges, nor the governors, nor the captain generals, nor the Inca himself could pervert them to the disadvantage of the vassals. They were as follows: the first and most important was that no one who was exempt from tribute could be obliged to pay it at any time or for any reason. All those of royal blood were exempt, as were all captain generals and other captains, even the centurions and their children and grandchildren, and all the *curacas* and their kinsmen. Royal officials who were commoners and held minor posts were exempted from paying tribute during their term of office, as were soldiers on active service and youths of under twenty-five since they were required to serve their parents until that age. Old men of fifty and upwards were exempt from tribute, and so were all women, whether married or maidens, spinsters or widows. The sick were exempt until they were completely recovered, and all the disabled, such as the blind, lame, limbless, and others who were deprived of the use of their limbs, though the deaf and dumb were allotted tasks for which they did not need to hear or speak.

"The second law was that all the rest apart from these were obliged to pay tribute unless they were priests or officials in the temples of the Sun or of the chosen virgins. The third law was that no Indian was ever obliged for any reason to pay anything instead of tribute, but only to pay in labor, with his skill or with the time he devoted to the service of the king and the state. To this extent rich and poor were equal, for none paid more or less than others. The word rich was applied to anyone who had children or family to help him in his work and so to finish his share of the tributary labor sooner: anyone who had no children or family, though he might be well off in other respects, was accounted poor. The fourth law was that no one could compel anyone to perform or undertake any craft but his own, unless it was the tilling of the soil or military service, two duties to which all were liable in general. The fifth law was that each should pay his tribute in whatever goods were found in his own province, without being forced to go abroad in search of things that did not occur where he lived: it seemed to the Inca a great injustice to ask his subjects to deliver fruits their own earth did not produce. The sixth law required that each of the craftsmen who worked in the service of the Inca or his chiefs should be supplied with everything necessary for his work: thus the smith was given gold, silver, or copper, the weaver wool or cotton, the painter colors, and all the other requirements of their respective callings. Each craftsman was therefore only obliged to supply his labor and the time needed for the work, which was two months, or at most three. This done, he was not obliged to work any more. However, if there was any work left unfinished, and he wished to go on working of his own free will and see it through, what he did was discounted from the tribute he owed for the following year, and the amount was so recorded by means of their knots and beads. The seventh law required that all craftsmen of whatever occupation should be supplied if they fell ill with all they required for food, clothes, comforts, and medicine, instead of having to pay tribute: if the Indian concerned was working alone, he alone was helped, but if he had brought his wife and children so as to finish the work sooner, they too were fed.

"In the allocation of such tasks, the question of time was not taken into consideration, but only the completion of the job. Thus if a man could take advantage of the help of his family and friends to complete two months' work in a week, he was regarded as having fully satisfied his obligation for the year, and no other tribute could be pressed upon him. This alone is sufficient to refute the contention of those who say that formerly tribute was paid by sons, daughters, and mothers, whoever they were. This is false, for although these all worked, it was not because the obligation to pay tribute was imposed upon them, but because they helped their fathers, husbands, or masters: if the man did not wish his dependents to share in his work, but preferred to work alone, his wife and children remained free to busy themselves about the house, and the judges and decurions were unable to bring any compulsion to bear on them, as long as they were not idle. It was for this reason that in the days of the Incas those who had many children and large families were accounted rich: those who had not were often taken ill owing to the length of time they had to devote to their work until their tribute was settled. In order to remedy this there was a law that those who were rich by reason of their families and the rest who had finished their tasks should help them for a day or two. This was agreeable to all the Indians."

CHAPTER XVI

The system of collecting tribute; how the Inca
rewarded the curacas for the precious
objects they offered him.

T HE EIGHTH LAW was about the collection of the tribute: this was done as we shall say, for there was order and reason in everything they did. At an appointed time the judges responsible for the collection and accountants or scribes who kept the knots and beads for reckoning the tribute assembled in the chief town of the province: the calculations and divisions were made in the presence of the *curaca* and the Inca governor by means of the knots on the strings and small stones, according to the number of householders in the province. The calculations were so exact that I hardly know whether to praise the more the accountants who made their reckonings without the use of figures and contrived to divide exactly very small quantities, a thing our mathematicians have great difficulty in doing, or the royal governor and officials who followed the process with perfect ease.

"The knots showed how much work each Indian had done, what crafts he had worked at, what journeys he had made on the instructions of his ruler or his superiors, and any other occupation he had busied himself with: all this was deducted from the tribute he was required to produce. The judges and the governor were then shown separately all the goods stored in the royal warehouses, consisting of supplies, peppers, clothes, footwear, arms, and all the other things the Indians supplied as tribute, including the gold, silver, precious stones, and copper, which were provided in separate portions for the king and the Sun. They also inspected the contents of the storehouses in each village. The Inca governor of each province was required by law to keep a copy of the accounts in his possession so that no deception could be practiced by either the Indian tribute payers or the official collectors.

"The ninth law was that any surplus in the amount of tribute after the royal expenses had been paid should be devoted to the general good and placed in the common storehouses against times of need. The king ordered that of precious objects such as gold, silver, and stones, the plumage of certain birds, colors for painting and dyeing, copper, and many other things that were presented to him by the *curacas* either annually or whenever they visited him, part should be set aside to satisfy the needs of his household and service and those of the royal blood, and the surplus given as a reward to the captains and lords of vassals who had brought them, for even though they possessed these objects in their own provinces they were not allowed to use them except by privilege and with the Inca's permission. This shows that the Inca kings reserved for themselves the smaller part of the tribute they imposed and turned the greater part over to the advantage of their subjects.

"The tenth law stated the various occupations the Indians were to engage in, both in the service of the king and in the interest of the villages and the commonwealth as a whole: these occupations were imposed instead of tribute and were to be performed collectively. They were clearing roads and paving them; decorating, repairing, or reconstructing the temples of the Sun and other sanctuaries of their idolatrous faith; and making anything else that was needed for the temples. They were obliged to make public buildings such as granaries and houses for the judges and governors; to repair bridges; to act as messengers, which they call *chasqui;* to plough the earth; to collect the crops; to graze cattle; to watch estates, sown fields and other public property; to provide lodginghouses to accommodate travelers; and to attend to the needs of guests from the royal stores. In addition, they were obliged to undertake anything else that was to their common advantage, or to that of the *curacas* or the king. But as there was such a vast number of Indians in those days, the amount of labor required of each of them was so small that they hardly felt it, for they all took their turns and were perfectly honest in seeing that none were more burdened than the rest. This law also required them to mend the roads and fortifications once a year, restore the bridges, and clean out the irrigation channels: all this they were required by law to do without payment, for it was to the general advantage of each kingdom and province and of the whole empire.

"Other minor laws we have omitted lest our account become wearisome: those we have mentioned were the principal laws relating to tribute."

Thus far Padre Blas Valera. At this stage I should like to ask one of the historians who says that the Incas imposed oppressive legislation requiring their subjects to pay them great levies and tributes, what was this oppressive legislation? For the laws we have mentioned, and others we shall refer to later were readily confirmed by the kings of Spain of glorious memory, as Padre Blas Valera himself says. We must now return to Prince Viracocha, whom we left involved in great difficulties to defend the honor and majesty of his ancestors, and his own.

CHAPTER XVII

Inca Viracocha has news of his enemies,
and of assistance coming to him.

WE ARE obliged by the great deeds of Inca Viracocha to leave other matters and to treat of them. We told at the end of the history of his father how the prince left the latter in Muina and returned to Cuzco, summoning the people who were scattered about the countryside, and how he left the city with the intention of dying in battle with the enemy rather than witnessing the outrages and profanities they would commit in the houses and temples of the Sun and in the convent of the chosen virgins, and in the whole of that city which the Incas held sacred. Now just to the north of the city, at a little over half a league's distance, there is a great plain. There Prince Inca Viracocha stopped to wait for the people who had followed him out of Cuzco and to bring together those who had fled across the countryside. These, added to the force he already had, gave him a force of more than eight thousand warriors, all Incas and all determined to die before their prince. At this place he learned that the enemy had halted nine or ten leagues from the city and that they were already crossing the great river Apurímac. The day after the arrival of this bad news there came more encouraging tidings for the Incas to the effect that reinforcements consisting of nearly twenty thousand warriors were approaching from Cuntisuyu and were only a few leagues away: they were men of the Quechua, Cotapampa, Cotanera, Aimara, and other tribes whose boundaries touched those of the rebel provinces.

Although their enemies did all they could to conceal their treachery, the Quechuas knew of it, for their territories touch those of the Chancas; and in order not to waste time, they did not send messengers to the Inca and await his commands, but raised all the people they could with all the dispatch the circumstances demanded, and so marched toward the city of Cuzco to succor it if possible or die in the royal service, for these were the tribes that had voluntarily submitted to the Inca Cápac's rule, as we mentioned in due place. They brought these reinforcements to show their attachment and also in their own interests, for there had always been hatred and enmity between Chancas and Quechuas for many years back, and the Quechuas raised this army rather than face a return to the tyranny of the Chancas if by any chance they should prevail. And to prevent the enemy from reaching the city first, they took a short cut to bring them out to the north of it, face to face with the rebels. Thus both friends and enemies came together almost at the same time.

Prince Inca Viracocha and all his men were greatly roused by the knowledge that reinforcements on so large a scale were arriving at so critical a moment; and their coming was attributed to the promise made by his uncle the phantom, Viracocha Inca, when he appeared in dreams and told him that in case of need he would assist him as one of his own flesh and blood and bring him all the help he might need. The prince remembered these words when help arrived in such good time, and repeatedly referred to them, assuring his followers that they were protected by their god Viracocha, whose promise was thus fulfilled. The Incas thereupon so took heart that they regarded their victory as assured, and though they had intended to receive the enemy and offer battle on the slopes and rough ground between the river Apurímac and the top of the Villacunca (using the advantage of high ground), on receiving news of the approach of assistance they resolved to hold firm where they were until their friends should have arrived, rested, and taken refreshment, leaving the enemy to come up with them.

Inca Viracocha and his kinsmen, who were his advisers, also considered that it would be better not to go too far from the city now that they were strengthened, so as to have their food and other military supplies close at hand and to succor the city rapidly in the event of danger. With this in view Prince Inca Viracocha remained on the plain until reinforcements of twelve thousand appeared. The prince received them with due appreciation of their attachment to their Inca, and gave great favors and rewards to the *curacas* of each tribe as well as all the other captains and soldiers, praising their loyalty and offering future rewards for their notable service to his cause. After having worshipped the Inca Viracocha, the *curacas* told him that a further five thousand warriors were approaching about two days' journey away, but that they had not waited for them in view of the urgent need of help. The prince again thanked them, and after consulting with his kinsmen he ordered the *curacas* to send to this new force and inform them of the state of affairs, telling them that the prince would wait on the plain with his army, and they were to make all haste toward some low hills and ravines there were nearby: here they were to hide and wait in ambush until the enemy showed his hand. If the enemy wanted to fight, they could rush in in the heat of battle and take him in the flank with every prospect of defeating him with ease. If the enemy did not want to fight, they would still have done their duty as good soldiers. Two days after the reinforcements arrived the vanguard of the enemy forces appeared over the top of the hill of Rimactampu. When they found that Inca Viracocha was five leagues away, they halted and passed the word back that the main force and rearguard were to hasten forward and rejoin the van. They thus advanced all that day, and all came together at Sacsahuana, three and a half leagues from where Prince Viracocha was, and the spot on which the battle between Gonzalo Pizarro and President La Gasca was to take place.

CHAPTER XVIII

*A very bloody battle; it is won
by a stratagem.*

INCA VIRACOCHA sent messengers to the enemy at Sacsahuana with
offers of peace and friendship and pardon for their past misdeeds. But
the Chancas had heard that Inca Yáhuar Huácac had retired and left the
city exposed, and though they knew that the prince, his son, was determined to defend it and that the message had come from him, they chose
to disregard it, thinking in their pride that as the father had fled, there
was nothing to fear from the son, and that the victory was theirs. In this
expectation they dismissed the messengers without heeding them. Early
next morning they left Sacsahuana and marched toward Cuzco, and
though they made all possible speed, they could not reach the prince's
camp before nightfall since they had to advance in close battle formation. They stopped about a quarter of a league away. Inca Viracocha now
sent fresh messengers: he had done this frequently during the day and
repeated his offer of friendship and pardon for their share in the rebellion. But the Chancas had been unwilling to listen: they only admitted
the last messengers, who arrived when they had already camped, and to
them they returned the scornful reply: "Tomorrow we shall see who deserves to be king and who can offer pardon."

After this rude reply both sides remained on the alert all night with
sentries posted. As soon as day broke, they took up their arms and advanced against one another with a great noise of shouting and yelling
and the sound of trumpets, drums, horns, and conches. Inca Viracocha
insisted on leading his men and was the first to throw his weapon: a
fierce fight then took place. The Chancas strove obstinately to win the
victory they had promised themselves, and the Incas did the same to save
their prince from death or dishonor. All the participants fought most
courageously till midday with cruel carnage and no perceptible advantage
to either side. Then there appeared the five thousand Indians who had
been lying in ambush, and they attacked the enemy on the right flank
with great daring and fierce yells. As they came fresh into the fray and
attacked with great force, they wrought great havoc on the Chancas and
forced them a long way back. Nevertheless, the latter encouraged one
another and succeeded in regaining what they had lost, fighting with re-

doubled fury at finding themselves so long cheated of their long-promised victory.

After this second onset, they fought more than two full hours without either side winning the advantage, but from that time the Chancas began to weaken as they became aware that new forces were constantly joining the fray. This was because those who had fled from the city and the inhabitants of the neighboring villages, on learning that Prince Viracocha Inca had returned to defend the house of the Sun, had collected in bands of fifty and a hundred, or more or less, as they chanced to come together, and resolved to die with their prince. Seeing the battle joined, they rushed in with ear-splitting yells which made them seem more numerous than they were. With the arrival of these reinforcements the Chancas began to lose hope of victory, thinking that they faced much greater odds, and thenceforward they fought to die rather than to conquer. The Incas were accustomed to embellishing their deeds with fables and false explanations which they attributed to the Sun; and on finding themselves thus reinforced, though not with large numbers, they did not fail to turn the incident to account, using the considerable skill they had in such matters. They shouted aloud that the stones and thickets of the plain were being turned into men to fight in the prince's service, on the orders of the Sun and their god Viracocha. The Chancas, being a superstitious people, were much discouraged by this invention, which at once rooted itself in the minds of the simple and credulous inhabitants of all that kingdom, as Padre Jerónimo Román says in Book II of his *Republic of the Western Indies* (ch. xi), where he uses the following words of this battle: "So that the field was the Inca's. Even today all the Indians, in speaking of this hard-fought battle, say that all the stones in the field turned into men and fought on their side, and that the Sun was responsible for this in order to keep his word to the valiant Pachacuti Inca Yupanqui, which was the name of this brave youth." Here ends our quotation from that learned researcher into republics, who deals briefly in the chapter quoted and the one succeeding with many of the matters we have mentioned and shall mention concerning the kings of Peru. Padre Acosta also mentions the ghost of Viracocha (though he gives different names to the Inca kings), and describes the battle with the Chancas and other matters we shall mention about this prince, though his account is brief and confused, as are all those the Indians give to the Spaniards, either because of the difficulty of the language or because they have lost the memory of their historical traditions, and hand down the substance of them confusedly and without respect for order or time. I am however glad to quote what he says, however he may have come by it, as proof that I am not inventing fables but that my ancestors did invent them, and the Spaniards also heard them, though they did not imbibe them with their mothers' milk as I did.

His Paternity then says the following, which is taken literally from his Book VI, ch. xxi:

Pachacuti Inca Yupanqui reigned sixty years and made great conquests. The origin of his victories was when his elder brother, who wielded power during their father's lifetime and acted as commander of the armed forces with his consent, was defeated in a battle against the Chancas, who are the tribe that occupied the valley of Andaquailas, a matter of thirty leagues from Cuzco on the Lima road. Thus defeated, he retired with only a few men; but his younger brother Inca Yupanqui, in order to obtain power for himself, invented and put about the story that the creator Viracocha had spoken to him while he was alone and greatly troubled, complaining that though he, Viracocha, was the universal lord and creator of all and had made the sky and Sun and the world and men, and all was in his power, no one paid him due obedience, but venerated equally the Sun, the thunder, the earth and other things which had no virtues but those he had endowed them with, adding that in heaven, where he lived, he was called Viracocha Pachayacháchic, meaning universal creator. So that the Indians might believe this was true, the prince was not to doubt, even though he was alone, he could raise men by using this title, for although the Chancas were so numerous and victorious, the god would give him victory over them and make him lord, by sending men to help him, even though he, Viracocha, was unseen. Thus the prince began to collect men using this name, and he brought together a great many, and won a victory, and became ruler, and deposed his father and brother. After this victory he decreed that Viracocha should be regarded as universal lord and that the statues of the Sun and thunder should bow down and respect him. From that time onwards the statue of Viracocha was placed above those of the Sun, the thunder, and the rest of the huacas. And although Inca Yupanqui assigned *chacras* and land and flocks to the Sun, the thunder, and the other huacas, he assigned nothing to Viracocha, giving as the explanation that as the latter was the universal lord and creator he did not need them.

After the victory over the Chancas, therefore, he told his soldiers that it was not they who had been victorious, but some bearded men sent by Viracocha, invisible to all but him: they had after been turned into stones, and his men were to look for them, for he would know them. Thus he collected a great quantity of stones from the hillsides which he selected and declared to be huacas. They were worshipped and sacrifices were made to them. The name given to them was *pururaucas,* and they were devoutly carried into battle, it being considered that victory was certain with their aid. This fictitious invention on the part of the Inca was so effective that he won very notable victories,

etc. Thus far Padre Acosta; and as his Paternity tells it, the fable is the same. To say that they placed the statue of Viracocha higher than that of the Sun is a new invention of the Indians to flatter the Spaniards, as if to imply that the Indian word for them was the name of the highest and most revered god they had: this was not so, for they had no more than two gods, who were Pachacámac, the unseen and unknown, and the Sun, visible and evident to all. Viracocha and the other Incas were held to be children of the Sun.

CHAPTER XIX

The liberality of Prince Inca Viracocha after the victory.

SEEING their enemies weaken, the Incas all called on the names of their uncle, the phantom Inca Viracocha, as their prince bade them, and attacked with great fury, carrying the Chancas before them. A great many of them were killed, and the few survivors took to their heels and fled for all they were worth. Having given pursuit for a while, the prince called his men back, and ordered the slaughter of the enemy to cease, since they were already vanquished. He personally visited the whole field of battle and had the wounded brought in to be cured and the dead to be buried. He had the captives released and let them return freely to their own countries, telling them that they were all pardoned. The battle, having been bitterly contested for more than eight hours, was extremely bloody: the Indians say that in addition to what was spilt on the field itself, a stream of gore ran down a dry watercourse that passes through the plain, and which was afterwards known as Yáhuarpampa, "field of blood." More than thirty thousand Indians died: eight thousand being Inca Viracocha's men and the rest members of the Chanca, Hancohuallu, Uramarca, Villca, Utunsulla, and other tribes.

The two field commanders and the Hancohuallu general were taken prisoner. The latter was wounded, and the prince ordered him to be treated with great care: all three were kept for the triumph he proposed to celebrate. A few days after the battle one of the Inca's uncles sternly rebuked the captives for having dared to attack the children of the Sun, who he said were invincible, since stones and trees turned into men fought on their side in obedience to the command of their father the Sun, as they themselves had witnessed and would witness again whenever they tried conclusions with the Incas. He told them many other fables to the Incas' advantage, and finished by bidding them render thanks to the Sun who bade his children treat the Indians with mercy and clemency. For this reason the prince would spare their lives and return their possessions to them and deal likewise with the other *curacas* who had rebelled with them, even though they deserved to die a cruel death. Thenceforward they were to be good vassals, if they did not want the Sun to punish them by bidding the earth to swallow them up alive. The *curacas* humbly thanked him for this generosity and promised to be loyal servants.

After winning this great victory, Inca Viracocha at once sent off three messengers. One was sent to the house of the Sun to report to their god the victory that had been won through his mediation and help—as though he would not have seen it. The fact is that although the Incas regarded the Sun as god, they treated him as if he were physically a man like themselves. Among the ways in which they dealt with him as if he were a man, they used to offer him drink, pouring his share into a golden bowl which they stood in the square where they held their celebrations, or in his temple: they placed it in the sun and whatever disappeared they said the Sun drank: in this way they were not far from wrong for it was consumed by his heat. They also used to put out plates of meat for him to eat. And when any great event occurred, such as this victory, they sent a special messenger to tell him what had happened and to offer their thanks. In conformity with this ancient custom, Prince Viracocha sent his messenger to the Sun with news of the victory and ordered the priests to bring back those who had fled and offer a thanksgiving with sacrifices to the Sun. Another messenger was sent to the virgins dedicated as brides of the Sun with news of the victory which he had granted through the prayers and merits of the chosen women. A third messenger or *chasqui* was sent to his father the Inca to tell him all that had happened and beg him not to move until the prince returned.

CHAPTER XX

*The prince pursues the enemy, returns to Cuzco,
has an interview with his father, and
dispossesses him of the empire.*

AFTER SENDING off the messengers, he ordered six thousand warriors
to be selected to accompany him in pursuit of the enemy, dismissing
the rest of his men with permission to return home and promising to reward the *curacas* for their services in due course. He appointed two of
his uncles to accompany him as commanders, and with this force he left
in pursuit of the enemy two days after the battle. His pursuit was not to
wreak vengeance on them, but to allay their fears of retribution for their
misdeeds. Thus all those who were found on the way, whether wounded
or not, were regaled and cared for, and some of the defeated were sent
as messengers to their own provinces and towns to proclaim that the Inca
was coming to pardon and comfort them, so that they were not to be
afraid. After taking these measures, he travelled rapidly ahead, and on
his reaching the province of Antahuailla, the home of the Chancas, all
the women and children came out with green branches in their hands
and acclaimed him with the words: "Unique Lord, child of the Sun,
lover of the poor, take pity on us and pardon us!"

The prince received them very mildly and had them told that their
husbands and fathers were to blame for their recent misfortune, that he
had pardoned all those who had rebelled, and that he had come to visit
them personally so that they should hear about their pardon from his
own mouth, and be more at ease and lose any fear they might have of
retribution for their crime. He ordered them to be given whatever they
needed, and to be treated with love and charity, with special regard for
the feeding of the widows and orphans of those who had died in the
battle of Yáhuarpampa.

He rapidly toured all the provinces that had been concerned in the rebellion, leaving behind governors with adequate garrisons, and then returned to the city, which he re-entered one moon (as the Indians say, for
they count months by moons) after he had left it. The Indians, both those
who were loyal and those who had recently rebelled, were astonished by
the mildness and clemency of the prince, which they had not expected to

find in one of such stern character: on the contrary they imagined that the victory would be followed by a great massacre. They said however that his god the Sun had bidden him change his character and resemble his ancestors. This much is certain, that the desire for honor and fame can influence generous spirits to the extent of changing a wild and savage nature or any other ill disposition to its opposite: this was the case with this prince, who thus left a good name among his people.

Inca Viracocha entered Cuzco on foot, so as to appear as a soldier rather than a king. He came down the hill of Carmenca surrounded by his warriors and marching between his two uncles, who had been his commanders, and followed by his prisoners. He was received with great rejoicing and loud acclamations from the multitude. The old Incas came out to welcome him and worship him as the child of the Sun, and after having shown him due respect, they mingled with his soldiers so as to participate in the triumph, implying that they wished they were young enough to fight under such a leader. His mother, Coya Mama Chic'ya, and the women who were his closest kin—sisters, aunts, and first and second cousins—with a great throng of other *pallas,* approached from another direction to welcome him with festive and joyous songs. Some embraced him, others wiped the sweat from his face, others brushed the dust off his clothes, and others strewed flowers and scented herbs. In this fashion the prince advanced to the house of the Sun, which he entered barefoot, according to their custom, to give thanks for the victory the god had given him. He then went to visit the virgins, who were the wives of the Sun; and after these two visits, he left the city to see his father, who had remained where he left him in the defile of Muina.

Inca Yáhuar Huácac received the prince, his son, not with the pleasure and joy that might have been expected after so great and unlooked-for a victory, but with a grave and melancholy expression that indicated grief rather than satisfaction. It is not known whether this was due to jealousy of his son's great achievement, or to shame of his own past cowardice, or to fear that the prince would depose him for having abandoned the house of the Sun, the virgins, the brides of the Sun, and the imperial city, or to a combination of all three motives.

Few words passed between them in public, but they later had a long conversation in private. The Indians do not know what was said, but suppose there was a discussion about which of the two, father or son, should rule, for the prince came away from this secret conversation determined that his father should not return to the city he had abandoned. And as ambition and the passion to rule drives princes to seize on any pretext, this was excuse enough to dispossess the father of the kingdom. The king indeed soon yielded to his son's determination for the whole court and capital approved of the prince's desire: in order to avoid strife and scandal, and especially because he had no alternative, he accepted all his son's demands. By agreement, therefore, a royal house was established for him between the defile of Muina and Quespicancha a pleasant spot, like all that valley, with the most delightful groves and gardens imaginable and ample facilities for the royal sports of hunting and fishing, since the Y'úcay River and many of its tributaries run not far to the east of the house. Having planned this house, the ruins and foundations of which can still be seen today, Prince Viracocha Inca returned to the city, and exchanged the yellow fringe for the red. But though he wore the latter, he never consented that his father should cease to wear his: for emblems are of little moment when the reality of power and command has been lost. When the house was finished, all the necessary servants and other facilities were installed, and this was done so amply that the Inca Yáhuar Huácac lacked nothing but the government of the kingdom. The poor king lived out the rest of his life in this solitary state, dispossessed of his kingdom by his own son, and banished among the fields to live among the wild beasts, as he had banished his son not long before.

The Indians used to say that his misfortunes were prognosticated by the evil omen of his having wept blood as a child. They added in conversing among themselves and recalling their past history that if when this Inca had first feared the ill nature of his son and sought to remedy it, he had thought of giving him a little poison (according to the custom of tyrants, and the practice of the witch-doctors of some of the provinces of his empire) he would probably not have been dispossessed. Others who spoke in favor of the prince did not deny that he had misused his father, but said that the latter would have been much worse off if he had fallen into the hands of his enemies, since he had already taken to his heels and deserted the capital: they would have robbed him of his life and his kingdom, the inheritance of his sons, so that all would have been lost; and all had been saved by the spirit and courage of the prince. Others would speak in praise of both kings, saying that the unfortunate Inca had not had any thought of using poison because all his race strove to abolish its use rather than to employ it. Others who considered themselves religious would magnify the nobility and generosity of the Incas, saying that though he had thought of the solution of poison, he had not employed it, for it was unworthy that the Incas, who were children of the Sun, should practice on their children what they forbade their subjects to practice on

strangers. Others added a great many other arguments in their conversations, according to their own opinions. With this we shall leave Inca
Weeping Blood, and speak no more of him.

CHAPTER XXI

On the name Viracocha, and why it was applied to the Spaniards.

To RETURN to the prince, we must mention that because of his dream
he was known as Viracocha Inca or Inca Viracocha, which is the
same thing, as the name Inca can be placed first or last without changing
the meaning. He was thus given the name of the phantom that had appeared to him and said that this was its name. As the prince said that it
had a beard, unlike the Indians who are usually without hair on the face,
and that it was dressed from head to foot while the Indians are clad differently and their dress does not go below the knees, the word Viracocha
was duly applied to the first Spaniards who entered Peru, who were seen
to be bearded and dressed from head to foot. And as the Spaniards soon
after their arrival arrested and put to death the usurper Atahuallpa who
had recently killed the legal heir Huáscar Inca and performed all sorts
of cruelties, which we shall describe in due course, on those of royal blood
without respect to age or sex, they regarded this as confirming the name
Viracocha as applied to the Spaniards, saying that the latter were the
children of their god Viracocha sent from heaven to relieve the Incas and
free the city of Cuzco and the whole empire from the tyrannies and cruelties of Atahuallpa, as Viracocha himself had done once before when he
revealed himself to Prince Inca Viracocha to save him from the Chanca
rebellion. They said that the Spaniards had killed the tyrant to avenge the
Incas and that this was ordained by the god Viracocha, the father of the
Spaniards, whence the name Viracocha was given to the first Spaniards.
And because they regarded the Spaniards as the children of their god,
they respected them so much that they worshipped them and scarcely defended themselves against them, as we shall see in describing the conquest, when six Spaniards, including Hernando de Soto and Pedro del
Barco, dared to make the journey from Cajamarca to Cuzco and beyond,

two or three hundred leagues distant, to behold the riches of that and other cities, being carried by the Indians in litters, as a mark of greater esteem. The Spaniards were also called Incas, children of the Sun, like the Indian kings. There is no doubt that great good would have been done if the Spaniards had replied to this vain superstition on the part of the Indians by explaining that they had been sent by the true God to save them from the tyranny of the Devil, which was much greater than that of Atahuallpa, and preached them the Holy Gospel with the good example that doctrine requires. But everything turned out very differently, as the Spanish historians themselves relate, and I can only refer to their accounts, for I myself may not say as much, or it will be thought that I speak with passion, as an Indian. It is true that all the Spaniards are not to be blamed, for most of them acted as good Christians, but among people so simple as those heathens the evil example of one destroyed what had been built by a hundred good examples.

The Spanish historians, every one of them, say that the Indians gave this name to the Spaniards because they had come from beyond the sea. They explain that *viracocha* means "fat of the sea," a compound of *vira* which they say is "fat" and *cocha,* "sea." They are mistaken both in the form of the compound and in its meaning, for their version would mean "sea of tallow," since *vira* is properly "tallow" and with *cocha,* "sea," it must mean "sea of tallow": in compounds of nominative and genitive the Indians always put the genitive first. Obviously therefore it is not a compound noun, but the proper name of the phantom which so described itself and was a child of the Sun. I mention this at this point for the benefit of those who may be curious to know the significance of this word which is in daily use, and to show how far astray those who have not been suckled in the city of Cuzco itself may go (even if they are Indians) in interpreting the Peruvian language: those who are not natives of Cuzco are just as rustic and strange in the language as the Castilians. Apart from the foregoing, we shall mention another reason of no less importance for the use of Viracocha in speaking of the Spaniards: this was because of the artillery and arquebusses they brought. Padre Blas Valera, in his interpretation of the word, translates it by the Latin *numen,* "the will and power of God." He does so, not because this is the meaning of Viracocha, but because of the divinity attributed by the Indians to the phantom, which was worshipped as a god and given the second place after the Sun, and after it they worshipped their Incas and kings, having no other gods.

Inca Viracocha was so highly esteemed among his kinsmen and vassals on account of the dream and of the victory that during his lifetime he was worshipped as a new god sent by the Sun for the salvation of his progeny and to save the imperial city and the house of the Sun and his virgins from destruction at the hands of their enemies. They therefore respected and revered him with new and profounder marks of adoration than those shown to his ancestors, as if there were a new and greater divinity in him than in them since he had brought to pass such strange and wonderful events. Although the Inca tried to forbid the Indians from worshipping him in preference to his uncle who had appeared to him, he was unable to do so. It was finally agreed that both should be worshipped equally and that when either of them was named, as the name was the same, it should be understood that both were meant. And Inca Viracocha built a temple, as we shall recount, to the greater honor and fame of his uncle the phantom and himself.

It may well be believed that the Devil, that master of all evil, produced the dream while the prince was sleeping, or that he appeared to him in that form while he was awake, for it is not known for sure whether he was asleep or awake. The Indians are inclined to assert that he was not asleep, but awake, lying under a rock. The enemy of mankind may have done this to increase the credit and repute of the idolatrous religion of the Incas: seeing that the Inca kingdom was steadily growing and that the Incas were imposing their vain law and heathen superstition so as to be considered as gods and obeyed as such, he would appear to them in that form as well as in other guises the Indians mention (though none so remarkable as that of Viracocha Inca since the phantom declared himself to be the child of the Sun and brother of the Incas). And it turned out that after the Chanca rising and the Inca's victory over them, the latter enjoyed very great authority and credit, and became a sort of oracle through which the Devil might thenceforward transmit his commands to the Indians.

Such was the fantastic god Viracocha said by some historians to have been regarded by the Indians as the chief of their gods and more greatly revered than the Sun. But the report given by the Indians is false and intended to flatter the Spaniards by leading them to suppose that the Indians called them by the name of their foremost god. The truth is that the only leading god was the Sun (unless it were the unknown god Pachacámac), and in order to confer the idea of divinity on the Spaniards, they first said that they were children of the Sun, like the phantom Viracocha.

CHAPTER XXII

*Inca Viracocha has a temple built in memory
of his uncle, the phantom.*

IN ORDER to do honor to his dream and to perpetuate it in the memory
of his people, Inca Viracocha ordered the building of a temple in
honor and reverence of his uncle the apparition. It was built at a village
called Cacha, sixteen leagues to the south of the city of Cuzco. He ordered
that the form of the temple should represent as far as possible the spot
where the apparition took place: it was to be open and roofless, like a
field, and to have a small chapel covered with stone, to recall the beetling
rock where he had been lying; it was also to have an upper floor or gallery[1] high above the ground, a plan that was quite different from anything built by the Indians before or since, for they never made any house
with an upper floor. The temple was 120 feet long and 80 wide. It was
of smooth masonry, the stone work being beautifully fitted, as is all the
work performed by those Indians. It had four gates, facing the four
cardinal points: three of them were shut, and existed only as portals for
the decoration of the walls. The gate facing east was used to enter and
leave the temple. It was in the middle of the façade, and as the Indians
did not know how to make arches to support an upper story, they built
walls of masonry to serve as supports: being of stonework they would
last longer than timber. These walls were spaced out at intervals of seven
feet and each was three feet thick. There were twelve passages between
these walls, which were covered over with stone slabs instead of floor
planks. These slabs were ten feet long and half a vara thick, and were
polished on all six faces. On entering the temple by the main gate, they
turned right down the first passage until they came to the wall at the
right-hand side of the temple; they then turned left down the second
passage and went on till they came to the opposite wall. There they turned
right again down the third passage, and by following the series of passages in the plan, went through the whole of the hollow part of the
temple, passage by passage, until they came to the twelfth and last, where
there was a staircase up to the upper floor.

Facing both ends of each passage there were loop-hole windows which
admitted sufficient light into the passages. Under each window there was

---

[1] *sobrado*: an upper story, often overhanging the street.

a niche in the wall in which a porter sat without taking away from the width of the passage. The staircase was a double one and could be ascended or descended from either side: the top of it was just in front of the high altar. The floor of the upper story was paved with shining black flagstones brought from a great distance, that looked like jet. Instead of a high altar there was a chapel twelve feet square covered in with the same black flagstones fitted into one another and rising in the form of a pyramid: this was the most notable part of the whole structure. Within the chapel tabernacle was made in the thickness of the temple wall, and it contained the image of the apparition Viracocha. There were also two other tabernacles in the side walls of the chapel, but there was nothing in them, and they served only for decoration and to set off the main chapel (*i.e.* the tabernacle). The walls of the temple reached three varas above the floor of the upper story and contained no window. They had a cornice of carved stone which ran round all four sides of the temple, both inside and out. In the tabernacle within the chapel there was a great pedestal, on which there stood a stone image which Inca Viracocha had had made in the same shape that he said the phantom had appeared to him.

The image was of a man of good height with a beard more than a span in length: he wore a long loose garment like a tunic or cassock, reaching to his feet. He held a strange animal of unknown shape with claws like a lion's and with a chain round its neck and the end of it in the statue's hand. All this was roughly done in stone; and as the stonemasons had never seen the original or any portrait of him, they failed to sculpture it as the Inca described it, so he himself dressed himself many times as the phantom had been dressed and assumed the attitude in which he had seen it. He refused to let anyone else do this, lest he should seem to be disrespectful to the image of the god Viracocha by permitting anyone but the king to represent him. Such was their reverence for their false gods.

The statue resembled the images of our most blessed apostles and especially that of Saint Bartholomew, who is depicted with the Devil fastened at his feet, like the figure of Inca Viracocha with his unknown animal. Spaniards, on seeing the temple and the statue as we have described it, have suggested that the apostle Saint Bartholomew might have reached Peru to preach to those heathens, and that the Indians made the statue and temple in his memory. Thirty years ago the mestizos of Cuzco had a fellowship of their own, into which they refused to admit Spaniards; they spent a great deal on their celebrations, and took the blessed apostle as their patron, declaring that as he was said to have preached in Peru, whether truly or falsely, they would have him as their advocate, though some malicious Spaniards, seeing the adornments they put on for the occasion, asserted that this was done for the Inca Viracocha, not for the apostle.

Why the Inca should have built the temple at Cacha and not at Chita where he saw the apparition or at Yáhuarpampa where he defeated the Chancas—either of which places would have seemed more appropriate than Cacha—the Indians cannot say, except that it was the Inca's will. We can only believe that there was some hidden reason. Although the temple was so curious in its construction, it was destroyed by the Spaniards, like many other notable works found in Peru, which they should have gone to the trouble and expense of preserving so that in future ages people might see the great things they had won with the strength of their arms and their good fortune. But they have pulled them down deliberately as if they were jealous of themselves, so that today only the foundations of the building remain: the same is true of many others, a thing which thinking people deeply deplore. The principal reason for destroying this work and all the others that have been pulled down was the rumor that there must certainly be a great deal of buried treasure under it. They first pulled down the statue, saying that there was a great deal of gold buried beneath its feet. They went on making trial excavations here and there in the temple down to the foundations, and in this way the whole was destroyed. The stone statue still existed a few years ago, though it was completely disfigured by the stones that had been flung at it.

CHAPTER XXIII

*A famous painting; the rewards
given to the Inca's allies.*

INCA VIRACOCHA was so proud and boastful of his deeds and of the new worship the Indians vouchsafed him that, not content with building this splendid temple, he made another shrine no less ostentatious and magnificent: it was just as pointedly to his father's discredit as to his own glory, but the Indians say that it was executed only after his father's death. This took the form of a painting on a very high pinnacle among the many rocks among which his father stayed when he deserted Cuzco. The painting was of two of the birds the Indians called *cuntur,* which are so large that many have been found five varas across from wing-tip to wing-tip. They are birds of prey and extremely fierce, though mother nature has tempered their ferocity by removing their claws: their feet are like those of chickens, but the beak is so sharp and strong that they can rip open the hide of a cow with a single gash, and two such birds will attack and kill a cow like wolves. They are colored black and white in patches like magpies. Of the pair of these birds that were painted, one was depicted with its wings closed and its head down, as even fierce birds stand when they want to conceal themselves: it was facing Collasuyu with its back turned to Cuzco. The other was painted quite differently, with the face boldly turned toward the city and its wings open as if in flight and prepared to swoop on its prey. The Indians explained that the first *cuntur* symbolized the Inca's father who had fled from Cuzco to hide in the Collas, and the second Inca Viracocha who had flown back to defend the city and empire.

The painting still existed in good condition in 1580. In 1592 I asked a creole priest who had come to Spain from Peru if he had seen it and what state it was in. He replied that it was very faint, and indeed scarcely perceptible at all, having been ruined by weather and water and neglect for the preservation of such antiquities.

So as to remain absolute lord of all his empire, to preserve the affection and respect of his subjects and to continue to be worshipped as a god, Inca Viracocha sought to establish his authority firmly from the outset and therefore attended to the peace and quiet of the country and the good government and welfare of his subjects.

His first action was to reward those who had brought him succor in the recent rebellion, especially the Quechuas of the Cotapampa and Cotanera tribes. As they were the main sources of his reinforcements he permitted them to wear their hair shorn and use the *llautu* as their headdress, and to have their ears pierced like the Incas, though the size of the hole was restricted as when the first Inca Manco Cápac established it with his first subjects.

The remaining tribes received other favors in the form of privileges that greatly satisfied them. He visited his domains so that the people should have the privilege of seeing him, one that was much desired by them all after the wonders that were related of him. And after spending some years on this visit he returned to Cuzco where, on the recommendation of his council, he decided to conquer the great provinces called Caranca, Ullaca, Llipi, and Chicha, which his father had left unsubdued so as to attend to the problem of his son's difficult character, as we have already said. Inca Viracocha therefore ordered thirty thousand warriors to be made ready for the following summer in Collasuyu and Cuntisuyu. He chose as captain general one of his brothers called Páhuac Maita Inca, meaning "flying Maita Inca," who was fleeter of foot than all his contemporaries and so received this nickname.

He chose four Incas as advisers to his brother and as field commanders. They left Cuzco and on the way collected the forces that had been summoned. They made for the provinces we have mentioned, two of which, Chicha and Ampara, worshipped the great cordillera of the snowcapped mountains on account of their grandeur and beauty, and because of the rivers that flow down to irrigate their fields. Some skirmishes and battles took place, though no considerable action. The enemy preferred to try their strength rather than attempt open war against the Incas, whose might was now such—especially since the recent fame of the deeds of Inca Viracocha—that their foes found themselves powerless to resist. For these reasons these great provinces were reduced to the empire of the Incas more easily and with less danger and loss of life than the prince had feared, for they are heavily populated with warlike people: nevertheless, it took more than three years to reduce and conquer them.

CHAPTER XXIV

*New provinces subdued by the Inca; and an
irrigation channel to water
the grazing land.*

INCA PÁHUAC MAITA and his uncles completed their expedition and left the necessary governors and officials for the indoctrination of the new subjects, returning to Cuzco, where they were received by the Inca with many festivities and great rewards and marks of favor, as befitted the completion of so great a conquest. Inca Viracocha had now extended his empire to the furthest possible limits, for to the east it stretched to the foot of the great range of snowcapped mountains, to the west as far as the sea, and southwards to the remotest province of the Charcas, more than two hundred leagues from the city. In these three directions there was nothing else left to conquer, for the way was barred on one side by the sea and on the other by the snowy heights of the Antis, while to the south there lay the deserts that separate Peru from the kingdom of Chile. Nevertheless as ambition to rule is insatiable, the Inca was beset by new preoccupations concerning the region of Chinchasuyu to the north. He desired to extend his empire as far as possible in that direction, and having informed his council, he had thirty thousand warriors raised and picked six of the most experienced Incas to accompany him. Duly provided with everything necessary, he left with his army by the road to Chinchasuyu, leaving his brother Inca Páhuac Maita as governor of the capital. He reached the province of Antahuailla, which belongs to the Chanca tribe, who on account of their treachery in rebelling against Inca Yáhuar Huácac, were nicknamed "the traitors": this name continued among the Indians today, who never say Chanca without adding *auca*, "traitor." The word also means "rebel, caitiff, perjuror, knave," and includes all the other properties of treachery and rebelliousness. This is *auca* used as an adjective; it also means "to make war" and "to give battle," which illustrates how many meanings are covered by a single word in the general language of Peru.

Inca Viracocha was received by the Chancas with such festivities and rejoicings as could be expected from a defeated race. He treated them all with great affability and rewarded their leaders with gifts and words, presenting them with garments and jewels so as to remove their sense of guilt for their past misdeeds, for as they had not been punished at the time in proportion to the enormity of their offence, they feared they had it coming to them sooner or later. In addition to the general favor he displayed to everyone, the Inca visited all the provinces, and supplied them with what he thought necessary. This done, he reassembled his army, which had been billeted in various provinces, and travelled toward those that were to be reduced. The nearest, called Huaitara, was very large and inhabited by wealthy and warlike people who had been on the side of the rebels. It surrendered as soon as Inca Viracocha sent his messengers to demand obedience of it, and they duly came out very humbly to receive him as their lord, for they were well chastened by what happened at the battle of Yáhuarpampa. The Inca received them very affably and bade them live quietly and peaceably, which was what most benefited them.

Thence he passed to another province named Poc'ra, or otherwise Huamanca, and others called Asancaru, Parcu, Pícuy, and Acos, all of which surrendered easily and gladly entered his empire, for Inca Viracocha was desired everywhere on account of the wonders he had done. After winning over these peoples, he dismissed his army. He gave such instructions as were necessary for the common welfare of his vassals, among them orders to construct an irrigation channel more than 12 feet deep and 120 leagues in length. It began in the peaks of sierras between Parcu and Pícuy, among some splendid fountains there, which are like great rivers. The channel ran toward the Rucanas, and served to irrigate the grazing land of those empty moors where are eighteen leagues across and almost as wide as Peru.

A similar channel crosses almost all Cuntisuyu and runs from the south northwards for more than 150 leagues among the highest sierras in those provinces until it reaches the Quechuas. It is used exclusively for watering the pastures when the autumn rains are delayed. There are many of these channels for irrigating pasture land in all the empire governed by the Incas, and the works are worthy of the greatness and political organization of these princes. Such channels can be compared with the greatest works in the world, and may be set before all the rest, when due consideration is given to the height of the sierras through which they passed, the immensity of the rocks that were demolished without any implements of iron and steel, only by breaking stone on stone with the strength of the human arm, and their ignorance of making vaults to carry the arches of bridges for spanning ravines and streams. If they were faced by a deep river to cross, they diverted it at its source, making a way for it round all the mountains that reared themselves before them. The channels were ten or twelve feet deep. So as to make way for the water they would dig into the very mountainside on the one hand, while on the outer side they protected the channel with great stone flags smoothed on all six surfaces, a vara and a half or two varas long, and more than a vara deep. These were set in a row, each set against the last, and strengthened on the outside with large turfs and a great deal of earth piled against the flagstones, so that the flocks should not chip off the edges of the stonework in passing.

The channel that passes through the whole region called Cuntisuyu empties into the province called Quechua which is at the limit of that district: it has all the things I have mentioned, and I have inspected it with great care. These works are certainly so great and wonderful that they exceed all the description and praise that one can devote to them. The Spaniards, as foreigners, have taken no notice of these marvels, either in caring for them, or esteeming them, or even referring to them in their histories. On the contrary, they seem to have let them go to rack and ruin either deliberately, or what is more probable, through complete indifference. The same may be said of the irrigation channels used by the Indians to irrigate their maize fields, two-thirds of which have been ruined. Today—and for many years back—the only channels in use are those which they cannot avoid maintaining because they are essential. There are still traces and relics of the large and small channels that have gone to ruin.

CHAPTER XXV

The Inca visits his empire; ambassadors come and offer him their vassalage.

AFTER HAVING established the plan for the great irrigation channel to water the pastures and having supplied what was necessary to build it, Inca Viracocha left the province of Chinchasuyu for those of Cuntisuyu, in order to visit all his domains in that expedition. The first provinces he visited were those called Quechua: of all those with this name the principal are two called Cotapampa and Cotanera. These he rewarded with special favors and grants for their great service in relieving him against the Chancas. He then went on to visit all the remaining provinces of Cuntisuyu, and was not content to visit only those of the mountains, but also the valleys of the plains and seacoast, so that no province remained in disfavor through his not having visited it as they all wished.

He made careful investigations to see if the royal governors and officials were doing their duty according to the responsibility of each. Delinquents were most rigorously punished, and he said that such deserved greater penalties and chastisement than bandits, for they abused the royal powers given them to promote justice and welfare among his subjects and vexed them with hardships and wrongs against the Inca's wishes and in contempt of his laws and ordinances.

After visiting Cuntisuyu, the Inca entered the provinces of Collasuyu, which he visited one by one, stopping at the principal villages, where as before he conferred many grants and favors both to the Indians in general and the *curacas* in particular. He visited the seacoast as far as Tarapacá.

While the Inca was in the province of Charca, ambassadors came from the kingdom called Tucma, which the Spaniards call Tucumán, which is two hundred leagues to the southeast of the Charcas. Coming before him, they said:

"Sapa Inca Viracocha, the fame and the deeds of the Incas, your ancestors; the strictness and fairness of their justice; the goodness of their laws; their government, so favorable to their subjects' welfare; the excellence of their religion; the piety, clemency, and mildness of your royal state; and the great marvels that your father the Sun has recently performed on your behalf have penetrated to the uttermost parts of our land, and even beyond. Aware of your great deeds the chiefs of all the kingdom of Tucma have sent us to beg you to deign to receive them into your empire and permit them to call themselves your subjects, in order that they may enjoy the benefits of your rule: they beg that you will condescend to appoint Incas of your royal blood to come among us and lift us up out of our barbarous customs and laws and teach us the religion we should observe and the laws we ought to respect. We therefore worship you as a child of the Sun and receive you as our king and lord in the name of our whole kingdom, in testimony whereof we offer you our persons and the fruits of our country, as a sign and proof that we are yours."

Saying this, they produced a great quantity of cotton garments, much excellent honey, *sara,* and other crops and vegetables from their region, bringing a little of everything so that the Inca might take possession of it all. They brought no gold or silver, for those Indians had none, nor has any been found there despite the great efforts that have been made to discover it.

After delivering these gifts, the ambassadors knelt before the Inca according to their custom, and worshipped him as god and king. He received them very affably and having received the presents as a token of his possession of the whole kingdom, he ordered his kinsmen to drink the health of the donors, a favor they regarded as inestimable. This done, he had them informed that the Inca was very glad that they had come of their own free will to accept the rule of the Incas and to offer their obedience: they would be more favored and better treated than the rest since they had deserved more by their goodwill and love than those who had to be coerced. He ordered them to be given a great number of woolen garments for their *curacas,* of the finest quality which was made for the Inca, and other precious articles made by the hands of the chosen virgins for the royal person and therefore considered sacred and divine: many gifts were offered to the ambassadors. He ordered that Incas, his kinsmen, should go to instruct the Indians in their idolatrous religion, to put an end to the follies and abuses that prevailed, and to teach them the laws and ordinances of the Inca which they were to observe henceforth. He ordered officials to be sent as experts in digging irrigation channels and cultivating the earth so as to augment the possessions of the Sun and of the king.

After attending court for several days in the Inca's presence the ambassadors were extremely satisfied with their treatment and astonished by the good laws and customs of the capital, and having compared them with those they had previously had, they declared that the former were the laws of men and children of the Sun and their own those of beasts without understanding. Full of enthusiasm, they addressed the Inca as follows:

"Sole Lord, so that no one in the world shall fail to enjoy your religion, laws, and government, we inform you that far beyond our country, between the south and west, lies a great kingdom called Chile, with a great population: we have no dealings with them because there is a great chain of snow-covered mountains between them and us, but the news of this land has been handed down to us by ancestors, and it seemed that we ought to inform you so that you may perhaps see fit to conquer it and bring it under your empire and let its inhabitants know your religion, and worship the Sun and enjoy the benefits of your rule."

The Inca ordered the report to be noted and gave the ambassadors permission to return to their own country.

Inca Viracocha continued his visit, as we were saying, and inspected all the provinces of Collasuyu, everywhere bestowing favors and honors on the curacas and commanders, councils and common people, so that all were doubly contented and satisfied with the Inca. In all these provinces he was received with very great rejoicings and festivities and acclamations such as had never hitherto been heard: as we have often had occasion to remark, the dream and the great victory of Yáhuarpampa had produced such respect and veneration for the Inca among the Indians that he was worshipped as a new god: and even today they hold in great veneration the rock under which they say he was lying when the phantom appeared to him. This is not from idolatry, for by God's mercy they are now quite undeceived about their former religion: it is out of respect for the memory of a king who did so much for them in war and peace.

After his visit to Collasuyu, he entered Antisuyu, where, though he was received with less display and ostentation, since the villages are smaller, the inhabitants did not fail to show him all possible attentions and festivities. They made triumphal arches of wood on the roads, covered with reeds and flowers, a very common thing among the Indians for great receptions. Moreover the roads along which the Inca passed were also strewn with flowers and reeds. In short, they made every possible demonstration of the vain adoration they wished to honor him with. Inca Viracocha spent three years in visiting the three parts of his empire, during which he did not fail to celebrate the feasts of the Sun called Raimi and and the one called Citua wherever he happened to be at the time. The ceremonies were less elaborate than at Cuzco, but they were nevertheless celebrated in order to fulfil the obligations of their vain religion. After completing the visits he returned to the imperial city, where he was as well received as he had been sincerely missed, for as he was its defender, protector, and, as it were, second founder, all the members of the court came out to welcome him with great festivities and new songs composed in honor of his great deeds.

CHAPTER XXVI

The flight of the brave Hancohuallu from the Inca empire.

THIS INCA visited all his kingdoms and provinces twice more after the manner already described. On the second visit it happened that, while travelling through the province of the Chichas, which is the furthest part of Peru toward the south, he was brought news of a strange occurrence which caused him great grief and regret. This was that the brave Hancohuallu, whom we have mentioned as the king of the Chancas, desired to obtain his liberty with the loss of all he possessed rather than continue to enjoy greater estates without his liberty. He had been deprived of none of his estates and jurisdiction, but remained as great a lord as ever, and the Inca had shown him every possible courtesy and kindness, yet his proud and generous spirit could not tolerate subjection and vassaldom to another after he had been absolute lord of all the subjects he had had, and his fathers and ancestors had conquered and reduced many tribes to their estate and power, especially the Quechuas, who were the first to bring aid to Inca Viracocha, and prevent Hancohuallu from winning the victory he had expected. Now he found himself equal to those he had considered as his inferiors, and he imagined, as was indeed reasonable, that on account of their good services his enemies were more highly esteemed by the Inca than he was and that he would count for less and less. These broodings were constantly in his fancy, though he saw that the government of the Incas was such that free lords and potentates submitted to it of their own volition. Yet he preferred to seek his liberty and abandon all he had, rather than forfeit his freedom and enjoy great estates. He therefore spoke to some of his own Indians and revealed what was in his mind, explaining that he wanted to forsake his native land and his own authority and avoid the overlordship of the Incas and their empire, seeking new lands to colonize and rule as absolute lord, or die in the attempt. In order to bring this about they were to pass the word on and leave the Inca's jurisdiction with their wives and children in small groups as best they could: he would give them passports so that no one could question them about their journey, and they were to await him on neighboring territory. They could not all leave together without the Inca becoming aware and preventing them, so he would follow them as soon as possible. This was the surest way to regain their lost liberty, for it was folly and nonsense to attempt a new rising since they were not strong enough to resist the Inca, and even if they had been, he would not have undertaken it so as not to appear ungrateful to one who had showered favors on him, or a traitor to one who had been so magnanimous. All he sought was liberty, and to do as little wrong as possible to so good a prince as Inca Viracocha.

With these words the brave and generous Hancohuallu persuaded the first who heard him, and they persuaded others, and they more. In this way because of the deep devotion all the Indians feel toward their natural lord, it was easy for the Chancas to persuade one another, and very soon more than eight thousand proven warriors went forth, not counting the common people and women and children. With this force the proud Hancohuallu forced a way through other people's lands by the terror of his arms and by dint of the name Chanca, whose ferocity and boldness was feared by all the tribes of the region. In the same way he frightened the natives into giving him supplies until he reached the province of Tarma and Pumpu, sixty leagues from his own country, where he had some encounters with hostile forces. Although he could easily have subdued these tribes and settled among them, he refrained from doing so, thinking them too near the Inca empire: it seemed as though the ambitious Incas would soon reach that district and he would fall into the same subjection and misery from which he had fled. He therefore decided to press on and get to a distance where the Inca would less easily reach him, at least during his own lifetime. So he went on, bearing to the right, and coming to the high mountains of the Antis, which he proposed to enter in search of a suitable place to dwell. His fellow tribesmen say that he did so at a distance of nearly two hundred leagues, but they do not know where he entered and settled, though they say he entered down a great river and established his people on the shores of some large and beautiful lakes. It is said that they performed great deeds there, though these seem to be fables invented in praise of their relatives the Chancas rather than true stories: nevertheless great deeds might be expected of the courage and bravery of the great Hancohuallu. We shall not repeat these matters as they fall outside our history: we have said all that concerns it.

CHAPTER XXVII

Colonies settled on Hancohuallu's lands; the vale of Y'úcay described.

INCA VIRACOCHA greatly regretted the flight of Hancohuallu, and would readily have prevented it; but it was now too late, so he consoled himself with the fact that the fault was not his. The Indians used to say that on due reflection he was glad that Hancohualla had gone, for it is quite natural for lords to take exception to vassals of such spirit and courage who are dangerous to them. He obtained detailed information about the flight and the state in which Hancohuallu's provinces had been left, and on learning that they were peaceful, he had them visited by his brother Páhuac Maita who had remained in Cuzco as governor and two other members of his Council who were to depart with a strong guard and visit the villages of the Chancas, quieting the minds of those who had been excited by the flight of Hancohuallu by kind and gentle treatment.

The Incas duly inspected those villages and the surrounding provinces, and as far as possible left them quiet and peaceful. They also visited two famous fortresses made in ancient times by Hancohuallu's ancestors and named Challcumarca and Suramarca. *Marca* is "fortress" in the language of those provinces. The exiled Hancohuallu had been there in the last days before his departure, as if to take leave of them, for according to his

Indians he regretted abandoning them more than all the rest of his domains.

Once the disturbance caused by the flight of Hancohuallu had been put down, and the Inca had completed his visit to his empire, he returned to Cuzco, resolving to settle in his capital for some years and attend to the government and welfare of his realms, until this second revolt of the Chancas should have been forgotten. His first action was to promulgate laws that seemed necessary to prevent the recurrence of any risings similar to those of the past. To the Chanca provinces he sent people whom they called migrants. They numbered ten thousand heads of families and were to settle and fill the places of those who had died in the battle of Yáhuarpampa and those who had gone off with Hancohuallu. Under Incas by privilege, who were appointed as their leaders, they were to occupy the abandoned lands. This done, the Inca had large and splendid buildings erected throughout his empire, especially in the Y'úcay valley, and lower down at Tampu. This valley excels all others in Peru, so that all the Inca kings from Manco Cápac, the first, to the last made it their garden and haunt of pleasure and recreation, where they repaired to seek respite from the cares and troubles that the duty of government always involves with its constant responsibilities of peace and war. It is four short leagues to the northeast of the city. The site is very pleasant with soft and fresh air, sweet waters, a climate of great moderation without extremes of either heat or cold and free of flies or mosquitoes or other noxious creatures. It lies between two great sierras: that to the east is the great chain of the Sierra Nevada, one of the curves of which reaches as far as this point. The crest of this sierra is covered with eternal snows, from which many streams drop down into the valley, supplying irrigation channels to water the fields. The middle of the sierra consists of very wild mountainside, and its foothills are full of rich and plenteous pastures, full of deer of all kinds, *huanucos,* vicuñas, and partridges, and many other birds, though the Spaniards have wastefully destroyed all its game. The bottom of the valley consists of fertile farms full of vines, fruit trees, and sugar plantations which the Spaniards have introduced.

The other range to the west is lower, though it is still more than a league high. At its foot runs the great Y'úcay River with its gentle flowing stream well stocked with fish and frequented by herons, ducks, and other water birds. For these reasons all the invalids of Cuzco who can, go to that valley to convalesce, for the city is too cold to be good for convalescence. Even nowadays the Spaniard who dwells in Cuzco is not regarded as prosperous unless he has a piece of this valley. Inca Viracocha was par-

ticularly attached to the spot, and therefore had many buildings erected
there, some for recreation and others to display majesty and greatness: I
saw parts of them. He extended the house of the Sun, endowing it with
riches, new buildings, and more serving-people, as befitted his magnanimity and the veneration and respect in which all the Incas held the
house, especially Inca Viracocha on account of the message he received
from the phantom.

CHAPTER XXVIII

He names his first-born, and prophesies the coming of the Spaniards.

INCA VIRACOCHA occupied himself with these matters for some years
while great peace and tranquility prevailed throughout the empire on
account of the good government he had established. His first-born son by
his legitimate wife and sister, Coya Mama Runtu, he required in his will
to be called Pachacútec (he had hitherto been known as Titu Manco
Cápac). This word is a present participle meaning "one who turns, or
overturns, or changes the world." There is a proverb, *"pácham cutin,"*
"the world changes," which is usually applied to important matters that
change for the worse: it is rarely used when they change for the better, for
they say that things more often go from good to bad than from bad to
good. In the light of this saying, Inca Viracocha meant to call himself
Pachacútec for he kept his empire intact and changed it from bad to good
after the rebellion of the Chancas and the flight of his father had changed
it from good to bad. But he could not assume the name himself, for all his
realms called him Viracocha after the phantom had appeared to him, and
he therefore gave the name Pachacútec which he had intended to assume
to the prince his heir, so that the memory of the father's deed might be
kept green by the son. Padre Acosta says in Book VI, ch. xx:

This Inca was criticized for calling himself Viracocha, which is the name of
god, and excused himself by saying that Viracocha himself had appeared to him
in dreams and bidden him take his name. He was succeeded by Pachacuti Inca
Yupanqui, who was a great conqueror and statesman and the inventor of most

of the rites and superstitions of their idolatry, as I shall soon have occasion to say.

He ends his chapter with these words. My own account is corroborated by the statement that the phantom appeared to him in dreams and that he took his name, as well as by the succession of the son called Pachacútec. His Paternity's statement in ch. xxi that Pachacútec took the empire from his father is a mistake for Inca Viracocha's taking it from his father Yáhuar Huácac; the account given by his Paternity is a generation out. In spite of this, I am glad to find the reference and make use of it.

The name of the queen, Inca Viracocha's wife, was Mama Runtu. This means "mother egg": she was so called because she was whiter than Indian women usually are. The comparison with an egg is an elegant figure of speech in their language: they meant she was a mother as white as an egg. Those interested in philology will be glad to hear these and similar prolixities, which will not seem so to them. Those who are not interested must excuse me.

The natives attribute to Inca Viracocha the origin of the prophecy known to the rulers of Peru, that after a certain number of them had reigned, people never before seen would come to that country and deprive them of their religion and their empire. This was the prophecy in brief, though it was expressed in confused words with double meanings which could not be understood. The Indians say that this Inca became an oracle among them after the dream of the apparition and that the *amautas,* or philosophers, and the high priest, together with the senior priests of the temple of the Sun who were the soothsayers, used to ask him what he had dreamed: the prophecy we refer to was drawn by Inca Viracocha in consultation with the priests from dreams, comets in the sky, various omens on the earth observed from animals and birds, and from superstitions and warnings drawn from their sacrifices. It was regarded as a major revelation and instructions were given that it should be preserved as a tradition in the memory of the kings, but not divulged to the common people, both because it was wrong to profane what was regarded as a divine revelation and because it was impolitic that it should be known or said that the Incas were ever to lose their empire and their idolatrous religion, or they would fall from the divinity in which they were held. So there was no more talk of this prophecy until the time of Inca Huaina Cápac; he revealed it in public shortly before his death, as we shall say in due course. Some historians refer briefly to what we have said, and state that the prophecy was given by an Indian god called Tici Viracocha. The version I have given I had from the old Inca who used to recount the ancient legends of their kings in my mother's presence.

Because Inca Viracocha had uttered this prophecy and because it was fulfilled by the coming of the Spaniards to Peru and their conquest of it with the overthrow of the Inca religion and the preaching of the Catholic Faith of our Holy Mother Church, the Indians applied the name Viracocha to the Spaniards. This is the second reason for using the name for them, the first being the belief that they were sons of the imaginary god Viracocha, and sent by him, as we have said, to assist the Incas and punish the rebel. We have mentioned this matter before its proper place so as to bring in this remarkable prophecy which the Incas knew so long ago: it was fulfilled in the time of Huáscar and Atahuallpa who were great grandchildren of this Inca Viracocha.

CHAPTER XXIX

The death of Inca Viracocha; the
author saw his body.

INCA VIRACOCHA died in the height of his power and majesty, and was universally mourned throughout all his empire, and worshipped as a god, a child of the Sun to whom they offered many sacrifices. As his heir he left Pachacútec Inca and many other sons and daughters, both legitimate ones of the royal blood and illegitimate. He won eleven provinces, four to the south of Cuzco and seven to the north. It is not known for certain how many years he reigned or lived, but it is commonly thought that his reign lasted more than fifty years. This was confirmed by the appearance of his body, which I saw in Cuzco at the beginning of 1560. When I was to come to Spain, I visited the house of Licentiate Polo Ondegardo, a native of Salamanca who was corregidor of the city, to kiss his hand and take leave of him before departing. Among other favors he showed me, he said: "As you are going to Spain, come into this room, and you shall see some of your ancestors whom I have exhumed: that will give you something to talk about when you get there." In the room I found five bodies of Inca rulers, three males and two females. The Indians said that one of them was this Inca Viracocha: it certainly corresponded to his great age and had hair as white as snow. The second was said to be the great Túpac Inca Yupanqui, the great grandson of Viracocha Inca. The third was Huaina Cápac, the son of Túpac Inca Yupanqui and great great grandson of Viracocha. The last two bodies could be seen to be of younger men: they had white hairs but fewer than those of Viracocha. One of the women was Queen Mama Runtu, the wife of Inca Viracocha. The other was Coya Mama Ocllo, mother of Huaina Cápac, and it seems probable that the Indians buried husband and wife together as they had lived. The bodies were perfectly preserved without the loss of a hair of the head or brow or an eyelash. They were dressed as they had been in life, with *llautus* on their heads but no other ornaments or royal insignia. They were buried in a sitting position, in a posture often assumed by Indian men and women: their hands were crossed across their breast, the left over the right, and their eyes lowered, as if looking at the ground. Padre Acosta, speaking of one of these bodies which he too saw, says in his Book VI, ch. xxi: "The body was so complete and so well preserved with a certain bitumen that it appeared to be alive. Its eyes were made of cloth of gold, and so well fitted that one did not notice the loss of the real ones," etc. I confess my own carelessness in not having examined them so closely, for in those days I had not thought of writing about them: if I had, I should have looked carefully at their state to see how and with what materials they were embalmed, for they would not have refused to tell me as a son of the Incas, as they have refused to tell the Spaniards, how it was done. Although close investigations have been made it has been impossible to get the Indians to tell this secret: this must be because the tradition has already been lost, as in the case of other things which we have mentioned and shall mention. Nor did I notice the bitumen, for they were so natural that they seemed to be alive, as his Paternity says. It is of course probable that they were so treated, for it is impossible that bodies should be dead for so many years and keep all their flesh so perfectly as this without some kind of application, though it was so skilfully done that it could not be noticed. The same author, in speaking of these bodies, says in Book V, ch. vi:

They first sought to preserve the bodies of their kings and lords, which remained whole without stench or corruption for over two hundred years. Thus the Inca kings were kept in Cuzco, each in his chapel or temple, whence the viceroy, Marqués de Cañete, had three or four extracted and brought to the city of Lima, in order to extirpate their idolatry, and it astonished those who saw human bodies, so perfect and with such beautiful complexions after so many years,

etc. Thus far Padre Acosta. It should be remarked that the city of Lima
(where the bodies had lain for nearly twenty years when his Paternity
saw them) has a very hot, wet climate which makes it impossible to keep
meat from one day to the next: in spite of which he says it astonished
those who saw human bodies, so perfect and with such beautiful complexions after so many years. How much better they would have been
twenty years earlier in Cuzco, where the climate is dry and cold and
flesh keeps without going bad until it is as dry as a stick. My own opinion
is that the main operation in embalming was to take the bodies above the
snow line and keep them there until the flesh dried, after which they
would cover them with the bitumen Padre Acosta mentions, so as to take
the place of the flesh that had dried away and leave the bodies as whole
as if they were still alive and in good health, lacking only the power of
speech, as the saying runs. I am led to this supposition by observing that
the pemmican the Indians make in all the cold countries is produced
simply by placing the meat in the open air until it has lost all its moisture.
No salt or other preservative is used, and once dried it is kept as long as
desired. This was the method for preparing all the Indians' meat supplies for time of war.

I remember having touched one of the fingers of Huaina Cápac, which
seemed like that of a wooden statue, it was so hard and stiff. The bodies
weighed so little that any Indian could carry them in his arms or his back
from house to house, wherever gentlemen asked to see them. They were
carried wrapped in white sheets, and the Indians knelt in the streets and
squares and bowed with tears and groans as they passed. Many Spaniards
took off their caps, since they were royal bodies, and the Indians were
more grateful than they could express for this attention.

I have said all I could find of the deeds of Inca Viracocha. The minor
doings and words of this famous king have been forgotten, and it is indeed a pity that the deeds of men so valiant should die and be buried for
lack of letters.

Padre Blas Valera records only one saying of this Inca Viracocha, who
he says used to repeat it very frequently: he mentions three Incas who told
him the tradition of it and repeated to him other sayings by other Inca
kings, which we shall mention. This is about the bringing up of children,
and as this Inca was reared so harshly and out of favor with his father,
with this in mind he warned his people how they ought to bring up their
children so that they would turn out well. He used to say:

"Fathers are often responsible for their children being ruined or
spoiled by letting them form bad habits in childhood. Some bring them

up with an excess of attentions and softness, and let them have their own way as though bewitched by the beauty and tenderness of the children, without giving a thought to what will happen to them later when they grow up. Others bring their children up with excessive harshness and chastisement which can also destroy them, for excessive punishment discourages them and dulls their spirits so that they lose the hope of learning and hate education: those who fear punishment can never make the effort to do anything worthy of men. The proper system is to bring children up by the middle way, so that they are strong and brave in time of war and wise and prudent in time of peace." With this saying Padre Blas Valera ends his account of the life of Inca Viracocha.

End of the Fifth Book

BOOK
SIX *of the*
FIRST PART

*It contains the furnishing and service of the royal palace
of the Incas; the royal obsequies; the hunting of the
kings; the system of messengers and method of reckoning by knots; the conquests, laws, and government of
Inca Pachacútec; the chief festival they celebrated; the
conquest of many of the coastal valleys; the extension
of the schools of Cuzco; and the maxims
of the Inca Pachacútec.
It contains thirty-six chapters.*

CHAPTER I

The fabric and adornment of the royal houses.

THE CONSTRUCTION and adornment of the royal palaces of the Inca kings of Peru were no less in grandeur, majesty, and spendor than all the other magnificent things they had for their service. In certain points, as the reader will note, their palaces surpassed those of all the kings and emperors that have ever existed, according to our present information. In the first place, the buildings of their palaces, temples, gardens, and baths were extraordinarily even: they were of beautifully cut masonry, and each stone was so perfectly fitted to its neighbors that there was no space for mortar. It is true that mortar was used, and it was made of a red clay which they call in their language *lláncac allpa,* "sticky clay," which was made into a paste. No trace of this mortar remained between the stones, and the Spaniards therefore state that they worked without mortar. Other writers assert that they used lime; but this is an error, for the Peruvian Indians never learnt the manufacture of lime or plaster, or tiles or bricks.

In many of the royal palaces and temples of the Sun they poured in molten lead and silver and gold for mortar. Pedro de Cieza confirms this in his ch. xciv, and I am glad to be able to adduce the evidence of Spanish historians in support of what I saw. These substances were used to add majesty to the buildings, which was the chief cause of their total destruction: as these metals were found in some of them, they were all pulled down by seekers for gold and silver, though the buildings themselves were so finely constructed of such solid stone that they would have lasted for centuries if they had been left. Pedro de Cieza, in his chapters lxii, lx, and xciv, confirms that they would have lasted a long time if they had not been destroyed. The temples of the Sun and the royal apartments, wherever they existed, were lined with plates of gold, and many gold and silver figures copied from life—of men and women, birds of the air and waterfowl, and wild animals such as tigers, bears, lions, foxes, hounds, mountain cats, deer, guanacos and vicuñas, and domestic sheep—were placed round the walls in spaces and niches which were left for the purpose as the work proceeded. Pedro de Cieza refers to this at length in his ch. xliv.

They imitated herbs and such plants as grow on buildings and placed them on the walls so that they seemed to have grown on the spot. They also scattered over the walls lizards, butterflies, mice, and snakes, large and small, which seemed to be running up and down. The Inca himself usually sat on a seat of solid gold called *tiana*. It was a *tercia* in height and without arms or back, but with the seat rather hollowed out. It was placed on a great square platform of gold. All the vessels for service in the palace, both tableware and dispensary and kitchen utensils, were of gold and silver. Similar pieces were kept in all the storehouses for the king's use when he was travelling: he did not therefore take his plate with him but every house on the road and in the various provinces was stocked with everything necessary for the Inca's use, whether he was accompanying his army or making a progress through the provinces. Therefore in the royal palaces also were baskets and bins, which the Indians call *pirua,* made of gold and silver: they were not intended for the storage of grain but merely to add grandeur and majesty to the house and its owner.

Similarly they always had a great stock of new robes and bed linen, for the Inca never wore a garment twice, but presented it to his kinsmen after use. The bed linen consisted of blankets and pelisses made from vicuña wool, which is so soft and fine that bedclothes made of it have been brought, together with other precious wares from Peru, for the bed of King Philip II. These blankets were used to lie on and as coverings. They did not think of, or rejected, the idea of mattresses: it can be supposed that they rejected the idea, for after having seen them on the beds of Spaniards they have never adopted them for their own, thinking them too luxurious and artificial for the natural life they seek to lead.

Tapestries were not used for the walls since, as we have said, these were covered with gold and silver. Their meals were extremely plenteous, since food was prepared for all the Inca kinsfolk who wished to come and eat with the king and for the numerous servants of the royal household. The hour of the main meal for the Incas and all the common people was in the morning between eight and nine. In the evening they had a light supper by daylight, and ate no more than these two meals. Generally they were poor trenchermen, by which I mean that they ate sparingly. They were heartier in drinking: they did not drink while eating, but they made up for it after the meal, for they would go on drinking until nightfall.

Such was the custom among the rich, for the poor, who were the common people, had only their bare needs in all things, though they did not want. They went to bed early, and got up very early to start their business.

CHAPTER II

They copied all sorts of objects in gold and silver
with which to adorn the royal palaces.

ALL THE royal palaces had gardens and orchards for the Inca's recreation. They were planted with all sorts of gay and beautiful trees, beds of flowers, and fine and sweet-smelling herbs found in Peru. They also made gold and silver models of many trees and lesser plants: they were done in natural size and style with their leaves, blossoms, and fruits, some beginning to sprout, others half-grown, and others in full bloom. Among these and other spendors, they made fields of maize, copying the leaves, cob, stalk, roots, and flowers from life. The beard of the maize husk was done in gold and the rest in silver, the two being soldered together. They made the same distinction in dealing with other plants, using gold to copy the flower or anything else of a yellow tint and silver for the rest.

There were also large and small animals carved or hollowed out of gold and silver—rabbits, mice, lizards, snakes, butterflies, foxes, and wild cats (they had no domestic cats). There were birds of all kinds, some perched on the trees as if they were singing, while others were flying and sucking honey from the flowers. There were, too, deer and stags, lions, tigers, and all the other animals and birds that bred in the country, each being set in its natural surroundings to give greater similitude.

In many palaces, or even in all of them, they had baths, consisting of great tubs of gold and silver, for washing in: water was brought to them through pipes of silver and gold. And wherever there were natural hot springs, they also made very rich and splendid baths. Their other wonders included piles and heaps of firewood, done in gold and silver, as if they were stocks for use in the palace.

Most of these riches were buried by the Indians as soon as the Spaniards arrived thirsting for gold and silver, and they were so carefully concealed that they have never been found, nor is it likely that they will be found unless they are come upon by chance, for it is clear that the Indians of today do not know the places where these treasures are, and their parents and grandparents chose not to tell them because the objects had been dedicated to the service of their kings, and they did not want them to be used by others. What we have said of the treasure and wealth of the Incas is mentioned by all the historians of Peru, each of whom dwells on them according to the information he has received. Those who write at greatest length on this matter are Pedro de Cieza de León in his chapters xxi, xxxvii, xli, xliv, and xciv, as well as in other parts of his history, and the accountant-general Agustín de Zárate, Book I, ch. xiv, where he uses the following words:

They held gold in great esteem, for the king and his chief followers used vessels and wore adornments made of it, and offered it in their temples. The king had a block on which he sat of 16-carat gold: it was worth over twenty-five thousand ducats, and was the article that Don Francisco Pizarro chose as a present for himself at the time of the conquest, for according to his contract he was to receive a present of his own choosing, in addition to his share in the booty as a whole.

When his first son was born, Huaina Cápac ordered a rope of gold to be made, which was so thick—as many Indians who are alive today affirm—that more than two hundred Orejón Indians could scarcely lift it. In memory of this remarkable ornament the child was called Huasca, meaning "rope" in their tongue, to which was added Inca, the word applied to all their kings just as the Roman emperors called themselves Augustus. I have mentioned this in order to eradicate an opinion that has been held in Castile by people with no experience of American affairs, to the effect that the Indians thought nothing of gold and were unaware of its value. They also had a great many granaries and barns made of gold and silver and large figures of men and women, of sheep, and all other sorts of animals and all kinds of plants that grow in those parts, with husks, beards, and shoots all copied from life, and a great quantity of blankets and slings interwoven with gold wire, and even a number of faggots, such as they used for burning, of gold and silver.

This is all taken from our author, who thus finishes ch. xiv of his *History of Peru.*

The gift he says Don Francisco Pizarro chose was part of the great ransom paid by Atahuallpa, and according to military law Pizarro, as general, was entitled to take whatever jewel he liked from the common booty. Although there were others of greater price, such as tubs and vats, he picked this because it was unique and was the king's throne (for on it the royal seat was placed), as if to forecast that the king of Spain would sit on it. We shall mention the rope of gold, which was quite incredible, in dealing with the life of Huaina Cápac, the last of the Incas.

What Pedro de Cieza says of the great wealth of Peru and the hiding of the rest of it by the Indians is as follows (this is from his ch. xxi, omitting the references in other chapters):

If what lies buried in Peru and these other countries could be recovered, its value would be so great as to exceed computation. I consider it would be so much that what the Spaniards have already got could hardly be compared with it. When I was in Cuzco taking down accounts of the Incas from the leading people there, I heard it said that Paulo Inca and other leading citizens used to assert that if all the treasure there had been in the provinces and in their huacas, or temples, and what was buried with the dead were gathered together, all that the Spaniards had collected would seem so insignificant by comparison that it might be compared with a drop of water from a great vessel. In order to bring home the point of the comparison they used to take a measure of maize and draw out a handful, saying: "The Christians have taken this much, and the rest is in places that we ourselves do not know." So that very great treasures have been lost in those parts, and all that has been found, or most of it, would certainly, if the Spaniards had not taken it, have been offered to the Devil and their temples and tombs where they buried their dead, for the Indians do not seek or desire gold for any other purpose. They do not use it to pay their warriors or to support the trade of cities and realms, but only decorate themselves with it while they are alive and take it with them when they die. Though to me it seems that we were obliged to do all this as a warning to them so as to acquaint them with our Holy Catholic Faith, and not merely for the sake of filling our pockets,

etc. All this is taken literally from Pedro de Cieza's ch. xxi. The Inca he calls Paulo was named Paullu and is mentioned by all the Spanish historians. He was one of the numerous children of Huaina Cápac: he proved valiant, served the king of Spain in the Spanish wars, was baptised as Don Cristóbal Paullu, and had as his godfather my lord Garcilaso de la Vega, who was also godfather to a legitimate brother of his called Titu Auqui, baptised as Don Felipe, out of respect for King Philip II, who was then prince of Spain. I knew both of them: they died shortly after. I also knew the mother of Paullu: she was called Añas.

What Francisco López de Gómara writes in his *History* of the wealth of the Inca kings is as follows, taken word for word from his ch. cxxi:

The whole service of his house, table and kitchen was of gold and silver, or at least of silver and copper, which is stouter. In his antechamber he had hollow golden statues like giants and life-sized figures of all the animals, birds, and plants the earth produces, and all the fish to be found in the sea and the fresh water in his kingdom. He had moreover ropes, hampers, baskets, and bins of gold and silver, and heaps of gold sticks that looked like fuel chopped for burning. In short there was nothing in the whole country that they did not have copied in gold, and it is even said that the Incas had a garden on an island near Puna where they went to rest when they wanted to be near the sea, and it had plants, trees, and flowers of gold and silver, a marvel never before seen. Apart from all this there was an infinite quantity of unworked gold and silver in Cuzco, which was lost at the death of Huáscar. The Indians hid it when they saw that the Spaniards were seizing it to send to Spain. Many have sought for it since that time, but have not found it,

etc. Thus far López de Gómara. The garden which he says the Inca kings had near Puna existed in all the royal residences throughout the country with the wealth and splendor he attributes to it: but as the Spaniards saw no other garden but that one still standing—it being where they first entered Peru—they could not describe the others. As soon as they made their appearance, the Indians removed the gardens and hid the treasure in places from which it has never been recovered, as this author and all the other Spanish historians assert. The infinite quantity of unworked silver and gold which he says existed in Cuzco in addition to the splendor and majesty of the royal palace was what was left over, and as they had no other use for it, it was allowed to accumulate. This will not be hard to believe for those who have seen all the gold and silver that has been brought from my country to Spain: for in 1595 alone thirty-five million in gold and silver crossed the bar at Sanlúcar in three consignments over a period of eight months.

CHAPTER III

The accounts of the royal household; and those who carried the king's litter.

THE ATTENDANTS in the royal service such as sweepers, water carriers, woodcutters, cooks for the courtiers' table (the Inca's food was prepared by his concubines), stewards, porters, keepers of the wardrobe and of the jewels, gardeners, major domos, and holders of all such other offices as exist in the households of kings and emperors, were not persons who undertook these functions as individuals, but natives of a certain village or two or three villages designated for each separate office. These villages were called upon to supply capable and faithful men in sufficient numbers to perform the necessary duties. These men worked in spells of so many days, weeks, or months, and their work counted as the tribute of the respective villages. Any carelessness or neglect on the part of any of these servants was looked on as a crime by the whole village, and all the inhabitants were punished more or less severely, according to the crime, for the fault of the individual. If the crime was that of *lèse-majesté,* the village was razed. When we speak of woodcutters, it is not implied that they went to the woods looking for fuel: their duty was to store in the palace the fuel that was brought by all the vassals for the royal use. The same may be said of the other offices, which were highly esteemed by the Indians because their holders served the royal person directly: and not only the Inca's household but also his person, which was what they prized above all, was entrusted to them.

The villages that supplied servants in this way to the royal household were those situated nearest the city of Cuzco, within a radius of five, six, or seven leagues, and they were the first that the first Inca, Manco Cápac, had colonized with the savages he reduced to subjection. By his special grace and privilege they called themselves Incas and received the right to wear the same insignia and dress and headwear as the royal person.

Two provinces were chosen to supply men to bear the royal person on their shoulders in the gold litter in which he was always transported. These two provinces shared the same name and were coterminous, but to distinguish them one was called Rucana and the other Hatunrucana, or "great Rucana." They contained more than fifteen thousand inhabitants, a strong, healthy race, all much of the same height. The inhabitants, on reaching the age of twenty, began to practice carrying the litters straight, without swaying or bumping them, and without falling or stumbling. This latter was regarded as a great disgrace to the unfortunate fellow who committed the blunder, and his captain, the chief litterbearer, would visit him with a public chastisement, like a public whipping or pillorying in Spain. One historian says that anyone who fell was punished with death. The vassals in question served the Inca in this task by turns, and this was the chief form in which they paid tribute. On account of it they were excused from other forms of tribute, and they themselves were enormously proud of a privilege which rendered them worthy of carrying their king on their shoulders. There were always twenty-five or more men support-ing the litter, so that if anyone did stumble or fall it should not be felt.

The consumption of food of the royal household was very great, es-pecially in meat, for all those of the royal blood who dwelt in the capital were supplied from the Inca's house, and the same was done wherever the royal person happened to be. The consumption of maize, which was their daily bread, was not so great, except among the indoor servants of the palace, for the outdoor servants all produced enough for the support of their families. Game, such as deer of all kinds, guanaco or vicuña, was not killed for the royal table or for those of any of the lords of vassals, except in the case of birds. Animals were preserved for the hunts which we shall describe in the chapter dealing with the chase: they were called *chacu*, and the meat and wool of the quarry was then divided among rich and poor alike. The drink consumed in the Inca's palace was in such quantity that it was almost impossible to keep check or measure of it. As the chief favor that was shown to those who came to serve the Inca, whether *curacas* or not, arriving on visits or bringing messages of peace or war, was to give them all liquor to drink, the quantity consumed was quite incredible.

CHAPTER IV

Halls used as meeting places and other
aspects of the royal palaces.

I N MANY of the Inca's houses there were large halls some two hundred paces in length and fifty to sixty in breadth. They were unpartitioned and served as places of assembly for festivals and dances when the wea-ther was too rainy to permit them to hold these in the open air. In the city of Cuzco I saw four of these halls, which were still standing when I was a boy. One was in Amarucancha, among the houses that belonged to Hernando Pizarro, where the college of the Holy Society of Jesus now is. The second was at Cassana, where by old schoolmate Juan de Cellorico now has his shops. The third was at Collcampata in the house formerly belonging to the Inca Paullu and his son Don Carlos, who was also a schoolfellow of mine. This was the smallest of the four halls, and the largest was that of Cassana, which was capable of holding three thousand persons. It seems incredible that timber could have been found to cover such vast halls. The fourth is that which now serves as the cathedral church. We should mention that the Peruvian Indians never built upper floors, but all their buildings were of one story. Nor did they join their rooms together, but made each separately and by itself: at most they would have one small apartment serving as antechamber on either side of a very large hall. Their dependencies were separated off by long or short fences to prevent communication between them.

It should also be noted that they left all four walls of masonry or sun-dried brick in any room or house, large or small, leaning together, since they did not know how to attach one apartment to another, or place joists from one wall to another, and they were ignorant of the use of nails. The timber that served as roof beams was laid on top of the walls and lashed down with strong ropes made of a long, soft straw like esparto grass, instead of being nailed. Over these main timbers they placed those which served as joists and rafters, binding them together in the same fashion. Over all this they placed the straw thatch which was so thick that in the royal buildings we are referring to it would be almost a fathom in depth, if not more. The same covering served as eaves to keep the damp out. It projected more than a yard beyond the walls so as to carry off the rain. Where the straw projected it was clipped very evenly. I saw a hall in the Y'úcay Valley made in this style, and it was more than seventy feet square and covered with a pyramidal roof. The walls were three times the height of a man and the roof more than twelve times the height of a man. It had two small chambers on either side. This building was not burnt by the Indians when they launched their general rebellion against the Spaniards because it had been used by the Inca kings to watch the chief festivities, which were performed in a very large square, or rather ground, in front of it. A great many very fine buildings in that valley were burnt, and I saw their walls.

Apart from these walls of masonry, they made them of sun-dried blocks, which were shaped in moulds, like bricks in Spain. They were made of trodden clay mingled with straw, and these adobes were made as long as they desired the thickness of the wall to be. The shortest would be a yard long and about six inches thick and six inches wide. They were dried in the sun, and afterwards piled up in rows under a roof and exposed to the sun and rain for two or three years so as to get thoroughly hard. They were laid in the same way as bricks, and the same clay as was used for the adobe slabs, trodden in with straw, served as mortar.

They did not make mud walls, nor do the Spaniards use them, since they have the adobes. If any of the grand Indian houses we have mentioned were burnt down, they never rebuilt them on the burnt walls, saying that as the fire had destroyed the straw in the adobe blocks, the walls would be weak, like loose earth, and would not support the weight of the roofing. But this must have been due to some superstition, for I saw many walls of such buildings that had been burnt down, which yet were in good condition.

As soon as the royal owner of a palace died, the apartment in which he used to sleep was shut, with all its gold and silver decorations still inside, as a sacred place, so that no one should ever again enter: this occurred in all the royal houses in the kingdom where the Inca had ever spent a night, even though it were only while on his travels. And they at once built new sleeping quarters for the Inca who succeeded him, at the same time carefully repairing the outside of the closed apartments to save them from deterioration. All the vessels of gold and silver that the king's hand had touched—jars, pitchers, bowls, and all the cooking-pots—and everything else normally used in royal palaces, and his personal clothing and jewels were buried with the dead king whose property they had been, and wherever similar objects existed in other royal buildings they also were buried, as if they were being despatched for him to make use of in the other life. The other riches which constituted the decoration and splendor of the royal palaces, such as gardens, baths, imitation fuel, and and other extraordinary things, were preserved for his successors.

The fuel, water, and other things consumed in the royal household when the Inca was in the city of Cuzco were brought in turn by the Indians of the four districts called Tahuantinsuyu, or to be exact by the villages of these four districts that were nearest the city, within a radius of fifteen or twenty leagues. If the Inca was absent the same duty was performed, but the quantities supplied were smaller. The water used to make their beverage called *aca* (pronounce the last syllable deep down down in the throat) was required to be thick and a little brackish, since they maintain that sweet and clear water makes the brew sour or bad, and gives it no flavor or bouquet. For this reason the Indians took little pains to find springs of good water, for they preferred it cloudy rather than clear; and the city of Cuzco itself has no good springs. When my father was corregidor there after the war against Francisco Hernández

Girón, in 1555 and 1556, they brought in what was called Tisatica water, from a spring a quarter of a league away from the city: it is very good and was brought down to the main square. I am told that it has since been diverted to the square of San Francisco, and another larger spring of very good water has been brought to the main square.

CHAPTER V

How the kings were buried; their
obsequies lasted a year.

THE OBSEQUIES for the Inca kings were extremely solemn and lengthy. The dead body was embalmed, though it is not known how this was done. The corpses remained so fresh that they seemed to be still alive, as we had occasion to mention in the case of the five bodies of Incas which were discovered in 1559. All their insides were buried in the temple they had in the village of Tampu, less than five leagues from the city of Cuzco down the river Y'ucay. There they had splendid buildings of masonry of which Pedro de Cieza states in his ch. xciv that he was told for certain that "somewhere in the royal palace or the temple of the Sun melted gold had been found instead of mortar, and this, together with the bitumen they used, held the stones firmly together." These are his words, letter for letter.

When the Inca or one of the leading chiefs died, his closest servants and favorite wives killed themselves and [or] allowed themselves to be buried alive, saying that they wished to serve their king and master in the other life—as we have already explained, they held in their pagan religion that this life was followed by another similar to it, corporeal and not spiritual. They either offered themselves for slaughter or died by their own hand, moved by their love for their masters. Some historians say that they were killed so as to be interred with their masters or husbands, but this is false: it would have been considered scandalous tyranny and inhumanity if, for the purpose of sending them with their masters, orders had been given to kill those who were hated by the latter. The truth is that they themselves volunteered to die, and often in such numbers that their superiors had to intervene saying that that was enough for the present, and the rest would, as they gradually came to die, have the opportunity of going to serve their masters.

After the bodies of the kings had been embalmed, they were placed before the figure of the Sun in the temple of Cuzco where a great many sacrifices were offered to them as being divine men regarded as children of the Sun. During the first month after the death of the king he was wept for daily with great feeling and loud cries by all the inhabitants of the city. Each ward of the city would go out in a group to the fields bearing the insignia of the Inca, his flags, his arms, and his clothes, or such part of them as they had not buried with him, but preserved for these rites. Their mourning included the recital in a loud voice of all the deeds he had done in war and of the favors and benefits he had performed in the provinces of which the mourners were natives. After the first month they repeated the ceremony fortnightly at each conjunction and at the full moon: this lasted throughout the year. At the end of the year they celebrated the anniversary of the king's death with all possible solemnity and the same kind of mourning. There were in fact famous and experienced mourners of both sexes who related the great deeds and virtues of the dead king in songs sung in sad and funereal tones. The practices we have mentioned as being followed by the common people of the city were observed by Incas of the royal blood, but with much greater solemnity and show, as befitted the difference between princes and plebeians.

The same rites were observed in every province of the empire, each lord seeking to express the greatest possible grief on account of the death of his Inca. They would visit the places where the king had stopped in their province to confer some benefit on them either while travelling or on a stay in some village, and they would mourn there. Such places were, as we have said, held in great veneration: the wailing and shouting was louder than elsewhere, and in particular they would recite the benefit or blessing he had performed at that spot. This must suffice for the royal obsequies, which were instituted to some extent in the provinces on the death of the caciques, and I remember in my childhood having seen something of the ceremonies. In one of the provinces called Quechua, I saw a great throng go out into the fields to mourn the death of the *curaca*. They had made banners of his clothes and their shouting caused me to ask what it was all about, and I was told it was the obsequies for Chief Huamanpallpa, the name of the deceased cacique.

CHAPTER VI

*The solemn hunting excursions made by the
kings throughout the country.*

A MONG MANY other demonstrations of royal greatness practiced by the
Inca kings of Peru, one was the holding of a solemn hunt from time
to time, which in their language was called *chacu,* "cutting off, intercep-
tion," for the game was intercepted. Throughout their domain it was forbidden to hunt any kind of game except partridges, doves, pigeons, and
other small birds used for the tables of the Inca governors and the *curacas*:
even these were only caught in small quantities and by express permission of the authorities. The hunting of all other game was prohibited, lest
the Indians become idle and abandon the care of their houses and land
from their attachment to the chase. Thus no one dared kill a bird for fear
of being killed himself for breaking the Inca's laws, which were not made
to be scoffed at.

The laws were in fact so strictly observed, and especially in regard to
the chase, there was so much game, both animals and birds, that it even
entered the houses. The law did not prohibit them from turning deer out
of their gardens and fields if they found them there, for it used to be said
that the Inca meant the deer and all other game for his vassals, and not
the vassals for the game.

At a certain time of the year, after the breeding season, the Inca went
out to the province that took his fancy, provided that the business of
peace and war permitted. He bade twenty or thirty thousand Indians present themselves, or more or less according to the area that was to be
beaten. These men were divided into two groups, one of which went out
in a line to the right and the other to the left, until they had made a great
enclosure which might consist of twenty or thirty leagues of land, or more
or less according to the area agreed on. They followed the rivers, brooks,
and valleys that had been fixed as the limits for the year's hunting and
avoided entering the area set aside for the following year. They shouted
as they went and observed all the animals they started. It had already been
arranged where the two lines of men were to come together to close the
circle and shut in the game they had collected. They also knew from observation where the beasts had stopped, and the country they chose was

clear of trees and rocks so as to facilitate the chase. Having enclosed the game, they tightened the circle forming three or four rows of men, and closed in until they could take the game with their hands.

With the game they caught lions, bears, many foxes, wild cats, which they call *ozcollo,* of two or three kinds, genets, and other similar creatures that do harm to game. They were all killed at once in order to rid the country of such vermin. We do not mention tigers because they were found only in the dense forests of the Antis. The number of deer of various kinds and of the large sheep they call *huanacu,* with coarse wool, and of the smaller vicuña, with very fine wool, was very considerable. Naturally in some areas they were more plentiful than others, but often more than twenty, thirty, or forty thousand head were taken, a very fine sight which gave rise to much rejoicing. That was in former times. Those in Peru can say how few have escaped the destruction and waste caused by the arquebus, for guanacos and vicuñas are now hardly to be found except in places where firearms have not reached.

All the game was taken by hand. Female deer of all kinds were at once released, as there was no wool to be got from them. The old ones which were past breeding were killed. They also released such males as were necessary as sires, picking the best and largest. The rest were all killed and their meat was divided among the common people. The guanacos and vicuñas were shorn and then also released. A tally was kept of the number of wild sheep as of the domesticated, and recorded on the *quipus,* the yearly accounts, noting the different species and the number of males and females. They also kept the score of the animals they killed, both noxious and useful: knowing how many head had been killed and how many released alive, they could tell at what rate the game had increased at the next hunt.

The wool of the guanaco, being coarse, was distributed among the common people. That of the vicuña, being prized for its fineness, was all set aside for the Inca, who shared it with those of the royal blood: no others were allowed to use the wool, under pain of death. It was also presented to the *curacas* as a special privilege and favor: otherwise they were not allowed to use it. The meat of the guanacos and vicuñas that had been killed was distributed among the common people, the *curacas* receiving their share together with part of the venison, according to the size of their families, not because they needed it, but in order that all might join in the merrymaking and joy of the hunt.

These hunts took place in each district every four years. The interval of three years was allowed to elapse because the Indians say that this is the space of time necessary for the vicuña's wool to grow to its full length, and they did not shear it before so as not to lose its quality. This also gives all the wild flocks time to multiply, and they are not so shy as they would be if they were hunted every year, a proceeding that would be to the detriment of the Indians and of the animals. But in order that there might be a hunt every year, and it seems that they did regard it as an annual undertaking, the provinces were divided into three or four parts (or "leaves," as country people say), so that each year they hunted over an area that had been undisturbed for three years.

The Incas hunted their domains according to this system, by which they preserved game and improved it for future use. The Inca and his court had their pleasure, and all his vassals were benefited: the same arrangements were applied throughout the empire. They said that wild animals should be treated so as to give the same profit as domestic, for Pachacámac or the Sun had not created them to be useless. Moreover noxious animals and vermin should be hunted and separated from the useful ones, just as weeds are removed from cornfields. These and other similar reasons were given by the Incas for their royal chase, called *chacu,* and they serve to illustrate the good government and system which the Inca kings adopted in matters of greater import, since they did all this to regulate the chase. From the wild flocks the bezoar stone that comes from Peru is obtained: it is said however that there are differences in its quality, and that that from certain species is better than all the rest.

The Inca viceroys and governors hunted in the same way in their respective provinces, being present in person, both as a recreation and in order to see that no injustice was done in dividing the meat and wool among the common people and the poor: that is, those disabled by old age or long illness.

The plebeians were in general poor in flocks, except the Collas, who had a great many. There was therefore a lack of meat, which they only ate by favor of the *curacas* or when they celebrated a great occasion by killing one of the rabbits they bred in their houses, called *coy.* In order to supply this general want, the Inca organised these hunts and had the meat divided among the common people. They turned it into pemmican which they call *charqui* and which lasts the whole year until the next hunt, for the Indians were very sparing with their food and kept their dried meat very parsimoniously.

In their dishes they eat all the herbs that grow in the fields, both sweet and bitter, provided they are not poisonous. Bitter herbs are boiled two or three times, dried in the sun, and kept until fresh herbs are not available. They do not spare the cresslike plants that grow in streams, which they also wash and preserve for use. They also eat some green herbs raw, as lettuces and radishes are eaten, but they never make salads of them.

CHAPTER VII

Posts and relays, and the messages they carried.

CHASQUI was the name given to the runners placed along the roads for the purpose of carrying the king's orders rapidly and bringing news and reports of importance from his domains and provinces, far and near. For this purpose, they had four or six young and athletic Indians stationed at each quarter of a league in two huts built to shelter them from inclement weather. They took turns to carry messages, first those in one hut, then those in the other. Some watched the road in one direction, and others in the opposite direction, so as to see the messenger before he arrived and be ready to take the message without loss of time. For this reason the huts were always built at high points, and in such positions that each was within sight of the next. The distance apart was a quarter of a league, which they said was how far an Indian could run at speed and in breath, and without being tired.

They were called *chasqui*, "to exchange," or "to give and take," it is all one. This was because they exchanged, gave, and took from one another the messages they bore. They were not *cacha*, "a messenger," as this name was used for an ambassador or envoy who personally goes from one prince to another or from lord to vassal. The message carried by the *chasquis* was a verbal one, since the Peruvian Indians could not write. The words were few, plain, and succinct, so that they should not be confused or be so numerous as to be forgotten. When the approaching messenger came within view of the hut, he used to shout, so that his relay could prepare to leave, just as a mail-post plays its horn so that the post-horses shall be ready. On coming within earshot, the message was transmitted, and repeated three or four times until the relay was sure of it: if he did not understand it, he would wait for the other to come up with him and deliver it to him formally. In this way it was transmitted from one runner to another until it reached its destination.

Other messages were carried not orally, but written down, so to speak, though, as we have said, they had no letters. These were knots in different threads of various colors, which were placed in order, though not always in the same order: sometimes one color came before another, and on other occasions they were reversed. This type of communication was a system of cyphers by which the Inca and his governors agreed on what was to be done, and the knots and colors of the threads implied the number of men, arms, or clothes or supplies or whatever it was that had to be made or sent or prepared. The Indians called these knotted threads *quipu*, "to knot, a knot," used as both verb and noun, and they were used for their accounts. Elsewhere, in a separate chapter, we shall describe what they were like and how they were used. If there was a rush of messages, they added more runners, and would place ten or twelve *chasquis* at each post. They also had another way of sending messages, by passing on smoke signals by day or flames at night. For this purpose the *chasquis* always kept fire and faggots prepared, and kept permanent watch by night and day in turns, so that they were always ready for any contingency. This method of sending messages by fires was reserved for any rising or revolt in any great province or kingdom, so that the Inca would know about it within two or three hours at most, even though it would be five or six hundred leagues away from the capital, and could take the necessary steps even before he received tidings about the exact province where the rising had occurred. Such were the duties of the *chasquis* and the messages they carried.

CHAPTER VIII

They counted by threads and knots; the accountants
were extremely accurate.

QUIPU means "to knot" and "knot," and is also used for reckoning, since the knots were applied to everything. The Indians made threads of various colors, some were of a single hue, others of two, others of three or more, for single or mixed colors all had separate significances. The threads were closely twisted with three or four strands, as thick as an iron spindle and about three quarters of a vara in length. They were threaded in order on a longer string like a fringe. The colors showed what subject the thread was about, such as yellow for gold, white for silver, and red for warriors.

Objects that had no special colors were arranged in order, beginning with the most important and proceeding to the least, each after its kind, as cereals and vegetables. For illustration let us arrange the plants that grow in Spain: first wheat, then barley, then chick-peas, beans, millet, etc. Similarly in dealing with arms, they placed first those they considered noblest, such as spears, then darts, bows and arrows, clubs and axes, slings, and the other weapons they possessed. If they referred to their subjects, they recorded first the inhabitants of each village and then those of each province combined: on the first thread they would enumerate the old people of sixty or more, on the second men in their maturity of fifty upwards, the third stood for those of forty, and so on in groups of ten years, down to babes and sucklings. Women were counted similarly by age groups.

Some of these strings had finer threads of the same color attached, serving as offshoots or exceptions from the general rules. For instance the finer thread on the string referring to men or women of a certain age, who were assumed to be married, would mean the number of widows or widowers of that age in a given year, for all their records were annual, and they never referred to more than a single year.

The knots were arranged in order of units, ten, hundreds, thousands, tens of thousands, and seldom if ever passed a hundred thousand, since as each village kept its own records, and each capital the records of its districts, the numbers never in either case went beyond a hundred thousand, though below that figure they made many calculations. If they had had to count hundreds of thousands, they would have done so, since their language has words for all possible numbers known in arithmetic. But as they had no cause to use larger numbers, they did not go beyond tens of thousands. These numbers were reckoned by means of knots in the threads, each number being divided from the next. But the knots representing each number were made in a group together, on a loop, like the knots found in the cord of our blessed patriarch St. Francis: this was not difficult to do, as there were never more than nine, seeing that units, tens, etc., never exceed nine.

The greatest number, say tens of thousands, was knotted at the upper end of the threads, the thousands lower down, and so on down to units. The knots for each number on each thread were exactly alike, precisely as a good accountant sets his figures to make a long addition. The knots or *quipus* were in the charge of special Indians called *quipucamayu,* meaning "one who has charge of the accounts," and although in those days there was little difference between good and bad among the Indians, since they were so well governed and had so little harm in them that they might all be described as good, nevertheless for these and similar duties they picked the best and such as had given longest proof of their aptitude. Offices were never obtained by favor, for among these Indians appointments were always made by merit and never out of favoritism. Nor were offices sold or leased, for as they had no money they could not lease, or buy, or sell. They did exchange some things, notably foodstuffs, but that was all, and there was no sale of clothing, houses, or land.

Although the *quipucamayus* were as accurate and honest as we have said, their number in each village was in proportion to its population, and however small, it had at least four and so upwards to twenty or thirty. They all kept the same records, and although one accountant or scribe was all that would have been necessary to keep them, the Incas preferred to have plenty in each village and for each sort of calculation, so as to avoid faults that might occur if there were few, saying that if there were a number of them, they would either all be at fault or none of them.

CHAPTER IX

*What they recorded in their accounts,
and how these were read.*

THESE MEN recorded on their knots all the tribute brought annually to the Inca, specifying everything by kind, species, and quality. They recorded the number of men who went to the wars, how many died in them, and how many were born and died every year, month by month. In short they may be said to have recorded on their knots everything that could be counted, even mentioning battles and fights, all the embassies that had come to visit the Inca, and all the speeches and arguments the king had uttered. But the purpose of the embassies or the contents of the speeches, or any other descriptive matter could not be recorded on the knots, consisting as it did of continuous spoken or written prose, which cannot be expressed by means of knots, since these can give only numbers and not words. To supply this want they used signs that indicated historical events or facts or the existence of any embassy, speech, or discussion in time of peace or war. Such speeches were preserved by the *quipu-camayus* by memory in a summarized form of a few words: they were committed to memory and taught by tradition to their successors and descendants from father to son. This was especially practiced in the villages or provinces where the event in question had occurred: there naturally such traditions were preserved better than elsewhere, because the natives would treasure them. Another method too was used for keeping alive in the memory of the people their deeds and the embassies they sent to the Inca and the replies he gave them. The *amautas* who were their philosophers and sages took the trouble to turn them into stories, no longer than fables, suitable for telling to children, young people, and the rustics of the countryside: they were thus passed from hand to hand and age to age, and preserved in the memories of all. Their stories were also recounted in the form of fables of an allegorical nature, some of which we have mentioned, while others will be referred to later. Similarly the *harauicus,* who were their poets, wrote short, compressed poems, embracing a history, or an embassy, or the king's reply. In short, everything that could not be recorded on the knots was included in these poems, which were sung at their triumphs and on the occasion of their greater festivals, and recited to the young Incas when they were armed knights. Thus they remembered their history. But as experience has shown, all these were perishable expedients, for it is letters that perpetuate the memory of events. But as the Incas had no knowledge of writing, they had to use what devices they could, and treating their knots as letters, they chose historians and accountants, called *quipucamayus,* ("those who have charge of the knots") to write down and preserve the tradition of their deeds by means of the knots, strings, and colored threads, using their stories and poems as an aid. This was the method of writing the Incas employed in their republic.

The *curacas* and headmen in the provinces resorted to the *quipucamayus* of their provinces to learn historical events concerning their ancestors or any other notable occurrence that had taken place in any given province. This was because the *quipucamayus* acted as scribes and historians in keeping the records, which were the annual *quipus* made of happenings worthy of memory, and were bound by their office to study constantly the signs and cyphers on the knots so as to preserve in their memories traditions about famous events of the past. Thus, like historians, they were supposed to narrate such matters when requested, and by reason of their office they were exempted from the payment of tribute and any other forms of taxation. Consequently they never let the knots out of their hands.

In the same way records were kept of their laws, ordinances, rites, and ceremonies. From the color of the thread and the number of the knots, they would tell what law prohibited any particular offence and what penalty was to be applied to anyone who broke it. They could say what sacrifice or ceremony was performed in honor of the Sun on such-and-such a festival. They could state what ordinance or privilege afforded protection to widows, or the poor, or wayfarers. In this way they could provide information on any other matters that had been memorized and handed down by tradition. Each thread and knot suggested the meaning attributed to it, rather like the commandments or articles of our Holy Catholic Faith and the works of mercy, which we can recall from the number assigned to them. Thus the Indians recalled by means of the knots the things their parents and grandparents had taught them by tradition, and these they treated with the greatest care and veneration, as sacred matters relating to the idolatrous religion and laws of their Incas, which they contrived to retain in their memories because of their ignorance of writing. The Indian who had not learnt by memory and tradition the account or whatever subject was recorded on the *quipu* was as ignorant of such matters as a Spaniard or any other foreigner.

I used the *quipus* and knots with my father's Indians and other *curacas* when they came to the city to pay tribute on St. John's Day or at Christmas. The *curacas* under the charge of others would ask my mother to send me to check their accounts, for they were suspicious people and did not trust the Spaniards to deal honestly with them in these matters until I had reassured them by reading the documents referring to their tributes which they brought me, and comparing them with their knots: in this way I came to understand the latter as well as the Indians themselves.

CHAPTER X

Inca Pachacútec visits his empire;
he conquers the Huanca tribe.

O N THE death of Inca Viracocha, he was succeeded by his legitimate
son, Pachacútec Inca, who after having solemnly observed the
obsequies of his father, devoted three years to governing his realms without leaving his capital. He then visited his provinces one by one in person, and although he did not find any faults to punish, since the governors
and royal officials tried to deal justly with their people at peril of their
lives, the Inca kings were always glad to make these general progresses
from time to time lest their ministers should become careless and tyrannical because of the long absence and neglect of their prince. Another reason was to allow their subjects to present complaints about injustices to
the Inca himself, face to face—they did not permit themselves to be
addressed through third parties, lest the latter should understate the guilt
of the accused or the wrongs of the complainant out of friendship for
those concerned or through bribery. Certainly the Inca kings took great
pains to see that no one should be wronged in the administration of
justice, which was dispensed according to natural law to great and small,
poor and rich. Because of the rectitude they observed they were so greatly
beloved, and will remain so for many centuries in the memories of the
Indians.

The Inca spent a further three years on this visit. On returning to his
court, it seemed to him only proper to devote part of his time to the exercise of war and not to spend it all in the idleness of peace under the pretext of administering justice, a mode of life that savored of cowardice.
He ordered thirty thousand warriors to be collected, with whom he
marched through the district of Chinchasuyu, accompanied by his brother
Cápac Yupanqui, a valiant prince worthy of the name. They proceeded
as far as Villca, the furthest point so far conquered in that direction.

From this place the Inca sent his brother out to make new conquests,
well supplied with everything necessary for the war. He entered the province called Sausa, a name the Spaniards have corrupted to Xauxa [Jauja],
a most beautiful province which had above thirty thousand families all of
the same stock and using the common tribal name of Huanca. They
boasted of their descent from a man and a woman they said had descended

from a spring. They were warlike, and they flayed those whom they captured in war. Some of the skins of their victims were stuffed with ashes
and placed in a temple as trophies of their successes; others were used to
make their drums, for they maintained that their enemies would take fear
on knowing that the drums were made of their compatriots and would
take to their heels as soon as they heard them. Their villages, though
small, were well fortified with their own style of fortifications, for
although they were all of the same tribe, they had a great many rivalries
and disputes over the farmlands and boundaries of the various villages.

In the ancient days of their heathendom, before they were conquered
by the Incas, they worshipped the image of a dog as their god. They had
dog idols in their temples, and so relished the flesh of the dog that they
would do anything for it: it may indeed be suspected that they worshipped the animal because they found its flesh so appetizing. In short,
their greatest celebration was to be invited to a dog, and in order to make
patent their devotion to dogs, they formed their skulls into a sort of horn
they played at their festivals and dances, producing a kind of music that
was very sweet to their ears. In time of war they played these horns to the
astonishment and terror of their enemies, declaring that these two opposite effects were produced by the special virtue of their god—to them
who honored it the sound was good, while their enemies were terrified
and put to flight by it. All these superstitions and cruelties were suppressed by the Incas, though they were permitted to make horns, no longer
of dogs' heads, but of those of deer of various kinds at their own choice,
out of respect for their ancient customs. Thus even now they play these
horns for their festivities and dances, and because of their former passion
for dogs as a delicacy, the tribe has received a nickname which still persists, and when anyone mentions the name Huanca, he adds "dog-eater."
They had, too, an idol in the form of a man. The Devil spoke through
him, ordering them to do what he wished and answering the questions
they put to him. This the Huancas were allowed to retain after their conquest, since it was a speaking oracle and did not conflict with the idolatry
of the Incas. The dog they suppressed, since they did not permit the
worship of idols of animals.

This powerful tribe of dog lovers was conquered by Inca Cápac Yupanqui, by dint of presents and flattery rather than by force of arms, for they
claimed to be masters of men's minds rather than of their bodies. Once
the Huancas had been put down, they were divided into three groups so
as to remove the rivalries that had previously existed, and their lands were
divided and their boundaries marked. One domain was called Sausa, the

second Marcavillca and the third Llacsapallanca. They all wore the same headdress, which they were allowed to keep, but were obliged to distinguish the groups by the use of different colors. The province was called Huanca, as we have said. The Spaniards however called it Huancavillca, I do not know for what reason. There is a province of Huancavillca near Túmbez, almost three hundred leagues away from this, which is close to the city of Huamanga, the one being on the seacoast and the other far inland. We mention that so that readers of this history shall not be confused; later on, in its proper place, we shall speak of Huancavillca, where strange events took place.

CHAPTER XI

Other provinces won by the Inca; their customs and the punishment of sodomy.

WITH THE same skill and order Inca Cápac Yupanqui conquered many other provinces in that district on both sides of the royal road. Among these the chief are those of Tarma and Pumpu, which the Spaniards call Bombón, both very fertile provinces. Inca Cápac Yupanqui reduced them very easily by dint of good management and subtlety and with gifts and promises, though as the people are warlike and brave, this was not done without some skirmishes with loss of life. But finally they yielded with only slight resistance in comparison with what it had been feared they might put up. The natives of these provinces of Tarma and Pumpu and of the surrounding ones used to celebrate marriage by means of a kiss which the bridegroom gave the bride, on the forehead or the cheek. Widows cut their hair as a sign of mourning and could not marry for a year. Men, when they observed fasts, ate neither meat, nor salt, nor pepper, and did not sleep with their wives. Those who devoted themselves to religion and formed a sort of priesthood fasted after their own fashion all the year round.

When Inca Cápac Yupanqui had conquered Tarma and Pumpu, he marched on and reduced many other provinces to the east, towards the Antis. These countries were like *behetrías* or independent communities, without order or government. They had no villages, worshipped no gods, and had no human acquirements. They lived like beasts, scattered about the countryside, the mountains, and the valleys, slaughtering one another for no particular reason, recognizing no lord or master, and having no names for their provinces. This state of affairs obtained over an area of more than thirty leagues from north to south and as many again from east to west. These people submitted and gave their obedience to Inca Pachacútec as a result of his policy of attraction, and like simple people, they duly went where they were sent, settling in villages and acquiring the teaching of the Incas. Nothing else of note requires to be added until the province called Chucurpu is reached; this was inhabited by warlike, barbarous, and uncouth peoples with savage practices, in conformity with which they worshipped a tiger for its ferocity and wildness.

Inca Cápac Yupanqui fought several actions with this tribe, which was so ferocious and barbarous that it prided itself on not heeding persuasion of any kind. In these engagements more than four thousand Indians were killed on both sides, but the savages at length surrendered when they had experienced the power of the Inca and also his clemency and mercy. For they realized that many times it was within his power to destroy them, yet he refrained from doing so, and the greater straits he reduced them to, the more mildly and mercifully he invited them to capitulate. They therefore thought it wise to give in and accept the rule of Inca Pachacútec, embracing his laws and customs, worshipping the Sun, and repudiating their tiger god, their idolatry, and their traditional way of life.

Inca Cápac Yupanqui rejoiced at the submission of this tribe, which had shown itself so fierce and intractable that he had feared it would be necessary either to destroy it utterly in order to conquer it, or to leave it in its original state of liberty, both of which courses would have harmed the reputation of the Incas. Thus with much flattery and dexterity and presents, peace was made with the Chucurpu province, where the Inca left such governors and officials as were necessary for the teaching of the Indians and the administration of the treasury of the Sun and of the Inca. He also left garrisons to secure what he had newly conquered.

He then crossed to the right of the royal highway, and with the same subtlety and skill—which we shall abbreviate in order to avoid repeating the same actions—he reduced two more very large and thickly populated provinces, one called Ancara and the other Huaillas. As in other places he left there officials for the government and treasury and the necessary garrison. In the province of Huaillas he inflicted very severe punishment on some perverts who very secretly practiced the abominable vice of sodomy. As no case of this crime had ever been heard of until then among the Indians of the mountains (though it was known among the coastal Indians, as we have said), its occurrence among the Huaillas caused great scandal, and gave rise to a saying among the Indians which is still used as a stigma on that tribe. It is *"Astaya Huaillas,"* "Go hence, Huaillas," implying that they still stink of their ancient sin, though it was little practiced and in great secrecy, and was well punished by Inca Cápac Yupanqui.

The latter, having taken the measures we have mentioned, thought that what he had won was sufficient for the time being, consisting as it did of an area sixty leagues long from north to south and as broad as the space from the coastal plain to the great chain of the snow-covered mountains. He therefore returned to Cuzco, three years after the date of his departure. He found his brother, Inca Pachacútec, there, and was received by him with great festivities: his triumph lasted a moon, which is the interval of time by which the Indians count.

CHAPTER XII

Buildings, laws, and new conquests made by Inca Pachacútec.

A FEW months after these celebrations and the bestowal of many favors on the generals, captains, and chiefs who took part in the conquests, not forgetting the soldiers who had signalized themselves above the rest and who all received their separate share of attention, the Inca decided to make a new progress through his domains, this being the greatest favor and benefit he could confer on them. During the course of this visitation he had temples built in the noblest and richest provinces to the honor and glory of the Sun, and also founded houses for the chosen virgins, for one was never established without the other. This was regarded as a great privilege by the natives of the provinces concerned, since it made them citizens and natives of Cuzco. In addition to the temples, they had many fortresses built on the frontiers of the regions that were still unconquered, as well as palaces in pleasant and delightful valleys or on the roads where the Incas could be accommodated when they had to journey with their armies. He similarly had many storehouses erected in individual villages for the purpose of laying by supplies for years of need, whereby the natives might be succored.

He promulgated many laws and local privileges, observing the ancient customs of the provinces to which they were to be applied, for the Inca kings were always content to allow every tribe to follow its traditional usages so long as they did not conflict with their idolatrous religion and the general laws of the kingdom. In this way it never seemed that the Incas tyrannized over their subjects, but rather that they brought them out of their savage existence and raised them to a human one, leaving everything that was not opposed to natural law, which was what the Incas most desired to observe.

After this progress, which lasted three years, the Inca returned to his capital, where he spent some months in festivities and rejoicing. But he soon took up with his brother, who was his alter ego, and the members of his council the question of new conquests in the provinces of Chinchasuyu, for it was only in that direction that there was any fertile land left to conquer: only wild forests were to be met with in the region of Antisuyu, under the shadow of the snowy cordillera. It was agreed that the Inca Cápac Yupanqui should resume the conquest, since he had given such good proof of his prudence and valor and all the qualities of a great captain in the last campaign. He was to be accompained by the heir to the throne, his nephew, a boy of sixteen called Inca Yupanqui, who had been made a knight that same year according to the rite of *huaracu,* which we shall have occasion to refer to at some length later. The boy was thus to acquire experience in the art of war, so much esteemed by the Incas. Fifty thousand warriors were made ready. The Incas, uncle and nephew, left with the first contingent and travelled as far as the great province called Chucurpu, which was the furthest confine of the empire in that direction.

Thence they sent the usual summonses to the natives of a province called Pincu, who, seeing that they could not resist the Inca's power and having heard how well his subjects fared under his laws and government, replied that they would be glad to receive the commands and laws of the Inca. At this response the Incas entered the province, whence they sent the same summons to other neighboring provinces: the chief of these are, among others, Huaras, Piscopampa, and Cunchucu. But these, instead of following the example of Pincu, did the opposite, and rose up in arms, calling on one another for help and dropping their private quarrels to rally to the common defence. Thus they gathered together and made reply that they would rather all die than receive new laws and customs and worship new gods: these they did not want, since they were well satisfied with the ones they had, which they had received from their fore-bears who had had them for many centuries. Let the Inca be satisfied with what he had seized, since he had usurped the authority of so many chiefs under pretext of religion.

Having given this reply and seeing that they could not resist the power of the Inca in open battle, they decided to withdraw to their fortresses, collect supplies, destroy the roads, and defend the difficult passes, all of which they did with great diligence and haste.

CHAPTER XIII

The Inca subdues the hostile provinces
by hunger and military strategy.

G ENERAL Cápac Yupanqui was not disconcerted by the arrogant and shameless reply of the enemy, for such was his magnanimous spirit that he was prepared to receive both good and bad words and events as well with an equal mind. Nevertheless he did not fail to make ready his men, and on learning that his foes were retiring to their fortresses, he divided his army into four forces of ten thousand men, sending each group against the enemy strongholds nearest at hand with orders not to engage in open battle but to force them to surrender by siege and starva-tion. He himself remained on watch with his nephew, ready to give suc-cor wherever it was needed. To provide against any lack of supplies—the enemy having taken what was available—in case the war should last long, he sent messages to the nearest provinces belonging to his brother, the Inca, that they were to despatch him double the usual amounts.

After taking these steps Inca Cápac Yupanqui awaited the outbreak of hostilities. The war was fought with great bitterness, and considerable loss of life on both sides, for the enemy stubbornly defended the roads and strong points, coming out when they saw that the Incas did not attack, rushing forward with desperate fury and falling on their adversaries' weapons. Each of the three provinces vied with the others to display the greatest spirit and outshine them in valor.

The Incas merely held their own, waiting until hunger and the other concomitants of war should reduce them to surrender. When they found women and children abandoned by the enemy in his withdrawal and wandering in the fields or the deserted villages, they treated them with care and kindness and gave them food; then as many as possible were collected together and guided to where their husbands and fathers were, so as to prove that the Incas had not come to take them captive, but to improve their laws and customs. It was also done as a military stratagem, so that the enemy should have more mouths to feed and a greater number to guard and protect than if they had remained unburdened with women and children and free to conduct the struggle without impedimenta. Moreover the hunger and sorrow of their children would affect them more than their own, and the weeping of the women would soften the resistance of the men, making them lose courage and aggressiveness, and so making them more ready to yield.

The enemy did not fail to notice the benefits done to his women and children, but his obstinacy and persistence were such that they left no room for gratitude. It even appeared that such acts of kindness merely steeled them to resist.

So both sides persisted in the struggle for five or six months, until the starvation and death of the weakest, the children and the more delicate of the women, made themselves felt, and as they mounted, forced the men to take thought lest death itself lay them low. Thus the captains and soldiers in the various strongholds decided by common consent to send ambassadors to approach the Incas in all humility, asking their pardon for what had happened and offering them obedience and homage for the future.

The Incas received them with their usual clemency and advised them in the gentlest terms they knew to return to their villages and houses and seek to be good subjects of their lord the Inca so as to deserve his favors: all that had gone before would be forgiven and never more brought to mind.

The envoys went back to their friends, much satisfied by the success of their mission, and when the reply of the Incas was made known, there was great rejoicing, and the people duly returned to their own villages where they were welcomed back and supplied with all they needed: the double supplies the Inca Cápac Yupanqui had called for at the beginning of the war proved highly necessary, since the vanquished enemy faced a whole year of scarcity owing to the destruction of all their crops, and they had to be supplied by the Incas. In addition to foodstuffs officials were provided to administer justice and collect taxes, and also to teach the idolatrous religion of the Incas.

CHAPTER XIV

*The good curaca Huamanchucu, and
how he was subdued.*

THE INCA continued his conquest and reached the borders of the great province called Huamanchucu, where there was a great lord of the same name, who was regarded as a person of great prudence and discretion. The usual summons and guarantees were despatched to him, offering peace and friendship, and better customs, laws, and religion. This tribe indeed was extremely barbarous and cruel in its habits, and its idolatry and sacrifices were particularly so, for it worshipped stones of various colors found by the rivers and brooks, such as jasper. The idea was that different colors could only be produced in the same stone by the influence of some great god within it, and in this stupid conviction they kept such stones in their houses as idols and respected them as gods. Their sacrifices were of human flesh and blood. They had no settled towns, but lived dispersed about the countryside in scattered huts, lacking any form of social organization or order. They lived like beasts. The good Huamanchucu would have liked to alter all this, but he dared not try lest his own followers should slay him, accusing him of disrespecting the religion and way of life of their ancestors with such reforms. This fear made him repress his good intentions, and he was therefore overjoyed with the Inca's message.

In the light of his own good sense he replied that he was overjoyed that the standards of the Inca empire should have been planted on his borders, for he had desired to have the Inca as his lord and king for many years, having heard excellent reports of their religion and administration. Because of the hostile provinces intervening and of his reluctance to forsake his own domains, he had not gone forth to seek the Inca and offer him homage and worship him as a child of the Sun, but now that his wishes had been realized, he would welcome the Incas with all the goodwill and desire he had felt to accept their overlordship, and he begged them to receive him in the same spirit as he offered himself, conferring on him and his subjects the benefits they had extended to the other Indians.

After receiving this friendly reply from the great Huamanchucu, Prince Inca Yupanqui and his uncle, the general, entered the province. The chief came out to welcome them with presents and gifts of all the produce of the country, and worshipped them with great reverence. The general received him most affably, and on behalf of the Inca, his brother, expressed thanks for his goodwill and affection. The prince had a great quantity of the garments that had been prepared for his father distributed among the chief, his relatives, and the headmen and nobles of the province. In addition to this favor, by which the Indians set great store, privileges and rewards of great value were conferred on them in return for the love they had shown toward the Inca. Indeed Inca Pachacútec and all his successors displayed great esteem and regard for Huamanchucu and his descendants, and greatly ennobled their province because of the way in which it had been added to their empire.

When the festivities on the occasion of their acknowledgment of the Inca as their lord had been completed, the great chief Huamanchucu spoke to the captain general begging him to take steps to raise the crude villages of his domains to a better way of life and to improve their religion, laws, and customs, realizing that those they had inherited from their forebears were beastly and ridiculous: he had wished to improve them, but did not dare for fear his people would kill him for contempt of their traditional laws. Though so brutish, his people were satisfied with their own ways. But now that good fortune had brought the Incas, the children of the Sun, to his land, he begged that they would improve it in every way, since he and his people had become their vassals.

The Inca was very glad to hear this and ordered that the hovels and cabins scattered about the countryside should be replaced by villages built on suitable sites in which the people would live in streets in neighborly fashion. He had a proclamation made that they were not to worship any god but the Sun, and that they were to cast out into the streets the colored stones they kept as idols in their houses, which were more suitable for children's playthings than as objects of human worship. They were to observe and fulfil the laws and ordinances of the Incas, and men were appointed to dwell in each village to indoctrinate them and teach them the new order of things.

CHAPTER XV

The people of Cajamarca resist,
but eventually surrender.

HAVING settled all this to the great satisfaction of the good Huaman-chucu, the Incas, uncle and nephew, advanced in their conquest until they reached the district of Cassamarca [Cajamarca], which came to be made famous by the imprisonment of Atahuallpa there. This was a large, rich, fertile province, thickly populated with warlike Indians who were sent the usual summons and offer of peace or war, so that they could not afterwards allege that they had been taken unawares.

The inhabitants of Cajamarca were greatly incensed by the message, though previously, on finding the zone of war nearing their own territory, they had, like a brave and warlike race, made ready their weapons and supplies, fortified themselves in their strongholds, and defended the diffi-cult places on the highroads. They therefore proudly replied that they had no need of new gods or a foreign overlord to give them other laws and strange privileges: they had what they needed, the laws and privi-leges established by their ancestors, and wanted no new-fangled ones. Let the Incas be satisfied with the obedience of those who wished to obey them and seek other vassals, for they did not want the Incas' friendship, much less their sovereignty, and would all die in defence of their liberty.

On receiving this reply, Inca Cápac Yupanqui entered the confines of Cajamarca, and the natives bravely barred his way at the difficult places, desiring to fight till death or victory. Although the Inca tried to avoid open warfare, this was impossible since he had to capture the enemy's strongholds by force of arms in order to advance. In these conflicts many perished on both sides in bitter fighting, and many more died in battles in the open country. But as the power of the Incas was such that their opponents could not resist them, the latter sought shelter in their fast-nesses, and the ravines and mountaintops where they proposed to hold out. From these places they sallied forth to attack, killing many of the Incas' warriors and also losing many of their own. This sort of warfare went on for four months, the delay being caused more by the Incas' desire to avoid annihilating their enemies than by the latter's own power, though they continued to resist with bravery and fortitude, even if not with the same energy as at first.

During the course of the war the Incas did all the good that was possible to their enemies so as to conquer them by kindness. Those captured in battle were released with kind words which they were to convey to their chiefs with offers of peace and friendship. The wounded were dressed, and on their recovery sent away with similar messages: they were told that they could return to fight, and as often as they were wounded and captured they would be healed and set free, since the Incas intended to prevail like Incas and not as cruel and tyrannical enemies. Women and children found in the fields and caves were tended and then returned to their parents or husbands with entreaties not to persist in their obstinacy, since it was impossible for them to defeat the children of the Sun.

After these and similar acts of kindness, repeated for a long time, the people of Cajamarca began to soften and lose their savagery and obduracy, and gradually to begin to ponder on whether they would not do well to submit to an enemy who could have put them to death, but chose instead to confer such benefits on them. They saw from experience, moreover, that the Inca's power mounted from day to day while theirs waned hourly, and they were now so sorely beset by hunger that they could scarcely expect to survive, let alone resist or defeat the Incas. Because of these difficulties, the *curaca* and his headmen decided, after due consultation, to accept the advances offered by the Incas, before their own obstinacy and ingratitude led to their withdrawal. They therefore sent ambassadors to say that, after experiencing the mercy, clemency, and mildness of the Incas, as well as the power of their arms, they were ready to admit that they deserved to be masters of the world, and that those who conferred such benefits on their enemies had every right to proclaim themselves children of the Sun: such acts constituted an assurance that the benefits would be even greater when the recipients became vassals of the Incas. Consequently, repenting of their obstinacy and ashamed of their ingratitude in not having responded earlier to the favors they had received, they begged the prince and his uncle, the general, to be so good as to forgive them for their rebelliousness and to become their sponsors and advocates, interceding with the Inca to accept them as vassals.

Scarcely had the envoys been able to reach the Incas than the *curaca* of Cajamarca and his headmen decided to present themselves in person to beg forgiveness for their faults, so as to move the Incas more readily to compassion. They thus approached with the greatest possible show of humility, and coming before the prince and the Inca general, worshipped them according to their usage and repeated the same words their envoys had used. Inca Cápac Yupanqui received them affably on behalf of his nephew, the prince, and informed them in very gentle terms that, in the name of his brother, the Inca, and his nephew, the prince, they were forgiven and received into the royal service like any other of the Inca's vassals. Their past misdeeds would never be recalled, but they must seek to do their best to deserve the Inca's favors, for His Majesty would not fail to confer the customary benefits on them and would treat them as his father the Sun had bidden him: let them depart in peace, returning to their villages and homes, and requesting whatever benefits they thought fit.

The *curaca*, accompanied by his friends, again worshipped the Incas and declared in the name of all his people that they had shown themselves to be true children of the Sun: his tribe held itself fortunate in having gained such masters, and they would serve the Incas like good vassals. This said, they took their leave and returned home.

CHAPTER XVI

The conquest of Yauyu, and triumph
of the Incas, uncle and nephew.

T HE INCA general valued the conquest of this province very highly, since it was one of the best in the whole of his brother's domains. He sought at once to improve it, replacing the scattered hovels with sizable villages and laying the foundations of a temple for the Sun and a house for the chosen virgins. These houses later reached such a high degree of decoration and were so well served that they became among the foremost in the whole of Peru. Teachers were appointed to inculcate their idolatrous religion and governors for the administration of the province and of the property of the Sun and of the king, as well as engineers to build water channels and extend the cultivated fields. He left a garrison to secure the conquest.

This done, he decided to return to Cuzco, but to reduce on the way a small area that he had passed by without conquering as it was remote from the route he had followed on his outward journey. This province, called Yauyu, is a rugged piece of territory peopled by warlike inhabitants, but he thought it could be reduced by a force of twelve thousand. He had these men picked and dismissed the rest, being unwilling to weary them without due cause. On reaching the confines of the province he sent forward the usual summons to peace or war.

The Yauyus met to discuss the matter, and opinions were divided. Some declared that they ought all to die defending their country, their liberty, and their ancient gods. Others were more prudent, and said that there was no reason to indulge in obvious and imprudent follies: it was clearly impossible for them to defend their country or their liberty against the power of the Inca, whose domains surrounded theirs on all sides. They knew that the Inca had reduced other provinces more powerful than their own and their gods could not take offence since they were irresistibly compelled to forsake them, and in this they committed no greater wrong than other tribes who had done the same. Let them remember that the Incas, according to report, treated their vassals in such a way that their rule was to be desired and sought after rather than avoided. From all this it seemed that they ought quickly to submit. Any other course would be patent folly and lead to the utter undoing of what they most wished to preserve since the Incas could, if they desired, cast down the surrounding mountain peaks on top of them.

This opinion prevailed, and thus by common consent they received the Incas with every possible ceremony and solemnity. The general conferred many favors on the *curaca*, and his kinsmen, captains, and nobles were given many of the fine garments called *compi*, while the common people received the inferior sort called *avasca*: all were delighted to have received such a king and lord.

The Incas, uncle and nephew, returned to Cuzco, leaving in Yauyu the usual officials for the government of the natives and administration of the royal estates. Inca Pachacútec came out to receive his brother and the prince, his son, with a solemn triumph and great festivities which had been prepared. He bade them enter on litters, which the Indians from the provinces conquered in the course of the expedition bore on their shoulders.

All the tribes who lived in the city and the *curacas* who came to take part in the celebrations marched in separate groups with their various instruments, drums, trumpets, horns, and shells, according to local usage, with various new songs composed in their own language in praise of the deeds and excellencies of the captain general, Cápac Yupanqui, and his nephew, Prince Inca Yupanqui. The good beginning made by the latter gave the greatest joy to his father, his kinsmen, and his vassals. After the courtiers and chief inhabitants marched the warriors, with their weapons in their hands, each tribe coming separately and singing the deeds the Incas had done in the war, uncle and nephew being treated as one person. The songs related the greatness and excellence of the pair: their boldness and valor in battle; their skill, diligence, and subtlety in the stratagems of war; their patience, wisdom, and mildness in suffering the follies of the ignorant and rash; their clemency, mercy, and charity towards the defeated enemy; their affability, liberality, and munificence towards their captains, their soldiers, and strangers; and their prudence and discretion in all they had done. The names of the Incas, uncle and nephew, were repeated many times: it was said that they fully deserved names of such majesty and grandeur by reason of their own virtues. After the warriors came the Incas of the royal blood, carrying their arms, both those who had come out of the city and those who came back from the wars, all grouped together without any distinction, for the custom was that any deeds performed by few or many of the Incas were made common to all, as if all had been present.

In the midst of the Incas went the general with the prince on his right hand. Behind them rode Inca Pachacútec in his golden litter. In this order they advanced till they reached the precincts of the house of the Sun, where the Incas alighted and all except the king removed their shoes. Then they entered as far as the gate of the temple where the Inca took off his sandals and entered the temple with the rest of those of the royal blood, but no others. Having worshipped the Sun and given thanks for the victories he had vouchsafed, they returned to the main square of the city where a festival was held with many songs and dances and much eating and drinking, which formed the main part of their festivities.

Each tribe rose from its place by order of seniority to dance and sing before the Inca according to the usage of their country. They brought with them their servants who played their drums and other instruments and accompanied the songs. After the dances, toasts were drunk, then others got up to dance, and then others, and so the dance lasted all day long. In this way the triumph was celebrated for a whole month: the previous triumphs were solemnized in the same way, but we have not described them because Cápac Yupanqui's was the most splendid and solemn hitherto seen .

CHAPTER XVII

Two valleys are subdued; Chincha
replies arrogantly.

A FTER these festivities, the Incas rested for three or four years without
waging any wars, but devoting themselves to the embellishment and
development of the provinces and kingdoms they had already won with
new buildings and the benefits of their administration. After this long
spell of peace, the Incas turned their attention to the conquest of the
coastal plains, where they had only reduced the area extending as far as
Nanasca. Having taken the opinion of their council of war, they had a
force of thirty thousand men equipped to depart at once on this conquest,
while as many again were prepared as a relief expedition, so that the
whole army could be changed every two months: this was rendered
necessary by the unhealthy climate of the plains, which is dangerous for
those born and bred in the mountains.

When the armies were ready, Inca Pachacútec gave orders for thirty
thousand men to stay in the surrounding villages ready to be called, while
the other thirty thousand went forth on the expedition. Three Incas went
with them, the king, Prince Inca Yupanqui and General Cápac Yupanqui,
and they travelled to the provinces called Rucana and Hatanrucana, where
the Inca himself decided to remain, so as to be close enough to the seat
of war to instil vigor into the operations while still attending to the administration of the realm.

The two Incas, uncle and nephew, advanced to Nanasca. Thence they
despatched messages to the valley of Ica, to the north of Nanasca, with
the usual summons. The natives asked for time before giving their reply,
and after some disagreement they decided to receive the Inca as their
lord, since they had heard and seen how mildly the Incas governed from
their long proximity to Nanasca. The people of the Pisco valley did the
same, though only after some difficulties. These were caused by their
closeness to the great valley of Chincha from which they thought of seeking protection and succor. They did not do so, thinking that such assistance would not be sufficient to defend them from the Inca, and they therefore resolved on the safer and wiser course of accepting the laws and
customs of the Incas and promising to worship the Sun as their god, and
repudiating and abhorring their present gods.

The Inca kings improved the Ica valley, which, like all these coastal valleys, is fertile, by building a very fine canal which brought down a great volume of water from high up in the mountains. In order to do this they very skilfully reversed the flow of the water, which had formerly run eastwards and was now made to flow westwards, taking advantage of a river that passed through the valley with only a small depth of water in summer, in consequence of which the Indians used to suffer greatly from drought in the maize fields, and many years, when it scarcely rained at all in the sierra, they lost their crops for lack of water. But now, with the aid of the canal, which was bigger than the river, they more than doubled the extent of their cultivable land, and thenceforward lived in great abundance and prosperity. All this caused the conquered and unconquered Indians to desire and love the Inca empire, whose care and attention was, they observed, always devoted to providing such benefits in the valleys.

It must be observed that in general the Indians of the coast for nearly five hundred leagues from Trujillo to Tarapacá, which are the northern and southern extremities of Peru, worshipped the sea (as well as the idols which each province had in particular). They worshipped it on account of the usefulness of its fish as food and as manure for their soil, which in some parts of the coast is fertilized with sardine heads. They therefore referred to the sea as Mamacocha, "mother sea," since it performed the part of a mother in feeding them. They also commonly worshipped the whale on account of its monstrous size, and some provinces worshipped some particular fish and others another, according to the value they attached to them and the quantity they caught. Such was, in belief, the idolatrous religion of the coastal Yunca Indians before the Inca empire was implanted.

Having conquered the two valleys of Ica and Pisco, the Incas sent their messages to the great and powerful valley called Chincha, from which the name Chinchasuyu is applied to the whole district, one of the four parts into which the Incas divided their empire. Their message was that the people of the valley should either take up arms or obey Inca Pachacútec, the child of the Sun.

The people of Chincha, confiding in the great host of warriors they had, tried to brazen it out. They said they wanted neither the Inca as their king nor the Sun as their god. They already had a god to worship and a king to serve: their common god was the sea, which as anyone could observe, was bigger than the Sun and gave them a great deal of fish, while the Sun did them no good at all, but merely harmed them with its excessive heat. Their land was a hot one, and they had no need of the Sun: let the mountain peoples who lived in cold climates worship him, since they had need of him. As to kings, they had one of their own stock and kind, and did not want a stranger, even though he were a child of the Sun: they had no need of the Sun or of his children either. They needed no warning to take up arms, for anyone who entered their province would always find them ready to defend it, together with their liberty and their gods, especially a god called Chincha Cámac who was the sustainer and creator of Chincha. The Incas would do better to return to their homes than to make war on the lord and king of Chincha, who was a most powerful prince. The natives of Chincha boasted that their ancestors had come from remote countries (though they did not say whence) with a captain general as devout as he was brave, so they said. They had won the valley by force of arms, destroying its previous occupants, a mean and feeble race which had accomplished nothing and perished to a man, leaving no survivors. They made a great many other boasts which we shall mention in due course.

CHAPTER XVIII

The obstinacy of Chincha; its final surrender.

O N RECEIVING this reply, the Incas travelled toward Chincha. The chief, who was also called Chincha, advanced out of his valley with a large force to skirmish with the Incas, but owing to the great quantity of sand neither side could fight and the Yuncas gradually fell back until they were again within their valley, where they resisted the Incas' advance, though without being able to avoid giving up enough ground for the enemy to build up a position. The battle raged with great fury, with losses of dead and wounded to both sides. The Yuncas were fighting to defend their country, and the Incas to extend their empire and increase their fame and glory.

The conflict went on for many days. The Incas many times offered the foe peace and friendship, but the Yuncas, obstinate in their resistance and confident that the heat of their climate would force the mountain people to withdraw, refused to receive any terms, on the contrary showing themselves daily more rebellious as they persisted in their vain hope. The Incas stood by their ancient custom of not destroying their enemies in war, but conquering them by kindness, and waited until the Yuncas should tire and give in of their own accord. As two months had now passed, they ordered the army to be relieved before the hot climate should have a disastrous effect on it: consequently the army that had been left behind in preparation was ordered to advance as far as possible so that those who had been fighting might depart before the heat laid them low with disease.

The commanders[1] of the reserve army advanced with all possible speed, and in a few days they reached Chincha. General Cápac Yupanqui welcomed them and dismissed the first army, ordering an equal number of soldiers to make ready to replace the second army if necessary. He also sent his nephew, the prince, to the mountains with the retiring army, lest his health and life be endangered on the coastal plain.

When all this had been done, the general began to intensify the war against the Chinchas, investing them more closely and laying waste their crops and the fruits of the field, so that they might be straitened by hunger. He had the irrigation channels destroyed, so that any land not laid waste by the Incas could not be watered. This had the greatest effect on the Yuncas, for as the country is so hot and the sun burns, the land has to be watered every three or four days or it will not bear fruit.

The Yuncas were hard set with the close siege and the destruction of their water channels. They had lost their former hope that the Incas might leave for the mountains for fear of the unhealthiness of the lowlands, and when they saw that a new army had arrived and realized that it could be relieved every three months, their arrogance began to abate, though not their stubbornness, for they held out another two months, refusing the offers of peace and friendship the Incas made them every week. On the one hand they resisted the enemy by force of arms, fighting for all they were worth and patiently supporting the hardships of war: on the other they besought the aid of their god Chincha Cámac, with great devotion and many promises, especially the women, who begged him with many tears and sacrifices to spare them from the Incas' power.

It should be mentioned that the Indians of the beautiful Chincha valley had a famous idol which they regarded as their god, and which they called Chincha Cámac. This god they adored like Pachacámac, the unknown

---

[1] *Maeses de campo*: a term applied to the commander of a Spanish *tercio*, or an officer directly under a commander-in-chief.

god, whom the Incas worshipped mentally, as we have described. The reason was that the natives of another great valley in front of Chincha (of which we shall speak later) had adopted Pachacámac as their god and erected a famous temple to him. As they knew that Pachacámac meant the "sustainer of the universe," it occurred to them that he had so much to sustain that he might neglect or be unable to sustain Chincha as well as its inhabitants desired. They therefore took it into their heads to invent a god who would sustain their country in particular, whom they therefore called Chincha Cámac: it was because of their confidence in this god that they obstinately refused to surrender, trusting that he, as their household deity, would save them from the Incas.

The latter suffered the weariness of battle and the persistence of the Yuncas with great patience: they were determined not to destroy the enemy, but short of killing them, they pressed and harassed them as much as they could.

Inca Cápac Yupanqui, on seeing how rebellious the Yuncas were, realized that it was a loss of his time and reputation to be so forbearing: he had already waited long enough to satisfy the merciful policy of his brother the Inca, and if he continued to display gentleness toward his enemies, it might be turned to cruelty against his own men, if they should succumb to disease, as was much to be feared from the great heat of those regions for such Indians as were not accustomed to it. He therefore sent a message to say that he had already fulfilled the orders of his brother, the Inca, to attract the Indians to his rule by kindness and not by cruelty, but that the more clemency he had shown, the more rebellious the enemy had become, attributing his mildness to cowardice: in consequence he was going to warn them to surrender and submit to the Inca's service within a week, after which he would, if necessary, have them all put to the knife and settle their land with new peoples brought from elsewhere. He ordered the envoys to deliver this message and return without awaiting an answer.

The Yuncas were alarmed at the message, since they saw that the Inca was quite right: he had suffered and waited long enough, and though he could have waged war with blood and fire, he had on the contrary shown great mildness, treating them as he had their fields which had not been laid waste completely. After discussion, they therefore thought that they ought not to provoke him to a display of greather wrath, but to do as he bade, since hunger and toil had reduced them almost to surrender. This agreed, they sent their ambassadors to beg the Inca to spare them and receive them as their subjects: thenceforth they would exchange

the rebelliousness they had shown for loyalty, and serve him as good vassals should. The following day the *curaca,* accompanied by his kinsmen
and other nobles, went to kiss the Inca's hands and to offer him their
personal obedience.

CHAPTER XIX

The ancient conquests and false boasting of the Chinchas

T HE INCAS rejoiced with the Chincha chief that so troublesome and
    difficult a war should be concluded. He received the great Yunca with
affability and said very gracious words about his pardon for the late revolt, since the chief displayed great grief and affliction for his offence.
The Inca bade him never to speak of it any more or even to remember it,
since his brother the king had already blotted it from his memory: to
prove that the chief had forgiven, various favors were granted him and
his friends in the Inca's name, and they also received the highly esteemed
garments and jewels from the Inca, at which they were all well satisfied.
    The Chincha Indians now boast a great deal of the great resistance they
put up against the Incas, declaring that they could not be reduced at the
first campaign, but had to be attacked twice, since the first time the Incas
withdrew and returned to their homes. This refers to the two armies sent
against their province, which took turns, as we have said. They also said
that the Incas took many years to conquer them, and that they finally reduced them with promises, gifts, and presents, and not by force of arms,
turning the mildness of the Incas to a proof of their own valor, though
the power of the Incas in those days was already such that they could
easily have defeated the Yuncas by main force if they had so desired. But
once the crisis is over, it is easy for anyone to brag.
    They also say that before the Incas reduced them they were so power-
ful and warlike that they often sallied forth on raids and brought back a
great deal of plunder: the mountain dwellers feared them and abandoned
their villages to them, so that they often reached the province of Colla.
All this is false, for most of the Yuncas are for the most part a soft-living
and idle race, and they would have had to travel nearly two hundred

leagues and cross bigger and more densely populated provinces than their own to get to the Collas. An even stronger proof is afforded by the fact that, since they live in a hot country where it never rains and they never hear the sound of thunder, if the Yuncas go up into the mountains and hear thunder, they almost die of fear, and not knowing where to hide themselves, they return hot-foot to their own country. This shows how convincing is the evidence the Yuncas bring on their own behalf against the mountain people.

Inca Cápac Yupanqui, while making the necessary arrangements and giving orders for the administration of Chincha, warned his brother the Inca of all that had happened, and begged him to send a new army to replace the one he then had and press forward with the conquest of the Yuncas. In dealing with the new laws and customs that were to be implanted in Chincha, the Inca learned that there were a large number of sodomites among them. He had them arrested and burned them all alive on the same day, giving instructions that their houses should be pulled down, their fields laid waste and their trees uprooted, so that no memory should remain of anything the sodomites had planted with their hands: women and children would have been burnt for the sin of their fathers, if this had not appeared inhumane, for the vice was one that the Incas abominated exceedingly.

Thenceforward the Inca kings greatly adorned the valley of Chincha. They built a splendid temple for the Sun and a house for the chosen virgins. The valley had over thirty thousand families, and is one of the loveliest in all Peru. And now, because the deeds and conquests of King Pachacútec were many and it is tedious to discourse constantly on the same theme, I have thought it best to divide my account of his life and deeds in two parts and place between them a description of two great festivals which these kings observed in the days of their idolatry; after this we shall return to the life of the Inca.

CHAPTER XX

*The principal feast of the Sun, and how
they prepared for it.*

T HE NAME Raimi corresponds to our greater festivals such as Easter or
Christmas. Of the four festivals celebrated by the Inca kings in the
city of Cuzco, which was their home, the most solemn was that held in
honor of the Sun in the month of June and called Intip Raimi, meaning
"the solemn feast of the Sun." It was usually simply called Raimi, with
no difference of meaning, and if the word was applied to other festivals
it was by extension from this, to which the name Raimi properly belonged. It took place after the June solstice.

The festival was dedicated to the Sun in recognition of their worship
of it as the sole, supreme, and universal god, who created and sustained
everything in the earth with his light and virtue. Out of regard for the
fact that the Sun was the natural father of the first Inca Manco Cápac and
of the Coya Mama Ocllo Huaco and of all the kings and their children
and descendants sent down to earth for the universal benefit of mankind,
the feast was a very solemn one. It was attended by all the military leaders who were retired or not actually engaged on a campaign and by all the
curacas, the lords of vassals, of the whole empire. They came not because
they were obliged to appear, but because they were glad to attend the observation of so great a feast, which, as it included the worship of their
god the Sun, and the veneration of their king the Inca, was attended by
absolutely everyone. When the *curacas* could not be present because they
were prevented by old age, ill health, or serious business in the royal
service, or because of the great distance, they used to send their sons and
brothers, escorted by the most noble members of their people, so that they
might represent them at the festival. The Inca was present in person, provided he was not prevented by some necessary war or visit to his provinces.

The king performed the first rites as high priest: although there was
always a high priest of the blood royal (since he must be a brother or
uncle of the Inca of legitimate descent on both sides), nevertheless as this
festival was dedicated especially to the Sun, the ceremonies were performed by the king himself, as the first-born child of the Sun and therefore primarily and principally obliged to solemnize the occasion.

The chiefs appeared in their best attire and adornments, some wearing plates of silver and gold on their garments and wreaths of the same on their heads, round their headdresses. Others came exactly as Hercules is depicted, clad in a lion's skin, with the Indian's head inside the lion's, since they boasted of their descent from a lion. Still others appeared in the guise in which angels are depicted, with the great wings of a bird called the *cuntur*. These are black and white, and so large that specimens have been killed by the Spaniards with a wing span of fourteen or fifteen feet. The Indians in question pretended to originate and descend from a *cuntur*.

Others, notably the Yuncas, came in masks devised with the most repulsive figures imaginable. They made their entry into the festivals grimacing and striking attitudes like fools, madmen, or simpletons, and they carried suitable instruments in their hands, such as ill-devised flutes or tamborines and pieces of skin of which they availed themselves for their follies. Other chiefs brought various other devices. Each tribe carried the weapons it used in time of war, some bows and arrows, other lances, darts, bolts, clubs, slings, and short single-handed axes or long double-handed ones. They carried representations of the deeds they had performed in the service of the Sun and of the Incas, carrying great drums and trumpets, and brought a great many performers to play them. In short each tribe came as well attired and attended as possible, each seeking to out-shine his neighbors and countrymen, or the whole assembly, if possible.

They generally prepared themselves for the Raimi of the Sun by observing a strict fast, eating nothing for three days but a little raw white maize, a few herbs called *chúcam,* and some plain water. During the whole time they lit no fires in the city and refrained from sleeping with their wives.

After the fast, the night before the feast, the Inca priests appointed to attend to the sacrifice had the sheep and lambs made ready, as well as the other offerings of food and drink that were to be presented to the Sun. When these arrangements were made it was known what people had come to the feast, since all the tribes had to share in the offerings, not only the *curacas* and ambassadors, but also all their kinsmen, vassals, and servants.

That night the women of the Sun busied themselves with the preparation of enormous quantities of a maizen dough called *çancu,* of which they made little round loaves the size of an ordinary apple, and it is to be noted that the Indians never ate their corn kneaded and made into loaves except at this festival and another called Citua: even so they did not eat these loaves during the whole meal, but only a few mouthfuls at the beginning. Their usual meal in place of bread is the *sara* roasted or cooked in the grain.

The flour for this bread, and especially that which was to be eaten by the Inca and the members of the royal family, was ground and kneaded by the chosen virgins, the wives of the Sun, who also prepared the rest of the food for the feast. The banquet seemed indeed rather a gift from the Sun to his children than from the children to the Sun, and for that reason the virgins prepared it, as wives of the Sun.

An infinite number of other women appointed for the purpose kneaded the bread and prepared the meal for the rest of the people. The bread, though it was for the community, was compounded with care and attention that at least the flour should be prepared by damsels; for this bread was regarded as something sacred and not allowed to be eaten during the year, but only at this festivity which was their feast of feasts.

CHAPTER XXI

They worshipped the Sun, went to his house, and sacrificed a lamb.

EVERYTHING being prepared, the following day, which was that of the festival, the Inca went out at daybreak accompanied by his whole kin. They departed in due order, each according to his age and rank, to the main square of the city called Haucaipata. There they waited for the sun to rise and stood with bare feet, attentively gazing toward the east. When the Sun began to appear, they all squatted (which among the Indians is as though they were to kneel) to worship it. This they did by raising their arms and placing their hands beside their faces, kissing the air, which is the same as kissing one's hand or the garment of a prince as a mark of respect in Spain. They worshipped the Sun with great affection and acknowledgment that he was their god and natural father.

The *curacas* who were not of the royal blood went to another square next to the main one, called Cussipata, where they worshipped the Sun in the same way as the Incas. Then the king stood up, the rest remaining squatting, and he took two great golden vessels which they called *aquilla*, full of the beverage they drink. He performed this rite in the name of his father, the Sun, as his first-born, and invited him to drink with the vessel in his right hand. This the Sun was supposed to do, and the Inca invited all his kinsmen to drink too. This custom of inviting one another to drink was the greatest and most usual demonstration of condescension on the part of the superior toward his inferior, and of the friendship of friends for one another. After the invitation to drink, the Inca poured the contents of the vessel in his right hand, which was dedicated to the Sun, into a gold basin, and from the basin it flowed along a beautifully made stone-work channel which ran from the square to the house of the Sun. It was thus as if the Sun had drunk the liquid. From the vessel in his left hand the Inca swallowed a draught, which was his portion, and then shared what was left among the other Incas, giving each of them a little in a small bowl of silver or gold which was ready to receive it. At intervals the vessel the Inca held was replenished, so that the first liquid which had been sanctified by the hands of the Sun or of the Inca, or both of them, should transmit its virtue to each of the recipients. All the members of the royal blood drank a draught of the beverage. The rest of the *curacas* in the other square drank of the same brew prepared by the women of the Sun, but not of the part that was sanctified, which was reserved for the Incas.

After this ceremony, which was a sort of foretaste of what was to be drunk later, they all went in order to the house of the Sun, and two hundred steps before they reached it they removed their shoes, with the exception of the king who only took them off at the very door of the temple. The Inca and members of the blood went in like natural children and worshipped the image of the Sun. The *curacas*, being unworthy of entering the high place, since they were not children of the Sun, stayed outside in a large square which today stands before the temple gate.

The Inca offered the vessels of gold used for the ceremony with his own hands. The remaining Incas gave their vessels to the Inca priests appointed and dedicated to the service of the Sun: those who were not priests, even though they were of the Sun's blood, were seculars and not permitted to perform the functions of priests. After offering up the vessels of the Incas, the priests went outside to collect the *curacas'* vessels. The *curacas* approached in order of seniority according to the period when their people had been incorporated in the empire, and they handed over their vessels and other objects of gold and silver which they had brought from their own provinces to present to the Sun, such as sheep, lambs, lizards, toads, serpents, foxes, tigers, lions, and a great variety of birds. In short they brought natural models in gold and silver of whatever was found most abundantly in their provinces, though each object appeared only in small quantities.

After the offering, they returned in order to their two squares. Then came the Inca priests with a great number of lambs, barren ewes, and rams of all colors, for the Peruvian sheep is found in all colors, like horses in Spain. All the sheep belonged to the Sun. They would take a black lamb, this being the color these Indians preferred above all others for their sacrifices, regarding it as having greater divinity. Their argument was that the black animal was black all over, while the white, though the whole of the rest of its body might be white, always had a black snout, which they held to be a defect, so that the white was always regarded as inferior to black. For this reason the kings usually dressed in black: when in mourning, they wore the natural grey-brown color of the wool.

The first sacrifice of the black lamb was intended to observe the auguries and omens of the festival. For in everything they did of importance, either for peace or war, they almost always sacrificed a lamb so as to inspect its heart and lungs and discover if it was acceptable to the Sun; that is, whether the expedition would be successful or otherwise, or whether the harvest that year would be good or bad. For some purposes they used a lamb for their auguries, for others a sheep, for others a sterile ewe, and whenever we say an ewe we mean a sterile one, for those capable of bearing were never killed and not even used for eating until they were past breeding.

They took the sheep or lamb, and placed it with its head facing the east. Its feet were not tied, but it was held by three or four Indians. While still alive, its left side was opened, and by inserting the hand they drew forth the heart, lungs, and entrails, which were plucked forth with the hand and not cut: the whole must come out together from the throat downwards.

CHAPTER XXII

The auguries of their sacrifices,
and the use of fire.

T HEY REGARDED it as a most happy omen if the lungs came out still quivering, before they had finished dying, as they put it, and if they obtained this good omen, they ignored the rest, even though they might be bad. They said that the excellence of this lucky omen would overcome the ill effects of all bad omens. Taking out the entrails, they inflated them by blowing and held the air in by tying up the main gut or nipping it with their fingers: they then inspected the passages whereby the air enters the lungs and the little veins along them to see if they were swollen or contained little air: the more swollen they were, the happier was the augury. They also inspected other things, but I cannot say what they were, for I did not observe them. I do remember what I have described for I witnessed it twice when, as a boy, I happened to enter a certain yard where old Indians who had not been baptised still performed this sacrifice—though not for Raimi, which was no longer celebrated when I was born. They had other special occasions for inspecting the omens and they then sacrificed lambs and rams as we have described for Raimi: what was done at private sacrifices was modelled on what took place at the chief festivals.

It was regarded as a most inauspicious augury if the beast rose to its feet while its side was being opened, forcibly overcoming those who were holding it down. It was also a bad omen if the gut broke while it was being plucked out, and did not come out whole. It was also a bad omen if the lungs were drawn out broken or the heart spoiled, together with other points which, as I have said, I did not ask about or notice. I remember those I have mentioned because I heard them spoken of by Indians engaged in making the sacrifices: they asked one another if the auguries were good or bad, and took no notice of me because of my youth.

To return to the celebration of the feast of Raimi, we should mention that if the augury did not appear favorable from the sacrifice of the lamb, they performed another with a ram; and if this was also unlucky, they made a third with a barren ewe. If this too was unpropitious, they went on with the feast, though sad at heart and inwardly grieving, saying that their father the Sun was angry with them for some fault or negligence which they had inadvertently committed.

The things they feared were bitter wars, the sterility of their crops, the death of their sheep, and similar evils. Yet when the auguries promised them good fortune, they celebrated their Easter with the greatest joy in the hope of coming benefits.

After they had sacrificed the lamb, a great quantity of other lambs, ewes, and rams was brought for the common sacrifice. This was not performed like the first offering by opening them while they were still alive: their throats were cut and they were flayed. Their blood and hearts were all kept and offered to the Sun, as in the case of the first lamb. Everything was burned to ashes.

The fire for the sacrifice had to be new, given by the Sun's hand, as they put it. To this end they used to take a large bracelet called a *chipana,* like those the Incas usually wore on their left wrists. It was kept by the high priest, and was larger than the usual size, and had on its front a highly burnished concave bowl like a half orange. It was placed against the sun and at a certain point where the rays reflected from the bowl came together, they placed a piece of well-carded cotton (not having tinder). This was quickly fired, as was only natural. By means of this fire, given by the Sun's hand, the sacrifice was burnt and all the meat slaughtered that day was consumed. The fire was carried to the temple of the Sun and the house of the virgins where it was kept alive throughout the year. It was a bad omen if it went out for any reason at all. If there was not enough sun on the eve of the feast, when everything was made ready for the next day's sacrifices, to produce new fire, it was obtained by means of two rounded sticks, as thick as the little finger and half a vara long, which were rubbed together. The sticks are cinnamon-colored, and were called *u'yaca,* which is also the word for "strike fire," the same word serving for noun and verb. The Indians use them instead of flint and steel, and carry them on their travels to produce fire when they camp in the uninhabited countryside. I have often seen them do this while travelling with them, and shepherds do the same.

It was regarded as an unfavorable omen to have to make fire for their festivals with this instrument: they said that the Sun was angry with them since he denied them fire from his own hand. All the meat for the sacrifice was burnt in public in the two squares and shared among all those who had been present at the festivity: Incas, *curacas,* and common people, according to their rank. They were all given it with the bread called *çancu,* which formed the first dish at their great feast and solemn banquet.

Then a great variety of foods was brought, and they ate, without pausing to drink, for it was the universal custom among the Indians of Peru not to drink while they were eating.

The customs we have described may be the source of statements made by certain Spanish writers to the effect that the Incas and their vassals communicated like Christians. We have simply described what the Indians did and leave each reader to draw what parallel he wishes.

After the meal, the Indians were brought drink in great abundance. This was one of the most conspicuous vices of the Indians, though today, through God's mercy and the good example set in this particular by the Spaniards, there are no Indians who get drunk, but they scorn and abominate it as a great infamy. If the example set by the Spaniards had been such in the case of all vices, they would have been truly apostolic preachers of the Gospel.

CHAPTER XXIII

How they drank to one another, and in what order.

SEATED on his chair of solid gold which was placed on a gold platform, the Inca used to send his relatives called Hanan Cuzco and Hurin Cuzco to drink in his name to the most eminent representatives of other tribes who were present. They would first toast captains who had proved themselves valiant in war, for they, even though they were not lords of vassals, were set before *curacas* on account of their valor: but if a *curaca* had been a captain in the wars as well as a lord of vassals, then he was honored on both counts. Secondly, the Inca invited the *curacas* of the neighborhood of Cuzco to drink with him: these were the people the first Inca Manco Cápac reduced to his service, and they were treated as Incas and regarded as occupying the first place after the Incas of the royal blood, and were set before the members of all the other tribes because of the great privilege Manco Cápac had conferred on them in giving them the name of Incas. The Inca kings never indeed thought of curtailing or suppressing any privileges or favor that their ancestors had conferred on their vassals in general or in particular; on the contrary, they would confirm and extend such favors.

In order to understand their manner of drinking toasts, it must be mentioned that all the Indians had and still have, according to their rank, matched drinking vessels in pairs. Whether large or small, they are of the same size and shape and of the same substance, gold, silver, or wood. This was done so that there should be equality in what was drunk. Whoever extended the invitation to drink carried the two vessels in his hands, and if his guest was of lower rank, he offered him the vessel in his left hand; if of higher or equal rank, the one in his right, exhibiting greater or less ceremony according to the degree or equality of each. Both then drank equally and the host, after recovering his vessel, would return to his place. In such festivities, the first invitation was always from superior to inferior, as a token of favor or regard. Afterwards the inferior invited his superior to drink, thus acknowledging his vassalage and servitude.

In obedience to this practice, the Inca began by first inviting his subjects to drink with him, following the order we have stated, and giving precedence to the captains over the other members of each tribe. The Incas who carried the beverage would say to the guest, "The Sapa Inca has bidden you to be invited to drink, and I have come in his name to drink with you." The captain or *curaca* would take the vessel very reverently, raising his eyes to the Sun, as if giving thanks for the unmerited favor conferred on him by the child of the Sun, and after drinking returned the vessel to the Inca, saying nothing, but making gestures of adoration with his hands and kissing the air with his lips.

It is worthy of note that the Inca never invited the whole of the *curacas* to drink together (though he did all the captains), but bade only certain ones in particular who were the most beloved of their vassals, the most devoted to the common good, this being the common aim of all, the Inca, *curacas,* and the royal officials for peace and war. The Incas themselves invited the remaining *curacas* to drink, carrying the vessels in their own names and not in that of the Inca. To be invited by any Inca was sufficient and accounted a great honor, for they were all children of the Sun like their king.

After the first round of drinking, the captains and *curacas* of all the tribes soon returned the invitation in the order in which they themselves had been invited, some to the Inca himself and others to the remaining Incas, each corresponding to the original invitation. They approached the Inca without speaking, merely offering him the silent adoration we have described. He received them with great affability and took the vessels they offered him, but as he could not, nor was it lawful for him to drink them all, he merely put them to his mouth. From some he drank a little, taking more from some and less from others according to the degree of favor he wished to show to their owners, corresponding to their merits and qualities. He also bade all the servants he had about him, who were all Incas by privilege, to drink on his behalf with the captains and *curacas*: these, having drunk, returned the vessels to their owners.

The vessels that the Sapa Inca had touched with his hand and with his lips the *curacas* held in the highest veneration as sacred objects. They neither drank from them nor touched them, but simply set them up as idols, so as to worship them in memory of their having been touched by the Inca. With regard to this it would be impossible to express adequately the love and veneration these Indians both felt in themselves and displayed outwardly toward their kings.

Having exchanged drinks, they all returned to their places. Then the dancers and singers of various kinds made their appearance, with the insignia, emblems, masks, and devices of each tribe. And while they sang and danced, they did not cease to drink, some of the Incas inviting others, and captains and *curacas* other captains and *curacas*, according to their personal friendships, the proximity of their provinces, and other connections between them.

The celebration of Raimi lasted for nine days, with the abundant feasting and drinking we have mentioned, and such rejoicing as each could show. But the sacrifices for determining the auspices took place only on the first day. As soon as the nine days were over, the *curacas* returned to their own countries, with the king's permission, very happy and satisfied at having celebrated the chief festival of their god, the Sun. When the king was occupied in war or in visiting his realms, the feast was celebrated wherever he happened to be on the appropriate day, though not with so much solemnity as when he was in Cuzco. In his absence the Inca governor, the high priest, and the remaining Incas of the royal blood carefully observed the festival, and on these occasions the *curacas* and envoys from the various provinces each repaired to the celebration that was nearest.

CHAPTER XXIV

How the Incas were armed knights, and the tests they were submitted to.

THE WORD *huaracu* occurs in the general language of Peru and is equivalent to arming a knight in Spanish, for it was applied to the granting of the tokens of manhood to lads of the royal blood, which qualified them to go to war and to set up house. Until they received these insignia of manhood they were not allowed to do either of these things, being, as the books of chivalry would say, mere squires who were not entitled to bear arms. In order to receive these insignia, which we shall describe later, the youths who were candidates underwent a very severe initiation, and were tested in all the hardships and emergencies that might occur in war whether its fortunes were prosperous or adverse. In order to explain this the better, we had best describe these solemn rites stage by stage: certainly for a barbarous race, these Indians had some remarkably civilized practices in military matters. The occasion was one of great rejoicing among the common people and of considerable honor and splendor among the Incas, whether old or young, already approved in the ordeal or still untested. For the honor obtained by the novices in passing the test, or the disgrace of failing it, was shared by their whole kin, and as the Incas formed a single family, consisting mainly of those of the royal blood of legitimate descent, the good fortune or misfortune of each of them affected all the rest, though especially those most nearly related.

More or less every year or every other year, according to circumstances, the young Incas (and it must be emphasized that we are referring to them and not to the rest, even to the sons of great lords) underwent the military ordeal. They had to be over sixteen years of age, and were assembled in a building built for the ordeal in the quarter called Collcampata: I myself saw it while it was still standing and witnessed some of the ceremonies, though they could only be described as a shadow of the past, as regards spendor and completeness. The old Incas, experienced in affairs of peace and war, who acted as masters of the novices, repaired to the house to examine them in the points we shall mention and others that are now forgotten. The candidates were required to observe a very strict fast for six days, receiving only a handful of raw *sara* (their corn) apiece and a jug of plain water, without anything else, either salt or *uchu* (which in

Spain is called Indian peppers), a condiment that flavors and enriches the poorest and meanest meal, even if it is only a dish of herbs: for this reason the novices were deprived of it.

Such a rigorous fast was not usually permitted for more than three days, but this period was doubled for the initiates undergoing their ordeal, in order to show if they were men enough to suffer any hunger or thirst to which they might be exposed in time of war. The fathers, brothers, and other close relatives of the candidates underwent a less rigorous, but none the less strictly observed, fast, praying their father the Sun to strengthen and encourage the youths so that they might come through the ordeal with honor. Anyone who showed weakness or distress or asked for more food was failed and eliminated from the test. After the fast they were allowed some victuals to restore their strength and then tried for bodily agility. As a test they were made to run from the hill called Huanacauri, which they regarded as sacred, to the fortress of the city, which must be a distance of nearly a league and a half. At the fortress a pennant or banner was set up as a finishing post, and whoever reached it first was elected captain over the rest. Those who arrived second, third, fourth, and down to the tenth fastest were also held in great honor, while those who flagged or fainted on the course were disgraced and eliminated. Their parents and relatives exhorted them as they ran, urging upon them the honor of victory and shame of failure, and representing that they would do better to burst than swoon by the wayside.

The next day they were divided into two equal bands. One group was bidden to remain in the fortress, while the other sallied forth, and they were required to fight one against the other, the second group to conquer the fort and the first defending it. After fighting thus for the whole day, they changed sides on the morrow, the defenders becoming the attackers so that they could all display their agility and skill in attacking or defending strongholds. In such struggles the weapons were blunted so that they were less formidable than in real warfare; nevertheless there were severe casualties which were sometimes fatal, for the will to win excited them to the point of killing one another.

CHAPTER XXV

*They were required to know how to make
their own arms and their shoes.*

A FTER THESE exercises in common, the candidates were required to
wrestle with one another, being matched according to their ages, and
to compete in jumping and throwing a large or small stone, a spear, dart,
and any other missile. They had to shoot at the mark with bows and arrows to prove the accuracy of their aim and their dexterity in handling
weapons, and they also competed at shooting for distance, to prove their
strength of arm and skill. Similarly they exercised with slings to test the
length of their shooting and the accuracy of their aim. They were further
tested in the use of all other weapons employed in warfare by the Indians,
in order to show their dexterity. They were required to keep vigil in
watches for ten or twelve nights, acting as sentinels, to prove if they were
the sort of men who could resist the force of sleep. They were summoned
without warning, and those who were found asleep were shamed with
severe reproaches, as being too childish to qualify for military insignia
of honor and dignity. They were harshly beaten with rods of osier and
similar plants on the arms and legs which the Peruvian Indians as they
usually dress leave bare, to see how they reacted to such blows; and if they
showed signs of pain in their expression or by shifting their legs or arms
ever so slightly, they were eliminated with the remark that those who
could not suffer the blows of such light rods would suffer even less the
blows and wounds of the hard weapons of their foes. They were expected
to stay as if they felt nothing.

Then they were placed in a double row, and an experienced captain
carrying a weapon like a two-handed sword or perhaps a club, which is
the nearest weapon to what the Indians call *macana,* or on other occasions
with a pike, which they call *chuqui,* would pass between the two files
brandishing either of these weapons with great dexterity round the candidates. The weapon would graze their legs, as if about to break them,
or sweep past their eyes, as if to blind them, and if any of them had the
misfortune to express any sign of fear by blinking their eyes or moving
a limb, they were rejected, and told that anyone who feared the blows of
weapons that they knew would not wound them would be much more
afraid of the arms of any enemy who they would be sure wielded them to

kill. They must therefore remain as motionless as rocks beaten by the sea and wind.

In addition, they were required to know how to make with their own hands all offensive weapons necessary for waging war, especially the commonest and those that did not require metalwork—such as the bow and arrows; a kind of projectile which might be described as a throwing-dart, being propelled by a stick or string; a spear, the point of which was sharpened instead of being tipped with iron; and a hempen or esparto sling —so that in case of need they could prepare and use all of these. They used no defensive weapons but a sort of shield or targe which they call *huallcana*. These they also had to be able to make of any material they could find. They also had to make the footwear they used called *usuta*: a sole of leather, esparto or hemp, like the rope-soled sandals worn in Spain. They did not know how to attach these to a welt, but fastened the soles to their feet with strings of hemp or wool which for brevity we may compare with the open shoes worn by the religious of the order of St. Francis.

The strings for this footwear are made of wool twisted on a little stick. They hold the wool in one hand to twist and the little stick in the other, and half a fathom of string suffices for each foot. It is as thick as the little finger, since the thicker it is, the less harm it can do the foot. Because of this custom of twisting strings for this particular purpose, one historian of the Indians, in speaking of the Incas, says that they spun, though he does not say how or what. He may well be pardoned this mistaken account he was given, like many others, to the prejudice of both Indians and Spaniards, for which he is not to blame, since he wrote far away from Peru and had to rely on various accounts by people with their own axes to grind. Generally speaking there were no more manly people, or prouder of it, among all the pagans than the Incas, nor any who so scorned feminine pursuits. All of them were high-minded and they set their thoughts on the greatest matters they knew: they boasted of being children of the Sun, and this boast urged them to heroic thoughts.

This style of twisting wool is called *milluy*. The verb alone, with no other word, implies twisting wool with a little stick to make strings for shoes or ropes for lifting things, which were also made of wool. As the work was performed by men, the verb was not used of spinning by women, or it would have suggested that they were men. Spinning by women was called *buhca*, a word meaning "to spin with a distaff" and also the "distaff." As this work was proper for women, the verb *buhca* was never applied to men or it would have implied they were women.

This is characteristic of their language, as we shall have occasion to note in the case of other verbs and nouns that those interested may be curious to see. Thus the Spaniards who write histories of Peru in Spain miss the subtleties of the language, while those who write histories in Peru disregard them and interpret them according to the Spanish language, involuntarily bearing false witness against the Incas.

To return to our theme, we repeat that the candidates were required to know how to make the weapons and footwear they would need in an emergency in time of war. This was required of them so that they should never be helpless in case of need, but always have the ability and skill to fend for themselves.

CHAPTER XXVI

The prince underwent the ordeal, and was treated more severely than the rest.

EACH DAY one of the captains and overseers of these rites made them an address, reminding them of their descent from the Sun; of the deeds done in peace and war by past kings and other famous men of the royal stock; of the courage and spirit they ought to show in wars to extend the empire; of patience and endurance under hardship as a proof of generosity and magnanimity; of clemency, pity, and mildness toward their subjects and the poor; of rectitude in the administration of justice; of the duty to prevent anyone from being wronged; and of liberality and open-handedness toward everyone, as befitted children of the Sun. In short they were taught all aspects of moral philosophy as they knew it, having regard to their divine origin and descent from heaven. They were required to sleep on the bare ground, eat little and badly, go barefooted, and do everything else likely to make them good soldiers.

The first-born son of the Inca who was the legitimate heir to the throne was also subjected to this ordeal, when he reached the proper age. It is noteworthy that in all these exercises he was tested with the same strictness as the rest, and was not exempted from any trial on account of his princely rank, except the contest for the pennant awarded to the fleetest of foot in the race for the captaincy: this was granted to him as part of his birthright. In all other exercises, fasting, military discipline, the making of weapons and shoes, sleeping on the ground, eating little, and going barefoot, the prince enjoyed no privileges of any sort, but was treated rather more harshly than they on the ground that, as he was to be king, it was only right that he should rise above the rest in anything he undertook, as he did in the greatness of his rank: if the royal person underwent experiences similar to his subjects', it would be unseemly that he should emerge below them. Both in prosperity and in adversity he must show his superiority, in spirit and in deed, and especially in military matters.

They would say that these excellences constituted his right to rule, much more than the fact that he was his father's eldest son. They would also say that it was highly necessary that kings and princes should experience the toils of war so as to be able to assess the merits of those who served them in the field and to reward them properly. During the whole period of the ordeal, which lasted from one new moon to the next, the prince went about clad in the poorest and vilest dress imaginable, consisting of wretched tatters, in which he appeared in public whenever necessary. It was said that this was so that in the future, when he became a mighty king, he should not scorn the poor, but remember that he had been one of them and had worn their uniform. He would thus be well-disposed to them and become charitable, so as to be worthy of the title Huacchacúyac, which they conferred on their kings, meaning "the lover and benefactor of the poor." After the examination, the candidates were qualified to wear, and considered worthy of, the insignia of the Incas. On their being declared true Incas and children of the Sun, their mothers and sisters came and shod them with *usutas* of raw esparto in witness of the fact that they had passed through the sharp ordeal of the military exercises.

CHAPTER XXVII

The Inca awarded the insignia to the leading
candidate, and a member of his
family to the rest.

AFTER THIS ceremony was over, the king was informed, and he appeared together with the eldest Incas of the royal blood, and standing
before the novices, he addressed them in a short speech, bidding them not
to be content merely to wear the insignia of knights of the royal blood
and to be honored because of them, but to exhibit the virtues of their
ancestors, especially in doing justice to all, and in showing compassion to
the poor and weak; and so to show themselves true children of the Sun,
whom they should resemble like a father in the splendor of their deeds,
to the common benefit of their subjects, since they had been sent from
heaven to earth to do good to them. After the speech, the novices came
one by one before the king, where they knelt to receive the first and principal token of knighthood, which was the boring of the ears. This was
a mark of royal and supreme distinction. The Inca himself pierced them
at the place where earrings are usually worn, performing the operation
with thick gold pins which were left in the ears so that the lobes should
heal and be enlarged, as they were to an incredible size.

The new knight kissed the Inca's hand to demonstrate that the hand
that conferred such an honor deserved to be kissed, as they said. He then
went on and stood before another Inca, a brother or uncle to the king,
second in authority to the royal person. This Inca removed the youth's
usutas of raw esparto, as a sign that the rigors of the ordeal were over,
and replaced them with splendid woollen ones such as the king and the
other Incas wore. This ceremony resembled the putting on of spurs in
Spain when knights of the military orders receive their habits. After
putting on the young man's *usutas*, the Inca would kiss him on the right
shoulder crying: "The child of the Sun, who has given such proof of
himself, deserves to be worshipped," for the verb to kiss also means to
worship, to revere, and to salute. After this ceremony the novice entered
a robing enclosure where other senior Incas invested him with the loincloth which was worn as a sign of manhood, and which until then he
was forbidden to don. This loincloth was made like a three-cornered
kerchief; two of these points were sewn to a cord about as thick as a

man's finger which ran around the waist, being tied behind to the right of the kidneys, so that the cloth hung over the private parts. The third point of the cloth was passed between the thighs and fastened to the same cord behind, so that even when they removed their clothes, they were sufficiently and decently covered.

The principal rite was the piercing of the ears, this being a royal insignia: the second was the putting on of the loincloth, which was the insignia of manhood. The putting on of the sandals was regarded as a ceremony performed as a reward for their exertions, but not as being essential to their honor and rank. The word *huaracu*, which alone covers all we have said of this solemn festival, is derived from the noun *huara*, "loincloth," since any man who merited the right to assume this was thereby entitled to all the other insignia, honors, and dignities that could be conferred on him then or later, in peace or war. Apart from the insignia we have mentioned, the heads of the youths were decked with two kinds of flowers, one called *cantut*, of very beautiful form and color, some yellow, some purple, and others red, and all three very brilliant. The other variety of flower is called *chihuahua*, and is yellow: it resembles the pinks of Spain. These two flowers could not be worn by the common people or the *curacas*, however great lords they might be, but only by those of the royal blood. They also wore on their heads a leaf of the herb called *uiñay huaina*, "always young": it is green, resembles the leaf of the lily and keeps its color for a long time, not even losing it when it is dried: hence the name.

The heir to the throne was given the same flowers, and the same leaf and all the other insignia as the other young Incas; for, as we have said, he was not distinguished from them in any way save by a band worn across the forehead from one temple to the other, and about four fingers in breadth. It was not round as the Spanish word *borla* suggests, but long like a fringe. It was made of wool (for the Indians had no silk) and was yellow in color. The emblem was worn only by the heir to the throne, and no one else could wear it at all, even one of his brothers, nor indeed the prince himself until he had passed his ordeal.

As a final royal device the prince was presented with a battle-axe which they called a *champi*, with a handle more than a braza in length. The blade consisted of an edge on one side and diamond-point on the other, and was exactly like a partisan except that it lacked the forepoint. As they took it up, they said "*aucacunápac.*" This is the dative plural and means "for the rebels, traitors, caitiffs, the cruel and perfidious," all of which, and much more, is contained in the word *auca*. This single word, according to the structure of their language, meant that this weapon was entrusted to them in token of their duty to chastise all such. The other token, the pretty and sweet-scented flowers, were taken to represent their clemency, pity, mildness, and the other royal virtues they were supposed to display to the good and loyal. As their father the Sun produced such flowers in the fields for the joy and satisfaction of mankind, so the prince should breed these virtues in his heart and mind for the benefit of all, so that he might worthily be called the lover and benefactor of the poor, and his name and fame would live for ever in the world.

After all this had been said by the officials of the knighthood in the presence of his father, the prince's uncles and brothers and all the members of the royal blood came and knelt after their fashion and worshipped him as the Inca's first-born. This ceremony was equivalent to swearing in the heir and successor to the empire, and the prince was given the yellow fringe. Thus the Incas ended the solemn ceremonies of making the young men knights.

CHAPTER XXVIII

The insignia of the kings and other Incas,
and the masters of the novices.

T HE KING wore the same headband, but it was red. In addition to this the Inca wore on his head two of the outer wing-feathers of a bird called *corequenque*. In the general language of Peru this word is a proper noun with no other meaning, though in the lost language of the Incas it must have had some meaning. The feathers have black and white bands and are about as big as those of a hen sparrow-hawk: they were required to be a pair, one from each wing. I saw the Inca Sairi Túpac wearing them. The birds from which they are taken are found in the desert of Villcanuta, thirty-two leagues from the city of Cuzco, on a small lake there, at the foot of that inaccessible snow-covered range. Those who have seen them state that only two are seen, one male and one female: if they are always unique, and where they come from or breed is not known, nor, according to the Indians, have any others but these been seen in all Peru, in spite of the fact that there are a great many snow-covered mountains, and deserts, and lakes large and small, like that of Villcanuta. It would appear to resemble the story of the phoenix bird, though I do not know that anyone has ever seen the latter, as they have the *corequenque.*

It was because only this pair of birds was to be found, and there was no news of any others in the world that the Inca kings wore their plumes, and esteemed them so highly that no one else was allowed to wear them under any circumstances, not even the heir to the throne. They declared that these birds, in their uniqueness, resembled their parents, the first Incas, who were only two, man and woman, when they came from heaven. It was therefore to keep the memory of these first ancestors that they used the plumes of these birds as their principal insignia and regarded them as sacred. I myself consider that there must be many more of these birds, for such a degree of rarity is not possible—the story of the phoenix is quite sufficient. They probably go about in solitary couples, as we have said, and the Indians would say what they do because of the parallel with the first Incas. Suffice it to say that the plumes of the *corequenque* were as highly esteemed as we have said. They tell me that nowadays many Indians wear them and assert that they are descendants of the royal blood of the Incas, while the rest make fun of them, since the blood of the Incas has almost completely disappeared. But the introduction of foreign fashions has caused them to confuse the insignia they used to wear on their heads as a mark of distinction, and has emboldened them thus and in many other ways: all of them now say they are Incas and Pallas.

The feathers were worn over the red fringe with the points upward, some distance apart, though meeting at the lower end. In order to obtain the plumes, the birds were taken as gently as possible, and when the two plumes had been removed, were released. Whenever a new Inca inherited the throne, they were caught again and had the feathers removed. The heir always took new insignia and never used the same as his father, since on the latter's death his body was embalmed and buried with the same imperial insignia as he had used during his lifetime. Such was the majesty of the *corequenque,* and the veneration and esteem which the Inca kings attached to its feathers.

Although this information has little or no importance for Spaniards, I have included it as belonging to the former kings. To return to our novices, we must add that on being awarded the insignia, they went out with them into the main square of the city, where they celebrated their success together for many days with singing and dancing. They also celebrated in their fathers' houses, where their nearest relatives foregathered to celebrate the victory of each novice. Their masters in the exercises and making of weapons and signals were their own fathers, who educated and trained them in all the necessary accomplishments as soon as they had left the tender age of childhood, substituting for childish ease the hardships of the military life, so that when they grew up they should acquit themselves like men in peace and in war.

CHAPTER XXIX

The surrender of Chuquimancu, lord of four valleys.

To RETURN to the life and conquests of Inca Pachacútec, we must mention that his brother General Cápac Yupanqui, after subduing the great *curaca* Chincha, sent to his brother the king to ask for a new army with which to conquer the valleys beyond Chincha. This army was sent off with some distinguished officers and great quantities of arms and provisions, in due proportion to the scale of the undertaking on which they were to engage. As soon as the new army appeared, accompanied by Prince Inca Yupanqui, who delighted in the exercises of war, the general left Chincha to repair to the beautiful valley of Runahuánac, "the chastener of men." It was so called on account of a large and turbulent river running through the valley which received this intimidating appellation because many people had been drowned in it. Many indeed have been drowned there through venturing to cross the stream instead of taking a detour of about a league to a bridge above the ford, thinking no doubt that as the river can be crossed in summer it may be likewise in winter, only to perish miserably. The name of the river is composed of the word *runa,* "people," and the verb *huana,* "to chasten": the final *a* gives the present participle "chastening, what chastens," hence "the chastener of men." The Spanish historians call the valley and its river Lunaguana, corrupting three of the letters. One of them says the name was derived from *guano,* "dung," which he says was much used in that valley for sown fields. This *guano* should be written *huano,* for as we explained at first, the general language of Peru has no *g*: it does mean "dung" but *huana* is a verb, meaning "to chasten." From this and many other instances we shall give, it will be seen how little Spaniards understand the language.

Even my fellow-countrymen, the mestizos, follow them in the pronunciation and orthography, for almost all the words they wrote down for me in what is, after all, their own and my own language are hispanized, according to the speech and spelling of the Spaniards. I have taken up the cudgels with them about this, but it does no good, since it is the common fate of languages to become corrupted after conquest and contact with other peoples.

In those days the whole of the valley of Runahuánac and another to the north called Huarcu, with more than thirty thousand inhabitants, was very thickly settled. So was Chinca, and others to their north and south. Nowadays the most populated has less than two thousand families, and there are some that are quite deserted of Indians but populated by Spaniards.

With reference to the conquest of the Yuncas, we should mention that the valley of Runahuánac and three others to the north of it, Huarcu, Malla, and Chillca, belonged all four to a lord called Chuquimancu, who was treated as king and claimed that all the peoples of the district feared him and recognized his superiority, though they were not his vassals. When he knew that the Incas were approaching his kingdom, as we shall call it because of the *curaca's* boast, he collected as many people as possible and went out to prevent them from crossing the river. There were several encounters in which many died on both sides, but at last the Incas, being supplied with a great many large and small rafts, forced a passage. The Yuncas did not defend it as completely as they might, for King Chuquimancu planned to wage war in the Huarcu valley, thinking this to be the strongest site, though his skill in military science was less than it might have been. He did not therefore resist as he could have done at Runahuánac, which turned out to be a mistake, as we shall see. The Incas installed their army, and in less than a month gained the whole of that splendid valley, owing to the wrong plan adopted by Chuquimancu.

The Inca left garrisons at Runahuánac to receive the supplies that were being brought up and to guard his rear. He then passed on to Huarcu, where there was a very fierce battle, since Chuquimancu, having assembled all his power in the valley, had twenty thousand warriors with him and was anxious not to lose his reputation. He therefore deployed all the forces he could against the enemy, using every possible stratagem and wile. On their side, the Incas did their best to resist and conquer without killing the Indians. This struggle lasted more than eight months, and bloody battles occurred. The Yuncas resisted so obstinately that the Inca renewed his army three times, some say four. To prove to the Yun-

cas that they would not go away until they were victorious and to show
that their soldiers were as much at ease as if they were in their own
capital, the place where the army was camped was called Cuzco and the
various camps were named after the principal quarters of the city. Because this name was given to the Inca camp, Pedro de Cieza de León
(ch. lxxiii) says that another city like Cuzco was founded when the Incas
found how pertinacious the enemy were, and that the war lasted more
than four years. This he states on the authority of the Yuncas themselves,
as he admits, and they exaggerated for his benefit in order to emphasize
the greatness of their deeds in its defence, which were indeed many. But
the four years must have been derived from the four times the Inca armies
were changed, and the city was the name they gave to the site of their
camp: in each case there was nothing more than what we have said.

After this long spell the Yuncas began to feel the cruel pangs of hunger, which is a thing that softens and tames even the most tough and
resistant warrior. Even before this set in, the natives of Runahuánac had
for days importuned their king Chuquimancu to give in to the Incas, since
they could no longer resist them, and to do so before the latter deprived
them of their houses and farms for distribution among their ancient
enemies the Chincas because of their obstinacy. Fearing this, when they
found that their king did not heed their request, they decided to flee and
return to their homes, informing the Inca of the state of the enemy's
forces and of their sufferings from starvation.

When Chuquimancu heard and saw all this, he was afraid lest all his
followers should desert and go over to the Inca, and therefore inclined
to do as they suggested, having displayed his soldierly spirit. He consulted
with his chief followers, and they all decided to go in person to the Inca,
not sending a mission, but acting as their own ambassadors. In this resolve all those who had been at the council went forward to the Incas'
camp, and kneeling before them, begged for mercy and forgiveness for
their misdeeds: they said they were glad to become vassals of the Inca,
since his father the Sun had bidden him to be lord over the whole world.

The Incas, uncle and nephew, received them mildly and said that they
pardoned them, sending them to their homes very satisfied with the usual
gifts of clothes and other presents.

The natives of these four provinces also boast, as the Chinchas do, that
the Incas could not subdue them in more than four years of warfare for
all their power, and that they founded a city and won them over with gifts
and promises and not by force of arms. This refers to the three or four
times the army was renewed so as to tame the enemy with hunger and

wear him down, rather than defeat him by force of arms. They tell a great many other tales of their valiant deeds, but as they do not affect our history, we shall omit them.

The Incas were proud of having subdued King Chuquimancu and prized the victory so much that they commemorated their own deeds in the war, as well as the valor of the Yuncas, by a perpetual trophy and monument in the shape of a fortress built in the valley of Huarcu, not of large size, but of marvellous construction. For this reason and for its situation, with the sea beating against its walls, it would have deserved to have been spared, and its workmanship was such that it would have lasted many years without repair. When I passed the place in 1560, one could still see what it had been, but it was a sad sight to the beholder.

CHAPTER XXX

*The valleys of Pachacámac and Rímac,
and their idols.*

AFTER KING Chuquimancu had been subdued and measures had been taken for the government and the laws and customs to be observed by him and his people, the Incas went on to conquer the valleys of Pachacámac, Rímac, Cháncay, and Huaman, which the Spaniards called La Barranca. All these six [*sic*] valleys were held by a powerful lord called Cuismancu, who also presumed to entitle himself king, though the Indians have no word for "king," but use a similar phrase *hatun apu,* "great lord." In order to avoid repetition, we shall say only what applies in particular to the valley of Pachacámac and the other valley called Rímac, which the Spaniards have corrupted to Lima.

We must mention that, as we have said before and shall have cause to say again, and as all the Spanish historians write, the Inca kings of Peru understood by the natural light that God gave them that there was a creator of all things whom they called Pachacámac, meaning "creator and sustainer of the universe." This doctrine originated with the Incas and spread throughout all their realms, either before or after their conquest.

They said that he was invisible, and never permitted himself to be seen. For this reason they did not make temples or sacrifices for him as they did for the Sun, but worshipped him usually with great devotion, which they disclosed by making signs with the head, eyes, arms, and body whenever they mentioned him. This doctrine had spread far and wide by report and had been embraced by all these tribes, in some cases before they were conquered and in others after. Those who embraced it before the Incas conquered them included in particular the predecessors of King Cuismancu, who made a temple to Pachacámac and applied his name to the valley where it was, which in those days was one of the most important in the whole coastal area. The Yuncas placed their idols in the temple: these were representations of fishes, but they also included the figure of a fox.

This temple of Pachacámac was very splendid, both as regards its buildings and their contents: it was unique in the whole of Peru, and the Yuncas made a great many sacrifices of animals and other objects, some with the blood of men, women, and children who were slaughtered on the occasion of the great festivals, following the practice in many provinces until the Incas conquered them. Here we shall say no more of Pachacámac since we shall include all that remains to be said on the subject in its proper place.

The Rímac valley is four leagues to the north of Pachacámac. The word *rímac* is a present participle meaning "he who speaks." The valley was so called on account of an idol there, in the shape of a man, which spoke and gave answers to questions, like the oracle of Apollo at Delphi and many others mentioned in the histories of the ancient heathens. Because of this, it was called "he who speaks" and the valley was given the same name.

The Yuncas held this idol in great veneration, as did the Incas after they had won that fair valley. It was here that the Spaniards founded the city they called the City of the Kings, because it was founded on the day of Epiphany, when our Lord appeared on earth. Thus Rímac, Lima, or the City of the Kings are all the same thing. Its arms are three crowns and a star.

The idol was kept in a sumptuous temple (though it was not equal to that of Pachacámac) whither the rulers of Peru went or sent ambassadors to consult on matters of consequence. The Spanish historians confuse the temple of Rímac with that of Pachacámac, saying that Pachacámac was "he who spoke" and making no mention of Rímac. This error, like many more in their histories, springs from insufficient knowledge of the language, and want of effort in ascertaining the truth: it may also arise from the proximity of the valleys, which are only four short leagues apart and were ruled by the same lord. This shall suffice for an account of these valleys, and having mentioned that the speaking idol was at Rímac and not at Pachacámac, we shall return to describe the conquest of the valleys.

Before General Cápac Yupanqui reached the Pachacámac valley with his army, he followed the usual practice of sending messengers to King Cuismancu, bidding him obey Inca Pachacútec and hold him as his supreme lord, observing his laws and customs, worshipping the Sun as his principal god, and casting down the existing idols from their temples and houses. If not, he must prepare for war, for the Inca would subdue him by hook or by crook, willingly or by force.

CHAPTER XXXI

They summon Cuismancu to capitulate;
his answer and the terms.

THE GREAT lord of Cuismancu was prepared for war. He had seen the approach of hostilities, and fearing the onset of the Incas against his own territories, he made ready to defend them. He thus received the Inca's envoys surrounded by his captains and soldiers, and replied that his subjects needed no other lord but himself. He was the only ruler his people and lands needed; their laws and customs were those they had inherited from their ancestors, who had been quite satisfied with them; they needed no other laws and did not wish to repudiate their gods, who were very mighty, since they worshipped among others Pachacámac, who they had heard was the maker and sustainer of the universe. If this were true, he must inevitably be a greater god than the Sun; and they had made him a temple wherein they offered him the best of everything they had, even sacrificing men, women, and children to his greater honor. Such was their veneration for him that they did not dare to set eyes on him, and when the priests and the king entered the temple they turned their back to the idol, and similarly on leaving it, so as not to have to look upon it. They also adored the Rímac, a god who spoke to them and answered their questions and foretold the future. Similarly they worshipped the fox for his cunning and sagacity. They had never heard the

Sun speak, or that he gave oracles like Rímac. They also worshipped
Mamacocha, the sea, who maintained them with her fish. The gods they
had were sufficient. They wanted no others, and certainly not the Sun,
since they needed no greater warmth than their land provided for them.
They begged or summoned the Inca to leave them alone: they had no
need of his empire.

The Incas were delighted to know that the Yuncas held in such veneration Pachacámac, whom they worshipped inwardly as the greatest god.
They therefore proposed not to wage war on the Yuncas but to reduce
them kindly, by persuasion, flattery, and promises, only resorting to arms
in the last instance if all else failed.

With this determination the Incas went to the valley of Pachacámac.
King Cuismancu came out with a strong force to defend his realms, and
General Cápac Yupanqui sent to urge him not to fight until they had
spoken at greater length about their gods, for he must know that the
Incas too worshipped Pachacámac as well as the Sun, although they made
no temple to him and did not know what he was like. But inwardly, in
their hearts, they revered him and held him in the highest veneration,
so much so that they never dared to utter his name except with the greatest adoration and humility. Since they all worshipped the same god it
was not right that they should quarrel or wage war: they should be
friends and brothers. And the Inca kings, in addition to worshipping
Pachacámac and regarding him as the creator and sustainer of the universe, would thenceforward regard the Rímac whom the Yuncas adored
as a sacred oracle. The Yuncas should therefore reciprocate in a brotherly
manner by worshipping the Sun, which deserved to be adored for his
benefits, beauty and splendor, instead of the fox and other beasts of the
earth and sea. Furthermore he begged them in peace and friendship to
obey his brother and lord, the Inca, the child of the Sun, considered as
a god on earth. The Inca was beloved by many peoples on account of his
justice, mercy, and clemency, and for the mildness of his laws and administration, and many of them had come freely and willingly to offer
their submission because of reports of his virtues and his majesty: it
would therefore be wrong for them to reject the Inca when he came to
seek them out in their own country to benefit them. He bade them consider all these matters calmly and follow the dictates of their reason: let
them not bring about by force and the surrender of the Inca's favor what
they could now accomplish with his entire approval, for there was nothing
on earth capable of resisting the power and force of his arms.

King Cuismancu and his followers heard the Inca's messengers and having made a truce, discussed the matter for many days, until finally, owing to the shrewdness and diligence of the Incas, peace was concluded on the following conditions.

The Yuncas agreed to worship the Sun like the Incas. They would build him a separate temple like Pachacámac's, and offer him their gifts and sacrifices, except those of human blood. Since it was against the natural law for one man to kill another to make a sacrifice, this practice was to be utterly abolished. The idols were to be removed from the temple of Pachacámac, for as he was maker and sustainer of the universe, it was not proper that idols of less majesty should stand in his temple and before his altar. They would worship Pachacámac in their hearts and without making any statue to him, for since he had not revealed himself, they did not know what form he took and could not portray him as they did the Sun. For the greater splendor of the valley of Pachacámac, they would found a house of chosen virgins, for two things that were very highly regarded wherever they existed were the houses of the Sun and of the virgins, since they recalled the two most splendid monuments of Cuzco. King Cuismancu was to keep his authority, and all the rest of the *curacas* theirs, but regarding the Inca as their supreme lord. He was to observe and obey the Inca's laws and customs, and the Incas were to esteem and venerate the oracle of Rímac and order all their kingdoms to do likewise.

Under these conditions peace was concluded between General Cápac Yupanqui and King Cuismancu, who was informed of the laws and customs the Inca would require to be observed. He accepted them with alacrity, since they seemed just and fair; similarly he accepted the ordinances of tribute that were to belong to the Sun and the Inca. When all this had been agreed and set in order, and the officials and garrison necessary for the security of the new territory had been appointed, Inca Cápac Yupanqui resolved to return to Cuzco together with the prince, his nephew, to report to his brother the Inca all that had occurred with the Yuncas in the course of his two conquests. He took King Cuismancu with him so that the Inca might make his acquaintance and favor him with his own hand as a friend and ally and not a conquered subject. Cuismancu was delighted to go and kiss the Inca's hands, and see the Inca's capital, the famous city of Cuzco.

Inca Pachacútec, who had remained in the province of Rucana at the beginning of the expedition, had returned to the imperial city on learning how well his brother was faring in the conquest of the coastal provinces. He now came forward to receive his brother and his son with the same demonstrations of joy and triumph as on the previous occasion, and greater if such were possible. Having welcomed them, he greeted Cuismancu with kind speeches, and ordered him to join the triumph among the Incas of the royal blood, since like them he worshipped Pachacámac. Cuismancu was extremely proud of this favor, for which he was envied by all the other *curacas*.

After the triumph, the Inca conferred many favors on Cuismancu, sending him home laden with honors, together with all his company. They returned to their own country full of satisfaction, declaring that the Inca was a true child of the Sun, worthy of the adoration and homage of the whole world. It is noteworthy that as soon as the Devil saw that the Incas were masters of the valley of Pachacámac and that the temple of Pachacámac was rid of all the idols it had held, he sought to possess himself of it and to have himself regarded as the unknown god whom the Indians so greatly honored. He thus hoped to be worshipped in many ways and to sell his wiles at a higher price in some places than in others, and to this end he used to address the priests of highest rank and repute in the corners of the temple, saying that he would do them the favor of answering their questions when they were alone: he would not answer them in general, for it did not befit his might and dignity to converse with men of low degree. His speech was only for kings and lords, and he would bid his servant, the idol Rímac, to speak to the common people and reply to their questions. Thus it was arranged that thenceforward royal and noble matters should be taken to the temple of Pachacámac, and common and popular business to that of Rímac. In this way the name of "speaker" applied to the latter idol was confirmed, for, as it had to answer everyone, it had a great deal of speaking to do. Padre Blas Valera also mentions this, though briefly.

Inca Pachacútec decided to desist from the conquest of new provinces for some years and to allow his own dominions a period of rest, since the raising of armies to relieve one another had caused some difficulties. He restricted his activities to the government of his realms, their embellishment with new buildings, the framing of laws and ordinances, and the regulation of rites and ceremonies, which he devised anew, reforming the ancient idolatry. Thus the significance of the name Pachacútec fitted him well, and his fame was immortalized as a great king in the administration of his dominions, a great priest in his vain religion, and a great captain in his conquests, of which he won more than any of his ancestors. In particular, he enriched the temple of the Sun, ordering the walls to be covered with golden plates, not only those in the temple itself but also those of the other apartments and of a cloister there was there, which still exists and is now richer in true wealth and spiritual goods than it then was in gold and precious stones. For on the very site of the temple where the figure of the Sun once was there now rests the Holy Sacrament, and the cloister serves as a walk for the annual processions and festivities. May the Eternal Majesty be praised for all His mercies: it is the convent of St. Dominic.

CHAPTER XXXII

They go to conquer King Chimu;
a cruel war is waged.

INCA PACHACÚTEC spent six years in the employments we have mentioned. After this, finding his realms prosperous and peaceful, he had an army of thirty thousand warriors made ready to conquer the valleys of the coast, as far as the district of Cajamarca, which constituted the frontier of the empire on the road to the sierra.

When the army was ready, he appointed six of the most experienced Incas as colonels or commanders and advisers to his son, Prince Inca Yupanqui. The latter was made general for the next conquest, for, as a pupil of such a great master and a soldier under so great a captain as his uncle Cápac Yupanqui, he had emerged so experienced in the art of war that any undertaking, however great, could be entrusted to him. The Inca's brother, whom he called "my right arm" on account of his great deeds, was to remain at court and rest from his past exertions. In reward for them and in witness of his own royal qualities, the Inca nominated him his lieutenant, second to him in peace and war, with absolute power and authority throughout the empire.

When the army was made ready, the prince Inca Yupanqui marched with the first regiment toward the sierra until he reached the province of Yauyu, which is in the neighborhood of the city of Lima. There he awaited the arrival of the whole army, and when it was gathered together he advanced to Rímac, where the speaking oracle was. According to the Indians, this prince Inca Yupanqui had the honor and fame of being the first of the Inca kings to set eyes on the Southern Sea and of being the one who conquered the most provinces on that coast, as we shall see in the account of his life. The *curacas* of Pachacámac, Cuismancu, and of Runa-huánac, called Chuquimancu, came out with their warriors to receive the prince and serve under him in the campaign. The prince thanked them for their zeal, and conferred great favors and rewards upon them. From the valley of Rímac he went to visit the temple of Pachacámac, which he entered without prayers or sacrifices other than the mental adoration the Indians accorded Pachacámac, as we have said. He then visited the temple of the Sun, where there were many sacrifices and great offerings of gold and silver. He likewise visited the idol Rímac to please the Yuncas, and in order to comply with the recent treaty, bade the priests offer sacrifices to the idol and consult it about the success of the present campaign. Having heard that it would prosper, he advanced as far as the valley the Indians call Huancu and the Spaniards La Barranca, whence he despatched the usual messages offering peace or war to a great chief called Chimu, who was lord of the valleys beyond La Barranca, as far as the city called Trujillo. There are five principal ones, named Parmunca, Huallmi, Santa, Huanapu, and Chimu (which is where Trujillo now is). All five are very beautiful valleys, very fertile and thickly populated, and the chief *curaca* was called the mighty Chimu, from the name of the province where his capital was. He was treated as a king and feared by all those whose territories marched with his to the east, north, and south, for to the west lies the ocean.

On receiving the Inca's summons, the mighty Chimu replied that he was ready to die, weapons in hand, in defence of his country, laws, and customs, and that he wanted no new gods: let the Inca take good note of this reply, for he would get no other. When he had received this intimation from Chimu, Inca Yupanqui advanced to the valley of Parmunca, where the enemy was awaiting him. The latter appeared with a large company of skirmishers to try the strength of the Incas. The strife continued for a long time, the natives endeavoring to defend the entrance to their valley. But they could not prevent the Incas from forcing an entry and gaining a foothold, though only at the cost of many dead and wounded on both sides. The prince, on seeing the resistance of the Yuncas, wished to prevent them from taking courage at the smallness of his force, and sent messengers to his father the Inca to report on what had happened and beg him to furnish twenty thousand warriors, not as a relief for his army as on previous campaigns, but to swell his forces and so shorten the war. He did not wish to give so much time to vanquishing this enemy as he had in the case of his former foes, because the Yuncas had shown themselves so arrogant.

Having despatched these messages, the Inca intensified the war on all sides. The two *curacas* of Pachacámac and Runahuánac proved very hostile to the mighty Chimu, since in the past, in pre-Inca times, they had had bitter conflicts with him about boundaries and grazing rights and the enslavement of members of those tribes, whom he had subjugated. Now with the powerful aid of the Inca, they wanted revenge for past slights and defeats, and Chimu resented this above anything else, and did all he could for his own defence.

The war among the Yuncas was very bloody: because of their ancient enmity, those serving the Incas strove more on their behalf than any other tribe, so that the whole valley of Parmunca was gained in a few days and its natives driven out to Huallmi, where also there were battles and skirmishes, but it could not be defended either, and the natives had to fall back on the valley called Santa, which was then the most beautiful on the whole coast, though today it is almost deserted, since the inhabitants have been destroyed, as in all the other valleys.

The people of Santa proved more warlike than those of Huallmi and Parmunca. They came out to defend their land, fought with valor and energy wherever an opportunity offered, resisted the full force of their enemies for many days without yielding them the advantage, and performed deeds of such courage that they won fame and honor from their very enemies. These efforts increased the hopes of their chief, the great Chimu, who was buoyed up by the bravery of his people and by certain ideas he put about, to the effect that the prince was a delicate and luxury-loving man who would soon tire of the hardships of war and be drawn back to the pleasures of his capital by amorous desires, while all his warriors would soon want to return to their homes and children: even if they did not, they would either be driven away by the heat or destroyed by it if they stayed. In these vain hopes the arrogant Chimu obstinately persisted in pursuing the war, without receiving or listening to the messengers the Incas sent him from time to time. On the contrary, in order to make patent his contumaciousness, he called up the inhabitants of the other valleys under his sway, and as they arrived the war grew daily in intensity. There were many dead and wounded on both sides. Each tried to force the victory, and the war was the bitterest so far waged by the Incas.

Nevertheless, the captains and leaders of Chimu, when they considered the state of affairs dispassionately, would have liked their chief to embrace the offers of peace and friendship made by the Inca, whose power they thought must sooner or later prove irresistible. However, in order to meet their lord's wishes, they suffered the toils of war with patience and energy, even witnessing the enslavement of their relatives, children, and wives, but not daring to tell their ruler what they felt.

CHAPTER XXXIII

The obstinacy and misfortunes of the great Chimu, and how he surrendered.

WHILE THE WAR was raging so bitterly and fiercely, the twenty thousand reinforcements the prince had requested arrived. With them he reinforced his army and checked the overweening arrogance of Chimu, which was already turning to melancholy and sadness as he saw his fond hopes frustrated. On the one hand, the power of the Incas was seen to be doubled, when it appeared to be faltering; on the other, Chimu sensed the discouragement of his own forces on seeing themselves faced by a new hostile army. For days past they had sustained the war more to comply with their master's obduracy than out of any hopes they might has entertained of resisting the Inca. Now that the latter's forces were strengthened, they at once faltered, and Chimu's leading kinsmen approached him and asked that his obstinacy should not continue until his men were utterly destroyed, but that he should consider that now was the time to accept the Inca's offers, if only to prevent his former rivals and enemies from battening on the spoils they daily took and from carrying off their wives and children as slaves. This state of affairs should be remedied without delay, before the havoc grew any greater, and before the prince shut the doors of his clemency and mercy against their obstinate resistance and visited them with fire and slaughter.

This speech, uttered in tones of reproach and menace rather than in those of good counsel and advice, made the brave Chimu feel that all was lost. He knew not where to seek remedy nor of whom to ask aid, for his neighbors, offended by his past arrogance and pride, had no cause to help him. His own men were dispirited, and the enemy was strong. Thus beset on all sides, he thought that he could accept the first advances of the Inca prince, but he would not ask for terms himself so as not to show lack of spirit or weakness. He therefore concealed his intention from his own people, but replied that he was not without hope and resources of resisting the Inca and, thanks to their courage, coming out of the war with fame and honor. Let them bestir themselves in defense of their country, for whose freedom and salvation they were obliged to die fighting: let them not show cowardice, for it was in the nature of warfare to be victorious one day and defeated the next. If some of their wives were carried off as slaves today, let them remember how many more they themselves had won from their enemies: he hoped he would soon set them free. Let them be of good cheer and show no weakness, for their enemies had shown none in the past and there was no call for them to do so now. Let them go in peace and be satisfied, for he thought more of his people's salvation than of his own.

With these tenuous hopes and feeble comfort, consisting more of words than facts, the great Chimu dismissed his friends. He was much afflicted to see them so despondent, but put on the best face he could muster, and sustained the war until he received the usual messages from the Inca offering forgiveness, peace, and friendship, as he had so many times before. On hearing this message, wishing to make a show of complete firmness, though in fact he had completely softened, he replied that he had no intention of accepting any terms, but that out of consideration for his people's salvation, he would consult them and do as they thought fit. He then summoned his captains and kinsmen, and put the Inca's offer before them, bidding them consider well the interests of them all, for he was prepared to obey the Inca for their sakes, even though it was greatly against his will.

The captains were very glad to find their chief somewhat shifted from his former rigid obstinacy, and they therefore plucked up courage to tell him squarely that it was very proper to obey and acknowledge the overlordship of so mild and clement a prince as the Inca, who still offered them his friendship, though he had almost reduced them to surrender.

This resolute opinion, delivered rather with the boldness of free men than with the subservience of vassals, proved to the mighty Chimu that his rebellious resistance was in vain, and to show that it was over, he sent his ambassadors to prince Inca Yupanqui asking him to beg the Inca not to withhold the mercy and mildness that the children of the Sun had displayed in all four quarters of the world they had subdued. They had spared all those who, like him, had been blameworthy and contumacious:

he acknowledged his fault and begged pardon, confiding in long experience of the clemency of all the ancestors of the Inca, and knowing that the Inca would not refuse it now since he so greatly prized his reputation as the lover and benefactor of the poor, and sought the same forgiveness for all his friends, who were less guilty than he, since they had resisted the Inca because of the *curaca's* obstinacy rather than of their own free will.

The prince was greatly pleased with this embassy, which put an end to the conquest and avoided the blodshed he had feared. He received the ambassadors very affably, had them rewarded, and told them to return to their chief and then bring him to hear the Inca's pardon from his own mouth, as well as receiving honors from the royal hands to his greater satisfaction.

The brave Chimu, his arrogance and pride now tamed, appeared before the prince with as much submission and humility, and grovelled on the ground before him, worshipping him and repeating the same request as he had made through his ambassadors. The prince received him affectionately in order to relieve the grief he was evincing. He bade two of the captains raise him from the ground, and after hearing him, told him that all that was past was forgiven, and much more would have been forgiven too. The Inca had not come to deprive him of his estates and authority, but to improve his idolatrous religion, his laws, and customs. In confirmation of this, if Chimu feared to have lost his estates, he would award them to him as an honor and favor to be possessed in all security, provided that the idols representing fish and animals were cast down, and they worshipped the Sun and served his father the Inca.

Chimu, cheered by the courtesy and kindness shown him by the prince in this encouraging speech, worshipped him anew and replied saying that his greatest grief was in not having obeyed the words of such a lord as soon as he had heard them. He himself would deplore all his life the misdeeds for which the Inca had forgiven him: for the rest, he would carry out with great love and goodwill the Inca's commands touching both religion and customs.

Hereupon peace was established and Chimu did homage, while the Inca offered presents of garments to him and his nobles. The prince visited the valleys of the new domain and ordered them to be improved and adorned with royal buildings and great new channels for irrigating and extending the cultivable fields far beyond their previous limits; storehouses were built for the revenues of the Sun and of the Inca as well as for the use of the natives in years of want, all of which the Incas used to have made by ancient custom. In the valley of Parmunca in particular, the prince had a fort built as a trophy in memory of the victory he had won over King Chimu, a victory he greatly prized because the war had been so bitterly fought on both sides. The fort was built in this valley, because the war had begun there. It was a strong building of admirable construction, handsomely adorned with pictures and other royal curiosities. But the newcomers have not respected any of this, or spared it from destruction. A few pieces still remain as survivors of the ignorance that caused them to be razed and as proof of their former greatness.

Having given instructions about all these matters and appointed the necessary officials for the administration of justice and the revenues, as well as the usual garrison, the prince left Chimu very satisfied with his situation and returned to Cuzco, where he was received with the solemn triumph and festivities we have mentioned in connection with other expeditions: they lasted a month.

CHAPTER XXXIV

*The Inca aggrandizes his empire; his
activities until his death.*

INCA PACHACÚTEC, having now grown old, decided to rest from any further conquests, having extended his empire by more than 130 leagues in length from north to south, and in breadth the whole distance from the great range of the snow-covered mountains to the sea, a matter of 60 leagues east and west in some places, and 70, more or less, in others. He busied himself with his usual activities, confirming the laws of his ancestors and framing new ones for the common good.

He founded many colonies of settlers in regions which had been sterile and uncultivated, but which by his industry were made fertile and productive through the use of irrigation channels.

He built many temples to the Sun in imitation of the temple at Cuzco, and many houses of the chosen virgins. He ordered many storehouses to be restored and new ones to be built on the royal highways, and stocked them with supplies, arms, and munitions for passing armies. He also built royal lodgings for the Incas to stay in when travelling.

He further had storehouses made in all the villages, large or small, where they did not already exist. These were for the purpose of succoring the inhabitants in years of want, and they were stocked from the royal revenues and from those of the Sun.

In short, the empire may be said to have been completely reformed, both as regards its false religion which received new rites and ceremonies, while many idols were removed from his vassals, and as to the behavior and customs of the people which were amended by new laws and pragmatics and the prohibition of many barbarous customs and abuses which the Indians had previously indulged in.

He further reformed the armed forces where he thought it was necessary, and proved himself as great a captain as king and priest, increasing the honors and favors granted to those who distinguished themselves. He especially embellished and extended the great city of Cuzco with new buildings and inhabitants. He built a palace for himself near the schools his great-grandfather Inca Roca had founded. Because of all this and of his gracious disposition and mild rule, he was loved and worshipped as a second Jupiter. He is said to have reigned for more than fifty years; some say for more than sixty. He lived in great peace and tranquility, as well obeyed as he was truly loved, and as well served as his goodness merited. When after this long time he died, he was universally lamented by all his vassals and placed among the number of their gods, as all the other kings before him had been. He was embalmed according to the Indian custom, and the mourning sacrifices and burial ceremonies lasted a year.

He left as his heir the Inca Yupanqui, his son by his legitimate wife and sister Coya Anahuarque. He also left more than three hundred other sons and daughters, and it is even maintained that in the course of his long life with a multitude of wives, he had more than four hundred legitimate and illegitimate children. The Indians affirm that even this large number is little for the children of such a father.

The Spanish historians confuse these two kings, father and son, applying the names of both to a single ruler. The father was called Pachacútec, which was his real name, the word Inca being used of all of them from the first Inca Manco Cápac. The grandson of the first Inca was called Lloque Yupanqui, and in recounting his life we explained the meaning of Yupanqui, a word which was used as a surname after his time. The two words together, Inca Yupanqui, are applied to all the Inca kings, unless their own name is Yupanqui: the two epithets are very appropriate for they are equivalent to the names Caesar Augustus given to all the emperors. When the Indians are relating the deeds of their kings and mention them by name, they say Pachacútec Inca Yupanqui, which the

Spaniards take to be the name of a single king, and omit the son and successor of Pachacútec, who used to be called Inca Yupanqui and used both titles as a proper name, giving the same name Inca Yupanqui to his heir. The Indians distinguished him from his father and indicate his excellent qualities by calling him Túpac ("he who shines") Inca Yupanqui, father of Huaina Cápac Inca Yupanqui, and grandfather of Huáscar Inca Yupanqui. All the other Incas can be called by this epithet. I have mentioned this so that those who read the histories may avoid confusion.

CHAPTER XXXV

He increased the number of schools, and made laws for their good government.

SPEAKING of this Inca, Padre Blas Valera sums up in the following words: "On the death of Viracocha Inca, who was worshipped by the Indians with their gods, he was succeeded by his son, the great Titu, known as Manco Cápac, a name he used until his father gave him the title of Pachacútec, 'reformer of the world.' He later justified this title by his distinguished words and deeds, to such an extent that his earlier names were forgotten and he was never called by them. He governed his empire with such industry, prudence, and fortitude in both peace and war that he not only extended the boundaries of all four parts of the kingdom they call Tahuantinsuyu, but also issued many laws and statutes, which have been very willingly confirmed by our Catholic kings, apart from such as refer to the worship of idols and to illicit marriages. More than anything else, this Inca enriched, extended, and honored the schools founded by Inca Roca in Cuzco. He increased the number of instructors and tutors, bade all the lords of vassals, the captains, and their children, and the Indians at large, whatever their occupation, whether soldiers or those of inferior rank, use the language of Cuzco: no post of authority, dignity, or command was to be given to anyone who did not know it well. And so that so useful a law should not have been made in vain, he appointed masters of great learning in Indian lore to teach the sons of the princes and nobility, not only those in Cuzco, but in all the rest of the provinces of his kingdom, to which he sent masters to teach the language of Cuzco to all those who served the state. It thus came about that the whole of Peru spoke the same tongue, though today owing to neglect (on whose part I cannot say) many provinces which used to know the language have completely forgotten it, to the great detriment of the preaching of the gospel. All the Indians who observed this law and still retain the language of Cuzco are more civilized and intelligent than the rest.

"Pachacútec forbade anyone but princes and their children from wearing gold, silver, or precious stones, or plumage of various colors, or vicuña wool, which is woven with extraordinary skill. He permitted them to adorn themselves within moderation on the first day of the moon and on other days of festivals and solemnities. This law is still observed by the tribute-paying Indians, who are satisfied with their common everyday clothes. Thus much of the corruption caused by gay clothing and finery is avoided. But the Indian servants of the Spaniards and those who dwell in the Spanish towns are very extravagant in this respect, and do grave harm to their consciences and their pockets.

"This Inca ordered his people to eat with great frugality, though they had more liberty in drinking, whether princes or plebeians. He established that there should be special judges to suppress idleness, and desired that everyone should busy himself at his trade or serve his parents or masters or work for the good of the commonwealth: even boys and girls of five, six, or seven were made to occupy themselves in some task suitable for their years. The blind, the lame and the dumb who were able to work with their hands were given various tasks. The old were required to scare birds off the tilled fields, and all drew ample supplies of food and clothing from the public stores. Lest they should be wearied and distressed by continuous toil, he made a law that there should be three days' holiday every month (which was counted by the moon), on which occasion various games of no great interest were played. He ordered there to be three fairs each month, one every nine days, so that the villagers and field workers, after spending eight days at their tasks, could come to market in the city on the ninth, where they would see and hear whatever the Inca or his Council ordained. Later this same king disposed that there should be daily markets, as there are today: they are called *catu*. He also ordered the fairs to be on feast-days for greater splendor. He made a law that every province or city should have definite limits enclosing heath, pasture, woods, rivers, lakes, and fields. These were to be assigned to the limits and jurisdiction of such-and-such a city or province in perpetuity. No governor or *curaca* was to make bold to diminish or divide them, or to apply any part to himself or to anyone else. The fields

were to be apportioned according to a fixed measurement, established
by law for the general and particular advantage of all the heads of families and other inhabitants of each province and city. The shares accruing
to the crown and the Sun were also fixed, as were the duties of ploughing,
sowing, and harvesting for the Indians themselves and for the state. These
duties went according to the division of the lands, which they were
obliged to till both severally and in common. This makes it clear that
there is no truth in the assertion frequently made that the Indians had no
rights of property with reference to their lands and estates, made by those
who have failed to realize that the division was made not on the basis of
the possession of land, but according to the amount of individual and
collective labor required to work it. This collective labor was a very ancient practice among the Indians, not only for public works, but also for
private works, which were undertaken and completed in common. For
this reason they measured the land, so that each might do what was allotted to him. The whole population would assemble, and till first their
own land, working in common and helping one another, and then the
lands belonging to the king. They followed the same practice in sowing
or harvesting and transferring the crops to the royal or common storehouses. They built their houses in about the same fashion. The Indian
who needed to build a house would go to the Council to appoint a day for
it to be built. The population would assemble with one accord to supply
their neighbor's want, and soon the house was finished. This custom had
the approval of the Incas and was confirmed in a law on the subject. To
this day many Indian villages observe this statute and greatly assist
Christian charity; but avaricious Indians, who think only of themselves,
do themselves harm, and are of no help to others, but rather offend
them."

CHAPTER XXXVI

Many other laws of Inca Pachacútec;
his words of wisdom.

IN SHORT, this king, with the approval of his councils, approved many
laws, regulations, and statutes, and privileges and usages for many

provinces and regions, to the advantage of the natives. He suppressed many others as being contrary to the peace and to his royal majesty and authority. He reformed many others, against blasphemers, patricides, fratricides, murderers, traitors to the Inca, adulterers (male and female), those guilty of removing daughters from their homes or violating maidens or touching the chosen virgins, robbers of any object whatever, those guilty of unnatural crimes or incest of parents with children, and incendiaries. He made many other decrees for the preservation of good customs and the regulation of the ceremonies in the temples and the sacrifices. He confirmed many more that had been made by previous Incas, such as the following: children should obey and serve their parents till they were twenty-five; no one should marry without the consent of his own parents and those of the bride; if they wed without consent, the contract was not valid and the children illegitimate, though if after having children and living together as husband and wife they obtained the approval and consent of their parents and parents-in-law, the marriage would be legalized and the children legitimate. He approved the inheritance of land and authority according to the ancient custom in each province or kingdom, and forbade judges to receive bribes from litigants. He made many other laws of less importance which I omit to avoid prolixity. Further on I shall refer to the laws he made to guide judges, to solemnize marriages, to make wills, to regulate the armed forces and to reckon the year. In our own days, Viceroy Don Francisco de Toledo modified and revoked many laws and statutes established by the Inca: and the Indians, astonished at his absolute powers, called him the second Pachacútec, meaning that he was the reformer of their first reformer. The reverence and respect in which they held this Inca was so great that they have still not forgotten him today."

This is from Padre Blas Valera. I found it among his mutilated papers, but the part in which he promises to speak of rules for judges, marriages, and wills, the armed forces, and the reckoning of the year has been lost, which is a great pity. On another sheet I found some of the wise sayings of this Inca Pachacútec. They are as follows:

"When subjects, captains, and chiefs willingly obey their king, the kingdom enjoys perfect peace and tranquility.

"Envy is a worm that grows and consumes the entrails of the envious.

"He who is envious and envied is twice tormented.

"It is better that others should envy you because you are good, than that you should envy others because you are bad.

"Who envies another harms himself.

"He who envies the good draws evil from them for himself, just as the spider draws poison from flowers.

"Drunkenness, rage, and madness are alike, but the first two are voluntary and revocable, and the third permanent.

"He who kills another without authority or due cause condemns himself to death.

"He who kills his fellow man must die, wherefore the old kings, our fathers, decreed that any murder should be punished with violent death, which we newly confirm.

"Thieves are in no wise to be permitted: they might gain property by honest toil and possess it rightfully, but they prefer to come by it by robbery, wherefore it is only right that thieves should be hanged.

"Adulterers who destroy the reputation and rank of others and take away their peace and happiness should be considered thieves, and therefore condemned to death without any reprieve.

"The noble and courageous man is known by his patience in adversity.

"Impatience is a sign of a vile and low mind, ill-taught and worse-trained.

"When subjects obey as best they can without any opposition, kings and governors should treat them with liberality and clemency, but otherwise with sternness and justice, and always with discretion.

"Judges who secretly take gifts from litigants and suitors should be regarded as thieves, and as such punished with death.

"Governors should attend to two things with great attention. The first, that they and their subjects should observe and fulfil perfectly the king's laws. The second, that they should consider with great vigilance and care the common and particular interests of their province. An Indian who cannot govern his house and family will be much less competent to govern a state; and he should not be set over others.

"The physician or herbalist who is ignorant of the virtues of herbs, or who knows the virtues of some but does not seek to know the virtues of all, knows little or nothing. He must work until he knows them all, whether useful or injurious, in order to deserve the title he lays claim to.

"He who seeks to count the stars before he can count the scores and knots of the *quipus* deserves derision."

These are the sayings of Inca Pachacútec. The reference to the scores and knots is because, having no letters to write with or figures to count with they used the knots and scores to reckon with.

End of the Sixth Book

BOOK
SEVEN *of the*
FIRST PART

*in which an account is given of the colonies founded by
the Incas; the upbringing of chiefs' sons; the third and
fourth of their principal festivals; the description of the
city of Cuzco; the conquests of Inca Yupanqui, the tenth
king, in Peru and in the kingdom of Chile; the rebellion of the Araucanians against the Spaniards, and the
death of Valdivia; and the fortress of
Cuzco and its wonders.
It contains twenty-nine chapters.*

CHAPTER I

The Incas established colonies;
they had two languages.

HE INCA KINGS used to transplant Indians from one province to another to live. Their motives were partly the good of their subjects, and partly their own advantage in securing their dominions from rebellions and risings. As the Incas proceeded with their conquests, they found some provinces which were naturally fertile and productive, but which were thinly populated and ill-cultivated for want of inhabitants. To them, so that they should not be wasted, they sent Indian settlers who were brought from places of similar climate and conditions lest they should be harmed by the change of surroundings. Sometimes they were moved when they had increased to such an extent that there was no room for them in their own provinces, and the Incas sought other similar ones where they could live: in this case half of the population, more or less, would be moved. They also shifted Indians from poor and sterile provinces to settle in fertile and productive ones, thus benefiting both those who were moved and those who remained behind, since, being related they could help one another by exchanging their crops. Such was the case throughout Collao, a province of over 120 leagues in length and containing many other provinces of different tribes, where the climate is too cold to produce maize or *uchu*, which the Spaniards call *pimiento*, though other plants and vegetables that do not occur in the hot zones, such as *papa* and *quinua,* grow in great abundance, and there are infinite flocks of sheep. From all these cold provinces they removed many Indians at their own expense and settled them to the east, that is toward the Antis, and to the west, in the direction of the coast where there were great fertile valleys capable of bearing maize, pimento, and fruit, a district which had been uninhabited before the time of the Incas, and which had remained as empty as a desert because the Indians had had neither the knowledge nor the skill to build canals to irrigate the fields. The Inca kings realized all this, and settled many of these untilled valleys with the Indians who happened to be nearest in either direction. The settlers irrigated the soil and levelled it so that the land might benefit: they were bidden by law to assist one another like kinsmen, exchanging their surplus produce and remedying one another's wants. The Incas also benefited from this by obtaining enough maize for their armies, since, as we have said, two-thirds of the sown land belonged to them: one-third belonging to the Sun and one-third to the Inca. In this way the kings had an abundance of maize in that cold and sterile land, and the Collas carried on their sheep commodities to exchange among their transplanted kinsfolk—a great quantity of *quinua* and *chuñu*, or dried potatoes, and much jerked meat or *charqui*—returning laden with maize, pimentos, and fruit which did not grow in their own country. These precautions were greatly appreciated by the Indians.

Pedro de Cieza de León, in speaking on this subject, in his ch. xclx, says:

When the year is good, all the inhabitants of Collao are happy and well supplied, but if it is sterile and waterless, they undergo great privations. Though in truth, as the Inca kings who ruled this empire were so wise and such excellent administrators and managers, they established their own system and imposed their own laws, without which indeed most of the peoples under their sway would have suffered great hardships and lived in dire need, as they had done until they were reduced by the Incas. I have mentioned this because the Collas and all the other valleys of Peru that are cold, and therefore less fertile and productive than the hot and wealthy regions, were required to produce from the many villages bordering on the great range of the Antis a certain number of Indians with their wives who had to appear at the places their chiefs indicated to labor in the fields and sow whatever nature had failed to provide, using fruit collected from their lords and captains. These were called *mitimaes*. To this day they serve under the chief *encomienda*, and grow and treat the much-valued coca. So that although maize is neither sown nor reaped in Collao, the chiefs there have no lack of it, nor have any others who apply the same arrangement: indeed they never fail to bring in loads of maize, coca, and fruits of all kinds, and a great deal of honey.

This far Pedro de Cieza, word for word.

Indians were also transferred for another reason. Whenever some war-like province had been conquered which was distant from Cuzco and peopled with fierce and restless inhabitants and might therefore prove disloyal or unwilling to serve the Inca peacefully, part of the population was moved away from the area—and often the whole of it—and sent to some more docile region, where the newcomers would find themselves surrounded by loyal and peaceable vassals and thus learn to be loyal themselves, bowing their necks under the yoke they could no longer throw off. In making these exchanges of Indians, they always used the Incas by privilege of the first king Manco Cápac, sending them forth to govern and teach the rest. All others who went with these Incas were honored with the same title, so as to be the more respected by their neighbors, and all such Indians thus transplanted were called *mítmac,* whether immigrants or emigrants: the word means equally "settlers" or "emigrants."

Among other things devised by the Inca kings for the good government of their empire, they bade all their vassals learn the language of their capital, which is what is now called the general language. To teach it, masters who were Incas by privilege were installed in each province. It should be added that the Incas had another private language which they spoke among themselves, and which the other Indians did not understand and were not allowed to learn, as it was a sacred tongue. I hear from Peru that this has been completely lost, having perished with the Inca state. The kings ordered the general language to be taught for two principal reasons. One was so as not to have to keep such a horde of interpreters as would have been necessary to understand and answer such a variety of tongues and tribes as existed in the empire. The Incas desired that their vassals should address them as man to man, or at least in person and not through a third party, and that their subjects should hear their decisions from their own mouths, since they understood how much more satisfaction and confidence comes from the word of a prince than from the same word uttered by an official. The second and chief reason was that foreign peoples, which, as we have said, held themselves as enemies and waged cruel war because they did not understand one another, might come to love one another as if they were of the same family and kinship by talking and revealing their inmost hearts to one another, thus losing the fear that arises from not understanding each other. With this device the Incas tamed and united a great variety of different tribes of conflicting religions and customs whom they brought into their empire and welded by means of the common language into such a friendly union that they loved one another like brothers. In this way also many provinces which were not incorporated into the Inca empire were so convinced of and attached to this benefit that they later learned the general language of Cuzco, and speak it themselves and use it to communicate with many tribes of different languages: through it they have become friends and confederates when they used to be mortal enemies. And on the other hand many tribes that used to know the language have forgotten it since the new dispensation, as Padre Blas Valera testifies in speaking of the Incas in the following words:

They commanded all to speak their tongue, though today, owing to neglect (on whose part I cannot say) many provinces which used to know the language have completely forgotten it, to the great detriment of the preaching of the gospel. All the Indians who observed this law and still retain the language of Cuzco are more civilized and intelligent than the rest.

Thus far Padre Blas Valera: perhaps later we may include a chapter of his in which he asserts that the general language of Peru should not be allowed to disappear, for once it is forgotten it will be necessary for preachers to learn many languages to preach the gospel, which is impossible.

CHAPTER II

The heirs of chiefs were brought up at court;
the reasons for this.

T HE INCA kings also disposed that the heirs of lords of vassals should be brought up at court and reside there until they inherited their estates so that they should be well indoctrinated and accustomed to the mentality and ways of the Incas, holding friendly converse with them so that later, on account of this familiar intercourse, they would love them and serve them with real affection. They were called *mítmac,* "settlers." This was also done to ennoble and dignify the capital with the presence and company of so many heirs of kingdoms and chieftaincies as there were in the empire. This dispensation helped them to learn the general language with greater pleasure and less toil and strain. As their servants and subjects took turns to wait on their masters in the capital, whenever they returned to their own countries they had learned something of the courtly tongue and were very proud to speak it among their friends, since it was the language of people they considered divine. This caused great competition among the rest to try to learn it, and those who knew a little sought to press forward with their study of it, conversing often and familiarly with the governors and officials of the royal treasury and judges who resided in their country. In this way they easily learned to speak the tongue of Cuzco without the usual labor with teachers throughout almost the whole of the thirteen hundred leagues won by the Inca kings.

In addition to the purpose of adding luster to their court with the presence of so many princes, the Inca kings had another motive, that of assuring their kingdoms and provinces against risings and rebellions, for as the empire was so far-flung, there were many provinces four, five, or six hundred leagues away from the capital, including the largest and most warlike, such as the kingdoms of Quito and Chile and their neighbors. Because of their remoteness and of the ferocity of their inhabitants it was feared that they might revolt on some occasion and seek to throw off the imperial yoke; and although each one separately had not the means, they might concert together in a league of many provinces and attack the kingdom from all sides, gravely menacing the authority of the Incas. In order to assure themselves against all these and other troubles that occur in such vast empires they took the course of bidding all the heirs to reside at court, where they were carefully treated with every favor whether the Inca were present or not, each one receiving the attentions his merits, rank, and estate entitled him to. The princes frequently reported these general and special favors to their parents, sending them the garments and jewels the Inca gave them from his own wardrobe, objects which were of incalculable esteem among them. The Inca kings sought thus to oblige their vassals to be loyal to them out of gratitude, or if they should prove so ungrateful that they did not appreciate what was done for them, at least their evil desires might be checked by the knowledge that their sons and heirs were at the capital as hostages and gages of their own fidelity.

With this and other similar discreet devices and through the fairness of their justice, the Incas kept their empire in such peace and quiet that during the whole time of their rule there were hardly any revolts or risings to put down or punish. Padre José de Acosta, speaking of the government of the Inca kings (Book VI, ch. xii), says:

Undoubtedly the reverence and affection of the people for their Incas was very great, and there is no record of the latter ever having committed treason against them, for they proceeded in their government not only with great authority, but also with much rectitude and justice, not consenting that anyone should suffer wrong. The Inca appointed governors to the various provinces, some of whom enjoyed full powers and were immediately below himself, while others were of medium standing, and others with only local powers, yet so strongly subordinated that none dared get drunk or steal a head of maize from his neighbor.

Thus far Padre Acosta.

CHAPTER III

The language of the court.

THE CHAPTER of Padre Blas Valera dealing with the general language of Peru to which we have referred was ch. ix of Book II of the *History,* as is seen from the mutilated remains. The chapter, with its heading as his Paternity wrote it, runs as follows:

"Chapter Nine. On the General Language, and Its Ease and Usefulness
"It remains for us to say something of the general language of the natives of Peru, for although it is true that each province has its own particular language which differs from the rest, what is called the language of Cuzco is uniform and general and in the time of the Inca kings was used from Quito to the kingdom of Chile and even as far as the kingdom of Tucma. Now it is used by caciques and the Indians whom the Spaniards have in their service and as officials in their affairs. The Inca kings from ancient times, as soon as they subdued some kingdom or province, gave various orders for the good of their subjects including one that they should learn the courtly language of Cuzco and teach it to their children. And in order that their orders might not be fruitless, they appointed Indians who were natives of Cuzco to teach them their language and the customs of the court. They were given houses and land in the various provinces and villages where they and their children were to settle permanently as teachers. And the Incas gave preference in the choice of governors for offices in their state, whether in peace or war, to those who spoke the general language best. Under this system the Incas governed their whole empire in peace and quiet, and the vassals of various tribes behaved like brothers, for they all spoke the same tongue.

"The children of these teachers from Cuzco are still to be found scattered in various places where their parents used to teach, but as they no longer have the authority formerly conceded to their elders, they cannot teach the Indians or oblige them to learn. Hence it has arisen that many provinces which, when the Spaniards first appeared in Casamarca, used this common tongue like the rest of the empire, have now completely forgotten it, for once the power and rule of the Incas was brought to an end, it never occurred to anyone to see to a thing so necessary for the preaching of the Holy Gospel. This neglect was due to the wars between the Spaniards and afterwards to many other causes, especially as I think to the various obstacles that the wicked Satan has sown to prevent so excellent a disposition from being put into effect. Thus the whole district of the city of Trujillo and many other provinces of the jurisdiction of Quito are completely ignorant of the general language they used to speak, and all the Collas and Puquinas are satisfied with their own speech and scorn that of Cuzco. Moreover in many places where the language of the court lingers on, it is now so corrupt that it seems to be almost a different tongue. It is also worthy of note that the multiplicity and confusion of tongues the Incas tried so carefully to resolve has reappeared so that at the present day there are more different languages among the Indians than there were in the time of the last emperor, Huaina Cápac. Because of this the like-mindedness that the Incas tried to inculcate among the Indians by means of a common tongue now scarcely exists, despite the fact that they are Christians.

"The use of the same or similar words almost always helps to reconcile men and unite them with the bonds of genuine friendship: but this fact was almost completely disregarded by the officials appointed by a certain viceroy to reduce many small Indian villages to larger ones, bringing members of many different tribes together in a single place so as to obviate the difficulty of preaching the gospel at great distances. This difficulty has however been greatly increased by the variety of peoples and tongues that have been brought together. It is indeed humanly speaking impossible that the Peruvian Indians shall be instructed in the faith and in good manners so long as this confusion of tongues endures, unless the priests can learn all the languages of the empire, which is impossible. Nevertheless a knowledge of the speech of Cuzco, however imperfect, is of great use.

"There are some who think it would be wise to oblige all the Indians to learn the Spanish language, so as to spare the priests the vain labor of learning the Indian language. Anyone who hears this argument will realize that it arises more from weakness of spirit than from dullness of understanding. For if the only solution is for the Indians to learn Spanish,

which is so difficult for them, why should they not learn the speech of
their own capital which comes easily and is almost natural to them? On
the contrary, if the Spaniards, who are sharpwitted and versed in learning, cannot, as they say, learn the general language of Cuzco, how can
they make the Indians, who are untutored and uninstructed in letters,
learn Spanish? The truth is that even though there were a great many
teachers ready to teach the Indians Spanish for nothing, the latter, being
uninstructed—and especially the common people—would have such difficulty in learning that any priest who tried would learn to speak fluently
in ten different Peruvian tongues before the Indians could talk Spanish.
There is therefore no reason why we should impose two such heavy penalties on the Indians as to bid them forget their own tongue and learn another so as to save ourselves the small task of learning the speech of their
court. It will suffice that they should be taught the Catholic faith in the
general language of Cuzco, which does not greatly differ from the remaining languages of the empire.

"The viceroys and other governors could easily put an end to the confusion of tongues that has arisen by adding to their duties that of seeing
that the children of the language teachers appointed by the Incas should
resume the teaching of the general language to the rest of the Indians as
they did before. It is easy to learn, so much so that a priest I knew who
both was learned in canon law, and piously desired the salvation of the
Indians of the *repartimiento* it was his duty to indoctrinate, carefully
studied the general language for the purpose of teaching them, and repeatedly begged and importuned his Indians to learn it. To please him
they studied so hard that in scarcely more than a year they could talk it as
if it were their mother tongue, which indeed it became, and the priest
learnt by experience how much more docile and ready to receive Christian
doctrine they were in that language than in their own. Now if this good
priest succeeded with average pains in attaining his object with the Indians, why should not the bishops and viceroys do as much? Indeed if all
the Indians of Peru from Quito to the Chichas are ordered to learn the
general language they will be governed and taught with the greatest of
ease. And it is worthy of note that the Indians whom the Inca ruled with
very few judges can now scarcely be governed by three hundred corregidores, and then only ineffectively and with great difficulty. The main reason for this is the confusion of tongues, which prevents intercourse.

"Many who have tried to learn the general language of Peru bear witness to how quickly and easily it can be picked up, and I have known
many priests who have become proficient in it with average pains. In

Chuquiapu there was a theologian who, as a result of the reports of third persons, hated the general language so much that he would grow angry at the very mention of it, thinking that he could not possibly learn it because of the great difficulty he had heard attributed to it. It happened that before the Jesuit College was founded in that village, a Jesuit father chanced to arrive and stayed there several days to teach the Indians and preach to them in public in the general language. Our priest went to hear the sermon, attracted by the novelty, and seeing many passages of holy scripture explained in the Indian tongue and the Indians marvelling and accepting the teaching as they listened, he felt some respect for the language.

"After the sermon he spoke to the Jesuit, saying: 'Is it possible that divine words, so sweet and mysterious, can be explained in so barbarous a tongue?'

"He was told that they could, and that if he would study the general language with care, he might do the same himself within four or five months. The priest, desiring to benefit the souls of the Indians, promised to learn it with all care and diligence, and after receiving some rules and advice from the Jesuit, worked so hard at it that six months later, he could hear the confessions of the Indians and preach to them, to his own immense delight and their great benefit."

CHAPTER IV

The usefulness of the language of the court.

HAVING SHOWN how easy it is to learn the language of the capital, even for Spaniards coming from Spain, we must point out how much easier it will be for the Indians of Peru to learn it, even though they are of various tongues, for to them it seems to be of their own race and proper to them. This is easily proved, for we notice how the common Indians who come to the city of Lima or Cuzco, or the City of La Plata, or the mines of Potosí, learn to speak the tongue of Cuzco fluently in a few months when they need to earn their keep and clothing by the work of their hands, merely by continuous habit and intercourse with the other Indians and without any instruction in grammar and pronunciation.

When they return to their homes, armed with the newer and nobler tongue, they seem themselves nobler, more cultured, and of better understanding. What means most to them is that the other Indians of their village honor and esteem them for their knowledge of the royal tongue. The Jesuit fathers noticed this in the village called Sulli, whose inhabitants are all Aymarás, and many other priests, judges and corregidores of these provinces assert the same, for the courtly language has this noteworthy property, that it has the same value to the Peruvian Indians as Latin to us.

"In addition to its use in commerce and negotiations, and other spiritual and temporal affairs, it makes them keener in understanding and more tractable and ingenious in what they learn, turning them from savages into civilized and conversible men. Thus the Puquinas, Collas, Urus, Yuncas, and other rude and wild tribes, who speak even their own languages ill, seem to cast off their roughness and savagery when they learn the language of Cuzco, and begin to aspire to a more civilized and courtly life, while their minds rise to higher things. Moreover they grow better adapted to receive the doctrine of the Catholic Faith, and of course preachers who know this tongue well take pleasure in standing up to discuss higher things, feeling that they can explain them to their hearers without the slightest trepidation, for just as the Indians who speak this tongue are of keener and more capacious intelligence, so also the language itself has greater scope and a wider variety of elegant ornaments. In this way the Indians of Cuzco, who speak it most elegantly and urbanely, admit the teaching of the gospel into their hearts and understanding most effectively and usefully. And although in many regions, even among the savage Uriquillas and ferocious Chirihuanas, divine grace has often wrought miracles without this aid, as we shall have occasion to tell, it is nevertheless evident that it usually works through such human media as this. And indeed among many means which the Divine Majesty has used to prepare and summon these barbarous and wild peoples to the preaching of the gospel we must mention the care and diligence taken by the Inca kings in indoctrinating their vassals with the light of natural law so that all should speak one tongue, which was to prove one of the chief vehicles to this end. And all the Inca kings—not without the guidance of Divine providence—paid particular attention to the spread of the language throughout the empire. But it is a pity that the work done by these barbarian pagans to dispel the confusion of tongues, in which they succeeded so well with their industry and skill, should have been so neglected by us, despite its value for teaching the Indians the doctrine of Our Lord

Jesus Christ. But governors who overcome difficult problems, including the most difficult one of reducing new tribes to subjection, might also effect this very simple measure so as to remove the wickedness of idolatry and the darkness of savagery from among Indians already converted to Christianity."

This passage is taken from Padre Blas Valera, and I have introduced it here since it seemed to me essential for the teaching of the Christian faith. His other remarks concerning the general language deal with the similarity of Peruvian and Latin, Greek, and Hebrew, of which he writes like a man skilled in many languages, though as this passage has nothing to do with the teaching of Christian doctrine, I do not include it here. While discussing the question of languages, I will mention what Padre Blas Valera says in another place in refuting the opinion of those who hold that the Indians of the New World descend from the Jews of the stock of Abraham and seek to demonstrate this by adducing some words from the general language of Peru which resemble Hebrew in sound, though not in meaning. In his refutation Padre Blas Valera remarks among other interesting observations, that the general language of Peru lacks the letters we have mentioned in our foreword, *b, d, f, g, j, x,* but the Jews, being so attached to their father Abraham that his name was always on their lips, could not have lacked the letter *b,* which appears so prominently in Abraham. We may add another argument, which is that Peruvian never has the group of two consonants called *muta cum liquida,* such as *bra, cra, cro, pla, pri, clla, cllo,* and others of the kind. Thus to say the name Abraham, the general language lacks not only the letter *b,* but also the syllable *bra.* There is therefore no justification to assume something which can obviously not be proved. Although it is true that my Peruvian mother-tongue has some words with the *muta cum liquida* such as *papri, huacra, rocro, pocra, chacra, llaclla, chocllo,* it should be made clear that in spelling out the syllables and pronouncing the words the *muta* is separated from the *liquida,* as *pap-ri, huac-ra, roc-ro, poc-ra, chac-ra, llac-lla, choc-llo,* and all others of the same kind. Spaniards do not notice this, but pronounce the words with whatever corruptions of letters and syllables they please. When the Indians say *pampa,* "place, square," the Spaniards say *bamba*; for *Inca* they say *Inga,* for *roc-ro, locro,* and so on. Scarcely a word is left without corruption, as we have explained at some length and shall have occasion to repeat. This said, we must return to our history.

CHAPTER V

The third solemn festival in honor of the sun.

T HE INCAS celebrated four solemn festivals a year in their capital. The
chief and most solemn was the festival of the Sun called Raimi, of
which we have spoken at length. The second and no less notable was
celebrated when young men of the royal blood were armed knights: we
have described it too. It remains to refer to the two remaining festivals,
with which we shall conclude our description of the festivals, for it
would be a lengthy and tedious matter to go into the ordinary festivals
celebrated each moon, and the special feasts held as a thanksgiving for the
great victories they won or on the occasion of some province or kingdom
willingly accepting the Inca's yoke. Suffice it to say that all such celebrations took place in the temple of the Sun, like the main festival, though
the others were done with much less ceremony and solemnity and without
going out into the market place.

The third festival was called Cusquieraimi. It took place after the sowing and when the maize had appeared. Many lambs, barren ewes, and
rams were offered up to the Sun, with prayers that he should not send
frost to spoil the maize, for in the valleys of Cuzco and Sacsahuana and
other neighboring districts, as well as in other parts with a similar climate,
the frost is apt to be very hard, and it effects maize more than any other
crop. Moreover in these valleys it freezes throughout the year, both summer and winter, whenever the sky is clear at nightfall. It freezes more on
St. John's day than at Christmas, for the sun is then furthest away. If the
Indians see that the sky is clear and cloudless at dusk, they fear there will
be a frost and set fire to piles of dung to produce smoke. Each family tried
to make smoke in their yard, saying that the smoke would prevent frost,
since it acted as a cover against it like clouds. I saw this in Cuzco, but do
not know if it is still done, nor do I know if it was true or not that the
smoke prevented frost, for as a boy I did not take any profound interest
in the doings of the Indians.

As maize was the chief food of the Indians and frost was so harmful
to it, the Indians would implore the Sun with sacrifices, feasts, dances,
and drinking to prevent the frost from damaging it. The flesh of the animals slaughtered in these sacrifices was all eaten by people who came to

attend the feasts, except the first lambs offered to the Sun and the blood and inwards of the other animals, all of which was burnt and offered to the Sun, as at the festival of Raimi.

CHAPTER VI

The fourth festival; the fasts; and their way of purging their ills.

THE FOURTH and last solemn feast celebrated by the Indians in their capital was called Citua. It was celebrated with great rejoicing by everyone for it represented the expulsion from the city and its district of all the diseases and other ills and troubles that man can suffer. It was like the explanation of the ancient pagans, when they purified themselves. The preparations for this festival included fasting and abstaining from women. The fast was held on the first day of the September moon after the equinox. The Incas had two strict fasts, the one more so than the other. The first consisted of only maize and water, the maize being uncooked and minute in quantity. As this fast was so severe, it lasted only three days: the other was milder, and roasted maize was permitted in rather larger quantities, together with uncooked herbs (as we eat lettuces and radishes) and *ají*, which the Indians call *uchu*, and salt, while they drank their beverage, but ate no meat, fish, or cooked vegetables. In both fasts they could only eat once a day. The fast is called *caci*, and the severer fast, *hatuncaci*, "the big fast."

After everyone—men, women, and even children—had made preparation with a day of rigorous fasting, they kneaded the bread called *çancu* the following night. It was cooked in balls in dry pots, for they had no ovens, and left half-baked and doughy. They made two kinds of bread. To the first they added the blood of boys or children of between five and ten, which they obtained by bleeding and not by killing the victims. The blood was obtained from between the eyebrows, above the nostrils, and the same bleeding was practiced in case of illness: I have seen it done. Each sort of bread was baked separately, as it was intended for different purposes. Relatives collected together for the ceremonies, repairing to the house of the eldest brother, or if they had none to that of their senior relative.

Shortly before dawn on the night of the baking, all those who had fasted washed their bodies and took a little of the dough mixed with blood and rubbed it on their heads, faces, chests and shoulders, arms and legs, as if cleansing themselves so as to rid their bodies of infirmities. This done, the eldest relative, the master of the house, anointed the lintel of the street door with dough, leaving some sticking to it as a sign that the ablution had taken place in the house and that their bodies had been cleansed. The high priest performed the same ceremonies in the house and temple of the Sun and sent other priests to do the same in the house of the women of the Sun and at Huanacauri, a temple a league from the city greatly venerated as the first place where Inca Manco Cápac stayed when he came to Cuzco, as we have already mentioned. They also sent priests to other places regarded as sacred, or where the Devil spoke to them in the guise of God. In the royal house the ceremonies were performed by the king's eldest legitimate uncle.

When the Sun came out they had adored him and begged him to banish all the ills, inward and outward, that afflicted them, they broke their fast with another loaf, kneaded without blood. After the adoration and the breaking of the fast, which took place at a fixed hour, so that the adoration of the Sun should be in unison, one of the Incas of the royal blood came out of the fort as a messenger from the Sun. He was richly dressed, wrapped in a blanket, with a spear in his hand garnished with a band about a *tercia* wide, made of feathers of various colors, which hung from the point of the spear down to the guard and was attached at places with gold rings, a device also used as a standard in wartime. He came out of the fort and not from the temple of the Sun because he was supposed to be the messenger of war and not of peace, and the fort was the house of the Sun as regards military affairs, while the temple was his dwelling for matters of peace and friendship. He came running down the slope from the hill called Sacsahuana to the middle of the main square brandishing his spear. There he was met by four other Incas of the royal blood, each with a spear in his hand adorned like the first, and their blankets wrapped round them as the Indians gird them when they are about to run or do anything of importance and want to move freely. The messenger touched the spears of the four Indians with his own, and told them that the Sun had bidden them to go forth as his messengers to expel the diseases and other ills there might be in the city and its neighborhood.

The four Incas ran down the four royal highways leading out of the city to the four quarters of the world, which they call Tahuantinsuyu. The inhabitants, men and women, old and young, came to the doors of their houses as the four ran by and shook their clothes as if shaking out dust, giving vent to loud cries of pleasure and rejoicing. They then ran their hands over their heads and faces, arms, legs, and bodies, as if washing themselves and driving all ills out of their houses so that the messengers of the Sun might expel them from the city. This was done not only in the streets through which the four Incas passed, but also throughout the city as a whole. The messengers ran with their spears a quarter of a league out of the city, where four other Incas, not of the royal blood, but Incas by privilege, took the spears and ran another quarter of a league, and then handed them to others, and so on until they were five or six leagues from the city, where the spears were stuck in the ground as a barrier to prevent the ills from re-entering the area from which they had been banished.

CHAPTER VII

A nocturnal rite for expelling ills from the city.

THE FOLLOWING night they went out with great torches of straw woven like the jackets for oil jars in round balls. These were called *pancuncu,* and took a long time to burn. Each was fastened to a cord a fathom in length, and they used to run through all the streets trailing the torches till they were outside the city, as if the torches removed the evils by night as the spears did by day. The burnt torches were finally cast into the streams that pass through the city, together with the water in which the people had washed the previous day, so that the running water might carry the ills they had driven out of their houses and out of the city down to the sea. If later any Indian, young or old, found any of these torches in a stream, he would flee from it as if from the flames, lest the evils that had been driven out should attach themselves to him.

Having made war on their ills and banished them by fire and the sword, they held great festivities and rejoicings for the whole of that quarter of the moon, as a sign of thanksgiving to the Sun for delivering them from their ills. They sacrificed many rams and lambs to him, and burnt their blood and inwards as an offering, while the flesh was roasted in the main square and distributed among all those present. During these days, and also at night, there was much dancing and singing and other expressions of rejoicing, both in the houses and in the public places, since they all in common enjoyed the good health and other benefits conferred by the rite.

I remember having seen part of this celebration in my childhood. I saw the first Inca come down with his spear, though not from the fort, which was already abandoned, but from one of the Incas' houses on the skirt of the hill where the fortress is. The place of this house is called Collcampata. I saw the four Indians running with their spears. I saw the common people shaking their clothes and making the other gestures, and saw them eat the bread called *çancu*. I saw the torches or *pancuncu,* but did not see the nocturnal rite, because it was very late and I had already gone to bed. I remember having afterwards seen a *pancuncu* in the stream running through the middle of the square. It lay near the house of my fellow pupil in the grammar school Juan de Cellorico, and I recall how the Indian boys passing down the street avoided it. I did not avoid it because I did not know why; if they had told me, I should certainly have fled too, for I was a child of six or seven. The torch I saw had been flung down within the city because in my time the rite was no longer observed with the strict reverence and solemnity of the days of the Incas. It was not performed to banish their ills, for they had already lost their belief in this, but as a memory of olden times: there were still many old people alive, who had spent all their lives in the pagan religion and had never been baptized. In Inca times they ran with the torches until they dropped them outside the city. The water in which they had washed their bodies was poured into the streams, even though they had to go a great distance from their homes to find them: they were not allowed to throw the water anywhere except in the streams lest the ills they had washed away should be left behind: it was supposed to be carried by the running water to the sea, as we have said above.

The Indians also performed another private ceremony, each in his own house. After having shut their crops in the granaries, which they call *pirua,* they burnt a little tallow nearby as a sacrifice to the Sun. The richer and nobler people burnt the tame rabbits called *coy,* as a thanksgiving for his having provided bread to eat during the year. They besought the Sun to bid the granaries to take good care of the corn he had provided for the support of men: these were the only prayers they made.

The priests made other sacrifices during the course of the year within the house of the Sun, but they did not bring them out into the market place or consider them as comparable with the four main feasts we have mentioned, which were like Eastertide: the common festivals were ordinary sacrifices made to the Sun every moon.

CHAPTER VIII

The description of the imperial city of Cuzco.

INCA CÁPAC was the founder of the city of Cuzco which the Spaniards honored with a longer title, though without removing its proper name. They called it the Great City of Cuzco, head of the kingdoms and provinces of Peru. They also called it New Toledo, but this other name was soon forgotten, since it was quite inappropriate: Cuzco is not girt by a river like Toledo, and does not resemble it in situation, for its population is centered on the slopes and folds of a high hill and stretches in all directions over a broad and spacious plain. It has long, wide streets and large squares, which is why the Spaniards in general, and royal scribes and notaries in public documents in particular, use the first title. For Cuzco in relation to its empire was like Rome to the Roman empire, and the two can be compared with one another, for they resembled one another in their nobler aspects. First, and in chief, both were founded by their first kings. Secondly, they resembled one another in the many different tribes they conquered and added to their empires. Thirdly, they had many excellent laws applied to the good government of the two states. Fourthly, they both bred many famous men and taught them good civil and military doctrine. In this Rome had the advantage over Cuzco, not because she reared her sons better, but because she was more fortunate in having attained the art of letters, whereby she perpetuated the fame of her offspring. They became indeed as illustrious in the sciences as they were excellent in the use of arms; and soldiers and writers honored one another, the first performing notable deeds in peace and war, and the latter writing them down to the honor of their country and the perpetual memory of all concerned. I do not know which did most, those who wielded their swords or those who wielded their pens, for the two activities are both heroic and occupy an equal place, as we see in the case of the great Julius Caesar, who exercised both professions with such talent

that it is hard to say in which he was the greater. Indeed it may be doubted
which of these two groups of illustrious men owed most to the other,
whether the warriors to the writers who set down their deeds and immortalized them, or the men of letters to the men of war, who daily provided them with such great deeds as to offer material for their whole
lives. Each group could allege many arguments in its own favor, but we
shall not repeat them, for we must return to the misfortune of my own
country whose sons, though they were distinguished in warfare and for
their great wisdom and understanding, and had great aptitude for learning, yet, having no knowledge of letters, left no memory of their great
deeds and wise sayings. Thus they all perished with their country. All
that has remained of their words and deeds is a feeble tradition passed
down by word of mouth from father to son. Even this has been lost with
the arrival of a new race, the imposition of a foreign rule and a change
of government: this indeed always occurs when empires fall.

I myself, moved by the desire to preserve the few shreds of the ancient
traditions of my country that have survived, lest they should completely
disappear, have undertaken the excessive labor that this work has oc-
casioned me, as far as I have gone, and that still faces me in continuing
the history of the ancient institutions till their end. And so that the city of
Cuzco, the mother and mistress of the ancient empire, shall not be forgotten, I have resolved to include a short description of it in this chapter,
following the traditions that I picked up as a native son of the city and
setting down what I saw with my own eyes. I shall give the traditional
names of its various wards which were retained until the year 1560, when
I left. Later some of these names were changed to correspond with those
of the parish churches built in some of the wards.

King Manco Cápac, having taken into account the advantages possessed by the valley of Cuzco—the flatness of the site, surrounded on all
sides by high sierras; the four streams (though none of them very large)
to irrigate the whole valley, and in the midst a splendid fountain of briny
water for making salt; fertile soil; and healthy air—decided to found
his imperial city on that site, in obedience to the will of his father the
Sun, who, according to the Indian belief, had bidden him set up his court,
which was to become the capital of his empire, at the place indicated by
the golden wand. The temperature of the city is cold rather than warm,
but not so cold as to oblige the inhabitants to light fires for warmth. They
have only to go into a room in which there is no current of air to shake
off the cold from the street. If they have a brazier, they keep very warm;
if not, they manage well without. Similarly with clothes; summer out-

doors dress is sufficient: winter outdoors dress is comfortable. In the same way for bedcovers a single blanket is enough, but three are not oppressive throughout the year, with no distinction between winter and summer. This is true of all the regions of Peru, which are constant throughout the year, whether hot, temperate, or cold. In Cuzco, which, as we have said, is cold and dry rather than hot and damp, meat does not go bad. A piece of meat hung in a room with the windows open will keep a week, a fortnight, or thirty or a hundred days until it is as dry as a bone. I have seen this done with the flesh of the Peruvian sheep. I do not know if it can be done with the flesh of the sheep introduced from Spain, or whether, as the Spanish sheep is more hot-blooded than the Peruvian sheep, its meat will keep in the same way or not stand such treatment. I did not see this, as in my time Castilian sheep were never killed because few of them were bred. Because of the coldness of the temperature there are no flies in the city, or very few, and such as there are live in the open air and do not enter the houses. Stinging mosquitos are not found, nor are other noxious creatures: the city is quite free of all of them. The first houses and dwellings in Cuzco were built on the slopes and folds of the hill called Sacsahuana, which is now between the east and north of the city. On the top of this hill the successors of the first Inca later built that spendid fortress, which was so little esteemed, but rather abhorred by its conquerors, that they pulled it down in a very short time. The city was divided into the two parts we mentioned earlier, Hanan Cuzco, which is upper Cuzco, and Hurin Cuzco, or lower Cuzco. They were divided by the Antisuyu road which leads eastwards, the part to the north of the road being Hanan Cuzco, and that to the south Hurin Cuzco. The first and most important district was called Collcampata. *Cóllcam* must have been a word from the special language of the Incas, whose meaning I do not know. *Pata* is "terrace," and also means a stair: as the cultivation terraces were made in the form of a staircase, this name was applied to them. It also means any kind of bench or seat.

It was on this terrace that Inca Manco Cápac founded his royal palace, and it was later occupied by Paullu, the son of Huaina Cápac. I saw a large and spacious hall which served as a public place for celebrating the great festivals in rainy weather: when I left Cuzco it alone was standing and a number of others like it, to which we shall refer, had all fallen in. Beyond Collcampata, moving toward the east, there lay another ward called Cantutpata, meaning the "terrace of pinks." *Cantut* is the name for a very pretty flower somewhat resembling Spanish pinks, though before the arrival of the Spaniards there were no pinks in Peru. The *cantut* has a stalk, leaf, and thorns like those of the Andalusian *cambronera* or box-thorn, and the plant grows in large thickets. The ward received its name from the very large quantity of these plants, which I saw when I was there. Still further round toward the east lies the ward of Pumacurcu, "the lions' beam," from *puma,* "lion," and *curcu,* "beam," referring to some large beams there were in this ward to which lions presented to the Inca were fastened until they were tamed and could be moved to their permanent quarters. Then followed another very large ward called Tococachi. The meaning of this compound I do not understand. *Toco* is "window" and *cachi,* "salt for eating," so that according to the rules of the language it ought to mean "window salt": I cannot understand what is intended unless it is a proper noun and has a different meaning which I do not know. In this ward stood the primitive building of the convent of St. Francis. Turning a little to the south, continuing the circle, follows the ward called Munaicenca, or "love-nose," from *muna,* "to love," and *cenca,* "nose." Why this name was given I do not know, but it must have been because of some anecdote or superstition, for names were never applied at random. Further toward the south follows another large ward called Rimacpampa, "the talking square," for it was there that some of the decrees issued for the government of the republic were announced. They were proclaimed from time to time so that the inhabitants might hear them and present themselves to carry out whatever obligations they entailed. As the square was in this ward, its name was given to the ward: from the square the royal highway leads out to Collasuyu. Beyond the ward of Rimacpampa lies another to the south of the city, called Pumapchupan, "lion's tail," for the ward tapers to a point between two streams that unite at a right angle. The name was also given to imply that this ward was the last in the city, and they therefore distinguished it with the name of "the lion's tail." Moreover, lions and other fierce animals were kept in it. At a distance to the west of this ward there was a village of over three hundred inhabitants called Cayaucachi. It stood more than a thousand paces from the last houses in the city. This was in 1560. As I write this, in 1602, I am told that it is already within the limits of Cuzco, the population of which has so multiplied that the city has surrounded the village on all sides.

To the west of the city, again a thousand paces away, there was another ward called Chaquillchaca, which again as a compound is a meaningless name, unless it is a proper noun. The royal highway to Cuntisuyu begins here. Near the road there are two streams of excellent water which are channeled underground. The Indians do not know where the water comes from, for the work is a very ancient one and traditions about these things are being forgotten. The channels are called *collquemachác-huay,* "silver snakes," for the water is as white as silver and the channels wind like snakes through the earth. I am told that the population of the city has also reached Chaquillchaca. Following the same circle and turning now from the west northwards there was another ward called Pichu, which was also outside the city. Beyond it lay another named Quillipata, likewise outside the city. Further on, to the north of the city lies the great ward of Carmenca, a proper name with no special meaning in the general tongue of Peru. The royal highway to Chinchasuyu begins there. Turning eastwards there follows the ward of Huacapuncu, "gate of the sanctuary," from *huaca,* which has many meanings, as we have explained, including that of "temple" or "sanctuary": *puncu* is "door, gate." The ward gets its name from the stream that runs through the main square of Cuzco. Beside the stream runs a long, wide street, and both of them traverse the whole city, meeting the royal highway to Collasuyu about a league and a half beyond it. This entrance is called the "gate of the sanctuary" or "of the temple" because in addition to the wards dedicated to the temple of the Sun and the house of the chosen virgins, which were the chief sanctuaries, they regarded the whole city as sacred, and it was one of their chief idols. For this reason they called this entry of the stream and the street the gate of the sanctuary while the place where the stream left the city was called "the lion's tail," indicating that the city was sacred according to their laws and their vain religion and a lion in their arms and warfare. The ward of Huacapuncu touches the limits of Collcampata, from which we began our tour of the wards of the city: we have thus come full circle.

CHAPTER IX

The city contained the description of the whole empire.

THE INCAS divided the wards according to the four parts of their empire, called Tahuantinsuyu. The division dated back to the first Inca Manco Cápac, who ordered that the savages he had subjugated should be settled according to their places of origin, those from the east to the east, those from the west to the west, and so on. The dwellings of the first subjects were thus disposed in a circle within the limits of the town, and those from newly conquered areas settled according to the situation of their provinces. The *curacas* built houses to live in when they came to the capital, each next to one another, but settling on the side nearest his own province. If a chief's province was to the right of his neighbor's, he built his house to the right; if to the left, he built it to the left, and if behind, he built his house behind. The result of this arrangement was that anyone who contemplated the wards and the dwellings of the numerous and varied tribes who had settled in them beheld the whole empire at once, as if in a looking glass or a cosmographic plan. In describing the site of Cuzco, Cieza de Léon makes the same observation in his ch. xciii:

And though the city was full of numbers of strange and remote tribes, such as Indians from Chile and Pasto, Cañaris, Chachapoyas, Huancas, Collas, and other peoples of these provinces, each race dwelt together in the place allotted to it by the governors of the city. The latter preserved the customs of their fathers, followed the usages of their provinces, and would easily have been recognized from the insignia they wore on their heads even though there were a hundred-thousand men gathered together,

etc. Thus far from Cieza de Léon.

The insignia they wore on their heads were a sort of headdress which served for identification, each tribe and province differing from the rest. This was not an invention of the Incas, but a custom of the various tribes. The Inca kings ordered it to be preserved to prevent confusion among the tribes and nations from Pasto to Chile. According to the same author (ch. xxxviii) the distance is more than thirteen-hundred leagues. So that the great ring of the outer wards was inhabited solely by the vassals of the whole empire and not by the Incas or members of the royal blood. These wards formed the suburbs of the city itself, which we shall now describe street by street from north to south, including the various wards and the houses between the streets: we shall mention the royal palaces and say to whom they fell in the distribution that took place after the Spanish conquest.

From the hill called Sacsahuana there runs a stream containing little water which flows north and south as far as the last suburb, called Pumapchupan. It divides the city from the wards. Further in the city there is a street now called St. Augustine which follows the same route from north to south, beginning from the palaces of the first Inca Manco Cápac and going straight down to the square called Rimacpampa. There are three or four more streets that cross the broad space between the street and the stream from east to west, and it was in this broad space that the Incas of the royal blood lived, divided into their *aillus* or clans, though all of them were of the same blood and stock. Although they all descended from King Manco Cápac, yet each claimed descent from the one or other of the kings, saying these descend from this Inca, those from that Inca, and so on for all the rest. This is what the Spanish historians refer to when they say confusedly that such and such an Inca founded one line, and another a different one, suggesting that these were different stocks. But the lineages were in fact all the same, as the Indians show when they apply the common name *Cápac Aillu,* "august lineage of the royal blood," to them all. They also apply the word *Inca,* meaning "a man of the royal blood," indiscriminately to all males of this lineage, and call the women *Palla,* "woman of the royal blood." In my day the residents in this street from the upper end downwards were, Rodrigo de Pineda, Juan de Saavedra, Diego Ortiz de Guzmán, Pedro de los Ríos and his brother Diego de los Ríos, Jerónimo Costilla, Gaspar Jara (who owned the houses on the site of what is now the monastery of St. Augustine the Divine), Miguel Sánchez, Juan de Santa Cruz, Alonso de Soto, Gabriel Carrera, Diego de Trujillo (one of the first conquerors and one of the thirteen companions who stood by Don Francisco Pizarro, as we shall relate in due course), Antón Ruiz de Guevara, Juan de Salas, the brother of the archbishop of Seville and inquisitor-general, Valdés de Salas, besides others whose names I do not recall. They were all lords of vassals and held allocations of Indians, being among the second conquerors of Peru. Apart from these, many other Spaniards who had no Indians dwelt in the same street. In one of the houses the convent of the divine St. Augustine was founded, though after I left the city. We use the term first conquerors for the 160 Spaniards who were with Don Francisco Pizarro at the arrest of Atahuallpa, and second conquerors for those who were with Don Diego de Almagro and Don Pedro de Alvarado who arrived in Peru almost at once. The aforesaid and no others were called conquerors of Peru: the second looked up to the first as such, despite the fact that some of the first were of lower rank and less estate.

To return to the top of the street of St. Augustine, whence we shall penetrate further into the city, at its upper end stands the convent of Santa Clara on a site that belonged first to Alonso Díaz, a son-in-law of the governor Pedro Arias de Ávila. To the right of the convent there are many houses belonging to Spaniards, including those of Francisco de Barrientos which later belonged to Juan Alvarez Maldonado. To the right of these were the houses of Hernando Bachicao and later of Juan Alonso Palomino. Facing these, to the south, stands the episcopal palace, which formerly belonged to Juan Balsa and afterwards to Francisco de Villacastín. Next follows the cathedral church, which gives onto the main square. Its site was occupied in Inca times by a fine hall which was used in bad weather as a place of assembly for festivities. It had been the site of the palace of Inca Viracocha, the eighth king, but I only saw this hall. When the Spaniards entered the city, they all lodged in it so as to be together in case of emergency. When I saw it it was covered with thatch, and later I saw it being tiled. To the north of the cathedral church, and across the street from it, there are many houses with gates giving onto the main square: they are used as shops by craftsmen. To the south of the cathedral, and across the street, stand the main shops of the wealthier merchants.

Behind the church are the houses that formerly belonged to Juan de Berrio, and others whose owners I do not recall.

Behind the chief shops are the houses that used to belong to Diego Maldonado called the rich, for he was wealthier than anyone else in Peru: he was one of the first conquerors. In Inca times the place was called Hatuncancha, "big ward." It had been the site of the palace of one of the kings called Inca Yupanqui. South of the house of Diego Maldonado and facing it stands the former house of Francisco Hernández Girón. Beyond this to the south are the houses of Antonio Altamirano, one of the first conquerors, Francisco de Frías, Sebastián de Cazalla, and many others on either side and behind. This ward is called Puca Marca, "the red ward," and the houses belonged to King Túpac Inca Yupanqui. Beyond this ward there is another very large ward to the south, the name of which I forget. It contains the houses of Antonio de Loaisa, Martín de Meneses, Juan de Figueroa, Don Pedro Puertocarrero, García de Melo, Francisco Delgado, and many others belonging to lords of vassals whose names escape my memory. Beyond this, still moving southward, is the square called Intipampa. This means "square of the Sun," for it lay before the house and temple of the Sun, and was the place where those who were not Incas, and could not therefore enter the house of the Sun, delivered their offerings. There the priests received them and presented them to the image of the Sun which they worshipped as god. The ward where the temple of the Sun stood was called Coricancha, "ward of gold, silver, and precious stones," since these treasures existed in that ward, as we have already stated. After this came the ward called Pumapchupan, which is already one of the suburbs.

CHAPTER X

The site of the schools, that of three royal palaces, and that of the chosen virgins.

TO ENUMERATE the remaining wards, we must return to Huacapuncu, the gate of the sanctuary, which stood to the north of the main square of the city. It was followed to the south by another very extensive ward, the name of which has escaped my memory. We might call it the ward of the schools, for it contained the schools founded by King Inca Roca, as we mentioned in describing his life. In the Indian language they are called *"yacha huaci,"* "house of teaching." The sages and teachers of the Inca state lived there, both *amautas,* "philosophers," and *haráuec,* "poets," who were much esteemed by the Incas and all their empire. They had with them many of their pupils, especially those who were of the royal blood.

Moving southward from the ward of the schools, we come to two others containing two royal palaces giving on to the main square. They filled the whole side of the square: one of them, to the east of the other, was called Coracora, "the pastures," for the place used to be pasture and the square in front of it was a swamp or marsh until the Incas had it transformed to its present state. Cieza de Léon confirms this in his ch. xcii. In this pasture King Inca Roca established his royal palace to favor and assist the schools, where he often went to hear the masters. I saw nothing of the house called Coracora, for it had been razed by my time. When the city was divided among the Spaniards it fell to Gonzalo Pizarro, the brother of the marquis Don Francisco Pizarro. He was one of its conquerors. I knew this gentleman in Cuzco after the battle of Huarina and before that of Sacsahuana, and he treated me as if I were his own son. I was then about eight or nine.

The other royal palace, to the west of Coracora, was called Cassana, "something to freeze." The name was applied to it out of wonder, imply-ing that the buildings in it were so large and splendid that anyone who gazed on them attentively would be frozen with astonishment. They were the palaces of the great Inca Pachacútec, the great-grandson of Inca Roca, who built his house near the schools his grandfather had founded. These two palaces had the schools behind them, and all adjoined one another without any gap. The main gate of the schools gave onto the street and onto the stream. The kings passed through the side door to hear the lec-tures of the philosophers, and Inca Pachacútec often gave them himself in explanation of his laws and statutes, for he was a great legislator. In my time the Spaniards built a street which divided the schools from the palace. I saw in my time a great part of the walls of the building called Cassana, which were of finely worked masonry, showing that it had been a royal dwelling, as also a splendid hall which the Incas used for festivals and dances in rainy weather. It was so large that sixty mounted men could easily joust with canes in it. I saw the convent of St. Francis established in this hall, for it was moved from the ward of Tococachi, where it had formerly been, owing to the great distance of the latter from the houses of the Spaniards. A large section of the hall, big enough to hold many people, was set apart as a church: then there were the cells, the dormitory and the refectory and remaining dependencies of the convent, and if the inside had not been roofed, a cloister could have been made too. The hall and all the necessary space was presented to the friars by Juan de Pan-corvo, one of the first conquerors, to whom the royal mansion fell in the distribution of the houses. Many other Spaniards had shares in them, but Juan de Pancorvo bought them all at the very first, when they were given away for a song. A few years later the convent was moved to its present site, as we shall mention elsewhere when dealing with the alms given by the inhabitants to the religious to buy a site to build a church. I also saw the hall destroyed, and the modern shops with doorways for mer-chants and craftsmen built in the ward of Cassana.

In front of these houses, which were formerly palaces, stands the chief square of the city called Haucaipata, "terrace or square of festivities and rejoicing." From north to south it would measure about 200 paces in length, or some 400 feet. From east to west, it would be a 150 paces wide as far as the stream. At the end of the square to its south, there were two other royal houses, one that was near the stream, and opposite it, called Amarucancha, "ward of the great snakes." It faced Cassana and was the palace of Huaina Cápac: it now belongs to the holy Society of Jesus. I remember seeing still a great hall, though not so large as that of Cassana.

I also saw there a very fine round tower which stood in the square before the house. Elsewhere we shall speak of this tower, which was the first lodging of the Spaniards in the city, and for this reason, apart from its great beauty, it would have been well if the conquerors had preserved it. I saw no other remains of this palace: all the rest was razed. In the first division the main part of this palace, giving on to the square, fell to Hernando Pizarro, the brother of the marquis Don Francisco Pizarro, who was also one of the first conquerors of the city. I saw this gentleman in the court of Madrid in 1562. Another part fell to Mancio Serra de Leguiçamo, one of the first conquerors. A further part was awarded to Antonio Altamirano, who had two houses when I knew him: he must have bought one of them. A further part was set aside as the prison for Spaniards. Still another part was given to Alonso Mazuela, one of the first conquerors, and later passed to Martín Dolmos. Other sections fell to others whom I do not recall. East of Amarucancha, across the street of the Sun, is the suburb called Acllahuaci, "the house of the chosen virgins," where stood the convent of the maidens dedicated to the Sun, of whom we have already given a full account. The part of the building that still existed in my time was divided between Francisco Mejía—who was given the part giving onto the square, which also is filled with merchants' shops—Pedro del Barco, Licentiate de la Gama, and others whose names I do not remember.

All the settled area of wards and palaces lay to the east of the stream that runs through the main square. We may note that it was here that the Incas had those three halls on the sides and in front of the square, so that they could celebrate their principal festivals even though it was raining on the appropriate days, which were at the new moon of certain months or at the solstices. When the Indians made their general rising against the Spaniards and burnt the whole city, they spared three of the four halls we have mentioned, those of Collcampata, Cassana, and Amarucancha. On the fourth, which was the lodging place of the Spaniards and is now the cathedral church, they threw innumerable burning arrows and the thatch was fired in more than twenty places. It was however extinguished, as we shall tell in due course, for God did not permit it to be burnt that night or any of the other nights or days when they sought to burn it; and because of these and similar wonders wrought by the Lord so that his Catholic Faith might enter the empire, it was won by the Spaniards. The temple of the Sun and house of the chosen virgins were also spared. All the rest of the buildings were set on fire in an attempt to burn the Spaniards.

CHAPTER XI

The wards and houses to the west of the stream.

THE PALACES and buildings of the city that we have already described
were all to the east of the stream that run through it. To the west of
the stream is the square called Cussipata, "the terrace of pleasure and joy."
In Inca times the two squares were one: the whole stream was covered
with broad beams, and great flags were laid over them to make a floor,
for so many lords of vassals rallied to the chief festivals performed in
honor of the Sun that there was no room for them in the main square; it
was therefore extended with another and rather smaller space. The stream
was covered with beams because they did not know how to make arches.
The Spaniards used the timber and replaced it with four bridges at intervals: they were also of wood, and I saw them. They later built three
arched bridges, which were standing when I left. In my time the two
squares were not divided, nor were there houses on the two banks of the
streams as there are now. In 1555, when my lord Garcilaso de la Vega
was corregidor, these houses were built and granted to private citizens of
Cuzco, for the city herself, who had once been lady and empress of that
mighty empire, had not a maravedi of income at that time—I do not
know if she now has. To the west of the stream the Inca kings had raised
no buildings, and there was nothing but the outer ring of suburbs. The
space had been kept for future kings to build their palaces as had been
done in the past, for though it is true that successors inherited their predecessors' palaces, they also had a new one built for themselves to add to
their greatness and majesty and perpetuate their names as builders. In
this respect, as in everything else, they preserved the names of the Incas
who had owned them, to the special greatness of these kings. The Spaniards built their houses on the spot, and we shall name them as we proceed from north to south, mentioning where they were and who were
their owners when I left Peru.

Following the stream down from the gate of Huacapuncu, the first
house belonged to Pedro de Orué. There followed those of Juan de Pan-
corvo where Alonso de Marchena lived, for although he had Indians of
his own, Juan de Pancorvo did not want him to live anywhere else because of their long and close friendship. Following the same direction
on the opposite side stood the house that belonged to Hernán Bravo de

Laguna, formerly owned by Antonio Navarro and Lope Martín, of the first conquerors. Other houses attached to this belonged to Spaniards whom we shall not name as they had no Indians. We have omitted mentioning such in dealing with the other wards, for any other procedure would lead to intolerable length. The house of Hernán Bravo was followed by those of Alonso de Hinojosa, formerly the property of Licentiate Carvajal, the brother of the factor Illén Suárez Carvajal, who is mentioned in the histories of Peru. Moving in the same north-south direction, there follows the square of Cussipata, now called Our Lady of the Mercies. In my time Indian men and women drove a miserable trade there, bartering various objects one for another. For in those days there was no minted coin, and there was none for another twenty years. It was a sort of fair or market, which the Indians call *catu*. Beyond the square to the south stands the convent of Our Lady of the Mercies covering a whole block bounded by four streets. Behind it and opposite there were other houses belonging to lords of Indians, but I do not mention them as I do not remember the names of the owners. This was the limit of the buildings in those days.

Returning to the ward called Carmenca, we descend another street of houses. Those nearest the Carmenca belonged to Diego de Silva who was godfather at my confirmation: he was the son of the famous Feliciano de Silva. Southward again, and opposite, was the dwelling of Pedro López de Cazalla, who was secretary to President La Gasca, and that of Juan de Betanzos, as well as many others on either side and behind them, whose owners had no Indians. Proceeding southwards, and opposite, there was the house that belonged to Alonso de Mesa, one of the first conquerors. It faces onto the square of Our Lady, and there are many others on either side of it and behind it which we need not mention. The house to the south of that of Alonso de Mesa and facing it belonged to my lord Garcilaso de la Vega. It had a long, narrow balcony above the main door which was used by the chief gentlemen of the city for watching the various spectacles that took place in the square, such as the *sortija*,[1] bullfighting, and jousting with canes. Before my father had it, it belonged to a nobleman called Francisco de Oñate, who had been one of the first conquerors and who died in the battle of Chupas. From the balcony, and other points in the city, one can see a snowcapped peak shaped like a pyramid, which is so high that, although it is some twenty-five leagues away, with other mountains between, a considerable part of the top is

[1] The *sortija* is a ring, and the spectacle consists of tilting at it with a lance.

visible. No crags or rocks are to be seen, but only pure and perpetual snow which never decreases. It is called Villcanuta, meaning "something sacred, marvellous or extraordinary," for the name *villca* is never used unless for things worthy of admiration: and indeed the pyramid is remarkable, exceeding any description one could possibly give. I appeal to those who have seen it, or may do so. To the west of my father's property stood that of Vasco de Guevara, one of the second conquerors. It later belonged to Coya Doña Beatriz, Huaina Cápac's daughter. To the south and opposite was the house of Antonio de Quiñones, which also projected into the square of Our Lady. Below that of Antonio de Quiñones stood that of Tomás Vázquez, one of the first conquerors. It had previously belonged to Alonso de Toro, who had been Gonzalo Pizarro's lieutenant general. He was killed by his father-in-law Diego González, out of pure alarm in the course of a domestic quarrel. West of Tomás Vázquez's was the house of Don Pedro Luis de Cabrera, which later belonged to Rodrigo de Esquivel. South of Tomás Vázquez's was that of Don Antonio Pereira, son of Lope Martim, a Portuguese. There followed the house of Pedro Alonso Carrasco, one of the first conquerors, south of which there were others of little consequence. They were the last in this ward, which was settled in 1557 and 1558. If we return to the skirts of Carmenca, we reach the house of Francisco de Villafuerte, one of the first conquerors and one of the thirteen companions of Don Francisco Pizarro, which was to the west of Diego de Silva's. Opposite stood a long, broad terrace with no houses on it, and to the south of this was another very fine terrace, where the convent of the divine St. Francis now stands. There is a large square before the convent, and to the south of this stands the house of Juan Julio de Hojeda, one of the first conquerors, whose son, Don Gómez de Tordoya, is still alive. West of the house of Don Gómez stood that formerly belonging to Martín de Arbieto: in 1560 there were no buildings beyond this in this direction. To the east of Martín de Arbieto's house lies a large level ground which was used for exercising horses in my time. At its extremity was built the rich and famous hospital of the Indians: it was founded in 1555 or 1556, as we shall mention. The inhabited area was that which we have described. The gentlemen I have mentioned in this discourse were all of very noble blood and distinguished in the exercise of arms, for they were the conquerors of that extremely rich empire. Most of them were known to me, and of the ones I have mentioned there were barely ten with whom I was not acquainted.

CHAPTER XII

Two donations made by the city for charitable purposes.

BEFORE TREATING of the foundation of the hospital and the first charitable grant that was made for it, I must mention another charity which the leading citizens of Cuzco bestowed on the religious of the divine St. Francis in order to buy the site and pay for the building of the church. This occurred before the other charity, and both took place during the time my lord Garcilaso de la Vega was corregidor of Cuzco. While their convent was still at Cassana, as we have said, the friars, for what reason I do not know, brought a suit against Juan Rodríguez de Villalobos, the owner of the site and the buildings on it, producing a letter and confirmation from the royal chancery instructing him to hand over the site in return for the appraised value of the two terraces and the part of the church that had been built. The whole was valued at 2,200 ducats. The provincial head of the Franciscans was then a religious of the recollects, called Fray Juan Gallegos, a man of holy life and excellent example, who handed over the compensation in my father's house. He paid the sum in silver bars, and it was my father who gave him possession. Those present were astonished that such poor friars could find so large a sum in so short a time for the order required that payment should be made before a stipulated date, and the friar answered:

"Gentlemen, do not wonder at this, for it is due to heaven and the charitableness of this city, which God protect. And to show how great is the spirit of charity here I can assure you that on Monday of this very week we had less than 300 ducats, and now by Thursday morning I have collected the sum you see here. During the last two nights so many prominent citizens who own Indians and gentlemen soldiers who have none have appeared bringing alms, such a quantity of alms that I sent many away when I saw that I had enough. Moreover for the last two nights they did not let us sleep for they kept coming to the porter's lodge with their alms and charity."

I myself heard the good friar say this of the liberality of Cuzco.

To turn now to the foundation of the hospital, I should say that this provincial was succeeded by another called Fray Antonio de San Miguel, of the noble family of this name in Salamanca: he was a great theologian and a true son of St. Francis in his life and teaching, by reason of which he later became bishop of Chile, where he lived with his usual sanctity, as the kingdom of Chile and Peru will testify. During the second of his three years, this holy man preached on Wednesdays, Fridays, and Sundays during Lent in the cathedral church of Cuzco, and one Sunday he suggested that the city should found a hospital for the Indians and that the town council should be its patron, as it already was of the church of the hospital for Spaniards. He said that such a house should be founded so that the Spaniards, both the conquerors and the rest, might have a means of carrying out their obligations, for none of them could avoid a greater or smaller share in this responsibility. He continued his argument in the other sermons of the week, and on the following Sunday he concluded by requesting the city for alms, saying: "Gentlemen, the corregidor and I will go out this afternoon at one o'clock to beg for alms for this work for the love of God: show yourselves as generous and liberal toward it as you were courageous and strong in gaining this empire." The two of them duly went out that afternoon to ask for alms, and noted down every contribution on a list. They went from house to house among the citizens who had Indians, and begged of no others all that day. At night my father returned home and bade me add up all the figures on his list, to find the total so far received: I made it 28,500 pesos, or 34,200 ducats. The smallest offering was of 500 pesos, or 600 ducats, and some reached 1,000 pesos. This was the sum for that afternoon, and it was collected in the space of five hours. On the following days they begged from *vecinos* and others alike, and all made very considerable offerings, so that within a few months more than 100,000 ducats had been contributed. As soon as the foundation of the hospital for the Indians was announced throughout the kingdom, a great sum in alms was offered that same year: some were gifts from living persons and others bequests. With this the work began and the Indians of the jurisdiction of Cuzco came forward with alacrity, knowing it was on their behalf.

My lord Garcilaso de la Vega, as corregidor, placed a gold doubloon of the kind they call double-headed, showing the Catholic monarchs Ferdinand and Isabella, under the first stone they laid in the building. This coin was placed there because of its remarkable rarity in Peru, where in those days there was no gold coin or any other, for no coin was then minted there, and the custom of the Spanish merchants was to barter their merchandise at a profit and not for gold or silver currency. Someone must have taken this doubloon to Peru as a curiosity from Spain (just as many other objects that do not exist in Peru have been taken out) and presented to my father on this occasion as a novelty (for I do not know how he came by it). It certainly was a novelty to all those who saw it that day, for it was passed from hand to hand among all the members of the city council and many other gentlemen who came to attend the stone-laying ceremony. Everyone said that it was the first minted money seen in Peru and that it might fittingly be used for this purpose on account of its singularity. Diego Maldonado of Salamanca, called "the Rich" because of his great wealth, as the senior regidor, put down a silver plate with his arms carved on it, and this poor beginning became the foundation of that rich edifice.

Since that time the Popes have granted many indulgences and pardons to those who die in that house. An Indian woman of the royal blood whom I knew was aware of this, and seeing herself near death, begged to be taken to the hospital to be cured. Her relatives begged her not to shame them by going to the hospital, since she had wealth enough to be treated in her own house. She replied that she did not seek to cure her body, which no longer needed it, but her soul, by means of the graces and indulgences the princes of the Church had granted to those who died in the hospital. She was thus borne thither, but refused to enter the infirmary, bidding them place her pallet in a corner of the hospital chapel. She begged them to dig her a grave near her bed, asked for the habit of St. Francis to be buried in, spread it on her bed, had the wax that would be used at her funeral brought and placed by her side, and received the Blessed Sacrament and extreme unction. She spent four days thus, calling on God, the Virgin Mary, and the whole Celestial Court, until she died. The city, on learning that an Indian woman had died such a Christian death, wished to mark the fact by honoring her funeral, so that the other Indians might be spurred to do likewise. Thus both councils, the ecclesiastical and the secular, attended the funeral, as well as the rest of the noble folk, and they buried her with solemn charity, which her kin and the rest of the Indians took as a mark of great honor, favor, and esteem. This said, we must now go on to tell the life and deeds of the tenth king, which will contain matters of great wonder.

CHAPTER XIII

King Inca Yupanqui seeks to make a new conquest.

THE GOOD Inca Yupanqui, having donned the scarlet fringe and thus observed the ritual for taking possession of the empire and also the obsequies of his parents, wished to show his affability and condescension by at once visiting all his realms and provinces, which, as we have already explained, was the most favorable and agreeable thing the Incas could do for their subjects, for as one of the superstitions of the Indians was that their rulers were gods, the children of the Sun, and not human beings, they so appreciated having the Incas in their own districts and houses that it would be impossible adequately to describe their sentiments. For this reason the Inca went out to visit his realms, where he was received and worshipped after their pagan fashion. Inca Yupanqui spent more than three years on this visit, and having returned to the city and rested from the long journey, he consulted with the members of his council about making a formidably difficult expedition into the Antis to the east of Cuzco. As the great chain of the Sierra Nevada formed the limit of his empire in that direction, he desired to cross it and reach the other side by following one of the rivers that run from the west side to the east, since the top of the range is impossible to cross because of the great depth of snow lying on it and perpetually falling there.

Inca Yupanqui had this desire to conquer the tribes in that area, reduce them to his empire, purge them of the barbarous and inhuman customs in which they lived, and teach them to worship his father the Sun as their god, as the Incas had done in the case of the other tribes they had conquered. The Inca had formed this desire because he and his predecessors had heard that in that vast expanse there were some inhabited regions, though others were unpopulated on account of their great mountains, lakes, marshes, and swamps, which made it impossible for anyone to live there.

He had heard that one of the best of the inhabited provinces was what the Indians call Musu and the Spaniards Los Mojos, which could be entered by a great river running through the Antis to the east of the city. It consists of many rivers that flow together at this point. There are five main courses each with a different name, as well as an infinity of little streams, all of which form a very great river called the Amarumayu. Where this flows out into the Northern Sea I cannot tell, but I suspect that, from its size and the general direction of its flow eastwards, it is one of the great rivers that joins with many others and forms the river Plate, so called because when the Spaniards who discovered it asked the natives of the coast if there were any silver in that province, they were told that there was none in those parts, but that there was a great quantity where that great river rose. From these words was derived its present name, and it is called Silver River even though it has none. It is so celebrated throughout the world that it occupies the second place among all the rivers discovered up to the present, the first being the river of Orellana.

In the Indian language the River Plate is called Parahuay. If the word is from the general language of Peru it means "rain me," and it might be interpreted in the diction of this language as if the river were boasting of its wonderful floods and said: "rain for me and you will see wonders." For, as we have said, it is characteristic of the language to express in a single significant word all the sense that can be compressed in it. If the word *parahuay* is from another language and not from the Peruvian I do not know what it signifies.

When the five great rivers flow together, each loses its separate name, and the single stream is called Amarumayu. *Mayu* is "river" and *amaru* the very large snakes that are found in the mountains there, which are as we have described them earlier. The river would be given this name on account of its extraordinary size, signifying that it is as great among rivers as the *amaru* among serpents.

CHAPTER XIV

The events of the expedition to Musu
until its completion.

K ING Inca Yupanqui decided to make his entry into the province of Musu along this great and hitherto little known river, since it was impossible to enter by land because of the wild mountains and numerous lakes, swamps, and marshes that abound in those parts. Having taken this decision he decided to cut a very great quantity of a timber that grows there. I do not know its name in the Indian language, but the Spaniards call it fig tree, not because it bears figs—it does not—but because it is as light or lighter than the fig.

It took almost two years to cut the wood, trim it, and build exceedingly large rafts with it. They made enough to hold ten thousand warriors and their supplies, and as soon as the men and their rations were ready and the general and other officers, who were all Incas of the royal blood, had been appointed, they embarked on the rafts, which each held thirty, forty, or fifty Indians, or thereabouts. The food was carried in the middle of the rafts on platforms or tables about half a yard high so that it should not get wet. Thus prepared, the Incas set off downstream, where they had great skirmishes and strife with the natives, called Chunchu, who lived on both banks of the rivers. These people appeared in great numbers on the rivers and its shores to prevent them from landing and to give battle afloat. They used bows and arrows as weapons of offence: these are the common weapons among all the tribes of the Antis. They appeared with their faces, arms, and legs painted red, and their whole body smeared with different colors, for as the climate is very hot there, they went naked except for loincloths, wearing feathered headdresses made of the plumes of parrots and macaws.

After many brushes with the Peruvians followed by various conferences, all the tribes of both banks of that great river submitted to the Inca, offering to serve and obey him. In acknowledgment of their vassalage they sent many presents to King Inca Yupanqui, consisting of parrots, monkeys, and macaws, honey, wax, and other products of that region. These presents were renewed until the death of Túpac Amaru, who was the last of the Incas, as we shall see in the course of our account of their lives and succession: he was beheaded by the Viceroy Don Francisco de Toledo. A village near Tono, twenty-six leagues from Cuzco, was settled with the Chunchu Indians who came to Peru as ambassadors, together with later arrivals. They asked the Inca to permit them to settle there and serve him from near at hand, and so they have remained until the present day. After the tribes of the banks of this river, which is commonly called Chunchu, after the province of Chunchu, had been reduced to the service of the Inca, they advanced and reduced many other tribes, until they reached the province called Musu, a region peopled by a great many warlike people and of great natural fertility. It is said to be two hundred leagues from the city of Cuzco.

The Incas say that when their forces reached this place, they were reduced to only a few, as a result of the many wars they had fought. Nevertheless they boldly persuaded the Musus to submit and serve the Inca, the child of the Sun whom his father had sent from heaven to teach men to live like men and not like beasts, and to worship the Sun as their god and give up the adoration of animals, and sticks and stones, and other unworthy objects. And finding that the Musus listened to them willingly, the Incas gave them a fuller account of their laws, privileges, and customs, and told them of the great deeds performed by their kings in past conquests, and how many provinces they had subdued, mentioning that many had submitted of their own accord, beseeching the Incas to receive them as vassals, and that they worshipped the Incas as gods. In particular they are said to have told the Indians about the dream of Inca Viracocha and his warlike deeds. All this astonished the Musus, who were delighted to receive the friendship of the Incas and to embrace their idolatry, laws, and customs, which they thought good, promising to be governed by them and to worship the Sun as their chief god. They did not wish to admit vassalage, because the Inca had not conquered them and subjected them by force of arms. They were, however, delighted to be his friends and confederates. As friends they would do anything in the Inca's service, but not as vassals, for they wished to remain free as their ancestors had been. By virtue of this friendship the Musus let the Incas settle in their country. There were little more than a thousand left when they arrived, for the rest had perished in the wars and amidst the hardships of the journey. The Musus gave them their daughters in marriage and were delighted to intermarry with them. Even today they hold the Incas in great veneration and are governed by them in peace and war. As soon as amity and kinship were established between the two peoples, ambassadors chosen from among the native nobility were sent to Cuzco to worship the Inca as the child of the Sun, and confirm the friendship and bond of blood between his people and theirs. Because of the roughness of the road, the wildness of the mountains and the swamps and marshes, they made a great détour to get to Cuzco, where the Inca received them very affably and with great favors and honors. He instructed them to be fully informed about the court, its laws, customs, and idolatry, whereupon the Musus returned to their own country with great content. This league and friendship lasted until the arrival of the Spaniards and their conquest of Peru.

In particular the Incas say that in the time of Huaina Cápac the descendants of the Incas who settled among the Musus wished to return to Cuzco, thinking that, if their only service was to stay quietly where they were, they would be better employed in their own country; but when they had all arranged to return to Cuzco with their wives and children, they heard that Inca Huaina Cápac was dead, that the Spaniards had won the country, and that the empire and sovereignty of the Incas was at an end. They therefore decided to remain where they were, and the Musus still hold them in great veneration and are governed by them in peace and war, as we have said. It is said that the river is six leagues wide thereabouts, and that it takes two days to cross it by canoe.

CHAPTER XV

Traces found of this expedition.

ALL WE have said in brief of the conquest and discovery carried out by King Inca Yupanqui down this river is told at length by the Indians, who boast of the prowess of their ancestors and describe the great battles that took place on the river and on its banks, mentioning the many provinces that were reduced as a result of these great exploits. But as some of these deeds seem to me incredible considering the small number of people involved, and as the Spaniards have never so far possessed the area the Incas conquered in the Antis, and one cannot point to it with one's finger as one can to all the rest of the area we have previously mentioned, I thought that I should not mingle fabulous matters, or what appear to be such, with true histories, for we have today no such full and clear description of that region as of the part we ourselves possess, though it is true that the Spaniards have recently found noteworthy traces of this expedition, as we shall see.

In 1564 a Spaniard called Diego Alemán, born at San Juan in the county of Niebla, and a citizen of La Paz, or New Town, where he had a small *repartimiento* of Indians, was persuaded by one of his chiefs that there was a great quantity of gold in the province of Musu, and guided by this chief, he set out with twelve other Spaniards in quest of it. They went on foot since the route was unsuitable for horses, and they hoped thus to avoid attention, merely discovering the province and noting the way thither, so as to obtain the formal right of conquest and then to return with a greater force to win it and settle it. They entered by Cocha-pampa, which is the nearest point to Los Mojos.

They travelled for twenty-eight days across heaths and wastes, at the end of which time they came in sight of the first village in the province. Although their own chief warned them to wait until an Indian came out whom they might silently seize as an informant and interpreter, they would not heed him. On the contrary, as soon as night fell, foolishly be-lieving that it would merely suffice for a Spaniard to raise his voice for all the village to surrender, they forced an entrance with as much to-do as possible so as to frighten the Indians with the idea that there were a great many Spaniards. But their plan misfired, for the Indians came out giving the alarm in reply to the Spaniards' war-cry, and seeing how few the latter were, fell upon them, slaughtered ten of them and captured Diego Alemán. The other two escaped under cover of darkness and repaired to the place where their guide had said he would await them, for he had wisely refused to accompany them when he saw how rash they were. One of those who escaped was a mestizo called Francisco Moreno, the son of a Spaniard and an Indian woman, born in Cochapampa. He recovered a cotton blanket which was hung up as a hammock or cradle for a baby: it was woven in patterns of various colors and had six little gold bells. As soon as dawn broke the two Spaniards and the *curaca,* who had hidden on a high hill, saw a band of Indians outside the village with spears and pikes and breastplates brightly glittering in the sun, and the guide told them that all they saw glittering was gold and that those Indians had no silver except what they might have obtained by barter from Peru. And to emphasize the greatness of this region, the guide took his cloak which was woven in stripes and said: "In comparison with this country Peru is no bigger than a stripe on this blanket in comparison with the whole." But the Indian had little knowledge of geography and was mistaken, though it is true that the province is very large.

It was later learned from the Indians who at rare intervals came to trade with the Peruvians that when Diego Alemán's captors learnt that he had an allocation of Indians in Peru and that he was the captain of the little band of misguided followers, they made him their captain general in a war against the Indians of the opposite bank of the Amaru-mayu, doing him great honor and holding him in the highest esteem because of the authority and advantage they derived from having a Span-ish general. The other survivor, who left with the mestizo Francisco Moreno, died from the hardships of the journey as soon as they reached

friendly territory: one of the greatest of these hardships was the passage
of some great marshes that could never have been crossed on horseback.
The mestizo Francisco Moreno gave a long account of all he had seen on
this expedition, and some adventurers were stirred by it to ask for the
right of conquest. The first of these was Gómez de Tordoya, a young
gentleman whose request was granted by the then viceroy of Peru, the
count of Nieva. But as a great many people collected for the undertaking
and it was feared that disorders would occur, the project was dropped,
and he was instructed not to raise any more men and to disband those he
had already enrolled.

CHAPTER XVI

Other unfortunate occurrences
in the same province.

TWO YEARS later, Licentiate Castro, formerly governor of Peru,
granted the same right of exploration to a citizen of Cuzco, a gentleman called Gaspar de Sotelo, who prepared a large crowd of gallant
volunteers for the expedition. His most notable stroke was an arrangement with Inca Túpac Amaru who was living in retirement at Villcapampa to go shares in the conquest. The Inca had promised to accompany
him and supply all the necessary rafts, the entry being made by the Villcapampa River to the northeast of Cuzco. But there is never a lack of rivals
in such undertakings, and the governor was persuaded to withdraw or
annul the rights he had granted to Gaspar de Sotelo and award them to
another citizen of Cuzco called Juan Alvarez Maldonado. This being
done, Maldonado gathered a force of 250 soldiers and more than 100
horses and mares, embarking them on large rafts on the river Amarumayu
to the east of Cuzco. When Gómez de Tordoya saw that the conquest he
had been deprived of had been awarded to Gaspar de Sotelo, and later
to Juan Alvarez Maldonado after he had wasted his own substance and
that of his friends on it, he greatly resented the slight and announced
that he had the right to carry out the expedition. The truth was that although his rights had been cancelled, he still held the document in which

they had been conceded. He thereupon summoned supporters together, but as the plan was in defiance of the governor's will, few presented themselves, barely sixty in all. With these he entered the province called Camata, to the southeast of Cuzco, though with great difficulty. Crossing great forests and swamps, he reached the river Amarumayu, where he learned that Juan Arias [Alvarez] had not passed by. Regarding him as his mortal enemy, he waited for him in trenches on the river banks, planning to attack and discomfit him, for though he had few companions, he trusted in their courage, since they were chosen men who were loyal to him, and each of them carried two well-primed arquebusses.

Juan Alvarez Maldonado meanwhile followed the stream until he reached the place where Gómez de Tordoya was waiting, and as they were rivals in the same enterprise they did not discuss terms or parley, though they might easily have joined company and both profited, for there was plenty for all. The ambition to rule admits neither equality nor submission, so they both fought. Juan Alvarez Maldonado was the first to attack, confiding in the advantage of numbers he had over his rival. Gómez de Tordoya awaited his onslaught, relying on the strength of his position and the double supply of arms his men had. The fighting lasted the whole day. Many died on both sides. They fought again on the second and third day, so bitterly and with so little regard for life or limb that almost all were killed, and the few survivors were hardly fit to fight. The Chunchu Indians, in whose territory they were, knew that the Spaniards had come to conquer them, and finding them in this state, assembled for the attack, fell on them and killed them all, Gómez de Tordoya among them. I knew the three gentlemen concerned, who were living in Cuzco when I left. The Indians captured three Spaniards, one was Juan Alvarez Maldonado, one a Mercedarian friar called Fray Diogo Martim, a Portuguese, and a smith called Master Simón López, an expert craftsman with arquebusses. Maldonado, who was known to be the leader of one of the Spanish factions, was treated with honor, and being too old to be of use, was set free to return to his own Indians in Cuzco. His captors led him as far as the province of Callavaya, where fine gold of twenty-four carats is extracted. The friar and the smith were kept more than two years. As Master Simón was known to be a smith, he was brought a great quantity of copper and bidden to make axes and adzes, on which he was kept busy during the whole time of his captivity. Fray Diogo Martim was venerated, because they knew he was a Christian priest and minister of God, and even when they gave him permission to depart for Peru, they asked him to stay among them and teach them the Christian faith, but he refused to do so. Many similar opportunities of preaching the Holy Gospel to the Indians without force of arms have been wasted.

After more than two years, the Chunchus permitted the two Spaniards to return to Peru, accompanying them as far as the Callavaya valley. On their return they told the story of the ill-fated expedition, reporting what the Incas had done on that river, and how Incas had settled among the Musus, who had recognized the Inca as their overlord, serving him and sending him many presents of their country's products every year. The sending of these presents continued until the death of Inca Túpac Amaru, a few years after the ill-starred expedition of Gómez de Tordoya and Juan Alvarez Maldonado. We have taken this out of its place and time to give evidence of King Inca Yupanqui's conquest on the great river Amarumayu and of the fact that the Incas who undertook the conquest settled among the Musus. Fray Diogo Martim and Master Simón brought back a full account of all this and told it to all those who were interested. The friar used to add that he particularly regretted not having remained among the Chunchus as they had asked him, saying that he had found himself without the necessary means of saying mass, or otherwise he would have stayed. He had often been on the point of returning alone, for it preyed on his conscience very much that he had not granted a request so earnestly made by the Indians and so just in itself. The friar also said that the Incas who had remained among the Musus would be of great help toward a Spanish conquest of the territory. But it is now time for us to return to the deeds of the good Inca Yupanqui, and to speak of the conquest of Chile, one of his greatest achievements.

CHAPTER XVII

*The Chirihuana tribe, its life
and customs.*

As THE chief object of the Incas was the conquest of men, kingdoms, and provinces, to acquire the glory of extending their empire and to gratify the ambition and desire to rule which is so natural among the powerful, Inca Yupanqui determined four years after sending his army down the river, as we have said, to embark on another conquest, which was that of a great province called Chirihuana, in the Antis to the east of Charcas. As this country was then unexplored, he sent spies to make careful and thorough observations of the land and its inhabitants, so as to provide more adequately for the expedition. The spies departed according to their instructions, and returned with the report that the land was extremely bad. It consisted of wild forests, swamps, lakes, and morasses, and very little of it was of any use for cultivation. The natives were utterly savage and worse than wild beasts, for they had no religion and did not worship anything at all, living without laws or good customs, like animals on the hillsides, having no villages or houses. They ate human flesh which they obtained by raiding neighboring provinces, devouring all their captives without regard for age or sex, and drinking their blood as they slaughtered them so as to lose nothing of their prey. They not only ate their neighbors' flesh, but consumed their own people when they were dying. After they ate the flesh, they pieced together the bones, and buried the victims in crannies in the rocks or hollow trees. They went naked, and felt no compunction in lying with their sisters, daughters, and mothers. This was the normal way of life of the Chirihuana tribe.

The good Inca Yupanqui—a title we apply to this prince because his own people usually call him so, and Pedro de Cieza de León also always refers to him in this way—on receiving this news, turned to the other Incas of the royal blood, his uncles, brothers, nephews, and other remoter kinfolk who were present, and said: "Our obligation to conquer the Chirihuanas is now greater and more pressing, for we must deliver them from the beastly and vile state in which they live, and reduce them to the life of men, for which purpose our father the Sun sent us here." After these words, he ordered ten-thousand warriors to be made ready, and sent them forth with generals and captains of his own kin, men of experience in peace and war and well versed in their duties. The Incas went, and on realizing how sterile and useless the land and province of Chirihuana was they sent messengers to the Inca to beg him to expedite the supplies they might want, for there were none in the province. This was done, but though the captains and their men did everything possible, after two years they finally abandoned the conquest, having failed to carry it through because of the difficulty of the country and the great number of morasses and swamps, lakes, and wild forests. They thereupon reported to the Inca everything that had happened to them. He bade them rest in anticipation of other expeditions and conquests he had in mind, which might prove more profitable than the last.

The Viceroy Don Francisco de Toledo, who governed Peru in 1572, wished to conquer the Chirihuanas, as Padre Acosta briefly mentions in his Book VII, ch. xxviii, and prepared many Spaniards and a great deal of equipment for the expedition. Many horses, cows, and brood mares were taken, but when he entered the province he soon discovered from experience how great were the difficulties. When his friends had pointed them out to him and advised him not to attempt an exploit the Incas had been unable to accomplish and had abandoned, he had refused to believe them; but he now fled, forsaking all his equipment so that the Indians might let him get away in their joy at such great booty. He followed such bad roads that the beasts could not carry his litter, which Indians and Spaniards had to take on their shoulders. The Chirihuanas pursued them shouting, among other insults: "Let the old woman out of the *petaca* (a closed hamper), and we'll eat her alive!"

The Chirihuanas are, as we have said, very fond of eating meat, for none exists in their own country, either wild or tame, on account of the badness of the soil. If they had kept the cows the viceroy left behind, these might have gone wild and multiplied, as was the case in the islands of Santo Domingo and Cuba, where the land is suitable. The Chirihuanas did lose a little of their savagery from their intercourse with the Incas during the past campaign, for it is known that they no longer eat their own dead as they used to, though they spare none of their neighbors and are so gluttonous and avid for human flesh that when they attack they have no fear of death and seem insensible, rushing on their enemy's arms for the purpose of seizing one of them. If they find shepherds grazing animals, they would rather have the shepherd than the whole herd of cattle or sheep. Because of their ferocity and inhumanity they are greatly feared by all their neighbors: a hundred or a thousand of the latter will not face ten Chirihuanas, and the name alone is enough to inspire fear and silence in children. The Chirihuanas also learned from the Incas how to make houses to dwell in. They are not private houses, but communal dwellings. They make a very large hall, with sections inside for each family. These sections are so small that there is only room for their persons. This is enough, for they have no furniture or clothing, as they go naked. Thus each of these halls might be described as a village. This shall suffice for a description of the beastly condition of life among the Chirihuanas: it would be a great wonder to be able to deliver them from it.

CHAPTER XVIII

Preparations for the conquest of Chile.

T HE GOOD KING Inca Yupanqui, though he saw how little fruit, if any, was to be gained from the conquest of the Chirihuanas, did not on this account lose the desire and intent to engage on other greater exploits. For as the chief boast and purpose of the Incas was to bring new races into their empire and reduce them to their laws and customs, and as they were already so powerful, they could not desist from engaging in new conquests, which indeed were necessary to keep their vassals occupied in increasing their estates and to use up their revenues, consisting of the supplies, arms, clothing, and footwear contributed every year according to the resources of each province. The gold and silver was, as we have already said, not presented by the vassals as tribute to the king, but offered, without being demanded, for the service and adornment of the royal palaces and the temples of the Sun. Seeing himself so well-beloved and obeyed and so mighty in wealth and men of war, King Inca Yupanqui resolved on a great undertaking, the conquest of the kingdom of Chile. To this end, he consulted his council and prepared everything that was necessary. Leaving in his capital all the officials necessary for the government and administration of justice, he went to Atacama, which is the last province settled by the Incas and subject to their empire in the direction of Chile, so as to encourage his men in their task from the nearest point: beyond this there is a great desert to cross before reaching Chile.

From Atacama the Inca sent scouts and spies into the desert to discover a road to Chile and report on its difficulties so that measures could be taken to circumvent them. The scouts were Incas, for matters of such great import were not entrusted by the Incas to any but their own kin. They were accompanied by Indians from Atacama and Tucma (from whom, as we have said, they had had news of the kingdom of Chile) who acted as guides. Every two leagues reports were sent back about what had been found, and this was necessary so that adequate steps might be taken. The scouts continued in this way, undergoing great privations in the desert, but leaving markers as they advanced so as to be able to find the road on their return and to enable those who came behind to follow them.

They came and went backwards and forwards like ants, reporting on whatever they found and carrying up supplies, which was the essential part of their task. By dint of their labors they penetrated eighty leagues across the desert between Atacama and Copayapú, which is a small but well-populated province surrounded by broad expanses of desert: beyond it in the direction of Cuquimpu there are a further eighty leagues of desert. When the scouts had reached Copayapú and obtained such information as they could of the province from inspecting it, they returned with all diligence to report to the Inca what they had seen. As a result of the report, the Inca had ten thousand warriors sent forward in their usual formation under a general called Sinchiruca and two commanders of the royal blood, whose names the Indians have not preserved. He ordered them to take sufficient supplies on beasts of burden, which were also to serve as rations since their meat is very good to eat.

As soon as Inca Yupanqui had sent off the ten thousand warriors, he had a similar number prepared and bade them follow the first in order to help their friends and fill their enemies with surprise and alarm. When the first army was approaching Copayapú, they sent forward messengers, according to the ancient Inca custom, bidding them surrender to the child of the Sun who had come to bring them a new religion, new laws, and customs so that they might live like men and not like beasts. If not, they should make ready for war, for willingly or unwillingly they must obey the Inca, the lord of the four quarters of the earth. Those of Copayapú were incensed by the message, and taking up arms, they prepared to resist the invasion of their country. There were some skirmishes and light conflicts, for each side was probing the other's strength and courage. But the Incas, obeying the orders of their king, avoided making war with sword and fire, seeking to hold off the enemy until he should surrender peaceably. The natives were perplexed as to how they might defend themselves. On the one hand they feared the divine power of the child of the Sun, thinking that they would fall under some great curse if they did not receive his child as their lord. On the other hand, they were stirred by the desire to retain their ancient freedom and their attachment to their own gods, having no desire for new things, but only to live as their forebears had lived before them.

CHAPTER XIX

The Incas win the regions as far as the valley called
Chile; the messages and replies they
exchanged with other new tribes.

IN THIS state of uncertainty they were found by the second Inca army
which had come to the aid of the first. On seeing it, Copayapú surrendered, thinking it impossible to resist such a large force and making
the best terms they could with the Incas about what they would keep and
what they would give up in their idolatrous religion. All this was reported to the Inca, who was delighted to find the road open and such a
good beginning made in the conquest of Chile, which was such a large
and remote kingdom that he had fears about being able to reduce it. He
was therefore very glad that the province of Copayapú should have fallen
into his hands by a peaceable agreement and not by bloodshed and war.
In order to follow up his good fortune he had informed himself of conditions there and sent forward another army of ten thousand men, with
all necessary supplies, who were ordered to assist the first two armies
and press forward with the conquest, at once requesting any further help
they might need. With the new reinforcements and the royal instructions,
the Incas pressed on a further eighty leagues, and after overcoming many
labors on the long journey, they reached another valley or province called
Cuquimpu, which they reduced. We cannot say if there was fighting, for
the Peruvian Indians do not know the details of a campaign that took
place on foreign soil so distant from their own land, except that the Incas
reduced the valley of Cuquimpu. They advanced beyond this, conquering
all the tribes between it and the valley of Chile which gives its name to
the kingdom. During the whole duration of the campaign, which is said
to have been more than six years, the Inca always took particular care
to supply his men with reinforcements, arms, and provisions, clothing,
and footwear, so that there was no want of anything: so well did he understand the importance to his honor and majesty that his men should
not be forced to take a step back. He thus came to have a force of over
fifty thousand warriors in Chile, as well supplied with everything they
needed as if they were in the city of Cuzco.

The Incas, after reducing the valley of Chile to their empire, advised their ruler of their success. Each day they sent an account of their hourly doings, and after making the usual arrangements for the administration of the region they had just won, they continued their advance southwards and conquered each valley and tribe until they reached the river Maulli [Maule], nearly 50 leagues from the valley of Chile. It is not known what battles they fought, but it is supposed that the area was reduced peaceably: it was indeed always the first object of the Incas in their conquests to attract the Indians by friendly means and not to resort to arms. The Incas were not content with having extended their empire the distance of more than 260 leagues from Atacama to the river Maule, part settled and part desert—from Atacama to Copayapú was 80 leagues, and from Copayapú to Cuquimpu almost 50 more; from Cuquimpu to Chile is 55 and from Chile to the river Maule nearly 50. Their ambition and desire to possess new provinces drove them to press on, and they therefore set up the administration of the area already won with their usual system and skill, leaving the necessary garrison and always taking every precaution against any reverse that might befall them. The Incas thus crossed the river Maule with twenty thousand warriors, and following their traditional usage, summoned the inhabitants of the province of Purumauca (whom the Spaniards call Promaucaes) to accept the Inca as their overlord or resort to arms. The Purumaucas, who had already heard about the Incas and were already prepared and allied with other neighboring tribes such as the Antalli, Pincu, and Cauqui, were all determined to die rather than lose their former liberty and replied that the conquerors should indeed be the overlords of the conquered, and the Incas would soon see how the Purumaucas obeyed them.

Three or four days after delivering this reply, the Purumaucas appeared with some of their confederates to the number of eighteen or twenty thousand warriors. That day they spent in establishing their camp within sight of the Incas, who sent new messages offering peace and friendship and protesting solemnly in the name of the Sun and Moon that they would not deprive the natives of their land and property, but would show them how to live like men, and acknowledge the Sun as their god and his child the Inca as their king and lord. The Purumaucas replied saying that they were determined not to waste time with words and vain reasonings, but would fight till they conquered or died. So let the Incas prepare for battle next day, and send no more messages, which they had no wish to hear.

CHAPTER XX

A cruel battle between the Incas and other
tribes; the first Spaniard who
discovered Chile.

T HE NEXT DAY both armies left their camp and attacked one another, fighting with great spirit, courage, and obstinacy. The battle lasted all day without any definite advantage to either side, though with many killed and wounded. At nightfall both armies retired to their quarters. On the second and third days they fought with the same cruelty and pertinacity, the one side for its liberty and the other for its honor. At the end of the third onset it was seen that on both sides more than half had died, and the rest were almost all wounded. On the fourth day, though both armies took up battle order, they did not emerge from their quarters, but made themselves strong there in case their adversaries should attack. This situation lasted the whole of that day, and two more days following. At the end of this time they withdrew toward their own districts, each side fearing the other had sent for reinforcements and had summoned them in all haste. The Purumaucas and their allies now began to think they had done wonders in resisting the arms of the Incas, who had hitherto proved so powerful and indeed irresistible. On this supposition they returned to their homes, singing victory and declaring that they had routed the enemy.

The Incas considered that it was more in keeping with the policy of their past and present rulers to give rein to the bestial fury of the enemy than to destroy them by calling up reinforcements which could have been summoned in a brief time. There were therefore consultations among the captains, and though some thought that the struggle ought to continued until the enemy was overcome, it was finally decided to return to the territory already conquered and to fix the river Maule as the limit of the empire, not passing beyond it until a report of what had happened had reached Inca Yupanqui and he had sent new instructions. The Inca's instructions were that they were not to conquer more lands but to devote great attention to the cultivation and improvement of what they had already won, always seeking the advantage of their vassals. In this way the neighboring Indians would realize that blessings of all kinds ensued from the rule of the Incas and would themselves also submit to it, as so many other tribes had done, and if they did not, they would lose more than the Incas. With these instructions the Incas made an end of their conquests in Chile, strengthened their frontiers, set up boundary marks and fixed the river Maule as the furthest limit of their empire toward the south. They attended to the administration of justice, the royal estates, and the property devoted to the Sun, to the special benefit of their vassals. The latter accepted the rule of the Incas, and their privileges, laws, and customs with true affection, and lived under these laws until the Spaniards entered Chile.

The first Spaniard who discovered Chile was Don Diego de Almagro, but he merely visited it and returned to Peru, undergoing innumerable hardships on the outward journey and the return. This expedition led to the general rebellion of the Indians in Peru, and to discord between the two governors and civil war between them, resulting in the death of Don Diego de Almagro after his capture in the battle of Las Salinas and the deaths of the marquis Don Francisco Pizarro and of Don Diego de Almagro the mestizo in the battle of Chupas. All this we shall recount at length if the Lord God spares us. The second Spaniard to enter the kingdom of Chile was Governor Pedro de Valdivia, who was accompanied by a powerful force of men and horses. He passed beyond the limits of the Inca occupation, and successfully conquered and settled the region until his good fortune brought about his death at the hands of his own vassals, the Indians of the province called Araucu, which he had chosen as his own in the distribution of that kingdom among its conquerors. This gentleman founded many cities and peopled them with Spaniards, including that which bears his name, Valdivia. He performed great deeds in the conquest of this kingdom, and governed it with much prudence and wisdom, to the great prosperity of himself and his followers, and with the hope of even greater good fortune had it not all been cut short by the stratagem of an Indian who broke the thread of his life. And since the murder of this governor and captain was one of the most notable and famous deeds done by the Indians in the Inca empire and indeed in all the Indies, after the Spanish conquest, and one of the most grievous losses suffered by the Spaniards, I propose to relate it here so as to include the plain facts about how the first and second news of this ill-starred struggle reached Peru: but to make it intelligible it will be necessary to give the beginnings and origin of the case.

CHAPTER XXI

The rebellion of Chile against Governor Valdivia.

IN THE conquest and division of the kingdom of Chile there fell to this gentleman, a worthy conqueror of empires, a rich *repartimiento* with much gold and many vassals producing more than a hundred thousand gold pesos a year in tribute; and as the hunger for gold is insatiable, the yearning for it grew greater the more the Indians produced. The latter were unused to the labor of extracting the gold and unable to stand the abuses they were subjected to to get it. Having always been independent of other lords, they were unable to bear the present yoke, and the Araucanians who belonged to Valdivia and other confederates of theirs decided to rebel. This determination was duly carried out, and they did everything they could to outrage and molest the Spaniards. Governor Pedro de Valdivia heard of this and advanced with 150 mounted men to punish the rising, paying no more attention to it than the Spaniards ever do to such Indian movements. Through this arrogance many have perished, as Pedro de Valdivia and his company did at the hands of those he had scorned.

The first news of his death that reached Peru was brought by a Chilean Indian to the city of La Plata. It was written on a scrap of paper without signature, date, or place and said: "Pedro de Valdivia and 150 lances that were with him were swallowed by the earth." The purport of this message, with the news that it had been brought by an Indian from Chile, soon ran the length and breadth of Peru to the great scandal of the Spaniards, who could not guess what the swallowing of the earth meant, since they would not credit that any Indians had the power to slay 150 mounted Spaniards, a power that had never existed hitherto. As Chile, like Peru, is a country of rough ground, full of mountains, valleys, and ravines, and is subject to earthquakes, they said that it might have happened that the victims were travelling through some deep cleft when part of the mountainside slipped and overwhelmed them. This opinion was generally accepted, for they could not imagine from past experience going back many years that the Indians were so strong or so bold as to have slain them in battle.

While the people of Peru were under this misapprehension, there finally arrived after sixty days a different and very full account of the death of Valdivia and his friends, and of the course of his last struggle with the Indians. I shall relate this as it was told in the report that came from Chile, which first referred to the rising of the Indians and the out-rages and crimes they had committed, and continued thus.

When Valdivia reached the place where the rebellious Araucanians were, he found 12,000 or 13,000 of them and fought a great many bitter-ly contested battles all of which were won by the Spaniards. The Indians were by now so terrified by the furious onrush of the horses that they dared not appear on the open field, for ten horses could disperse a thou-sand Indians. The latter held out only in the mountains and heaths where the horses could not master them: there they did what havoc they could, refusing to receive any of the envoys sent to them, and obstinately pre-ferring to die rather than become subjects or vassals of the Spaniards. This state of affairs lasted for many days, and the news of their lack of success spread daily into the Araucanian country, where it came to the ears of an old captain who had been famous in the science of war, but was now living in retirement in his home. He duly set off to find out what miracle enabled 150 Spaniards to hold off 12,000 or 13,000 war-riors so that they could do nothing with them. He could not believe it possible unless the Spaniards were demons or immortal, as the Indians at first believed. In order to discover the truth about this, he wished to go to the scene of hostilities and behold the course of events with his own eyes. He reached a height from which he could observe both armies and noted that the Indian position was broad and extensive, while that of the Span-iards was small and compact, and he spent a long time pondering over the reason why so few could overcome so many. After a close study of the position, he returned to his people and summoned a council, and after a lengthy discussion of everything that had taken place, he formu-lated the following questions:

Were the Spaniards mortal men like themselves or were they immortal like the Sun and Moon? Did they feel hunger, thirst and fatigue? Did they need sleep and rest? In short, were they of flesh and bone or of iron or steel? He asked the same questions about the horses. When the answer was given that the Spaniards were men as they were, and of the same composition and nature, he had replied. "Then go and rest, all of you, for tomorrow we shall see on the field of battle who acquit themselves the more like men, they or we." The council then broke up, and at day-break next morning the alarm was sounded. The Indians responded with louder war cries and a greater sound of trumpets and drums and other instruments then on previous occasions, and the old captain at once disposed thirteen companies, each of a thousand men, and sent them out in a line, one after another.

CHAPTER XXII

A new order of battle; the stratagem of the old Indian captain.

ON HEARING THE Indian war cry, the Spaniards advanced splendidly armed, with great plumes in their helmets and the head-pieces of their horses and breastplates jingling with bells. When they saw the Indian companies divided, they took them less seriously, thinking that it would be easier to disperse many small bands than one large one. As the Spaniards entered the field the Indian captain told the members of the first company:

"Go out brothers, and fight those Spaniards. I don't bid you defeat them, but only do what you can on your country's behalf. When you can do no more, take flight, for I will succor you in good time. But those who have fought in the first company and are driven back must not mingle with the second, nor those of the second with the third: when you are driven back, go to the rear and I will give orders about what you are to do."

With this the old captain sent his men to fight the Spaniards, who resisted the first company, and though the Indians did all they could to defend themselves, they were driven off. The same happened with the second, third, fourth, and fifth companies who were easily dispersed, though not without causing many wounds and some deaths among the Spaniards and their horses.

As the first companies went into the fray and were worsted, the Indian captain gradually put the others into the battle in due order. Behind the whole force he had a captain who reformed the Indians who had retreated from the fight into new companies, and gave them food and drink and rested them until their turn came to go back into the line of battle. When the Spaniards had repulsed five companies they looked up to see how many remained and beheld eleven or twelve more in front of them. And though they had been fighting for over three hours, they braced themselves, and calling on one another for a new effort, attacked the sixth company as it came up to relieve the fifth, and broke it, and also the seventh, eighth, ninth, and tenth. But neither they nor their horses were now fighting with their original vigor, for they had been at it fully seven hours without a moment's respite. The Indians did not let them rest as a group or individually, for hardly had one company been dispersed than another attacked, and those who were driven off left the field to rest and form new companies. Then the Spaniards looked upon their enemies and saw that they still had ten companies on their feet. With invincible spirit they strove to carry on the fight: though their strength was dwindling and their steeds flagging, they fought their best so as not to show any sign of weakness before the Indians. The latter hourly took courage as the Spaniards weakened, for they sensed that the enemy was no longer resisting as he had at the outset and even in the middle of the engagement. So both sides continued until two in the afternoon.

Then Governor Pedro de Valdivia, seeing that there were still eight or nine companies of Indians to fight, and that even though they repulsed them the Indians would form afresh, thought that if this new system of attack were continued he would be given no rest by night any more than by day, and decided that he had better retreat before the horses were completely worn out. His object was to fall back on a narrow pass about a league and a half in the rear: if he reached it, he thought he would get away, for two Spaniards on foot could defend the place against all their enemies.

Thus resolved, though it was late, he called to his followers as he came upon them in the fray, and said: "Fall back, gentlemen, and withdraw gradually to the narrow defile; and pass the word on." This was done and they all gradually retired, still facing the enemy, but in an attitude of defence rather than of attack.

CHAPTER XXIII

*The Indians prevail owing to a treacherous plan
executed by one of their number.*

AT THIS point an Indian who had been brought up since boyhood with
Governor Pedro de Valdivia and was called Felipe, or by the Indians
Láutaru, the son of one of his caciques, influenced more by faithlessness
and attachment to his country than by his duty to God and his master,
heard the Spaniards call the retreat, and as he understood their language
because he had been reared among them, feared that his people would let
them get away from joy at their retreat. So he went to the Indians crying: "Do not give up, brothers. These brigands are on the run and they
have set their hopes on getting to the defile. So see to the liberty of our
country and the death and destruction of these traitors." With these
words, he encouraged his followers with his example, and taking a spear
from the ground, placed himself in the van to attack the Spaniards.

The old Indian captain who had thought out the new stratagem saw
the direction the Spaniards were taking and heard Láutaru's warning.
Realizing what the enemy was proposing to do, he at once ordered two
fresh squadrons to march forward briskly and in good order by a short
cut, and occupy the defile that the Spaniards hoped to hold, remaining
there quietly until the main body came up. After giving these orders, he,
with the rest of his troops, marched in pursuit of the Spaniards, sending
companies and reinforcements forward from time to time, partly to keep
up the fighting and prevent the enemy from resting, and partly to allow
the Indians who were exhausted time to recover and re-enter the fray. In
this way the Spaniards were remorselessly pursued and harassed, and
some of them killed, until they came to the defile. When they reached the
place, it was nearly sunset. They found that what they had hoped would
prove a refuge and defence was instead occupied by the enemy, and they
then lost all hope of saving their lives. As their fate was assured, they
sought to die like Christians, and called on the names of Christ, Our
Lord, the Virgin, their mother, and the saints they held in greatest devotion.

Finding them now so weary that neither they nor their horses could
stand out, the Indians, both those who had pursued them and those who

had held the pass, fell on them in a mass. Fifteen or twenty of the ruffians seized each horse by the tail, legs, and mane, and others clubbed mounts and riders wherever they could, bringing them to earth and slaughtering them with the greatest possible cruelty and fury. Governor Pedro de Valdivia and a priest accompanying him were taken alive and each tied to a stake until the battle was over, when their captors could decide at leisure what to do with them. Thus far we have followed the second account of the defeat and death of Valdivia which, as we have said, came from Chile to Peru immediately after the event and was brought by friendly Indians who had been present at the battle. There were three of them who escaped by hiding in some bushes under cover of darkness. And when the Indians retired to celebrate their victory they came out of the undergrowth, and, knowing the way well and showing more loyalty to their masters than Láutaru had done, they made off to inform the Spaniards of the defeat and destruction of the famous Pedro de Valdivia and all his companions.

CHAPTER XXIV

Valdivia slain; the war has continued for fifty years.

THE MANNER in which the Araucanians put Governor Pedro de Valdivia to death was later told in different ways, for the three Indian survivors had not seen it and could not therefore describe it. Some said that Láutaru, his own servant, had found him fastened to a stake and slain him, saying: "Why are you keeping this traitor?" and that the Governor had begged and persuaded the Indians not to kill him until his servant Láutaru should appear, hoping that, as he had been reared by him, he would try to save his life. Others affirmed—and this was truer—that an old captain had killed him with a club. This may have been the same who devised the stratagem that defeated him. The Indian killed him with sudden violence lest his companions should accept the offers made by the wretched governor while he was tied to the stake, and set him free. The other Indian leaders were indeed inclined to trust Valdivia's promises and give him his liberty, for he had offered to leave Chile himself and to withdraw all the other Spaniards there, and never return. The old captain sensed the state of mind of his friends and realized that they were disposed to believe the governor, so he rose up among them while they were listening and quietly dispatched the poor gentleman with a club he was holding, cutting short the debate with the words: "Shame on you for being so weak and foolish as to trust the words of a slave who is captured and bound. Tell me, what will a man in such a state as this not promise, and what will he fulfil once he is free?"

There were other accounts of Valdivia's death, one by a Spaniard born in Trujillo and called Francisco de Rieros, who was then in Chile, where he had Indians. He came to Peru soon after the disaster and said that the Indians had passed the night following their triumph in great celebrations with dances to solemnize the achievement, and that for each dance they cut off a piece of Valdivia and a piece of the priest who was tied by him, and roasted and ate them in front of their victims. He declared that while this cruel torment was being practiced, the good governor confessed his sins to the priest and they both died in the ordeal. It is possible that after the captain had slain the governor with his club the other Indians may have eaten him, not because they were accustomed to eat human flesh, for such was never the case, but to display their fury against him for bringing so many tribulations and so much strife and death upon them.

Thereafter it was their custom to form a great many separate companies in fighting with the Spaniards, as Don Alonso de Ercilla mentions in the first canto of his *Araucana*. They have carried on the war that arose from this rebellion for forty-nine years. It began in the last days of 1553, the year of Don Sebastián de Castilla's rebellion in the towns of La Plata and Potosí and Francisco Hernández Girón's in Cuzco.

I have given this unadorned account of the battle and of the death of Governor Pedro de Valdivia as it was written and told in Peru in those days by people from Chile itself: the reader may accept whatever version he wishes. I have anticipated it in time and place because it is one of the most noteworthy events that have occurred in the Indies and I do not know if another opportunity will occur to refer to Chile: I fear too that I may never conclude so lengthy a task as that of recounting the Spanish conquest of that kingdom.

CHAPTER XXV

New misfortunes in the kingdom of Chile.

I HAD reached this point when I received new reports of lamentable disasters that occurred in Chile in 1599 and in Peru in 1600. Among other calamities, reports from Arequipa refer to great earthquakes and a shower of ashes from an erupting volcano which lasted twenty days and left an ashy deposit more than a vara deep in places, and in places more than two, and more than a cuarta at the very least. The result was that the vineyards and maize and wheat fields were buried, and the orchards and other trees were stripped and bore no fruit, while all the animals died for lack of pasture. The ash covered the fields for thirty leagues around Arequipa in some directions and for over forty in others. Herds of five hundred cows were found dead, and flocks of sheep and goats and bands of swine were buried. Houses collapsed under the weight of the ash, and those that survived were saved because their owners hastened to clear off the deposit. There were great flashes of lightning and claps of thunder that were heard for thirty leagues round Arequipa. For many days the sun was so obscured by fog and falling ash that lights had to be lit in the middle of the day so that men could see what they were doing. These and similar events have been reported to me as having happened in Arequipa and its neighborhood. I have mentioned them in passing, abbreviating the account sent from Peru, for historians who deal with the events of the period will be obliged to relate them at greater length.

We shall describe the misfortunes of Chile as they have reached us from that country, for they are relevant to what we have said about the Araucanian Indians and their exploits since the rising of 1553 which still continues in the year now beginning, 1603. We cannot tell when it will come to an end; it appears indeed that it is increasing in impetus and vigor from year to year, since after forty-nine years of rebellion and after sustaining perpetual war with fire and the sword, they have performed the deeds we shall now describe, following word for word a letter written by a citizen of Santiago de Chile, which came together with the account of the calamities of Arequipa. These accounts were brought to me by a gentleman, a friend of mine, who was in Peru and served as a captain in putting down the rebellion in Quito against the imposition of the sales tax, during the course of which he performed great services to the Spanish crown. His name is Martín Zuazo. The title of the misfortunes of Chile is called "News from Chile," and it begins as follows:

When the above news had just come from Arequipa, others of very great grief and sorrow arrived from Chile. The news is as follows, related in the same way as it was received from those parts.

Report of the loss and destruction of the city of Valdivia in Chile, which occurred on Wednesday, November 24, 1599. At daybreak on this day the city was set upon by a force of about five thousand Indians from the neighborhood and the districts of La Imperial, Pica, and Purén, three thousand mounted and the rest on foot. They were said to have brought more than seventy arquebusiers and more than two hundred coats of mail. They arrived unperceived at daybreak, having been guided by double spies from the city. They came in organized bands because they knew the Spaniards were sleeping in their houses and were guarded by only four men with two others to go the rounds: and fortune had blinded the Spaniards with the success of two *malocas*—which is the same as raids—carried out twenty days earlier, in the course of which they overran an Indian fort on the plain and marsh of Paparlén with the death of many natives. So great were their losses that it was thought that not a single Indian could be found for eight leagues round. But by bribing the double spies, the Indians performed the bravest exploit that savages ever carried through, secretly surrounding each house with sufficient men to cope with the number of Spaniards known to be inside. Taking possession of the ends of the streets, they advanced up them, assaulting the unfortunate city, setting fire to the houses and occupying the gates so that no one could escape or come to the aid of the rest. Within two hours the town had been sacked by fire and the sword, and the Indians had captured the fort and artillery since there was no one within. Those who surrendered or were killed numbered four hundred Spaniards, men, women, and children. Three hundred thousand pesos' worth of goods were robbed, and nothing was left standing and unburnt. The ships of Vallano and Villarroel and another belonging to Diego de Rojas sailed off down the river. A few people escaped in this way in canoes: otherwise no one would have got away with the news.

The savages acted in this ruthless way because of their losses in the two raids we have mentioned in which most of their women and children were captured and sold to the merchants for transportation from their native districts. Their behavior was in spite of the fact that they had been subdued for more than fifty years, all having been baptized and having priests among them to teach them Christian doctrine during all this time. The temples were the first to be burnt, and the images and saints were destroyed, smashed to pieces with sacrilegious hands.

Ten days after the occurrence the good Colonel Francisco del Campo reached the gates of the city with reinforcements of three hundred men sent by his Excellency from Peru to assist the cities of Chile. He ransomed his son and daughter, both young children, whom he had left in the hands of a sister-in-law and who had been captured in the assault with the rest of the inhabitants. Then, seeing the pitiful ruins of the city, he bravely landed his men to succor the towns of Osorno, Villarrica, and the ill-starred Imperial, of which there was no news except that it had been surrounded by the enemy for a year: it was thought that they must all have starved to death, for there was nothing left to eat but dead horses, dogs, cats, and leather. This became known through a message from the city brought by a spokesman who made his way down the river to beg for help with the most pitiful pleas on behalf of those unfortunate people. As soon as the colonel had landed, he determined first to succor the city of Osorno, knowing that the enemy had overrun Valdivia and, inspired by this victory, were preparing to finish off Osorno. He did relieve Osorno and achieved other successes. At the time of writing, news has been received that the inhabitants of La Imperial all perished of hunger after being besieged for a year. Only twenty men escaped, and their fate was worse than death, for they were driven by hunger to go over to the Indians. At Angol they killed four soldiers: their identity is unknown. May the Lord have pity on us, amen. From Santiago in Chile, March 1600.

All the above news came, as I have said, in reports from Peru and Chile, and has been a great affliction to the people there. Moreover, Padre Diego de Alcobaça, whom I have already mentioned more than once, speaks of the kingdom of Chile in the following terms in a letter about various matters concerned with the empire he addressed to me in 1601:

Chile is in a very bad state, and the Indians are so skilled and cunning in warfare that any of them will fall with spear and horse on any Spanish soldier, however brave. Every year forces are raised in Peru to fight there: many go and none come back. They have sacked two Spanish towns, slain all their male inhabitants and carried off their poor daughters and wives after killing their fathers and sons and servants. Recently they slew Governor Loyola in an ambush—he was married to a daughter of Don Diego Sairi Túpac, the Inca who came down from Villcapampa before you left for Spain. God have mercy on the dead and save the living.

Thus far from Padre Alcobaça, who has sent me other deplorable news which I shall not repeat, for it is too grievous: he mentioned the disasters at Arequipa, one of which was that wheat was sold for ten or eleven ducats that year, and maize for thirteen.

In addition to what we have already said about Arequipa, its ordeals have been multiplied by the inclemencies of all four elements, as is made plain by the reports that the Jesuit fathers there sent to their general about the notable events of Peru in 1602. They state that the misfortunes of Arequipa are still not at an end, but they say in the same report how much greater are those of the kingdom of Chile following the events we have already described. These reports were given me by Padre Francisco de Castro, a native of Granada, who is prefect of the schools and professes rhetoric in the holy college here at Córdova this year of 1604. The report on Chile copied literally, with its title, is as follows:

On the revolt of the Araucanians.

Of the thirteen cities that existed in this kingdom of Chile, six have been destroyed by the Indians—Valdivia, La Imperial, Angol, Santa Cruz, Chillán, and La Concepción. They destroyed and laid waste the habitation of the houses, the honor of the temples, the devotion and faith that shone in them, and the beauty of the fields, and perhaps the greatest suffering arose from the fact that the Indians were stimulated and emboldened by these successes to commit greater pillaging and burning, and to lay waste, sack, and destroy cities and monasteries. They elaborated all sorts of cunning and treacherous tricks. They surrounded the city of Osorno, and the Spaniards lost strength and withdrew into a fort, where the Indians have kept them in a state of almost continuous siege. Those inside have sustained themselves on the seeds of herbs and a few turnip leaves, and even these were only obtained by dint of fierce fighting. In one of the sieges of the city the images of Our Lord, Our Lady, and the saints were broken, wherein God showed his invincible clemency through his infinite patience: while he did not lack the power to chastise the deed, his goodness was too great to permit it. In the last attack the Indians made against this fort, they killed the sentries unperceived by the Spaniards, and entered it in safety, taking possession of it with inhuman savagery. They put all the children to the knife and manacled the women and nuns, intending to take them off as their captives. But they were so greedy for plunder that they fell into disorder as they busily collected the spoils, and gave the Spaniards the opportunity to recover their courage and God was pleased to give our people the advantage when they returned to the fray. The women and nuns, all but a few who were carried off, were saved, and the Indians were put to flight. The last victory gained by the Indians was the capture of Villarrica, which was razed with great loss of life to the Spaniards. The enemy set fire to it on four sides: they slew all the religious of St. Dominic, St. Francis, and Our Lady of the Mercies, as well as the priests who were present. All the women, who were numerous and of high rank, were taken captive, and thus a very wealthy city was wiped away and a place known for its illustrious nobility succumbed to an unhappy fate.

Thus far the report from Chile, which arrived at the beginning of the present year of 1604. Of all this I know not what to say, except that these are secret judgments of God who knows why He permits such things. With this we shall return to the good Inca Yupanqui, and add what little remains to be said about his life.

CHAPTER XXVI

The peaceful life and occupations of King Inca Yupanqui until his death.

KING Inca Yupanqui, after settling the affairs of the provinces conquered by his captains in the kingdom of Chile, as regards religion, the government of his new subjects, and the administration of the estates of the crown and of the Sun, decided to abandon completely the idea of gaining new territories, considering that those won by himself and his captains were already many. His empire now exceeded a thousand leagues in length, and he therefore preferred to devote the rest of his life to embellishing and ennobling his kingdoms and estates. To commemorate his great deeds, he ordered the construction of many fortresses and of large new buildings to serve as temples for the Sun and houses for the chosen virgins. He built royal and common storehouses for the royal line, and had great irrigation channels dug and numerous terraces raised. He added wealth to what already existed in the temple of the Sun at Cuzco, for although there was no need for such in the temple, he thought it his duty to add all the adornement he could to show himself a true son of his father. In short, he left undone none of the good works in which his ancestors had engaged for the ennoblement of the empire. In particular he applied his attention to the fortress of Cuzco, which his father had planned, leaving a vast accumulation of stone and rock toward this splendid building which we shall soon describe. He visited his realms to study the needs of his subjects with his own eyes and provide remedies: he attended to them with such care that he earned the title of pious.

In these employments the prince passed some years in great peace and quiet, served and beloved by his subjects. At the end of this time he fell ill, and feeling the approach of death, summoned the heir to the throne and his other sons: in place of a testament, he urged them to preserve the idolatry and laws and customs of the Incas, to act with justice and rectitude towards their vassals and to seek to benefit them. He then bade them remain in peace, for his father the Sun was calling him to rest. He then died full of great deeds and trophies, having enlarged his empire by more than 500 leagues southward from Atacama to the river Maule and more than 140 northwards along the coast from Chincha to Chimu. He was mourned with deep regret, and his obsequies lasted a year, according to the Inca custom. He was made the tenth of their gods, the children of the Sun, as he was their tenth king. Many sacrifices were offered up to him. He left as his successor and universal heir Túpac Inca Yupanqui, his eldest son by his wife and sister Coya Chimpu Ocllo. The queen's name was Chimpu: Ocllo was a sacred title among the Incas, and not a name. He left many other legitimate and illegitimate sons and daughters, exceeding 250, though this is not a large number considering the multitude of chosen brides these kings had in each province. And as this Inca began the building of the fortress of Cuzco, we may properly describe it now after dealing with its founder, so that it may serve as a trophy, not only to him, but also to his forebears and followers, for the monument was so great that it might serve to lend fame to all the Inca kings.

CHAPTER XXVII

The fortress of Cuzco; the size of its stones.

THE INCA kings of Peru made marvellous buildings, fortresses, temples, royal palaces, gardens, storehouses, roads, and other constructions of great excellence, as can be seen even today from their remaining ruins, though the whole building can scarcely be judged from the mere foundations.

The greatest and most splendid building erected to show the power and majesty of the Incas was the fortress of Cuzco, the grandeur of which would be incredible to anyone who had not seen it, and even those who have seen it and considered it with attention imagine, and even believe, that it was made by enchantment, the handiwork of demons, rather than of men. Indeed the multiplicity of stones, large and small, of which the three circumvallations are composed (and they are more like rocks than stones) makes one wonder how they could have been quarried, for the Indians had neither iron nor steel to work them with. And the question of how they were conveyed to the site is no less difficult a problem, since they had no oxen and could not make wagons: nor would oxen and wagons have sufficed to carry them. They were in fact heaved by main force with the aid of thick cables. The roads by which they were brought were not flat, but rough mountainsides with steep slopes, up and down which the rocks were dragged by human effort alone. Many of the pieces were brought a distance of ten, twelve, or fifteen leagues, in particular that stone, or rather rock, which the Indians call Saicusa, "the weary," because it never reached the site. This rock is known to have been brought from a place fifteen leagues from the city and through the Y'úcay river, which is only a little narrower than the Guadalquivir at Córdova. The nearest source of stone was Muina, five leagues from Cuzco. And if one went on to wonder how such large stones could be fitted together so that the point of a knife could scarcely be inserted between them, there would be no end to our pondering. Many of them are so closely set that the seam is scarcely visible. To lodge them in this way it would have been necessary to lift each stone and lower it on the one below a great many times, for they had no set-square or even a ruler to help them to put it in place and see if it fitted. Neither did they know how to make cranes or pulleys or any other device to help them raise and lower masonry, though the pieces they handled are terrifyingly large, as Padre José de Acosta says in speaking of this very fortress. I appeal to the authority of this great man since I have no exact measurements of the size of many of the stones, for although I have asked my former schoolfellows for information and they have sent it to me, their account of the dimensions of the biggest stones is not as clear as I would have liked: they sent me the measurements in fathoms, though I wanted them in varas and ochavas. I would also like to have had attested evidence of this, for the most wonderful thing about the fortress is the incredible size of the stones and the extraordinary labor that was necessary to raise and lower them until they were finally adjusted to their present positions: it is indeed incomprehensible how this could have been done with no assistance but men's hands. Padre Acosta says in his Book VI, ch. xiv:

The edifices made by the Incas—fortresses, temples, roads, country houses, and others—were numerous and wrought with vast labor, as the ruins and fragments that still exist today clearly prove. In Cuzco, Tiahuanaco, Tambo, and elsewhere there are stones of immense size, and one cannot conceive how they were cut, carried, and set in their places. A vast quantity was brought from all the provinces for the buildings and fortifications the Inca had made in Cuzco and in various parts of the kingdom. The task is an astonishing one. They did not use mortar and had no iron or steel for cutting and working the stone, nor engines or instruments for shifting it, yet the surface of the wall is often so smooth that in many places the joint is scarcely visible. And many of the stones used are so large that anyone who had not seen them would regard the thing as incredible. In Tiahuanaco I measured a stone thirty-eight feet long and eighteen broad, and it must have been six feet thick. The wall of the fortress at Cuzco, which is of masonry, contains many stones that are even larger. The most remarkable thing is that though the stones in the wall are not cut to size, but are extremely irregular in size and shape, they nevertheless fit together with incredible exactitude without the use of mortar. All this was carried out with great masses of workers who patiently toiled to lay one stone on another, a task that required many trials, for most of them were not level or uniform,

etc. These words are extracted literally from Padre Acosta, and show with what difficulty and toil the fortress was built in the absence of instruments or engines.

The immensity and majesty of this monument seems to show that the Incas intended to demonstrate the greatness of their power. It was indeed made to impress rather than for another reason. They also wished to exhibit the skill of their masons and builders, not only in dressing the smooth masonry (which the Spaniards are never tired of praising) but also in rough stonework, which they executed with no less mastery. They sought also to exhibit their knowledge of military science in the plan of the fortress, including everything necessary for its defence against the enemy.

The fortress was built on a high hill to the north of Cuzco, called Sacsahuana, at the foot of which begin the outskirts of the city that spread around for a great distance in all directions. On the side toward the city the hill is steep, almost sheer, so that the fort is secure from enemy attack from that direction, whether by companies in regular formation or any other system. Nor is there any room to install artillery, though the Indians had never heard of it until the arrival of the Spaniards. Owing to the natural strength on this quarter it was thought that any defence, however slight, would suffice, and so they merely set up a thick freestone wall, carefully wrought on all five sides except what masons call the extrados. This wall was more than two hundred fathoms long. Each line of stone was at a different height, and every stone in each line was alike and

set in a row and excellently fitted on all four faces so that there was no
room for mortar. They did not indeed use mortar made of sand and lime,
for they were unacquainted with lime. They did however employ a mortar
consisting of a paste of sticky red clay, which was used to fill up the gashes
and pits caused in working the stone. This defence was both stout and
smooth, for the wall was thick and carefully polished on both sides.

CHAPTER XXVIII

The three circumvallations, the most
remarkable part of the work.

O N THE other side, opposite this wall, there is a large level space.
From this direction the ascent to the top of the hill is a gradual one
up which an enemy could advance in order of battle. The Incas therefore
made three concentric walls on the slopes, each of which would be more
than two hundred fathoms long. They are in the shape of a half moon,
for they close together at the ends to meet the other wall of smooth masonry on the side facing the city. The first of these three walls best ex-
hibits the might of the Incas, for although all three are of the same workmanship, it is the most impressive and has the largest stones, making the
whole construction seem incredible to anyone who has not seen it, and
giving an impression of awe to the careful observer who ponders on the
size and number of the stones and the limited resources of the natives for
cutting and working them and setting them in their places.

I for my part consider that the stones are not quarried, for there are
no signs of their having been cut, but that the Indians took loose boulders
(what quarrymen call *tormos*) which lay strewn about the mountainside
and seemed suitable for the work. They would use them as they found
them, some being concave on one side, convex on another, and skew-
pointed on a third; some have sharp edges and others none. The natives
made no attempt to remove what was not required or supply what was
wanting, except that where a big rock had a concave side they would fit
into it the convex part of another rock, as large or even larger, if they
could find such, or similarly they would match the flat edge or slope of

one rock with that of another, and if they used a rock with a corner missing they would supply the want by introducing another, not using only a small piece which would suffice to add the missing corner, but setting up another large rock with a projecting corner. This shows that the aim of the Indians was not to insert small stones into the walls, even to supply gaps in the larger ones, but to use only big rocks of remarkable size and to fit them together so that they served to strengthen one another and fill one another's gaps, to the greater grandeur of the whole structure. This was what Padre Acosta meant to emphasize when he said: "the most remarkable aspect of the whole work is the fact that though the stones are not cut to a size, but are very unequal in shape and dimensions, they are fitted together with incredible exactitude without the use of mortar." While the arrangement of the rocks is thus quite haphazard, they are none the less as carefully set as smooth stonework. The surface of each rock is only very roughly worked: they are almost left in their original state except that the stone is very carefully worked for about four fingers' breadth at the edges. This careful working of the seams, together with the roughness of the surface and the uneven arrangement of the rocks gives a bold and striking appearance to the whole.

A priest from Montilla who went out to Peru since my return to Spain and soon came back told me, in speaking of the fortress, and in particular of the monstrous size of the stones, that before seeing them he would never have believed that they could have been so large as he had been told, and that when he saw them they seemed even bigger. There then occurred to him an even more difficult problem—he could not believe they could have been set up unless by diabolic art. He was indeed right to wonder how the rocks could have been set in place even with the aid of the devices that architects and engineers have in Europe, and how much more so without their aid. To this extent this fortress surpasses the constructions known as the seven wonders of the world. For in the case of a long broad wall like that of Babylon, or the colossus of Rhodes, or the pyramids of Egypt, or the other monuments, one can see clearly how they were executed—whether of brick and bitumen, like the wall of Babylon, or of copper and bronze like the colossus of Rhodes, or of stone and mortar like the pyramids, one perceives how, by summoning an immense body of workers and accumulating more and more material day by day and year by year, they overcame all difficulties by employing human effort over a long period. But it is indeed beyond the power of imagination to understand how these Indians, unacquainted with devices, engines, and implements, could have cut, dressed, raised, and lowered great rocks, more like lumps of hills than building stones, and set them so exactly in their places. For this reason, and because the Indians were so familiar with demons, the work is attributed to enchantment.

Almost in the middle of each wall there was a gate, and these gates were each shut with a stone as high and as thick as the wall itself which could be raised and lowered. The first of these was called Tiupuncu, "gate of sand," since the plain is rather sandy or gravelly at this point: *tiu* is "sand," or "a sandy place," and *puncu,* "gate, door." The second is called Acahuana Puncu, after the master mason, whose name was Acahuana, the syllable *ca* being pronounced deep down in the throat. The third is Viracocha Puncu, dedicated to the god Viracocha, the phantom we have referred to at length, who appeared to Prince Viracocha Inca and forewarned him of the rising of the Chancas, as a result of which he was regarded as the defender and second founder of Cuzco, and therefore given this gate with the request that he should guard it and defend the fortress as he had guarded the city and the whole empire in the past. Between each of the three walls and extending the full length of them, there is a space of twenty-five or thirty feet. Each space is levelled off to the top of the wall in front, but I cannot say if the earth so contained forms part of the slope of the hill or if it was filled in by man's handiwork; it was perhaps a mixture of both. Each wall had its parapet, which was more than a vara high: behind this the defenders could fight with greater security than in the open.

CHAPTER XXIX

Three towers, the master masons, and the Weary Stone.

WITHIN this triple row of walls there is a long narrow space containing three strong towers arranged in an elongated triangle as the site requires. The chief of these towers, which was in the middle, was called Móyoc Marca "the round fortress," for it was circular in shape. Within it was a spring with a copious supply of excellent water brought underground for a long distance. The Indians do not know whence it comes nor by what route. The tradition of such matters was kept secret by the Inca and the members of the supreme council. It was in this tower that the Inca kings lodged when they went up to the fortress for repose. All its walls were adorned with gold and silver, with animals, birds, and plants imitated from life and fitted into the wall, serving as a kind of tapestry. There was similarly a great deal of plate and the other objects we have described as existing in the palaces.

The second tower was called Páucar Marca and the third Sácllac Marca: both were square, and contained many rooms for the soldiers on guard, who relieved one another in due order. They were required to be Incas by privilege, and no other people could enter the fortress, for it was considered a house of the Sun for arms and warfare, just as the temple was a house of the Sun for prayer and sacrifice. It had a captain general as its governor, and he was required to be a legitimate member of the royal blood. He had deputies and specialists for various duties—for the training of the soldiers, the delivery of supplies, the care and keeping of the weapons, and the control of the store of military clothing and footwear that existed in the fortress.

The towers went as far below ground as they did above it. There were tunnels between them so that one could pass from one to the others below ground as well as above it. The tunnels were made with great skill. There were so many underground passages, large and small, twisting and turning in all directions, with so many doors, all of the same size, but some opening on one side and some on the other, that anyone entering the maze soon lost his way and was at a loss to find the way out. Even the most experienced dared not enter without a guide, which consisted of a skein of thick cord tied to the door of entry so as to show the way back. When I was a boy, I often went up to the fortress with others of my own age, and though the stonework part of the building was already ruined— I mean the part that was above ground and even a good deal of the part below the surface—we never dared enter certain parts of remaining vaults except as far as the light of the sun penetrated lest we should get lost inside, which was the fear the Indians taught us.

The Incas could not make a vaulted arch. When dressing stone for walls they prepared corbels for lining underground tunnels; on top of these, in place of beams, they set long flagstones, dressed on all six sides, which stretched from wall to wall and were tightly fitted together. The whole structure of the fortress was of stonework, either rough-hewn or dressed, most skilfully done. In this the Incas demonstrated their knowledge and ability, intending this work to surpass in size and art everything they had accomplished hitherto, as the trophy of their trophies, and it was

thus the last of their achievements, for only a few years after its completion the Spaniards entered their empire and put a stop to the building of
other projects no less grand.

Four master masons were employed on the construction of the fortress.
The first of these, to whom fell the planning of the work, was Huallpa
Rimachi Inca, and to show that he was the chief, he was called Apu, "captain" or "chief" in any occupation. The second was Inca Maricanchi, and
the third Acahuana Inca, to whom is attributed a great part of the mighty
buildings of Tiahuanacu, which we have already mentioned. The fourth
and last of the masters was called Calla Cúnchuy. It was in his time that
the Weary Stone was brought, to which the master mason gave his own
name in order to preserve its fame: its size, like that of other similar rocks,
is incredible. I should be glad to be able to set down its exact circumference and height, but I have not been able to find precise information:
I can only refer the matter to those who have seen it. It stands on a level
space in front of the fortress, and the Indians said that after the great
labors it experienced on the way there, it grew weary and wept blood, and
could not reach the building. The stone is not dressed but rough, as it was
lifted out of the ground where it was embedded. A considerable part of
it lies under the ground. I am told that it has subsided further than when
I saw it, for it was thought that a great treasure lay beneath it and tunnels
were dug to get it out, but before the supposed treasure was reached, the
great rock sank down and the major part of its immense size disappeared:
thus today it is mostly underground. At one of its peaks it has a hole or
two, which, if I remember aright, pass through from one side to the other.
The Indians say that these holes are the stone's eyes, through which it
wept blood. A reddish mark or sign has been produced by the earth
(which is red thereabouts) that has stuck in the holes and the rain water
running down the stone, and the Indians say that this mark was left when
the stone wept blood. They handed down this fable in so many words,
and I have often heard it.

The historical truth, as the Inca *amautas* (their wise men, philosophers,
and doctors in all matters concerning their pagan beliefs) affirm, is that
more than twenty thousand Indians brought this stone up, dragging it
with great cables. Their progress was very slow, for the road up which
they came is rough and has many steep slopes to climb and descend. Half
the laborers pulled at the ropes from in front, while the rest kept the rock
steady with other cables attached behind lest it should roll downhill and
come to rest where it could not be recovered.

On one of these slopes, as a result of carelessness on the part of the bearers who failed to pull evenly, the weight of the rock proved too much for the strength of those controlling it and it rolled over down the slope and killed three or four thousand Indians. Despite this disaster the rock was drawn up and deposited on its present site. The blood it shed is the blood they said it wept, meaning that they wept it. As it was never placed in the building, they say that it grew weary and could not be got there, for they grew weary of moving it: so that their own failings passed as an attribute to the rock. They had a great many similar fables that they taught by tradition to their children and grandchildren in order to serve as a memorial of the most notable events that occurred among them.

The Spaniards, though they should have maintained this fortress even if they had had to restore it at their own expense, so as to demonstrate to future ages the great strength and courage of the conquerors and to provide an everlasting monument to their great deeds, were as if envious of the remarkable achievements of the Incas, and not only failed to preserve the fortress, but even demolished it to build private houses in Cuzco. And to save themselves the expense, effort and delay with which the Indians worked the stone, they pulled down all the smooth masonry in the walls. There is indeed not a house in the city that has not been made of this stone, or at least the houses built by the Spaniards.

The large slabs that formed the roof of the underground passages were taken out to serve as lintels and doorways. The smaller stones were used for foundations and walls, and for the steps of the staircases they sought slabs of stone of the size they needed, pulling down all the stones above the ones they wanted in the process, even though there might be ten or twelve rows or many more. In this way the majesty of the fortress was brought to the ground, a monument worthy of being spared such devastation, which will cause everlasting regret to those who ponder on what it was. It was pulled down with such haste that all that was left in my own time was the few relics I have mentioned. The three walls of rock were still standing when I left, for they could not be demolished on account of their size. Nevertheless, I have been told that part of them was pulled down in the search for the chain or cable of gold made by Huaina Cápac, which they supposed or guessed was buried there.

The good king Inca Yupanqui, the tenth of the Incas, began the construction of this inadequately portrayed and insufficiently praised fortress, though others assert that it was his father Pachacútec Inca. They say this because he left the plan and the model, and collected a vast quantity of rock and stone, the only available material for the work. It took more than fifty years to complete the task, until the time of Huaina Cápac. The Indians even say that it was unfinished, for the Weary Stone had been brought for another great construction that was planned but cut short, like many others throughout the empire, by the civil wars that soon broke out between the two brothers Huáscar Inca and Atahuallpa, during which the Spanish invasion occurred, so that all the work was stopped and the monuments were reduced to their present ruinous state.

End of the Seventh Book

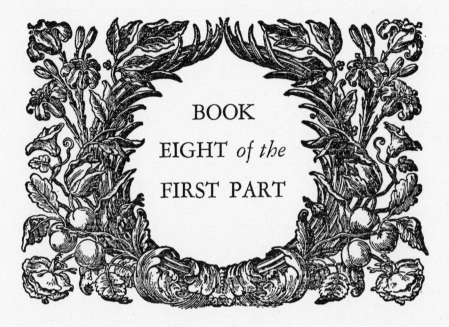

BOOK
EIGHT *of the*
FIRST PART

*in which are seen the many conquests undertaken by the
eleventh ruler Túpac Inca Yupanqui, and the three marriages of his son Huaina Cápac; the testament and death
of the said Túpac Inca; the domestic and wild animals,
crops and vegetables, fruits and birds; the four famous
rivers; the precious stones, gold, and silver; in short
everything there was in the empire before
the arrival of the Spaniards.
It contains twenty-five chapters.*

CHAPTER I

The conquest of the province of Huacrachucu,
and the meaning of its name.

s SOON as his father died, the great Túpac Inca Yupanqui (whose name Túpac means "he who glows or shines," a title this prince merited by his great deeds) assumed the scarlet fringe; and after carrying out the usual obsequies and performing the other ceremonies and sacrifices due to dead kings, which occupied the first year of his reign, he went out to visit his kingdoms and provinces. This was always the first act of Inca rulers on inheriting the throne, for they wished to know and be known and loved by their subjects and also to permit the municipalities and villages as a whole, as well as each individual in them, to ask them personally for whatever they saw fit, and to prevent the governors, judges, and older ministers of justice from neglecting their subjects or oppressing them in the Inca's absence. He spent four full years on this visit, and when he completed it, left his subjects very satisfied with his magnanimity and royal qualities: he then gave orders for the raising of forty thousand warriors to pursue the path of conquest that his ancestors had pointed out to him, for the chief glory of the Incas and the veil with which they covered their ambition to expand the empire was to give out that they were moved by the desire to uplift the Indians from the inhuman barbarism of their present existence and to reduce them to a moral and political way of life through the knowledge and worship of their father the Sun, whom they regarded as God.

When the force had been made ready and a deputy had been appointed to take the Inca's place in the city, he himself marched to Cajamarca, thence to enter the province called Chachapoya, which, according to Padre Blas Valera, means "place of strong men." It lies to the east of Cajamarca, and was inhabited by many brave people, remarkable for the spirit of the men and the extreme beauty of the women. These Chachapoyas worshipped snakes and regarded the *cuntur* as their principal god. Túpac

Inca Yupanqui desired to reduce the province to his empire on account of its great fame. It then had more than forty thousand inhabitants, and is extremely inaccessible.

The Chachapoya Indians wear a sling as a typical headdress, which serves to mark them out from other tribes. The sling is of a different type from those used by the other Indians, and it is the principal weapon they use in warfare, as did the Majorcans of old.

Before the province of Chachapoya there is another called Huacrachucu. This province is large and the country very difficult, and its people extraordinarily ferocious and warlike. They are, or rather were—for all these things are now confused—distinguished by wearing on their heads a black woolen band with white speckles surmounted by the tip of a deer's horn. Hence the name Huacrachucu, "headdress or hat of horn": from *chucu,* "headdress," and *huacra,* "horn." The Huacrachucus worshipped serpents before they were subdued by the Incas, and there were paintings of serpent idols in their temples and houses.

It was necessary for the Inca to conquer this province of Huacrachucu before passing on to Chachapoya, and he therefore marched his army against it. The natives prepared to resist, emboldened by the great difficulty of their country, and confident of victory since they regarded it as inexpugnable. In this spirit of confidence they advanced to occupy the passes, where there were hard-fought battles with many dead on both sides. When the Inca and his council saw this, they felt that if the war were continued with fire and the sword, it would result in heavy losses to themselves and the total destruction of their enemies. When they had won some of the enemy strongholds, they therefore sent to offer peace and friendship, according to the custom of the Incas. They bade the enemy recall that the Inca was more concerned with benefiting them, as his predecessors had benefited all the other Indian peoples reduced to their empire, than with lording it over them or deriving such profits as he might expect from them: let them bear in mind that he would not deprive them of any of their lands and possessions, but rather extend them with new irrigation channels and other improvements. The *curacas* would retain their existing authority, for all that the Inca desired was that they should worship the Sun and give up the inhuman practices in which they indulged. The Huacrachucus discussed all this, and though there were many of them who thought that they should receive the Inca as their ruler, no agreement was reached, for the younger people, who were least experienced and most numerous, opposed it persistently and had their way. They pursued the war with great fury, considering themselves obliged to conquer or perish to a man, since they had flouted the advice of their elders.

The Inca, in order to show the enemy that his invitation to make peace was inspired not by pusillanimity or lack of strength, but by the humanity and mildness traditionally displayed by his ancestors, ordered the war to be intensified, and the enemy to be attacked on all sides, dividing his army into regiments so as to distract the Huacrachucus and weaken their military strength and spirit. At the Inca's second attack he won more strongholds and passes, and pressed the enemy so hard that they had no option but to sue for mercy. The Inca received them with great clemency, following the usual practice of the rulers of Peru, who prided themselves greatly on this virtue, and hoping to appeal to the neighboring peoples in this way. He therefore ordered his minsters to treat the Huacrachucus as if they were brothers, and gave instructions for quantities of the fine clothes called *compi* to be given to *curacas* and of the other clothes, *avasca*, to the common people. They were also to be furnished with great quantities of provisions, since their whole year's supplies had been squandered in the war; and because of this the newly conquered Indians were extremely satisfied and set aside the fear of punishment that they anticipated after their rebellious obstinacy.

The Inca did not wish to pursue this conquest, since he thought he had done enough that summer by winning a province so inaccessible and peopled by such warlike inhabitants: moreover the region is extremely rainy. He ordered his army to be billeted in the frontier district, and also gave instructions for twenty-thousand more men to be made ready for the following year, since he did not intend that his next conquests should take so long as the last.

He had the newly reduced peoples instructed in their vain religion and in the laws and moral customs of the Incas which they were to keep and fulfil. He further had them given directions for the digging of irrigation channels, the construction of terraces, and the levelling of hillsides and rough places that were suitable for sowing crops. The land was in fact a fertile one, but it had hitherto remained undeveloped and sterile for lack of skill. The natives acknowledged that all these measures were greatly to their advantage.

CHAPTER II

The conquest of the first villages
in the province of Chachapoya.

WHEN SUMMER arrived and his reinforcements were gathered, the great Túpac Inca Yupanqui ordered his army to take the field and advance forward toward the province of Chachapoya. A messenger was sent forward according to the traditional Inca custom to offer peace or war. The Chachapoyas resolutely replied that they were ready to take up arms and die in defense of their freedom; let the Inca do as he would, they would not be his subjects.

After the receipt of this reply, both sides engaged in a cruel war, with many dead and wounded on both sides. The Incas were determined not to retreat. The Chachas (for the tribe also uses this name) were resolved to die rather than yield any advantage to their enemies. Because of the obstinacy of both parties, the conquest was attended by great bloodshed: moreover, the Chachas, having seen the Inca empire approach their province—which we might well call a kingdom, since it is more than fifty leagues long and twenty broad, apart from the part that projects to Muyupampa, a length of thirty leagues more—had made preparations for defence some years earlier. They had built many forts in strong places, as can still be seen from the surviving remains, and they had blocked many defiles in order to increase the natural difficulty of the country, which is so rugged that on some roads the Indians slide down ropes a distance eight or ten times the height of a man, for there is no other way of advancing.

Owing to these difficulties the Incas suffered great loss of life in gaining a few fortified passes and a number of forts, to which they attached great importance. The first of these forts were on a slope, rising two and a half leagues, which is called the hill of Pías, from a village of this name which lies beyond it. It is one of the chief places in the province, situated eighteen leagues from the frontier at the point where the Incas made their entry. All this intervening area was won with the greatest difficulty. The village was found unoccupied, for though it stood in a strong position, the inhabitants had fortified other and even stronger sites.

At Pías the Incas found some useless old men and women who could not climb into the mountains with the young people, together with many children whom their parents had been unable to take to the fortresses. The great Túpac Inca Yupanqui ordered them all to be treated with mercy and care.

From the village of Pías the army advanced, and at a certain gap of pass in the snow-covered mountains, called Chirmac Cassa, "the harmful pass," because of the great harm it does to those who cross it, three hundred picked men sent ahead by the Inca to reconnoiter perished when they were caught in a great snowfall, which buried them all and froze them to death without a single one being able to escape. Owing to this misfortune the Inca was unable to cross the pass for several days and the Chachapoyas, thinking that this was caused by fear, spread reports throughout their province that he had retreated and fled.

When the fury of the snowstorm had abated, the Inca pursued his conquest, advancing inch by inch amidst great diffculties as far as Cuntur Marca, another important village, and gradually reducing at the same time many smaller places on either side of the royal highway, a laborious task because of the difficulty of the country and the fortifications recently set up by the inhabitants. In the village of Cuntur Marca the numerous inhabitants made a great resistance: they fought valiantly and sustained the conflict for many days, but as the power of the Incas was by then such that resistance was hopeless, and the Chachas had nothing to support them but their own valor and resolution, they were overrun by the mass of men bearing down on them, so that they were obliged at last to submit to the Inca's will. He received them with his usual clemency and bestowed on them gifts and favors so as to pacify their spirit and also to induce those who had not surrendered to do so.

Leaving officials in Cuntur Marca to govern the area he had recently won, the Inca advanced and conquered the villages and fortresses that stood in his way, though with less toil and bloodshed than hitherto. Most of the natives followed the example of Cuntur Marca and gave in, while the rest fought with diminished obstinacy. In this way he came to another of the chief towns called Cajamarquilla, eight leagues from Cuntur Marca, by a very rugged road through wild mountain ranges. At Cajamarquilla the numerous and warlike population put up much resistance, but after some encounters in which the Chacas came to realize the power of the Incas, they decided that, as most of their province had already been subdued, they would submit also.

CHAPTER III

The conquest of other villages and of other barbarous tribes.

FROM Cajamarquilla the Inca advanced to another important village called Papamarca, "potato village," from the size of the potatoes produced there. The Inca conquered this village in the same way as the others. Then he advanced eight leagues beyond this, reducing all the villages on the way until he came to another place of note called Raimipampa, "field of the chief festival of the Sun," *Raimi,* of which we have spoken at length in a special chapter. The name was given, and the original name suppressed, because after Túpac Inca Yupanqui had taken the place, which stands in a very beautiful valley, he celebrated this festival there, since, as we have said, it was the custom of the Incas to celebrate it as best they might wherever they happened to be at the season, leaving the high priest and other Incas who were in Cuzco to celebrate it there with every solemnity.

Having won Raimipampa, he went on to another place three leagues beyond, called Suta, which he also conquered easily, since the natives no longer resisted on finding the greater part of the province in the Inca's hands. From Suta the army marched to another large place called Llauantu, the last important village in the province of Chachapoya. It surrendered like the rest on finding that it could not resist, and the Inca thus remained the master of the whole of that great province. The chief places are those we have mentioned, in addition to which it then had a great multitude of small villages. The conquest of this province was very difficult, and cost the Inca many men, partly because of the rugged and difficult nature of the land, and partly because the people were so spirited and warlike.

From Llauantu the great Túpac Inca Yupanqui sent part of his army to conquer and reduce a province called Muyupampa, to which the gallant Hancohualla retreated when he forsook his own country to avoid acknowledging the supremacy of the Incas, as we have mentioned in telling the life of Inca Viracocha. This province is in the Antis, and recognized the sovereignty of the Chachas either as vassals or as friendly confederates, a point on which the Indians disagree. This region lies nearly thirty leagues to the east of Llauantu.

The natives of Muyupampa, on learning that the whole province of Chachapoya was subject to the Inca, soon surrendered, swearing to embrace the Inca idolatry and their laws and customs. Those of the province called Cascayunca did likewise, and other provinces of less renown in the area followed suit, all surrendering to the Inca with little or no resistance. The latter took the necessary steps for implanting his vain religion and the worship of the Sun, and for attending to the good of the inhabitants. He had irrigation channels dug and new land brought under cultivation so as to make the provinces more productive. He also gave the *curacas* many garments, which they greatly esteemed. He then suspended the war until the following summer, putting the army into winter quarters and bringing up a great store of provisions for the warriors and his newly conquered vassals who were in straits for food after the late wars.

When summer came, Túpac Inca Yupanqui went with an army of forty thousand men against the province of Huancapampa, a large and thickly-peopled area with various tribes and differing languages. They lived apart, each tribe by itself, with no peace or friendship between them and no overlord or state or settled towns. They warred against one another like wild beasts, for their quarrels were not about sovereignty since there was none, and they did not even know what a lord was. Neither did they wage war over the possession of property, since they had none, and most of them went naked, not knowing how to make clothes. The prize of the conqueror was the wives and daughters of the defeated: they took all of them they could, and the men ate one another like wild beasts.

They were as beastly in their religion as in the moral life, or more so: they worshipped many gods. Each tribe, each captaincy or band, and each house had its own. Some worshipped animals, others birds, others herbs and plants, others hills, springs, and rivers, each according to his fancy. About this there were also great battles and much strife, in common and in particular, about which of the gods was the best. Because of the state of political independence in which they lived, without any common norms, they proved very easy to conquer, since their only defence was to fly like beasts into the heaths and the rugged mountains, to caves and nooks in the rocks where they might hide. Hunger brought most of them out of these places and reduced them to the Inca's service and obedience. Others, fiercer and more brutish, allowed themselves to starve in the wilderness.

King Túpac Inca Yupanqui had them carefully brought together and appointed teachers to show them how to settle in villages, till the soil, and cover their nakedness, making them clothes of wool and cotton. Many large channels were dug for the watering of the fields, and the province was cultivated so thoroughly that it became one of the best in Peru. Later, it was embellished by the foundation of a temple of the Sun, a house for the chosen virgins and many other buildings: their gods were ordered to be overthrown and they were bidden to worship the Sun as their only and universal god, and not to eat human flesh under pain of death and total destruction: they were given priests and men skilled in laws and customs for their instruction, and they proved so docile that they were soon civilized, and those two provinces Cascayunca and Huancapampa were among the best in the Inca empire.

CHAPTER IV

The conquest of three large, warlike,
and recalcitrant provinces.

IT IS not known how many years passed after the conquest of the great province of Huancapampa before the Incas went on to conquer three other provinces, which also contain many different tribes, though, unlike the foregoing peoples, these lived in a civilized fashion, having villages and strongholds, and a system of government, and met together from time to time to discuss matters of advantage to them all. They did not recognize any lord, but by common consent elected governors for times of peace and captains for their wars, respecting and obeying them with great veneration while they exercised these offices. These three provinces, which were the principal ones, were called Cassa, Ayahuaca, and Callua. As soon as the Inca reached their confines he sent to summon the natives to receive him as their lord or prepare for war. They replied that they were prepared to die in defence of their liberty, for they had never had any lord and did not desire one. At this, war flared up and was bitterly contested by both parties, for the offers made by the Inca with peace and clemency were of no avail. To this the Indians replied that they wanted no peace from anyone who claimed to make them his vassals and deprive them of their present freedom, that they begged him to leave them free and go away in peace, since this was the greatest favor he could confer on them. The provinces rallied to one another's assistance in their hour of need with great promptness; they fought like men and killed many of the Inca's forces, which exceeded eight thousand men. On seeing this the Inca pressed them hard with fire and bloodshed using all the rigors of war; but the enemy suffered all this with great courage in order to preserve their liberty, and when some of their strongholds were reduced, those who escaped withdrew to others, and thence to others, and others, forsaking their own hearths and lands and heedless of their wives and children, for they preferred to die rather than see themselves subjected to an alien.

The Incas gradually gained ground from them until they were driven into the remotest part of their territory, where they fortified themselves and prepared to die resisting. There they were so tightly pressed that they were reduced to the last extremity, though they remained ever firm in not submitting to the Inca. When this was seen by some of their more prudent captains, they realized that they would all perish without cause while other tribes that had been as free as they had surrendered to the Inca, only to increase their possessions instead of being deprived of them. All the captains therefore discussed this among themselves and decided to submit to the Inca and give in, which was done, though not without a disturbance on the part of the soldiers, some of whom mutinied: but seeing the example of the captains and heeding the summons addressed to them to obey, they all surrendered.

Túpac Inca Yupanqui received them kindly and with regrets that they should have allowed themselves to reach a state of such extreme need. He gave instructions that they should be cared for as if they were his own children, and since many had perished in the war and left the land seriously underpopulated, he ordered colonists to be brought from other provinces to settle and till the area. Having provided everything necessary for its administration and for the introduction of their idolatry, he returned to Cuzco much wearied and strained by the war, though less on account of its hardships than because of the obstinacy and destruction of the Indians: he often said that if other provinces to be conquered in the future might not have been set a bad example by these stubborn tribes, he would have desisted from reducing them for the time being and waited until they were more ready to receive the authority of the Incas.

The great Túpac Inca Yupanqui spent some years in visiting his kingdoms and in embellishing them with special buildings for each village or province, such as royal palaces, fortresses, storehouses, irrigation channels, and temples of the Sun and for the chosen virgins, as well as other works of general importance for the whole kingdom, such as the royal roads he built, of which we shall speak at greater length elsewhere. In particular he took great pains with the works of the fortress of Cuzco which his father, Inca Yupanqui, had begun.

After spending some years in these peaceful occupations, the Inca returned to the conquest of the provinces to the north, called Chinchasuyu, so as to incorporate them in his empire. He marched on the province called Huánucu, which contains many separate tribes that waged cruel war on one another. They lived scattered across the land with no villages or civic organization. They had a few fortresses on the tops of hills, where they took refuge in defeat. The Inca conquered these tribes without difficulty, by showing his usual clemency, though the people of Huánucu proved warlike and recalcitrant in some encounters at the beginning of the campaign. Because of this the Inca's captains punished them severely, putting many of them to the knife, until the Inca restrained them, bidding them remember the law of the first Inca Manco Cápac, who bade them reduce the Indians to their rule with blandishments and presents and not by force of arms.

The Indians, chastened by the punishments they had received and tempted by the benefits and promises of the Incas, submitted without more ado and settled in villages and accepted the religion and rule of the Incas. The latter, who esteemed this beautiful province for its fertility and good climate, soon greatly advanced it: they made it the capital of many other provinces in that region, built there a temple to the Sun, a thing that was only done as a great favor in the most famous provinces, and founded there also a house for the chosen women. These two houses were served by twenty thousand Indians a year by rotation: the area was so thickly populated that some say there were thirty thousand. Pedro de Cieza, in his ch. lxxx, speaks of Huánucu in these words which are taken literally from that chapter (omitting other important matters):

In what is called Guánuco there was a royal palace of admirable construction, for the stones were large and carefully dressed and laid. This palace or dwelling place was the capital of the provinces nearest the Antis, and near it there was a temple of the Sun with a number of virgins and officials. It was so important in Inca times that there were more than thirty thousand Indians constantly serving it in shifts. The Incas' stewards undertook the collection of the ordinary tribute, and the surrounding districts pooled their services for this palace.

Thus far Cieza de León.

After the conquest of Huánucu, which we have related very summarily

(as we shall tell all the succeeding episodes unless there is anything remarkable to add, for I wish to finish off the conquests of the Inca kings
and describe the wars between Huáscar and Atahuallpa, the grandsons
of this Inca Túpac Yupanqui), the Inca had a powerful army summoned
together for the following year, proposing to conquer the great province
called Cañari, the capital of many others, and the abode of numerous
brave and warlike inhabitants. They wore their hair long as a distinguishing mark. It was piled up on top of the head and then twisted into a knot.
The nobler and more elegant wore as headgear a perforated hoop, about
three fingers high in the middle, through which colored skeins were
passed.

The poorer people and those less careful in their dress substituted a
similar strip from a gourd for the hoop and for this reason the whole
Cañari tribe was known to the other Indians for the insulting name of
matiuma, "gourd-head." By these distinguishing marks, and other similar
tokens which the Indians wore on their heads, it was possible in Inca
times to tell to what province and tribe each belonged. In my own time
they all still wore these tokens, but I am told that they are now quite confused. The Cañaris and their wives went scantily dressed and almost
naked before the Incas came, except that they all covered their private
parts. They had a great many lords, some of whom were allied together.
The latter were the lesser lords who united for defence against the greater,
who used their power to subject and tyrannize over the weaker.

CHAPTER V

The conquest of the Cañari province; its riches and its temple.

TÚPAC Inca Yupanqui went to the province of Cañari, and on the way
conquered the intervening region called Palta, whence the rich and
succulent fruit called *palta* was brought to Cuzco and to the hot valleys.
The Inca won the province very easily, by means of kindness and flattery
rather than by force of arms. The people are warlike, yet princes can
achieve much by clemency. The tribe's distinguishing mark is the flatten-
ing of the head: when a child is born a small board is placed before its

forehead and another behind its nape and the two are fastened together and daily drawn a little tighter. The baby is kept lying on its back and the boards are not removed until it is three years old: the result is a very ugly deformation of the head. Thus any Indian whose forehead was broader than usual or whose nape was flat would be scornfully referred to as *palta uma,* "Palta head." The Inca went on, leaving officials to attend to the spiritual and temporal administration of the province. On reaching the frontier of the Cañaris, he sent them the usual summons to surrender or resort to arms. The Cañaris held various views, but they at last agreed to obey the Inca and accept him as their lord, realizing that they could not offer resistance to him on account of their quarrels and differences. They came forward with great rejoicing to present their obedience to the Inca; and their example was followed by all the other *curacas* who readily gave in. The Inca received them with great affability and granted them favors: he had them provided with garments, of which they stood in great need, and ordered them to be instructed in the worship of the Sun and political system of the Incas. Before Inca times the Cañaris had worshipped the moon as their principal god and secondarily great trees and large stones that stood out from the rest, especially if they were mottled. After being taught by the Incas they worshipped the Sun, for whom they built a temple and a house of the chosen women, as well as many palaces for the kings.

The Incas had storehouses built for the royal revenues and for the vassals, extended the cultivated fields, dug irrigation channels, and in short carried out in that province everything they used to do when they made a conquest, though in this case with greater effect since the character of the country lent itself to all the improvements they undertook. The Cañaris were delighted and became excellent subjects, as they proved in the wars between Huáscar and Atahuallpa, though later, when the Spaniards appeared, the example of one of the Cañaris who went over to them was sufficient to cause the rest to love the Spaniards and hate the Incas, as we shall tell in due course. It is the way of the world to say "long live the winner!"

After the conquest of the Cañaris the great Túpac Inca Yupanqui established order among the many various tribes that are included under the title of Cañari. As a mark of greater regard he chose to be present in person at the indoctrination and the teaching of the idolatry and laws of the Incas. He spent much time about this in order to leave the province well settled and in peace, and thus cause the provinces so far unsubdued to become attached to the Inca empire and accept the rule of the Inca gladly. Among those tribes there was one called Quillacu. These are a very vile folk, so mean-spirited that they are afraid of having their land, their water, and even the very air taken away from them. This gave rise to an Indian saying which has found its way into Spanish: to say "he is a Quillacu" is to stigmatize a person for meanness or some other vile characteristic. The Inca gave special instructions that these pitiable people were to pay tribute in lice so as to oblige them to keep themselves clean and not allow themselves to be consumed by vermin.

Túpac Inca Yupanqui, and later his son Huaina Cápac greatly improved these provinces of the Cañaris and that known as Tumipampa with royal buildings and palaces, the inner walls of which were decorated with natural models of plants and animals in gold and silver: the doorways were covered with gold plates with precious stones, emeralds, and turquoises set in them. They built a famous temple to the Sun which was similarly plated with gold and silver, for these Indians strove to make a great display of their loyalty to their rulers and to please them bestowed all the treasure they could find on the royal palaces and temples.

Pedro de Cieza, in his ch. xliv, speaks at length of the splendor of the temples and royal lodgings in the provinces of the Cañaris as far as Tumipampa (which the Spaniards call Tome Bamba, altering the letters quite unnecessarily). In addition to this splendor Pedro de Cieza says there was a vast quantity of treasure in jars, basins, and other vessels, as well as a great quantity of fine clothing adorned with silver ornaments and *chaquiras*. In his history he recounts many episodes in the conquests we have mentioned. *Chaquira* is the name the Spaniards give to some very small gold beads, finer than seed-pearls, which the Indians make with such exquisite delicacy that the best silversmiths I met in Seville asked me how it was that the Indians contrived to solder the joints of such tiny pieces. I brought a small quantity of this work with me to Spain, where it was looked on as a great wonder. After speaking at length of the treasures of the Cañari privinces, Pedro de Cieza says: "Finally I cannot say anything that would not fall short of the truth in extolling the wealth the Incas displayed in their royal palaces." And speaking of the dwellings and the temple of Tumipampa in particular he adds:

Some Indians suggested that the greater part of the stones from which these dwellings and the temple of the Sun were built had been dragged by means of heavy ropes from the great city of Cuzco on the orders of King Huaina Cápac and the great Tupa Inca, his father. If so, it would be no small wonder, on account of size and great number of the stones and the great length of the road.

These are the words of the historian copied literally, and though they reflect his doubt of the truth of the Indian account by reason of the magnitude of the task, I myself, speaking as an Indian well aware of the powers of the Indians, will make bold to assert that it was so. For the Inca kings would order the stones to be conveyed from Cuzco as a mark of great favor and condescension toward this province, since, as we have often remarked, the Indians regarded stones and anything else from Cuzco as sacred objects. Thus, as it was a great favor for any of the country provinces to be given permission to build a temple of the Sun, since it made the natives of that province citizens of Cuzco, and as this favor was held in such high esteem among the Indians, it was without any exaggeration a vastly greater favor when the Inca ordered stones to be taken from Cuzco so that this temple and the palaces should not only resemble those of the capital, but be in fact the same, since they were made of the same stones and materials. And in order to enjoy such honors, which they regarded as divine, the Indians would think nothing of all the hardships to be undergone dragging the stones over the long and rocky road that stretches from Cuzco to Tumipampa, which must measure little less than four hundred leagues. The roughness of the road will be incredible to those who have not travelled over it, and I shall therefore not enlarge upon it here. And the report the Indians gave to Pedro de Cieza to the effect that the greater part of the stones with which the palaces and the temple of the Sun were built had been brought from Cuzco was rather with the object of boasting of the great favor shown them by the Inca kings than in order to emphasize the toil it had cost to bring them so far. This is clearly seen from the fact that our author does not refer anywhere else in his history to a similar incident relating to buildings. The above must suffice to show the richness and splendor of the royal palaces and temples of the Sun in Tumipampa and the whole of Peru.

CHAPTER VI

*The conquest of many other large provinces
as far as the confines of Quito.*

H AVING MADE provision for all the foregoing with regard to the provinces of the Cañaris, the Inca returned to Cuzco where he spent some
years in the task of governing his realms, conducting himself like a great
prince. But as the Incas, following the natural tendency of the powerful,
felt so great an ambition to extend their empire, it went against the grain
with them to spare much time from their campaigns. The Inca consequently raised a famous army and marched with it to the borders of
Tumipampa, where he began his conquest, winning many provinces between that point and the confines of the kingdom of Quito, a distance of
just under fifty leagues. The most famous of these provinces are: Chan-
chan Moca, Quesna, Pumallacta (this means "land of lions," which are
commoner there than in the neighboring districts, and are worshipped
as gods), Ticsampi, Tiucassa, Cayampi, Urcollasu, and Tincuracu, not to
mention many others of less note. These provinces were easily won, for
most of them are infertile regions thinly settled by very simple people
with no lords, system of government, civilization, laws, or religion: each
worshipped whatever he fancied as his god, and many of them did not
even know what worship was. They thus lived like wild beasts scattered
about the countryside, and it was consequently more difficult to instruct
them and reduce them to a civilized way of life than merely to subdue
them. They were taught to wear clothes and shoes, to till the soil, and to
dig irrigation channels and construct terraces to increase its fertility. In all
these provinces the Incas established storehouses for their armies and
lodgings for the king along the royal highways; but they did not build
temples to the Sun or houses for the chosen virgins because of the primitive and barbarous character of the inhabitants; in particular the tribute
of lice was imposed on them.

While Inca Túpac Yupanqui was busy with the conquest and indoctrination of the provinces mentioned above, other tribes to the west of these,
on the borders of the province the Spaniards call Puerto Viejo, sent ambassadors to him with presents and the request that he should receive them
as his vassals and subjects, and send them captains and teachers to show
them how to build villages and till the fields so that they might live like

men: in exchange they promised to be his loyal vassals. The originators of this mission were the members of the tribe called Huancavillca. The Inca received them very kindly, bestowed favors on them, and gave orders that all their requests be granted. Teachers were sent to instruct them in the religion of the Incas and in their customs, and engineers to dig irrigation channels, till the fields, and settle them in villages. Later they killed all the teachers and engineers, utterly ungrateful for the benefits they had received and scorning the promises they had made to the Inca. This is also related by Pedro de Cieza de León in his *Demarcation*, and as what he says is relevant to what we have often repeated in our history in speaking of the clemency and kindness of the Inca kings and of what they taught the Indians they reduced to their empire, I considered it appropriate to introduce here his very words on this matter so as to show that what we ourselves say of the Incas is said likewise by the Spanish historians. In his ch. xlvii, speaking of these provinces, he says as follows:

Returning then to the subject, I must add that, according to what I have heard from old Indians who were captains under Huaina Capac, in the days of the great Topa Inca Yupanqui there came certain captains with a force of men drawn from the ordinary garrisons that existed in many provinces of the kingdom and attracted these people by dint of persuasion and devices to make friends with Topa Inca Yupanqui and enter his service. Many of the chief people went to the province of the Paltas to do obeisance to the Inca, taking presents with them. He received them kindly and with much love, offering some of his visitors rich pieces of woollen cloth woven in Cuzco. And as he found it necessary to return to the upper provinces where he was so highly regarded that the people called him father and honored him with titles of distinction (and indeed he displayed such benevolence and love towards everyone that he acquired perpetual fame among the Indians), he departed in order to settle various matters referring to the government of his realms and was therefore unable to visit these provinces in person. However he placed there various governors who were natives of Cuzco and could explain to the Indians how to live so as to emerge from their primitive barbarism and attain various other advantages. But the Indians not only rejected the good intentions of those appointed by Topa Inca to reside in their provinces and set them on the path of civilization and social order and teach them agriculture so as to raise their standard of living: they even repaid the benefits they would have received if they had not been so ungrateful by killing all the Inca's officials, none of whom was left within the whole of the area, though they had done nothing to deserve such a fate by harming or oppressing the natives. It is said that Topa Inca heard of this act of cruelty, but that for important motives he dissimulated, being unable to undertake the punishment of those who had so treacherously slain his captains and vassals.

Thus far Pedro de Cieza, who ends his chapter here. The Inca, after the conquest of these provinces, returned to Cuzco to rest from the toils and anxieties of the war.

CHAPTER VII

The Inca conquers Quito; Prince Huaina Cápac is present.

AFTER Túpac Inca Yupanqui had spent some years in the enjoyment of peace and quiet, he resolved to embark on the conquest of the kingdom of Quito, on account of its fame and extent. It is seventy leagues long and thirty broad, an abundant and fruitful land well adapted for any agricultural and other improvements that might be carried out on behalf of the natives. He therefore had a force of forty thousand warriors made ready and went with them to Tumipampa, which is on the confines of the kingdom of Quito. Thence he despatched the usual summons to King Quito, whose name was the same as that of his country. The king was by nature very rude and barbarous, and consequently warlike and cruel, and feared by all his neighbors for his great might and the extent of his domains. Confident in his strength, the king retorted arrogantly that he was a lord and would not recognize any other. He wanted no new laws for he laid down for his vassals such laws as he saw fit, nor would he forsake his gods which had come down from his ancestors and suited him very well: they were deer and large trees which provided the meat and fuel on which his tribe supported itself. On hearing this reply the Inca refrained from provoking an immediate outbreak of war in the hope of attracting the natives with kindness and attentions, according to the practice of his ancestors. But the greater the restraint shown by the Inca, the more arrogantly those of Quito behaved. Because of this the war lasted many months and years, and many were killed and wounded on both sides in skirmishes, encounters, and minor engagements.

When Túpac Inca Yupanqui saw that the conquest was dragging out, he sent for his eldest son called Huaina Cápac, who was the heir to the throne, so as to give him the opportunity of gaining experience in the art of war. He gave orders for him to bring twelve thousand warriors with him. The prince's mother, the queen, was called Mama Ocllo: according to the Inca custom she was his father's sister. The prince was called Huaina Cápac, and this is commonly interpreted by the Spanish historians as being the words that mean "rich youth." This interpretation seems to be incorrect according to the popular language, but in giving titles and epithets to their ruler these Indians had, as we have said, a different meaning and a more elegant turn of speech than that of the common people. They would carefully study the signs their princes gave in boyhood of the royal virtues they seemed to promise for the future, and would consider likewise their great and generous deeds when they grew to manhood, thus deriving an appropriate title. And as this prince very early gave signs of a truly royal and magnanimous character, they called him Huaina Cápac, which as a royal title signifies: "rich in magnanimous deeds from boyhood." For the first Inca Manco Cápac received the name Cápac meaning "rich, not in worldly wealth, but in excellence and greatness of spirit," on account of his treatment of his first vassals, and the word was thereafter applied only to the royal house, which was called *cápac aillu,* or the royal lineage and descent. *Cápac raimi* was the name given to the chief priest of the Sun, and, to descend lower, *cápac runa,* "vassals of the rich one," was a phrase applied with reference only to the Inca and not to any other lord of vassals, however many he might have and however wealthy he might be. And many other things were similarly dignified with the word *cápac.*

Among the other great qualities of this prince, which caused his subjects to grant him the title Cápac so early, was a practice he always observed, both as prince and as monarch, and one that was esteemed by the Indians above all others. This was that he never denied any request made him by any woman, of whatever age, rank, or condition. He would reply to each suppliant according to her age: if she were older than the Inca he would say to her: "Mother, what you require must be done." If she were of about the same age, he would say: "Sister, what you wish shall be done." And if she were younger: "Daughter, what you request shall be granted." In all cases he would place his right hand on their left shoulder as a mark of regard and in confirmation of the favor he was granting. And he was so constant in his magnanimity that he would persist in it even in matters of the greatest moment that ran counter to his own majesty, as we shall see.

This prince, who was now about twenty years old, pressed on with the war and gradually conquered the kingdom of Quito, always offering the peace and friendship that the Incas habitually extended, though the enemy, being simple, naked, and uncivilized people, refused to accept them.

Seeing the prince's skilful conduct of the war, Túpac Inca Yupanqui returned to Cuzco to attend to the government of his realms, leaving Huaina Cápac with absolute powers in the field. With the aid of his good captains, the latter gained the whole kingdom in the space of three years, though the inhabitants of Quito maintain that it took five: this must include the period of nearly two years that Túpac Inca Yupanqui spent on the conquest before calling on his son to take over: for this reason the Indians say they both conquered Quito. The campaign lasted so long because the Incas, both father and son, were reluctant to make war with fire and the sword, but took the land gradually as the natives withdrew and abandoned it to them. It is said that the campaign would have gone on even longer if the king of Quito had not died at the end of the five years. His death was caused by grief at the loss of the greater part of his domains and by his awareness of his own inability to defend the rest: he dared not trust in the Inca's clemency or accept the offers extended to him, thinking that his past rebellious actions did not merit any pardon. Thus plunged into grief, the poor king despaired and died. His captains soon fell on the mercy of Inca Huaina Cápac, who received them with great kindness and presented them with a great quantity of the apparel that was so much esteemed by the Indians, as well as other much cherished gifts. He also gave orders for the common people to be treated with kindness and friendship. In short, he displayed every possible generosity toward the inhabitants in order to make patent his mildness and clemency, and he soon bestowed on the land itself proofs of his affection for it as the scene of his first conquest, for as soon as the war was done he gave orders for the building of a temple of the Sun and a house of the chosen virgins, with all the richness of adornment such houses and temples usually had, in addition to the provision of irrigation channels and all the other customary benefits for the greater fertility of the soil. The natives received very great advantages. The region had a great store of gold that had been extracted for its ruler and much more was later produced for Prince Huaina Cápac, since the natives were aware of his regard for them. This regard increased thereafter to such an extent that he performed favors far beyond anything previously undertaken by the Inca kings. This was the cause of the ruin of the Inca empire and finally of the extinction of the royal line.

Huaina Cápac went beyond Quito and reached another province called Quillacenca, "iron-nose," so called because the inhabitants bored the membrane between the nostrils and wore an ornament of copper, gold, or silver hanging over their lips like an earring. The Inca found them in a very primitive and filthy condition, ill-clad and consumed by vermin which they did not trouble to remove, with no religion and no idea of worship except that one might say they adored meat, since they are so inordinately fond of it that they will steal any animals they can lay hands on. Even today they eat with the greatest pleasure any horse, mare, or other beast they find dead, however rotten it may be. They were easily subdued, being a wretched race hardly better than wild beasts.

Thence the Inca passed to another province called Pastu [Pasto] inhabited by people no less vile than the last, but so different in their attitude toward meat that they never touched it, and if urged to do so, would say that they were not dogs. They were easily attracted to the service of the Inca, and given teachers to educate them toward a better way of life. Among the other physical benefits conferred on them was the tribute of lice which was imposed on them to prevent them from perishing from the vermin. From Pasto he went on to another province called Otavallu [Otavalo], inhabited by a more civilized and warlike race than the last. They made some resistance to the Inca, but soon gave in when they saw that they could not defend themselves against so powerful a prince. Imposing the necessary order on these people, the Inca passed on to another great province called Caranque, inhabited by a people of great savagery in their life and customs. They worshipped tigers, lions, and great serpents, offering human hearts and blood in their sacrifices. These they obtained from their neighbors, against all of whom they were at war for the mere pleasure of fighting and for the sake of having enemies to capture and slay for eating. At the outset they resisted the Inca with great ferocity, but they were disillusioned after a few days and surrendered. Huaina Cápac appointed teachers to instil them with his religion and morality; he deprived them of their idols, their blood sacrifices, and their cannibal practices. The latter they greatly resented for they were gluttons for human flesh. This was the last conquest among the provinces bordering in that quarter on the kingdom of Quito.

CHAPTER VIII

The three marriages of Huaina Cápac; the death
of his father; his sayings.

Túpac Inca Yupanqui, having completely abandoned warfare, devoted himself to the government of his empire. He visited the various provinces in turn in order to give pleasure to his vassals, who regarded it as a mark of the most signal favor to have the Inca in their country. He busied himself seriously with the building of the fortress of Cuzco, which his father had planned and begun. The work had been going on for many years, and more than twenty thousand Indians were engaged on it with such order and harmony that each tribe and province applied itself to the task and duty assigned to it like the servants in a well-ordered household. His governors made tours of inspection of the kingdom of Chile every two or three years: he sent a great deal of fine clothes and personal ornaments to the *curacas* and their families together with quantities of common clothes for their vassals. The caciques sent him a great deal of gold, plumage, and other products of those parts; and this went on until Don Diego de Almagro entered Chile, as we shall see.

After completing the conquest of the kingdom of Quito and the provinces of Quillacenca, Pasto, Otavalo, and Caranque, and taking the necessary steps for the administration of the whole frontier area, Huaina Cápac returned to Cuzco to report to his father what he had accomplished in his service. He was received in the greatest triumph. On his arrival he contracted his second marriage with his second sister, Rava Ocllo, for he had no children by his first wife and eldest sister, Pillcu Huaco, and in order that the heir to the throne should be legitimate on both the father's and the mother's sides, as the Inca law and custom required, he now married his second sister. He also contracted a legitimate marriage according to Inca law and custom with his cousin Mama Runtu, the daughter of his uncle Auqui Amaru Túpac Inca, his father's second brother. Auqui is a word meaning prince applied to the second sons of kings and by extension to all those of the royal blood, though never to the common people however great lords they might be. Amaru is the name of the very large snakes that exist in the Antis: the Incas took such names of animals, plants, or flowers implying that as these latter surpassed other things of their own kind, the bearers of such names were similarily remarkable among men.

King Túpac Inca Yupanqui and all the members of his Council decreed that these two women should be regarded as legitimate wives and treated as queens, like Huaina Cápac's first wife, and not as concubines, so that their children could succeed in due order to the throne. This step was taken because of the sterility of the first wife, which caused great scandal; and the third marriage was with his cousin because Huaina Cápac had not a third sister who was legitimate on both sides. For lack of a suitable sister he was given his cousin to wife as the female nearest the royal stem. By his sister Rava Ocllo Huaina Cápac had Huáscar Inca. Huáscar is an epithet, the meaning of which we shall explain in due course: Huáscar's real name was Inti Cusi Huallpa. By his cousin and third wife he had Manco Inca, who also succeeded to the throne, though only in name, for by then the royal power had been lost, as we shall see.

After living some years in peace and quiet, Túpac Inca Yupanqui fell ill and felt the approach of death. He sent for Prince Huaina Cápac and the rest of his children, who were extremely numerous, exceeding two hundred sons and daughters. To them he addressed the usual discourse which the Incas delivered instead of a testament. He urged them to maintain peace and justice and seek the welfare of their vassals, recommending them to show themselves in all things true children of the Sun. In particular he urged his heir to proceed with the conquest and reduction of the barbarians, attracting them to the worship of the Sun and to civilized practices. He bade his successor always to follow the example of his ancestors. Finally he entrusted him with the duty of punishing the treachery of the inhabitants of Puerto Viejo and the neighboring provinces, especially the Huancavillcas who had slaughtered the teachers and other officials sent by the Incas at their own request to educate them and raise them out of their previous savage way of life, for previously they did not know how to till the fields or cover their nakedness. It was wrong, he said, that such ingratitude should go unpunished lest other vassals might follow their bad example. He bade them remain in peace, for he was going to the other life whither his father the Sun was calling him to rest.

Thus died the great Túpac Inca Yupanqui, leaving among his people a perpetual memory of his piety, clemency, and mildness and of the many benefits he had performed for the whole empire. Because these last he was given, in addition to the epithets applied to the other kings, the title of Túpac Yaya meaning "shining father." By his legitimate wife Mama

Ocllo he left five sons in addition to the heir: the second was called Auqui Amaru Túpac Inca after his father [uncle] in order to keep the latter's name always alive: the third was called Quéhuar Túpac; the fourth Huallpa Túpac Inca Yupanqui, who was my maternal grandfather; the fifth, Titu Inca Rimachi; the sixth, Auqui Maita. His body was embalmed, and when I saw it in 1559 it seemed still to be living.

Padre Blas Valera refers to this Inca in the following words, which I have translated literally from his Latin into the vernacular.

Túpac Inca Yupanqui said: "Many say that the Sun is alive and is the maker of all things; it is proper that he who makes anything should be present with what is made, but many things are made when the Sun is not present; therefore he is not the maker of all things. It is clear that the Sun is not alive from the fact that it does not grow weary from its continuous burning; for if it were a living thing it would tire as we do, and if it were free, it would visit other parts of the sky where it is never seen. It is like a tethered animal that always goes round in a circle, or like an arrow which goes whither it is sent and not where it desires." It is also said that he often repeated a saying of Inca Roca, the sixth king, which seemed of great importance to the state: this was: "It is not right that the children of plebeians should be taught knowledge that is only suitable for the nobles, lest the lower classes rise up and grow arrogant and bring down the republic: it is enough that they learn the trades of their fathers, for governing is no matter for them, and it is discreditable to power and to the state that they should be entrusted to the common people." He also said: "Avarice and ambition prevent men from being able to moderate themselves and others, for avarice distracts the mind from the public and private good, and ambition limits the understanding so that it cannot receive the good counsel of the wise and virtuous, but only follows its own fancy."

Thus far Padre Blas Valera on the sententious sayings of Túpac Inca Yupanqui.

And as we are now approaching the time when the Spaniards arrived to conquer the empire, we must in the following chapter turn to the things that existed in Peru for the support of human life: we shall then proceed to the life and deeds of the great Huaina Cápac, and afterwards mention the things that were not found in Peru but were brought by the Spaniards, so that there may be no confusion between the one and the other.

CHAPTER IX

Maize and what they call rice, and other seeds.

T HE FRUITS of the earth on which the natives of Peru lived before the
Spaniards came were of various kinds, some of which grew above
ground and others below it. Of the fruits that grew above ground the
most important was the grain the Mexicans and the inhabitants of the
Windward Islands call maize and the Peruvians *sara,* for it is their bread.
It is of two kinds, one hard kind called *murchu,* the other soft and very
tasty, called *capia.* They eat it instead of bread, roasted or boiled in plain
water. The seed of the hard maize is the kind that has been introduced
into Spain: the soft sort has not been brought here. In some provinces it
is softer and tenderer than in others, especially in the province called
Rucana. For their solemn sacrifices, they used, as we have mentioned, a
maize loaf called *çancu,* and they made the same bread to eat as an occasional delicacy; they they called it *huminta.* The two names were applied, not because the bread was any different, but because one kind was
used for sacrifices and the other simply for eating. The flour was ground
by the women on broad flat stones. They laid the grain on one of these
and applied to it another stone, shaped like a rather elongated half moon,
though not rounded. It would be about three fingers broad, and the
women held it by the two points of the half-moon and moved it to and
fro on the maize. In this clumsy way they ground their corn and anything
else they needed to grind: because of the difficulty of the process they did
not eat bread regularly.

They did not grind with pestle and mortar, though they had these implements. Grinding in a mortar is done by the force of blows, but the
moon-shaped stone grinds whatever comes under it by its own weight and
the Indian women can easily handle it because of its shape, rocking it to
and fro and occasionally heaping the grounds in the middle of the flat
stone with one hand so as to grind them over again, while the other hand
is left free to hold the grindstone, which we might reasonably describe as
a *batán* from the strokes given alternately by the two hands. This method
of grinding is still in use. They also made porridge, which they call *api,*
and ate it with great relish, because it was only consumed on rare occasions. To complete our account, the flour was separated from the bran

by pouring it on to a clean cotton cloth and smoothing it over with the hand. The pure flour is so fine that it sticks to the cloth while the bran, being coarser, remains detached and is easily removed. The fine flour is collected in the middle of the cloth and poured out; then more is put on the cloth until the necessary quantity has been sifted. The sifting of flour was intended for the bread consumed by the Spaniards rather than for Indian use, since the latter were not so particular as to turn up their noses at bran, and the bran is not so rough, especially that from soft maize, as to need to be removed. The sifting was done in the fashion we have described for want of sieves, which only arrived from Spain with the introduction of wheat. I have seen all this with my own eyes, and until I was nine or ten years old I was brought up on *sara* or maize, the bread of which is known by three names—*çancu*, bread for sacrifices; *huminta*, special bread for celebrations; and *tanta* (the first syllable pronounced in the palate), common bread. Roast *sara* is called *camcha*, "toasted maize," a word that includes both the adjective and the noun: the *m* should be pronounced, for if the word were written with *n*, it would mean "ward, suburb," or "large enclosure." Cooked *sara* is called *muti* (by the Spaniards *mote*): the word includes both the noun maize and the adjective cooked. With maize flour the Spaniards make little biscuits, fritters, and other dainties for invalids and the healthy. As a remedy in all sorts of treatment experienced doctors have rejected wheat flour in favor of maize flour. The same flour is mixed with plain water to brew their beverage, which can be soured in the Indian fashion to make a very good vinegar. An excellent honey is made from the unripe cane, which is very sweet. The dried canes and their leaves are of great value, and cattle are very fond of them. The leaves from the ear of maize and the stalks are used by those who make statues who thus avoid weight. Some Indians, who are more intent on getting drunk than the rest, place the *sara* in steep and keep it there until it begins to sprout. They then grind it and boil it in the same water as other things. Once this is strained it is kept until it ferments. A very strong drink, which intoxicates immediately, is thus produced. It is called *viñapu*, or in another language *sora*. The Incas forbade its use since it at once produces drunkenness, but I am told that it has recently been revived by some vicious people. Thus the advantages I have mentioned are all derived from the various parts of the *sora*, and there are many other medical derivatives, both beverages and plasters, as we shall have occasion to mention later.

The second most important of the crops that are grown above ground is that called *quinua*, or in Spanish "millet" or "little rice" which it rather resembles in the color and appearance of the grain. The plant is rather like the wild amaranth in stalk, leaf, and flower: it is the latter that produces the *quinua*. The Indians eat the tender leaves in cooked dishes, for they are very tasty and nourishing. They eat the grain in pottages prepared in many different ways. The Indians also brew a drink from the *quinua*, as they do from maize, but it is only produced in regions where maize does not grow. The Indian inhabitants use flour made of *quinua* in various illnesses. In 1590 I was sent some of the seeds from Peru, but they were dead, and though planted at different times never sprouted.

In addition, the Peruvian Indians have three or four kinds of beans, shaped like broad beans but smaller: they are quite good to eat, and are used in cooked dishes. They are called *purutu*. They have lupins like those in Spain, though rather larger and whiter: they are called *tarui*. Apart from the edible types, there are others not suitable for eating: they are round and look like cut turquoises, though they have many different colors and are about as big as chick-peas. The general word for them is *chuy*, but they are given various names according to the color. Some of these names are comic and others are appropriate, but we shall not include them so as to avoid prolixity. They are used in many different games played by boys and by grown men: I remember taking part in both sorts.

CHAPTER X

The vegetables that grow in the earth.

MANY OTHER plants grow underground. They are sown by the Indians and afford them sustenance, especially in the provinces that do not produce *sara*. The principal one is called *papa* [potato] which serves as bread. It can be eaten boiled or roasted and is also put in stews. After exposure to the frost and sun for preservation according to the method we have already mentioned, it is known as *chuñu*. Another type is called *oca* which is very tasty: it is as long and thick as the big finger of a man's hand, and is eaten raw, since it is sweet, or cooked in stews. It is placed in the sun to make it keep, and without the addition of honey or sugar becomes like jam, for it possesses a great deal of sweetness. It is then called *cavi*. There is another like it in shape, though not in taste:

it is rather the opposite, for it borders on bitterness and can only be eaten cooked. It is called *añus;* and the Indians say that it reduces the procreative powers, but in order to prevent it from harming them, those who prided themselves on their gallantry used to hold a little rod or stick in one hand while they ate it, saying that in this way it lost its peculiar property and did them no harm. I heard them give the explanation and often saw them do this, though they implied that it was intended rather as a joke than as a serious acceptance of the foolish tradition of their elders.

What the Spaniards call *batatas* [sweet potatoes] and the Peruvian Indians *apichu* are found in four or five colors: some are red, others white, yellow, or purple, but there is little difference in taste. Those that have been brought to Spain are the least good. They also have the calabashes or melons known as Roman calabashes in Spain and in Peru as *sapallu*. They grow like melons, and are eaten boiled or stewed, but cannot be eaten raw. There are many good calabashes for making vessels, and they are called *mati*. The edible kind and those grown in Spain were unknown until the Spaniards arrived. There is another fruit that grows underground which the Indians call *inchic* and the Spaniards *maní* [peanuts]—all the names the Spaniards apply to the fruits and vegetables of Peru are taken from the language of the Windward Islands and have now been adopted in Spanish, which is why we give them. The *inchic* is very like almonds in consistency and taste. It is bad for the head if eaten raw, but tasty and wholesome if toasted. With honey it makes an excellent marzipan. An excellent oil useful for many illnesses is also extracted from *inchic*. In addition to these fruits another that grows underground is called by the Indians *cuchuchu*: I do not know that the Spaniards have yet given it a name, for this fruit does not occur in the Windward Islands, which have a very hot climate, but only in Collao, a very cold region. It is sweet and tasty, is eaten raw, and is very wholesome for weak stomachs. The roots are much larger than those of anise. The plant has no leaves, but the surface of the soil where it grows appears greenish, and it is thus that the Indians know that there is *cuchuchu* below. When the greenness disappears, the root is ready and is dug up. This plant and the *inchic* are luxuries for epicures rather than staple foods of the common people, though they do collect them and present them to the rich and powerful.

CHAPTER XI

The fruit of larger [plants and] trees.

THERE IS another excellent fruit which the Spaniards call cucumbers, because they rather resemble these in shape, though not in taste or in their wholesomeness for those suffering from fever or in the ease with which they are digested: in these ways they are rather the opposite of the Spanish cucumber. I do not recall the Indian name, though I have often racked my brain for days on end, and when I reproved memory for failing to retain so many words in our language it offered as an apology the word *cácham,* for cucumber. I do not know if my memory, relying on my inability easily to rectify its mistakes because of the distance that separates me from my own people, is indeed deceiving me: my relatives, the Indians and mestizos of Cuzco and the whole of Peru, shall be the judges of this piece of ignorance on my part and doubtless of many others in my work. I hope they will forgive me, for I am all theirs and have only undertaken a task so out of proportion with my feeble strength as this book, and without any hope of reward from anyone, in order to serve them. The cucumbers are of three sizes: the smallest are heart-shaped and are the best. They grow in small clumps. Another fruit called *chili* reached Cuzco in 1557. It has an excellent taste and is a great delicacy. It grows on a low plant which almost rests on the ground. It has berries like the arbutus, and is of the same size, though instead of being round it is rather elongated in the shape of a heart.

There are many other fruits that grow on tall trees; those we have already described rather resemble vegetables. Some occur in very hot zones, such as the coast and the Antis. Others are found in more temperate areas, like the hot valleys of Peru. But as all are obtainable and eaten everywhere, it is hardly necessary to deal with them separately, and I will mention them as they occur to me. To begin with, there are what the Spaniards call *guayavas* and the Indians *savintu.* These are round and about the size of the average apple, which they resemble in having a skin but no rind: inside, the pulp has a great many round seeds or pips rather smaller than those of a grape. Some are yellow outside and others red, and the red ones are found in two varieties, one so bitter as to be inedible and the other sweet with a very good taste. Still others are green outside and white within, and are much superior to the red variety, though in many of the coastal provinces the red are on the contrary regarded as better than the white. The Spaniards have made preserves of this and other fruits since the time when I left Peru, when such things were not made. I have seen a preserve of *savintu* in Seville. A passenger who was a friend of mine brought it from Nombre de Dios and invited me to take some because it was a fruit of my country.

Another fruit is called *pácay* by the Indians and *guavas* by the Spaniards. It grows in green pods more or less a cuarta long and two fingers broad. Inside the pod there are some little white wads exactly like cotton, which they resemble so closely that there have been cases of newly-arrived Spaniards who were unfamiliar with the fruit quarrelling with the Indians who offered them it because they supposed they were being made fun of by being given cotton to eat. They are very sweet, and if exposed to the sun can be kept a long time. Inside the wads or pods there is a black pip like small beans, which is inedible.

The fruit the Spaniards call pears, because they resemble Spanish pears by their green color and shape, are called *palta* by the Indians, since they spread from a province of this name to the rest of Peru. They are twice or three times the size of large Spanish pears. They have a thin and tender rind under which is the pulp, about a finger in thickness. In the middle there is a stone, or kernel, as sticklers for accuracy will prefer to call it. It is pear-shaped and as big as a common Spanish pear. No investigations about its uses have been carried out, but the fruit is very palatable and wholesome for invalids: eaten with sugar it makes a very rich preserve.

There is another coarser fruit which the Indians call *rucma* and the Spaniards *lucma*, so as not to except it from the usual corruption they give to all Indian names. It is a rough fruit, with nothing rich or delicate about it, though it is sweet rather than sour or bitter, and there is no proof that it is harmful. Nevertheless it makes poor and coarse eating. The fruit is the shape and size of oranges: in the middle of the pulp it has a stone very like a chestnut in color, size, and contents, which are white, but bitter and inedible. There was a sort of plum which the Indians call *ussun;* they are sweet and red: the day after they are eaten they discolor the urine which becomes so red that it seems tinged with blood.

CHAPTER XII

The mulli tree and the pimento.

AMONG THESE fruits we may include that of the tree called *mulli,*
which grows wild in the countryside. It produces long, narrow
bunches of fruit in the form of red berries the size of dry coriander seeds.
The leaves are small and evergreen. When ripe the outside of the berry
is sweet and soft and very tasty, but beyond this the rest is very bitter. A
beverage is prepared from these berries, by gently rubbing them with the
hands in hot water until all the sweetness has been extracted: care must
be taken not to get to the bitter part or the drink is spoilt. The liquid is
strained and kept for three or four days until it is ready. It makes a delightful drink, being full of flavor and very wholesome for diseases of
the urine, and side, kidneys, and bladder. If mixed with the maize beverage, the latter is improved and made more appetizing. If the water is
boiled until it thickens a very pleasant syrup is left. The liquid, if placed
in the sun with the addition of something or other, becomes bitter and
provides a splendid vinegar. We have said elsewhere how excellent the
milk and resin of *mulli* is for wounds. The liquid made by boiling the
leaves in water is good for washing the body and limbs and for curing
eczema and healing old wounds. The tender branches make excellent
toothpicks. I remember that the valley of Cuzco used to be adorned with
innumerable trees of this valuable variety, but within the space of a very
few years it was almost stripped of them, the reason being that they provide excellent charcoal for brasiers. Though the wood emits many sparks
on first being lit, when it has caught it burns on until nothing but ash is
left.

With these fruits—and at the head of them all according to the taste
of the Indians—we might include the condiment they invariably take
with everything they eat, whether stewed, boiled, or roasted. They call it
uchu, and the Spaniards say *pimiento de las Indias,* though in America
it is called *ají,* a word from the language of the Windward Islands. The
inhabitants of my own country are so attached to *uchu* that they will eat
nothing without it, even for instance a few uncooked herbs. Because of
the pleasure they obtain from it, they used to prohibit the eating of it
when they were observing a strict fast, which was thereby rendered the
stricter, as we have said elsewhere. The pimento is found in three or four

varieties. The commonest is thick, rather long, and not pointed. It is called *rócot uchu,* "thick pepper," to distinguish it from the next sort: it is eaten either ripe or green, that is before it takes on its final red color; others are yellow or purple, though I have only seen the red kind in Spain. There are other peppers about a *geme* long and as thin as the bigger finger, which were regarded as nobler than the others and therefore used in the royal household and among all the royal kin: I cannot remember its separate name. It is also called *uchu,* but the adjective escapes me. Another small round pimento resembles exactly a cherry with its stalk. It is called *chinchi uchu.* It is incomparably stronger than the rest, and only small quantities of it are found, wherefore it is the more esteemed. Poisonous creatures avoid the pimento and its fruit. I heard a Spaniard from Mexico say that it was very good for the sight, so he used to eat two roast peppers as a sort of dessert after every meal. All the Spaniards who come to Spain from the Indies are accustomed to it and prefer it to Oriental spices. The Indians esteem it so highly that they set it above all the other fruits we have mentioned.

CHAPTER XIII

The maguey tree and its uses.

AMONG THESE fruits we may include that of the tree the Spaniards call *maguey* and the Indians *chuchau,* for it has numerous uses which we have already mentioned. But Padre Blas Valera refers to many other virtues of the *chuchau* which cannot properly be omitted, though we shall describe them more briefly than does his Paternity. He says that the plant is ugly to look at and that its wood is light: it has a bark and grows to a height of twenty feet and a thickness like that of a man's arm or leg. The pith is spongy and very light, and is used by painters and carvers of images. The leaves are thick and about half a fathom long; they all sprout from the foot of the plant like those of the garden thistle, for which reason the Spaniards call the plant *cardón.* The leaves might more properly be called sheaths:[1] they have spines like those of the thistle. They yield a very bitter juice, which can be used for removing stains from

[1] *Penca*: a fleshy leaf.

clothing, or for curing cancerous sores or inflamed wounds, or for getting worms out of sores. The same juice when boiled with the roots in rain-water is excellent as a wash for relieving tiredness and for various medi-cinal purposes. The leaves that are left to ripen and dry at the foot of the stem yield a very strong hemp used for making the soles of shoes and ropes, halters, and cables, and other tough products. The leaves that are cut before they dry are crushed and put in a running stream so as to wash away their viscosity: they then produce a different hemp which is not so coarse as the former. It serves to make slings which are worn round the head, and clothing whenever there is a lack of wool or cotton. It re-sembles the Anjou canvas that comes from Flanders or the rougher bur-lap made in Spain. A finer hemp than either of these is also produced and it makes an excellent line for nets used by birdcatchers: these nets are stretched across certain narrow defiles between two hills and attached to trees. The Indians examine the bottom of the net to see what birds they have taken, for the birds are scared by the people and fall into the nets, which are extremely fine and dyed green so that they are quite in-conspicuous against the green of the ground and the trees and the birds fall into them more easily. Nets are made six, eight, twelve, fifteen, or even twenty fathoms or more across. The leaves of the *maguey* are con-cave and they collect rainwater, which is useful for various diseases. The Indians collect it and make a very powerful drink by mixing it with maize or *quinua* or the seed of the *mulli* tree. They also make honey and vinegar with it. They grind the roots of *chuchau* and make little cakes of soap which the Indian women use for washing their heads, relieving headaches, removing blotches from the face, and for strengthening the hair and dyeing it black. Thus far Padre Blas Valera: I have added only the size of the nets, a point that is worthy of note, but which he omits. We shall now say how they make their hair grow and dye it black, a fearsome and barbarous procedure.

The Indian women of Peru all have long, loose hair and wear no headgear, or at most a band as broad as the thumb round their heads. The only exception is the Collas, who cover their heads because the climate is so cold in their district. As the Indian women wear their hair uncovered they are naturally very fond of having it very long and black. If it goes brown or splits or falls out when combed, they boil a cauldron of water with herbs in it over the fire. One of the herbs must be the root of the *chuchau* mentioned by Padre Blas Valera, but I have seen it made on more than one occasion with several ingredients, though I was too young to notice how many or what herbs they were. In order to get her hair in the cauldron which was boiling away with this decoction on the fire, the woman would lie on her back with some protection so that she did not burn her neck. They also took precautions against the boiling water touching the head and scalding the flesh. The hair that was not covered with water was wetted so that it too should enjoy the virtues of the brew. They would submit to this voluntary torment for, I was going to say, nearly two hours, though as I was a boy at the time I did not take note so carefully that I could now assert exactly how long. I did not however fail to wonder at the ordeal, which seemed to me a severe one for those who submitted to it. However in Spain I have ceased to wonder, after seeing what many ladies do to bleach their hair by perfuming it with sulphur, wetting it in gilder's aqua fortis, exposing it to the sun at midday in the dog-days, and other processes they have contrived. I do not know which treatment is worse and more injurious to the health, the Indian or the Spanish. The Indian women, after washing their hair again to remove the scum from the boiling, appear with their hair blacker and more lustrous than the feathers of a newly-moulted raven. This and much more will the longing for beauty induce people to undergo.

CHAPTER XIV

The banana, the pineapple, and other fruits.

To RETURN to the fruits, we shall now refer to some of the most remarkable that grow in the Antis of Peru which are the hottest and dampest districts. We shall not mention them all to avoid prolixity. The first place must be given to the tree and fruit the Spaniards call *plátano,* the plantain, or banana. It resembles the palm in shape and in having broad, green leaves growing at the top. The trees grow wild and require a rainy climate like that of the Antis. The fruit is found in bunches of such size that, as Padre Acosta says in his Book IV, ch. xxi, some have been encountered with three hundred bananas. The banana has a skin which is neither rind nor bark, and is easily removed. They are about a cuarta long and three fingers in thickness.

Padre Blas Valera, who has also written about bananas, says the bunches are cut when they begin to ripen lest their weight should pull down the tree, which is soft and delicate and useless for wood or even as fuel. The bunches are ripened in jars and covered with a certain herb that helps them to mature. The inside is tender, soft, and sweet. If exposed to the sun, it becomes like a preserve. It is eaten raw or roasted, boiled, or stewed in pottages, and tastes very good in all these styles. Various preserves are made of the banana with a little honey or sugar (only a little is needed). The bunches that ripen on the tree are sweeter and tastier. The trees are about two varas high, some more, some less. There are other smaller bananas called Dominicans to distinguish them from the larger variety. In this case the skin is white when the bunch appears, and when the fruit is ripe it is black and white in patches. It is half the size of the other kind and much superior, though there are not so many of this sort.

Another fruit is what the Spaniards call *piña* because in appearance and shape it resembles a Spanish pinecone, though there is no other connection between the two plants. The Peruvian *piña,* when the rind is removed with a knife, reveals a very tasty white pulp, all of which can be eaten. It has a faintly acid taste which makes it even more palatable. In size they are twice as big as pine cones. There is also in the Antis another fruit which the Spaniards call *manjar blanco,* since when cleft in two it resembles two bowls of *manjar blanco* in color and flavor. It has inside black pips like small almonds, which are not edible. In size the fruit is like a small melon. It has a hard rind like a dry calabash and almost as thick. Inside the much-esteemed pulp is found. It is sweet but with a slight bitter tang which makes it luscious.

Many other fruits grow wild in the Antis, such as what the Spaniards call "almonds" and "walnuts" because of some slight resemblance with those of Spain. For the first Spaniards who went to the Indies had a mania for applying the names for Spanish fruits to American fruits with very little likeness and no real connection. Indeed when compared the fruits are seen to differ in far more respects than they resemble one another, and some are even the opposite, not only in taste but in their properties, as are these walnuts and almonds, which are of little importance and which we shall dismiss together with other fruits and vegetables of the Antis to turn to others of greater worth and note.

CHAPTER XV

The precious leaf called coca, and tobacco.

IT WOULD not be right to pass over the herb the Indians call *cuca* and the Spaniards *coca,* which was and still is the chief source of wealth of Peru for those who are engaged in the trade: we should indeed give a full account of it, such is the esteem in which the Indians hold it by reason of the many remarkable virtues they had discovered in it of old, and the many more that the Spaniards have found in applying it to medicine. Padre Blas Valera, a close observer who spent many years in Peru and left it more than thirty years after I did, writes of both kinds of use, as one who had personal experience of them: I shall simply repeat what his Paternity has to say, and later add the few points he omitted, so as not to run to length by going into detail. He says:

Coca is a certain small tree as big and as high as a vine. It has few branches, but many delicate leaves as broad and half as long as one's thumb. They have a good, but not a soft smell. Indians and Spaniards alike call the leaves *cuca.* It is so agreeable to the Indians that they prefer it above gold, silver, and precious stones. They display great care and diligence in planting it and greater in harvesting it. They pluck the leaves by hand and dry them in the sun; and when so dried they are eaten by the Indians, but they do not swallow them, merely savoring the taste and swallowing the juice. The great usefulness and effect of coca for laborers is shown by the fact that the Indians who eat it are stronger and fitter for their work: they are often so satisfied by it that they can work all day without eating. Coca protects the body from many ailments, and our doctors use it in powdered form to reduce the swelling of wounds, to strengthen broken bones, to expel cold from the body or prevent it from entering, and to cure rotten wounds or sores that are full of maggots. And if it does so much for outward ailments, will not its singular virtue have even greater effect in the entrails of those who eat it? It has another great value, which is that the income of the bishop, canons, and other priests of the cathedral church of Cuzco is derived from the tithe on the coca leaf, and many Spaniards have grown rich, and still do, on the traffic in this herb. Nevertheless, some people, ignoring these facts, have spoken and written strongly against this little bush, moved only by the fact that in former times the heathens offered coca to their idols, as some wizards and diviners still do: because of this it is maintained that the use of coca should be completely suppressed and prohibited. This would certainly be good counsel if the Indians merely offered this herb and nothing else to the Devil. But the former heathen (and the idolaters of today) sacrificed crops, vegetables, and fruits that grow below ground and above, and offered their drink and cold water, and wool, and their garments, and cattle, and a great deal else, in short all they might possess, and as they cannot be deprived of all these things, neither can they of coca. They should be instructed to abhor superstition and serve truly one God, availing themselves of all these things in a Christian fashion.

Thus far Padre Blas Valera.

To supply what is missing for full measure, we may add that the bushes are as high as a man. They are grown by placing the seed in a nursery as is done with greenstuffs. Small holes are dug for the plants, as for vines, and they are layered like the vine. Great care is taken that no root however small is bent, for this is enough to cause the whole plant to wither. The leaves are plucked, each branch being taken separately between the fingers, which are run along it as far as the new shoot, which must be left or the whole branch shrivels. Both sides of the leaf are exactly like that of the arbutus in color and shape, but they are very thin and it would take three or four of them to equal the arbutus in thickness. I am glad to find objects of Spain that can be so appropriately compared with those of my own country yet which do not exist there: it is thus much easier for those on both sides to understand and know one another. When the leaves have been plucked they are dried in the sun; they are not completely dried or they lose most of their greenness which is much prized, and turn to dust because of their delicacy; nor must they remain very damp, or they grow moldy and rot in the baskets in which they are packed for carriage. They must thus be dried to a point between these extremes. The baskets are made of split canes of which there are plenty, both large and small, in those provinces of the Antis. The outsides of the baskets are covered with the leaves of the thick canes, which are more than a *tercia* broad and more than half a vara long: thus the coca is prevented from getting wet; for water soon damages it. The baskets are woven with a special kind of hemp that grows in the district. When one considers the quantity of each of these things that is necessary to turn the coca to account, one is rather inclined to give thanks to God for supplying everything wherever it is needed than to attempt to describe it, for it seems incredible. If it were necessary to bring all these requirements from outside, the labor and cost would outweigh the value of the product. The herb is plucked every four months, or thrice yearly, and if the ground is carefully weeded so that all the plants that grow in that hot, wet soil are removed, each harvest is brought forward by a fortnight, so that there are nearly four a year. For this reason a greedy tithe collector bribed the overseers of the most important and wealthiest estates in the district of Cuzco to see to it that the fields were frequently weeded. In this way he deprived the collector for the following year of two-thirds of the tithe on the first crop. This led to a bitterly-contested suit between them, the result of which I never knew, for I was only a boy at the time.

Among the other virtues of coca, it is said to be good for the teeth. With regard to the strength it gives to those who chew it I remember a tale I heard in Peru from a gentleman of quality and merit called Rodrigo Pantoja, who, while travelling from Cuzco to Rímac, came across a poor Spaniard (for there are also poor people over there as there are here) who was walking along with a little daughter of two years old on his back. Pantoja knew him and they fell into conversation.

The gentleman asked: "Why are you burdened like that?"

The other replied: "I have no means to hire an Indian to carry the little girl, so I'm carrying her myself."

At this Pantoja looked at the man's mouth and saw it was full of coca, and as in those days the Spaniards abhorred everything the Indians ate and drank as if they were idolatries, and especially chewing coca (which seemed a vile thing to do), Pantoja asked: "Then if your need is so great why are you chewing coca as the Indians do, when Spaniards hate and detest the stuff?"

The soldier replied: "Sir, I used to abominate it no less than the rest, but necessity forced me to imitate the Indians and chew it, and I can tell you that if I didn't chew it I couldn't carry this burden. It is because of it that I feel strong and vigorous enough to cope with the task."

Pantoja was surprised at hearing this and repeated the story in many different places. Afterwards the Spaniards were inclined to believe the Indians when they said that they ate the herb because they needed it, and not from greed. And this can be credited, for its taste is not pleasant. Later we shall say how it is transported to Potosí and describe the trade in coca.

We have spoken elsewhere of the bush the Spaniards call tobacco and the Indians *sairi*. Dr. Monardes writes wonders of it. Sarsaparrilla needs no one to sing its praises, for its effects against the buboes and other diseases in both the Old World and New speak loud enough. There are many other herbs in Peru of such virtue for medicinal purposes that, as Padre Blas Valera says, if they were all known there would be no need to bring herbs from Spain or elsewhere; but the Spanish doctors set so little store by them that even those which used to be known to the Indians have in the main been forgotten. Because of their vast numbers and their smallness it would be difficult to mention all the herbs: suffice it to say that the Indians eat them all, sweet and bitter alike; some they consume raw, like lettuces and radishes, others are put in stews and pottages and form the staple diet of the common people who have no great abundance of meat or fish as the wealthy do. Bitter herbs such as the leaves of the bushes they call *sunchu* and others like them are cooked in two or three waters, dried in the sun, and kept for the winter when there is a lack of such things. They go to such pains to seek and store herbs to eat that none are over-looked: even the waterweeds and creatures that grow in rivers and streams are collected and prepared for food.

CHAPTER XVI

Their tame animals: the flocks they kept.

THE DOMESTIC animals that God gave to the Indians of Peru were, according to Padre Blas Valera, conformable to the mild character of the Indians themselves. They are indeed so tame that a child can drive them anywhere, especially those that are used as beasts of burden. They are of two sorts, one larger than the other. In general the Indians call them by the name llama, "cattle": the shepherd is *llama michec,* "grazer of flocks." To distinguish, the larger are called *huanacullama* because of their similarity to the wild animals called guanaco from which they only differ in color, the tame animals being of all colors, as horses are in Spain, while the wild guanaco has only one color, a polished chestnut with the flanks of a lighter brown. These creatures are as tall as European deer, and resemble no other animal so much as the camel, without its hump and without a third of its bulk. They have long smooth necks, the skin of which the Indians flayed and greased with tallow till it was soft and appeared to have been tanned, when it was used for the soles of their shoes. But as it was not really tanned, they used to take their shoes off to cross streams or when there had been heavy rains, otherwise they became like tripe when they got wet. The Spaniards used the skin for making fine reins for their horses, similar to those brought from Barbary. It serves likewise for bands and cruppers for saddles, and for whips and thongs, and straps for girths and light riding saddles.

The llama is also used by Indians and Spaniards for the transport of merchandise to all parts, though they travel best between Cuzco and Potosí where the land is flat. The distance is of nearly two hundred leagues; and they also go between the mines and many other places with all sorts of supplies, Indian garments, Spanish wares, wine, oil, preserves, and everything else that is used in the mines. The chief article they bring to Cuzco is the herb called coca. In my time there were in Cuzco flocks of six hundred, eight hundred, and a thousand and more head for the carriage of these goods. Flocks of less than five hundred were thought nothing of. The weight they can carry is three or four arrobas; and they can cover three leagues in a day, for they are not capable of heavy work. They must not be pressed beyond their usual pace or they tire: they then lie down on the ground and there is no getting them up whatever one does, even if the burden is removed. One can then flay them, and there is no way of getting them to move. If one persists in trying to get them to rise and goes up to them to lift them, they defend themselves with the dung they have in their maw which they bring up and spit at the person nearest to them, aiming it as his face for preference. They have no other weapon of defence, not even horns as deer have. Despite the great difference between them and European animals, the Spaniards call them rams and sheep. To avoid tiring them, each flock has forty or fifty unladen animals, and whenever any beast is found to be flagging its burden is at once removed and transferred to another, before it lies down; for once it does this, there is no solution but to have it killed. Their meat is the best in the world: it is tender, tasty, and wholesome. The meat of the four- or five-month-old lamb is recommended by doctors for invalids in preference to chicken.

In the time of the Viceroy Blasco Núñez Vela, in 1544 and 1545, there appeared various plagues in Peru including that known to the Indians as *carache* or llama-mange. It was a very dire disease, hitherto unknown. It afflicted the flank and belly and then spread over the whole body, producing scabs two or three fingers high, especially on the belly, which was the part most seriously affected and which came out in cracks two or three fingers deep, such being the depth of the scabs down in the flesh. Blood and matter issued from the sores, and in a few days the animal withered and was consumed. The disease was highly contagious, and to the horror of both Indians and Spaniards it accounted for two-thirds of all the animals, both *paco* and *guanaco*. From them it was transmitted to the wild varieties, the *guanaco* and *vicuña*, but it was not so severe on them because of the colder zone they frequent and because they do not collect in such numbers as the tame animals. Even the foxes were not spared: indeed they suffered terribly, for in 1548, when Gonzalo Pizarro was in Cuzco after his victory in the battle of Huarina, I saw many foxes suffering from the plague: they crept into the city by night and lay about in the streets and squares, some alive and some dead, with two, three or more holes through their bodies caused by the disease. I remember that the Indians, who are very superstitious, foretold from the foxes the death and destruction of Gonzalo Pizarro, which occurred soon after. When the outbreak began, one of the desperate remedies that occurred was to slaughter or bury alive the victim. This is mentioned by Padre Acosta in Book IV, ch. xli. But it continued to spread, and neither Indians nor Spaniards knew what to do to stop it, so they tried to cure it with artificial fire by boiling together corrosive sublimate, brimstone, and other powerful substances which they fancied might avail, but the animals only died the sooner. They tried applying boiling lard, but still with fatal results, and many other remedies which I have forgotten were attempted, all without success, until gradually it was discovered by experience that the best cure was to rub affected parts with warm pig's lard and to prevent the animals from scratching their flanks, which is where the mange first appears, and so cure it before it spread. In this way the disease was greatly curbed and its contagiousness much reduced, for it has never reappeared in so virulent a form as on this first occasion. The virtues of their lard enhanced the value of pigs, which breed so greatly that they would otherwise be of little value. It is worthy of note that though the plague was so general it did not affect deer of any kind, which must be of a different complexion. I remember too that in Cuzco they adopted St. Antoninus as advocate and defender against this plague, and a great feast was held every year in his honor: it must still continue.

Although the flocks are so large and the distances so great, the animals do not put their owners to any expense by way of food, lodging, shoes, packsaddles, trappings, girths, cruppers, or any of the numerous other requirements that carriers need for their beasts. When they reach the place where they are to spend the night, they are unloaded and turned loose in the fields where they graze on whatever grass they find. They keep themselves in this way for the whole journey and require neither grain nor straw. They will eat maize if given it; but the creature is so noble that it can manage without even when working. It does not wear shoes, for it is cloven-footed, and has a pad instead of a hoof. No packsaddle is needed, for their wool is thick enough to take the weight of their load, and the carriers take care to arrange the packs on either side, so that the strap does not touch the spine, which might prove fatal. The packs are not attached with the cord carriers call twine [*lazo*], since as the animal carries no frame or saddle, the weight of the burden would cause it to cut the flesh. The packs are therefore sewn together by the canvas, and though the sewing rests across the backbone, it does no harm provided the strap is kept aside. The Indians have twenty-five animals to load and unload, but they help one another, for as the packs are fastened together one alone could not cope with them. The merchants take their own tents and set them up wherever they decide to pass the night, piling their merchandise inside. They do not sleep in the villages, for it would waste a great deal of time to have to take the llamas out of the village and bring them back. The journey between Cuzco to Potosí takes four months, two going and two coming back, without allowing for the time taken to dispose of the merchandise. A choice llama was worth eighteen ducats in Cuzco, and an inferior one twelve or thirteen. The chief articles of merchandise they carried were coca and Indian textiles. All this was true when I was there and I saw it with my own eyes: I do not know what happens nowadays. I met many of the wayfarers, and on some routes they could sell a basket of coca for more than thirty pesos of assayed silver. Although carrying burdens of such value and returning with loads of silver amounting to thirty, forty, fifty, or a hundred thousand pesos, neither Spaniards nor Indians ever feared to sleep in the open with no other company or security than their comrades, for there were no thieves or bandits. The same security existed in dealing with the merchandise to be carried, or the crops collected for the Spanish landowners, or loans of money. However great the amount of the sale or loan, there was no written document or obligation—everything was done verbally, and those concerned always kept their word. It often happened that a Spaniard would gamble away a sum owed him by another who was in some distant place, and he would say to the winner: "Tell so-and-so that he is to pay you the sum he owed me, because you have won it from me." This was sufficient for the winner to be trusted and claim the debt, however large. Such was the faith then placed in the word of a merchant, a landowner who was a lord of Indians, or a soldier. This credit, confidence, and security on the highway was common to all of them. It might be called the golden age, and I suppose it still prevails.

In peacetime when there was no fighting, many soldiers, very noble gentlemen, avoided idleness by engaging in this trade of bringing coca and Indian textiles to and from Potosí and selling it wholesale and retail. In this way men, however noble, could employ their resources in carrying on business: they did not deal in Spanish cloth, which is sold by the vara in shops. Many of them delighted in accompanying their possessions, and because of the slow movement of the flock, they would take with them a pair of hawks, retrievers, greyhounds, and their arquebus, and while the flock pursued its unhastening march, they would make off in one direction or another and hunt, so that by the time they stopped for the night, they would have caught a dozen partridges, or a guanaco or vicuña or deer, for the land has wide, open spaces and is well stocked. In this way they amused themselves during the journey, which was rather an excuse for hunting and diversion than for trading; and the rich and powerful landowners greatly esteemed the noble soldier who did this. Padre José de Acosta (Book IV, ch. xli) speaks at length in praise of the animal and its merits.

Of the smaller stock, the *pacollama*, there is less to say, for they are of no use for transport or any other service, but only to eat, their flesh being slightly inferior to the other, and for their wool, which is long and excellent. It is used for making the three types of textiles we have mentioned. The colors are excellent—for the Indians are expert dyers—and never fade. The Indians do not use the milk of either kind of animal either to drink or for cheese-making. They do in fact produce very little milk, only enough to bring up their own young. In my time cheeses were sent from Majorca to Peru, and no others. They were much esteemed. The milk was called *ñuña*, and the teat and to suckle and give suck also *ñuña*.

Of the Indian dogs we should mention that they had not the differences that European pedigree dogs have. They only had what are called mongrels here: they were large and small. The general word for them was *alco*, "dog."

CHAPTER XVII

The wild flocks and other creatures.

BEFORE the arrival of the Spaniards the Indians of Peru had only the two types of domestic cattle we have mentioned, *paco* and guanaco. They had more wild cattle, but treated it like the tame, as we have said in speaking of the periodical hunts that were held. One of the wild varieties was called guanaco, a word also applied to the larger tame llama which resembled it in size, shape, and the quality of its wool. The flesh of the wild guanaco is good, though inferior to that of the tame kind. They are, in short, very much alike. While the females browse in the valleys, the males keep watch on the high hills and give warning by whinnying like horses if they see people. If they are approached, they take flight, driving the females in front. Their wool is short and coarse, but is also used by the Indians for textiles. In my time they were hunted with greyhounds and many were killed.

There is a wild animal called vicuña which resembles the smaller domestic animal, the *paco*. It is a delicate creature with little flesh, but much fine wool. Of its medicinal virtues Padre Acosta writes at great length, as he does in dealing with other animals and birds found in the Indies; but as his Paternity is writing of the whole of the New World, it is necessary to pay special attention to his passages referring particularly to Peru. I refer to him in much of what I am saying. The vicuña is taller than the largest goat. The color of its wool is very light chestnut, or what is called *leonado*. It runs so fast that no greyhound can catch it, and it must be killed with arquebusses and by trapping, as in Inca times. It grazes in the highest deserts, near the snowline. The flesh is edible, though less so than that of the guanaco. The Indians appreciated it because they had little meat.

There were deer in Peru, though they were much smaller than those of Spain. The Indians call them *taruca*. In the times of the Incas they were so common that they came into the villages. There are also smaller or fallow deer. All these wild animals yield the bezoar stone, though in my time this was never thought of. There are wild cats of two or three kinds, called *ozcollo*. There are foxes, much smaller than the Spanish kind, called *átoc*. There is another kind of animal smaller than a domestic cat which Indians call *añas* and the Spaniards *zorriña*. They have such a stench that if they were scented as much as they stink they would be more prized than ambergris and musk. They visit the villages at night, and even though windows and doors are shut one can still catch their stench, even though they are a hundred paces or more away. There are not many of them: if there were, the world would be poisoned. There are domestic and wild rabbits which differ in color and taste. They are called *coy*, and are also different from Spanish rabbits. The tame kind have been brought to Spain, but are little esteemed: the Indians, being poor in meat, regard them highly and eat them as a great treat. Another type of rabbit is the *vizcacha,* with a long tail like a cat's. They breed in desert places where there is snow, though this does not prevent men from going there to kill them. In the times of the Inca kings and for long afterwards (for I have seen this myself), the hair of the *vizcacha* was used and spun so as to vary the colors of the fine textiles they made. Its color is a light ashy-grey, and it is soft and smooth in texture. It was very much esteemed by the Indians and only used for the clothes of the nobles.

CHAPTER XVIII

Lions, bears, tigers, and monkeys.

THERE ARE lions, though they are not numerous. They are neither so large nor so fierce as the African kind: they are called *puma.* There are also bears, but they are quite rare. As the whole of Peru is free from thick forests[1], these fierce animals do not occur: also the Incas, as we have mentioned, ordered them to be killed in the royal hunts. They call the bear *ucumari.* The only tigers are in the Antis where the forests are thick, and there are also the great snakes called *amaru* which reach twenty-five or thirty feet in length and are thicker than a man's thigh. There is also a multitude of other smaller snakes called *machác-huay,* as well as poisonous vipers and many other harmful creatures, of all of which Peru is free. A Spaniard I knew killed in the Antis on the edge of the province of Cuzco a great lioness that was crouching in a high tree: he brought it down with four darts and found in its belly two whelps by a tiger, for they had the father's stripes. I have forgotten the name for the tiger in the general language of Peru, although it is the fiercest animal there is in my country. When I reproach my memory for its negligence, it asks me why I chide it for something I myself am guilty of and reminds me that it is forty-two years since I spoke or read the language. I hope this excuse will serve if anyone blames me for having forgotten my own tongue. I think the tiger is called *uturuncu,* though Padre Acosta gives the name to the bear in the form *otoroncos,* thus corrupted in Spanish. I do not know which of us is wrong, but I think his Paternity. There are other creatures

---

[1] *Montañas bravas: montaña* is applied in Peru not to the mountain chain of the Andes (the Sierra), but to the foothills and forests to its east.

in the Antis resembling cows; they are as big as small cows and have no horns. The skin is extremely strong for leather, and some writing in praise of it say it is tougher than mail. There are wild boars that partly resemble domestic pigs. All these animals are rare in the side of the Antis bordering Peru, and I do not propose to deal with the more distant Antis.

Monkeys of various kinds, large and small, are numerous; some with tails, others without. We might say a great deal of their characteristics, and as Padre Acosta writes of them at length in his Book IV, ch. xxxix, and his account coincides with what I have heard the Indians say and in part with what I have seen, I shall reproduce here what he has to say, as follows:

There are innumerable *micos* throughout the forests of the islands, the main, and the Antis. They are of the monkey kind, but differ from them in having a long tail and including some varieties three or four times as large as ordinary monkeys. Some are black all over, some bay, some grey, some striped, and mixed. Their quickness and cunning is remarkable, for they seem to have discourse of reason; and when they move through the trees, they seem almost to be imitating birds. In Capira, passing from Nombre de Dios to Panama, I saw one of these *micos* jump from one tree to another on the other side of the river, which astonished me. They grip a branch with their tail and hurl themselves where they like. If the space is so great that they cannot cross it at a leap, they have an amusing trick of taking one another's tails to make a sort of chain: then they all sway or swing until the first, helped by the momentum of the rest, can jump and grip the branch and support the rest as they arrive, clinging to one another's tails.

Their tricks, cunning and pranks would take a long time to describe. Their ingenuity when pressed by need seems hardly to belong to brute beasts but to come from human understanding. I saw one at Cartagena in the governor's house and the things I was told of it hardly seem credible, such as that when they sent it for wine to the tavern, they put the money in one of its hands and the wine-jug in the other and it could never be made to give up the money until it had been given the jug with the wine. If the boys in the street shouted at it or threw things, it would place the jug on one side and pick up stones and throw them back at the boys until the coast was clear and it could pick up its jug again. Moreover, though it was quite a tippler—I saw it drink wine which its master poured for it from a height—it never touched the jug unless it was allowed. I was also told that if it saw women dressed up it would pull their hats off and upset them. Some of this may have been exaggeration, for I did not see it all, yet I do not think there can indeed be any animal that understands and adapts itself to human intercourse as does this variety of monkey. So many tales are told of them that rather than seem to give credit to fables, or that others should consider them to be fables, I think it best to leave the subject, merely giving praise to the Author of all creatures who seems to have made one kind of animal that does nothing but laugh or cause laughter for the amusement, delight, and entertainment of mankind. Some have written that Solomon received these monkeys from the West Indies, but I consider that they came from the East Indies.

Thus far Padre Acosta.

I might add that monkeys carry their young on their backs until they are of an age to fend for themselves: they cling with their arms round their mothers' necks and their legs round their bodies. The forming of chains that Padre Acosta mentions is done to cross streams or rivers that are too large to jump across. They suspend themselves, as he says, from a tree facing another tree and swing to and fro until the lowest monkey contrives to seize a branch of the other tree; he then climbs up it until he is level with the top monkey, whereupon he shouts to the other to let go. This is done, and they are thus all enabled to cross the river. They use their skill and resources in emergencies like seasoned soldiers. As they understand one another's cries (as I believe all animals and birds do after their own kind), the Indians say that they can talk and that they keep their language a secret from the Spaniards lest the latter should make them dig for gold and silver. They also say that monkeys carry their children on their backs in mockery of the Indian women, and they tell a great many jokes about them, but this must suffice for monkeys.

CHAPTER XIX

Land and water fowl, tame and wild.

THE PERUVIAN Indians had no domestic fowl except a variety of duck, which are very like those in Spain and are called ducks by the Spaniards. They are middle sized, not so large or tall as Spanish geese, nor so short and small as ducks. The Indians call them *ñuñuma,* derived from *ñuña,* "to suckle," for they gobble as they eat as if they were sucking. There were no other tame fowl in my country. Birds of the air and water- and seafowl we shall mention as they occur to us, though their number and variety is so great that we can hardly mention a half or a quarter of them. There are all sorts of eagles, royal and otherwise, though they are smaller than in Spain. There are hawks of many kinds, some resemble those of Europe and others not. In general the Indians call them *huaman*. Some of the smaller ones I have seen brought to Spain, where they are much esteemed. Those called *neblíes* in Peru are very strong fliers with very sharp claws: they are nearly black in color. In Cuzco in 1557 a gentleman from Seville who prided himself on his falconry did everything within his power to tame a *neblí*. It would come to hand and to the lure from a great distance, but he could never get it to pounce on its prey and he thus despaired of the task.

There are other birds that can be included with the birds of prey. They are extremely large and are called *cuntur,* or by the Spaniards condor. Many have been killed by Spaniards and measured so that their size can be accurately quoted. Some have been found to measure fifteen or sixteen feet from wing-tip to wing-tip, or in yards five varas and a third. They have no claws as eagles have: nature did not give them to them, to temper their ferocity. Their feet resemble those of chickens, but their beaks are sufficient, and are strong enough to pierce the hide of a cow. A pair of them will attack a cow or a bull and devour it. It has been known for one of them to attack boys of ten or twelve and eat them. They are black and white in patches like magpies. They are rare, otherwise they would destroy the flocks. On their foreheads they have a smooth crest like a razor, not with points like a cock's. When they drop from a height they make an astonishingly loud buzzing noise.

Padre Acosta, in speaking of the birds of the New World, especially of the condor, in his Book IV, ch. xxxvii (to which I refer anyone who wishes to read wonderful things), says: "Those called condors are of immense size and such strength that they can not only open and eat a sheep, but even a calf."

In contrast to the condor his Paternity refers to other little birds found in Peru which the Spaniards call *tominejos* [hummingbirds] and the Indians *quenti*. They are of a golden blue, like the most delicate part of a peacock's neck, and they feed like bees, sucking the juice or honey of flowers with their long bills. They are so tiny that his Paternity says of them: "In Peru there are those called *tominejos* which are so minute that I have wondered when watching them in flight if they were bees or butterflies, but they are really birds," etc. After hearing of these two extremes of birds in Peru, the reader will not be surprised by those that come between them. There are what the Indians call *suyuntu* and the Spaniards *gallinaza* [turkey-buzzards]. They are very fond of meat and so greedy that if they find a dead animal in the fields they will eat so much of it that though they are quite light, they cannot take flight from the ground because of the weight of what they have eaten. But if they find they are pursued, they scuttle off vomiting what they have eaten so as to lighten themselves for taking off. It is amusing to see their haste and anxiety to cast up what they have just as hastily and anxiously eaten. If one hurries, one can catch them and kill them, but they are inedible and useless except for cleaning the streets of refuse. For this reason they are not killed, even when it can easily be done. They are not birds of prey. Padre Acosta holds that they are a kind of crow.

Like these there are sea birds which the Spaniards call *alcatrazes* [pelicans]. They are a little smaller than bustards, and live on fish. It is enjoyable to watch them fishing. At certain hours of the day, in the morning and evening, which must be the hours when the fish rise or when the birds are hungriest, they collect in flocks in the air, perhaps as high as two towers, whence they drop with wings folded, like trained hawks, to catch the fish, diving under water until they succeed. Sometimes they spend so long under the surface that they seem to have drowned. This must be because the fish try their best to escape. When one really begins to think they have disappeared, they emerge with the fish in their mouths and swallow it as they fly in the air. It is interesting to watch them drop and to hear the blows as they strike the water, while others emerge with their prey and take flight, and still others break off in the middle of the dive and fly up again, having lost their prey. In short, it is like watching two-hundred trained hawks rising and dropping in turns like a blacksmith's hammer.

Apart from these, there are many flocks of sea birds which occur in such multitudes that anyone who had not seen them would find a description of them incredible: they are of all sizes—large, medium and small. I often watched them carefully when sailing down the Pacific. Some of the flocks were so vast that I should think they would extend over a distance of more than two leagues from the first birds to the last. They flew in such close formation that one could not see through the mass of them. While in flight some would drop down to the surface of the water to rest and others would rejoin them after resting. It is certainly wonderful to see how numerous they are, and one is stirred to give thanks to the Eternal Majesty which created such an infinite number of birds and sustains them with an infinite number of fish. This shall suffice for the sea birds.

To return to the waterfowl of the earth, there is an infinite number of these in the rivers and lakes of Peru—herons, egrets, ducks, and coots, and what are called flamingoes in Europe, as well as many other varieties which I cannot describe as I have not observed them closely. These are large birds, bigger than storks, which feed on fish. They are pure white and have very long legs. They go about in pairs and are very beautiful, but they seem quite rare.

CHAPTER XX

Partridges, pigeons, and other lesser birds.

T HERE ARE two sorts of partridges in my country; one is like a laying chicken and breeds in the deserts the Indians call *puna.* The other is smaller than the European bird and has excellent flesh, more palatable than that of the larger variety. Both are of a greyish color, with white bills and feet. The smaller rather resemble quails in the color of their plumage, except that they do not have white specks. They are called *yutu,* from the sound of their song, which is "yut-yut." Not only partridges, but many other birds are named after their song, as we shall say in this chapter: similarly with many other things which will be mentioned when they occur. I have not heard that Spanish partridges have ever been introduced into Peru.

There are ringdoves resembling those of Spain in size, plumage, and flesh. They are called *urpi,* "dove." The Indians call the tame pigeons introduced from Spain *Castilla urpi,* "Castilian doves," from their origin. There are turtles as in Spain, though perhaps a little larger: they are called *cocohuay,* the first two syllables of which are taken from their song and are pronounced down in the throat so that the name may resemble the song more exactly. There are other smaller turtledoves, of the size and color of common or crested larks. They breed on rooftops as sparrows do, and also in the fields: they are not common. There are small grey birds the Spaniards call sparrows, alluding to their size and color, though they differ in having a very sweet song: the Indians call them *paria pichiu.* They breed in the sides of houses wherever there are clumps of plants growing in the walls: they also breed in the fields. There are small reddish birds the Spaniards call nightingales from the similarity of color, though their song is as different as white from black: the Peruvian bird sings very badly, so much so that the Indians of old regarded their song as of ill omen. There are little black birds the Spaniards call swallows, but they are more like martins than swallows. They appear at certain seasons and lodge in the gutters of roofs in groups of ten or twelve. These birds live in the villages and are on closer terms with human beings than any others. I never saw swallows or swifts, at least in the highlands of Peru.

The lowland birds are the same except that the sea birds are different. There are no woodcocks, grouse, thrushes, cranes, or bustards. There are certainly others in their place which I do not remember. In the kingdom of Chile, which also belonged to the empire of the Incas of Cuzco, there are ostriches which the Indians call *suri*. Their color is between grey and white. Their plumes are neither so fine nor so showy as those of Africa. They do not fly in the air, but are very speedy on the ground, running with the aid of their wings faster than a horse. The Spaniards have caught them with relays of horses, for the breath of one horse alone or even two is not sufficient to tire the birds. In Peru there are also *sirgueros* which the Spaniards call thus because they have two colors, yellow and black: they go about in bands. The Indians call them *chaina,* taking the name from their song. There are many other sorts of birds, large and small, which I cannot describe because of their great numbers and the inadequacy of my memory.

I remember there are kestrels, like those of Spain, but they are braver and some stoop for small birds. I saw two of them flying at a bird in the Y'úcay plain: they pursued it for a long way until it took refuge from them in a large thick tree that grows in the plain. The tree, which was still standing when I left, was held sacred by the Indians because their kings used to stand under it and watch the festivities that took place in this beautiful valley. One of the kestrels displayed its natural sagacity by going into the tree after the bird, while the other climbed up in the air above the tree to watch for it as it came out. As soon as the little bird emerged the kestrel fell on it like a falcon, and it returned to the tree, whereupon the second pursuer went into the tree to get it out and the first sailed up in the air to occupy the watching position. In this way the two attackers took turns and entered and left the tree four times, the small bird avoiding them as often and defending its life with great spirit, until at the fifth assault it fled to the river and got away among some walls of ancient buildings, to the great pleasure of four or five Spaniards who had been watching the chase, astonished at the way in which nature teaches all its creatures, even the smallest birds, to protect their lives, some by attacking others, and some by escaping with such skill and cunning as we have seen.

There are various sorts of wild bees. The domestic kind kept in hives were unknown to the Indians, and the Spaniards have not taken the trouble to breed them. The wild bees breed in nooks and crannies in rocks and hollow trees. In the cold zones they feed on poor plants and produce little honey, and it is disagreeable and bitter, while the wax is black and useless. In warm or hot areas they live on good plants and make an excellent honey, clear, white, fragrant, and very sweet: if transported to a cold climate it solidifies and resembles sugar. It is much esteemed, not only to eat, but for use in various medicines, for which purpose it is of great efficacy.

CHAPTER XXI

Varieties of parrots; their talkativeness.

PARROTS breed in the Antis. They are of many kinds, large, middling, lesser, small, and tiny. The tiniest are smaller than larks and the biggest like large falcons. Some are all of one color, others of two colors—green and yellow or green and red—others are of many various colors, especially the large ones the Spaniards call *guacamayas* which are of all hues and very delicately colored. The tail feathers are extremely long and showy and are much prized by the Indians for adorning themselves at festivities. From the beauty of these feathers the famous Boccaccio took the argument for the amusing story of Frate Cipolla. The Spaniards give parrots various names to distinguish between the various sizes. The very smallest are called *periquillos*; others a little larger *catalinillas*; and bigger ones that talk better, *loros*. The biggest are *guacamayas*. These last are difficult to teach to speak and in fact never talk: they serve only to be looked at on account of their beautiful colored feathers. The other varieties of parrots have been brought to Spain and are kept in cages for the enjoyment of their talking. There are other kinds too which have not been brought, probably because they talk little. In Potosí, in 1554 and 1555, there was a *loro* that spoke so well that when the Indian men and women passed by in the street it would call them by their respective tribes, saying

"Colla," "Yunca," "Huairu," "Quechua," and so on, without any mistakes, as if it realized the meaning of the different headgear they used to wear in Inca times to distinguish themselves. One day a beautiful Indian woman passed down the street where the parrot was: she was attended by three or four servants, who treated her as a lady *palla,* or member of the royal blood. When the parrot saw her, it shrieked and laughed: "Huairu, Huairu, Huairu!" the name of a tribe that is looked down on by all the rest. The woman was very much humbled in front of the bystanders, for there was always a crowd of Indians listening to the bird. When she was opposite it, she spat at the bird and called it *súpay,* "devil." The Indians said the same, for it recognized the woman though she was disguised as a *palla.* In Seville in the Caldefrancos, a few years ago, there was a parrot that, whenever it saw a certain doctor who was unworthy of the name, go past, used to abuse him so scandalously that he was forced to bring a suit against the bird. The magistrate ordered its owner not to keep it in the street, under pain of being forced to surrender it to the plaintiff.

The Indians call them in general *uritu,* "parrot," and because of the great and wearisome noise they make as they fly about in large flocks, the word is applied as an epithet for a boring speaker, who, as the divine Ariosto says in his twenty-fifth canto, knows little and talks much. To such the Indians appropriately say: "Hush, parrot!" The parrots come out of the Antis at the time when maize (of which they are inordinately fond) is in season throughout the main part of Peru. They do great damage to the crops. They fly very strongly at a height. The *guacamayas,* being heavy and slow, do not leave the Antis. They go about in bands, as we have said, but those of different varieties do not consort together, each bird keeping to its own company.

CHAPTER XXII

Four famous rivers; the fish found in Peruvian rivers.

I HAD forgotten to describe the fresh-water fish which the Peruvian
Indians find in their rivers. These rivers are, as is well known, numerous and very large, and we shall only name the four largest of them in
order not to weary the hearer. The so-called Río Grande, otherwise the
Magdalena, which enters the sea between Cartagena and Santa Marta,
is eight leagues wide at its mouth according to the chart: it rises in the
mountain ranges of Peru. It comes down with such impetus that it flows
ten or twelve leagues out to sea, pushing back the waters of the ocean,
which despite their immensity cannot resist the fierce onrush of the river.

The Orellana, which we call by this name to distinguish it from the
Marañón, is 54 leagues wide at the mouth, more rather than less, according to the same chart. Though some writers say it is 30 leagues, others less,
and still others from 40 to 70, I have preferred to accept the opinion of
seafarers, which indeed is not opinion but experience, for in that floating
republic on the waters of the sea, the citizens must never trust to opinions,
but carry in their hands the pure and simple truth. Those who say the
river is 70 leagues at its mouth are measuring it obliquely from one point
of land to another: but they are not level, for the left bank of the river
goes far further into the sea than the right, and so by measuring obliquely
one can truthfully arrive at 70 leagues from point to point, though the
straight distance does not exceed 54 leagues as the pilots know. The head-
waters of this famous river rise in the district called Cuntisuyu, between
the west and south of Cuzco, or as sailors say to the southwest. It runs
eleven leagues to the west of the city. Even close to its source it cannot be
forded, for it carries much water and is very rough, running hidden under
high peaks, that rise thirteen, fourteen, or fifteen leagues from the bottom to the snowy peaks, almost in a sheer cliff. This is the biggest river
in Peru. The Indians call it the Apurímac, "the speaking captain or
leader": *apu* has two meanings covering a leader in peace or a leader in
war. It is also given another name to its greater praise, Cápac Mayu:
mayu is "river" and *cápac* the title given to kings, so that the name means
that this was the prince of all the rivers in the world. It keeps these names
until it leaves the confines of Peru: whether it is known by them down

to the sea or whether the tribes that live in the mountains through which it passes give it another name, I do not know.

In 1555, during the heavy winter rains, a large piece of the mountainside fell into the river and blocked it with rock and earth so that for three days the stream failed to run, until the weight of water held back threw down the dam. Those who lived downstream thought that the end of the world was coming when they saw so mighty a stream dry up so suddenly. The dam stretched 14 leagues up the river, as far as the bridge on the royal road from Cuzco to the City of Los Reyes.

This river Apurímac flows from south to north for more than 500 leagues from its source to the equator: it then turns east and flows almost under the equator for 650 leagues more as the crow flies, until it reaches the sea. With all its twists and bends, it flows more than 1,500 leagues to the east, as we are told by Francisco de Orellana, who first sailed down it when he went with Gonzalo Pizarro to discover what they called the Land of Cinnamon, as we shall mention. The 650 leagues from west to east (without the bends) can be seen from the mariners' chart, for although seafarers do not usually describe what is inland, but only the sea and its shores, they have made an exception in the case of this river because it is the largest in the world and to explain the fact that when it enters the sea it is several leagues across and produces a freshwater sea in the gulf it pours into, with a size of over a hundred leagues. Thus according to Orellana's account, which is confirmed by López de Gómara in his ch. lxxxvi, adding the 500 leagues we have mentioned, the river is 2,000 leagues long including all its bends. It enters the sea exactly under the line. It is called Orellana's River because this gentleman sailed down it in 1543, though the Pinzóns of Seville discovered it in 1500. The name it was given, the River of the Amazons, was because Orellana and his companions observed that the women of the riverside tribes fought as bravely as the men, a fact we have noticed in certain passages of our history of Florida. It did not mean that there were Amazons on the river, though because of the bravery of the women it was implied that there were. There are many islands in the river, large and small. The tide goes up it for more than a hundred leagues. This must suffice for this famous emperor of rivers.

What is called the Marañón enters the sea just over 70 leagues to the south of the Orellana. It is three degrees south of the line, and is more than 20 leagues across at the mouth. It springs from some large lakes at the back of Peru, to the east. These lakes are formed by the great flow of water from the great chain of snowcapped mountains that runs down

Peru. As these two great rivers enter the sea so near one another, their waters join and are not separated by the sea. This makes the freshwater sea even larger and the Orellana even more famous, for it is credited with the whole. By this junction of the waters I suspect that the Orellana is called the Marañón, borrowing both its waters and its name and making one river of the two.[1]

It remains to mention the river the Spaniards call the River of Silver and the Indians the Parahuay. We have mentioned how the Castilian name was given and what the Indian word means. Its first waters rise, like those of the Marañón, in the incredible range of snow-covered mountains that runs the length of Peru. It has enormous spates that submerge the fields and villages and force the inhabitants to spend three months of the year living on rafts and in canoes moored to the trunks of trees until the floods have abated, for there is nowhere else to go. It runs into the sea at 35° south, and is more than 30 leagues across at the mouth, though the land pinches it here, for 80 leagues upstream the river is 50 leagues wide. Thus if one adds the breadth of these four rivers together, one might say that they are 130 leagues wide where they enter the sea— which in itself constitutes one of the many marvels of Peru. So great are these four rivers. There is an infinity of others, which enter the sea in all directions, as can be seen from the mariners' charts, to which I refer the reader. If they were all joined together, they would make other rivers as large as those we have mentioned.

Despite the existence of all these waterways, which would suggest the existence of large fisheries, there is in fact little fish, at least in the parts of the rivers that fall in Peru, which is all I claim to speak of, for I am not concerned with the rest. It is thought that this is due to the fierce currents and the lack of pools. The few fish there are are quite different from European river fish, and seem to belong all to the same kind. They have no scales, only skin. The head is broad and flat like a toad's and they therefore have very wide mouths. They are tasty, and the skin can be eaten, for it is so delicate that there is no need to remove it. They are called *challua*, "fish." Few fish enter the rivers that run into the sea down the Peruvian coast; most of these rivers are small and very rapid, though in winter they flow with great fury and cannot be forded.

---

[1] Garcilaso's geography is surprisingly accurate. Only in his account of the Marañón River does he show confusion. The Marañón, a tributary of the Amazon which rises and flows to the west and north of the Apurímac, obviously does not fit his description. He was probably referring to the Mamoré, another large tributary of the Amazon which rises to the east and southeast of Cuzco. The Pará, which enters the Atlantic south and east of the Amazon, takes its origin in the interior of Brazil, not in the Andes.

There are a great many fish in the great lake of Titicaca. Although it is the same shape as the river fish, the Indians distinguish it with the name *suchi*. It is very fat, and needs no grease but its own for frying. There is also another smaller fish in the lake which the Spaniards call *bogas* [rowers]: I have forgotten the Indian name. They are small, ugly, and ill-tasting: so far as I remember, they have scales: they are so small they might better be called sprats. Both sorts of fish breed in quantities in this great lake, for there is plenty of room and good feeding in the waste brought down by five large rivers that flow in, as well as other smaller ones and many streams. This shall suffice for the rivers and the fish found in Peru.

CHAPTER XXIII

Emeralds, turquoises, and pearls.

THE PRECIOUS stones that existed in Peru in the time of the Incas were turquoises, emeralds, and much fine crystal, though they did not know how to work it. Emeralds are found in the mountains of the province called Manta, in the jurisdiction of Puerto Viejo. The Spaniards have never, despite many efforts, succeeded in discovering the mineral that produces them, and there are now almost no emeralds from that province, though it formerly produced the best in the empire. From New Granada so many have been brought to Spain that they are now almost disregarded, not without cause, for in addition to their great number (which in everything leads to loss of value), they are many carats inferior to those of Puerto Viejo.

The emerald grows to perfection in its mineral, gradually acquiring the green color, as a fruit ripens on a tree. At first it is a dusky white with a greyish or greenish tinge. It begins to ripen or attain perfection on one of its four sides, probably that facing the east, as is the case with fruit with which I have just compared it: the good color then spreads from one side until it covers the whole emerald. It remains in the state in which it is mined, whether perfect or imperfect. In Cuzco I saw two emeralds in particular, among the many I saw there: they were as big as average walnuts, perfectly round and with holes in the middle. One of them was quite perfect on all sides. The other was a mixture: one side was very beautiful and as perfect as possible, the two flanks were not quite perfect, but were approaching the beauty and perfection of the first: the last, the opposite side, was ugly, for it had taken a very little of the green color and the contrast with the beauty of the other side made it look worse; it seemed like a piece of green glass fitted into the emerald. Its owner decided therefore to cut out this piece which spoilt the rest, and did so, though some amateurs blamed him afterwards, saying that he should have left the jewel, which was valuable as proving how the emerald gradually ripens by sections in its mineral. As a boy I was given the rejected part, and still have it in my possession; it has lasted so long because it has no value.

The turquoise is blue: some are of a prettier color than others. The Indians did not think so highly of them as they did the emeralds. Pearls were not used in Peru, though they were known, for the Incas, who always paid more attention to the well-being of their vassals than to the accumulation of what we call riches (which they did not consider such), seeing the toil and danger caused by fishing for pearls, prohibited it; and pearls were therefore not used. Since then they have been found in such numbers that they have become common, as Padre Acosta says in ch. xv of his Book IV, where he writes the following, word for word:

Since we are discussing the chief source of wealth brought from the Indies, it would be improper to forget pearls, which the ancients called margarites. They were at first so highly esteemed that they were considered to belong only to those of royal rank. Now there are so many of them that even negresses wear pearl necklaces,

etc. In the last third of the chapter, after having repeated notable anecdotes from ancient history about famous pearls in the world, his Paternity says:

Pearls are found in various parts of the Indies. They are fished most in the Pacific, near Panama, where the islands therefore called the Pearl Islands are. But the greatest and best are fished in the Caribbean, near the river called the Hacha. It was there that I saw the operations which give great toil and labor to the poor divers, who go down six, nine, and even twelve fathoms in search of the oysters, which are usually found clinging to rocks and reefs under the sea. They are torn off, carried to the surface and thrown into canoes, where they are opened and the treasure within extracted. The coldness of the sea at that depth is very great, and the labor of holding the breath even greater, for at times it takes a quarter or even half an hour to do the fishing. So that they are able to hold their breaths, the poor divers are made to eat little and only dry food, and to practise great continence. Thus covetousness also causes abstemiousness, even though it is practiced unwillingly. Various types of pearls are worked (this is a printing error for fished) and they are pierced for stringing. There is now a great superfluity of them everywhere. In 1587 I saw in a report of what was brought from the Indies to the king. 18 marks of pearls and three crates of them besides. Private persons imported 1,264 marks of pearls, in addition to which there were seven more sacks of unweighed pearls, a quantity that would earlier have seemed fabulous.

Thus far Padre Acosta, who finishes his chapter here.

To his Paternity's remark that the quantity would have seemed fabulous I will add two tales that occur to me about pearls. One is that in about 1564, more or less, so many pearls were brought for His Majesty that they were sold in a heap in the India house at Seville just as if they were some kind of seed. While the crier was announcing the pearls before the bidding, one of the royal officials said: "Anyone who offers so much as a starting price shall have six thousand ducats commission." On hearing this a wealthy merchant who knew the trade well, for he dealt in pearls, at once offered the price. Despite the large commission it was easily covered in the final bid, and the merchant was very satisfied to have earned six thousand ducats by uttering a single word, while the purchaser was even more pleased, expecting an even greater profit from the great quantity of pearls, the size of which can be imagined from the commission.

The other tale is that in Spain I knew a youth of humble family who lived in need, for though he was a good goldsmith he had no capital and worked as a journeyman. He was in Madrid in 1572 and 1573, and lived in my lodgings. He was passionately fond of chess at which he used to lose all he earned at his trade; I often chided him, telling him he would be reduced to great straits by betting, but one day he replied: "They can't be any greater than the straits I've been through, for I reached this capital on foot with only fourteen maravedis in the world." This poor youth tried to escape from his misery by embarking for the Indies to engage in the pearl trade, of which he knew something. He was so successful in his travels and in the trade that he accumulated more than thirty thousand ducats. For his wedding (I also knew his wife), he had a large skirt of black velvet made with a border of fine pearls a sesma broad running down the front and round the whole hem, a very grand and original style. The embroidery was valued at more than four thousand ducats. I mention this to show the incalculable quantity of pearls brought from the Indies, in addition to those we have mentioned in our history of Florida (Book III, ch. xv and xvi), which were found in many parts of that great country, and especially in the rich temple of the province of Cofachiqui. The eighteen marks of pearls which Padre Acosta says were brought for His Majesty, as well as three chests more, were those chosen as the finest, for from time to time the best of the pearls are set aside in the Indies and presented to His Majesty as the royal fifth. In this way they enter the royal store chamber, whence they are distributed for divine service to which His Majesty devotes them. I saw them on a mantle and skirt for the image of Our Lady of Guadalupe, and on a complete set of vestments with cape, chasuble, dalmatics, altar cloths, stoles, maniples, and the skirts and albs and sleeve ends all embroidered with very fine large pearls, the mantle and skirt being completely covered like a chessboard, the white squares being square patches of pearls bulging out in mounds, while the colored squares consisted of rubies and emeralds set in enamelled gold. The alternate squares were so beautifully done that the makers had clearly shown for whom the work was intended, and the Catholic king on whom he bestowed his treasure, which is certainly so great that none other but the emperor of the Indies could embark on so magnificent, grandiose, and heroic a work.

To realize the great wealth of this monarch, it is well to read the fourth book of Padre Acosta, and the rest, wherein all the wonders that have been discovered in the New World are unfolded. Among them, I can, without straying from my subject, tell a thing I witnessed in Seville in 1579, a pearl brought from Panama by a gentleman called Don Diego de Témez and dedicated to King Philip II. It was the size and shape of a good-sized pear. It had a neck rising into a nipple, like that of a muscadine pear, and even had the small hollow at the bottom. The round part would be as big as a large pigeon's egg at the broadest. When it came from the Indies it was valued at 12,000 pesos, or 14,400 ducats. Jacomo de Tresso of Milan, an excellent craftsman and his Catholic majesty's lapidary, said it might be worth 14,000 or 30,000 or 50,000 or 100,000 ducats, declaring that it was beyond price as it was unique in the world. It was therefore called the Peregrine, and people in Seville went to see it as a marvel. An Italian gentleman was then in the city buying the biggest pearls possible for a great lord in Italy. He brought a long string of them, but when compared with the Peregrine and set against it they looked like pebbles from rivers. Those who knew about pearls and precious stones said it exceeded all other known pearls by 24 carats: I do not know by what reckoning this was calculated and cannot therefore explain it. It was found in the fishery by a Negro boy who, his master said, was not worth a hundred reals, and the shell was so small that they nearly threw it back into the sea as worthless, for it seemed so unpromising. The slave was set free as a reward for his good fortune, and his owner was rewarded with the office of alguacil-mayor of Panama.

Pearls are not worked, for the substance cannot be touched except for the purpose of drilling. They are worn in the condition they occur in the shells. Some are quite round and others less so: some are elongated and others bellied, with one half rounded and the other half flat. Others are shaped like pears, and they are the most esteemed on account of their rarity. When a merchant has one of these pear-shaped pearls or a large round one of good quality, and he finds another like it in someone else's possession, he tries to buy it at all costs, for if they are paired and both are identical, each doubles the other's value: if each of them alone was worth 100 ducats, when it is matched each is worth 200, and the pair together 400, for they can now be used as earrings, the purpose for which they are most esteemed. It is impossible to work them because they consist of layers of leaves like an onion, not of solid matter. The pearl ages with them, like all other corruptible things, losing the beautiful clear color it had in its youth, and growing dusky and smoky. Then the top layer is removed and the one below is exposed, showing the same color as it had at first; but this does the jewel great harm, for it removes at least a third of its size. This rule does not apply to those called *netas* [pure] because they are very fine.

CHAPTER XXIV

Gold and silver.

SPAIN is a good witness to the wealth of gold and silver that is mined in Peru, since for more than twenty-five years past, without counting the previous period, more than twelve or thirteen millions of gold and silver are brought here without counting other articles that are not included: each million is ten times a hundred-thousand ducats. Gold is found throughout Peru: it is more abundant in some provinces than others, but in general it occurs throughout the kingdom. It is found on the surface of the earth and in streams and rivers where it is carried down by spates after the rains. It is obtained by washing the earth or sand, as silversmiths in Spain wash the sweepings of their shops. The Spaniards call what is thus recovered "gold dust" because it is like filings; there are a few bigger grains of two or three pesos or more. I have seen grains of more than twenty pesos: they are called *pepitas* or nuggets. Some are flat like the seeds of melons or calabashes, others are round. Some are as big as eggs. All the gold from Peru is 18 to 24 carat, or rather more or less. That which is extracted from the mines of Callavaya or Callahuaya is extremely fine, of 24 carats, and it is even claimed to be finer, according to what I have heard from some goldsmiths in Spain. In 1556 in a corner of one of the mines of Callahuaya there was discovered one of the stones that occur with the metal, as big as a man's head. In color it resembled a lung, and even in shape, for it was riddled with large and small holes that ran right through it. In all of them points of gold could be seen as though molten gold had been poured over it: some of these points projected from the stone, others were level with it, and others were inside it. Those who understood mining said that if it had not been extracted, the whole stone would in the course of time have turned to gold. In Cuzco the Spaniards regarded it as a marvellous thing. The Indians called it *huaca*, which, as we have said, has among other meanings that of a remarkable thing, something admirable for its beauty or also something abominably ugly. I saw it with both Indians and Spaniards. Its owner was a rich man who decided to come to Spain, bringing it as it was as a present for King Philip II, for the gem was a strange one and very estimable. From others who came in his fleet I heard when I was in Spain that his ship was lost with a great deal of other treasure.

Silver needs more work to mine than gold, and is more costly to refine and purify. In many parts of Peru silver mines have been, and are still, found, though none like those of Potosí, which were discovered and explored in 1545, fourteen years after the arrival of the Spaniards there. The hill where they are is called Potocsi, such being the name of the place: I do not know if it has a meaning in the special language of that province, for it has none in the general language of Peru. It stands on a plain and is shaped like a sugarloaf: it is a league round at the base and a quarter of a league at the top. The top of the hill is round. It is beautiful to see, for it stands alone, and nature decked it so that it might be as famous in the world as it now is. Some mornings the hill appears covered with snow, for the site is a cold one. The place used to belong to Gonzalo Pizarro's allocation, which later passed to Pedro de Hinojosa. We shall say later how he got it, if we may without odium delve into and reveal the secret deeds that are done in time of war, for historians usually omit many things for fear of the odium they may arouse. Padre Acosta writes in his Book IV at length of the gold, silver, and quicksilver that have been found in the empire of Peru, and more is discovered every day: I shall therefore not describe all this, but merely refer to a few notable facts of those times, and say how the Indians obtained and founded the metal before the Spaniards discovered the use of quicksilver. I should mention that the mines of the hill of Potosí were discovered by certain Indians in Spanish service called in their language *yanacuna,* which means a man obliged to act as a servant. They enjoyed the use of the first vein they found for some days as friends and partners, keeping their discovery secret; but as its wealth was so great that they could not or would not conceal it from their masters, they then revealed it. The first vein was explored and the rest were then discovered. Among the Spaniards present was one called Gonzalo Bernal, who was later steward to Pedro de Hinojosa. Soon after the discovery, speaking in the presence of Diego Centeno, a famous gentleman, and many other noble people, he said: "The mines promise such wealth that when they have been worked for a few years iron will be worth more than silver." I saw this forecast fulfilled in 1554 and 1555 when, during the war of Francisco Hernández Girón, a horseshoe was valued at five pesos, or six ducats, and a mule's at four: two nails for shoeing cost a tomin or fifty-six maravedis. I saw a pair of buskins sell for thirty-six ducats, a quire of paper for four, and a vara of fine Valencian scarlet for sixty; fine Segovia cloth, silks, linen, and other Spanish wares were in proportion. The war produced this dearth, for during the two years it lasted no fleets reached Peru bringing goods from Spain. It was due also to the great quantities of silver extracted from the mines, for three or four years before this time a basket of the herb we call coca had reached thirty-five ducats, and maize the same, and a measure of wheat twenty-four and twenty-five. Maize was the same, and clothes and footwear in proportion. The first wine, until it was available in abundance, sold at two hundred ducats and more the jar. And despite the richness of the land and its abundance of gold, silver, and precious stones, as all the world knows, the natives are the poorest and wretchedest people in the universe.

CHAPTER XXV

Quicksilver, and how metal was founded before the use of quicksilver.

As we have said, the Inca kings knew of quicksilver and admired its brightness and mobility, but found no use for it. There was nothing indeed in their service to which it could be applied, and they felt that on the other hand it was dangerous to the lives of those who mined it and handled it, since they noticed that it caused them to tremble and lose their senses. For this reason, these kings who paid such attention to the welfare of their subjects and merited the title of lovers of the poor, prohibited the mining of quicksilver by law and ordered it to be forgotten; and the Indians so abhorred it that its very name was obliterated from their memory and from their language. They have indeed no word for quicksilver, unless they have invented it since its discovery by the Spaniards in 1567. As they had no writing, they rapidly forgot any word that was not in current use. The Incas used, and permitted their vassals to use the scarlet color of incredibly fine quality which is found in powder form in the ore of quicksilver: the Indians call it *ichma* (the word *llimpi* given by Padre Acosta refers to another purple color which is not so fine and which is obtained from other minerals, for these occur in Peru in all colors. As the Indians became so attached to the color *ichma,* which certainly is enough to inspire passionate attachment, that they would go to all lengths to get it, the Incas feared they would come to harm in the caverns, and prohibited its use by the common people, restricting it only to women of the royal blood. It was not used by men, as I myself saw, and only by young and beautiful women, not by the older ones, for it was rather an adornment for the young than an ornament for mature people. Even the girls did not put it on their cheeks as they do rouge here, but applied it with a little stick like henna between the corner of the eyes and the temple. The line they drew was about as broad as a stalk of wheat and looked very well. The *pallas* used no other cosmetics but powdered *ichma,* and that not every day but only occasionally on feast days. They kept their faces clean, as did all the women of the common people. Those who prided themselves on the beauty of their complexions used to apply a white milk which they made of I know not what so as to preserve their coloring. The stuff was left on for nine days, at the end of which time it was removed from the face and had formed a skin, which came off in pieces, leaving the complexion much improved. The color *ichma* was used as sparingly as I have mentioned in order to spare the vassals the danger of mining it. Painting or staining the face with various pigments in wartime or for feasts, which is mentioned by one author, was never practiced by the Incas or the Indians as a whole, except by a few tribes who were regarded as the most savage and primitive.

It remains to describe how silver ore was founded before quicksilver was introduced. Near the hill of Potosí there is another small hill of the same shape as the first. The Indians call it Huaina Potocchi, or Potocchi Junior, to distinguish it from the other which, after the discovery of the lesser one, was known as Hatun Potocsi, or Potocchi—it is all one—saying they were father and son. The silver ore is extracted from the larger, as we have said, but it proved at first very difficult to smelt, for instead of running, it burnt and spent itself in smoke. The Indians did not know the cause of this, though they had mastered other metals. But need or covetousness is a great teacher, especially when gold or silver is in question, and they made so many attempts with different remedies that they at length found a solution. In the small hill there was a base ore consisting almost entirely of lead and when this was mixed with the silver ore it made it melt. It was therefore called *surúchec,* "what makes one slip." The two ores were mingled in due proportion, with so many pounds of silver ore to so many ounces of lead ore, the quantities being varied according to the lessons of daily experience, for not all the silver ore is of the same kind. Some has more silver than others, even though it comes from the same vein, and the proportion of silver varies from day to day, so that the *surúchec* has to be added according to the quality and richness of each ore. Thus tempered, the ore is smelted in small portable furnaces, like clay ovens. They did not smelt with bellows or by blowing down copper tubes, which, as we have said elsewhere, they used when they wanted to melt gold and silver for working them: although they often tried this, the ore would not run and they could not find out the cause. They therefore smelted their ore with the aid of the wind. But it was also necessary to temper the wind; if it was very strong it wasted the charcoal and cooled the metal. If it were soft, it had not enough force to heat the fire. Consequently the little ovens were taken out at night and set on high or low points on the hillsides, according to the strength of the wind, which was more or less tempered according to whether the site was sheltered or not. It was a pretty sight in those days to see eight, ten, twelve, or fifteen thousand little furnaces blazing away on the hillsides. The first smelting was done in this way. The second and third were carried out indoors with copper pipes to purify the silver and separate the lead; for the Indians had none of the Spanish devices with acids and other substances to separate gold from silver or copper, or silver from copper and lead, and could only refine by repeated smeltings. In this way, the Indians smelted the silver of Potosí before quicksilver was found; they still practice this to some extent, though nothing like on the scale they did.

The mine owners found that this system of open air smelting spread their treasure among many hands and enabled many others to share their wealth; and they sought to remedy this state of affairs and to keep the metal to themselves by making their own foundries and employing the Indians by the day. Previously the Indians had worked on their own account and undertook to deliver to the owner so much silver for each hundredweight of ore that was mined. Stirred thus by avarice, the owners had great bellows made which blew onto the ovens from a distance like the wind. As this proved useless, they built machines and wheels with sails, like windmills, which were driven by horses. However, this also was of no avail, and they therefore gave up these devices and went on following the system invented by the Indians. Twenty-two years went by, until in 1567 by the ingenuity and skill of a Portuguese called Henrique Garcés quicksilver was found. It was discovered in the province of Huanca to which for reasons I do not know is added the epithet -*villca*, "greatness, eminence," unless the reference is to the abundance of quicksilver that is mined. Apart from what is wasted, eight thousand quintals, or thirty-two thousand arrobas, are extracted yearly for his majesty. Despite its discovery in such quantities, no one knew how to turn it to account for this purpose until 1571, when a Spaniard called Pedro Fernández de Velasco arrived in Peru, after having been in Mexico, where he saw the process of extracting silver with quicksilver, as Padre Acosta reports at length in a curious account to which I refer anyone who is interested in acquiring remarkable and important information.

End of Book Eight

BOOK
NINE *of the*
FIRST PART

It contains the mighty and magnanimous deeds of
Huaina Cápac; the conquests he accomplished; his punishment of various rebels; his clemency toward the
Chachapoyas; the creation of his son Atahuallpa king
of Quito. He receives tidings of the Spaniards; explanation of the prophecy about them; the things the Spaniards took to Peru and which were unknown there before their arrival; and the wars of the two brothers
Huáscar and Atahuallpa, the misfortunes
of the first and cruelties of the second.
It contains forty chapters.

CHAPTER I

*Huaina Cápac orders a golden cable to be made;
the reason for this and its purpose.*

HE MIGHTY Huaina Cápac, now absolute master of his empire, spent the first year of his reign in performing his father's obsequies. He then went out to visit his domains to the very great applause of his vassals. Wherever he passed *curacas* and people came forth and strewed the ways with flowers and reeds and made triumphal arches of the same. He was received with great acclamation and many repetitions of the royal titles, especially of his own name: "Huaina Cápac! Huaina Cápac!" This seemed to be the title that did him most honor, for he had merited it since childhood, and by uttering it they adored him as if he were a god, while he was still on earth. Padre José de Acosta, in speaking of this prince, says in his Book VI, ch. xxii, among other great things he sets down in the Inca's praise: "This Huaina Cápac was worshipped by his people as a god while he was still alive, a thing which the old people say was never accorded to any of his predecessors," etc.

In the early stages of this journey Inca Huaina Cápac had news of the birth of his heir, who was after known as Huáscar Inca. As this prince had been so greatly desired, his father wished to be present at the celebration of his birth, and he therefore returned to Cuzco with all possible speed, being welcomed there with every manifestation of joy and pleasure that the circumstance required. The festivities lasted twenty days, and after they were over Huaina Cápac was so overjoyed with his new son that he began to devise all kinds of great and novel celebrations for the day when he should be weaned, and have his hair cut for the first time and receive his own name. This was, as we have said already, one of the most solemn occasions not only for the Incas, but for everyone down to the poorest of the poor, such as their regard for their first-born. Among other marvels devised for these celebrations was the cable of gold, which is famous throughout the world, but has still never been seen by any stranger, though many have desired it. In devising it the Inca availed himself of the following custom. Each of the provinces of Peru had a different style of dancing from the others, by which each tribe could be recognized as clearly as by their headdress. The dances were traditional ones, and never changed. The Incas themselves had a solemn and dignified dance without any leaps or skips such as the rest had. It was danced by men, and women were never admitted to it. The men took one another's hands, but each dancer gave his hand not to the one immediately in front of him but the next one. They all did this, thus forming a chain. Two- or three-hundred men would dance together, or more according to the solemnity of the occasion. The dance was begun at a distance from the prince in whose honor it was performed. All the dangers commenced together and took three steps in time, the first stepping backward and the next two forward, after the fashion of the steps in the Spanish dances called *dobles* and *represas*. These steps to and fro carried them gradually forward till they were disposed in a half-circle round the Inca. They took turns to sing in groups, lest they should tire if they all sang together. The songs were to the rhythm of the dance and were composed in praise of the present Inca and his ancestors and others of the royal blood who were famed for their deeds in war or peace. The Incas standing by joined in the singing, so that the festival should be a universal one. The king himself sometimes danced in the solemn festivals in order to add to their solemnity. From the custom of linking hands to form a chain, Inca Huaina Cápac conceived the idea of making the cable of gold, since it seemed more decent, solemn, and majestic that the dancers should be united by the chain and not by holding hands. I heard this fact both from popular report and in particular from an old Inca, my mother's uncle, whom I mentioned at the beginning of this history as having recounted the ancient traditions of his ancestors. When I asked him how long the cable was, he told me that it stretched along two sides of the great square of Cuzco, that is, the length and breadth of it, where these major festivities were held. The Inca had had it made thus to his own greater glory and to add splendor and dignity to his son's festivity, whose birth he wished to celebrate as solemnly as possible, though it was not necessary that it should have been so long for the sake of the dance. There will be no need to mention the size of this square, which the Indians call Haucaipata, to those who have seen it. For the benefit of those who have not seen it, I should say that from north to south it would be 200 ordinary paces of 2 feet in length and 150 east and west as far as the stream, including the space now taken by the houses which the Spaniards built along the stream in 1556 when my lord Garcilaso de la Vega was corregidor of that great city. By this reckoning the golden cable would thus be 350 paces long, or 700 feet. When I asked the same Indian about its thickness, he raised his right hand and showing his wrist declared that each link was so thick. The treasurer Agustín de Zárate in his Book I, ch. xiv, whose authority I have already invoked in speaking of the incredible wealth of the royal palaces of the Incas, says remarkable things about these treasures. I will mention here what he says about this cable in particular. It is literally as follows:

When a son was born to him, Guainacava [Huaina Cápac] had a cable of gold made, so that, according to the report of many living Indians, when two hundred Indian warriors [*orejones*] grasped it together they had some difficulty in lifting it up. In memory of this remarkable treasure his son was called Guasca, which means "rope" in their language, with the title of Inca, the name given to all their kings, as the Romans were called Augustus,

etc. Thus far this historian of Peru. This superb and valuable piece was hidden by the Indians with the rest of the treasure which was spirited away as soon as the Spaniards came in, to such purpose that no trace of it has been found. As this superb object was first used when the prince was shorn and named, they added to his own name, which was Inti Cusi Huallpa, the title of Huáscar, thus giving greater splendor to the treasure. *Huasca* means "rope." They had no word for chain, but used the word for rope, adding the name of the metal of which it was made, as we might say gold, silver, or iron chain. And in order that the word should not sit ill on a prince because of its meaning, this was disguised by adding the final *r*. So written it has no meaning, and they wished him to have the name of *Huasca* without the implication of "rope." In this way the name Huáscar was applied to the prince, and became so closely associated with him that his vassals used it for preference to his own name Inti Cusi Huallpa. *Huallpa* means "sun of joy." In those days the Incas were at the height of their power, and as power usually incites men to vanity and arrogance, they did not care to apply to their prince any of the titles they had hitherto taken as marks of greatness and majesty, but chose rather to lift themselves up to heaven and take the name of what they honored and adored as god and impose it on a man calling him *inti*, "Sun." *Cusi* means "joy, pleasure, content, delight." This shall suffice for the names and titles of Prince Huáscar Inca. To return to his father Huaina Cápac, we should mention that after devising the cable and other remarkable in-

ventions for the ceremony of shearing and naming his son, he resumed
the tour of his domains he had already begun, and spent more than two
years in it, until it was time to wean the child. He then returned to Cuzco,
where such celebrations as can readily be imagined took place, and the
name and title Huáscar were applied to the child.

CHAPTER II

Ten of the coastal valleys give in of their own free will, and Túmbez surrenders.

A YEAR after these celebrations, Huaina Cápac ordered the massing of
forty thousand warriors, with them he went to the kingdom of
Quito. On the journey he took as his concubine the eldest daughter of the
ruler who had been deprived of the kingdom of Quito: she had been for
some days in the house of the chosen women. By her the Inca had Atahuallpa and other sons and daughters, whom we shall mention in the
course of our history. From Quito the Inca descended to the llanos, or
seacoast, wishing to conquer it. He reached the valley called Chimu, which
is now Trujillo, the limit of the conquests of his grandfather, the good
Inca Yupanqui, whose additions to the empire we have already described.
Thence he despatched the usual summons to accept peace or war to the
inhabitants of the valley of Chacma and Pacasmayu, which lies beyond.
These, having been neighbors of the Inca's vassals for a number of years
and being, therefore, aware of the mildness of their rule, had long desired their sovereignty and accordingly replied that they were delighted
to become the Inca's vassals and to obey his laws and observe his religion.
The example of these valleys was followed by eight more between Pacasmayu and Túmpiz [Túmbez]—Saña, Collque, Cintu, Tucmi, Sayanca,
Matupi, Puchiu, Sullana. It took two years to conquer them, mostly in
order to cultivate the land and dig channels for irrigation: it took little
time to subdue them, for most of them submitted very willingly. During
this period the Inca had his army replaced two or three times: the replace-
ment of the soldiers by others was caused by the danger to health which

the uplanders experience when they leave their own cold climate for the hot coastal region.

After completing the conquest of these valleys, the Inca returned to Quito where he spent two years improving the kingdom with sumptuous buildings, great irrigation channels and many other benefits that he conferred on the inhabitants. After this interval, he had an army of fifty thousand warriors made ready and went down with them to the coast as far as the valley of Sullana, which reaches the sea near Túmbez, whence he despatched the usual summons to peace or war. The people of Túmbez were richer and stronger than any of the other coastal tribes so far conquered by the Incas. They wore as a distinguishing mark a headdress like a garland, which they call the *pillu*. Their chiefs had jesters, comedians, singers, and dancers for their entertainment. They practised sodomy, worshipped lions and tigers, sacrificed men's hearts and human blood, and were diligently served by their own people and much feared by the rest. Nevertheless, they dared not resist the Inca, whose great power they in turn feared. They replied that they would readily receive him as their lord and obey him. The same answer was received from others of the coastal valleys and tribes of the hinterland called Chunana, Chíntuy, Collonche, Yácuall, and many others of the region.

CHAPTER III

The punishment of those who killed the officials left by Túpac Inca Yupanqui.

THE INCA entered Túmbez, and among other royal works ordered the building of a fine fortress, where he left a garrison of warriors. A temple of the Sun and a house for the chosen virgins was built. This done, he marched inland to the provinces that had massacred the captains, lawgivers, and teachers his father Túpac Inca Yupanqui had sent to educate these tribes, as we have mentioned above. The provinces were alarmed by the recollection of their misdeeds, and when Huaina Cápac sent them messengers bidding them confess and receive the chastisement they deserved, they did not dare resist, for they felt themselves accused by their own ingratitude and treachery and daunted by the Inca's might. They therefore came submissively to beg for mercy for their crimes.

The Inca bade them assemble all the chiefs, ambassadors, and counsellors, captains, and nobles, who were responsible for recommending and carrying out the embassy they sent to his father to request the sending of the officials they later slew. He said he wanted to address them together, and when they had collected, one of his commanders delivered, on his instructions, a harangue reprimanding them for their treachery and cruelty, and reminding them how, when they should have worshipped the Inca and his officials for the benefits these had conferred on them by lifting them out of their brutal state and making men of them, they had cruelly slain them and disrespected the Inca, the child of the Sun. On this account they merited a punishment worthy of their wickedness, and indeed if they were punished as they deserved, none of all the tribes would be spared either on account of age or sex. Yet Inca Huaina Cápac, desiring to display his natural clemency, and taking pride in his title of Huacchacúyac, "lover of the poor," would spare all the common people; and as to those who were there present and who had been the authors and executors of the treacherous act, and therefore deserved death, they too would be pardoned, except that one in ten among them would be executed as a record and punishment of their crime. To this end they were to draw lots by tens, and the least fortunate should die, lest they should have occasion to say that the Incas had picked on those they most hated out of anger or rancor. Furthermore the Inca ordered that in the case of the chiefs and leaders of the tribe of Huancavillca, who had been the chief authors of the embassy and the ensuing treachery, each of them, and each of their descendants forever, should have four teeth removed, two from the upper and two from the lower jaw, as evidence of the fact that they had broken the promises of fidelity and vassalage they had made to his father, the great Túpac Inca Yupanqui.

The punishment was carried out and justice was done. All the tribes accepted it with great humility, counting themselves fortunate, since they had feared they would all be put to the knife for their treachery. Indeed no crime was punished so severely as that of rebellion after submission to the sway of the Incas, for the latter took it as a grave offence if their subjects, instead of showing thankfulness for the many benefits they received, proved so ungrateful as to rebel and slaughter the royal officials. The whole Huancavillca tribe accepted the punishment with greater humility and submission than the rest, for, as they had been responsible for the late insurrection, they had feared they would be visited with total destruction. But when they saw so light a punishment wreaked on so few, and understood that the tooth-pulling was to be limited to their chiefs and captains, the whole tribe regarded themselves as favored rather than punished. So all the inhabitants of the province, men and women alike, by common consent adopted the penalty inflicted on their captains as a token or emblem, simply because it was the Inca's order, and they had their teeth extracted, and thenceforward had those of their sons and daughters extracted as soon as their second set had grown. Like rude and barbarous people, they showed greater appreciation of the punishment they had escaped than of the excess of benefits bestowed on them.

An Indian woman of this tribe whom I knew in Cuzco in my father's house told me this tale at length. The Huancavillcas of both sexes used to bore the membrane between their nostrils so as to wear a little jewel of gold or silver hanging from it. I remember as a child having seen a chestnut horse belonging to a landowner from my town who owned Indians and was called something-or-other de Coca: the horse was a very good one, but as it got out of breath, they bored its nostrils above the vents. The Indians were astonished at this novelty and duly called the horse Huancavillca, implying that it had had its nostrils bored.

CHAPTER IV

The Inca visits his empire, consults the oracles, and gains the island of Puna.

INCA Huaina Cápac, after reducing to his service and punishing these provinces and leaving an adequate garrison there, made his way up to the kingdom of Quito whence he turned south again and visited his whole empire as far as the city of Cuzco and thence to the Charcas, a distance of more than seven hundred leagues. He had the kingdom of Chile inspected, whence he and his father obtained much gold. This visit took nearly four years, and he passed two more resting in Cuzco. At the end of this time he gave orders for an army of fifty thousand warriors to be raised in the provinces of Chinchasuyu, to the north of Cuzco. They were to assemble in the confines of Túmbez, and he himself marched down to the plains, visiting the temples of the Sun in the chief provinces there.

He visited the rich temple of Pachacámac, whom they worshipped as the unknown god. He had the priests consult the demon who spoke there about the conquest he was preparing to undertake. The answer given was that he should undertake it or any other he wished, for in any case he would be victorious, having been chosen to be lord of the four quarters of the world. He thereupon went to the Rímac valley where was the famous talking idol. He had it consulted about the campaign in order to fulfil his great-grandfather's promise to the Yuncas that the Incas would always venerate the idol. Having received its reply which was a long rigmarole full of flattery, he went on and visited the valleys between that place and Túmbez. On arriving here, he sent forward the usual invitation to peace or war to the natives of the island called Puna, a place of great fertility and abundance not far from the mainland. The island is twelve leagues round, and its lord, who was called Tumpalla, was very proud because neither he nor his predecessors had ever acknowledged any superior, but had always presumed their own superiority over their neighbors on the mainland. They had therefore had wars with them and this discord had made them unable to resist the Inca; for if they had all been in agreement they could have defended themselves for a long time. Tumpalla, who was not only arrogant but rich and luxurious, had many wives and boy loves, and sacrificed human hearts and blood to their gods, who were lions and tigers, as well as the common god worshipped by all the coastal Indians—the sea and the kinds of sea fish they most used for food. Tumpalla received the Inca's message with great sorrow and regret, and before replying summoned together all the leading people of the island and addressed them with much grief as follows:

"We now have a foreign tyranny at the very doors of our houses, which he threatens to take from us. Us ourselves he will put to the knife if we do not receive him willingly, and if we accept him as our lord, he will deprive us of our ancient liberty, dominion, and authority, which our ancestors have bequeathed to us from remote times. He will not trust our loyalty, and will make us build towers and fortresses to harbor his garrison, which he will maintain at our expense so that we shall never aspire to liberty. Our most valued possessions will be taken away from us, together with our most beautiful wives and daughters, and what we shall feel most deeply will be the loss of our ancient customs and the imposition of new laws on us; the obligation to worship strange gods and the overthrow of our own deities who are familiar to us. In short we shall be made to live in perpetual servitude and vassalage, which I think is perhaps worse than that we should die here and now. Since this applies to all of you, I bid you consider what we should do and advise me what you deem to be the best course."

The Indians talked for a long while among themselves. They deplored the paucity of their strength against so powerful a tyrant and lamented that the inhabitants of the mainland were ill-disposed on account of their own wars and not obliged to succor them. Finding themselves deprived of any hope of sustaining their liberty and thinking that they would all perish if they sought to defend it by force of arms, they agreed to choose what they considered the lesser of two evils, and obediently submit to the Inca with feigned and dissimulated affection, biding time and opportunity to free themselves from his empire when they might. In view of this, the chief Tumpalla not only replied to the Inca's messengers peacefully and submissively, but sent his own ambassadors with valuable presents to offer in his name and in that of his territory the promise of obedience and vassalage the Inca had demanded, and to beg him to confer on his new subjects and on the whole of their island the favor of his royal presence which would constitute all the felicity they could desire for themselves.

The Inca thought himself well served by the chief, and gave instructions that his people should take possession of the island and make all preparations for his army to cross over. This was duly accomplished with all possible speed, though with less ostentation and display than Tumpalla and his friends would have wished. The Inca went over to the islands, and was welcomed with solemn feasts and dances, and the singing of new chants in praise of the great deeds and qualities of Huaina Cápac. He was lodged in a newly built palace, at least as far as his own person was concerned, for it was not decent for the royal person to sleep in a chamber where anyone else had slept. Huaina Cápac spent some days on the island, establishing the form of government according to his laws and ordinances. He bade the natives and their neighbors on the mainland, who formed an independent region with various tribes and languages (they had also submitted to him) to abandon their gods, to give up sacrificing human blood or flesh, or eating the latter, to forsake sodomy, to worship the Sun as the universal god, and to live like men by the light of reason and justice. All this he ordered as the Inca, the child of the Sun, and legislator of that great empire, bidding them not to infringe his orders in whole or in part under pain of death. Tumpalla and his neighbors said that they would fulfil the Inca's commands.

After the solemn ceremonies of receiving the Inca's law and teaching, the *curacas* gradually realized how rigorous these were and how directly opposed they were to their own laws and to all their old pleasures and pastimes. Foreign rule seemed harsh and heavy to them, and they desired to return to their vile practices. The inhabitants of the island therefore conspired with those of the mainland to slay the Inca and all his followers by treachery at the first opportunity that offered. They then consulted their overthrown gods, which they secretly restored to decent places in order to recover their friendship and seek their favor. Many sacrifices and great promises were made to them, and they were asked for advice about the undertaking and whether the outcome of the deed would be successful or the reverse. The demon told them to attack, for they would succeed in their plan, having the favor and protection of their own natural gods. At this, these savages were so filled with arrogance that they would have attempted the deed without further delay, had their witch doctors and soothsayers not prevented them by bidding them await an occasion of less danger and greater certainty, such being the advice of their gods.

CHAPTER V

The people of Puna kill Huaina Cápac's captains.

WHILE THE *curacas* were plotting their treachery, Inca Huaina Cápac and his council were attending to the government and political system of their tribes, for it usually took longer to arrange this than to subdue them. For this purpose it was necessary to despatch certain captains of the royal blood to the mainland tribes to indoctrinate them, as well as the other inhabitants of the empire, in their vain religion and laws and customs. They were bidden to take with them warriors for the garrisons and for any military emergency that might arise. The natives were ordered to transport these captains by raft to a river mouth where they could conveniently land to perform these duties. Having given these instructions, the Inca returned to Túmbez to attend to other important administrative matters, for these princes studied only to do good to their vassals, because of which Padre Blas Valera very properly calls them fathers of their families and devoted guardians of their wards: he may have used these words as interpretations of a title we ourselves have mentioned as applied by the Indians to their Incas, that of lover and benefactor of the poor.

As soon as their king had left the island, the captains made arrangements to execute their mission. They ordered rafts to be brought to ferry them over the sea. The *curacas* who were in the conspiracy perceived the opportunity to carry out their treachery and therefore did not produce all the rafts they could have done, so as to take the Inca captains over in two journeys and thus carry out their plan more safely, which was to slay them at sea. Half of the soldiers embarked with the captains: both these and the men were chosen from all the military forces available. They wore many decorations as befitted men who were close to the royal person. All of them were Incas, either by blood or by privilege of the first Inca. On reaching a certain place where the natives had decided to execute their treachery, they loosed and cut the cables by which the poles were attached to the rafts and suddenly threw the captains and all their men into the sea. The Incas, who trusted the seamen, were taken unawares and slain to a man with the oars and their own weapons, which were turned against them. None were taken alive and though they tried to escape by swimming (for the Indians can usually swim), it was of no avail: the coastal Indians with their experience at sea were as superior to them above and below the water as sea animals to land animals. Thus the islanders were victorious and won a great quantity of valuable booty, which caused them to congratulate one another on their feat, shouting from raft to raft in their delight and triumph, for they imagined, like rude and savage people, that they were not only free from the Inca's rule, but that they were powerful enough to deprive him of his empire. In this vain presumption they returned to collect the captains and soldiers remaining on the island, and with complete dissimulation, they conveyed these to the same point as the first party and killed them as well. Those who had stayed on the island and in the other provinces that were in the plot and those who had been appointed as governors, magistrates and officials in charge of the estates of the Sun and of the Inca were dealt with in the same way, being slain with great cruelty and utter disrespect for the royal person. Their heads were exposed at the temple gates, and their hearts and blood offered up to the idols. In this way the natives fulfilled the promises they had made at the outset of their revolt if the demons should grant them their help and favor in this treacherous enterprise.

CHAPTER VI

The punishment of the rebels.

WHEN Inca Huaina Cápac heard of this misfortune, he displayed great grief at the death of so many nobles of the royal blood and of such great experience in war and peace, whose bodies were left unburied and cast away as food for the fishes. He put on mourning to show his sorrow. These kings wore the grey color known in Spain as *vellorí* for mourning. After the period of grief, he began to display his anger, summoning his people and, when he had gathered the necessary force, marching in all haste on the rebel provinces of the mainland. These were easily subdued for they had too little military spirit or organization to defend themselves, and insufficient forces to face those of the Inca.

After reducing these tribes, he crossed to the island. The natives showed some resistance at sea, but so little that they soon acknowledged defeat. The Inca ordered the arrest of all the principal perpetrators and authors of the revolt and of all the most notable captains and soldiers who had been present at the execution of his governors, officials, and magistrates. One of the Inca's commanders then delivered a harangue before them in which he emphasized their cruel treachery and wickedness toward those who had studied to benefit them and tried to raise them above their previous beastly existence and teach them human ways. In these circumstances the Inca could not exhibit his natural clemency and mercy, for his sense of justice would not allow it and the wickedness of the crime was such that no mitigation was possible. He therefore ordered them to be punished with the death they deserved for their treachery. On the announcement of this sentence, execution was done. The guilty suffered various deaths, corresponding to those inflicted on the Inca's officials: some were thrown into the sea with great weights attached to them; some were transfixed with pikes in punishment for their having exhibited the heads of the Incas at their temple gates on spears and pikes; others were beheaded and quartered; others were slain with their own arms, as they had slain the captains and soldiers; others were hanged. Pedro de Cieza de León, after recounting the story of this rebellion and its punishment at greater length than any other deed of the Incas, gives the following final summary in these words in his ch. liii:

And thus many thousands of Indians were killed in different ways, and many of the leading counsellors were impaled and drowned. After having carried out this great and fearful punishment Huaina Cápac ordered that reference to their wretched deed should be preserved in their songs, in dire and mournful rhythms. And indeed the Indians recite these events with other matters in their own languages like dirges. The Inca then ordered that an attempt should be made to build a causeway over the river at Guayaquil, which is very wide. To judge by the few pieces that are left, this must have been a mighty work, but it was never finished or completed as he desired. It is called "the passage of Huaina Cápac." After inflicting the punishment and ordering all the natives to obey their governor who was at the fortress of Túmbez, and making other dispositions, the Inca left the region.

This is all from Pedro de Cieza.

CHAPTER VII

The mutiny of the Chachapoyas, and
Huaina Cápac's magnanimity.

WHILE KING Huaina Cápac was preparing for his return to Cuzco and to visit his domains, many caciques arrived from those coastal provinces he had reduced to his empire with great presents of all the best products of their respective regions. Among other things he was brought a most ferocious lion and tiger, which the Inca greatly esteemed and which he ordered to be kept and tended with great care. We shall later recount a marvel performed by our Lord God in favor of the Christians with the aid of these animals, as a result of which the Indians worshipped them and said that they were children of the Sun. Inca Huaina Cápac left Túmbez, after making the necessary civil and military arrangements, and then visited the full length of half his kingdom, as far as the Chichas, who are at the limit of Peru. He intended to return through the other half further to the east, and from Chichas he sent inspectors to the kingdom of Tucma, which the Spaniards call Tucumán, and also to the kingdom of Chile. He ordered both missions to take great quantities of the Inca's garments and many other of his personal valuables for presentation to the governors, captains, and royal officials in those parts and also for the native chiefs, so that they should be honored by these gifts, which they so greatly esteemed, in the Inca's name. On both journeys, as he passed through Cuzco, he visited the fortress, the building of which was now in its final stages: he himself laid hands on certain parts of the work so as to encourage and honor the architects and laborers who were toiling there. After completing his tour of inspection, which lasted more than four years, he raised an army in order to carry his conquests along the seacoast to the north of Túmbez. But while the Inca was in the province of the Cañaris, whence he had intended to go to Quito and then descend to the coast and conquer it, he received news that the great province of Chachapoya, on finding him busily engaged in wars and conquests of such import, had rebelled, relying for success on the possession of a large and warlike population and a rough and difficult country. They had killed the Inca's governors and captains under pretence of friendship, and slain many of the common soldiers and captured many more, intending to use them as slaves. Huaina Cápac was very distressed on learning this, and ordered that the warriors who were marching toward the coast in various directions should return toward the province of Chachapoya, where he hoped to inflict severe punishment on the natives. He himself went to the point where the soldiers were to gather, and while his men were assembling, he sent messengers to the Chachapoyas to offer them forgiveness if they returned to his service. But instead of giving a fair answer, the Chachapoyas abused the messengers with foul words and threatened them with death. This made the Inca extremely angry; he accelerated the rallying of his men, and marched with them to a great river, where a great many rafts of a very light wood known in the general language of Peru as *chuchau* had been made ready.

It seemed to the Inca unbecoming to himself and to his army that they should cross the river on rafts in sixes and sevens, so he ordered the rafts to be turned into a bridge by making a chain of them across the water. The Indian warriors and camp followers worked to such good purpose that in the space of a day and a night the bridge was made. The Inca crossed with his army in formation, and hastily marched on Cajamarquilla, one of the chief towns of the province. His intention was to raze it and lay it waste, for this prince prided himself on being always as severe and rigorous toward obstinate rebels as he was gentle and merciful toward his humble subjects.

On realizing the wrath of the Inca and the might of his army, the rebels perceived too late the gravity of their crime, and began to fear the punishment that was now near at hand. Not knowing what course to take, since they imagined that, in addition to their principal offence, their impertinent refusal of the Inca's approach would have closed the gates of his mercy and clemency to them, they resolved to forsake their villages and homes and take flight into the wilderness. All those who could did so, but the old people, who remained behind with the rest of the non-combatants, remembered from experience Huaina Cápac's generosity and the fact that he never refused a request from a woman. They therefore had recourse to a Chachapoya matron, a native of the village of Cajamar-quilla who had been one of the many concubines of the great Túpac Inca Yupanqui, and assured her with all the earnestness and weeping their plight prompted to them that they had no other remedy or hope of saving themselves and their wives and children, all their villages and whole province from destruction, except that she should go and beg her son the Inca to forgive them.

The matron saw that she herself and all her kin without exception were exposed to the same peril, and therefore departed in all haste, accompanied by many women of all ages, but with no men to escort them. They went out to meet the Inca, whom they found nearly two leagues from Cajamarquilla. Prostrating herself at his feet, she addressed him with great spirit and valor:

"Sole Lord, where are you going? Do you not see that you are going in anger to destroy a province that your father conquered and added to your empire? Do you not realize that you are going against your own clemency and mercy? Do you not stop to think that tomorrow you will regret having indulged your rage and will wish you had not done so? Why do you not recall your title of Huacchacúyac, or lover of the poor, in which you take such pride? Why not take pity on these poorly advised wretches, for this, as you know, is the direst of all the forms of poverty? And even if you do not think these wretches deserve your clemency, remember your father who conquered them so that they should be your subjects. Remember that you are the child of the Sun. Do not let a fit of wrath stain your great deeds, past, present, and future, and shed the blood of people who have already surrendered to you in order to carry out a useless punishment. Do not forget that the greater the wrongs and the guilt of these wretched people, the more brightly will your clemency and mercy shine. Remember the clemency of all your ancestors and the great pride they took in it. Consider that you are the sum of them all. I beg you, as the child of the Sun you are, to forgive these wretches, and if you will not deign to grant my request, grant at least that I, as a native of this province that has offended you, shall be the first on whom the sword of your justice shall fall, that I may not witness the total destruction of my compatriots."

Having spoken these words, the matron was silent. The other women who had come with her raised doleful cries and wailing, repeating many times the Inca's titles, and saying: "Sole Lord, child of the Sun, lover of the poor, Huaina Cápac, have mercy on us and on our fathers, husbands, brothers, and sons."

The Inca was silent a long while, considering the argument of the *mamacuna*, and as she fortified her words with the same clamor and tears as the other women were pouring forth, his natural clemency asserted itself over the fires of his just anger, and he took pity on them. He went to his stepmother, raised her from the ground and said to her:

"You are indeed a Mamánchic (which is 'a common mother,' *i.e.*, my mother and the mother of your own people) since you watch over my honor from afar and advise me what behoves my honor and the memory of my father's majesty. I am deeply grateful to you, for there is no doubt as you say that tomorrow I should have regretted indulging my anger today. And you have acted as the mother of your own people, since you have redeemed their lives and their dwelling places to such good purpose; and since you have shown yourself so good a mother to us all, it shall be done as you require, and you may think if you have any other request to make of me. Return with my blessing to your people and pardon them in my name, and do them any other favor that you think fit. Tell them to be grateful to you, and as further proof that they are forgiven take four Incas with you, my brothers and your sons, who shall take no soldiers with them, but only the officials necessary for the restoration of peace and good government."

This said, the Inca returned with all his army, which was again directed toward the coast, as he had first intended.

The Chachapoyas were so convinced of their own guilt and of the Inca's mercifulness, that they were thenceforward very loyal subjects. In memory of his magnanimity toward them, which they greatly venerated, they built a wall round the spot where Huaina Cápac had had the conversation with his stepmother, so as to keep it as a sacred place because so great a deed had been done there, and neither men, nor animals, nor even birds, if possible, were to set foot there. Three walls were built, the first of very smooth masonry with a frieze at the top, the second of rough masonry to protect the first, and the third of baked mud to protect the other two. Some remains of these walls can still be seen: they were so built that they might have lasted many centuries, but human covetousness prevented this, and they were all overthrown in the search for buried treasure.

CHAPTER VIII

The gods and customs of the Manta tribe;
their subjugation and that of
other savage peoples.

H UAINA CÁPAC directed his march toward the seacoast for the conquest he desired to undertake there. He reached the borders of the
province known as Manta, the district in which the port the Spaniards
call Puerto Viejo lies: we mentioned the reason for this name at the
beginning of our history. The natives of this region and of the whole
coast for many leagues to the north had the same customs and the same
form of idolatry. They worshipped the sea and the fish they caught in
greatest numbers for food: they worshipped tigers and lions, the large
snakes, and other beasts, as the fancy took them. Among the objects they
worshipped in the valley of Manta, which was as it were the capital of
the whole region, was a great emerald, said to be almost as large as an
ostrich's egg. It was exhibited in public on their greater festivals, and the
Indians came from great distances to worship it and sacrifice to it, bringing gifts of smaller emeralds, for their priests and the cacique of Manta
put it about that it was a very agreeable offering for their goddess, the
great emerald, to be presented with smaller emeralds, which were her
daughters. By means of this covetous doctrine they collected a great
quantity of emeralds in this place, where they were found by Don Pedro
de Alvarado and his companions, one of whom was my lord Garcilaso
de la Vega, when they went to conquer Peru. The Spaniards broke most
of the stones on an anvil, thinking, like very unskilled lapidaries, that if
they were fine stones they would not break however hard they were struck
and that if they broke that they were only glass and not fine stones at all.
The emerald that was worshipped as a goddess was spirited away by the
Indians as soon as the Spaniards entered that kingdom: and it was so
carefully hidden that, despite much search and the application of many
threats, it has never reappeared. In the same way an infinite quantity of
other treasure has been lost in Peru.

The natives of Manta and its surrounding region, especially the coastal
Indians, though not those of the interior called *serranos,* practised sodomy
more openly and shamelessly than all the other tribes which we have so

far noted as having indulged in this vice. They made it a condition of marriage that the bridegroom's relatives and friends enjoyed the bride before he did. They flayed the prisoners they took in battle and filled their skins with ashes, so that they looked as they were before: they hung the bodies at the gates of their temples and in the squares where they held their festivities and dances as a sign of victory.

The Inca despatched the usual summons to them, that they should either prepare for war or surrender to his authority. The people of Manta had for long realized that they could not resist the Inca's power, and though they had tried to form an alliance with the many neighboring tribes for their mutual defence, they had been unable to reduce them to conformity, for they were mostly independent and anarchical and had no law or government. For this reason they all surrendered to Huaina Cápac with great ease. The Inca received them affably, bestowing presents and favors on them and appointing governors and officials to instruct them in his idolatrous beliefs and laws and customs, while he himself passed on to the conquest of another great province called Caranque. There are many tribes in this district, and all independent, without any law or government. They surrendered easily, for they did not aspire to defend themselves, and could not have done so had they wished, since the Inca's power was now so great that none could stand up against him. As in previous conquests, the Inca appointed teachers and governors and continued with his conquests. He then reached peoples who were more savage and beastly than any of those he had hitherto conquered in the coastal region, men and women who disfigured their faces with sharp flints, and deformed their children's heads from birth by placing boards on the forehead and nape and tightening them daily until the children were four or five years old, by which time the head had been flattened across the front and narrowed from front to back. And not content with this broadening process, they also clipped the hair from the scalp, crown, and nape, leaving that at the sides: the hair that remained was never combed or smoothed, but left rough and unruly to add to the monstrous appearance of the face. They lived by fishing, being great anglers, and on herbs, roots, and wild fruit. They went naked, and worshipped the same objects as their neighbors. These tribes were called Apichiqui, Pichunsi, Sava, Pecllansimiqui, Pampahuaci, and others. Having reduced them the Inca went on to another people called the Saramissu, and thence to others called Passau who live exactly on the equator. The people of this province are far more savage than any others conquered by the Incas. They had no gods and no idea of what worship was; they had no villages or houses, but lived in hollow trees in the mountains, which are very wild in those parts; they had no acknowledged wives and did not know which were their own children; they were open sodomites; they did not know how to till the land, or do anything else to their own advantage; they went naked and in addition to piercing their lips inside and out, smeared their faces in quarters with different colors, one yellow, one blue, one red, and one black, each one varying the colors as he saw fit; they never combed their heads, but wore their hair long and tangled, full of straw and dirt and anything that fell on them: in short they were worse than beasts. I saw them with my own eyes when I came to Spain in 1560, for our ship stopped there three days to take on water and fuel, and a great many of them came out on reed rafts to haggle with those on the ship. The trade was in large fish which the natives caught with spears before our eyes, and they fished with such skill and dexterity (for such savage people) that the Spaniards would buy the fish before they were caught for the pleasure of watching the process. They asked for biscuit and meat for their fish, and refused money. Their private parts were covered with cloths made of the bark or leaves of trees. This was done more out of respect for the Spaniards than from any natural sense of shame. They were indeed as rank savages as one could imagine.

Inca Huaina Cápac, on seeing and realizing the wretchedness of this rough and sorrowful land and the bestiality and brutishness of the filthy inhabitants, knew that it would be a waste of effort to try to reduce them to civil order, and is said to have remarked: "Let us retire, they do not deserve to have us as their masters." This said, he bade his army return, leaving the natives of Passau as brutish and ignorant as before.

CHAPTER IX

The giants of those parts and how they met their deaths.

BEFORE leaving this region, we should mention a very remarkable story which the natives have received as a tradition handed down by their ancestors for many centuries. It refers to some giants who they say arrived in their country from over the sea and landed at the point now

called Santa Elena, a name given to it because it was first seen by Spaniards on this saint's day. As Pedro de Cieza de León is the Spanish historian who speaks of these giants at greatest length, having received his
version in the very province which the giants visited, it seemed best that
I should follow his account word for word, for although Padre José de
Acosta and the accountant general Agustín de Zárate say the same, their
version is very brief. Pedro de Cieza's fuller account in his ch. lii is as
follows:

As there is in Peru a story of some giants who landed on the coast at the point
of Santa Elena, in the vicinity of the city of Puerto Viejo, I have resolved to
mention what I was told about them, as I understood it, without taking into
account the opinions of the common people and their various anecdotes, for
they usually magnify events larger than life. The natives, repeating a story received from their forefathers from very remote times, say that there arrived
from across the sea on reed rafts that were as large as big ships some men who
were so big that an ordinary man of good size scarcely reached up to their
knees: their members were in proportion to the size of their bodies, and it was
a monstrous thing to see their enormous heads and their hair hanging down
about their shoulders. Their eyes were as large as small plates. They say that
they had no beards and that some of them were clad in the skins of animals
and others only in the dress nature gave them. There were no women with them.
On reaching this point, they set up their camp like a village (and even in these
times there is a memory of the site of their houses). As they found no supply
of water they remedied the lack by making some very deep wells, a labor certainly worthy of record, being undertaken by such strong men as these must
have been, to judge by their size. They dug these wells in the living rock until
they came to the water, and afterwards they built the wells in stone from the
water line upwards so that they would last for ages. In these wells the water is
excellent and it is always so cold that it is very pleasant to drink.

When these great men or giants had thus made their settlement and dug
these wells or cisterns, they destroyed and ate all the supplies they could find
in the neighborhood. It is said that one of them ate more than fifty of the natives of the land; and as the supply of food was not sufficient for them to maintain themselves, they caught much fish with nets and gear that they had. They
lived in continuous hostility with the natives, because they slew the latter's
women in order to have them, and they also slew the men for other reasons.
But the Indians were not numerous enough to kill these newcomers who had
occupied their land and lorded it over them; and although they held great discussions about this, they never dared attack them.

After some years the giants were still in this region, and as they had no
women of their own and the Indian women of the neighborhood were too
small for them, or else because the vice was habitual to them and inspired by

the demon, they practised the unspeakable and horrible sin of sodomy, committing it openly and in public without fear of God or personal shame. The natives say that our Lord God, unwilling to conceal so wicked a sin, sent them a punishment suited to the beastliness of the crime, and when all the giants were together engaged in this accursed practice there came a fearful fire from heaven to the accompaniment of a great noise, in the midst of which a shining angel appeared holding a sharp, bright sword with which he slew them all at a single stroke, and the fire consumed them leaving only a few bones and skulls, which God allowed to remain unconsumed as a token of the punishment. This is the account they give of the giants, and we believe that it happened, for it is said that very large bones have been found and still are found thereabouts and I have heard Spaniards say they have seen pieces of teeth which they thought must have weighed half a pound when whole, and who had also seen a piece of a shin-bone of wonderful size, all of which bears witness to the truth of the incident. In addition to this one can see the places where the sites of their villages were, and also the wells or cisterns they made. I cannot state whence or how these giants came there.

In the present year of 1550 when in the city of Lima, I heard that when his excellency Don Antonio de Mendoza was viceroy and governor of New Spain, certain bones of men as big as these giants, and even bigger, were found there. I have heard too that in an ancient sepulcher in the city of Mexico or somewhere else in that kingdom certain bones of giants have been found. Since so many people saw them and attest having done so, it can therefore be credited that such giants did exist and indeed they may all have been of the same race.

At this point of Santa Elena, which is as I have said on the coast of Peru and in the district of the city of Puerto Viejo, there is a remarkable penomenon: the existence of certain wells or seams of pitch of such excellent quality that it would be possible to tar all the ships one wished with it, since it flows from the earth. This pitch must be from some seam passing through that place: it comes out very hot,

etc. Thus far Pedro de Cieza, whose history we have followed to show the Indian tradition about the giants, and the well of pitch at the same place, for it too is remarkable.

CHAPTER X

What Huaina Cápac said about the Sun.

As we have seen, King Huaina Cápac ordered his army to return from the province called Passau, which he established as the furthest limit of his empire in that direction, *i.e.*, to the north. Having disbanded his men, he returned toward Cuzco, visiting his kingdoms and provinces and conferring favors and administering justice to all those who asked him for it. He arrived back in Cuzco from this tour of inspection in a certain year in time to celebrate the chief feast of the Sun called Raimi. The Indians say that on one of the nine days the feast lasted, he availed himself of the newly acquired liberty of looking at the Sun (which was formerly prohibited as disrespectful), and set his eyes on it or near it, where the Sun permits, and spent some time gazing at it.

The high priest, one of his uncles, was by his side and said: "What are you doing, Inca? Do you not know it is unlawful to do that?" The king then lowered his eyes, only to raise them shortly after with the same liberty and fix them on the Sun. The high priest said: "Sole Lord, look what you are doing, for not only is it forbidden for us to look freely on our father the Sun, as disrespectful, but you are setting a bad example to the whole court and your whole empire, which is concentrated here duly to venerate and worship your father as their sole and supreme lord."

Huaina Cápac then turned to the priest and said: "I wish to ask you two questions in reply to what you have just said. I am your king and universal lord: would any of my subjects dare to make bold to bid me rise from my place and make a long journey at his behest?"

The priest replied: "Who could be so mad as that?"

The Inca answered: "And is there any *curaca* among my subjects, however rich and powerful, who would not obey me if I bade him go by road from here to Chile?"

The priest said: "No, Inca, there is none who would not obey you to the death in everything you bid."

Then the king answered: "Then I tell you that our father the Sun must have another greater lord more powerful than himself, one who bids him undertake this journey he daily performs without stopping; for if he were the supreme lord, he would every now and then desist from his journey, and rest at his ease, even though there were no need for him to do so."

Because of this saying and others they heard the Indians repeat about this prince, the Spaniards used to say that if he had chanced to hear Christian doctrine, he would have readily embraced the Catholic faith on account of his good understanding and subtle wit. A Spanish captain who must have been one of the many who heard this anecdote about Huaina Cápac (for it was public knowledge in Peru) adopted it as his own and told it as such to Padre Acosta, and indeed it may have been his. His Paternity includes it in Book V of his history of the New World (ch. v). After this, he adds the saying of Huaina Cápac, without naming him, for it also came to his notice, and observes:

It is told that one of these Inca kings, a man of very subtle wit, seeing that all his ancestors had worshipped the Sun, declared that he did not think that the Sun was God, or could be. For God is a great Lord, and goes about his affairs quietly and supremely and the Sun never stops moving, so that it seemed to him unlikely that such a restless body could be God. He spoke rightly, and if the Indians hear their errors and ignorance explained to them gently and reasonably, they are soon convinced and accept the truth.

Thus far Padre Acosta, who finishes his chapter here. The Indians, being so superstitious and easily alarmed, took this king's innovation in looking freely at the Sun as a bad omen. Huaina Cápac took this liberty because he had heard his father Túpac Inca Yupanqui say almost the same of the Sun, as we have mentioned in speaking of him.

CHAPTER XI

The revolt of the Caranques; their punishment.

WHILE Inca Huaina Cápac was visiting his domains on the last tour of inspection he made, he received news that the province of Carangue (which, as we have mentioned, he had conquered on the extreme confines of the kingdom of Quito and which was populated by cruel and barbarous savages who ate human flesh and offered up as sacrifices the blood, heads, and hearts of those they killed) could no longer bear the Inca's yoke, especially in regard to the law that forbade them to eat human flesh, and had risen in revolt together with other provinces which shared their customs and also feared the empire of the Incas. The latter indeed now extended to their very gates and threatened to impose the same prohibitions on them as on their neighbors, particularly in regard to the things they cherished most for their beastly practices and pleasures. For this reason they were easily drawn into the plot and with great secrecy prepared a large force to slay the Inca's governors and officials and the garrison forces residing among them. Until the time they had fixed for the execution of their treacherous attack they served the Incas with the greatest submission and every possible display of feigned affection, so as to be able to take them unawares and kill them without risk to themselves. The day arrived, and the natives butchered them with the greatest cruelty, offering their heads, hearts, and blood to their own gods in gratitude for having freed them from the Inca's sway and restored their ancient customs. They ate the flesh of all their victims with great voracity and relish, swallowing it unchewed as a result of having been forbidden to touch it for so long under pain of punishment if they did so. They committed every possible kind of outrage and insult.

When Huaina Cápac heard of this, it caused him great grief and anger: he ordered captains and men to make ready to go and punish the wickedness of these savage beasts, and he himself followed behind to observe events. The captains reached the Caranques and before beginning to make war on them sent messengers in the Inca's name, offering to pardon them for their offence if they would beg for mercy and bow to the will of their king. The rebels, like true savages, not only refused to give in, but even replied quite shamelessly and misused the messengers almost to the point of killing them. When Huaina Cápac learned of this new outrage on the part of these brutes, he joined his army so as to open operations in person. He ordered his followers to make war with blood and fire, and many thousands were killed on both sides, for the enemy fought stubbornly like rebels, and the Inca's men, in order to avenge the outrage on their ruler, acquitted themselves like true soldiers. But as there was no possible resistance to the Inca's power, the enemy shortly weakened. They no longer gave open battle, but made sudden attacks in prepared ambushes, defending the difficult passes, the mountaintops and strong places. But the Inca's might overcame them and brought his enemies low. Many thousands of them were taken captives. The guiltiest, including those responsible for the rising, numbered two thousand, some of them the Caranques who had rebelled and others their allies who had not previously been conquered by the Inca. All were visited with an exemplary and rigorous punishment: they were to be beheaded in a great lake that lies on the borders of the districts of the Caranques and the rest, and so that its name should preserve the memory of their guilt and chastisement it was called Pahuarcocha, "lake or sea of blood," for the lake was turned into blood on account of the quantity that was spilt. Pedro de Cieza refers briefly to this incident in his ch. xxxvii, saying that twenty thousand were put to death: he must have meant this as the number who died in the war on both sides, for the fighting was bitter and cruel.

After this chastisement, Inca Huaina Cápac went to Quito, grieving greatly that such inhuman and atrocious acts of treason should occur in his reign, demanding severe and cruel punishment, so alien to his own character and indeed to that of all his predecessors who had prided themselves on their clemency and mercy. He regretted that these risings should have taken place in his own time and so rendered it unhappy, rather than in the past, for there was no memory of any other such occurrence except that of the Chancas in the days of Inca Viracocha. But, duly considered, these things seem rather to have been auguries and prophecies threatening the approach of an even greater rebellion, which would cause the loss of their empire to a race of strangers and the total destruction of their royal blood, as we shall soon see.

CHAPTER XII

Huaina Cápac makes his son Atahuallpa king of Quito.

As we have already noted Huaina Cápac had his son Atahuallpa by the daughter of the king of Quito, who was to succeed her father in that kingdom. This son displayed a ready intelligence and understanding, and was astute, sagacious, and prudent: his mettle was brave and warlike, his bearing noble and his features handsome, as those of all the Incas and Pallas usually were. Because of these gifts of body and mind his father loved him tenderly and always took him with him. He would have liked to leave his whole empire to the boy, but could not deprive his first-born, Huáscar Inca, of his legitimate rights, and therefore sought, against the custom and constitution of all his ancestors, to deprive the heir of the kingdom of Quito, giving the proceeding the appearance of justice and restitution. To this effect he summoned Prince Huáscar Inca who was in Cuzco, and on his arrival held a great gathering of his sons and many captains and *cuaracas* who were with him, and addressed his legitimate heir in the presence of all of them in the following terms:

"It is notorious, prince, that according to the ancient custom that our first father Inca Manco Cápac bequeathed to us to observe, this kingdom of Quito belongs to your crown, for this is what has been done hitherto, and all the kingdoms and provinces that have been conquered have been annexed and incorporated in your empire and subjected to the jurisdiction and control of our imperial city of Cuzco. But because I love your brother Atahuallpa very dearly and I regret to see him in poverty, I should be glad if you would consent that, of all the domains I have won for your crown, the inheritance and succession of the kingdom of Quito—which belonged to his ancestors on his mother's side and would today have been his mother's—should be left to him so that he can live in royal estate as his virtues well merit, for being a good brother as he is, and having resources, he may serve you better in all you require than if he were poor. And in recompense and satisfaction of the little I now ask of you, you yourself will still find many other broad kingdoms and provinces around your own possessions which you can conquer, wherein your brother will serve you as a soldier and captain, and when the time comes for me to go and rest with our father the Sun, I shall go happily from this world."

Prince Huáscar Inca readily replied that he would be exceedingly glad to obey his father the Inca in this matter and in anything else he demanded of him, and if it were his father's pleasure to take away other provinces so as to give more to Atahuallpa, he would willingly do so to make him happy. Huaina Cápac was very satisfied with this reply. He ordered Huáscar to return to Cuzco, and began to place Atahuallpa in possession of his domains, giving him other provinces in addition to Quito. He also provided him with experienced captains and part of his army to serve and accompany him. In short he bestowed every possible favor on Atahuallpa, even to the disadvantage of his heir. He behaved like a father smitten with passionate love for his son, and wished to spend the rest of his life in Quito and its district, taking this decision partly to favor and further Atahuallpa's reign, and partly to subdue and pacify the newly won provinces of the coast and interior, which had still not settled down under the rule and administration of the Incas, but behaved like warlike, though savage bestial people. For this reason it was necessary to shift many of these tribes to other provinces, and bring in quiet and peaceful races in their stead, the remedy that those kings usually resorted to to secure themselves against rebellion, as we explained at length in speaking of the emigrants, called *mítmac*.

CHAPTER XIII

Two famous roads in Peru.

I T IS proper that in recounting the life of Huaina Cápac we should refer to the two royal highways that run from the north to the south of Peru, since they are attributed to him. One of them passes through the llanos, that is by the seacoast, while the other goes inland by the sierra. They are dwelt on at some length by the historians, but they represent an achievement so great as to defy description, and as I cannot myself describe them as well as they have done, I shall quote each of the historians word for word. Agustín de Zárate (Book I, ch. xiii), speaking of the origin of the Incas, says:

By the succession of the Incas power devolved upon one of their number called Huaina Cápac (which means "Rich Youth") who won more lands, extended their sway more widely, and governed with greater justice and right than all the rest. He raised Peru to such a degree of political consciousness that one would have thought it impossible for an uncivilized and illiterate people to be governed with such regularity and order or to display such love and obedience towards its rulers. And in his service they built two roads which are so remarkable that they should certainly not be overlooked, for none of the monuments that ancient writers referred to as the seven wonders of the world was built with such difficulty, labor, and expense as these. When this Huaina Cápac marched with his army from the City of Cuzco to conquer the province of Quito, a distance of about five hundred leagues, he had great difficulty on the mountain road because of the roughness of the way and the ravines and cliffs he encountered. The Indians therefore thought it fitting to build a new road for his triumphant return once he had reduced the province of Quito, and they made this smooth, broad highway the whole length of the mountain chain, cutting through the rock and levelling it wherever necessary and filling the ravines with rubble. In some places it was necessary to raise the surface fifteen or twenty times the height of a man, and this road runs for a distance of five hundred leagues. And it is said that when finished the road was so smooth that a wagon could have run along it, though since those times, owing to the wars of the

Indians and of the Christians, the rubble-work has been broken down in many places in order to hold up the advance of enemy forces. The difficulty of the feat will be appreciated by anyone who watches the labor and expense of leveling two leagues of mountain road in Spain between El Espinar near Segovia and Guadarrama, a task that has never been completely finished in spite of the fact that it is the route continually used by the kings of Castile and their court and household whenever they come or go from Andalusia or from the kingdom of Toledo to this side of the passes.

And not satisfied with executing this noteworthy work, when Huaina Cápac again decided to visit the province of Quito, to which he was much attached because he himself had been the conqueror of it, he returned by the coastal plains and the Indians built for him another system of roads no less difficult than the mountain highway; for in every valley when the road came to the fresh river sides with their groves of trees, which, as we have said, normally extend for a distance of a league, they made thick mud walls on either side nearly forty feet apart and four or five bricks deep; and when the road left these valleys it was continued across the sandy deserts, where stakes and rods were driven in so that no one could miss the way or stray to right or left. And this road also runs for five hundred leagues, just like the mountain highway, and though the stakes in the deserts are destroyed in many places, having been used for fuel by the Spaniards in time of war or peace, yet the walls in the valleys are still standing in most places and they suffice to give an idea of the great scale of the whole work. Thus Huaina Cápac went by one road and returned by the other, and wherever he passed the way was always covered and strewn with branches and sweetly-smelling flowers.

Thus far Agustín de Zárate. Pedro de Cieza de León on the same subject refers in his ch. xxxvii to the mountain highway as follows:

From Ipiales the road goes to a small province called Huaca, and before reaching the latter, one sees the Inca highway, which is as famous in those parts as the road Hannibal made through the Alps when he descended on Italy, and may be regarded as even more remarkable, both because of the great lodging places and storehouses built all along it and because of the great difficulty in driving it through such steep and craggy mountains. It is an astonishing sight.

Pedro de Cieza says no more than this of the mountain highway, but further on, in his ch. lx, he refers to the coastal road as follows:

In order to arrange my work in due order, I intend, before concluding with the description of the upland provinces, to comment on the coastal plains, a subject of great importance, as has been said elsewhere. Here I shall describe the great highway built through the middle of this area by order of the Incas. Although this is now broken and destroyed in many places, one can still see how great it was and how powerful were its builders. Huaina Cápac and Túpac Inca

Yupanqui, his father, are reputed by the Indians to have come down through all this coastal region and to have visited the valleys and provinces of the Yuncas, though some of the Indians also say that Inca Yupanqui, the grandfather of Huaina Cápac and father of Túpac Inca, was the first to see the coast and traverse the plains. And in these coastal valleys the caciques and chiefs built, on the Inca's orders, a road fifteen-feet wide with a wall along it higher than a man and very substantially constructed. Through its whole length the road was level and shaded by groves of trees, from which boughs laden with fruit often hung over the way. And in the woods the trees were full of many kinds of birds and parrots,

etc. Further on, after mentioning the storehouses and the stocks kept for the armies along the road, which we have already described, he says:

The walls that ran along either side of these roads continued until the ground was too sandy to permit the Indians to build foundations for them. Thereafter, lest the traveller should be lost or lest he should forget the greatness of the builder of the highway, long and heavy stakes, as big as beams, were driven into the ground at intervals. And just as they took pains to keep the road clear and rebuild the walls if they crumbled or fell, they also paid attention in case any of the stakes or beams in the desert fell and duly replaced them. Thus this surely marked road was a great work, though not so great a labor as the other. There were some fortresses and temples of the Sun in these valleys as I shall mention in their due place,

etc. Thus far Cieza de León, word for word. Juan Botero Benes also mentions these roads and includes them in his reports as marvels, and though he writes briefly, his descriptions are excellent:

From the city of Cuzco there are two roads or royal highways two thousand miles long, one following the coastal plains and the other the mountain peaks, so that in order to bring them to their present state it was necessary to raise the valleys, cleave the stones and the living rock, and humble the pride of the hills. They were twenty-five feet wide. A work that incomparably excels the constructions of Egypt and the monuments of Rome,

etc.

So speak these three authors in referring to the two famous roads, which each of the historians have extolled as best he could, though all their words fall short of the greatness of the work, and it is sufficient to emphasize its continuity for a distance of five hundred leagues, including slopes two, three, four, or more leagues long, to show that no description can do justice to it. In addition is is worth mentioning that on the mountain highway they built level spaces on either side of the road at the highest points with the broadest views. These platforms were approached by stone steps and were for the porters to set down the litters and rest and for the Inca to enjoy the view in all directions over these high mountains and their foothills, some covered with snow and others bare, a most wonderful panorama, for from some points, according to the height of the ranges the road crosses, one can see fifty, sixty, eighty, and a hundred leagues. Some of the crests are so high that they seem to touch the sky, and the valleys and ravines are so deep that they appear to go down to the middle of the earth. Of all this great structure all that remains is what time and war has failed to consume. On the coastal road, with its sandy deserts, which are very extensive with their hills and hillocks of sand, high poles have been set up at intervals, so that each can be seen from the last and they thus serve as a guide to prevent travellers from losing their way, for the surface of the road disappears with the movement of the sand which covers it completely when the wind blows, and there is no certainty in taking the sandhills as a guide for they too disappear and change their place if the wind is strong. For this reason the stakes by the roadside are necessary for the guidance of wayfarers, and they have been preserved because it would be impossible to do without them.

CHAPTER XIV

Huaina Cápac heard that the Spaniards were off the coast.

WHILE Huaina Cápac was thus engaged at the royal palace of Tumipampa, one of the most splendid in Peru, he received news that strange people, never before seen in those parts, had arrived in a ship off the coast of the empire and were asking what land they had come to. This news roused in Huaina Cápac a new preoccupation, that of ascertaining what people these were and whence they came. Now this ship belonged to Vasco Núñez de Balboa, the discoverer of the Pacific Ocean, and these Spaniards were those who applied the name Peru, as we said at the outset, to the Inca empire. This was in 1515, the discovery of the Pacific having taken place two years before. One historian says that the Spaniards in this ship were Don Francisco Pizarro and his thirteen companions, whom he describes as the first discoverers of Peru. But this is an error and confuses the conquerors with the discoverers. There is also an error in the date, for sixteen or more years elapsed between the discovery and the conquest: the first discovery of Peru and the application of this name date from 1515, while Don Francisco Pizarro and his four brothers and Don Diego de Almagro entered Peru to conquer it in 1531. Huaina Cápac had died eight years earlier in 1524, after reigning forty-two years, as the torn and tattered papers in which that great investigator, Fray Blas Valera, wrote the ancient deeds of these kings, testify.

Huaina Cápac spent the eight years between the first news of the discoverers and his death peacefully governing his domains. He did not wish to embark on new conquests but preferred to wait and see what might come from over the sea. The news of the arrival of this ship worried him greatly, and he pondered on an ancient oracle the Incas had, to the effect that after a certain number of kings had come and gone, a strange race, never before seen, would deprive them of their kingdom and destroy their race and religion. As we shall see, this prophecy was due to be fulfilled with the present Inca. Moreover, three years before the arrival of this ship off the coast of Peru, an ill-omen or portent occurred in Cuzco and greatly alarmed Huaina Cápac and terrified the whole empire. This was that, during the celebration of the solemn festivity dedicated every year to their god the Sun, they saw a royal eagle, which they call *anca*, approach, pursued by five or six kestrels and other little hawks of a variety which is so handsome that many specimens have been brought to Spain where they are called *aletos*: in Peru they are known as *huaman*. These in turn fell on the eagle, brought it down and dealt it mortal blows. The eagle could not defend itself and sought refuge by dropping into the middle of the main square of the city, among the Incas. The latter picked it up and found it stricken and covered with scales, like a scurf, and almost denuded of its under feathers. They fed it and tried to cure it, but to no avail, and within a few days it died, unable to rise from the ground. The Inca and his companions took this as an ill omen, and the soothsayers interpreted the significance of it using many of the explanations they keep for such occasions. All of these however threatened the ruin of the empire and the destruction of the Inca state and religion. There were also great earthquakes and tremors, and though Peru is greatly subject to this scourge, it was noted that the tremors were much worse than usual and that many high hills fell down. They learnt from the coastal Indians, moreover, that the tides of the sea greatly exceeded their normal limits, and they saw that many fearful and horrifying comets appeared in the air. Among these wonders and alarms, they noticed one clear calm night that the moon was surrounded by three large rings, the first the color of blood; the second, further out, greenish-black; and the third smoky-looking. A soothsayer or magician, called by the Indians *llaica,* having seen the rings around the moon, came to Huaina Cápac and with a sad and tearful countenance, almost unable to speak, declared:

"Sole Lord, know that your mother the Moon is warning you like a loving parent that Pachacámac, the creator and sustainer of the world, threatens your royal blood and your empire with great plagues with which he will visit you and your people. The first ring round your mother the Moon, which is the color of blood, means that after you have gone to rest with your father the Sun there will be cruel war between your descendants and much shedding of your royal blood, so that in a few years all will be finished; and for this reason she would fain burst with weeping. The second black ring threatens us with the destruction of our religion and our state and the loss of your empire in the midst of the wars and the slaughter of your people. Then all will be turned to smoke, as the third and smoky ring indicates."

The Inca was greatly distressed, but said to the magician in order not to show weakness: "Come, you must have dreamed this nonsense last night, and you say these are revelations from my mother."

The magician answered: "In order that you shall believe me, Inca, you may go out and see your mother's tokens with your own eyes, and you shall bid the other soothsayers appear and you shall know what they say of these omens."

The Inca came forth from his apartment, and after seeing the signs, he ordered all the magicians who were in his court to be assembled, and one of them, of the Yauyu tribe, who was regarded as superior by the rest, also contemplated the rings and said the same as the first. In order that his followers should not be discouraged by such sad auguries, even though they only confirmed what was in his own breast, Huaina Cápac pretended not to believe them and told his soothsayers: "If Pachacámac himself does not tell me so, I do not propose to give credit to what you say, for it is unthinkable that my father the Sun should so abhor his own blood as to permit the total destruction of his children." Whereupon he dismissed the soothsayers. However, on considering their words, which so closely followed the ancient oracle that had been handed down from his ancestors, and associating them with the strange wonders that the four elements daily revealed, and further with the arrival of the ship bearing unknown people, Huaina Cápac lived in fear and anguish. He was always accompanied by a good army of experienced veterans chosen from the garrisons in these provinces. He ordered many sacrifices to be made to the Sun and bade the soothsayers and wizards, each in their own provinces, consult their familiar devils, particularly the great Pachacámac and the devil Rímac who gave out answers to questions. They were to ask whether the new wonders that had been seen on the sea and in the other elements boded well or ill. From Rímac and other places obscure and confused answers were brought, which neither failed to promise some good nor to threaten much ill. Most of the wizards gave bad auguries, so that all the empire feared some great adversity. But as none of the new things feared occurred in the first three or four years, their former confidence was restored and they lived without care for a few years until the death of Huaina Cápac.

Our account of these prophecies is derived both from popular tradition general to the whole empire and in particular from two captains of Huaina Cápac's guard, each of whom survived to the age of over eighty. Both were baptized: the elder was called Don Juan Pachuta. He took as his surname the name he had before he was baptized, as most of the Indians have done. The other was called Chauca Rimachi: his Christian name has gone from my memory. Whenever they told of these prophecies and the events of those times, these captains dissolved in tears and it was necessary to change the subject to make them cease to weep. The testament and death of Huaina Cápac and everything else that followed it we shall tell from the version of the old Inca called Cusi Huallpa, and for a great part of it, particularly the cruelties that Atahuallpa performed on those of the royal blood, I shall draw on the account given by my mother and a brother of hers called Don Fernando Huallpa Túpac Inca Yupanqui, who were in those days children of under ten years of age and were in the midst of his savagery during the two and a half years it lasted, until the Spaniards entered Peru. In due course we shall say how they and the few of their line who escaped were saved from Atahuallpa's executions, by favor of their own enemies.

CHAPTER XV

*The testament and death of Huaina Cápac and the
prophecy of the arrival of the Spaniards.*

WHEN Huaina Cápac entered the kingdom of Quito, during the last
days of his life, he went into a lake to bathe for pleasure and refreshment. He came out with a chill, which the Indians call *chucchu,* "trembling," and as it was followed by a fever, which they call *rupa* (soft *r*),
he felt that his illness was fatal, for he had had intimations of it for the
past two years drawn from the witchcraft, omens, and divinations so
general among these heathens. These prophecies, especially those refer-
ing to the royal person, were said by the Incas to be revelations of his
father the Sun in order to give authority and credit to his idolatry.

In addition to the prophecies that had been drawn from these wizard-
ries or revealed by the demons, fearful comets appeared in the air, including one very large and alarming one of a green color, and the thunderbolt we have mentioned as having fallen on the house of the Inca
himself, together with other prodigies that greatly terrified the *amautas,*
who were the wise men of the Inca state, and wizards and priests. Being
so intimate with the Devil, they were able to foretell not only the death
of the Inca Huaina Cápac, but also the destruction of his royal blood, the
loss of his kingdom and other great calamities and misfortunes, which
they said all in general and each in particular were to suffer. These things
they dared not publish so as not to alarm the land to such an extent that
the people would die of terror, so timid were they and so ready to believe
new things and fatal wonders.

Feeling himself stricken, Huaina Cápac called together the children
and relatives he had around him and such of the governors and captains
of the army from the nearer provinces who could arrive in time, and said
to them:

"I am going to rest in heaven with our father the Sun, who revealed to
me some days ago that he would call me from a lake or river, and as I
came out of the water with this present indisposition, it is a certain sign
that our father the Sun is calling me. When I am dead, you shall open
my body, as is the custom with royal corpses. My heart and entrails, and

all the inner parts, I order to be buried in Quito as a mark of my love for that place, and the body you shall bear to Cuzco and place it with those of my ancestors. I recommend to you my son Atahuallpa, whom I love so dearly, who remains as Inca in my place in this kingdom of Quito and in all the other places he may conquer by force of arms and add to his empire; and, captains of my army, I bid you in particular to serve him with the fidelity and love you owe to your king for I recommend him to you as king so that you may obey him in all things and do what he bids you, which will be what I shall reveal to him by order of our father the Sun. I also recommend you to show justice and clemency toward the vassals, so that the title we have received of lover of the poor shall not be lost, and I bid you act in all things like Incas, children of the Sun."

After making this speech to his sons and relatives, he bade the other captains and *curacas* who were not of the royal blood to be called, and urged on them loyalty and good service to their king, concluding:

"Many years ago it was revealed to us by our father the Sun that after twelve of his sons had reigned, a new race would come, unknown in these parts, and would gain and subdue all our kingdoms and many others to their empire. I suspect that these must be those we have heard of off our coasts. They will be a brave people who will overcome us in everything. We also know that in my reign the number of twelve Incas is completed. I assure you that a few years after I have gone away from you, these new people will come and fulfil what our father the Sun has foretold, and will gain our empire and become masters of it. I bid you obey them and serve them as men who will be completely victorious, for their law will be better than ours and their arms more powerful and invincible than ours. Remain in peace, for I am going to rest with my father the Sun, who is calling me."

Pedro de Cieza de León, in ch. xliv, mentions this prophecy that Huaina Cápac made about the Spaniards, that after his time the kingdom was to be ruled by a strange race like that which came in the ship. This author says that the Inca told this to his followers at Tumipampa, near Quito, where he says that he had news of the first Spaniards who discovered Peru.

López de Gómara (ch. cxv), in telling of the conversation that Huáscar had with Hernando de Soto, who was later governor of Florida, and with Pedro del Barco when the two went along from Cajamarca to Cuzco, as we shall say in due course, gives among other statements by Huáscar, who was then a captive, the following, which we reproduce word for word: "And finally he told him that he was the true lord of all those realms and

Atabáliba a usurper, and that he therefore wished to inform and see the captain of the Christians who was undoing the other's wrongs and would restore him to his liberty and domains. For his father Huaina Cápac had bidden him in the hour of his death to be a friend to the bearded white people who had come, since they were to be the masters of the land," etc. So this prophecy of the king was published throughout Peru, and as such is recounted by the historians.

All the above was left by Huaina Cápac instead of a testament, and the Indians therefore held it in the greatest veneration and adhered to it literally. I remember how one day, when the old Inca was speaking in the presence of my mother and relating these things and the arrival of the Spaniards and how they won Peru, I said to him: "Inca, how is it that as this land is naturally so rough and rocky, and you were so numerous and warlike, and powerful enough to gain and conquer so many other provinces and kingdoms, you should so quickly have lost your empire and surrendered to so few Spaniards?" In order to answer this he repeated the prophecy about the Spaniards which he had told us some days before, and explained how their Inca had bidden them obey and serve the Spaniards since they would prove superior to them in everything.

Having said this, he turned to me with some display of anger that I should have criticized them as mean-spirited and cowardly, and answered my question by saying: "These words, which were the last our Inca uttered, were more effective in overcoming us and depriving us of our empire than the arms your father and his companions brought to this country." The Incas said this so as to show how much they honored whatever their kings bade them do, and in especial the dying words of Huaina Cápac, the most beloved of their rulers.

Huaina Cápac died of that illness. In fulfilment of his commands his followers opened the body, embalmed it, and removed it to Cuzco, leaving the heart buried in Quito. Wherever they passed along the roadside, his obsequies were celebrated with a very great display of weeping and wailing and shouting, on account of the love in which he was held. On arrival at the imperial city, the full obsequies were celebrated, which according to the custom of those kings, lasted a year. He left more than two hundred sons and daughters, or over three hundred, as certain Incas affirmed in emphasizing Atahuallpa's cruelty, for he killed almost all of them. And as we proposed to say here the things that were lacking in Peru and have been introduced since, we shall tell them in the following chapter.

CHAPTER XVI

Mares and horses; how they were bred in the
early days and their great value.

As it will be agreeable for those of this and future generations to know
what things were not found in Peru until the Spaniards conquered
it, I have thought fit to devote a separate chapter to them, so that the
reader may see and understand how many things that are apparently necessary to human life the Indians were able to do without. And they were
very satisfied without them. In the first place, they had neither horses nor
mares for warfare or festivities; neither cows nor oxen for ploughing and
sowing; neither camels, asses, nor mules as beasts of burden; neither the
coarse Spanish sheep nor merinos for wool and meat; neither goats nor
pigs for dried meat and leather; nor even pedigree dogs for hunting, such
as greyhounds, beagles, retrievers, setters, pointers, spaniels, whippets, or
mastiffs to guard their flocks, or even the pretty little creatures called lap
dogs. There were a great many of what in Spain are called curs, large and
small. Neither had they wheat nor barley, nor wine nor oil, nor fruit nor
vegetables of the Spanish varieties. In each case we shall say how and
when these were introduced into Peru.

In the first place, the Spaniards brought mares and horses with them,
and with their aid they completed the conquest of the New World; for
the Indians, being born and bred in the country, are more agile than the
Spaniards in flight and pursuit and in climbing up and down and running
among the rough and craggy places of Peru. The race of horses found
throughout all the Indian kingdoms and provinces that have been discovered and conquered by the Spaniards since the year 1492 is the Spanish breed, and more particularly, that of Andalusia. The first were taken
to the islands of Cuba and Santo Domingo, and then to the other Windward Islands as these were discovered and conquered. Here they bred in
great abundance, and were taken thence for the conquest of Mexico and
Peru, etc. In the beginning, partly because of the neglect of their owners,
and partly because of the almost incredible difficulty of the mountains
there, some of the mares strayed into the wilderness and were lost. A great
many of them were gradually lost in this way; and their owners, seeing
that they bred freely in the mountains and came to no harm from wild
beasts, even released tame animals to go with them. In this way the islands

came to possess a race of wild horses that fled like deer from human beings, yet multiplied rapidly on account of the fertility of the country,
which is hot and damp and never lacking in green grass.

When the Spaniards living in these islands saw that they needed horses
for the conquests they thereafter undertook, and that this breed was a very
good one, they began to raise them on their estates and were very well
paid for them. There were men who had thirty, forty, or fifty horses in
their stables, as we said in speaking of them in our history of Florida. In
order to catch the colts they build wooden enclosures in the hills, along
the paths by which the horses come and go to graze on the clearings.
These clearings in the islands are two, three, or more leagues long and
wide and are called savannas. The animals come out of the woods to
pasture at certain hours, and watchers who are sitting up in the trees make
a signal, whereupon fifteen or twenty men appear on horseback and drive
the wild horses into the enclosures. Mares and colts are penned up indiscriminately. Then the three-year-old colts are lassoed and fastened to
trees, and the mares let loose. The colts stay tied up for three or four days,
and kick and leap until they are so tired and hungry that they cannot stand
and some of them swoon. When their mettle has been broken, they are
saddled and reined, and mounted by youths, while others lead them by
the halter. They are treated in this way night and morning for fifteen or
twenty days until they are broken in. The colts, like animals bred for the
express purpose of serving man, respond nobly and loyally to whatever
he demands of them, so much so that within a few days of being broken
in they can be used for the *juego de cañas* [tilting with canes]. They
turn out excellent mounts. More recently, as the number of new conquests
has dropped off, the old style of horse breeding has disappeared, and
farmers have taken to breeding cattle for their hides, as we shall say
further on. When I think how much good horses cost in Spain and how
excellent those of the islands are in size and color, I have often wondered
why they are not brought here, if only in repayment of the benefits conferred by Spain in introducing them into service. If they were brought
from the island of Cuba they would be most of the way here already, and
the ships are for the most part empty. Peruvian horses mature earlier
than Spanish horses: the first time I played at *cañas* in Cuzco it was on a
young horse not yet three years old.

At first, when the conquest of Peru was still proceeding, horses could
not be bought. If one was ever sold on account of the death of its master
or because he was leaving for Spain its price was excessive—four, five,
or six thousand pesos. In 1554 when the marshal Don Alonso de Al-

varado was pursuing Francisco Hernández Girón, before the battle called Chuquinca, a Negro was holding a splendid horse, excellently harnessed, ready for its master to mount, when a rich gentleman who was much taken by the horse said to the owner: "I'll give you ten thousand pesos for the horse and slave as they stand"—that is twelve thousand ducats. The owner refused, saying that he wanted the horse in order to take part in the battle which they were expecting to have with the enemy. And indeed the horse perished in the fray and its owner was severely wounded. The remarkable thing is that the would-be purchaser was wealthy, having a good allocation of Indians in Charcas, while the owner of the horse had no Indians. He was a famous soldier, and therefore in order to appear to advantage on the day of the battle, refused to sell the horse, notwithstanding the excessive price he was offered. I knew the two men, and they were both noble gentlemen.

Since those days prices have abated in Peru, for horses have greatly multiplied. A good horse is now worth three or four hundred pesos and a nag thirty or forty. The Indians are usually greatly afraid of horses, and on seeing one gallop they lose their heads to such an extent that instead of taking to one of the walls and letting the animal pass, they feel that the horse will trample them down wherever they are just as if they were lying on the ground, no matter how wide the street. So as soon as they see a horse running they take flight and run backwards and forwards two or three times across the street. As soon as they reach one wall, they think they would have been safer at the other and run back to it. They are so blinded and bewildered with fear that it has often happened—and I myself have seen this—that they rush toward the horse in order to get away from it. They never felt themselves secure unless they had some Spaniard in front of them, and even then they were never quite at ease. It would be difficult to exaggerate the panic they used to feel in my time. Now, owing to long habit, their fear is less, but it has never declined to the point when any Indian has had the courage to become a blacksmith; and though they have become great experts in the other crafts they have learned from the Spaniards, they have never tried to learn to shoe horses, in order to avoid coming into close contact with them. It is true that even in those days there were many Indian servants of Spaniards who combed and groomed horses, but they never dared to mount them—I have never seen an Indian riding—or even to lead them by the rein unless the animal was as quiet as a mule. This was lest the horse should rear, for blinkers were not used, not having arrived in America then, nor were headstalls for controlling horses: everything was dependent on the skill and effort of the tamer and the master. But it may be added that the horses are of such noble character that if they are skilfully handled without the use of violence, they readily do what is required of them. At the beginning of the conquest, moreover, the Indians throughout the New World believed that rider and mount were all in a piece, like the centaurs of the poets. I am told that there are now some Indians who do dare to shoe horses, but that there are very few of them. With this we pass on to tell of other things that did not exist in my country.

CHAPTER XVII

Cows and oxen; their prices, high and low.

COWS ARE thought to have been introduced immediately after the conquest, and to have been brought in in large numbers, so that they soon spread over the whole country. The same could be said of pigs and goats, which I remember having seen as a child in Cuzco.

Like horses, cows could not be bought at first when there were very few of them, for the Spaniards who imported them for breeding were reluctant to sell. I cannot therefore say what their value was until later when they had multiplied. The first man who had cows in Cuzco was Antonio de Altamirano, a native of Extremadura, the father of Pedro and Francisco Altamirano, two mestizos who were at school with me. They soon died, to the great regret of the whole city, which had built up great expectations of their strength and good qualities.

The first oxen I saw ploughing were in the valley of Cuzco in about 1550. They belonged to a gentleman called Juan Rodríguez de Villalobos, a native of Cáceres, and were only three yokes. One of the oxen was called Chaparro, one Naranjo, and one Castillo. I was taken to see them by a whole army of Indians who gathered from all sides for the purpose, amazed and bewildered by so monstrous a spectacle, which was as new to them as it was to me. They said that the Spaniards were too lazy to work and forced these great animals to perform their labors for them. I remember this very well, for the excursion to see the oxen cost me two dozen of the best—half administered by my father because I had not gone to school and the rest by the master because I had skipped his lessons. The land that was being tilled was a very fine terrace standing above another where the convent of St. Francis has now been founded: this house, or rather the nave of the church, was paid for by the said Juan Rodríguez de Villalobos and dedicated to St. Lazarus, to whom he was deeply devoted. The Franciscan Friars bought the church and the two terraces some years later, for at the time I saw the oxen ploughing there were no houses either Spanish or Indian at the spot: we have spoken elsewhere at length of the purchase of the site. The laborers who were ploughing were Indians. The oxen had been tamed at a farm outside the city, and when they were fully broken they were brought to Cuzco: I really believe that the solemn triumphs of Rome in all its glory were no more admired than the oxen that day. When cows began to be sold they fetched 200 pesos: the price dropped gradually as they multiplied, and later fell suddenly to the present level. At the beginning of 1554 a gentleman I knew called Rodrigo de Esquivel, a *vecino* of Cuzco and native of Seville, bought ten cows in Lima for 1,000 pesos, or 1,200 ducats. In 1559 I saw them bought in Cuzco for 17 pesos or 20½ ducats, rather less than more. The same was true of goats, sheep, and pigs, as I shall have occasion to say in showing the fertility of the country. Since 1590 I learn from letters from Peru that cows sell at 6 or 7 ducats in Cuzco, when bought singly or in pairs; but when bought in a herd the price is lower.

The cattle became wild in the Windward Islands in the same way as the mares, and almost in the same region. Some are kept in folds for the use of their milk, cheese, and butter, but otherwise they are found in greater numbers on the hillsides. They have multiplied in a manner that would be incredible if the number of hides brought every year to Spain did not bear witness to it: according to Padre Acosta (Book IV, ch. xxxiii): "the fleet of 1587 brought 35,444 hides from Santo Domingo and 64,350 were brought from New Spain, giving a total of 99,794." In Santo Domingo, Cuba, and the other islands the cattle would have multiplied even more if they had not been so molested by the packs of hounds and mastiffs which were introduced in the early days: these have also gone wild and increased to the point where men dare not travel unless in groups of ten or twelve together: a reward is given for killing them, as if they were wolves.

In order to kill the cattle the Spaniards wait until they come down to the savannas to graze: the animals are pursued on horseback with lances, which have a metal crescent called a *desjarretadera* instead of a point. The blade is on the inside and on overtaking the beast it is struck on the hock and hamstrung. The rider who does this has to take care to strike the animal on the right leg if it is running on his right, or on the left if it is running on his left, since it will turn its head to the side on which it is wounded, and unless the rider takes this precaution, his horse will be caught by the horns of the cow or bull, having no time to avoid them. There are men so skilled in this occupation that they can bring down twenty, thirty, or forty beasts in a run of two arquebus shots. The whole Spanish fleet could be supplied from the meat that is wasted on the islands, but I fear that this cannot be dried owing to the heat and damp of the region, which causes it to rot. I am told that in Peru there are already unclaimed cows wandering about the countryside, and that the bulls are so fierce that they attack travellers on the road. Soon they will become wild like those of the islands, which now seem to have recognized the benefit Spain conferred on them in introducing these cattle and repay it by providing such an abundance of hides every year.

CHAPTER XVIII

Camels, asses, and goats; their prices
and their breeding in Peru.

B EFORE, there were no camels in Peru, but now there are some, though only a few. The first who introduced them—and I do not think that anyone has taken any since—was Juan de Reinaga, a man of noble birth from Bilbao, whom I knew. He was a captain of infantry in the war against Francisco Hernández Girón and his followers and served his majesty well in that campaign. Don Pedro Puertocarrero, a native of Trujillo, paid him 7,000 pesos, or 8,400 ducats, for seven she-camels and one male he had imported; but the camels bred little or not at all.

The first donkey I saw was in the district of Cuzco in 1557. It was purchased in the city of Huamanga and cost 480 ducats of 375 maravedis. My lord Garcilaso de la Vega had it bought for breeding mules from his mares. In Spain it would have been worth 6 ducats, for it was a poor small creature. Another was bought later by Gaspar de Sotelo, a nobleman from Zamora whom I knew, for 840 ducats. Mules have since been bred in great numbers for the carrying trade, and are much used owing to the roughness of the roads.

I do not know how much goats were worth when they were first introduced. Years later I saw them sold at 100 and 104 ducats. There were very few for sale, and these were only obtained by friends as a favor, and then only in ones and twos. Ten or a dozen were collected to form a herd for grazing. This applies to Cuzco in 1544 and 1545. Since then they have multiplied so much that they are not esteemed except for their leather. The she-goat usually produced three or four kids, as I myself have seen. A gentleman told me that in Huánucu, where he lived, he saw many bear five kids.

CHAPTER XIX

Pigs: their great fertility.

A T FIRST when they were newly introduced the price of sows was much greater than that of goats, though I cannot say for certain exactly how high it was. The chronicler Pedro de Cieza de León, a native of Seville, in his *Demarcation of the Provinces of Peru* (ch. xxvi), says that the marshal Don Jorge Robledo bought from the estate of Cristóbal de Ayala, who was killed by the Indians, a sow and a boar for 1,600 pesos or 1,920 ducats. He adds that the sow was eaten a few days later at a banquet he attended in the city of Cali, and that unborn sucking-pigs were bought for 100 pesos (or 120 ducats) or more. Anyone who wishes to know the excessive prices at which goods were sold among the Spaniards should read this chapter and he will see how little value was then attached to gold and silver in terms of things from Spain. These and similar excesses were caused by the attachment of the Spaniards of the New World to the country of their birth, for in the early days if anything was brought from Spain they bought it and bred it without regard for the price, as though they could not live without it.

In 1560 a good fat pig was worth ten pesos in Cuzco. Now they fetch six or seven, and would sell for even less were it not for the lard, which is esteemed for its value in curing mange among the Peruvian sheep, and also because the Spaniards, lacking olive-oil, which cannot be obtained, use lard for cooking on Fridays and in Lent. Sows have proved very prolific in Peru. In 1558 I saw two in the great square of Cuzco with thirty-two sucking pigs, each having put down sixteen. The piglets would be just over thirty days old when I saw them, and they were so fat and healthy that people were amazed that the sows could rear so many at once and feed them all. The Indians call pigs *cuchi,* and have introduced this word into their language for a pig from hearing Spaniards say *"coche! coche!"* when calling them.

CHAPTER XX

Sheep and domestic cats.

CASTILIAN sheep—as we call them to distinguish them from the Peruvian kind, which the Spaniards quite improperly also call sheep, though they do not bear the slightest resemblance to one another—were first introduced at an unknown date. I do not know what price they fetched or who first brought them in. The first I saw were in the district of Cuzco in 1556, and were sold at forty pesos a head as a flock, though selected ones cost fifty pesos, or seventy ducats. Like the first goats, they were only obtained as a favor. In 1560, when I left Cuzco, Castilian lambs were still not weighed at the slaughterhouse. According to letters I have received since 1590, it is reported that a sheep is worth eight reals in the market of that great city, or ten at most. Sheep have dropped within the last eight years to four ducats or less. At present there are so many of them that their value is very low. They usually give birth to two lambs, and many have three. Their wool is also so plentiful that its value has fallen to three or four reals the arroba. I have not heard that coarse-woolled sheep have reached Peru. There were no wolves before and are still none, for they have no use or value and have therefore not been introduced.

Nor were there any domestic cats before the arrival of the Spaniards. They are found nowadays, and the Indians call them *micítu,* because they have heard the Spaniards say *"miz, miz"* to call them: the word *micítu* for a cat has now been introduced into the Indian language. I mention this lest Spaniards should assume that, as cats have a different name in Peru from the Spanish *gato,* they may have existed before the conquest, as is often supposed in the case of chickens, which Spaniards assumed to have existed in Peru before the conquest because the Indians call them *atahuallpa,* as one historian says, arguing that the Indians gave names in their language to all the things they had before the Spaniards came, and that as they call chickens *gualpa* they must have had them before the arrival of the Spaniards. The argument may well convince anyone who does not know the derivation of the name *gualpa.* Chickens are not called *gualpa* but *atahuallpa.* The origin of this is an amusing one, and we shall give it in discussing the domestic birds that were not found in Peru before the Spanish conquest.

CHAPTER XXI

Rabbits and pure-bred dogs.

RABBITS were also not found in Peru, either the wild Spanish variety or the domestic rabbit. They have been introduced since I left. The first person who brought them to the district of Cuzco was a priest called Andrés López, a native of Extremadura, though I cannot discover of what city or town. This priest had two rabbits, one male and one female, in a cage. On crossing a stream sixteen leagues from Cuzco, passing through an estate called Chinchapucyu that belonged to my lord Garcilaso de la Vega, the Indian who was carrying the cage set it down in order to rest and eat. When he picked it up again to resume his journey, he found one of the rabbits missing: it had got out because one of the bars of the cage was broken, and it made its way to a wild covert of alders or poplars that grows along the whole course of this stream. It happened to be the female rabbit, which was pregnant and gave birth in this place. The Indians took care not to kill the first rabbits, which multiplied to such an extent that they spread over the land and have been taken thence to many other places. They grow very large owing to the fertility of the country, and this has occurred with everything else that has been taken from Spain to Peru.

This doe happened to find a good region with a temperate climate, neither too hot nor too cold. They have spread up the stream where the climate grows gradually colder as far as the region of perpetual snow, and they also went down the stream to the hotter zones, until they reached the

river called Apurímac, the hottest part of Peru. The story about the rabbits was told me by an Indian of my country who knew that I was writing
these things down: for its truth I must refer to the stream which will
show if there are or are not rabbits. In the kingdom of Quito there are
rabbits almost like those of Spain, except that they are much smaller and
darker in color, for the whole center of the back is black: otherwise they
are like the Spanish rabbits. There were no hares, and I have not heard of
their being introduced.

Pure-bred dogs of the breeds we have mentioned did not exist in Peru,
but were brought in by the Spaniards. Mastiffs were the last to be introduced, for they were not necessary in Peru as there were no wolves or
similar wild beasts. Once imported, they came to be much esteemed by the
owners of flocks of sheep, not so much because they fulfilled a need, as to
make the flocks resemble as far as possible those of Spain. So great was
this sort of anxiety in the early days that for no other reason than the sake
of appearance a Spaniard brought a mastiff puppy barely a month and a
half old all the way from Cuzco to Lima, a distance of 120 leagues by a
very rough road. He carried it in a bag hanging from the front of his
saddle, and at the end of each day's journey he had the task of finding
milk to feed the puppy. I saw this myself, for I was travelling in the Spaniard's company. He said he had brought the dog in order to give it as a
valuable present to his father-in-law who owned flocks and lived 50 or 60
leagues from Lima. Such, and even greater, were the pains taken by the
Spaniards to bring in Spanish things in the early days, though they later
grew weary of them, as has happened in many cases.

CHAPTER XXII

Rats; their great numbers.

I T REMAINS to speak of rats, which also arrived with the Spaniards and
did not exist until they came. López de Gómara writes in his *General
History of the Indies* (among other things that either exceed or fall short
of the truth as he was told it) that there were no mice in Peru until the
time of Blasco Núñez Vela. If he had said rats, meaning the large Spanish kinds—and this is probably what he had in mind—he would have

been right, for these did not exist in Peru. They are now found on the coast in such quantity and of such size that no cat dare look them in the face, let alone attack them. They have not found their way up to the mountain towns, nor it is feared that they will do so, on account of the cold and snow between, unless they find some way of going past under cover.

Small mice were numerous. They are called *ucucha*. In Nombre de Dios, Panama, and the cities of the Peruvian coast poison is used against the infinity of rats. At certain times of the year the town-crier announces that everyone is to put down realgar [*i.e.*, arsenic monosulphide] against rats. It is therefore necessary to take great care that all food and drink, and especially water, is kept safe, lest the rats should poison it. All the inhabitants put down the poison on the same night in fruit and other things rats are fond of. Next day innumerable rats are found dead.

When I reached Panama on my way to Spain, this poison must just have been applied, for one afternoon when I went out to walk by the shore, I found so many of them dead on the edge of the water that there was no room to stand for a distance of a hundred paces long by three or four deep. The heat of the poison drives them to seek water, and the sea water finishes them off the more rapidly.

With regard to their great quantity, I can repeat a strange tale which shows how numerous they are in ships, especially in old hulks. I make bold to repeat it on the good faith of a nobleman called Hernán Bravo de Laguna, who is mentioned in the histories of Peru and had Indians at Cuzco: I heard him tell it, and he had seen it. It occurred on a ship going from Panama to Lima which put in at Trujillo. Those on board went ashore in search of fresh supplies and relaxation on the day of its arrival and the day following. No one stayed on the ship except a sick man who remained behind because he could not walk the two leagues from the port to the city, but the ship was quite safe either from storms, for the sea is quite calm off that coast, or from corsairs, for Francis Drake, who showed how to navigate the high seas and taught shipping to beware of corsairs, had not yet made his appearance. When the rats realized that the ship was empty, they came out and scoured the place, and finding the sick man on deck, they attacked him and prepared to eat him, for it has often happened in these parts that a sick man has been left alive at nightfall, and having died unnoticed with no one to attend him, has been found in the morning with his face and parts of his body and limbs bitten away, for the rats attack from all sides. These rats had the same intention, and the man, in great fear of the attacking army, got up as best he could, armed himself with a pan from the galley, and returned to bed, not to sleep, which would have been unsafe, but to keep watch and defend himself from the enemy when it attacked; and he stayed on guard the rest of that day and the following night and the next day till quite late when his companions returned. And they found 380-odd rats slain with the pan round the bed, on the deck and in corners, not counting many others that were wounded. The sick man recovered, either from the terror he had undergone or from joy at the victory he had won, and had great things to tell of his battle with the rats.

Up to 1572 there were on three occasions great plagues of rats and mice in different years and in different places. They bred in infinite numbers, overran the land, and destroyed the crops and standing plants such as fruit trees, by gnawing the bark from the ground to the shoots: in this way the trees died and had to be replanted, and people feared they would have to leave the towns. This would indeed have happened, so great was the scourge, had not God in his great mercy mitigated it when it had reached its peak. Incredible damage was done, which we shall not describe in detail to avoid prolixity.

CHAPTER XXIII

Fowls and pigeons.

WE MUST refer to the birds that have been introduced into Peru, though they are not numerous, consisting only of chickens and domestic doves of the kind called goblins [*duendas*]. I am not aware that pigeons bred in dovecotes called *zuritas* or *zuraras* [*i.e.,* stock-doves] have yet been introduced. One writer maintains that chickens existed in Peru before the conquest; and there are those who have striven to prove as much by advancing such proofs as the fact that the Indians have words in their language for the chicken, *gualpa,* and the egg, *ronto,* and their use of the same epithet as the Spaniards, in calling a man a chicken, meaning that he is a coward. We can settle these arguments by giving the facts of the case.

Leaving the word *gualpa* till the last and taking the word *ronto* (which should be written *runtu,* the *r* being pronounced softly, for there is no double *rr* either at the beginning or in the middle of words), this is a common noun meaning "egg," not the egg of the chicken in particular, but that of any bird whether wild or tame, and when the Indians wish to make it clear what bird the egg belongs to they name the bird and the egg as we do in Spanish when we say chicken's or partridge's or pigeon's egg, etc. This is sufficient to dispose of the argument about the word *runtu.*

The epithet chicken applied to a coward has been taken by the Indians from the Spaniards in the ordinary course of daily contact and is an imitation of their speech precisely in the same way as Spaniards who have been in Italy, France, Flanders, and Germany intermingle words and phrases they have picked up from foreigners in their Castilian speech after they have returned to their own country. The Indians have done the same, though the Incas have an epithet for a coward which is even more appropriate: they say *huarmi,* "woman," using the word figuratively. The proper word for a "coward" in their own language is *campa,* and *llanclla* is "pusillanimous and weakhearted." So the epithet of chicken for a coward is appropriated from the Spanish and does not exist in the Indian language: I, as an Indian, can vouch for this. The name *gualpa* which the Indians are said to apply to chickens is written corruptly and shorn of two syllables: it should be *atahuallpa,* and is not a name for a chicken but for the last Inca of Peru, who, as we shall say in dealing with his life, displayed greater cruelty toward those of own kith and kin than all the wild beasts and basilisks in the world. He was a bastard, but he cunningly and treacherously captured and killed his elder brother, the legitimate heir called Huáscar Inca, and usurped the kingdom, destroying the whole of the blood royal, men, women, and children, with unheard of tortures and cruelties. The children being weaker and frailer, he visited with the cruelest torments that can possibly be imagined, and not sated with the destruction of his own flesh and blood, he went on to display his inhuman rage and savagery by slaughtering the closest servants of the royal houses, who, as we have said, were not private persons, but whole villages, each of which performed a special task such as porters, sweepers, woodcutters, water carriers, gardeners, cooks for the royal table, and so on. All these villages which were round Cuzco at a distance of four, five, six, or seven leagues, were destroyed, and not content with killing the inhabitants, he razed their buildings. These cruelties would have gone even further if the Spaniards had not cut them short by arriving in Peru when they were at their height.

As the Spaniards arrested the tyrant Atahuallpa on their arrival and soon put him to death by shamefully strangling him in the public square, the Indians said that their god, the Sun, had sent the Spaniards to take vengeance on the traitor and chastise and bring to book the tyrant who had slain their children and destroyed their blood. Because they had executed him the Indians obeyed the Spaniards as if they were envoys of their god, the Sun, deferring to them in everything and not resisting them in the conquest as they might have done, but rather worshipping them as children and descendants of their god Viracocha, the child of the Sun, who had appeared in dreams to one of their kings who was therefore called Inca Viracocha: the same name they therefore applied to the Spaniards.

This mistaken idea they had formed of the Spaniards became confused with an even greater misconception: as the Spaniards introduced cocks and hens among the first things brought from Spain to Peru, the Indians, when they heard the cocks crow, said that these birds were perpetuating the infamy of their tyrant and abominating his name by repeating "Atahuallpa!" when they crowed, and they used to pronounce the word imitating the crowing of the cock.

And when the Indians told their children these fictions as they always did in order that their traditions should not be lost the Indian boys, whenever they heard a cock crow, would repeat the same tones saying "Atahuallpa!" I remember how many of my fellow pupils, and I among them, the sons of Spaniards and Indian mothers, used to sing these syllables together with the little Indians in the streets.

And to illustrate our song more clearly, imagine four notes in two bars of part-song with the word *atahuallpa* sung to them. Anyone who hears this will see that they copy the usual crow of the cock: they are two crotchets, a minim, and a semibreve, all on the same note. And they remembered not only the usurper in this way, but all of his chief captains who had names with four syllables, such as Challcuchima, Quilliscacha, and Ruminaui, which means "eye of stone," for he had a film in one eye. This was the cause of the application of the word *atahuallpa* to cocks and hens from Spain. Padre Blas Valera, after telling in his regrettably half-destroyed papers how Atahuallpa came to his sudden end and having dwelt at length on his qualities, which, towards his vassals, were considerable, as in the case of all the Incas, though he displayed unheard-of cruelty toward his own relatives, enlarges on the affection in which his vassals held him and adds the following words in his elegant Latin:

Thus it came about that when the news of his death was known among the

Indians, in order that the memory of so great a man should not be forgotten they consoled themselves with the idea that whenever the cocks the Spaniards had brought with them crowed, they were mourning the death of Atahuallpa and that they perpetrated his memory by naming him in their song. For this reason they called the cock and its crow *atahuallpa*. In this way the name has been received by all the Indian tribes in all their languages, and not only they, but the Spaniards and the preachers always use it,

etc. Thus far Padre Blas Valera, who heard his account in the kingdom of Quito from the vassals of Atahuallpa himself, and as they were attached to their native king they said that the cocks mentioned him to his greater glory, while I heard it in Cuzco where he committed great cruelties and misdeeds and those who had suffered at his hands declared that the cocks uttered his name to his everlasting shame and disgrace. Everyone describes the fair according to how he has prospered at it.

I think that the foregoing deals with the three suggested "proofs" and show clearly that there were no chickens in Peru before the Spanish conquest. Having settled this point, I should like to be able to deal with a great many other errors and omissions which arise in the history of that country, owing to the incorrectness of the accounts given to the historians.

In addition to the hens and pigeons brought from Spain to Peru, we may mention that turkeys also were taken there from Mexico and were not found in Peru before. And it is worthy of note that hens did not raise chicks in the city of Cuzco or its valley despite every possible care, for the climate of the place is cold. Those who spoke of this said that the reason was that the chickens were strangers to the country and had not become acclimatized in the region, for in other warmer areas such as Y'úcay and Muina, four leagues away from the city, they reared many chicks. The sterility of the Cuzco chickens lasted more than thirty years, for in 1560, when I left, there were still none. Some years later a gentleman called Garci Sánchez de Figueroa wrote to me to say that hens were then raising chicks in Cuzco in great abundance.

In 1556 a gentleman from Salamanca called Don Martín de Guzmán returned to Peru after a visit home and took with him some fine harnesses and other curiosities, among which was a cage containing one of the little birds called canaries, because they came from those islands. It was greatly esteemed because of its beautiful song, and people were astonished that so tiny a bird should have crossed so many leagues of ocean and land between Spain and Cuzco. We mention these small matters so that people may be encouraged to introduce more useful and valuable birds, as for example Spanish partridges and other domestic fowls which have not yet been taken to Peru, but which would readily acclimatize themselves as other creatures have done.

CHAPTER XXIV

Wheat.

H AVING given an account of the birds, we should pass on to deal with the crops, plants, and vegetables, that were not found in Peru. The first who introduced wheat into my country—and I describe the whole of the former empire of the Incas as so—was a noble lady called María de Escobar, married to a gentleman called Diego de Chaves, both of whom were natives of Trujillo. I knew her in my own town where she settled many years after arrival in Peru: I never knew her husband, who died in Lima.

This lady, who deserves every honor, introduced wheat into Peru at the city of Rímac. The gentiles worshipped Ceres as a goddess for doing as much, but the inhabitants of my country set no store by this matron for her deed. I do not even know in which year she brought it in, but the quantity of seed was so small that it was kept and increased for three years before any bread was made. The original quantity was not half an almud, and some say even less. During the first three years the grain was divided out at twenty or thirty seeds a settler, and even so those who received them were only the closest friends of the owner.

On account of the benefit that this worthy lady bestowed on Peru, and of the services of her husband, who was one of the first conquerors, she was granted a good division of Indians in the city of Lima, though it disappeared when they both died. In 1547 there was still no wheaten bread in Cuzco, though there was wheat, for I remember that the bishop of the city, Don Fray Juan Solano, a Dominican and a native of Antequera, was received in my father's house with fourteen or fifteen companions after the defeat of Huarina, and my mother fed them on maize bread; but the Spaniards were so famished that while supper was being prepared they took handfuls of the uncooked maize that was brought for their horses and ate it as if it were sugared almonds. It is not known who introduced barley, but it is believed that some grains came in with the wheat. However much these two seeds are kept apart, they are never completely separated.

CHAPTER XXV

The vine; the first man to grow grapes in Cuzco.

T HE HONOR of introducing the plant of Noah belongs to Francisco Caravantes, one of the lordly conquerors of Peru, a noble gentleman from Toledo. When the land was somewhat settled, he sent to Spain for plants, and his agent, in order to get fresher plants, brought black-grape vines from the Canaries. Thus almost all the grapes were dark, and the wine is all claret and not completely red. Although other vines have been introduced since, and even muscatels, there is still no white vine.

Although the gentiles worshipped the famous Bacchus as a god for doing no more than this gentleman did in Peru, he received small thanks for his benefaction. Wine is now cheap in Peru, but the Indians do not care for it, and are satisfied with their traditional beverage of maize and water. In addition to what I have said above, I heard from a reliable source in Peru that a Spaniard had made a nursery of seedlings from currants brought from Spain, and that a few of the seeds of the currants germinated and produced shoots, though they were so delicate that it was necessary to keep them in the nursery for three or four years till they were strong enough to be planted out: the currants happened to be from black grapes, so all the wine in Peru has turned out red or claret, for it is not completely red like Spanish *vino tinto*. Both accounts may be true, for the anxiety of the Spaniards to have the things of their own country transplanted to the Indies was so strong that no danger or trouble seemed great enough to prevent them from trying to realize their desires.

The first to grow grapes and bring them into the city of Cuzco was Captain Bartolomé de Terrazas, one of the first conquerors of Peru, who went to Chile with the *adelantado* Don Diego de Almagro. I knew this gentleman, who was of noble character, magnificent, liberal, and full of other mighty qualities. He planted a vine on his allocation called Achanquillo in the province of Cuntisuyu, and in 1555 he showed the fruits of his labors and the liberality of his mind by sending thirty Indians laden with splendid grapes to my lord Garcilaso de la Vega, an intimate friend of his, with instructions to distribute part to all the gentlemen in the city so that they might enjoy the result of his labors. The gift was a great one, since the fruit was newly come from Spain, and a magnificent gesture, for if the grapes had been sold they would have fetched more than four or five thousand ducats. I enjoyed my full share of the grapes, for my father chose me as ambassador for Captain Terrazas, and I and two Indian pages carried two bowls of them to each of the principal houses.

CHAPTER XXVI

Wine; the first man to make it in Cuzco; its price.

IN 1560, when I was on the way to Europe, I passed through an estate belonging to Pedro López de Cazalla, a native of Llerena, who had settled at Cuzco and had been secretary to President La Gasca. This place is called Marcahuaci, and is nine leagues from the city, and I reached it on January 21. I found there a Portuguese steward called Afonso Vaz, an expert on agriculture and a very good person. He showed me over the whole estate, which was covered with excellent grapes; but did not offer me a single bunch, though it would have made a splendid gift to a travelling guest, especially to one such as myself who was no less attached to the fruit than I was to the man. However, he did not offer me any, and noting that I had observed his meanness, he asked me to excuse it since his master had bidden him not to touch a single grape because he intended to make wine of them, even if they had to be crushed in a kneading-trough. And this was done, as a fellow student of mine told me later in Spain, for they had no press, nor any of the other equipment, and this friend saw the trough that had been used. The reason for this was that Pedro López de Cazalla wanted to win the prize that the Catholic monarchs and the emperor Charles V had offered as a reward from the royal treasury to the first person who newly introduced into any Spanish colony a Spanish crop such as wheat, barley, wine, or olive oil, and produced a specific quantity of it. Those princes of glorious memory offered these rewards to stimulate Spaniards to cultivate the land and bring in such Spanish crops as were not found there.

The reward consisted of two bars of silver worth three hundred ducats apiece, and the quantity of wheat or barley produced had to be half a *cahiz,* or in the case of wine or oil, four arrobas. Pedro López de Cazalla did not wish to make wine out of covetousness for the sake of the prize, for he could have sold the grapes for much more than its value, but simply to have the honor and fame of becoming the first to produce wine from his own vineyards in Cuzco. Other Peruvian cities, such as Huamanga and Arequipa had wine much earlier, and it was all claret. When I was talking in Córdova to a canon from Quito about these matters we are discussing, he told me that he had known a Spaniard in the kingdom of Quito who was very interested in agriculture, and especially in vinegrowing, and had been the first to bring the plant from Rímac to Quito. He had a fine vineyard on the banks of the river Mira, which is on the equator and has a hot climate. He told me that the owner had shown him the whole vineyard and in order to prove his interest in its cultivation exhibited twelve sections in one corner of it, each of which was pruned during a certain month, and in this way he obtained fresh grapes all the year round. The rest of the vineyard he pruned once a year as did his Spanish neighbors. Vines are irrigated everywhere in Peru, and in the region of this river the climate is consistently hot, as it is in many parts of Peru. It is therefore not surprising that the seasons have their effect on plants and crops at any month in the year according to whether water is supplied or not. I have seen almost the same effect with maize in certain valleys where in one plot it was being sown, in another it was half grown, in a third in the cob, and in a fourth already gathered. And this was not done experimentally, but in obedience to the requirements of the Indians according to the value of the Indians' land and their ability to improve it.

Until 1560, when I left Cuzco, and for some years after, it was not usual for the *vecinos*—who are those who own Indians—to give table wine to ordinary guests, unless they needed it for their health. In those days wine drinking seemed rather a luxury than a necessity: the Spaniards had won that empire without the aid of wine or similar comforts and they seemed to wish to lend support to these excellent beginnings by not drinking it. And guests were also inhibited from taking it even when it was offered by its extremely high cost, for it fetched 30 ducats the arroba at its cheapest. I knew it at this price after the war of Francisco Hernández Girón. In the days of Gonzalo Pizarro and earlier it often reached 300,

400, or 500 ducats: and in 1554 and 1555 there was a great shortage of it everywhere in Peru. In Lima it grew so scarce that there was none even to say mass with. The archbishop Don Jerónimo de Loaisa, a native of Trujillo, had a search made, and half a jar of wine which was found in a house was kept for mass. This scarcity lasted days and even months, until a ship came into port. It belonged to two merchants I knew, but whom I will not name out of respect for their families. The ship carried 21,000 jars of wine, and when they found how scarce it was they sold the first at 360 ducats and the last at 200 or more. I heard this from the pilot in charge of the ship, for he brought me from Lima to Panama in her. Because of its excessive rarity it was therefore not possible to offer wine at table every day.

One day in those times a gentleman who had Indians invited one who had not to dine, and while half a dozen Spaniards were eating amicably the guest asked for a cup of water to drink. The owner of the house ordered wine to be brought for him, and when the other replied that he did not drink it, said: "Well, if you don't drink wine, come and dine and sup here every day." He said this meaning that the cost of all the rest, setting apart the wine, was as nothing. And even the cost of wine was less important than the total lack of it that often occurred, since it was brought so far from Spain across two such great oceans, for which reason it was esteemed as greatly as we have said in those early days.

CHAPTER XXVII

The olive; its first importer into Peru.

IN THE same year of of 1560 Don Antonio de Ribera, formerly a *vecino* of Lima, who had some years before been made procurator general of Peru in Spain, took back with him some young olive plants from Seville, but in spite of every precaution only three were still alive when he reached Lima, out of more than a hundred cuttings in two large vats. He planted these three survivors in a fine walled estate he had in the valley where he had already produced grapes, figs, pomegranates, melons, oranges, limes, and other fruits and vegetables from Spain, which had been sold as novelties and brought him a large sum of money, believed for certain to have exceeded 200,000 pesos. Don Antonio de Ribera planted the olives in this place, and surrounded them with a great army of more than a hundred Negroes and thirty dogs who watched his precious cuttings night and day so that not even a leaf could be removed and planted elsewhere. But it happened that someone was wider awake than the dogs, or else managed to secure the consent of some of the Negroes by bribery, as was strongly suspected; and one night one of the trees was spirited away, to make its appearance a few days later in Chile, six hundred leagues from Lima, where it propagated so successfully for three years that every shoot that was taken from it, however small, soon developed into a fine tree.

At the end of three years, as a result of the numerous comminations Don Antonio de Ribera had issued against the thieves, the migrant tree was returned to him and appeared in the very place from which it had been removed, and was restored with such skill and secrecy that he never found out who had taken it or who had returned it. In Chile the olives flourished better than in Peru, probably because they were not so upset by the difference of latitude, Chile lying like Spain between thirty and forty degrees. In Peru this tree grows better in the mountains than in the coastal plain. At first three olives, no more, were offered to a guest as a great feast and a tremendous display of luxury. Now oil has been imported from Chile to Peru. This is what has happened to the olive trees taken to my country: we will now deal with other plants and vegetables not formerly found in Peru.

CHAPTER XXVIII

The fruits of Spain and the sugarcane.

THERE WERE no figs, pomegranates, citrons, oranges, sweet or bitter limes, apples of any kind, quinces, peaches, apricots, or any of the many kinds of plums found in Spain. There was in fact only one variety of plum, quite different from those found in Europe, though the Spaniards use the word *ciruela* for it: the Indians call it *ussun*. I mention this to avoid confusion between it and the Spanish plum. There were no melons, and no Spanish cucumbers, or the gourds that are eaten cooked. All these fruits and a great many others that I cannot call to mind are now found in Peru in great abundance, and are no more prized than the live-stock. Moreover they grow so much larger than in Spain that Spaniards who have compared the same fruit in the two countries are amazed.

In Lima, as soon as pomegranates were produced, one was carried in the litter with the Holy Sacrament in the procession for Corpus Christi and it was so large that all who saw it were amazed. I dare not say how large they told me it was for fear of scandalizing the ignorant who never believe that there is anything bigger in the world than what comes from their own village, though it is a pity to refrain from describing the marvels attained by the works of nature in Peru for fear of simple people. To return to our fruits, let me say that they have all grown to an extraordinary size, especially the first named: the pomegranate was bigger than one of the jars made in Seville for carrying oil to the Indies, and many bunches of grapes have been seen weighing eight or ten pounds, and quinces the size of a man's heart, and lemons half the size of a pitcher. This shall suffice for the fruits of Spain and we will turn to the vegetables, which will cause no less amazement.

I would like to have found the names of those who introduced these plants, so as to mention them, their place of origin, and the year, in order that each may receive the praise due to him for such benefits. In 1580 a Spaniard called Gaspar de Alcocer, a wealthy merchant who had a fine estate at Lima, brought in cherry trees and mazards. I have since been told that they failed despite every kind of precaution to help them survive. Almonds have been introduced, but I do not know if walnuts have yet been brought in. Previously there was no sugarcane in Peru, but nowadays owing to the care taken by the Spaniards and the great fertility of the country there is such an abundance of all these things that a sort of surfeit has been produced, and whereas at first they were greatly esteemed they are now disdained and held of little or no account.

The first sugar mill in Peru was in the region of Huánucu [Huanaco], and belonged to a gentleman I knew. One of his servants, an intelligent and foresighted man, perceiving that a great deal of sugar was imported into Peru from the kingdom of Mexico and that the price of the sugar his master produced was held down by the large quantities thus imported, suggested loading a ship with sugar in Peru and sending it to New Spain, so that the Mexicans, on seeing sugar arrive from Peru, should think that there was too much there already and stop sending it. This was done, and the plan was effective and profitable: as a result the numerous sugar mills that now exist were built.

Some Spaniards have taken such an interest in agriculture, as I have been told, that they have grafted Spanish fruit trees on those of Peru, producing wonderful fruit to the great astonishment of the Indians on finding that one tree can be made to bear two, three, or four different fruits in the same year: these curious results, and others much less surprising, fill the Indians with wonder because they never attempted such things. Farmers might (if they have not done so already) graft olives on the trees the Indians call *quíshuar,* whose wood and fruit closely resemble the olive: I remember when I was a boy hearing Spaniards say on seeing a *quíshuar*: "Olives and the olive oil that come from Spain grow from a tree like that." It is true that the Peruvian tree bears no proper fruit: it flowers like an olive and the blossom then falls. We used its shoots to play *cañas* in Cuzco, for canes did not grow there owing to the coldness of the climate.

CHAPTER XXIX

Garden plants and herbs; their size.

NONE OF the vegetables eaten in Spain existed in Peru, such as lettuces, endives, radishes, cabbages, turnips, garlic, onions, eggplants, spinach, beets, mint, coriander, parsley, garden or wild artichokes, and asparagus (there were however pennyroyal and purslane). Nor were there carrots or any of the herbs used in Spain. As regards seeds, there were no chick-peas, beans, lentils, anis, mustard, rocket, caraway, sesame, rice, lavender, cuminseed, marjoram, fennel, or oatmeal, or poppies, or clover, or garden or wild camomile. Nor were there roses, or any of the various sorts of Spanish carnations, or jasmine, lilies, or musk-roses.

All the flowers and herbs we have mentioned, and others I have failed to recall, now exist in such abundance that many of them are regarded as weeds, for example turnips, mustard, mint, and camomile, which have thriven to such an extent in some valleys that they have defeated human effort and ingenuity in every attempt to extirpate them. They have in fact multiplied so much that they have overgrown the original names of the valleys and imposed their own as in the case of Mint Valley on the seacoast, which was formerly called Rucma, and others. In Lima the first endives and spinach grew so high that a man could hardly reach their shoots with his hand, and a horse could not force its way through them. The monstrous size and abundance attained at first by some vegetables and other crops was incredible. Wheat often produced 300 or more *fanegas* for each *fanega* that was sown.

When I was on my way to Spain in 1560 I passed through a village in the valley of Huarcu that was newly settled by a order of the viceroy Don Andrés Hurtado de Mendoza, marquis of Cañete, where I was taken by one of the colonists, a former servant of my father's called Garci Vázquez, to his house to dine, and he said to me: "Eat some of this bread, for it is part of a yield of more than three hundred for one. That will give you something to tell in Spain." I was astonished at this abundance, for the usual yield that I was accustomed to fell far short of this, but Garci Vázquez said to me: "You need not find it difficult to believe, for I am telling you the truth, on the word of a Christian: I sowed 2½ *fanegas* with wheat, and I have garnered 680, and have lost as much again because I had no reapers to help with the harvest."

When I told this story to Gonzalo Silvestre, of whom I wrote at length in my history of Florida, and shall again in this history if we reach his own times, he told me that it was not a great deal, for he had harvested four or five hundred for one the first year he had sown some land he owned in the province of Chuquisaca, near the river Pilcomayo. In 1556 when Don García de Mendoza, the son of the above viceroy, was going as governor of Chile, he put in at the port of Arica, where he was told that nearby, in a valley called Cuzapa, there was a radish of such remarkable size that five horses had been tethered under its leaves. They wanted to bring it for him to see, but he replied that they were not to pull it up: he would go and see it with his own eyes for it would make a tale worth telling. And so he went with many others who accompanied him and they saw that what they had been told was true. The radish was so thick that a man could scarcely embrace it in his arms and so tender that it was afterwards taken to Don García's lodgings, and many of the company ate it. In the place called Mint Valley many stalks have reached two and a half varas in length: and the man who measured them and by whose account I write these words is now staying in my house.

In the holy cathedral church of Córdova, in the month of May 1599, I was talking to a gentleman called Don Martín de Contreras, a nephew of Francisco de Contreras, the famous governor of Nicaragua, and mentioned that I had reached this part of our history saying that I was afraid to mention the size of the new crops and vegetables that were produced in Peru, because anyone who had never left his own country would not believe it, and he said:

"Don't desist from writing what has actually happened on that account: let them believe what they will, all you have to do is tell the truth. I am an eyewitness to the size of the radish in the valley of Cuzapa, because I was one of those who travelled with Don García de Mendoza and I can give my word as a gentleman that I saw the five horses fastened to it, and I afterwards ate the radish with the rest. And you can add that on the same expedition I saw in the valley of Ica a melon that weighed four arrobas and three pounds, and testimony to this effect was taken before the notary so that so monstrous a thing should be credited. And in the valley of Y'úcay I ate a lettuce that weighed seven and a half pounds."

This gentleman told me a great many similar things about crops, fruits and vegetables, but I have not included them so as not to bore the reader.

Padre Acosta in his Book IV, ch. xix, in dealing with the vegetables and fruits of Peru, says the following copied word for word:

I have not found that the Indians ever had gardens with different kinds of greenstuffs: in the country they cultivated their land in pieces with their own vegetables such as what they call *frijoles* and *pallares* which they use instead of chick-peas, beans, and lentils. And I have not discovered that these and other kinds of European vegetables existed before the arrival of the Spaniards, who brought various kinds from Spain which have done extraordinarily well there. In places the fertility is greatly superior to that of Spain, as for example the case of the melons of the valley of Ica in Peru, where the root forms a stock and lasts for years, giving melons annually, and it is pruned exactly like a tree, a thing which does not occur anywhere in Spain,

etc. Thus far Padre Acosta, whose authority strengthens my resolve to describe without fear the great fertility of Peru when Spanish plants were first introduced and reached such a fantastic and incredible development. This is not the least of the wonders of Peru, as recorded by Padre Acosta. And we may add that the melons had another quality in those days: none of them turned out bad, provided they were allowed to ripen, a further proof of the fertility of the country and if anyone takes observations, he will find that this is still true.

The first melons that were grown in Lima gave rise to an amusing incident which illustrates how simple the Indians were in pre-Christian times. A *vecino* of that city called Antonio Solar, a nobleman who was one of the first conquerers, had an estate at Pachacámac, four leagues from Lima, with a Spanish steward who looked after the property. This man sent his master ten melons which were carried by two Indians on their backs, after their custom, together with an accompanying letter. On their departure the steward told them: "Don't eat any of these melons, because if you do, this letter will say so."

They went on their way, and in the middle of the journey unloaded themselves to rest. One of them was tempted by gluttony and said to the other: "Shall we not know what these fruits from my master's country taste like?"

The other replied: "No, because if we eat any, this letter will say so, as the steward said."

"Well," answered the first, "let's put the letter behind that wall, then it won't see us eat and won't be able to tell our master anything."

His companion found this suggestion convincing, and they at once put it into effect, eating one of the melons. In those early days the Indians did not know what writing was, and thought that the letters Spaniards wrote to one another were like spies who might report what they saw on the way: for this reason one of these men said to the other: "Let's put it behind the wall so that it won't see us eat."

When the Indians wanted to continue their journey, the one who was carrying the five melons on his back said to the other: "We are making a mistake. We must even up the two loads, because if you have four melons and I have five, they will suspect we have eaten the one that is missing."

His companion said: "That is quite true." So to cover one misdeed they committed a second, and ate another melon.

They presented the remaining eight to their master, and when he read the letter he said to them: "What happened to the two melons that are missing?"

They both replied: "Sir, we were only given eight."

Antonio Solar answered: "Why do you lie? This letter says you were given ten, and you have eaten two."

The Indians were completely lost when they heard their master accuse them of what they had done in such secrecy. Confused and convicted, they had to admit the truth. They concluded that the Spaniards were rightly called gods, using the word Viracocha, since they could penetrate such complete secrets. López de Gómara tells of a similar incident that occurred in Cuba soon after its conquest. And it is not to be wondered at that the same ingenuousness should be found in different places and among different tribes, for all the Indians of the New World were equally simple about things that were outside their experience. Anything in which the Spaniards excelled them, as in riding horses, breaking in cattle and ploughing with them, building mills and bridges over great rivers, shooting with the arquebus and killing at a distance of a hundred or two hundred paces, and so forth, all this was attributed to divine powers, and led them to call the Spaniards gods, as in the case of this letter.

CHAPTER XXX

Flax, asparagus, carrots, and aniseed.

FLAX WAS also unknown in Peru. Doña Catalina de Retes, a native of the town of Sanlúcar de Barrameda, who was the mother-in-law of Francisco de Villafuerte, one of the original conquistadores and a *vecino* of Cuzco, herself a very noble and religious woman and one of the original founders of the convent of St. Clara in Cuzco, was expecting a quantity of flax which she had sent for from Spain, together with a loom for weaving linen for domestic use, in 1560, though as this was the year in which I left Peru, I did not hear whether she received them or not. I have since heard that a great deal of flax has been gathered, but I do not know how well my Spanish and mestizo relatives have turned out as spinstresses, for in my time as they had no flax I never saw them spinning, but only sewing and stitching. They had of course fine cotton and excellent wool, which the Indian women spun marvellously. They used to card these between their fingers, for the Indians never invented teasels, and the Indian women had no spinning wheels. If they did not turn out great spinners of flax they have some excuse, for they had no means of working it.

To return to the great esteem that existed in Peru for Spanish things, however ordinary, in the early days (though not necessarily later), I remember how in 1555 or 1556 García de Melo, a native of Trujillo, who was then treasurer of His Majesty's estate in Cuzco, sent my lord Garcilaso de la Vega three Spanish asparaguses with a message inviting him to eat this Spanish fruit which was new in Cuzco and was sent to him because it was the first to be grown there: I do not know whence it came. The asparaguses were magnificent, two of them were thicker than a man's fingers and more than a *tercia* long. The third was thicker and shorter, and all three were so tender that they came to pieces in one's hand. In order to celebrate fittingly this Spanish herb, my father ordered it to be cooked in his own room over the brazier he kept there, in the presence of seven or eight gentlemen who supped at his table. When the asparagus had been cooked, oil and vinegar were brought and my lord Garcilaso divided the two largest with his own fingers and gave a mouthful to each of his guests. He ate the third himself, asking to be excused for exercising his prerogatives for once, since it was something new from Spain. In this way they ate the asparagus with more rejoicing than if it had been the phoenix bird, and though I served at table and called for all the concomitants, I did not get any.

At about the same time Captain Bartolomé de Terrazas sent my father three carrots sent from Spain. These were a great gift and were put on the table whenever there was a new guest, and a single root was offered as a most munificent gesture.

Aniseed also made its appearance in Cuzco at about this time, and was put in bread as a thing of the greatest rarity such as the nectar or ambrosia of the poets. Everything from Spain was similarly appreciated when it first made its appearance in Peru. I have written about these matters, though they are not of great importance, because in future times, which is when history acquires most value, people may be glad to know about these beginnings. I do not know whether asparagus has flourished or if carrots have yet been grown in Peru, though other plants and animals have multiplied abundantly as we have said. They have also planted mulberries and taken silkworms, which also did not exist in Peru: but silk cannot be manufactured owing to a serious difficulty in the process.

CHAPTER XXXI

New names for various racial groups.

WE WERE forgetting the best imports into the Indies, namely the Spaniards, and the Negroes who have since been taken there as slaves, for they were previously unknown in my country. These two races have mingled [with the Indians] in various ways to form others which are distinguished by the use of different names. Although I spoke a little about this in the *History of Florida,* I have decided to repeat it here, as being the proper place. Thus any Spanish man or woman who arrives from Spain is called a Spaniard or Castilian, the two words being quite interchangeable in Peru; and I have used them indifferently in this history and in the *Florida.* The children of Spaniards by Spanish women born there are called *criollos* or *criollas,* implying that they were born in the Indies. The name was invented by the Negroes, as its use shows. They use it to mean a Negro born in the Indies, and they devised it to distinguish those who come from this side and were born in Guinea from those born in the New World, since the former are held in greater honor and considered to be of higher rank because they were born in their own country, while their children were born in a strange land. The parents take offence if they are called *criollos.* The Spaniards have copied them by introducing this word to describe those born in the New World, and in this way both Spaniards and Guinea Negroes are called *criollos* if they are born in the New World. The Negro who arrives there from the Old World is called Negro or Guineo. The child of a Negro by an Indian woman or of an Indian and a Negro woman is called *mulato* or *mulata.* Their children are called *cholos,* a word from the Windward Islands: it means a dog, but is not used for a thoroughbred dog, but only for a mongrel cur: the Spaniards use the word in a pejorative and vituperative sense. The children of Spaniards by Indians are called mestizos, meaning that we are a mixture of the two races. The word was applied by the first Spaniards who had children by Indian women, and because it was used by our fathers, as well as on account of its meaning, I call myself by it in public and am proud of it, though in the Indies, if a person is told: "You're a mestizo," or "He's a mestizo," it is taken as an insult. This is the reason why they have adopted with such enthusiasm the name *montañés* which some potentate applied to them, among other slights and insults, instead of the word mestizo. They do not stop to consider that, although in Spain the word *montañés* is an honorable appellation, on account of the privileges that have been bestowed on the natives of the Asturian and Basque mountains, if it is applied to anyone who is not from these parts, it assumes a pejorative sense derived from its original meaning "something from the mountains." This is brought out by our great master Antonio de Lebrija, to whom all good Latinists in Spain today are indebted, in his vocabulary. In the general language of Peru the word for a mountaineer is *sacharuna,* properly "savage," and whoever applied the word *montañés* was privately calling them savages: those of my own generation, not understanding this malicious implication, took pride in the insulting epithet, when they should rather have avoided and abominated it, using the name our fathers bestowed on us rather than accepting new-fangled indignities.

The children of a Spaniard and a mestizo, or vice versa, are called *cuatralvos,* meaning they have one part of Indian blood and three of Spanish. The children of a mestizo and an Indian, or vice versa, are called *tresalvos,* meaning that they have three parts of Indian blood and one of Spanish. All these names, and others which we omit to avoid tedium, have been devised in Peru to describe the racial groups that have come into existence since the arrival of the Spaniards, and we can therefore say that they were brought in together with the other things not previously found in Peru. With this we return to the Inca kings, the children of the great Huaina Cápac, who are calling us to relate great events that occurred in their time.

CHAPTER XXXII

Huáscar Inca demands that his brother
Atahuallpa shall do homage to him.

ON THE death of Huaina Cápac, his two sons reigned for four or five years in peaceful possession of their domains, without engaging in new conquests, or even attempting to do so, for King Huáscar found his realms barred on the northern side by those of the kingdom of Quito, belonging to his brother. Beyond this there were new conquests still to be made, though on the other three sides everything between the wilderness of the Antis and the sea, from east to west, had already been subdued, and the kingdom of Chile to the south had also been conquered. Inca Atahuallpa also refrained from attempting new conquests because he wished to attend to the welfare of himself and his subjects. But those who are called upon to rule can never tolerate an equal or a rival, and after passing these few years in peace and quiet, Huáscar Inca began to imagine that he had done amiss in obeying his father's orders to the effect that the kingdom of Quito should go to his brother Atahuallpa, for in addition to the loss of so great a kingdom to his empire, he realized that its separation blocked the continued progress of his conquests, while his brother was free to expand his own domains to the north, so that in time Atahuallpa's kingdom might come to exceed Huáscar's, and he, though he was called to be monarch, as the name Sapa Inca, or sole lord, implies, would in due course come to have another equal or perhaps superior to himself, and as his brother was ambitious and restless, when he had become powerful he might aspire to deprive him of the empire.

These imaginings increased from day to day, and caused such turmoil in the breast of Huáscar Inca that, when he could stand it no longer, he sent a relative as his messenger to his brother Atahuallpa, saying that, as Atahuallpa knew, by the ancient constitution of the first Inca Manco Cápac, which had been observed by all his descendants, the kingdom of Quito and all the other provinces belonged to the imperial crown of Cuzco, and that though he, Huáscar, had conceded what his father bade him, it had been from enforced obedience to the latter rather than out of a consciousness that it was right and just, for it was on the contrary prejudicial to the crown and the rights of his successors. For this reason his father should not have bidden him accept the division, and he was not obliged to fulfil it. However, as his father had ordered it and he had consented, he would gladly accept the situation under two conditions, first, that Atahuallpa should not add an inch of land to his realms, for all that was still unconquered belonged to the empire, and second, that Atahuallpa should do homage to him and become his vassal.

Atahuallpa received this communication with all the humility and submissiveness he could feign, and three days later, after considering his own interests, he replied with great astuteness and cunning to the effect that he had always had it in his heart to recognize the authority of his lord the Sapa Inca, which he now did, and he would not add anything to the kingdom of Quito, but if his majesty wanted it, he would give it up, abdicate, and live privately at Huáscar's capital, like any other of his kinsmen, and serve him in war and peace, and obey him, as he should obey his prince and lord in anything he wished. Atahuallpa's reply was sent to the Inca by the usual runner, as Huáscar himself had ordered, so that it would arrive sooner than if the envoy brought it himself, and the latter remained in Atahuallpa's court to await the Inca's instructions.

Huáscar received the answer with great satisfaction, and answered saying that he was very glad that his brother should remain in possession of what his father had left him, and that he would confirm him in his position provided that he would come to Cuzco within a certain period and offer him obedience and make the usual oath of fidelity and loyalty. Atahuallpa replied that he was delighted to know the Inca's wishes, the better to fulfil them, and that he would appear within the stated time to offer his obedience. Furthermore, so that the oath should be taken with greater solemnity and completeness, he begged his majesty to give permission for the provinces of his estate to accompany him to Cuzco to celebrate the obsequies of his father, Inca Huaina Cápac, according to the traditional usage in the kingdom of Quito and the other provinces. When this rite had been performed, he and all his vassals would take the oath together. Huáscar Inca granted all that his brother requested of him, and bade him make whatever arrangements he wished for their father's obsequies: for his part, he would be satisfied if they should be solemnized in Quito according to the local tradition and that Atalhuallpa should come to Cuzco at his own convenience. At this both brothers were very content, the first because he was far from imagining the treacherous design that was being prepared to deprive him of his life and empire, and the other, cunningly engaged in the deepest plot to relieve him of both.

CHAPTER XXXIII

Atahuallpa's devices to allay his brother's suspicions.

K ING Atahuallpa ordered it to be publicly announced throughout his kingdom and all the provinces he possessed that all able-bodied men should prepare for the expedition to Cuzco, which would depart within so many days to celebrate the obsequies of the great Huaina Cápac, his father, according to the traditional usage of each tribe, and to swear the oath of homage to their monarch Huáscar Inca. For both purposes they were to take all their accouterment and adornments, since he desired that the celebrations should attain the greatest possible solemnity. At the same time he secretly bade his captains to select the bravest warriors and bid them secretly take their arms, for he needed them not for obsequies but for war. They were to travel in troops of five or six hundred Indians, more or less, and to pretend that they were engaged on civil and not on military duties: each band was to march two or three leagues from the last. The first captains were to reduce the length of the day's march when they came within ten or twelve days of Cuzco, so that those behind might close up with them, while the bands in the rear were to double their marches when they came to this region, so as to catch up with the first. In this order King Atahuallpa sent off more than thirty thousand warriors, most of them chosen veterans left him by his father, with famous and experienced captains who had always attended him. The leaders were two generals, one called Challcuchima and the other Quízquiz, and the Inca announced that he would journey with the rearmost.

Huáscar Inca confided in his brother's words and more especially in the long experience among the Indians of respect and loyalty towards the Inca, especially on the part of his brothers and the other members of his family, which is described in the following words by Padre Acosta in his Book VI, ch. vi: "The reverence and affection of these people for their Incas was undoubtedly very great, and the latter were never known to have been betrayed by their own people," etc. For this reason Huáscar Inca not only did not suspect the treachery that was being prepared, but on the contrary very liberally ordered his people to welcome Atahuallpa's vassals and supply them with food, like their own brothers who were coming to his father's obsequies and to take the oath due to him. Such was the conduct of the two sides, Huáscar's followers acting with all their natural simplicity and goodness, and Atahuallpa's with all the malice and cunning they had learnt in his school.

Atahuallpa Inca resorted to this cunning and subtle ruse against his brother because he was not strong enough to declare war on him openly. He expected more from deceit than from his own strength for, by taking King Huáscar unawares, as in fact he did, he could not fail to win: if he had given his brother a chance to prepare, he would have lost.

CHAPTER XXXIV

Huáscar is warned and calls up
his warriors.

IN THIS way, the forces from Quito marched nearly four-hundred
leagues and came to within a hundred leagues of Cuzco. Certain old
Incas, the governors of the provinces through which they made their
way, men who had been captains and had great experience in peace and
war, were disturbed by the movement of so many men: to their minds
five or six thousand men, or ten at the outside, would have been enough
to celebrate the obsequies, while the presence of the common people was
not necessary for the purpose of taking the oath, which was done only
by the *curacas* or lords of vassals, the governors, and military leaders,
and King Atahuallpa, their leader. But no peace or good-fellowship was
to be expected from his astute, restless, and warlike spirit; and as their
suspicions and fears were aroused they sent secret messages to King
Huáscar, begging him to beware of his brother Atahuallpa since it did
not seem good to them that he should be accompanied by such large
forces.

Thus warned, Huáscar Inca roused himself from the dream of heedless confidence in which he had been slumbering. He despatched urgent
messengers to all the governors of the provinces of Antisuyu, Collasuyu,
and Cuntisuyu, and bade them repair to Cuzco in all haste with whatever
warriors they could raise. He sent no messengers to Chinchasuyu, the
largest and most warlike of the provinces, because it was cut off by the
invading army now marching across it. Atahuallpa's followers, aware of
the unpreparedness of Huáscar and his men, increased daily in courage
and cunning, and the vanguard reached a point forty leagues from the
capital, where they slowed their rate of advance, while those behind accelerated, so that in the space of a few days there were more than twenty
thousand warriors ready to cross the river Apurímac, which they did
without opposition. Beyond this point they advanced like open enemies
with banners unfurled and arms and badges revealed: they came on
slowly, in two main formations, the vanguard and the battle array, until
they were joined by the rear guard consisting of ten thousand more men.
Thus they came to the top of the hill of Villacunca, six leagues from the
city. Atahuallpa remained on the borders of his own kingdom, and dared

not approach until he saw the result of the first battle, on which he had placed all his hopes, relying on the good faith and unpreparedness of the adversary as well as on the courage and spirit of his captains and veterans.

While the army approached, King Huáscar Inca called up his warriors with all possible speed, but his men could not arrive in time to be of use on account of the great extent of the district of Collasuyu, which is more than two hundred leagues long. As to those from Antisuyu, they were few in numbers, for the area is thinly populated on account of its great mountains. Cuntisuyu, the most settled and thickly populated district, produced thirty thousand men with all their chiefs, but they were ill-practiced in war since they had had no training during the long period of peace. They were raw recruits with no military instinct. Inca Huáscar took all his kinsmen and the men who had obeyed the summons, amounting to nearly ten thousand men, and sallied forth to collect his forces to the west of the city. They were approaching from this direction, and he intended to gather them all here and wait for such other troops as would arrive.

CHAPTER XXXV

The battle of the Incas; Atahuallpa's
victory and his cruelties.

ATAHUALLPA'S captains realized from experience that delay would compromise their chance of victory and that an immediate issue would guarantee it: they therefore went in seach of Huáscar Inca so as to offer battle before more forces rallied to him. They found him on a wide plain two or three leagues to the west of the city. A fierce engagement took place there, without any preparation or forewarning on either side. The battle was fought with great cruelty, the attackers seeking to seize the Inca Huáscar, who was an inestimable prize, and the others not to lose their beloved ruler. The struggle lasted the whole day with great loss of life on both sides, but finally the absence of the Collas and the fact that Huáscar's army was new and unskilled in war told in favor of Inca Atahuallpa, whose seasoned soldiers were each worth ten of their adversaries. In the encounter Huáscar Inca was captured, this being the main

object of his enemies, who would not have considered they had accomplished anything if he had escaped them. He tried to make his escape with
about a thousand men who gathered about him and they all died in his
presence, some killed by the enemy and some taking their own lives when
they saw that their king had been captured. In addition to his royal person, those taken prisoner included many *curacas,* lords of vassals, many
captains, and a great number of nobles who were wandering like sheep
without a shepherd, neither seeking flight nor knowing where to betake
themselves. Many of them could have escaped, but knowing that their
Inca had been taken prisoner, allowed themselves to be arrested with
him out of love and loyalty toward him.

Atahuallpa's forces were full of content and joy at so great a victory
and so rich a prize as the imperial person of Huáscar Inca and all the leaders of his army. They guarded him extremely closely, appointing four captains and the most trustworthy soldiers in their army to take turns on
guard, not losing sight of him by day or by night. They then ordered the
announcement of his capture to be made throughout the empire, so that
if any forces were on the way to join him they would disband on learning
that he was already under arrest. They sent the news of the victory and of
the arrest of Huáscar posthaste to King Atahuallpa.

Such was the sum and substance of the war between these two brothers,
the last kings of Peru. Other battles and skirmishes related by the Spanish
historians were incidents that took place in different parts of both kingdoms between captains and garrisons, while Atahuallpa's so-called arrest was an invention which he himself caused to be spread about so as to
lull the suspicions of Huáscar and his supporters. He later put it about
that after his arrest his father the Sun had turned him into a snake so
that he could escape through a hole in his cell, a tale that was intended to
bolster up his authority and make his usurpation popular by causing the
common people to believe that their god, the Sun, had favored his cause
by freeing him from the power of his enemies. And the people were so
simple that they readily believed any fairy story that the Incas put forward concerning the Sun, since these were held to be his children.

Atahuallpa made very cruel use of his victory. He made a false pretence that he intended to restore Huáscar and summoned together all
the Incas in the empire, both governors and other civil ministers, and
generals, captains, and soldiers. They were all to appear within a certain time in Cuzco, where he said he wished to draw up with them certain privileges and statutes that should thenceforward be observed by
both kings so that they might live in peace and brotherhood. At this news

all the Incas of the royal blood assembled: only those who were prevented by sickness or age, and a few who were too far away or who could not or dared not come or did not trust the victorious Atahuallpa, were missing. When they were all assembled, Atahuallpa ordered them all to be killed in various ways so as to make sure that they would never plan any revolt against him.

CHAPTER XXXVI

The cause of Atahuallpa's atrocities and their most cruel effects.

BEFORE continuing we should refer to the motives for Atahuallpa's cruelty toward those of his own line. It should be recalled that according to the statutes and regulations of the kingdom which were in use and regarded as inviolable from the time of the first Inca Manco Cápac to that of the great Huaina Cápac, Atahuallpa not only could not inherit the kingdom of Quito, since all conquests belonged to the imperial crown, but was also incapable of possessing the kingdom of Cuzco, for each heir was required to be the son of the legitimate wife and sister of the king, so that he might inherit the kingdom through his mother and father equally. Failing this, the king was to be at least a legitimate scion of the royal stock, the son of a *palla* with no admixture of any other blood. Such sons were regarded as entitled to inherit the crown, but those of mixed blood had no such right to succeed, or even to dream of such a thing. As Atahuallpa thus lacked all the requisites necessary for him to be Inca, for he was neither the son of a *coya* (or queen) nor of a *palla* (a woman of the royal blood), his mother being a native of Quito, and as the kingdom of Quito could not be detached from the empire, he decided to remove the dangers that might in future ensue from such violent beginnings, fearing that once the present wars were over the whole empire would by common consent demand an Inca with the proper qualifications who might be elected and raised up by the inhabitants over his head: Atahuallpa would not be able to prevent this because it was established in the vain religion and idolatry of the Indians as a result of the doctrine taught by the first Inca Manco Cápac and observed as an example by all his descendants. Finding no better solution, he therefore resorted to the cruel destruction of the whole of the royal house, not only of those who might have a right to the succession of the empire, through the legitimacy of their blood, but also of all the rest, who were as incapable of succeeding as he was himself, lest anyone of them should do as much as he had done, for he had opened the door to all of them by his bad example. This same solution has usually been sought by kings who have seized the realms of others by violence, for it seems to them that in the absence of a legitimate heir to the throne their vassals will have no one to appeal to and no one to restore, and in this way they will be secure in conscience and justice. Ancient and modern histories give us ample evidence of this, which we shall omit to avoid prolixity: suffice it to mention the evil custom of the Ottoman house, by which the successor to the empire buries all his brothers with his father for his own security.

But the cruelty of Atahuallpa was greater than that of the Ottomans and he was even more avid for the blood of his own family. Not sated with that of two hundred of his brothers, the children of the great Huaina Cápac, he went on to drink that of his nephews, uncles, and other kinsmen up to and beyond the fourth degree, so that no member of the royal blood, legitimate or bastard, escaped. He had them all killed in different ways. Some were beheaded; some hanged; some were thrown into rivers and lakes, with great stones about their necks, so that they were unable to swim and drowned; others were flung from high crags and precipices. All this was done with as much haste as his ministers could apply, for the usurper could not feel safe until he saw or knew that all his rivals were dead. For despite his victory, he still dared not pass beyond Sausa, which the Spaniards call Jauja, ninety leagues from Cuzco. He spared poor Huáscar from immediate execution, keeping him as a defence in case of a rising, for he knew that he had only to send Huáscar to bid them be still, and his vassals would at once obey. But to the greater misfortune of the unhappy Inca, he was forced to witness the slaughter of his kinsfolk, and he died with every one of them, for he would have thought it a lesser thing to die himself than to see them all slain with such cruelty.

Nor could such inhuman cruelty allow the other prisoners to go unpunished. So, to chasten all the *curacas* and nobles of the empire who were affected to Huáscar, they were taken, with their hands bound, to a level space in the valley of Sacsahuana (where the battle between President La Gasca and Gonzalo Pizarro later took place) and forced to stand in a long double line. The wretched Huáscar Inca, clad in mourning and with his hands tied behind his back and a rope round his neck, was then driven down the lane between his men. When they saw their prince so fallen, they prostrated themselves on the ground to worship and revere him with great shouts and cries, since they could no longer free him from so great a misfortune. All those who did this were slain with axes and small single-handed clubs called *champi* (they have also other larger axes and two-handed clubs). In this way almost all the *curacas* and captains and nobles who had been arrested were put to death, and scarcely a man of them escaped.

CHAPTER XXXVII

The same cruel treatment is extended to the women and children of the royal blood.

WHEN Atahuallpa had killed the males of the royal blood and the vassals and subjects of Huáscar, he went on to swallow the still unspilt blood of the women and children of the same stock—cruelty is thus not sated, but grows hungrier and thirstier the more flesh and blood it consumes. The tenderness of youth and weakness of sex, which might have deserved some compassion, stirred the tyrant on the contrary to a greater rage. He ordered all the women and children of the royal blood who could be found, of whatever age and condition, except those who were dedicated as wives of the Sun in the convent of Cuzco, to be assembled and slaughtered in batches outside the city with various cruel tortures, so that they took a long time to die. The ministers of his cruelty carried out these orders wherever victims were found. All the women who could be found throughout the kingdom were collected together, and intensive search was made lest any escape. A great many children were rounded up, both legitimate and otherwise, for the lineage of the Incas was the largest and most numerous in the empire on account of their power to have as many wives as they wished. They were all put in the plain called Yáhuarpampa, "the field of blood," a name that was applied because of the bloody battle between those of Cuzco and the Chancas, which took place there, as we have mentioned. It lies almost a league to the north of the city.

There they were kept, and escape was made impossible by the construction of a triple fence. The first consisted of warriors who were lodged round them, to act as a guard and protection for Atahuallpa's forces against the city and to instill terror into his enemies. The other two circles consisted of sentries, some placed further away than others, who were to watch night and day so that no one could enter or leave unseen. They wrought their cruelty on their victims in many ways. They fed them on nothing but a little raw maize and herbs: this was the strict fast that the Indians observed in their heathen religion. The women, Atahuallpa's sisters, aunts, nieces, cousins, and stepmothers, were hanged from trees and from many high gallows built for the purpose: some were suspended by the hair, some under the arms, and others in other vile ways, which for decency's sake I do not mention. They were given their little children to hold in their arms, and when they dropped them, the soldiers beat them with clubs. Some were suspended by one arm, some by both, some by the waist, so as to prolong the torment and put off the hour of death, for a quick death was a great mercy which the unfortunate victims begged for with loud cries and screams. The boys and girls were killed off gradually, so many each quarter of the moon, and great cruelties were inflicted on them as on their fathers and mothers, though their tender years might have earned them mercy. Many of them died of hunger. Diego Fernández deals briefly with the tyranny of Atahuallpa and some of his cruelties in the *History of Peru,* (Part II, Book III, ch. xv). The following are his words letter for letter:

There were great differences between Huáscar Inca and his brother Atahuallpa about who should be master and ruler of the kingdom. While Atahuallpa was in Cajamarca and his brother Huáscar in Cuzco, the former sent two of his chiefs, captains called Chalcuchimau and Quízquiz, who were brave leaders and were accompanied by a great many men, with the object of arresting Huáscar. This was planned because once his brother had been arrested Atahuallpa would become lord and could do whatever he liked with Huáscar. This force marched on its way, conquering caciques and Indians and placing everything under Atahuallpa's control. When Huáscar received news of what was happening he made ready and departed from Cuzco for Quipaipan, which is a league from Cuzco, where the battle took place. Although Huáscar had many men, he was at last defeated and captured. Many were killed on both sides, so many that it is stated for certain that the number exceeded 150,000. After this they entered Cuzco in triumph, and killed many people: men, women, and children. All those who admitted they had been supporters of Huáscar were slain, and all his sons were sought out and put to death, likewise such women as were pregnant by him. One of Huáscar's wives, called Mama Uárcay succeeded in escaping with one of his daughters called Coya Cuxi Uárcay, who is now the wife of Xaire Topa Inca, of whom we have written at length in this history,

etc. Thus far our author, who then goes on to speak of the ill-treatment given to poor Huáscar in prison; we shall in due course quote his very words which are indeed harrowing. Coya Cuxi Uárcay, whom he says became the wife of Xaire Topa [Siari Túpac], was called Cusi Huarque: we shall speak of her later. The name of the battlefield which he gives as Quipaipan is a corruption: it should be Quepaipa, and is the genitive, meaning "out of my trumpet," as though that was the place where Atahuallpa's trumpet sounded loudest, according to the Indian phrase. I have been in this place two or three times with other boys who were fellow pupils of mine: we used to go hawking there with the little Peruvian falcons that our Indian hunters bred for us.

In this fashion the whole of the royal blood of the Incas was extinguished and stamped out within the space of two and a half years. It could indeed have been annihilated earlier, but the murderers avoided this so as to prolong the pleasure they derived from their cruelty. The Indians used to say that the name of Yáhuarpampa, "field of gore," was confirmed by the royal blood that ran there: it was much greater in quantity and incomparably so in quality than that of the Chancas, and it caused greater pity and compassion because of the tender age of the children and the natural weakness of the women.

CHAPTER XXXVIII

Some members of the royal blood escape Atahuallpa's cruelties.

A NUMBER escaped this butchery, some because they did not fall into Atahuallpa's power, and others because his own followers were filled with pity to see the extermination of the blood they had considered divine and, weary with the merciless carnage, permitted some of the victims to escape from the ring in which they were kept, and even drove them forth, removing their royal robes and giving them ordinary garb so that they should not be recognized; for, as we have explained, the rank of the wearer was known from the quality of his dress. All those who were spared in this way were boys and girls of ten or eleven years or less. One was my mother and a brother of hers called Don Francisco Huallpa Túpac Inca Yupanqui, whom I knew: he has written to me since I have been in Spain. All that I have written about this disastrous end of the Incas is derived from the account I have many times heard them tell. In addition I know a few others who escaped. I knew two *auquis,* or princes. They were sons of Huaina Cápac, one called Paullu, who was already an adult at the time of the catastrophe and is mentioned by the Spanish historians, the other Titu, a legitimate member of the royal blood: he was a boy at the time. I have written elsewhere about their baptism and the Christian names they adopted. Paullu had descendants with Spanish blood, for his son Don Carlos Inca, who was my fellow pupil and studied grammar with me, married a noblewoman born in Spain, the daughter of Spanish parents. They had a son, Don Melchor Carlos Inca, who came to Spain last year, in 1602, partly to see the capital and partly to receive the grants he was supposed to be awarded in Spain in return for his grandfather's services in the conquest and pacification of Peru and against the rebels, as can be seen from the histories of that empire. But he was chiefly entitled to these rewards as the direct descendant of Huaina Cápac in the male line, for he is the most famous and distinguished of the few surviving members of the royal family. He is at present in Valladolid, awaiting the grants he is to receive: however great they are he will deserve better.

I have not heard that Titu left issue. Of the *ñustas,* or princesses, the daughters of Huaina Cápac known to be legitimate by blood, one was called Doña Beatriz Coya: she married Martín de Bustincia, a nobleman who was treasurer or factor of the estates of the emperor Charles V in Peru; they had three sons who were called the Bustincias and another called Juan Serra de Leguiçamo, who was a fellow pupil of mine in the primary and grammar school. The other *ñusta* was Doña Leonor Coya, who married first a Spaniard called Juan Balsa, whom I did not know, for it was when I was a child, and had a son of the same name who was at school with me; and secondly Francisco de Villacastín, one of the first conquerors of Peru, who had also been a conqueror of Panama and other places. A historical anecdote about him occurs to me and is worth repeating: I take it word for word from the history of Francisco López de Gómara, (ch. lxvi):

Pedrarias settled Nombre de Dios and Panama. He drove the road from the former to the latter with the greatest difficulty, for it goes through thick jungle and steep mountains: in these parts, it is said, there were numberless lions, tigers, bears, and leopards, and such a multitude of monkeys of various shapes and sizes that when they were annoyed they deafened the workers with their cries: they climbed the trees and threw stones at anyone who approached.

Thus far López de Gómara. A conquistador of Peru has written a marginal note in a copy of the book I have seen, and he says at this point:

One wounded a crossbowman called Villacastín with a stone and knocked two of his teeth out: he was afterwards a conqueror of Peru and owner of a good allocation of Indians called Ayauiri. He died in prison in Cuzco, for he took Pizarro's part at Xaquixaguana; after he had surrendered one of his enemies slashed him in the face with a knife: he was a good man and helped many, though he died in poverty and deprived of his Indians and his land. Villacastín killed the monkey that wounded him, for he managed to fire his crossbow exactly as the monkey threw the stone.

Thus far the conquistador's note: I will add that I saw the broken teeth, which were the two front teeth of the upper jaw; and it was generally known in Peru that they had been broken by the monkey. I have included this here together with the evidence, as a thing worthy of mention: I always like to be able to quote my sources whenever possible in such cases.

I knew other Incas and Pallas of the royal blood, of less consequence than the foregoing: there would not be more than two hundred altogether. I have referred particularly to these because they were children of Huaina Cápac. My mother was his niece, the daughter of one of his brothers, legitimate on both his father's and his mother's side, called Huallpa Túpac Inca Yupanqui.

I knew a son and two daughters of King Atahuallpa. One of the daughters was called Doña Angelina, by whom the marquis Don Francisco Pizarro had a son called Don Francisco, a great rival of mine, as I was of his, for when we were both eight or nine his uncle Gonzalo Pizarro used to make us compete at running and jumping. The marquis also had a daughter called Doña Francisca Pizarro: she turned out a fine lady and married her uncle Hernando Pizarro. Her father the marquis had her by a daughter of Huaina Cápac called Doña Inés Huaillas Ñusta, who afterwards married Martín de Ampuero, a *vecino* of Lima. These two children of the marquis and one of Gonzalo Pizarro called Don Fernando came to Spain, but the boys died young, to the great sorrow of all who knew them, for they promised to be worthy sons of such parents. I do

not remember if the name of Atahuallpa's other daughter was Doña
Beatriz or Doña Isabel: she married a gentleman from Extremadura called
Blas Gómez and secondly a mestizo gentleman called Sancho de Rojas.
The son was called Don Francisco Atahuallpa: he was a handsome boy in
body and features, as were all the Incas and Pallas: he died young. I shall
later include a story about his death, which I had from the old Inca, my
mother's uncle, which concerns the cruelties of Atahuallpa we are describing. Huaina Cápac left another son whom I never knew: he was
called Manco Inca, and was the legitimate heir to the empire, as Huáscar
died without male issue: we shall refer to him at length later on.

CHAPTER XXXIX

*Atahuallpa's cruelty extends to the
servants of the royal house.*

T O RETURN to the inhuman deeds of Atahuallpa, we should add that,
not content with those he had inflicted on the members of the royal
family and the lords of vassals, captains, and nobles, he ordered the servants of the royal houshould to be put to the knife—that is those who
performed all manner of duties within the palace. They were, as we have
explained in dealing with them, not chosen as individuals, but the inhabitants of certain villages which were required to find persons who
took turns in performing such duties. Atahuallpa's hatred toward them
rose from the fact that they were servants of the royal household and also
from their having the title of Inca, on account of the privilege awarded
to them by the first Inca, Manco Cápac. His knife entered into these villages more or less deeply in proportion to the proximity to the royal person of the service they performed. Those who had the closest offices, such
as porters, jewel-keepers, butlers, cooks, and so on, were the worst treated,
for he was not content with executing all the inhabitants of both sexes and
all ages, but also burnt down and razed the villages and houses and
palaces in them. Those less intimately connected with the royal person,
such as woodcutters, water carriers, gardeners, and others, suffered less:
some were decimated, that is one in ten of the inhabitants, young and old,
were put to death; in others one in five; and in still others one in three.

So no village within five or seven leagues of Cuzco failed to suffer a special persecution in that cruel tyranny, in addition to the general oppression that was felt throughout the empire, for everywhere there were burnings, robberies, raids, rape, bloodshed, and other evils, as usually occur when military liberty gives way to licence. Nor did villages and provinces remote from Cuzco escape, for as soon as Atahuallpa heard of the capture of Huáscar he ordered war to be made with fire and the sword on all the neighboring provinces, especially the Cañaris who had refused to obey him at the beginning of his rebellion. Later, when he found himself powerful, he wreaked a terrible vengeance on them, as Agustín de Zárate tells in his ch. xv in the following words:

And on reaching the province of the Cañaris, he killed sixty-thousand men there because they had opposed him, and laid waste the towns of Tumibamba with fire and the sword. It stood on a plain on the bank of three rivers and was formerly very large: then he proceeded with the conquest of the whole land, and of those who sought to defend themselves he left not one alive,

etc. López de Gómara says the same, in almost the same words. Pedro de Cieza's version is longer and more emphatic: after referring to the lack of men and excess of women in the province of the Cañaris in his time and mentioning that the burdens of the Spanish armies were carried by Indian women instead of by men, he gives the reason why in the following words in his ch. xliv:

Some Indians say that this is due most to the greater lack of men and the abundance of women arising from the great cruelties performed by Atahuallpa on the natives of this province when he entered it after having defeated and killed Antoco, his brother Huáscar Inca's general, at Ambato: they say that although men and boys came forth with green boughs and palm leaves to beg mercy, he angrily ordered his captains and soldiers to slay them all with great severity. Thus a great number of men and boys were killed, as I say in the third part of this history. For this reason those now alive say that there are fifteen times as many women as men,

etc. Thus far Pedro de Cieza: and this shall suffice for the cruelty of Atahuallpa: we shall leave the greatest of them until its proper place.

From these cruelties there arose the tale I promised to include about Don Francisco, the son of Atahuallpa, who died a few months before I came to Spain. Early in the morning the day after his death, the few remaining Incas came to visit my mother before the funeral, and among them came the old Inca we have mentioned before. Instead of offering condolence, for the dead man was my mother's nephew, her cousin's son, he congratulated her, wishing that Pachacámac might preserve her for many years so that she should see the death of all her enemies, and he followed these remarks with other similar words of satisfaction and rejoicing. I, not having realized the reason for this contentment, said to him: "Inca, why should we rejoice over the death of Don Francisco, who was so closely related to us?"

And he turned on me in a rage, and taking the edge of the blanket he wore instead of a cloak, he bit it, which is a sign of the greatest anger among the Indians, and said to me: "Do you want to be the kinsman of an *auca,* the son of another *auca* (which is 'tyrant' and 'traitor'), who destroyed our empire? And one who killed our Inca, who consumed and extinguished our blood and descent, who performed so many cruel deeds, so unlike those of the Incas, our ancestors? Give me him dead as he is, and I will eat him raw without pepper, for the traitor Atahuallpa, his father, was not the son of Huaina Cápac, our Inca, but of some Indian from Quito with whom his mother betrayed our king. If he had been an Inca, he would not only not have committed the cruelties and abominations he did, but not even have imagined them; for the teaching of our ancestors was that we should never harm anyone, even our enemies, let alone our kinsfolk, but that we should confer good on all. So do not say that one who went against all our ancestors was our kinsman: you do them and us and yourself much wrong if you call us kinsmen of an inhuman tyrant who made those few of us who escaped his cruelty slaves instead of kings."

All this and much more the Inca said, stirred to wrath by the memory of the destruction of all his line, and the thought of the great and abominable wrongs done by Atahuallpa turned the joy they felt at the death of Don Francisco to bitter weeping. Don Francisco himself in his lifetime was aware of the hatred the Incas and all the Indians in common bore him, and he would not have to do with them or even leave his house: the same was true of his two sisters who heard the name *auca* at every step, a name so pregnant with tyranny, cruelty, and wickedness that it forms a proper title and device for those who earn it.

CHAPTER XL

The surviving descendants of the royal blood of the Incas.

MANY DAYS after finishing this ninth book I received certain information from Peru, from which I have compiled the following chapter, for I thought that this matter belonged to my history and I have therefore added it here. The few Incas of the royal blood who survived the cruelties and tyrannies of Atahuallpa and other later oppressions have more descendants than I had imagined, for at the end of the year 1603 they all wrote to Don Melchor Carlos Inca and to Don Alonso de Mesa, the son of Alonso de Mesa who was a *vecino* of Cuzco, and also to me, to ask us to beg His Majesty in the name of them all to have them exempted from the tribute they are paying and from other vexations that they undergo in common with the rest of the Indians. They sent the three of us powers to act together on their behalf with proofs of their descent, including details of which of them descended from which king, with all their names, and which from which other king, down to the last of their line; and for clearer proof and demonstration they included a genealogical tree showing the royal line from Manco Cápac to Huaina Cápac painted on a *vara* and a half of white China silk. The Incas were depicted in their ancient dress, wearing the scarlet fringe on their heads and their ear ornaments in their ears; only their busts were shown. This message was directed to me, and I forwarded it to Don Melchor Carlos Inca and Don Alonso de Mesa who reside at court in Valladolid: for I myself could not undertake their case because of this occupation, though I would be glad to devote my life to it, for it could not be better employed. The letter the Incas sent me is written in a fair hand by one of them, and the turn of language they use partly follows their own tongue and partly the Spanish, for they are all now Castilianized. It is dated April 16, 1603. I do not reproduce it here so as not to cause the reader pain with the miserable account they give of their life. They write with great confidence, which we all entertain, that when His Catholic Majesty knows their plight, he will relieve them and will confer many privileges on them, as befits the descendants of kings. After depicting the figures of the Incas, they have written the list of descendants against each headed: Cápac Aillu, "august or royal lineage." This title is used by them all in common and implies that they all descend from the first Inca Manco Cápac. Then they put another title in particular for the descent of each king with different names, to show that each comes from a certain king. The descent of Manco Cápac is called Chima Panaca, and consists of 40 Incas. That of Sinchi Roca is called Rauraua Panaca and embraces 64 Incas. That of Lloque Yupanqui, the third Inca, is called Hahuanina Aillu; it has 63 Incas. Those of Cápac Yupanqui are called Apu Maita, and number 56. Those of Maita Cápac, the fifth king, are Usca Maita, and number 35. Those of Inca Roca are Uncaquirau: they number 50. Those of Yáhuar Huácac, the seventh king, are called Ailli Panaca, and are 51. Those of Viracocha Inca are called Socso Panaca, and are 69. The descent of Inca Pachacútec and his son, Inca Yupanqui, are put together and called Inca Panaca, and the number of descendants is thus doubled and reaches 99. The descent of Túpac Inca Yupanqui is called Cápac Aillu, or imperial descent, confirming what I said above about this title, and numbers only 18. The descent of Huaina Cápac is called Tumi Pampa, after a very solemn feast that Huaina Cápac dedicated to the Sun at that place, which is in the province of the Cañaris. It had a royal palace, storehouses for the warriors, a house of the chosen women, and a temple of the Sun, all as grand and noble and full of splendor as anywhere in Peru, as Pedro de Cieza relates, with all possible emphasis, in his ch. xliv; and, appearing to think that he has fallen short of the truth, he concludes with the words: "Finally, I cannot say anything that does not fall short of a true description of the great wealth the Incas had in these palaces," etc. Huaina Cápac wished the memory of this solemn festivity to be preserved in the name of his descendants, and they are therefore called Tumi Pampa: they number only 22; for as the lines of Huaina Cápac and his father Túpac Inca Yupanqui were the closest to the royal tree, Atahuallpa did his utmost to extirpate them even more thoroughly than the rest, and very few therefore escaped his inhuman cruelty, as the list shows. The total number of Incas is 567 persons, and it should be noted that this is the descent by the male line, for the female line is, as we have said, ignored by the Incas, unless they are the sons of Spanish *conquistadores* who won Peru, for these too are called Incas, in the belief that they are descendants of their god, the Sun. The letter they wrote to me was signed by eleven Incas, one for each of the eleven lines, each signing for the whole of his line and giving his baptismal name and the names of his ancestors. I do not know the meaning of the names assumed by the other lines, except the two last, for they are names drawn from the special language used by the Incas in talking among one another and are not in the general language spoken in the capital. It remains to speak of Don Melchor Carlos Inca, the grandson of Paullu and great grandson of Huaina Cápac, who, as we have said, came to Spain in 1602 to receive grants. At the beginning of the present year of 1604 the result of his request was made known, and he was awarded 7,500 ducats in perpetuity payable from the royal chest of His Majesty in Lima, together with a subsidy to bring his wife and household to Spain, a habit of Santiago and the promise of a post in the royal household: the Indians he had inherited from his father and grandfather in Cuzco were to go to the crown, and he was not to return to the Indies. I am told by letter from Valladolid that all this was in the award: I do not yet know—it is now the end of March—if anything has been done, so I cannot include it here. We now enter the tenth book, in which we describe the incredible and heroic deeds of the Spaniards who won the empire of Peru.

End of the Ninth Book